D0090822

Politics and the Military in Modern Spain

Stanley G. Payne

1967
Stanford University Press
Stanford, California
London: Oxford University Press

Stanford University Press
Stanford, California
London: Oxford University Press
© 1967 by the Board of Trustees of the
Leland Stanford Junior University
Printed in the United States of America
L.C. 66-17564

For Julia

Preface

THE MILITARY have played a more important role and provoked more comment than any other institutional force in modern Spain save perhaps the Catholic Church, yet no serious study has ever been undertaken of the Army either as an institution or as a political influence. The purpose of this book is to help fill that gap, at least so far as the political dimension is concerned. In preparing this study, I have drawn on a great variety of materials. The documentation is less complete in some instances than one might wish, in part because the Spanish military archives for the recent period are closed to investigators, and in part because of the slippery nature of the topic. I do not pretend that this work is definitive. It is simply an attempt to open up one of the most important topics concerning modern Spain—a topic that has hitherto been untouched.

The importance of the theme was perhaps first made plain to me in a conversation with Jaime Vicens Vives in Barcelona in December 1958. Much of the research was subsidized by a Guggenheim Fellowship in 1962–63, and previous work was supported by smaller grants from the Social Science Research Council and the American Philosophical Society. Other expenses have been met with the assistance of the Senate Research Committee of the University of California, Los Angeles, and, in 1961–62, the University of Minnesota. I am indebted to a number of friends in Spain, particularly Francisco Javier de Lizarza Inda, Antonio Villar, and Federico Fernández de Castillejo, for aiding my work there. Professor Juan J. Linz of Columbia University made valuable suggestions for improving the manuscript.

I would like also to acknowledge the generous assistance of the staff of the Reference Department of the Research Library of the University of California, Los Angeles, in securing certain arcane printed materials. The heirs of John Whitaker and Arturo Barea have kindly allowed me to quote at length from the works of these authors. Nancy Donovan of Stanford University Press has labored long and valiantly to wrestle the manuscript into shape. My wife, to whom this book is dedicated, has provided invaluable aid by bearing up through many months of research in Spain and offering sound advice on the form and organization of the manuscript. It need scarcely be mentioned that I alone am responsible for whatever shortcomings the book may possess.

STANLEY G. PAYNE

August 1966

Contents

Maps

Chronology of Principal Political and Military Events in Spain, 1808–1939

1808	French invasion. Beginning of War of Independence.
1812	First Liberal constitution.
1813	Expulsion of French forces from the peninsula.
1814	Restored king, Ferdinand VII, seizes absolute power.
1820	Constitutional government restored.
1821–23	Civil war.
1823	Absolute monarchy restored. Purge of Liberals in regular Army.
1833	Death of Ferdinand VII. Succession of Isabella II.
1833–40	First Carlist War.
1834	Conservative charter promulgated.
1835	Abortive Liberal revolt in Madrid.
1836	Sergeants' revolt at La Granja. 1812 constitution restored.
1837	New Liberal constitution.
1841	Espartero elected regent. Conservative military revolt fails.
1843	Espartero overthrown. Narváez key political general till 1853.
1845	New Moderate constitution.
1846–49	Second Carlist War.
1854	Successful Liberal revolt.
1856	O'Donnell restores 1845 constitution.
1859–60	Hispano-Moroccan War.
1866	San Gil Artillery mutiny in Madrid.
1868	Monarchy overthrown by Prim and Serrano.
1868–78	Ten Years' War in Cuba.
1869	First democratic constitution.
1869–76	Third Carlist War.
1870–73	Brief reign of Don Amedeo of Savoy.
1873–74	Federal Republic.
1874	Bourbon monarchy restored by Army revolt.
1876	New restricted constitution.
1883	Unsuccessful military revolts.

1886	Abortive Villacampa rebellion in Madrid.
1893–94	Hispano-Moroccan border conflict.
1895–98	Final Cuban revolt.
1905	*Cu-cut* incident.
1906	Law of Responsibilities enacted.
1909	"Tragic Week" in Barcelona. Border conflict in Morocco.
1913	Establishment of Spanish Protectorate in Morocco.
1917	Creation of Military Defense Juntas.
1921	Disaster in Morocco, at Annual.
1923	Primo de Rivera pronunciamiento.
1925	Joint Spanish and French operations regain initiative in Morocco. Primo de Rivera's Military Directory becomes civilian-military dictatorship.
1927	Moroccan rebellion finally quelled.
1930	Resignation of Primo de Rivera.
1931	Collapse of the monarchy. Second Republic proclaimed.
1932	Unsuccessful revolt by conservative military elements.
1934	Revolutionary outbreak in Asturias quelled by Army.
1936–39	Civil War.

The Institutional Weakness of Modern Spain

How DIFFICULT it is," wrote the Duke of Wellington, "to understand the Spaniards exactly." He later remarked, "Spain is the only country where two and two do not make four." The singularity of the Spanish temper, which disconcerted the Iron Duke, has puzzled historians as well. It is not easy, for example, to explain why a country that showed such energy, enterprise, and even organizational ability in the sixteenth century should in more recent times have found it almost impossible to achieve national unity and institutional cohesion. In the nineteenth century, Spain's institutional framework, which a hundred years earlier had shown its ability to survive economic and military collapse, broke down. Only then was the weakness of the national edifice revealed. Nearly all nineteenth-century Spanish political history is a record of the search for a viable structure of government.

Traditionally there were two significant institutions in Spanish life—the monarchy and the Church. For more than three hundred years after Ferdinand and Isabella, the Spanish remained devoutly monarchist; and the various reforms of the eighteenth century only helped to solidify royal strength. But during the reign of Charles IV (1788–1808), the advance of the Bourbon regime was halted. The incompetence of the king, the baneful influence of the queen, the unpopularity of an intelligent but overly ambitious favorite, opposition by aristocratic and provincial interest groups, political polarization encouraged by the French Revolution, a weak and disastrous foreign policy—all combined to shatter the apparent unity forged by enlightened despotism. The "two Spains" of the nineteenth century—one liberal and anticlerical, the other absolutist and clerical—took shape.

The year 1808 was a turning point in Spanish history, not merely because of the Napoleonic invasion, but also and more significantly because of the internal collapse of the Spanish monarchy, which was divided between king and heir, centralists and regional oligarchs. The political failure of Charles IV had more domestic than foreign causes. His deposition by the *fernandista* faction—highlighted by the first riot of the common people against the king in recent Spanish history— preceded the invasion, and prepared the way for it. National autonomy was regained by the War of Independence (1808–14), but the institutional unity that the monarchy had provided for three centuries could not be restored.

The religious decline was more gradual and at first less perceptible, but the generation of 1790–1815, which saw the questioning of traditional political values, also witnessed the encroachment of rationalistic thought upon the spiritual monopoly of the Church—at least among part of the small cultured class. In the 1830's came the economic assault of the upper and middle classes on Church lands, almost all of which were confiscated during the two decades that followed, as well as the first signs of radical lower-class resentment against the social and economic order. In the larger towns, this resentment found its most intense expression in vengeful hatred of the Church, which was accused by revolutionaries throughout the nineteenth century of spiritual prostitution.

The turmoil of nineteenth-century Spain was not, however, caused by rebellious liberal elements alone. The role of the traditionalist right, which accepted nothing that happened after 1808, was perhaps even more important, for the one mass movement during this period was not liberalism, Republicanism, or syndicalism, but reactionary peasant Carlism. No less than five civil wars, large and small, were precipitated by the intransigent traditionalists.

The pressures of Carlism and liberal rebellion were aggravated by the civic apathy of the bulk of the population, whether literate or not, and by the extraordinary persistence of regional loyalties, which excluded any nationalism in the modern sense of the word. The various regions of Spain—Catalonia, the Levant, the Basque country, even Galicia and Andalusia—had never been fully integrated in a political and administrative union. They had merely been federated under a common dynasty. When that authority faltered, the regionalism of the Middle Ages returned. During the War of Independence, the country as a whole reverted to its medieval structure, in which towns and provinces, separated from one another by military operations, sometimes operated as autonomous cantons. After the war, they remained disunited. Geographic factors were partly to blame for this, since Spain is divided by severe mountain ranges and veritable deserts, but more significant than geography was the lag in civic and economic development. The uneven pattern of industrial and commercial growth during the nineteenth century did not bring the regions closer together but drove them further apart, for the coastal areas enjoyed most of the prosperity.

Civic irresponsibility was not due to the absence of a middle class (for the middle strata of society in Spain were almost as large as those in Italy) but to the absence of vigor, determination, enterprise, and independence among its members. The Spanish middle classes were sunk in routine and apathy, more concerned with maintaining the status quo and avoiding responsibility than with winning an effective voice in government or creating new economic opportunities. The upper classes had no more social conscience, and frequently even less energy, whereas the peasants and workers were quick to learn from modern ideas and to demand more than society was giving them. From the sixteenth century onward, Spain has had a floating population of unemployed persons amounting to three or four per cent of the population, and in the nineteenth century this element capitalized on any opportunity for agitation.

These vertical and horizontal splits, caused by a combination of regional, ideological, economic, and social factors, gave rise to sixty years of kaleidoscopic politics. The struggle between various ideas and interests produced half a dozen civil wars, and as many different constitutions and types of government.* Ultimately, such divisions could be reconciled only by force. Out of this situation came a new arbiter for the country's affairs—the Army. It became a central factor in politics, not necessarily because the military were ambitious or greedy, but because Spanish political society had broken down.

In modern Western states, the military has customarily been charged with defending the country from foreign attack or interference and with maintaining internal security. This latter function, which receives subordinate emphasis in the contemporary Western constitutional system, was nevertheless a primary reason for the development of the hierarchically ordered and disciplined modern army, which, after it began to take shape in the late Middle Ages, was in practice used almost as much to cement the domestic foundations of

---

* A chronological chart of this confusion is provided on pp. xii–xiii.

the monarchist state as to fight foreign wars. In this process the early modern monarchist state managed to retain reasonably firm institutional control of its military forces.

Modern militarism, under which organized military forces strive to achieve independent ends and in turn influence or dominate other sectors of the state, first emerged during the French Revolution, encouraged by the appearance of new pressure groups that were unable to realize their goals by normal civic means. However, as the liberal forces in Western Europe increased in influence during the first half of the nineteenth century they vigorously reduced the role, influence, size, prestige, and financial resources of the military. On the other hand, in most of the larger European states—Russia, Prussia, and the Hapsburg Empire, for example—the military still played a major domestic role in maintaining governmental authority. If the role of the Army in Spanish affairs seems anomalous when Spain is compared with France, Britain, or the United States during the nineteenth century, it seems less so when one calls to mind the political and military realities of central and eastern Europe—though Spain differed from the eastern states in that the latter retained outwardly strong monarchical institutions which their military nominally served, whereas elements of the Spanish military felt called upon to supplement an inadequate government.

The history of the Spanish Army as a political institution spans one hundred and twenty-five years, from 1814 to 1939, reaching its climax in the Civil War of 1936–39 and the long *pax armata* of Francisco Franco that has followed. The prominence of the Army in public affairs was due not to the wisdom of its leaders or to the efficiency of its organization, but simply to the fact that it was an armed force capable, at least temporarily, of sustaining or repressing other factions. Yet the Army found it difficult to serve as a moderating power because of inherent deficiencies in education, discipline, and unity. Before we examine the role of the Spanish Army in politics, we must consider the Army's own institutional problems.

CHAPTER ONE

The Disarray of the Spanish Army

PRIOR TO THE War of Independence against Napoleon, the Spanish Army had no political complexion, and no political record other than that of complete obedience to the monarchy. Originally created by the Catholic Kings, it had remained invincible throughout the sixteenth century.[1] During Spain's Golden Age it had been technologically the most advanced military force in Europe, well-organized and comparatively well-disciplined save when pay was in arrears. A clear distinction had been drawn between the Army and the provincial police in the late fifteenth century, and consequently the Army was rarely involved in questions of domestic order. Military careers were much sought after by aristocrats and commoners alike.

However, the esteem enjoyed by the Army during the reigns of Charles V and Philip II dwindled with the energy and ambition of the Spanish people themselves. Even under Philip II, most of the "Spanish Army" in the Low Countries was composed of non-Spanish mercenaries. Only five of the thirty-one brigades (*Tercios*) created during the reign of Philip III were composed predominantly of Spaniards.[2] Seventeenth-century commentators speak of the efforts of the common people to avoid military service; and the English ambassador wrote in 1635: "The infantry [are] . . . unwilling to serve, as they are carried like galley slaves."[3] The practice of quartering troops on the civilian population became widespread, and led to violent hostility between townspeople and military units. More and more the Army was looked upon as a place for vagabonds and criminals, which honest subjects might somehow hope to avoid. Just as the mood of apathy and depression undermined national self-confidence, so the ruin of the economy and the decadence of the state corroded the effectiveness of Army organization. The classic structure of the Tercios did not survive the demise of the Hapsburgs at the close of the seventeenth century. During the eighteenth century the Spanish military lacked the authority and prestige that the armies of most other continental European countries enjoyed. After Philip V, no Spanish ruler of the eighteenth century was personally identified with the armed forces, and military careers no longer proved generally attractive.

The organization of the modern Spanish Army dates from the institutional reforms introduced by the ministers of the Bourbon dynasty in the latter part of the eighteenth century. The loose brigade structure was reorganized into the regimental and corps formation of the French Army of that period. Several new military academies were established, and the Officer Corps was set up on a regular, coordinated scale, with ranks from second lieutenant (*alférez*) to Captain General roughly corresponding to those in the French system. The district Captain Generals* represented the executive power of the Crown, and might exercise the ultimate civil as well as military authority in their districts, especially in those cases where they were appointed to the post of president of the provincial court.[4] The traditional *fuero militar,* or separate judicial jurisdiction of the military, was preserved, but the Army remained completely subordinate to royal authority. Political rebellion or insubordination was unheard of. During the reign of Charles III (1759–88) the recruitment system was reorganized in a way that was not fundamentally altered until 1936. Lists were made of the available young men in each district, and one-fifth of each year's total were selected by lot, causing the draft units to be known popularly as "fifths" (*quintas*). Numerous exemptions were granted, but the term of service for those selected was eight years. In some parts of the country this recruitment program was unpopular from the very beginning. There were riots against the quintas at Barcelona as early as 1773, and Navarre and the Basque provinces insisted that such a draft countermanded their treasured *fueros,* or regional privileges.[5]

In the eighteenth century the Army had no regular reserve, but a provincial militia system was set up in 1735. Those enrolled were to be trained three days a year by regular officers, with equipment provided by the Army administration and uniforms paid for by the provincial governments.[6] In addition, during the 1760's a total of 33 companies of urban militia were organized in the larger towns.

* Since the Middle Ages, Spain and its outlying districts had been divided into a series of territorial Captain Generalcies for purposes of defense and military administration. The district Captain General was an administrative appointee, and did not necessarily hold the regular rank of Captain General, the highest in the military hierarchy.

Spain thus made at least a partial comeback as a military power under Charles III, but the Army, like other public institutions, declined in effectiveness during the reign of Charles IV. The initial campaign of the Revolutionary Wars in Roussillon did not go badly for the Spanish, but subsequent efforts were disheartening.[7] After 1800, the Army absorbed approximately forty per cent of the Crown's annual expenditures, but equipment, organization, and training all deteriorated. Furthermore, the military hierarchy was disoriented by special promotions and favoritism.

The ten-year military alliance with France was unpopular, and the Napoleonic agreement of 1808, which placed Joseph Bonaparte, Napoleon's brother, on the throne of Spain, was infinitely more so, yet the military hierarchy was so accustomed to strict political subordination that it made no effort to oppose the French takeover. Two Artillery officers tried to organize a general military revolt to throw the French out, and helped lead the Madrid populace against the Imperial forces on May 2, 1808, but this was a spontaneous, popular rebellion that carried the conspirators along with it.[8] The main Army command, having little or nothing to do with anti-Napoleonic machinations, was taken by surprise, and did nothing to support the revolt.*

The War of Independence that began with the Madrid revolt was a people's war—the first modern guerrilla war—and the regular Army was completely caught up in its maelstrom. When the fighting began, there were only about 28,000 trained and fully equipped troops in the peninsula, but it was a portion of these, reinforced with provincial militia and new recruits, that defeated and captured General Dupont's corps at Bailén on July 19, 1808.[9] When massive French reinforcements poured in, Spanish military organization fell apart.†

The new Army that emerged several years later had been revolutionized by the struggle. In many parts of the country, resistance against the French was maintained primarily by local peasant bands who waged an irregular guerrilla war against the invaders. Some of these

---

* Since Spain lacked a regular government, and since the king had given no orders to combat the French, hundreds of officers never joined the patriotic struggle. When King José (Napoleon's brother) was forced to leave Madrid temporarily, he was accompanied by five Spanish generals. In 1813, according to French records, some 830 Spanish officers accompanied the Bonaparte government into exile. Vigón, *Cien años*, p. 163; Artola, *Los afrancesados*.

† Theoretically, the Spanish Army numbered 108,000 troops at this time—but this figure included thousands of troops in America, others in northern Europe, recruits in training, and a good many more who existed only on paper. See Vigón, *Historia*, II, 50, on military strength in 1808.

groups acted independently until the very end of hostilities, though they were nominally incorporated into the expanded Army organization, which on paper amounted to 226,354 men by 1811.[10] Most of the guerrilla leaders were self-made men, and some had risen from the common people. The rule that an officer must be of noble birth had never been fully observed, and the Cádiz Cortes of 1811 suppressed it altogether. What counted was energy, cunning, and force of leadership. Francisco Espoz y Mina, "the little king of Navarre," had been an independent peasant farmer. Juan Martín, "El Empecinado," a typical guerrilla leader, had been a peasant charcoal burner. Juan Díaz Porlier began the war as a young marine guard, and ended it as commander of the Seventh Corps of provincial troops. Pablo Morillo was promoted by successive stages from NCO to major general.

Neither during nor after the war were the various contingents and their commanders integrated into an effective modern Army. Wellington lamented with disgust: "In this army there is no general capable of commanding a corps or even of administering it; there is no General Staff nor supply and, worst of all, there is not even anyone ashamed of such things and capable of making the slightest effort to remedy them."[11] The restored absolutism of Fernando VII was unable to remedy this situation, for the government itself suffered from extreme administrative disorder. The keynote of military administration was supposedly economy, yet this was practiced with utter caprice. Favored regiments were luxuriously equipped, though other units were unable to leave their barracks for lack of shoes.

After the fighting ended in 1813, supernumerary troops were dismissed, but the disposition of the large number of wartime officers presented a thornier problem. From this time forward, the bloat in the Officer Corps was one of the Spanish Army's major organizational dilemmas.[12] Since most officers were comparatively young men, few could be encouraged to accept premature retirement in a sluggish society that offered little alternative employment. Budgetary decisions led to the suppression of many regiments; the remaining ones were cut from three to two battalions, and the number of officers per company was reduced from five to three. About 75 per cent of the officers—between 11,000 and 12,000—were left with no assignment at all. So many were attached as adjutants to the remaining regiments that it was said with scant exaggeration that certain units had as many officers as men. Amid this glut, prospects for promotion were almost nil. Moreover, many officers on active duty did not receive their full salaries, and some found that they could guarantee regular payment only by kicking back eight or ten per cent to the chief quartermasters or royal finance officials.[13]

The absolute monarchy proved incapable of prosecuting the war against the rebellious American colonies. By 1820 there were less than 60,000 troops in the peninsula, and even this number was too much for the treasury to maintain. Most officers showed little zest for a colonial campaign. The government offered promotion to the next rank for all volunteers, but this merely confirmed the suspicion of the majority that the American campaigns were extremely difficult and probably hopeless.

The political turmoils of 1820–23 completed the disorganization of the Army. An attempt by the constitutional regime in 1821 to reorganize the military was largely frustrated, and efforts to combat the French intervention of 1823 collapsed.* The drastic purge that was carried out by the second restoration of the absolute monarchy resulted in the virtual dissolution of the Army.

When the First Carlist War began in 1833, no more than 10,000 trained and equipped troops could be put into the field. This civil war between liberals and traditionalists dragged on for seven dreary, bloody years because neither side could develop an effective modern army. Napoleon had observed that though the Spanish were very warlike, they were not very military. Admittedly the Carlists were difficult antagonists, for their peasant bands in the northeast turned against the Spanish government the same guerrilla warfare that had wasted the French. An effort was eventually made to seal off their base in the Basque country, but the means employed were inadequate and Carlist columns ranged far and wide, threatening Madrid itself in 1837.[14] The final victory of government forces in 1840 was due largely to the effects of attrition.†

The Army was greatly expanded in size during the Carlist War, but it was commanded not so much by an officer corps as by a congeries

---

* New laws of 1821 temporarily imposed recruitment on all social classes in equal measure, dissolved the special regiments of foreign troops, and deprived the regional Captain Generals of their political functions. Critiques of this reform effort are given in *Reflexiones* and in Andrés, pp. 22–29. The constitutional government tried vainly to build up its forces with volunteers, but only 7,000 stepped forward in 1822. Before the invasion, some 80,000 "reservists" were mobilized on paper, but many never actually served. See Vidart, *La fuerza armada*, p. 31.

† According to Fernández San Román, *Statistique*, pp. 290–92, total fatalities in the regular Army from 1833 to 1840, including those who died of wounds and illness, numbered about 64,250. The Carlist losses were possibly only half as great, but it would appear that altogether the war cost the lives of approximately 100,000 Spaniards.

of petty cliques and groups whose interests, efficiency, and loyalties varied greatly. Rapid promotion of large numbers of officers from obscure stations, sudden expansion of old units or the swift creation of new ones, battle casualties, the near-impotence of government, lack of cadres for administration or supply, interference or importuning by politicians—these factors made it extremely difficult for a sense of unity, institutional solidarity, or even common discipline to develop. Among the officers of certain units there might be firm adherence to an outstanding general; among others, at least a limited sense of professional identity. But the leaders of many sections shared little more than confusion and resentment.

The aftermath of the First Carlist War left the Army as disorganized as it had been after 1814. At the beginning of 1840 there were, theoretically, 11,300 officers and 209,000 men—a much healthier ratio than in earlier years. But after peace arrived, recruits were dismissed en masse while most officers were retained. By 1843, the number of troops under arms had fallen to little more than 50,000, but there were at least 9,000 officers nominally on active duty.[15] That meant one officer to every five or six men—the most grotesque disproportion in any European armed force at that time.

After the Moderates took over the government in 1843, some effort was made to tighten up the Army, but the esprit de corps and organization necessary to an efficient military machine were so lacking that only a genuine revolution could have knit the Army together—and the Moderates were anything but revolutionaries. Any serious attempt to change the situation met strong opposition from entrenched and conflicting interests.

The basic organizational code, insofar as it was effective, was still the one promulgated in 1768 by Charles III.[16] Territorial assignment of forces was often arranged not in terms of logical use of military strength or strategic distribution but simply to satisfy political pressures from different parts of the country. No existing garrison town could be deprived of its garrison, for the ensuing loss of business or prestige would be likely to create a local political storm. The twelve administrative Captain Generals had almost complete control over supply and training in their areas. To move recruits from one district to another required an official order from the Minister of War himself. The General Staff, organized as a separate Corps and limited to matters of routine and theory, exercised no supervision over the other sections of the Army.[17] Each of the separate Corps—Infantry, Cavalry, Artillery, Engineers, Supply—had its own Director General, who frequently could not or would not cooperate with his fellows. A leading general lamented in later years:

Since the military family doesn't exist in Spain, the fraternity that ought to unite the various Corps of the Army is unknown, and consequently they do not lend each other the indispensable support that ought to be given. . . . In the facultative Corps [Artillery and Engineers] . . . there exists an antiquated and harmful preoccupation with maintaining their own particular rules—of which there are a disgracefully large number—at lance-point, in defiance of the other Corps. . . . But the most serious problem . . . is that the Ministers [of the Army and Navy] do not represent the nation, but rather the interests of their respective Corps, and that they make common cause with their subordinates out of . . . form and loyalty . . . even when they are convinced that the subordinates are in error![18]

Limited improvements were made by Narváez and other Moderates in the 1840's. The budget and some aspects of military administration were centralized in Madrid. Though the Army's share of government expenditures, which had averaged 37 per cent during the years 1840–43, was reduced to an average of 28 per cent during the years 1844–49, more funds were actually available because of increased efficiency in accounting and administration.[19] The largest single item in the budget was officers' salaries. Even by present-day Spanish standards, these officers were not ill-paid,[20] and troops serving in the overseas garrisons drew from 250 to 350 per cent more than those stationed in the peninsula.[21] On the other hand, retirement income was too low at most ranks to live on, and during the periods of intermittent personnel contraction officers were frequently placed on the inactive list at half pay. Ultimately, the resentment aroused by this treatment found expression in political rebellion. Too little money was budgeted for equipment and training expenses. Spain lacked the industry to equip a modern army itself, and there were never sufficient funds to purchase abroad all the matériel needed, so that the technological gap between the Spanish Army and other Western European forces continued to widen.[22]

During the middle decades of the nineteenth century the Army numbered slightly less than a hundred thousand men.[23] This force was backed up by a theoretical reserve of two hundred and fifty thousand— the number of Spaniards of reasonably active age who had previously served in the Army.[24] The most positive single reform to eliminate waste would have been a drastic reduction in the size of the Officer Corps. Limited efforts were made in the mid-1840's, in 1851, and in

1863 to encourage earlier officer retirement, but they accomplished little. A royal order of February 1, 1866, directed that a proportion of vacancies be left unfilled until the total number of Infantry officers had been reduced by 2,055.[25] Changes of government prevented this order from being carried out, and General Narváez stated during his last ministry in 1867 that there were still at least 1,350 superfluous officers on the active list of the Infantry Corps alone.[26]

Special influence and favoritism were rampant, and created much discontent. After tendering his resignation as Minister of War in 1865, Lt. Gen. Fernández de Córdova wrote:

It was necessary to abolish favoritism, which had always caused great havoc in the service, and which, if it continued to dominate, would ruin whatever was done to improve the Army's situation and to raise the spirit of the officers. I therefore found myself extremely embarrassed, from the first days of our rise to power, because of the great barrage of recommendations and demands made by the most important personages of our country, who asked not only for constant changes in assignment to improve the situations of friends and relatives but also for promotions, decorations, and the most important posts, without the slightest indication of what merit or service could support the pretensions of such favorites. How is it possible to please politicians and other leading personalities without completely disgusting the bulk of the Army? "My dear friend," a Cabinet minister wrote to me one day in a private letter, "permit me to insist on my recommendation of Don N. N., since it is a matter of great importance in the electoral results of my district. If the legal restrictions on your Ministry do not allow you to promote him to captain, I pray you to give him something, in order that his family may have some indication of the good intentions of the candidate, which are none other than my own." It is clear that if one responded to this kind of pressure it would not be possible even to think of reorganization of the Army.[27]

Narváez had put his own concern succinctly in 1862: "The Army is the only thing that worries me—it is contaminated to the core."[28]

During the nineteenth century the Spanish Army was used almost exclusively to quell disturbances and to maintain domestic order. Almost all its fighting was done trying to repress the civil wars of 1821–23, 1826–27, 1833–40, 1846–49, and 1869–76, and the various Cuban rebellions, the most serious of which were those of 1868–78 and 1895–98. There were a few minor expeditionary efforts, such as temporary intervention in Portugal on behalf of the liberal monarchy in 1834 and 1847, the transfer of a detachment to Rome in support of the Pope in 1849, participation in the French expedition to Cochin China during 1859–63, and the unsuccessful repression attending the "reannexation" of Santo Domingo from 1861 to 1865.[29] However, between 1814 and 1898 the only military activity of any significance against a foreign power was the brief but successful Moroccan War of 1859–60, which provided perhaps the only genuine laurels won by the Army during the nineteenth century.[30]

The importance of the military in settling political and constitutional disputes, and the resulting development of political interests by many leading commanders, made it easy for some officers to overlook the Army's own institutional chaos and military weakness. By the middle of the century the idea was sometimes advanced that amid civic disunity the Army was the only truly national institution. As one military journal put it in 1852, "The Army can and should be the regenerator of our society."[31] The particular interests of various segments of the Army with regard to national policy were represented in the period from 1835 to 1882 by no less than thirty-four military newspapers. These were not official Army publications, but were put out by small groups associated with various branches of the Army. The effect of these ephemeral journals seems to have been negative, for they merely served to divide the Army further and to distract the attention of the officers from their primary responsibilities.[32] In any event, the Army could not lead and regenerate Spanish society—even if that were desirable—until it had unified and regenerated itself.

CHAPTER TWO

The Era of Pronunciamientos, 1814–68

D URING the nineteenth century, portions of the Army were used to accomplish almost every major institutional change in Spain. Absolute monarchy was restored at the invitation of the military hierarchy in 1814, but a series of minor, abortive rebellions against absolutism during the next five years led to the first successful liberal revolt in 1820. After French intervention helped restore absolute monarchy in 1823, the only serious efforts to reimpose constitutionalism during the following decade were the military-inspired rebellions in 1830 and 1831. When the succession to the throne was disputed in 1833, the great bulk of the Army rallied round the main branch of the dynasty and ultimately defeated the Carlist reactionaries in a seven-year civil struggle (the First Carlist War, 1833–40). During this conflict, military pressure helped gain a minimal guarantee of constitutional government in 1834, and a revolt in 1836 restored the original 1812 constitution. Under the three-year government of the Progressive caudillo General Baldomero Espartero (1840–43), the liberal forces seemed to achieve their maximum power. After the more conservative sectors of the Army had established the rule of the Moderate oligarchy in 1843, a dozen efforts were made by other military leaders during the next quarter of the century to reverse that decision. The two-year interlude of Progressive government, 1854–56, was sparked by an Army revolt, and the military led the rebellion of 1868 that overthrew the Bourbon dynasty.

Military intervention took several different forms. In general, such gestures were called *pronunciamientos,* or "pronouncements," after a term first used by Major Rafael de Riego in a speech to his troops on January 3, 1820, before he led them away in rebellion. The pronunciamiento was sometimes oblique and indirect, consisting of no more than strong statements, encouragements, or threats by powerful generals intended to influence the government's policy. However, the most spectacular and important pronunciamientos were those that involved some form of force. Ordinarily, the armed pronunciamiento was a revolt by one section of the Army—sometimes a very small section—which raised the flag of rebellion in its district and hoped that its example would lead other units to rally round, or would at least break the government's nerve. The pronunciamiento might take the form of a barracks revolt, or *cuartelazo,* in which the insurgent forces would simply hole up and await events. On the other occasions rebel units took to the road in order to maneuver, do battle, or draw other forces to their side. A less frequent form of the pronunciamiento was the classic coup d'état.[1]

That the institution which sustains a monopoly on force and organized violence should assume the lead in a disordered land is not in itself surprising, but the generally "liberal" orientation of the Spanish military during much of the nineteenth century merits further attention. A variety of factors may have been responsible: the misery and disorganization of the Army itself, which often was blamed on the ruling clique; political ideals held by the most energetic, imaginative, or altruistic, who sometimes supported progressivism for patriotic reasons; ambition, which could see political progressivism as more likely to offer careers to the talented; the insistent pressures of civilian politicians; the widespread influence of Masonry, at least in the first decades of the century; the unprivileged social background of most of the officers;* and the sometimes demagogic appeal of popular or lower-class interests among the NCO's—though these occasionally led to mutinies which in turn provoked a sharp reaction toward conservatism among the officers.

Conversely, if a significant minority of military activists directly supported political liberalism, there was an equally determined minority opposing this trend, or at least its fullest expression. Most commanders were naturally anxious to maintain discipline and hierarchy, the principles upon which military institutions are founded. There was a tendency for some Army officers to carry such attitudes over into civic affairs as well. Moreover, there existed the obligation of the armed forces to guarantee the security of the state—a fundamentally

---

* After 1814 the absolutist regime attempted to restore the requirement of noble birth for entrance into the Officer Corps, but even under Don Fernando this was never fully observed. The requirement was ended once and for all in 1835. Otero, *La nobleza*; Comisión Oficial de Heráldica, *Estatuto nobiliario*, pp. 369–414.

conservative task taken seriously by the majority of Spanish officers. There was also the concern of the senior commanding hierarchy to preserve and promote its own authority against threats from below or from without—a factor which in some cases aided liberal causes, but in the long run helped to hold the conservative line. In addition, either by temperament or by conviction a small minority of officers had reactionary principles. A very important factor in the ultimate rejection of the more democratic causes by many military men was the formation of volunteer civilian units that attempted to preempt the regular Army's role in moments of political flux. Furthermore, the political complexion of the Spanish Army has usually depended upon a comparatively small minority of activists. Even during the most chaotic years of the nineteenth century, most officers made no effort to intervene in politics, but simply obeyed the orders of their commanders, like officers in any army. In general, it can be said that the bulk of the Officer Corps eventually became champions of conservative order in reaction to the excesses or failures of political progressivism.

A significant minority of officers espoused constitutionalism during the War of Independence. There were no less than 66 Army and Navy officers among the liberal deputies at the Cádiz Cortes of 1811–12.[2] However, Spain's first modern elective assembly was on its guard lest members of the senior military hierarchy attempt to impose a military dictatorship in the king's absence. Several of the most powerful generals had been appointed to the Regency Council that governed before the elective Cortes met, and others, such as the Captain General of New Castile, had felt that a general or a committee of generals—perhaps the district commanders—should direct affairs, so that order and continuity might be ensured. Therefore, the Cádiz Cortes tried to freeze wartime promotions, and favored the new guerrilla chiefs and the younger officers above the senior professionals.

Most of the professionals responded with scornful hostility toward both the 1812 constitution and the irregulars who had been incorporated into the Army.* By the time the French had been driven from the country, much of the population hoped to reestablish the old

---

* General Castaños, the victor of Bailén, wrote to General Murillo of the *guerrilleros* as "a caste of bandits who are devastating the country." Gómez de Arteche, an Army officer and the leading Spanish military historian of the War of Independence, wrote: "The guerrillero is the faithful, unmistakable image of Iberian personalism, revealing its sinister face among our family dissensions and advancing to spread farther and farther the flame of disorder and the fear of its dreadful activity." Quoted in Vigón, *Milicia y política*, p. 255.

order, which was identified with the popular authority of the king. When the returning monarch, Don Fernando, reached Valencia on April 15, 1814, the Captain General of that district, Francisco Javier Elío, officially handed him the baton of command, contrary to the instructions of the Cortes.[3] Encouraged and supported by the senior Army hierarchy, the king dropped his pretenses, and on May 4 declared the constitution null and void. In Madrid, General Eguía (commonly known as "Pigtail," since he insisted on wearing his hair in the pre-revolutionary style) closed down the Cortes.[4]

The military hierarchy made certain that its loyalty to the king was fully noticed. After returning absolute authority to Don Fernando, Elío stressed the importance of the "well-deserving" military: "After having abundantly watered with their blood the soil they have liberated, [they] see themselves neglected, in want, and, even worse, insulted [by the Cortes], but are confident that you, my lord, will do them justice."[5] Don Fernando restored the authority of the senior hierarchy and promoted those officers most zealous on his behalf. Elío was given the rank of lieutenant general and Eguía soon became Minister of War in the first of a long series of special promotions that followed successful pronunciamientos.[6] In addition, the monarchy set up a number of military commissions, directed by senior "ultra" officers, to investigate and root out liberals.

In 1814, most Army officers, like most Spaniards, had no precise political convictions. Most of the military leaders had greeted the king's return with enthusiasm, and even some of the younger, more popular officers from the lower classes had been among the anticonstitutionalists. Only a few months were needed, however, to show that ex-guerrilla chiefs were viewed by the court circle as upstarts. The older generals had no desire to give permanent senior rank to men who lacked regular professional credentials. Having virtually held the power of life and death in their districts for years, these young commanders would inevitably feel snubbed.

Resentment spread not merely among ex-guerrilla chiefs but also within the most aristocratic section of the Army, the Artillery Corps. The Artillery zealously guarded its class origins for years after other sections filled up with middle- and lower-class officers; and in 1814–15 it received so many special attentions from the king that at least one senior general protested. However, Fernando's favor soon took the form of meddling with the Corps' command hierarchy. This and other aspects of his capricious absolutism were deemed intolerable by the aristocratic Artillerists, who wanted to control their own affairs. They showed their disdain by pointedly refusing to attend official functions and by abstaining from other court activities whenever possible.[7]

Lack of recognition from the king encouraged young firebrands to identify their interests with those of civilian liberals, repression of whom was ordinarily in the hands of the older officers. In the late summer of 1814 the popular guerrilla leader Juan Martín, "El Empecinado" (the Incorrigible), presented a memorandum to the king requesting him to grant the liberties he had promised when he first set foot in Spain, as well as to declare a general amnesty for the liberals.[8] Don Fernando did not deign to reply.

The most outstanding of the guerrilla chiefs was Francisco Espoz y Mina. He was one of the few men sufficiently talented to fill the responsibilities of regular Army command, and he expected a prominent assignment from the king. Instead, he was deprived of his own division and sent back to Pamplona as a mere brigadier. This, together with the insults he said had been flung at him by Don Fernando's entourage, was too much. He launched the first attempted military revolt near Pamplona in September 1814. Though Mina had not previously been known for his political convictions, his frustrated rebellion became associated with an appeal for restoration of the 1812 constitution.[9] The other pro-liberal revolts of the years 1815–19 were also led by young generals who had earned rapid promotions during the war but afterward had come to hold personal and professional grievances against the government.[10]

An important factor that encouraged political liberalism and subsequent revolt among Spanish officers during these years was the rise of Masonic lodges. Masonry apparently came to Spain from France and Britain. Its fraternal and idealistic spirit appealed to young officers, as did its secret organization. In 1814 no less than 4,000 Spanish officers emerged from captivity in France, and a significant number of them had been initiated into the lodges while under internment. Proselytization was especially directed toward the younger officers. This increased the sense of division between the younger and older generations, which was so strong that some of the younger men referred to older generals as *civiles*, asserting that only the more active merited the title of *militares*. During the first years of Don Fernando's reign, Masonic affiliation was most common in the Andalusian garrisons, where the lodges took on some of the functions of a trade union or mutual-aid society. Politically, these lodges were on the side of liberalism.[11]

It has recently been estimated that there were between 1,500 and 2,000 Masons in the Spanish Officer Corps during these years. This was little more than 15 per cent of all Spanish officers, but it was from such elements that most of the rebels of the years 1817–20 were drawn. In 1824 a purge list of all known Masons was compiled. It named about 2,000 men, half of them officers of senior rank. A later list bore the names of approximately 1,300 officers holding the rank of captain or above.[12] Since there was no regular investigative procedure, such statistics cannot be substantiated, but for the most part they are borne out by other evidence.

More important than the secret societies was the general neglect the Army suffered under Don Fernando. By the fall of 1819, between 15,000 and 20,000 troops were crowded together in unhealthy, primitive camps near Cádiz, waiting to be shipped to South America. Without proper shelter, supplies, or sanitary facilities, decimated by infectious disease and lacking any desire to fight Venezuelans or Colombians, many of the officers and men found it easy to believe that their predicament was somehow caused by the whims of absolutism. The pronunciamientos of 1814–18 had been no more than romantic gestures by individual commanders, lacking support from civilians and military subordinates, but Major Rafael de Riego now found a receptive audience among the unpaid expeditionary corps when he and a few confederates launched their rebellion in the first days of 1820. Though almost all of Riego's troops deserted during the slow, meandering march to the north, several other provincial garrisons eventually announced their support. Don Fernando finally capitulated and restored the constitution—not so much because of the force of the revolt as because of the weakness of his own government.[13]

In 1820 most of the Army did not rebel; it simply accepted the collapse of an incoherent absolutist regime. During the next two years all the military, except for some of the most conservative senior generals, served the new liberal regime faithfully and helped suppress the armed rebellion of provincial traditionalists.[14] Contrary to opinion at the time, the revolt of the Royal Guards in July 1822 was apparently not aimed at the restoration of absolutism, but instead was a forlorn attempt by one of the more conservative sectors of the armed forces to install a moderate government that would prevent the radicals from seizing power.[15] Although the Army never turned against the constitutional regime, the disorders of 1822–23 sapped its morale, and when the French intervened on the side of the absolutists, most of the mili-

tary made only a token effort to resist the reaction. The debility of
the Spanish Army in 1823 was at least as much the consequence of
weak and divided government as it was of faulty military leadership.
The effects of Army intrigue at this time were not so damaging in
Spain as they were in Peru, where dissidence among young liberal
generals undermined both the authority of the Viceroy and what remained of Spanish military power in South America.[16]

Since military leaders had ushered in the brief constitutional regime, the reaction of 1823 all but dissolved the Army organization.[17]
Encouraged by the French, provincial traditionalists formed a peasant
militia called the Royal Volunteers. The Volunteers cost almost nothing to maintain: the organization was thoroughly decentralized, the
men provided many of their own needs during brief periods of drill,
and extra expenses were met by local subscription. Because of their
zeal, officers of the Volunteers were sometimes placed at the head of
purge commissions charged with rooting out liberals and regular officers of questionable political allegiance.[18] Yet after a year or two, the
king and his advisers came to realize that an autonomous provincial
militia of this sort was less trustworthy than a centrally organized army.
The peasants who made up the Volunteers were mainly interested in
defending their native provinces, which meant more to them than the
central government did. Together with their leaders from the gentry
class, they were in some ways more reactionary than the king. They opposed centralized control, whether by a middle-class constitutionalist
oligarchy or by the bureaucrats of royalist despotism. Some of their
leaders talked of reestablishing a corporative, medieval-style Cortes,
and some demanded the return of the Inquisition. This ran counter
to the notions of Don Fernando, who began to perceive that an authoritarian monarchy could not be secure without the support of a regular, disciplined army that could hold in check all popular pressures,
whether liberal or reactionary.

Almost all the professional officers resented the creation of the
Royal Volunteers. Even liberal commanders returning from the American campaigns were more than willing to serve absolutism so long as
the king would rely on the Army rather than on the traditionalist
peasant militia. The first effort by the Minister of War to bring the
Royal Volunteers under Army control was foiled in 1825, but soon
after that the purge commissions were dissolved and the Infantry
Corps reconstituted.[19] Until Don Fernando's death in 1833, the remaining cadre of professional officers was the principal support of

absolute monarchy in Spain, checking efforts to overthrow the regime from both the left and the right.[20]

During the First Carlist War (1833–40), another civilian militia force emerged at the opposite end of the political spectrum, when the weak regency permitted the pro-liberal "Urban Militia" to be organized. The Militia was authorized only in towns of more than 300 people, and was not to exceed one per cent of the population of any district. The original decree of 1834 stated that every member must be at least 21 years old, and employed or the owner of property.[21] Under the pressure of civil conflict and Progressive influence, these qualifications were not always observed. The ultra-liberal militia forces of the southern and eastern cities became a constant source of disturbance, often leading riots and sometimes even assassinating district Army commanders.

So long as the struggle to establish the regency for Isabel II continued, the territorial Captain Generals and other leading commanders were more important in politics and administration than they might otherwise have been. Since a more liberal political orientation made it easier to deal with civilian politicians, a number of apolitical, professional military men transformed themselves into "liberal generals." Strong letters from two formerly conservative senior commanders advising slight concessions to constitutionalism were influential in preparing the way for the Charter of 1834.[22] This charter was highly circumscribed in nature, and small military cliques were encouraged by radical politicians to press for greater liberalization. This led to the abortive revolt by Captain Cardero in January 1835, during which the Captain General of New Castile was killed by the rebels; and to the mutiny of noncommissioned officers at the summer palace of La Granja in August 1836, which forced the queen regent to restore the Constitution of 1812.[23]

During the later years of the First Carlist War, both Moderate and Progressive politicians devoted a great deal of energy to attracting leading generals to their cause. Normal political life was nearly impossible, and little could be accomplished by civil means; the support of a leading general and his troops was much more meaningful. Sometimes both factions bargained for the aid of the same figure, as in the cases of Espartero and Narváez. The Ministry of War became a political football that constantly changed hands.[24] During 1837 discipline was near complete collapse: there were many riots among the troops, and several generals were assassinated. In August of that year conservative officers attempted an abortive pronunciamiento to restore the Moderates to power.[25] General Baldomero Espartero, commander of the main field army and also Minister of War for a brief period, restored discipline with an iron hand, and eventually led the Army to victory against the Carlists in 1839–40. Though he himself espoused the cause of the Progressives, he ended the conflict in the Basque country by a compromise peace—the 1839 "Abrazo de Vergara," which pledged noninterference with Basque privileges and offered commissions in the regular Army to all Carlist officers who desired them.[26]

By 1840 Espartero had become the arbiter of Spanish affairs. Supported by most of the Army and by the Ayacuchos, a group of pro-liberal companions from the South American campaigns, he ended factional strife by forcing the queen regent into exile and taking charge of the government himself. A newly chosen Progressive assembly elected Espartero regent in the spring of 1841. There is little question of Espartero's personal devotion to the liberal ideal, but he possessed virtually no political talent or understanding. He was the product of a period of civil war and national chaos, and had little or nothing to contribute to the creation of viable new institutions. His rule was personal, capricious, and authoritarian. A rebellion by conservative officers in October 1841 narrowly missed success, and Espartero was determined that the only one of its leaders to be captured, the romantic and respected cavalry general Diego de León, should be condemned to death. The dilemma of military authority in politics was well expressed by General Grasés, one of the minority who recommended clemency, when he lamented: "If León is to die for having rebelled, by what justice are we not to hang ourselves with our own sashes?"[27]

One of Espartero's major problems was to reduce the Army and its budget to size. Several thousand officers had to be let go after the war ended, and were pensioned off at a fifth of their regular salary. Lacking careers or alternative employment, some were even reduced to begging in the streets. It is easy to see why these ex-officers were attracted by the anti-Espartero conspiracies of Moderate politicians. Progressives, to guarantee the support of the troops still under arms, actively proselytized among the noncommissioned officers, to the disgust of the regular hierarchy. Within two years, over a thousand officers had resigned in protest.[28] With each passing month, Espartero's government became more narrowly restricted to his Ayacucho clique, as the regent lost touch not merely with civilian opinion but with the military as well. By 1843, even the Progressives were turning against him.[29]

Espartero was overthrown by a new pronunciamiento in 1843 that temporarily united most elements of the military and political oligarchy of Spain. It was led by General Ramón María Narváez, who proved to be the mainstay of the Isabeline monarchy for the next quarter of a century. The short, dark, nervous Narváez, a liberal in his youth, had been purged in 1823 and ostracized from the Army for ten years, until the beginning of the First Carlist War. Throughout his life he considered himself a liberal, but in fact he became the outstanding example of the sort of nineteenth-century Spanish general who bitterly opposed Carlism yet distrusted representative government and feared popular disorder. Such men were fundamentally pessimistic about the feasibility of civil liberty and suffrage in a land that lacked creative minorities, a tradition of self-government, economic interests consonant with constitutional liberalism, literate masses, and civic education.

Narváez had come to the fore during the middle years of the Carlist War, and was identified with the Moderates, who opposed regionalism, absolutism, and clericalism, and believed in political centralization and a limited constitutional system that restricted power to a small oligarchy of the wealthy and educated. Support among the Army grew slowly from 1836 until 1843, but the riots and mutinies of 1836–37, and the forced sale of Church land, helped array many professional officers against the ultra-liberals, as did such incidents as the fate of the rigorous General Quesada. Forced out of his post as Captain General of New Castile by the Progressives in 1836, Quesada was captured and murdered by radicals, who cut off one of his hands and used it to stir the punch bowl in the cafe they frequented.[30] Narváez's opposition to the Progressives had forced him into exile by 1838,[31] but in France he worked tirelessly for the overthrow of Espartero, and helped to organize a secret society called the "Orden Militar Española," which used oaths and ceremonies similar to those of the Masons in order to win the attention and allegiance of officers at home and abroad in opposition to the Progressives.[32] After establishing his leadership over the successful military rebels of 1843, he became for a time the arbiter of Spanish politics.

Narváez first served as Prime Minister in 1844–45, and played a significant role in the formulation of the 1845 Moderate Constitution, which limited suffrage to a tiny oligarchy and permitted only minimal civil liberties (though with considerable latitude for the press). It also set up an appointive Senate, in which a number of recently promoted pro-Moderate lieutenant generals received lifetime seats: thus the veto power of the Army was guaranteed, and the military interests represented. This semi-authoritarian framework, in which the government was responsible to the queen rather than to the Cortes, stood until the dynasty was overthrown in 1868.

Narváez could not brook opposition, and obviously lacked the temperament of a constitutionalist. He has been credited with saying, "I do not think that all men with advanced ideas are rogues [*pillos*], but I do think that all rogues have advanced ideas, just as half of those who do not have advanced ideas are rogues anyway."[33] Newspaper criticism always infuriated him. On May 5, 1845, the Madrid daily *El Espectador* published a caricature of him brandishing two huge pistols, with a sword and another pistol stuck in his belt. A satirical poem accompanied the sketch. Narváez wrote in high dudgeon to the capital's Captain General: "It is not enough to pick up the copies of the newspapers—you have to kill the newspapermen."[34]

Narváez and his colleagues repressed minor rebellions in 1843,[35] 1846, and 1848, as well as a long-smoldering peasant revolt in the northeast from 1846 to 1849 that is often called the "Second Carlist War" and several minor disturbances not worth naming.[36] However, to maintain civil order, more than mere military discipline was needed. The First Carlist War had revealed that there was violent dissatisfaction among some of the northern peasants, and the landless Andalusian rural proletariat was sinking deeper into misery as its population expanded and the extent of latifundia increased. To suppress jacqueries and riots, Narváez created in 1844 the classic institution of public order in modern Spain, the Civil Guard. It began as a special rural police force whose regulations were modeled on those of the French gendarmerie and whose duties were to eliminate the banditry so widespread in the south, to protect property, and to maintain order. Its members were much better paid than ordinary soldiers, and its officers were usually drawn from among the most iron-fisted military men—a former Carlist general, José Antonio Zariátegui, was one of the first directors.[37]

Narváez's only plan was to maintain order: he lacked the understanding and imagination to grasp the wider problems in Spanish affairs and to propose creative solutions. Unlike General Espartero, who on certain occasions was hailed by mammoth crowds in the larger towns, he was never a popular figure. Scorning all the "lawyers," as he called civilian politicians, Narváez never developed any sort of organized following. Jaime Balmes, the leading Catholic thinker of mid-nineteenth-century Spain, observed: "What frustrates his work is principally his lack of political thought. From this proceeds his fluctuation between absolutist and liberal tendencies. Thus we see him today trying to act like a parliamentarian and tomorrow, saber in hand, menacing the parliament. His instincts, his ideas, his sentiments, and his interests are in perpetual conflict."[38] In the long run, Narváez proved to be an administrative rather than a political success.[39]

Yet it should be emphasized that neither Narváez nor any other political general of the reign of Isabel II tried to govern as a military dictator. There was no such thing as an "Army" position in politics or an "Army government," at least before 1874. Rather, individual political generals dominated the government by force of will and personality, as well as by the hint of potential military intervention that always lingers behind a powerful general. That individual generals, or a small clique of them, could be so influential was due to the disunity of the Moderate politicians. Had the civilian oligarchy been a coherent force that developed strong leaders, Narváez and his peers would not have been needed. Indeed, generals who became prime ministers were overthrown with little difficulty whenever a civilian faction developed enough unity and determination of its own to gain the ear of the queen. The average life of the seven Narváez cabinets between 1844 and 1867 was only a little over a year each, and, with one notable exception (the second O'Donnell ministry), the same was true of the other governments in which a general was prime minister.

The strongest-minded civilian prime minister during the reign of Isabel II was Antonio Bravo Murillo, who took office in 1851. He was determined not only to subordinate the military but also to establish a more authoritarian constitution, and thus create such tight political control that the support of political generals would be unnecessary. He is said to have remarked in 1852: "If the reform is approved and I continue to enjoy the confidence of the Crown, I shall demonstrate to the Spanish people that with no emblem other than this frock coat I can see to it that the generals are hanged with their own sashes."[40]

The openly authoritarian designs of Bravo Murillo's group and its heavy-handed efforts to impose its will on the lieutenant generals brought strong opposition from nearly all Army leaders, including Narváez.* Bravo Murillo was defeated and turned out of office, but the *polacos,* as the narrow faction of right-wing Moderates was popularly called, made the capital mistake of continuing to work against the interests of the leading political generals and of arousing strong resentment in those with pro-constitutional principles. Even Narváez opposed clerical reactionaries. When both ambition and idealism were appealed to, the military usually reacted.

The leader who arose to right the balance in 1854 was Lt. Gen. Leopoldo O'Donnell, the subtlest politician of all the military figures of those years. In planning the pronunciamiento of 1854, his goal seems to have been to broaden the base of oligarchy just enough to restore a degree of compromise that would enable the country to live under the constitution of 1845. Subsequently one of his chief associates, Lt. Gen. Domingo Dulce, wrote this justification for military rebellion *in extremis*:

The Army is the name of a group of armed men, ruled by special statutes, which has the sole and exclusive duty of maintaining the laws in their most complete state of integrity.

Now this definition, as logical as it is philosophical, demonstrates that the armed forces are the strong arm of the law.

Some say, with Ciceronian aplomb, that the Army ought not to think, or to be enlightened, and should limit itself to obeying the government blindly. This is an elastic, high-flown saying of colossal dimensions, behind which are hidden the immoral, the cowardly, and the treacherous. Treacherous, because they betray the law, which is more than the government because it was created before the latter and gives it life and action; immoral, because they sacrifice their dearest affections and most sacred duties to the shameful preservation of a miserable career; and cowardly, because they lack the courage to cast in the faces of corrupt governments the anathema of active resistance with which a man of spirit responds to abuses of power. . . .

When a government, whatever its name may be, ignores the laws whose conservation is entrusted to it—laws which oblige the government's own obedience before that of others—when it violates and tramples them, has it

---

* Bravo Murillo broke the unwritten rule that only a lieutenant general could become Minister of War by appointing Major General Lersundi, an ex-Carlist and one of the Army's most reactionary commanders, who had led the suppression of the 1848 revolt. The ensuing squabble over jurisdiction led to the resignation of the Director General of Infantry, Leopoldo O'Donnell, and the Captain General of New Castile, Juan de la Pezuela, two of the most powerful Moderate lieutenant generals, and helped turn the political balance against the government.

not broken both in theory and in fact the bonds that unite it with the rest of the society of which it formed a part? . . .

When one proceeds by degrees from supplication to energetic opposition by the elected representatives of the people and the Crown, without obtaining any result, what resource is left to a great people whose most sacred rights are oppressed, vilified, and insulted? War marches in the rear guard of the reasoned discussions of diplomacy. . . .

Can a government under representative institutions claim the right to ignore the law, but demand its rigorous observance by the people . . . ? If we admit such mournful principles, soon, very soon, we will have nothing but an absolute system, because the Army will be reduced to the simple condition of a machine of force, mobile at the will of the government, and the consequences of this are easy to foresee.[41]

Such appeals against injustice have always been the customary rationale for military rebellion.

The pronunciamiento by Army dissidents in July 1854 was very nearly a failure. Rebel units marched out of Madrid in the early morning hours, fought an inconclusive skirmish with loyal troops some miles east of the capital, then were forced to retreat south, calling on other Army comrades and patriotic Spaniards to rally to their support. The government was toppled, not by the Army, but by a popular insurrection of Progressive forces in Madrid and several other large cities.[42] Though the rising of the urban lower and lower-middle classes saved the pronunciamiento, its effects were greater than O'Donnell had foreseen. Espartero was recalled from retirement to serve as Progressive prime minister, and a new Progressive Cortes was elected, which drafted a more liberal constitution. The Urban Militia, dissolved by Narváez a decade earlier, but reorganized now as the sword and buckler of Progressive government, found itself in sharp competition with the regular Army leadership.

Within two years these forces came to the parting of the ways. An armed clash between the Army and the Militia in Madrid in 1856 brought the defeat of the latter, and enabled O'Donnell to succeed Espartero as Prime Minister, dissolve the Militia outright, abrogate the new constitution, and restore the one of 1845.[43] O'Donnell's first government lasted scarcely a year, but after a brief Narváez ministry, he returned to power in 1858 and presided over a delicately balanced coalition that remained in office for four and a half years—a record for the Isabeline era. The Moderate party had never been more than a loose and vague grouping, and had long since disintegrated. O'Donnell endeavored to create a new coalition, called the Liberal Union, based mainly on the support of important lieutenant generals and on the more liberal factions of the old Moderate groupings. During his long ministry, O'Donnell also tried to distract political and military attention by a series of comparatively spectacular foreign adventures—the Moroccan War, naval intervention off the coast of South America, participation in the French expedition to Cochin China, and the attempted reannexation of Santo Domingo.* However, half a decade of political attrition, the accustomed absence of broad support and consensus, and the intrigue of court factions and the caprice of the queen, finally combined to bring O'Donnell down early in 1863.[44]

In retrospect, it seems clear that the Liberal Union was the last practicable attempt to make the narrowly oligarchical Isabeline regime function. By the mid-1860's the government was once more the prey of court cliques and tiny factions of favorites, and was out of touch not merely with the country but with much of the political and military leadership as well. In its last years, the Isabeline monarchy relied almost exclusively on a half-dozen senior generals whose function was to assure the loyalty of the Army and repress civil disorder. Responsibility for the narrow, artificial structure of government went far beyond the queen, but she did absolutely nothing to improve the situation. Sensual, superstitious, fickle, and of only mediocre intelligence, she had almost no understanding of Spanish problems. Rather than working to harmonize discordant political interests and give voice to the needs of her subjects, she confined her attention to a narrow circle of favorites and court manipulators. By the mid-1860's even Moderates were beginning to doubt the viability of constitutional monarchy with such a figure on the throne.

In this situation the outstanding Spanish political general of the century came to the fore. Don Juan Prim y Prats was, according to one of his biographers, a "statesman caudillo." At the climax of his career he made the most serious and constructive effort of the period to achieve democratic constitutional monarchy while preserving public order. The son of an Army officer, Prim enlisted in the ranks at an early age during the First Carlist War, and after several wounds and decorations was made a colonel at the age of twenty-six. He was Captain General of Puerto Rico, won more combat laurels in Morocco than any other Spanish commander, and in 1861–62 bore himself with

---

* At the conclusion of the Moroccan campaign, five of the Liberal Union lieutenant generals were given new aristocratic titles that raised them to the rank of *grandes de España*. This was one of the means by which O'Donnell endeavored to hold his coalition together.

restraint and sagacity as head of the Spanish contingent of the Anglo-Hispano-French expedition to collect international debts at Veracruz. He became the darling of public opinion in the larger Spanish towns. A lifelong Progressive, he assumed the vice-chairmanship and general direction of that party in 1864.[45]

After the regime had made clear that it would never permit the Progressives to share power by constitutional means, Prim based all his plans for political change on a military pronunciamiento. Between 1865 and 1868 he showed that he was the most determined, and probably the most skillful, military conspirator in Spanish history, yet he failed several times to achieve a successful revolt. The most unsettling of these abortive rebellions, from the military point of view, was the sergeants' mutiny at the San Gil Artillery barracks of Madrid in 1866. Even among political officers it was usually considered virtual treachery to proselytize among the NCO's. Baltasar Hidalgo de Quintana, the only Artillery officer to work with the mutineers, had previously tried to resign his commission in order to avoid setting the example of an officer subverting the military hierarchy. The sergeants, on the other hand, were disgruntled because amid the slothful routine of the nineteenth-century Spanish Army it was they who actually administered and cared for their companies. Not only did they receive no official recognition for their efforts, but their free time had been reduced by a recent order. When the mutiny finally broke out it was quelled very quickly, but not before several Artillery officers had been shot down by their subordinates and bloody casualties had been sustained in a day-long pitched battle. The experience was startling for the Artillery officers. Heretofore they had been generally liberal in their political orientation, but this revolt had a distinctly sobering effect on their political attitudes. Nor, for that matter, did Prim, with his strong sense of order, approve of mutiny as a mode of political rebellion.[46]

The September Revolution of 1868, headed by Prim, finally resulted in the overthrow of Bourbon power. This revolt could not have been successful, however, without civilian unrest, which reached a high point after the economic crisis of 1866–67 and the regime's mistake of alienating most of the lieutenant generals who had previously supported O'Donnell. In the 1868 rebellion, a strong minority of the officers supported the Army liberals, a larger minority remained on the sidelines, and only a handful rallied to the defense of the regime. After a brief pitched battle near Córdoba, the loyalist forces collapsed.[47] Francisco Serrano, one of the leading political generals and a former lieutenant under O'Donnell, became Prime Minister, but Prim acted as Minister of War and was the guiding spirit of the new regime.

The constitution of 1869 was the most progressive document that Spain had ever known. It provided for universal male suffrage, full civil liberties, and a ministry responsible to a directly elected unicameral legislature. The monarchical form of government was carefully preserved, and the problem of Prim's interim government of 1869–70 was to find an acceptable constitutional monarch to replace the capricious, discredited Isabel. After many soundings, the choice fell upon Amedeo, a younger son of the Italian royal family. On December 24, 1870, Prim brought about the election of Amedeo of Savoy as king of Spain by a margin of one vote.

During a snowy evening three days later, Prim was mortally wounded by a gang of shotgun-wielding assassins on a side street in the very heart of Madrid. He died within seventy-two hours. Prim's murder was the greatest unsolved crime of nineteenth-century Spain.[48] It was a national tragedy, for during the two and a half years preceding his death, he had accomplished much more than any previous caudillo in laying the basis for an orderly representative government in Spain.[49] Without him the new regime had no strong leadership. Perilously exposed to the omnipresent factionalism of Spanish politics, it survived little more than two years.

CHAPTER THREE

The Overthrow of the First Republic

THROUGHOUT 1871 the great majority of the military proved obedient to the new democratic monarchy of Don Amedeo of Savoy. The Army was vitally necessary to this regime because of the Cuban rebellion that had begun in 1868 and the Carlist outbreak that started a year later. But Spain's brief essay in democratic monarchy soon came under the domination of the extreme left forces in the Cortes—the Radicals (successors to the Progressives) and the new Federal Republicans.

Contrary to the desires of the moderate-minded Savoyard king, the government blundered into a severe conflict with the Artillery Corps in 1872. The center of the storm was the ultraliberal Artillery officer Hidalgo de Quintana, who had encouraged the San Gil mutiny of 1866. To his fellow officers he was anathema, for they viewed his action as flagrant disloyalty to the Corps, but the government appointed him to important commands at Pamplona and then at Barcelona. After 300 Artillery officers resigned in protest, the Radical-dominated Cortes supported a plan to reorganize the entire Corps, and to replace all officers who had resigned with NCO's. This crisis, coming during a three-front civil war—against Carlists, Cuban rebels, and Federalist incendiaries in the provinces—was too much for the Italian-born king. Convinced that he could not escape the factionalism of Spanish politics and the pressures of extremists, he resigned on February 11, 1873.

The abrupt collapse of the democratic monarchy shifted political emphasis sharply to the left. The Federal Republicans, who had gained strength among the lower and lower-middle classes, especially in the east and in the south, joined with the Radicals to establish by simple parliamentary decree a unicameral Republican regime—the first in

Spanish history. The Federalists soon took over the government altogether, setting up a kind of revolutionary dictatorship.

The new regime was antimilitary from its inception. Perhaps the most popular plank in the Federalist program was its promise to abolish the draft system and drastically reform the Army. Because of the widespread resentment against the conscription system, this proposal struck at the weakest link in the relations between the Army and Spanish society. No serious effort had ever been made to regularize the capricious selection of military manpower, and recruits were still chosen by lot. Throughout the nineteenth century, anyone who had enough money to pay a redemption bounty (*redención a metálica*) could avoid Army service. Many others were spared through "legal exemption." For example, of the 97,000 men chosen by lot in 1862, 33,000 paid bounties or in other "legal" ways escaped induction. It is no wonder that the minority who were finally drafted felt they had been discriminated against for lack of money or influence.[1] Resentment among the lower and lower-middle classes had been rising steadily since the 1830's, and the Federalists' pledge to abolish the quintas was possibly the most important single factor in attracting a large following for them in the eastern and southern towns.[2]

In 1868, when the old dynasty was overthrown, the Federalists had organized 40,000 militiamen as "Volunteers for Liberty." They broke into military arsenals in search of arms, and fought pitched battles with Army units sent by Prim to impose discipline. Few things could have done more to arouse the Army's apprehensions and to unite it politically than this determination to create a separate, anti-Army militia. But that did not deter the Federalists; on the very day of Don Amedeo's resignation, they announced the reorganization of the Volunteers for Liberty throughout Spain.

Because of their antimilitary policy, one of the Federalists' key problems was to find Army commanders who could be counted on to serve the new regime faithfully. "Only two generals were of known Federal sympathies—the equally incompetent Contreras and Nouvilas; and both were despised by the regular officers and disliked for their Intransigent [ultra-Federalist] contacts."[3] In mid-February, the Federalists appointed a new Minister of War, and named their protégé Contreras to the vital post of Captain General of Barcelona. The incumbent commander, Gaminde, had been sent to the Catalan capital four years earlier to quell the Federalist militia. Hoping to remain in command, he tried to seize the civil government of Barcelona on February 21, but was foiled by the militia. Three weeks later the regular Army forces in Catalonia were dissolved. After an abortive revolt by Moderates in Madrid on April 23, the Federalists tightened their hold on the Ministry of War by promoting nearly all the pro-Federalist officers they could find (about 145 in all).[4]

On February 22 the Federalist regime abolished the quintas. They proposed to replace it with eighty volunteer battalions, called Free Corps, which were expected to total 48,000 men. No recruiting problem was expected, for the Federalists idealistically theorized that there should be a natural outpouring of enthusiasm to protect the new republic from the Carlist bands forming in the northeast. To encourage enlistments, the pay of volunteers was raised above that of regular soldiers, though strong protests from the Army soon brought pay increases for them as well. Yet neither of these incentives proved attractive to young Spaniards. After four months, only 10,000 volunteers had been recruited, and most of these were militarily worthless—insubordinate and riotous.[5]

By the summer of 1873 the Federalist dictatorship had completely alienated the Army, and was beset by such a host of enemies from both left and right that political order collapsed. Establishment of a Republican regime in Madrid had given strong impetus to the regrowth of Carlism, and a full-scale civil war was launched in the northeast.[6] The Cuban rebellion still smoldered; and on the left, the authority of the government was undermined by a general revolt of provincial extremists who achieved the reductio ad absurdum of Federalist ideology by attempting universal regional separatism. On July 12, and in the days immediately following, lower-middle-class rebels seized most of the major towns in southern and eastern Spain and established autonomous "cantons."

The second Republican president within five months resigned on July 18, and was replaced by a Federalist moderate, Francisco Salmerón, who accepted the obvious fact that the previous policy had failed. Since the government could no longer survive without a reliable military force, Salmerón held a conference on July 20 with most of the generals currently stationed in Madrid. He promised to restore the organization of the Artillery Corps and to reestablish the traditional Code of Military Justice, making possible the resumption of courts-martial.[7]

As commander in chief in the south, Salmerón chose General Manuel Pavía, one of Prim's associates in the conspiracies of 1865–68 and a man with even more advanced political ideals than his martyred chief. Pavía was no Federalist, but he agreed with other Army liberals such as Serrano that a moderate republic under central control was Spain's best hope. Salmerón remarked to him: "If you can get a soldier to fire his gun against one of the cantonalists, order will be saved."[8] Few troops actually deserted to the cantonalists, except at Cartagena, for most of the peasant draftees felt relatively little sympathy for the revolutionaries. Moreover, the cantonalists lacked training and discipline, and in most areas they could not offer determined resistance. With only about 2,000 troops, Pavía occupied Córdoba on July 23 and Seville on July 30, took Cádiz on August 1, and was in Granada by the middle of August.[9] After a tough struggle, Major General Arsenio Martínez Campos had occupied Valencia on August 8.

Soon the only towns holding out were Cartagena and Málaga. The former was heavily defended, protected by its geographical location and by its own little "navy," which engaged in acts of piracy in the western Mediterranean. Málaga would have been much easier to take if its leader had not been staunchly supported by one of Salmerón's ministers, who threatened to bring down the government if the Army occupied the town. In reply, Pavía declared that he himself would resign—and risk the collapse of order in the south—if the government would not allow the Army to restore discipline in Málaga. Faced with this dilemma, on September 6 Salmerón gave up. Emulating two recent predecessors, he tendered his resignation.[10]

The next president was the golden-tongued orator Emilio Castelar. One of the most moderate of all the Federalists, Castelar might be better described as a pragmatic democratic liberal. He was horrified at the anarchy he saw growing in Spain. Twenty years later he gave us this description of the faults of the first Republic:

Let us evoke the period never emphasized with enough insistence—the fateful year of 1873. There were days during that summer when we thought our Spain had completely dissolved. The idea of legality had been lost so completely that any petty employee of the Ministry of War might assume full powers and notify the Cortes afterward; those whose duty it was to obey the laws ignored them, rebelling or jeering in unison against legality.... Efforts were made to divide our Fatherland into a thousand pieces, as occurred after the fall of the Caliphate of Córdoba. The strangest and wildest ideas came from the provinces. Some spoke of reviving the Crown of Aragon, as if the formulas of modern law were no more than a medieval imprecation. Others spoke of creating an independent Galicia under British protection. Jaén prepared for war against Granada. Salamanca feared the closing of its glorious university and the eclipse of its scientific leadership in Castile. Rivalries not calmed by the passage of centuries surged up as though we had regressed to the age of . . . Castros and Laras, of Capulets and Montagues, of universal war. Insignificant towns, scarcely discernible on the map, summoned constituent assemblies. The rebellion was directed against the most federalist of all possible ministries, and at the very moment when the Assembly was preparing a new constitution, whose worst defects were due to lack of time and patience.

And then came what we would like to have forgotten: daily riots, mobs everywhere, military indiscipline; popular republicans murdered in the streets; peaceful villages seized by fever and excited to revolt; demagogical dictatorship in Cádiz; bloody rivalry between men and families in Málaga that caused the flight of nearly half the population; disarming of the Granada garrison, after very costly battles; bands from one city who went to fight and die in another without knowing why, or for what, like medieval raiders; burnings and massacres in Alcoy; anarchy in Valencia; feuding in the Sierra Morena; the canton of Murcia dominated by demagogy, and that of Castellón by the apostólicos; Castilian towns calling from behind their barricades for a war by the municipalities, as if Charles of Ghent had disembarked on the northern coast; a horrible scene of strife and violence between cantonalist emissaries and government defenders in Valladolid; the capital of Andalusia up in arms; Cartagena in delirium; Alicante and Almería bombarded; the Spanish fleet passing from the red flag to a foreign flag; the coast divided up into sectors; boats in as much danger as if piracy had returned to the Mediterranean; insecurity everywhere; our parks going up in smoke and our Navy sinking into the sea; the ruin of our soil; the suicide of our party [the Federalists]; and finally, the lightning flash of total madness in that black night . . . as the sinister Carlist hosts surged up, like nocturnal birds of prey greedily devouring carrion, gaining advantage from our ills, ready to consummate our slavery and our dishonor, and to divide between theocracy and absolutism the torn remnants of unhappy Spain.[11]

Castelar took a more positive view of the political role of the Spanish military than most Federalists did. On one occasion he had said: "Without the generals, we are so weak that we cannot survive."[12] During a speech to the Cortes on February 22, 1869, he had said of the previous pro-liberal pronunciamientos, "Viewed in the light of positive law, the lapses in discipline are perhaps grave errors; but viewed in the eternal light of the human conscience, which blesses the heroes of liberty, those military rebellions are the guideposts marking the progress of Spain."[13]

Castelar feared disorder almost more than reaction, and for months had been pressing reconciliation with the Army. By the close of 1873, he stood on better terms with the officers than any government leader since Prim. On the other hand, he began to lose the support of his own party, which believed that Castelar had jeopardized the existence of the Federal Republic by appointing conservative generals to important commands. The Cortes, which had adjourned on September 20, 1873, was due to reconvene on January 2, 1874, and there was every indication that it would turn out of office the fourth Republican president in less than a year.

On December 24, Pavía, now the Captain General of Madrid, urged Castelar to postpone reopening the Cortes, but the President refused to delay the normal course of the constitutional system. After this interview, Pavía considered taking matters into his own hands. He contacted the principal commanders of units in the field to see if they would support a coup against the Federalists should Castelar be overturned. They seemed willing, at least in principle. On January 1, 1874, Pavía warned Castelar that his overthrow by the Cortes would mean the disintegration of both the military and the political structure of Spain. That same day Sagasta, a former Prime Minister and a leader of the moderate liberals, told Pavía that both the Radicals and the moderates would support a preventive coup against the Federalist intransigents.[14]

The Cortes met on the night of January 2. Pavía remained at a late supper in his own residence, accompanied by a select group of officers on whom he could rely, to await the results of the parliamentary deliberations. Very late that night, the Federalist Cortes overturned the government. As soon as word reached Pavía, he gave the order for troops to move into the streets. Immediately afterward, however, he was informed that because of the difficulty of finding a successor, the Cortes might reelect Castelar when the next session opened early in the morning. Upon hearing of this possibility, Pavía hurriedly canceled his command.

After a few hours of sleep, the deputies reassembled at 7 the next morning. It was soon made clear that the chamber did not intend to authorize a new Castelar government. Pavía then gave the command for occupation of the Cortes building. A regiment of Infantry left the nearby barracks and began their march through the chilly streets. When word reached the Cortes that troops were on their way, consternation broke out. Some deputies made ready to use their pistols; others prepared to climb out the windows. A panicky vote of confidence was given to Castelar, but when the ex-President was told of it, he observed simply, "It is too late." The Civil Guard occupied the chamber without bloodshed.[15]

The Federal Republic was the only new political regime of nine-teenth-century Spain born without benefit of military intervention, but it was brought to a close by one of the simplest and most direct coups ever effected. It is significant that this pronunciamiento was the first to enjoy the nearly unanimous support of the Army. Previous pronunciamientos had used a portion of the Army to further specific political goals not directly shared by a majority of the officers. But the turmoils of 1873–74 had welded a spirit of political unity among the military—at least in the sense that they refused to countenance further Federalist extremism and anarchy. Pavía's coup was thus the first apolitical pronunciamiento, expressing one interpretation of the Army's duty to save the country from disunity, corruption, and the schemes of professional politicians. In this sense it was a forerunner of the more famous rebellions of 1923 and 1936.

Like all nineteenth-century Spanish regimes, the Federal Republic had been a minority government. Its failure did not lie in that fact, however, but rather in its absolute inability to make government function. Moreover, its policy toward the Army had been unwise in the extreme. Under the liberal monarchy in 1871 there had been five different Ministers of War, but under the Federal Republic in 1873 there had been ten—an all-time high. The senior officers believed that the Republican politicians had attempted to subvert military institu-tions and incite mutiny. No previous liberal government had been accused of this sort of interference in Army affairs. The experience with the Republic left even some of the most liberal officers disillus-ioned with politics. They, and almost all their companions, accepted a corporate role for the Army as arbiter of an impossible civic situa-tion. After 1874 it would become much less common for individual generals or lesser officers to employ the Army for particular political ends. New pressures against the military, as well as the increasing diffi-culty of their own problems, encouraged a stronger identity among officers. Henceforth they would be more concerned with promoting their own interests as military men above or outside party conflicts, and less willing to be the tools of political factions.

However, this trend was only beginning in 1874, and after Pavía closed the Cortes the position of the Army was far from clear. No section of the armed forces questioned the validity of his action, but Pavía had no intention of establishing a military government. He had intended only to overthrow a Cortes dominated by the Federalists, not to displace the Republic. His only goal was to create a workable coalition government, and to this end he called a meeting of the leaders of all parties save the Federalists and Carlists. Pavía's summons was rejected only by the monarchists (*alfonsinos*).* With the Federalists proscribed and the alfonsinos abstaining, the two principal groups at the meeting were the Radicals and the Unionists (or Conservatives). The Unionist group was led by the sixty-three-year-old Serrano, the most active political general remaining, and since the Army was now the ultimate basis of power, Serrano assumed a dominant position. He was quickly accepted as interim President of a Unitary Republic, presiding over an uneasy coalition government composed mainly of Radicals and Unionists.[16]

Serrano's government was divided from the start, for the Radicals hoped to strengthen the Unitary Republic by winning over Federalists, whereas the Unionist moderates hoped to accomplish the same goal by shunning the left in favor of more conservative elements who would otherwise support the alfonsinos. After only four months, disputes over policy and appointments led to the breakdown of the compromise ministry in May 1874. Serrano's Cabinet was packed with members of his clique, military and civilian, and functioned as a sort of liberal dictatorship. The only other general who had previously served as head of state—Espartero—had been elected to that office by a fairly free Cortes and had acted as executive for a monarchy with a written constitution. Serrano's government, on the contrary, lacked direct legal justification, and could not in any way be considered a "national government." It did not win the enthusiasm even of the military, for Army commanders were neither oblivious to the question of legitimacy nor eager to be dominated by a single military faction. Pavía was sorely disillusioned by the outcome of events, yet his frustration has been a common experience among naïve generals who intervene to establish apolitical governments.[17]

With the discrediting of the Progressive and Republican forces, the political situation favored supporters of the young Bourbon heir, Don Alfonso. For five years, a restoration junta in exile had been led by several ultraconservative senior generals who had resigned their commands. Until the collapse of regular government in Spain, their efforts had seemed unimportant, for even under the most favorable conditions monarchy could only be restored from within Spain, not by conspiracies of exiled generals with no troops to follow them.

* The *alfonsinos* took their name from Don Alfonso, son of Isabel II and pretender to the throne.

When the anarchy of cantonalism was at its height, this rather hollow military junta had given way to a civilian monarchist committee, headed by the experienced politician and part-time historian Antonio Cánovas del Castillo, to whom the former queen delegated full powers to prepare for the restoration. Cánovas was undoubtedly one of the three or four major public figures of nineteenth-century Spain. He had intellectual and political talents of a high order, great energy, and considerable determination. He lacked faith in the possibility of a genuinely representative, self-responsible government for Spain, and his extensive historical study only added to his pessimism about the civic potential of his people. For Cánovas, a more realistic goal was a truly constitutional monarchy, balanced and moderate in form, based on the rule of law, and at least slightly broader and less exclusive than the Isabeline regime had been.[18]

He had no illusions about the importance of the military, and was well aware that recent experiences had made the officers more determined than ever to maintain their unity and discipline. On January 8, 1874, after the formation of the Serrano government, he wrote to the queen of the Army's "predisposition . . . to act with unity and not to be separated from its commanders," and added that the Army would henceforth be "master of the entire situation."[19] This did not mean that Cánovas wanted to rely primarily on the military. On the contrary, he hoped that a well-prepared monarchist regime would put an end to overt military intervention in politics, and would bring the era of pronunciamientos to a close. Cánovas realized that Serrano could not be overthrown without pressure from other parts of the Army, but he wanted to avoid using the military until civilian political support had been fully prepared. Relations between Cánovas and the ultramonarchist generals both inside and outside Spain were not fully harmonious. Monarchist generals distrusted him to some extent because they were apprehensive about his personal political schemes and ambitions; and Cánovas was determined that the monarchy should not fall captive to an Army clique.

Meanwhile, the Serrano regime extended Castelar's policy of restoring to command experienced (and usually conservative) generals—in part to win their support for the Unitary Republic, in part because competent leaders were needed for the struggle against the Carlists, which was going badly. In the spring of 1874, the main Army of the North was placed under General Manuel Gutiérrez de la Concha (Marqués del Duero), who had been one of the principal political generals of the Isabeline regime. Now in his sixties, Concha was still a hard-driving commander, and had retained the respect of his troops. He apparently hoped that a smashing victory over the Carlists would place him in a position to force the restoration of the regular Bourbon dynasty, but after several successes he was killed by an enemy sharpshooter during a crucial battle at Abárzuza (Navarre) that ended in the rout of the government forces.[20]

The disillusioned Pavía, named commander of the Army of the Center (the Levant and southern Aragon) in July, felt that current military difficulties were due mainly to the structure and leadership of the Army itself. Although Serrano was daring and resolute in moments of physical danger, he was lax and ineffective as head of the government, and did not seem able to improve Army organization.[21] Thus far, the field forces had had little strength or cohesion. The cadres born in 1853–55 had already been called up, but this provided only about 90,000 men during the first months of the year, or just enough to cover losses. On July 18, three weeks after the Abárzuza disaster, a special draft was decreed of all able-bodied bachelors between the ages of 23 and 30. This affected more than 125,000 men, but the customary special exemptions limited the number of those actually inducted to about 40,000.

The Radicals and Republicans had abandoned the political scene, and the monarchists busily rallied moderates and conservatives to their side, arguing that restoration of the Bourbon dynasty would deprive the Carlists of much of their right-wing support and restore national unity. Several ardent monarchists holding commands inside Spain seemed eager to initiate a coup, but Cánovas did all he could to restrain them until the proper situation had been prepared. Late in the autumn of 1874, he met with several of the monarchist generals, and sounded out the principal district commanders. A majority were in favor of the restoration, but Cánovas wanted near-unanimity and said the time was not quite ripe. It was rumored that he was trying to hold back the extremists until he could arrange for more moderate generals to organize pressure against Serrano. Under the guidance of Cánovas, the heir to the throne, twenty-year-old Don Alfonso, issued his "Sandhurst Manifesto" from the British military academy where he was studying. In this manifesto Don Alfonso pledged to abide by the principles of constitutional monarchy and affirmed that he was "a man of the century, a liberal." This maneuver gave the restoration specific political content and possibly broader appeal as well. By the beginning of December, rumor had it that Cánovas was trying to obtain guarantees from Primo de Rivera, the Captain General of Madrid, and Jovellar, Pavía's replacement as head of the Army of the Center, that they would throw their support behind a moderate, civilian-led restoration.[22]

These rumors brought a strong reaction from Army conservatives, who had no intention of being bypassed politically. Some of them also may have been genuinely convinced that only direct action by the Army could ensure the success of the restoration.[23] At any rate, the lead was taken by Maj. Gen. Arsenio Martínez Campos, who had distinguished himself in the recent Cuban and Carlist campaigns. His pronunciamiento was to make him the most influential political general of the next two decades. Martínez Campos was forty-three years old, of medium height, and rather slender. He wore the moustache of the period and an imperial-style beard. His eyes, behind thick brows, were lively and intelligent. Courtly and emotional by nature, he nonetheless tried to avoid excessive display. He had taught briefly in the Staff college during the 1850's, then served as Prim's aide in Mexico in 1861.[24] Brave and capable in the field, Martínez Campos had a reputation for concern about the well-being of his troops, but he had never been thought of as more than a reliable brigade commander, and it was not believed that he possessed leadership qualities of a high order. Like many active generals, he had been enraged and humiliated by the laxity of military discipline under the Federalists, and, although he was promoted to the rank of major general, he had resigned command of the Catalan front on January 23, 1874, disgusted with the continuing political disunity.

Martínez Campos did not have much of a reputation as a political general, but his anger and ambition were inflated by the encouragement of his wife and the pressure of military conservatives. Most of the senior monarchists either were out of the country or had not held active posts in recent years, so that shortly after the death of Concha, Martínez Campos became the most active leader of alfonsino conspiracy in the Army. After the Sandhurst Manifesto was issued, he received the support of approximately twenty other generals. Yet none of these wanted to be the first to act, and Martínez Campos, who was not at all a reckless man, also grew more cautious. Though the government knew that he and other officers had been conspiring in Madrid, the Captain General, Fernando Primo de Rivera, refused to arrest him, swearing on his "word of honor" and his "good faith as a gentleman" that Martínez Campos would never rebel and saying: "To doubt him is to doubt myself."[25]

Shortly before Christmas, Martínez Campos' hesitations were overcome by his devout, impetuous wife and his closest associates. Fellow conspirators arranged for him to take command of an Infantry brigade at Sagunto, near Valencia, to begin the pronunciamiento. On December 21 he wrote to Don Alfonso for permission to seize the initiative; he did not bother to wait for a reply.[26] On December 28, 1874, at a village close to Sagunto, Martínez Campos proclaimed the restoration of the Bourbon dynasty in the person of Don Alfonso. The pronunciamiento was quickly seconded by other Army units in the Valencia region, with the exception of the Artillery, and the local commanders at Valencia and Sagunto, who prided themselves on never having participated in political rebellion.[27] After a few days, what was left of Serrano's Republican dictatorship collapsed. Serrano had recently assumed personal command of the Army of the North, but its officers refused to take up arms against their comrades in support of his regime. Neither would the forces at Madrid, where Primo de Rivera came out for the monarchy.[28]

At first Cánovas was nonplussed and even worried, because he had explicitly asked that the generals not make a pronunciamiento on their own initiative. Martínez Campos insisted that he had only done what was necessary, and stressed that he firmly intended not to accept "a command, or a promotion, or a title, or any reward at all."[29] This, of course, was not the way things were done, and within a few days Martínez Campos had been promoted to lieutenant general. However, true to the nineteenth-century pattern of Spanish military intervention, the rebels did not try to form a military regency. Once the pronunciamiento had been completed, power was transferred to Cánovas, who formed a temporary coalition cabinet to prepare for the return of Don Alfonso and for the election of a constituent Cortes.

In the monarchist pronunciamiento of December, as in the "apolitical" coup of January, no part of the Army had resisted; nearly all the officers agreed that there must be an end to disunity, indiscipline, and insecurity. They accepted the return to a more conservative order with little objection, in order that the Army might concentrate on winning the civil war rather than becoming involved in the complications of political quarrels. That the six-year liberal interregnum of 1868–74 had been both begun and ended by military revolt was not so paradoxical as it might seem. The pro-liberal Spanish Army officers of the mid-nineteenth century were creatures of their time. For the most part, they were professional functionaries from the middle classes, and they responded to the political goals espoused by the bourgeois elite of their era. The limited constitutional liberalism of the first half of the century did not seem antipathetic toward military institutions. Only in 1868 had such liberalism begun to include political democracy. Once the trend of politics began to diverge toward mass demagogy and social revolution, a gulf opened between most politically minded officers and the new popular forces. Revulsion from "Federalist democracy" brought the Army nearer than ever before to a unified, if negative, position in political affairs. By 1874, the Army no longer seemed to be the "liberal" champion it had so frequently been in the past. Nearly half a century would pass before a large number of officers would again become united in support of a dissenting political opinion. Though no one could have been sure of it at the time, Martínez Campos had led the last of the major nineteenth-century pronunciamientos.

CHAPTER FOUR

The Army during the Restoration Era, 1875–95

D ON ALFONSO arrived in the peninsula early in 1875 to be crowned King Alfonso XII. A constituent Cortes was chosen by a greatly reduced electorate, and drew up a constitution providing for a bicameral legislature and for civil guarantees and electoral privileges only slightly more liberal than those prevailing under the Isabeline regime. However, the seven years since the expulsion of Isabel II had not been entirely fruitless. The turmoil of 1868–75 had convinced most elements in the dominant oligarchy that some liberalization was necessary, had discouraged most of the left and made the right more tractable, and had left middle-of-the-road forces even more willing to compromise than before. By the time the new constitution was completed at the beginning of 1876, it appeared that the new regime had a better chance of surviving than had most of its predecessors.

During the next decade, the Spanish government was dominated by Cánovas del Castillo. It was based on a small oligarchy of the politically conscious and economically powerful, drawn mainly from the upper and upper-middle classes but including some middle-class professional men. The same social strata provided support for both of the two main parties, Cánovas' Liberal Conservatives and Sagasta's Liberals. Political organization—insofar as it existed—was structured loosely around *caciques* (bosses) in each province. The Liberals suggested broader suffrage, greater control over the Church, and a slight extension of civil liberties, but neither party had a social program. For the next generation, the country's political exhaustion and apathy were so great that this system governed almost by default.

Cánovas hoped to neutralize the influence of the military as much as possible. A royal order of February 4, 1875, declared:

The rigor of military statutes and of military discipline is and ought to be even greater in the upper ranks of the Army than in the lower.... Commanders, officers, and troops are to abstain from taking part in the contests of parties, and so should the generals themselves, no matter how high their rank. Good military principles require this, as does public law, even in normal times, and today the dangerous state of war in which the nation finds itself demands it even more.... In case of disobedience, those guilty should be arrested.[1]

Yet Cánovas knew that the new regime was viable only so long as it retained the support of established pressure groups. Since the backing of influential generals could be an important factor in maintaining prestige, the customary round of politically inspired promotions took place during 1875.[2] Martínez Campos and a number of other leading generals were given lifetime seats in the appointive sector of the Senate. As it turned out, the orders forbidding military men to participate in political agitation applied more to ordinary officers than to key generals, and were interpreted broadly. During the years to come, it would be rare to find generals attending public political speeches, for that would identify them with "partisan politics" or "agitation." But it was deemed quite all right for certain "safe" generals to be elected to the Cortes from boss-ruled districts, to debate in parliament, or even to write articles. These last activities, rather than being proscribed as "political," were deemed "services to the Fatherland."

Identification with the restored monarchy was further encouraged by the fact that Don Alfonso showed himself more Army-minded than any Spanish monarch since Philip V, who had died in 1746. The young king frequently dressed in uniform; he took to the field with his troops against the Carlists during the first year of his reign; and in later, peacetime years he inspected barracks, occasionally attended maneuvers, and apparently learned passages of the Military Code by heart. However, Don Alfonso was by no means a genuine soldier-king; his association with the Army had a certain operetta quality, as though it were membership in a national sports club with romantic overtones. Having spent his adolescent years in exile, the king harbored few illusions of grandeur and did not envision an aggressive role for the Spanish Army. Politically, he lived up to Cánovas' expectations, avoided many of his mother's errors, and proved to be, after Don Amedeo, the most constitutional-minded sovereign the country had yet seen. Don Alfonso's association with the Army thus did not encourage dangerous new political ambitions among the military, but rather enabled it to adjust more comfortably to the restoration system.

The main task of the Army in 1875–76 was to mobilize all possible resources to put down the Carlists. The disorders of the Republican period were still being overcome, and one of the more perspicacious lieutenant generals, Pedro Ruiz Dana, wrote with mournful accuracy: "Our Army does not really deserve the name if compared with the armies of the other nations of Europe."[3] What was lacking in quality was eventually made up for in quantity, and once more the traditionalists of the northeast were ground down through attrition. By the beginning of 1876, three corps theoretically totaling more than 100,000 men—the largest force in Spanish history—were assembled in the Navarrese mountains. They were able to bring Carlist resistance to an end by the close of the year. This bloody conflict had lasted as long and had taken almost as many lives as the seven-year struggle of the 1830's, so that it has been estimated with scant exaggeration that the three Carlist outbreaks cost the Spanish people nearly a million casualties, including the wounded and sick on both sides.[4] Yet the war of 1869–76 was less extensive in geographical scope than that of the 1830's, for there was no fighting at all in most of the country. The role of the Army had been more or less restricted to purely military functions, and the great majority of the officers had become less involved in ideological issues than during the earlier conflict. Espartero had not hesitated to have virulently pro-Carlist priests in the rebel zone shot, but the politically more cautious Army of the 1870's treated such elements more respectfully.

The Cuban rebellion was not ended until two years later, when Martínez Campos arranged the Zanjón peace agreement of 1878.* By the time peace had finally returned to all parts of the Spanish world, Army administration was faced with the same structural blight that had beset it in 1814 and 1840—a grotesquely swollen Officer Corps. There were still no precise criteria for commissioning and promoting officers during time of war: to fill temporary positions, many corporals and sergeants had been promoted from the ranks on the basis of seniority, and several hundred other officers had been incorporated from provincial militia. Moreover, there was such an enormous list of claims for special compensation and decoration that the Ministry of War, it is said, reviewed no less than 16,000 petitions between the years 1875 and 1878.[5]

---

* The Cuban rebellion is treated in Chapter 5.

More than ever, the Army was in need of drastic reform; but this could not come from the military hierarchy, most of whom jealously guarded the status quo. Nor would the politicians take a hand, for if the civil leaders of the restoration hoped to avoid military intervention in politics, they felt a corresponding obligation to abstain from overt interference in Army affairs. Consequently there was no significant institutional change in the Army after the wars of the 1870's. The civil government did take an interest in Army expenditures, however, and on May 5, 1876, a government circular discussed "reductions and economies" to be made after the fighting ended.[6] Some of these were eventually carried out: troops were licensed and purchasing strictly limited. The most expensive single item, officers' salaries, could not be reduced without a drastic streamlining of the Corps, and this could hardly be attempted under existing circumstances. As late as 1884 there were 27,000 officers on the payrolls, and their number was slow in diminishing. However, in 1880 an expanded Reserve Officer Corps was created into which the oldest or those in ill health might pass. This was especially useful in trimming the number of generals on the active list, which fell from the grotesque figure of 617 in 1879 to 461 in 1881, and 282 in 1889.[7]

Though no organic changes of any significance took place, an effort was made to reorganize and improve the military academies. In 1882 the General Military Academy was opened in Toledo. Its function was to provide several years of common training in military fundamentals and professional attitudes for cadets in all branches of the Army and so help to overcome the disunity and rivalry among the various Corps. This academy, an attempted revival of an earlier institution that had existed at Segovia, was closed down in 1893 owing to budgetary difficulties. In the same year a compensating effort was made to improve the quality of instruction in the separate academies which existed for the various Corps. General field maneuvers, previously rare in the Spanish Army, were held on a sizable scale in 1886 and 1891. Despite the failure of the General Academy, there was greater evidence of a common esprit de corps than in earlier decades, probably because of the harsh experiences of the seventies and the three-pronged civil war. The founding of new professional journals devoted to technical matters rather than politics also reflected somewhat greater concentration on military duties.[8]

Though the literature on military reform, and with it the demands for a volunteer Army, diminished after 1875, they did not disappear altogether.[9] A new military recruitment law was passed in 1877, but its terms only slightly modified the preceding statutes. The length of service for draftees was set at three years on active service and eight years on the reserve list, but budgetary limitations made it impossible to keep most recruits in the ranks longer than twenty-four months. Articles 91 to 93 established all manner of exemptions for persons in specialized employment, for only sons, for grandsons supporting grand-parents, and even for illegitimate children supporting their parents. But for those who could not otherwise qualify for exemption, draft redemption was set at 1,200 pesetas.[10] This was a high price in terms of the low average income, but was not entirely beyond the reach of the middle classes. During the next few years, only 11 or 12 per cent of the Army recruits were provided through volunteer enlistment, and a sig-nificant minority of those drafted—10,000 in 1882—bought their way out. By 1883 this practice was said to produce as much as 77 million pesetas a year in revenue. The majority of the young men who bought their way out of service did not come from the upper classes, but from the middle classes, for whom the 1,200-peseta fee was a great financial sacrifice. Yet living conditions in the Army were still so poor that any privation was deemed worthwhile to save a son from military service.[11]

Despite the renewed effort to professionalize the Army and keep generals out of politics, by 1879 two generals had already served briefly as prime ministers under the new regime. General Jovellar headed a brief three-month transition ministry in the fall of 1875, and Martínez Campos was chief of the council of ministers in 1878 and 1879.[12] How-ever, both these ministries had been formed with the blessing (and through the machinations) of Cánovas, who found it convenient oc-casionally to shift political burdens onto the shoulders of trusted mon-archist generals. Martínez Campos was now the most important single figure in the military hierarchy, as much on account of his pronunci-amiento and the favor he enjoyed at court as for the laurels gained by the pacification of Cuba. It may indeed be true that the victor of the Antilles was not eager to become Prime Minister, but frequent quarrels made it impossible for Cánovas to remain in office, and the young king appointed his favorite general to the post. Cánovas and his colleagues approved, for such a nomination helped maintain the unity of their party, cowed extremists, and let a politically inexperienced general bear the onus of any new administrative adjustments. After Martínez Campos' Cuban settlement was approved by the Cortes, Cánovas replaced him as Prime Minister in December 1879. The brief experiences of Jovellar and Martínez Campos set the norm for other generals who became prime ministers under the restored monarchy. Later nominees, such as Azcárraga, who served for two months in 1897 and for a similarly brief term in 1900, and López Domínguez, who held the post for a few months in 1907, presided over transition ministries that no regular politician wanted or was able to fill. Rather than dominating the government, political generals were now being used by it. Martínez Campos felt, not altogether incorrectly, that the parliamentary rug had been pulled from beneath him when he no longer served Cánovas' purposes. In 1880 he and several other leading political generals, including Jovellar and Pavía, left the Conservatives to join Sagasta's Liberals. Their influence helped establish the first Liberal ministry in 1881.[13]

The equivocal nature of the politicians' attempt to "civilianize" government under the restored monarchy is illustrated not merely by the compromising policy of Cánovas but also by the attitude of one of the more progressive and reform-minded young Liberal deputies of the 1880's, José Canalejas. In five different speeches between October 24 and November 25, 1881, he noted, among other things, that there had already been 81 military revolts in nineteenth-century Spain; and he made strenuous appeals for the development of an Army designed to handle international, not internal, problems. He condemned perpetuation of the draft redemption system as wasteful and undemocratic. Finally, Canalejas turned his attention to Martínez Campos, then serving as Sagasta's Minister of War. He questioned the general about the influence of the military in current affairs, and urged him to encourage the Army to concentrate on professional matters.[14]

But Canalejas, like all the Liberals collaborating in the restoration regime, was a man of order. He feared the Spanish potential for violent political disturbance, and like most parliamentary leaders he agreed that the Army must play a vital role in civic affairs when subversion threatened. As he said in a speech at the beginning of 1883:

Great social problems created by hatred between classes, great problems of race that unfortunately cannot be resolved save by force, and finally, historical circumstances that connect the life of a people to dynastic interests, necessarily create a situation of violence; and since the resolution of any irruption of violence requires a powerful army, from this general condition of Europe and modern life we cannot and certainly ought not to except ourselves.[15]

Neither Canalejas nor any other leading politician denied the right of the military to "intervene" in moments of great danger for the country,

but he insisted that such critical moments arrived only when the orderly system was threatened wih subversion.[16]

Throughout the 1880's, a small group of Republican conspirators,
led by the former Prime Minister Ruiz Zorrilla, persisted in efforts to
overthrow the restored monarchy. Their plots relied mainly on a minority of the Army officers who remained distinctly liberal in their political sympathies despite the disillusion of the preceding decade. Small
conspiracies had been organized in 1877 and 1878 among both extremist pro-Republican junior officers and slightly more moderate generals
who wanted to replace the political leadership of Cánovas with a more
liberal one. These maneuvers had come to nothing owing to lack of
leadership and organization.[17]

The last nominal Republican president, General Serrano, made
his peace with the monarchy and was awarded a lifetime Senate seat on
condition of swearing loyalty to the regime. In a Senate speech of December 6, 1882, the aged Serrano affirmed full loyalty to the person of
Alfonso XII. In the twilight of his life he became a leader of a political
splinter group called the Dynastic Left, which championed the return
of the democratic monarchist constitution of 1869 within the framework of the existing regime.[18] The attitude of Serrano offered no encouragement to Republican conspirators, but the secret meetings of
pro-Liberal generals in 1880 and 1881, and their influence in the first
Sagasta government, had the opposite effect.

In 1880, Ruiz Zorrilla's exiled Republican Progressive Party set up
a secret association called the ARM (Asociación Republicana Militar).
It hoped to enroll officers from all ranks down to and including sergeants. During the years from 1877 to 1879, hundreds of junior officers
and NCO's had been transferred from the former Army of the North
to provincial garrisons, or brought back from Cuba. Fiscal pressures
had left many without regular pay for as long as twelve or fourteen
months. Since 1878 hundreds of supernumerary officers for whom no
positions were available had been drawing half salary on the "replacement list," and only a minority of the surplus manpower could be absorbed at four-fifths pay into the newly organized reserve. The Republicans found many sympathizers among these elements, but most of the
disgruntled ARM members were junior officers without influence, and
the conspiracy was sore beset for lack of funds. Moreover, it appears
that during the winter of 1882–83 another secret Republican military
organization was formed, parallel to ARM but not associated with it.
This second group was centered in the Madrid garrison, but had
branches elsewhere.[19]

At all events, by 1883 ARM leaders claimed to have organized cells in twenty-two garrisons, and to have approximately 3,000 members, including half a dozen generals.[20] A Republican pronunciamiento was planned for the summer, with the center of conspiracy in Barcelona, where the atmosphere was decidedly more liberal than in Madrid. At the end of June it was decided to delay the coup until August 5, so that it might be coordinated in five different centers. On the eve of the target date, the pronunciamiento was delayed once more, but the leaders failed to get word to the Badajoz garrison, which was one of the keys to the operation. At dawn on the fifth of August, 38 officers and 30 sergeants in Badajoz brought their troops out in open rebellion against the government. The thousand men at their disposal took over the entire town, including an arsenal containing 30,000 rifles—enough for a small Republican army—but during the course of the day, the rebels saw they were alone, and that their collaborators elsewhere had failed to act. On the morrow, August 6, more than 900 rebel officers and men crossed the Portuguese border into exile.[21]

After news of the Badajoz rebellion reached Madrid and Barcelona, however, ARM leaders sent out word for their supporters in other provincial garrisons to second the revolt, no matter where they might be. Amid the resultant confusion, the only groups to respond were in two small rural garrisons in the northeast. On August 8, officers at Santo Domingo de la Calzada in La Rioja called out their men, but the leader was shot by one of the ordinary soldiers, and the revolt broke up.[22] On the following day, a detachment at Seo de Urgel in northwestern Catalonia rebelled, but had to flee across the Pyrenees in less than forty-eight hours.[23]

Poor timing and communications had resulted in ignominious failure, and many ARM members began to lose heart. Second Lieutenant Miguel Pérez, who served as organizational secretary under the pseudonym of "Siffler," attempted to obtain the main records of the organization, in order to sell them to the government. But he had already drawn the suspicion of Ruiz Zorrilla, who kept all the records in Geneva, and could therefore give the authorities only the individual names he could remember.[24]

During the year that followed, a purge and a series of trials were conducted. Many members of the ARM were arrested, including four generals, and in one regiment alone thirty-five affiliated officers were discovered.[25] Most of the leaders of the revolt of August 1883 had escaped abroad, but 173 death sentences, mostly in absentia, were passed by the Spanish courts. While the purge was carried out in 1884, two more isolated revolts—which failed totally—were sparked by Ruiz Zorrilla. The two officers who instigated the more important of these, at Gerona, were quickly tried and shot.[26]

During 1884 the Minister of War issued the usual round of circulars requesting that all officers refrain from engaging in any political activity that might be prejudicial to public order. Latent discontent, however, remained near the surface, especially among frustrated, low-paid junior officers, and also among some dissatisfied generals. The political agitation of Ruiz Zorrilla was an important catalyst, but was not the only factor at work. This was shown by the abortive revolt of a detachment of marine infantry at the Cartagena naval base on October 31, 1885, and by another independent outbreak, led by a few officers in January 1886. These were very limited affairs and seem not to have been connected in any way with the Republican Progressive Party.[27]

The last of this round of abortive pronunciamientos took place in Madrid in July 1886. The Republican general Villacampa slipped back into the country after several years of exile, and, supported by two regiments and a small group of Republican enthusiasts, barricaded his forces in the capital's south railway station, hoping that other units would come over to the rebel side; but the government quickly summoned reinforcements and the rebels had to surrender.[28] In the court-martial that followed, Villacampa, a young lieutenant, and four sergeants were condemned to be shot, and three hundred soldiers were sentenced to life imprisonment. However, amid the political apathy currently prevailing in Madrid, there was no feeling of general resentment against the rebels. The decision of Sagasta and María Cristina, the queen regent,* to commute the death sentences won the widowed queen a certain amount of popularity.[29] A major victim of this affair was Pavía, at that time Captain General of Madrid, who had failed to take adequate precautions against the revolt and now fell into disgrace, ruining what remained of his career.

Not a single one of these attempted rebellions had come even remotely close to success, and one political wit in Madrid observed that the old-style Spanish military conspirators were to be compared with antediluvian creatures incompatible with the fauna of the late nineteenth century. Castelar, who had made his peace with the moderate restoration system, did not take the rebellions so lightly, but lamented

---

* An Austrian, María Cristina had been the head of state since the death of her husband Alfonso XII in 1885.

that this persistent agitation dishonored Spain before the civilized world, placing her on the level of "Bulgaria, Haiti, or the Congo." He no longer considered military rebellion the vanguard of liberty, and plainly took comfort in the relative impotence of the rebels.

Yet if the figures later published by ARM members can be accepted, at least 10 per cent of the Officer Corps was involved in the conspiracies. One of the most intelligent young politicians in the country had complained after the 1883 rebellion: "The damage done is not an accidental crime by a few dozen officers, but is rather the sign of an inner coldness, a dry and enervating positivism, that is diffused throughout the whole substance of the Army."[30]

Indeed, the restored monarchy, whose political system was based on narrow oligarchy, boss rule, and corrupt elections, elicited little genuine enthusiasm. In the long run, the Cánovas structure was too weak to remove the Army from politics altogether. Rather, it avoided successful pronunciamientos by keeping the lieutenant generals on its own side. Promotions, financial emoluments, Senate memberships, and important influence within the two official political parties wedded the senior military hierarchy to the system. Most of the dominant military men, following the lead of Martínez Campos and Jovellar, preferred to be identified with the Sagasta Liberals rather than the Cánovas Conservatives. This was due partly to the lingering effects of the progressive ideology of the earlier generation of generals, and partly to resentment against Cánovas because he was the chief political boss.

Nor was it impossible for a high-ranking general to try to carve out a third political position, so long as it was not leftist or anti-dynastic. By the late 1880's, the leading "independent" political general was José López Domínguez, conqueror of the canton of Cartagena and nephew of Serrano. After Serrano died in 1885, López Domínguez became his political heir. In the following year he formed a new faction, the Reformist Party. Its coleader was the former radical Romero Robledo, a frequent Minister of the Interior, who for ten years had been Cánovas' chief political henchman, but had broken with him for personal reasons. Romero Robledo had won a lurid reputation as the most expert electoral manipulator of his generation. The Reformist Party had few reforms to promote, and was motivated largely by the personal ambitions of its leaders. They soon began to quarrel among themselves, which precipitated the disintegration of the faction.

The post of Minister of War, the key political appointment for the Army command, ordinarily fell to one of the big names associated

with the group in power,* or was given to some senior general unlikely
to cause trouble. The successive ministries were interested mainly in
avoiding the issue of Army organization. During the 1880's budgetary
limitations made it necessary to release half of each year's contingent
of conscripts, and effective military manpower fell below 100,000.
This made the proportion of officers to troops even more ridiculous.
At the end of 1886 the current Minister of War, General Castillo,
obtained approval of a plan to reduce the number of officers and encourage early retirement. This measure was similar to a law of 1851
that had specified that a certain proportion of new vacancies were
not to be filled, and had offered seniority credits to officers willing to
retire early.[31]

Soon afterwards, Sagasta found it expedient to accept Castillo's
resignation and to replace him with a quiet, reliable general who
would not disturb the people or the government with any new ideas
of reform. His choice was Manuel Cassola, a staff officer with a fine
professional reputation who seemed unlikely to cause difficulty.[32]

Seldom was Sagasta's political intuition more sadly mistaken. Cassola was indeed an intelligent officer, and a high-minded one. During
his career he had had ample time to reflect on worthwhile organizational changes. His entry into the Cabinet gave him a long-awaited
opportunity for action. On April 22, 1887, he presented a series of
proposals to the Cortes. These did not suggest an organic reform of
the training and equipment of the Army, which would have been
much too difficult and expensive. Instead, Cassola proposed only to
amend some of the most inadequate and unjust aspects of Army personnel policy. He intended to enlarge and reactivate the nation's
highest board of military policy, the Junta Suprema, which had ossified
into a useless honorary body. The Crown already held the right of
military promotion, subject to ministerial approval, but Cassola proposed that it also be allowed to make organic changes in the Army
"consonant with the existing laws and regulations." The new minister
then addressed himself to the draft question, suggesting that at the age
of twenty all healthy male Spaniards be potentially subject to twelve
years of domestic military service (an extension of the present term)
or eight years of service overseas. Draft redemption would be increased
to 2,000 pesetas and would be accepted in lieu of overseas service only.

---

* For example, Martínez Campos was Minister of War under the first Sagasta government.

Several different proposals were included to suppress favoritism and corruption in the matter of promotions, as well as to alleviate the many discomforts and dissatisfactions of the junior officers. First, all peacetime promotions up to the rank of colonel were to be made on the basis of strict seniority. This was already the case in the "closed scales" of the Artillery and Engineering Corps, but their ranks ended at colonel, so that members of these Corps could only be promoted to general on the lists of other Corps (hence an Artillery colonel might also be a major general of Infantry). Cassola proposed to end this dualism by establishing proportionality of all Corps at the rank of general. Moreover, he intended to fuse the scales of officers serving at home and overseas in a single system of peacetime promotion by seniority and merit promotion during war years. The ordinary career would end with the rank of colonel, and all further advancement would take place by special election. If nothing could be done to raise salaries or speed promotion among the miserably paid second lieutenants at the bottom of the list, marriage would be forbidden to any lieutenant under the age of twenty-five; and lieutenants twenty-five or over would be permitted to wed only if they possessed private capital equivalent to 40,000 pesetas. Finally, Cassola proposed total reorganization of the General Staff. As currently arranged, the Staff was a separate Corps with few specific duties, and Cassola wanted to divide it into several branches, each serving a particular Corps.[33]

This amounted to much less than a radical reorganization, but it was the most ambitious attempt at patching that the Army had seen in decades. Though some generals supported it, the Cassola program met a storm of protest from most members of the hierarchy and from political leaders. It attempted to eliminate political promotions, removed part of the protection enjoyed by sons of the wealthy, changed the regional distribution of units into new groupings, and slightly shifted the balance of control in the separate Corps. Sagasta was shocked at the controversy this provoked. His colleagues quoted him as lamenting: "What a disappointment, gentlemen! Danger is where one least expects it. . . . The most scrupulous precautions are futile."[34]

Cassola made a strong impression on the political world, for he was an excellent orator and had an attractive public personality. Yet these qualities only made him appear more formidable and menacing to the established military hierarchy, which redoubled its opposition. The middle classes, particularly the students, were vociferously opposed to

universal military service. Artillery officers resisted en masse, because
the reforms deprived them of a completely separate closed scale and
of the duality of rank enjoyed by their senior officers. At an Artillerists'
banquet in the spring of 1888 a major recited this impromptu verse:

Lo queremos todo o nada:	We want all or nothing:
dualismo, escala cerrada	dualism, closed scale,
y ascenso hasta general.	and promotion to general.

He was afterward arrested for inciting discontent.[35]

Opposition was so strong that Cassola was unable to force his colleagues to take a vote of confidence on the reforms during the 1887–88
session of the Cortes. The climax of the "Cassola affair" came over an
absurd incident of protocol in the late spring of 1888. While the queen
was absent at the Barcelona Exposition, Martínez Campos thought it
his prerogative as current Captain General of Madrid to give the daily
santo y seña, or military watchword, from the royal palace. But Cassola ordered Martínez Campos to receive it instead from the Infanta
Eulalia (sister of the late Alfonso XII), who was still in residence. This
was a severe blow to the pride of Martínez Campos, who was already
vexed by Cassola's "pretensions." Arguing that the Infanta's royal
husband was a cavalry officer who only held the rank of major, and
that therefore she had no right to take precedence over the Captain
General of Madrid in military ceremonies, Martínez Campos broke
with the ministry and resigned his post. In the resultant crisis Cassola's
fellow ministers refused to support him against Martínez Campos.
The Cabinet was reorganized and a less ambitious general chosen as
Cassola's successor.[36]

Though Sagasta had not given his Minister of War much support
he had identified his government with the notion of military reform.
However, during the remainder of Sagasta's regime few changes
were made, and at the beginning of the 1888–89 session of the Cortes,
Sagasta stressed that the crux of Army reform lay in the dispositions
for promotion. These he defined as suppression of dualism, strict
seniority promotion, unification of ranks serving at home and overseas, proportionality of generalship among the various Corps, and
termination of the regular Army career with the rank of colonel.

Hostility to the reforms among the hierarchy was intense, whereas
lesser officers sent messages of support. There were reports of new Republican conspiracies and rumors centering about the possibility of
a pronunciamiento organized by Cassola.[37] On December 28, 1888, the
Director-General of Infantry, General Chinchilla, ordered Infantry

officers to refrain from writing about politics in news media or magazines. On January 15, 1889, Cassola declared in the Cortes:

I affirm that the army of a nation which has still not consolidated its constitution—since there are parties and forces that combat the government with both words and arms—ought to have a political consciousness of its own being and its functions, and educate the nation so that it will have a sense of the reality in which it lives.[38]

That same day, Antonio Pacheco, editor of one of the most widely circulated military newspapers, *El Ejército Español,* published an editorial entitled "Cultivate Your Memory." It threatened politicians and generals with dire consequences if the reforms were not passed.

Within a matter of hours Pacheco was placed under arrest by a platoon of soldiers, even though he was a civilian and not subject to military discipline. It was held by the Captain General of Madrid and other senior members of the hierarchy that Pacheco was liable to prosecution by a military court for "disrespect" under Article 13 of the Code of Military Justice, which stated that crimes of "violation and disrespect for military authority" were subject to the "exclusive jurisdiction of military courts." This was maintained despite the 1881 press law which stated specifically that libel, inciting to subversion, and other offenses committed by newspapers were to be tried before civil tribunals. Shortly after the passage of that law, the Army's Supreme War Council had had to release a major general arrested for writing a newspaper article that was critical of the Captain General of his district. However, Army leaders pointed out that the current Code of Military Justice had been approved by the Cortes on September 30, 1886, following the Villacampa rebellion, and should take precedence over earlier laws. Most of the more liberal politicians, including Cabinet members, disagreed with this interpretation. Specific civil decisions during the past three years had contravened military jurisdiction, and during his tenure as Minister of War Cassola had issued an order to remand such cases to the civil courts.[39] Yet when the public debate was resumed on January 21, Canalejas, the Minister of Justice, who did not believe in tampering with military prerogatives, concurred in the interpretation given by the Captain General. He cited another law, one dating from 1884, whose ambiguous wording seemed to grant the Army the right to prosecute those who criticized it publicly.[40] Though Pacheco was soon released, the hierarchy had demonstrated its power.

Opposition remained so entrenched that only one aspect of the reforms was carried out during that year: a royal decree of October 17, 1889, established that normal peacetime promotion up to the rank of colonel be made by seniority alone, save in the case of officers on overseas duty. The Minister of War appointed in the next reorganization of Sagasta's cabinet, General Bermúdez Reina, tried to push through the Cortes session of 1889–90 proposals to reduce and reorganize the overseas units, to suppress the present structure of the Captaincies General, and to shrink the Officer Corps. The usual strong protests were heard. One of the leading political generals, Luis Dabán, published "A Cry of Alarm" in *El Ejército Español* on March 30, 1890, and strongly criticized Bermúdez Reina in the Cortes.

Dabán's tone was so heavy and menacing that it could not be ignored even by the easygoing Sagasta. On March 31 the Prime Minister observed in the Cortes: "In other countries, perhaps unjustly, when a general shows disrespect and lack of discipline regarding the civil authorities, they do not say, 'He is a bad general,' but . . . 'He is a Spanish general.' "[41] There were further protests, after which Dabán and another general were arrested to await court-martial. However, Dabán had been one of Martínez Campos' intimates in the pronunciamiento of Sagunto, and after special pleading both generals were pardoned.

The main work of the Sagasta government during the first part of 1890 was not the endless question of Army reform, but the passage of a bill to restore universal male suffrage. It proved easier to win the vote for illiterate peasants than to change the status of district Captain Generals, and after this basic political reform had been approved, the Sagasta government was nearing the end of its fifth year in office. Under the compromise system of restoration politics the regime could not last much longer. Martínez Campos lent his support to the formation of a Conservative government in a Senate speech on July 1, and Sagasta, realizing that the time had come to retire temporarily, resigned a few weeks later.

Cánovas returned to power once again, Martínez Campos became president of the Senate, and the Army reform projects were quietly buried. To protect military prerogatives from civilian criticism, a new version of the Code of Military Justice was approved on September 27, 1890, which assigned jurisdiction over all "crimes of violation and disrespect of military authority," by whatever means inflicted, to the military courts. However, the Civil Supreme Court overruled one portion of this decree, stating that the military courts could have no jurisdiction over questions arising from civilian publications, which frustrated Army efforts to obtain powers of press censorship.*

Despite the reaffirmation of authority in Spanish institutions during the 1880's, the Republican conspirator Ruiz Zorrilla had never ceased his attempts to incite military rebellion. On April 10, 1890, he issued a manifesto in which he accused the constitutional monarchy of persistently refusing to grant junior officers (his main contacts) wages commensurate with their dignity and responsibility. He insisted that a truly patriotic regime would raise annual salaries all the way down the line, with increases ranging from 1,000 pesetas for colonels to 300 pesetas for lieutenants.[42] It was perhaps not entirely coincidental that the new military budget for 1890–91 brought salaries for majors and colonels up to the level demanded by Ruiz Zorrilla.

The last Spanish Army reform effort of the nineteenth century was made in 1892 and 1893 by General José López Domínguez, who became Minister of War when the Sagasta Liberals next took over the government. Since there was considerable pressure for reduction of military expenditures, López Domínguez introduced a so-called "peace budget" which lowered Army expenditures by about 5 per cent, from 141 million to 134 million pesetas. During the past twelve years officers' salaries had been increased approximately 20 per cent,[43] though prices remained more or less stable. This helped to pacify the officers professionally and politically, but officers' salaries still devoured about a third of the military budget. Since the officer hierarchy had proved politically untouchable, the only place to cut expenses was in the rank and file. Expenditures for pay, equipment, and training were already at a bare minimum, and costs per soldier could not be lowered. The budget could be reduced 5 per cent only by recruiting 10 per cent fewer troops, which would cut total manpower by 10,873.[44] Any hope of raising the armament of the Spanish Infantry—much less the Artillery—to the standards of contemporary Western armies had to be relinquished.[45]

López Domínguez offered special seniority credits to encourage early retirement of supernumerary officers and enforced strictly limited admission to the Reserve Officer Corps. During its twelve years of existence, this Corps had become a haven for invalids and elderly offi-

---

* On May 20, 1897, the Minister of War, General Azcárraga, introduced a bill to endow the military courts with jurisdiction over newspaper criticism of the Army, but the measure failed to carry. Such special authority was not granted courts-martial until passage of the notorious Law of Jurisdictions of 1906, which is discussed in Chapter 6.

cers as well as for NCO's directly promoted from the ranks. López Domínguez ruled that henceforth only NCO's advanced by merit during time of war could become Reservists. Regular officers were excluded; if no longer fit for active duty, they were to be retired.[46]

López Domínguez also tried to reorganize the unit structure of the Army in accord with the divisional organization of modern European forces. His plan to regroup the regiments and brigades stationed in the peninsula into seven divisions entailed the reduction of the number of territorial Captaincies General from twelve to seven, and would have brought some slight savings in administrative expense, but announcement of the proposed change led to furious protests by citizens in four of the five cities that would have lost their status as seats of Captaincies General. In Vitoria, military headquarters of the Basque region, martial law had to be invoked temporarily.[47] Yet, like most nineteenth-century Spanish military reforms, these changes did not go to the heart of the matter, and after the 1893 incident in Morocco and the start of the final Cuban rebellion two years later they were largely forgotten.

It was not because of their sympathy for the Army that political leaders lacked zeal for military reform, but simply because they were becoming more and more convinced that the Army was indispensable in maintaining order and repressing class struggle. It was during the years 1889 through 1893 that bomb-throwing anarchists became regular fixtures of the Spanish scene. The rebellions and government changes of earlier decades had lacked a consistent class basis, but by the 1890's portions of the working class in Catalonia and Andalusia had developed sufficient organization and self-consciousness to make revolutionary demands and underscore them with violence. Faced with this alarming trend, middle-class political leaders had no interest in feuding with the military hierarchy, whose strength and authority constituted the ultimate defense of the status quo. Cánovas declared in Madrid's Ateneo in 1890: "The Army will remain for long, perhaps forever, the robust support of the social order and an invincible dike against the illegal attempts of the proletariat, which will accomplish nothing by violence but the useless shedding of its own blood."[48]

The urban lower classes had been anti-militarist for half a century, but the development of organized working-class movements helped to focus hatred against the Army as a repressive institution. This in turn encouraged the shift in many politically minded officers' thinking from liberalism or progressivism toward a more conservative attitude that stressed national unity and order above other goals. Further, reaction to the rise of the regionalist movements in Catalonia and the Basque provinces aroused a more conscious sense of Spanish nationalism—or at least an exaggerated patriotism—among the military. Even the very inability of Army leaders to answer the critics of Spanish military institutions seemed to encourage a corporate spirit among many officers.

In the late 1880's and 1890's the Officer Corps became more and more independent and outspoken, and rebuked the various political factions for selfishness and weakness. José Gómez de Arteche, the leading military historian of the period, spoke for many when he said that it was because of civilian selfishness and ignorance that wars were prolonged. In contrast, said Gómez de Arteche, the Army, disciplined and responsible, was "the panacea for all the ills that afflict Spain."[49]

In July 1891 a rebellious corporal attempted to assassinate the Captain General of Andalusia. A month later a group of revolutionaries attacked a barracks in Barcelona in an unsuccessful effort to win the rank and file over to their cause. During the summer of 1892, troops had to be called out to protect the town of Jerez de la Frontera from more than a thousand peasants aroused by the teaching of local anarchists. In Barcelona there was an unprecedented wave of bomb throwing during the following year. Martínez Campos, Barcelona's Captain General, was wounded when two bombs exploded at the feet of his horse during a parade. Execution of the would-be assassin was accompanied by cries of "Viva la anarquía!" from sympathizers. After one shattering explosion caused extensive loss of life in the Barcelona opera house, theaters were left almost empty. Since Spanish cities still did not have effective police systems, it was up to the Army to restore order. The wounded Captain General was replaced by the most rigorous commander available, Valeriano Weyler Nicolau, who had gained some distinction combating Carlists[50] and Cuban rebels and had served as Captain General of the Philippines.[51] Only a few months earlier he had restored order in Vitoria. Under Weyler, the repression in Barcelona was stringent, even brutal, and terrorism was brought under control.

In the meantime, attention was diverted from domestic violence by the outbreak of hostilities in Morocco. In recent decades Spanish policy in Africa had been relatively unambitious compared to that of other European imperial powers. The internal weakness and division of the country naturally discouraged a strong outward-looking

orientation. At the end of the Isabeline regime a mood of disenchantment regarding Spain's Moroccan interests had followed the euphoria
of O'Donnell's campaign, but after the restoration signs of interest re-
appeared. The Spanish Association for the Exploration of Africa was
founded in 1877, and in 1882 Colonel Navarrete's *Las llaves del
Estrecho* (*The Keys to the Straits*) aroused some response with its call
for the recovery of Gibraltar and expansion into Morocco. One of the
terms of the 1860 treaty was finally carried out in 1883 when Morocco
officially ceded to Spain the sparsely settled Atlantic coastal enclave
of Ifni. No attempt was actually made by the Spanish government to
occupy Ifni, but a royal decree of December 26, 1884, created the protectorate of Río de Oro, which embraced a large section of the western
Sahara that lay south of Morocco and extended some distance inland
from the Atlantic coast. This was soon called "the Spanish Sahara."
Shortly afterward a smaller protectorate was established much farther
down the African coast, under the name of Río Muñi (Spanish
Guinea).[52]

The 1860 treaty had also granted Spain a slightly extended zone
of occupation around the small Spanish town of Melilla on the Mediterranean coast of Morocco. At length the restoration regime decided
to occupy this additional strip of land, and in 1891 it dispatched a
boundary commission to demarcate the area. The construction of a
network of small forts and blockhouses along the periphery was
planned as insurance against the border incidents that had intermittently plagued Ceuta and Melilla. One of these defenses was built at
a spot called Sidi Auriach, in close proximity to a local Muslim shrine.
The neighboring Berber kabyle (tribe) protested, but General Margallo, military governor of Melilla, went ahead with the construction
on September 28, 1893. Work done on the first day was immediately
torn down by the Moors, and on the second of October the Spanish
workmen were forced to quit Sidi Auriach altogether.

This provoked a sensation in the Spanish press. When the Sultan
was handed a note of protest in Marrakesh he replied, with considerable candor, that the central government was unable to control all its
subjects. During the month of October reinforcements were sent
across the straits, together with a "technical commission" to study the
problem. On October 27, an effort was made to resume work under
Army protection, but heavy pressure from Berber irregulars forced
the entire Spanish contingent to retreat. Margallo moved his advance

forces part of the way back to Melilla, withdrawing for the night into the fort of Cabrerizas Altas. Before morning this post was completely surrounded by tribesmen, and when Margallo went out to survey the situation he was shot in the head by a Moorish marksman and died almost instantly.*

Considerable public feeling against Morocco was whipped up in Spain, and was shared even by sectors of the proletariat. There was also widespread criticism of the government for being caught off guard without sufficient strength at hand. The Minister of War, López Domínguez, decided that the existing forces in the peninsula were not adequate, and called up thousands of men from the First Reserve. The Reserve was made up primarily of men who had served in the Army during recent years. It was not a trained, organized force, nor was there equipment and transportation readily available for the units. In order to avoid withdrawing large numbers of men from a few cities or provinces, the War Ministry chose to summon smaller contingents from many sections of the country. This completely confused the structure of units; it took at least a month for many of the Reservists to be assembled, and after reporting they were in some cases shunted around to two or three different mobilization centers before finding the right unit. Consequently significant reinforcements did not arrive in Melilla until two or three months had passed. The assignment of officers was as erratic as the mobilization of troops. It has been said that by the close of 1893 there were 30 generals and 248 other officers in the Melilla region who lacked specific duties.[53]

López Domínguez was determined that he should be named to replace Margallo and direct Spain's retaliatory action. He informed his fellow ministers that he would resign from the Cabinet unless he were chosen. But there was at least one political general more influential than López Domínguez. The command was given to the monarchy's darling, Martínez Campos—and López Domínguez did not resign.[54]

The selection was logical, for Martínez Campos had shown fifteen

---

* There was a rumor to the effect that Margallo was actually killed, not by the Moors, but by one of his own subordinates, Lt. Miguel Primo de Rivera (nephew of one of the leading political generals, Fernando Primo de Rivera), who was incensed because Margallo's corrupt administration had permitted Spanish Army weapons to be sold under the counter to Moroccans. Though there is abundant evidence of an extraordinary degree of corruption within the Army commissary in Morocco, and though weapons were indeed sold to Moors, this melodramatic explanation of Margallo's death is entirely without foundation.

years earlier in Cuba that he knew how to reach a peaceful settlement. By the end of the year there were 22,000 troops in the Melilla area, but they were scarcely called upon to fight at all. Once the Spanish made a strong display of force, much of the Moorish belligerence vanished. Work on the fort recommenced before the close of November, and after another month the local kabyles asked for a truce. From Madrid López Domínguez urged Martínez Campos to incite resistance and crush the offending tribesmen by force,[55] and on December 31, the Foreign Minister, Segismundo Moret, sent a strong note to the general saying that the Spanish forces should not be dissuaded by Moorish blandishments.[56] However, Martínez Campos well knew that an extension of hostilities was not in Spain's interest at the time. He accepted the request for a truce, then traveled to Marrakesh to sign a new treaty with the Sultan on March 5, 1894, which pledged an indemnity of 20 million pesetas to Spain. The Sultan also promised to disarm the tribesmen in the vicinity of Melilla, punish hostile kabyles, and allow Spain to station troops on adjacent territory technically under Moroccan sovereignty.[57]

This campaign saved national honor and achieved its goals, but militarily it was most unimpressive, and so far as patriotic sentiment was concerned, it was emotionally unsatisfying. Martínez Campos admitted to reporters that he was not surprised by the cold reception that greeted his return to Madrid in the spring of 1894. The mobilization had revealed the weakness of the Spanish Army and had undermined López Domínguez' "peace budget," but there was no indication that this example would lead to genuine military reform. Army leaders blamed the poor performance of the military machine on inadequate expenditure rather than on lack of planning and incompetent organization.

The terms of Moroccan concessions were reduced in subsequent negotiations during the winter of 1894. On January 31, 1895, the Sultan's representative in Madrid was struck on the shoulder by a flailing blow from a demented Reservist brigadier named Miguel Fuentes, who shouted "I am Margallo!" before being carried away.[58] Military hierarchs issued vociferous assurances that the insane Fuentes did not in any way represent the Army, but the incident nevertheless contributed to the weakness of Spain's bargaining position.

The poor showing of the Army in the Moroccan affair was soon rivaled by an inexplicable disaster in the Navy. After returning the Sultan's envoy to Africa, the new Spanish cruiser *Reina Regente* was never heard from again. It apparently ran into a sudden storm near Gibraltar on the short return trip, keeled over, and sank with all hands on board. This minor disaster was made all the more depressing by the fact that the *Reina Regente* had been one of the few important new additions to the obsolete Spanish fleet.[59] Within a few years, the disappearance of the *Reina Regente* became in the eyes of many a grim symbol of the grotesque ineptness of Spain's military organization throughout the restoration era.

CHAPTER FIVE

The Colonial Disaster

B Y THE MIDDLE of the nineteenth century Spain's colonial empire had diminished, and included only Cuba, Puerto Rico, the Philippine Islands, and a few scattered Pacific archipelagoes and Moroccan enclaves. Of these, Cuba was by far the most important because of its expanding sugar and tobacco economy. Income from Cuban taxes was of considerable importance to the Madrid government. Appointments to administrative posts on the island were much sought after, and Cuba was the main goal of enterprising Spanish émigrés, especially those from Catalonia and the north, who formed the basis of the new nineteenth-century Cuban middle class.

The Army's role was fundamental in the government of Havana, San Juan, and Manila, for in each case the Captain General of the city also held the ultimate civil authority in his territory. From the middle of the century onward, military leaders often took a tolerant, enlightened approach to social and political problems in Cuba, where friction between classes was most acute. For example, a Captain General of Havana, Juan de la Pezuela, who was considered one of the most conservative of the Isabeline political generals, had enforced closure of the Cuban slave trade in 1853 and 1854. However, this humane behavior drew strong protests from the Cuban oligarchy and Pezuela was recalled from his command.[1]

The resources of the Army were put to a severe test by the Ten Years' War of 1868–78. Prim conceded privately in 1869 that, after the rebellion had been quelled, Spain would have to work toward Cuba's autonomy and eventual independence. His first appointee as Captain General during the Ten Years' War, Domingo Dulce, offered amnesty and fair treatment to the insurrectionists, but was literally driven out of Havana by zealots of the *partido españolista*, or ultra-right party, who insisted on a Spanish Cuba at all costs and without quarter. The recalling of Pezuela in 1854 and that of Dulce in 1869 were not the only instances in which the government acceded to the wishes of the Cuban oligarchy at the expense of its own officials. Political representation was severely restricted, and even a visiting Turk might well have been shocked by the corruptness of the island's administration. The turmoils of the radical interregnum within Spain were reflected in the chaos of Cuban government: between 1867 and 1876 there were ten different Captain Generals.

The Army made a poor showing in its efforts to quell the insurrection of creoles and Negroes in eastern Cuba. Adequate resources were seldom available, and incompetence was rife. Emilio Mola, one of the leading political generals of twentieth-century Spain, has written:

In Cuba our military incapacity was made manifest and reached shameful extremes in every aspect, especially with regard to the care of personnel. The medical service, for example, was so deficient that the terrible Cuban vomit decimated whole battalions. The food service was nonexistent, and the troops were forced to live off the country. To cap it all, the payment of wages and allowances was suspended—a measure of accommodation adopted by those in power in order to balance the accounts of the Ministry of Finance—and this shameful state lasted so long that it was feared it would become chronic, not ending till some time after the "Pact of Zanjón" [which ended the war].[2]

The struggle in Cuba should not, however, be viewed in the context of the ordinary colonial campaigns of nineteenth-century European states, in which well-equipped professional western armies defeated backward, disorganized forces of disunited or disintegrating societies. The Cuban conflict was the first of the "dirty wars" of colonial emancipation. The insurgents—clever, fanatical, and inflamed with the desire for national independence—were supported to some degree by the colonial society, and it was difficult for the Spanish to achieve victory by purely military means. When the revolt began in 1868 there were about 21,000 troops in Cuba, but because of corruption, maladministration, and poor hygiene only 7,000 troops were available for combat duty.[3] The rebel forces were never large, but regular armies ordinarily require a numerical superiority of ten to one to repress guerrilla fighters effectively. Not only did the Spanish contingents fail to build up adequate military and numerical strength, but most of their officers never adjusted to the special terms of irregular combat in the tropics.[4]

By the time the civil wars in Spain had been brought under control in 1876, the Cuban struggle had lasted eight years. The Madrid government finally sent its most reliable political general, Martínez Campos, to bring the insurgents under control. Though he headed a force of 70,000 men—the largest army that Spain had ever assembled in Cuba—a military triumph was not the new commander's goal. The long conflict had wasted the ranks of the rebels, who had never been able to rouse the majority of the Cuban population to active resistance; and Martínez Campos relied upon the effects of attrition to implement his "policy of attraction," which offered amnesty, freedom for runaway slaves in the insurgent ranks, and the same sort of autonomy for the provincial government that had been granted to Puerto Rico (though with the hint of greater concessions in the future). In 1878 the rebel leaders finally accepted these terms in the Pact of Zanjón, and the Ten Years' War came to an end.[5] It had cost Spain an enormous amount of money and the lives of at least 50,000 men.[6]

Throughout the torpid years of the restoration, the unsettled problem of Cuba and the other overseas possessions remained as a disturbing specter in the background. A flare-up in Oriente Province was quelled in 1879–80,[7] but aside from the abolition of slavery, which was completed in 1886, no reforms were instituted in Cuban government or administration. The authority of Madrid, though identified with the conservative sector of the plantation-owning oligarchy, was undermined by an almost incredible degree of corruption on every level of Cuban administration. During his brief tenure as Minister of War, Cassola had planned reforms to improve military efficiency on the island, but these were blocked by the Army hierarchy. The only Captain General who seemed to be making headway in reform was Manuel Salamanca, but he died of fever in 1890 after holding his command for less than a year.[8] Another of the more competent Captain Generals, Camilo Polavieja, resigned his post in 1892 as a protest against the widespread bribery in Cuba, and on account of new military regulations which reduced the Captain General's military powers and increased the number of appointments controlled by the clique of political generals in Madrid.[9] Though military leaders were sometimes in favor of political reforms, especially concessions generous enough to forestall another insurrection, Madrid politicians were too much under the influence of the extreme right and the economic oligarchy to do anything effective.[10] The only real attempt at reform, Antonio Maura's local autonomy measure of 1893, was smothered in the Cortes, and its author was forced out of the Cabinet. Furthermore, owing to constant juggling between factions there were twelve different Captain Generals in Havana during the decade 1885–95.

Spain's other major colonial problem was the Philippines. Local administration was largely in the hands of the Spanish religious orders, and the southern islands of the archipelago had never been brought firmly under control. After the late 1880's rebellion became endemic in the Philippines, and there was also an uprising in the Caroline Islands. Small military expeditions were dispatched from the peninsula in 1890 to punish rebels in both archipelagoes, yet nothing was done to prepare the Army for the long-range task of maintaining control of the colonies against the insurrections that would inevitably result from the government's intransigence. Though the vast majority of deaths suffered in the Ten Years' War were due to rampant disease rather than to enemy action, the Army had taken few measures to improve its medical services and supply system. For years every aspect of preparedness was slighted, and finally, at the end of 1894, the garrison in Cuba was reduced, for budgetary reasons, to less than 16,000 men.*

Since the 1870's the independence movement had gathered extensive support in the island. Even moderates despaired of an adjustment of differences with Madrid. The sad spectacle of Spanish mobilization for the Melilla campaign, in which several months were required to dispatch 20,000 troops across the straits, further lowered Cuban respect for Spanish military effectiveness. With each passing year the island's garrison dwindled and the prospects for the success of a new revolt increased.

The final Cuban rebellion against Spain began on January 28, 1895. Calleja, Captain General of Havana, tried to buy off the insurrectionists with the customary promises of reform. Led by an ex-colonial officer from Santo Domingo, Máximo Gómez, the rebels had no intention of compromising; they were ready for a fight to the death.[11] Though Calleja did not immediately ask for reinforcements, it was soon necessary to bring in 9,000 troops from Spain.

Nearly all officers serving in colonial areas were volunteers, for the Army command had always been reluctant to assign officers to Cuba by administrative decree. On March 13, 1895, the Madrid daily *El Resumen* reported that the refusal of junior officers to volunteer for

* Altogether, the Spanish Army at this time numbered 18,562 officers (including 494 generals) and 98,446 troops, according to the *Anuario Militar* for 1893–94.

the Caribbean pesthole would soon force the command to assign colonial posts by lot. This account, though apparently true, was taken by young lieutenants lounging around Madrid as a slur on the honor of the Spanish Army. Civilian criticism throughout recent years, the hoots provoked by the 1893 campaign, and the hard, uncertain challenge of the new rebellion were encouraging a psychology of resentment and contempt in military minds. Several young officers formed a gang and smashed up furniture in the offices of *El Resumen*. When the newspaper *El Globo* published word of this vandalism the next day, the same gang sacked its office and was prevented from destroying its press only by the intervention of the Captain General of Madrid. *El Globo* retaliated on March 15 by demanding that justice be rendered. The Officers' Club, Madrid's Casino Militar, was in a state of intense excitement. A delegation of rebellious junior officers marched to the government building and angrily demanded to see the War Minister, López Domínguez, who broke up a meeting of the Cabinet to speak with them. They subsided only after López Domínguez had agreed to appoint Martínez Campos as Captain General of Madrid, and had accepted two formal petitions from the officers—one demanding suppression of both newspapers, the other requesting that all "attacks" and "insults" against the Army be transferred to the jurisdiction of military courts.[12]

The Sagasta ministry had been going through the motions of preparing a new Cuban autonomy bill, but the spread of the insurrection and this new pressure from Madrid officers forced it from power. It was replaced by what was to be the last Cánovas government. The *El Resumen* incident was a milestone on the road to extension of the *fuero militar* over civilian censorship. By this time the Cassola orders of 1887–88 against military participation in newspaper polemics had for practical purposes become a dead letter. The most bitter critics of Army administration were often not civilians but dissenting military men who wrote in the unofficial Army newspapers. The Army hierarchy responded with efforts to bring its critics, both civilian and military, under direct censorship. López Domínguez spoke in the Cortes about the need for a special press fuero for the Army,[13] and Martínez Campos went on record as believing that all newspapers should fall under the jurisdiction of the Code of Military Justice when dealing with Army matters.[14] Yet the spirit of constitutionalism was still strong enough in Spain to prevent this kind of suppression, and during the next three bitter years the Spanish press continued to speak vigorously on many aspects of Army policy.

By April 1895 the Cuban rebellion was completely out of control. Martínez Campos was relieved of his recent appointment as Captain General of Madrid and sent back to the island to repeat his feat of 1877–78. After a few months, the new commander, a mellowed sexagenarian, realized that this revolt would be far more difficult to suppress than that of the 1870's had been. In a general manifesto on July 1, 1895, Gómez made it clear that this time the insurgents would stop at nothing in their attempt to drive the Spanish out. If necessary, said Gómez, they would burn down plantations and sugar mills, ruin the island's economy, and make Cuba virtually uninhabitable. There could be no easy compromise: either the rebels' demands would have to be granted, or a harsh and bloody campaign would have to be waged to crush them.

This was too cruel a dilemma for the fundamentally humane and politically minded Martínez Campos. He tried to conduct his operations with restraint, exercising great care to avoid destruction of property, offering amnesty to anyone who would lay down his arms, and releasing most captured rebels who swore not to take up arms again. This policy proved completely ineffective; the insurgents increased in numbers and boldness with every passing month. On July 25, 1895, Martínez Campos wrote to the Prime Minister:

I, the representative of a civilized nation, cannot be the first to give an example of cruelty and intransigence. . . .

I could force the rural families into towns, but would then need strong forces to defend them, and already few men in the interior are willing to volunteer. . . . The misery and hunger would be horrible; I would have to distribute rations, and in the last war this meant taking care of 40,000 people daily. . . . Perhaps I may arrive at such measures, but only as a last resort, and I do not think that I have the qualities for such a policy. In Spain, only Weyler has them, for he combines intelligence, valor, and knowledge of war. Reflect, my dear friend, and if, talking with him, you prefer his system, do not hesitate to replace me. We are dealing with the fate of Spain, but I have scruples that come before everything else and forbid shootings and analogous acts. . . .

Even if the insurgents are beaten in the field or forced into submission, my loyal and sincere opinion is that, since this island will not support the war and cannot stand to see us here, with or without reforms, offering pardon or extermination, we will have another war within ten years; and if we still did no more than shed our blood, there would be another and another. Can Spain afford to go on like this? That is not a problem to be solved immediately. At the moment, the only concern is defeating [the rebels], whatever it may cost, but to statesmen like yourself, who have to look to the future, it ought to be a matter of concern to find ways of avoiding [future rebellions].[15]

By August 37,000 new troops had been shipped to Cuba, but the Spanish units were as weak as ever, for 80 per cent of the reinforcements were put out of action by yellow fever and dysentery. Any officer, regular or Reservist, received an automatic promotion for volunteering for Cuban duty. Sergeants in their third term of enlistment who were willing to volunteer were commissioned second lieutenants on the Reserve list. Since regular officers were reluctant to go, about 80 per cent of the lieutenants and captains who eventually served in Cuba were technically Reservists.[16] Pro-Spanish auxiliaries had played a considerable role in the Ten Years' War, but there were relatively few Cuban volunteers in 1895 and the burden on the regular units was heavy indeed.[17]

As it had been during the earlier rebellion, in 1895 the eastern end of the island was left largely in the insurgents' hands.* At no time during the Ten Years' War had the rebels managed to move in force into the richer, more populous western provinces, but in December 1895 a flying column almost succeeded in capturing Matanzas, in central Cuba, near Martínez Campos' own headquarters. When the Captain General tried to launch a punitive expedition, only 2,500 battleworthy troops could be freed from garrison duty. By the close of the year, the Spanish forces could only guarantee the security of the larger towns and the area immediately adjacent to Havana. From April 1, 1895, to January 12, 1896, a total of 80,219 troops were shipped to Cuba, but there were no more Spanish soldiers on their feet and able to bear arms than there were troops in the rebel camp.[18] According to captured reports, there were perhaps 40,000 armed insurgents ready to do battle. Furthermore, on January 22, 1896, one of the rebel leaders entered Mantua, at the western tip of Cuba, having marched almost unmolested all the way across the island. Despite hyperbolic reports from field commanders, the failure of Martínez Campos' moderate approach was obvious.[19] Cánovas had already ordered the Captain General to apply greater rigor, but the latter could not face so harsh a task. Newspaper opinion in Spain was strongly critical of Martínez Campos' command, and the government decided to recall him.[20] The old champion of Sagunto had held the limelight in Army politics for the past two decades, but the challenge of total war against colonial rebellion proved too much for him, and his removal from Havana virtually marked the end of his military and political career.

The Army had been expanding rapidly since General Azcárraga's

---

* This area, Oriente Province, was also Fidel Castro's stronghold in the 1950's.

appointment as Minister of War in September 1895, and Spain was rapidly approaching a state of general mobilization.[21] By the spring of 1896 there were approximately 140,000 troops in Cuba, most of them regularly (if inadequately) equipped, and their numbers were increasing daily. Losses were correspondingly heavy, though many more died from tropical illness than from Cuban bullets or machetes.

The new Captain General of Havana, who blanched at very little, was Valeriano Weyler. Small and wiry, scarcely over five feet tall, Weyler was the descendant of a German émigré who had settled in the Balearics generations earlier. He had steel-blue eyes, was full of energy and endurance, and had a reputation for efficiency and ruthlessness gained in action on nearly every front where Spanish troops had been engaged during the past generation. He had made his way to the top more through work than politics, and was one of the few Spanish generals who tried to keep up with contemporary European military literature. Save for his sexual promiscuity, Weyler's personal habits were almost ascetic. He neither drank nor smoked, and when on campaign he shared the lot of his men, sleeping on regular infantry field cots and living for days on bread and canned sardines. Weyler was a hard man, but most of the lurid Cuban propaganda about his so-called "atrocities" was fabricated. His main faults seem to have been excessive rigidity and an exaggerated sense of self-sufficiency.[22]

When he landed in Cuba, Weyler had few illusions about his task and calculated that the repression of the rebels would take at least two years. He planned a reorganization of the Spanish forces to make them more mobile and versatile in coping with guerrilla tactics. However, purely military measures would not suffice so long as the insurgents enjoyed shelter and support among the rural population. Resurrecting a policy first attempted in the 1870's, Weyler ordered the establishment of *reconcentraciones,* or concentration groups, for the population of the westernmost province, Pinar del Río, which was the easiest area to seal off from the rebels. Concentration of the peasantry had, in fact, been begun by the insurgents, whose widespread destruction of sugar plantations, mills, and other economic resources had already made it impossible for some villagers to continue to live in the countryside. Weyler's plan was to draw together in concentrated, supervised groups more and more of the peasants, who otherwise might give aid and shelter to the insurgents. This has since become a commonplace of counter-insurgency warfare, for the only effective way to deal with a tough, vigorous guerrilla force that is supported by, or coerces, the local population is to gain physical control of that population, or offer it full protection. This usually involves relocation or concentration. Weyler was the first commander to cope with this problem on a large scale, and by 1897 his efforts had become the subject of an enormous volume of atrocity propaganda ground out by the well-financed Cuban revolutionary junta in Tampa, New York, and Washington.* This, the first mass propaganda campaign in modern history based on supposed enemy atrocities, was promptly seconded by the so-called "yellow press" in the United States.[23]

There is at least as much evidence of "atrocities" by the Cuban rebels as by the Spanish military during these years, but misdeeds on the part of the Cubans drew scant international attention. Most of the substantiated incidents against which the insurgents complained seem to have been committed by the pro-Spanish Cuban auxiliaries, rather than by Spanish troops themselves. Most of the suffering in the *reconcentraciones* was caused by the Army's inability to care for the needs of the relocated population rather than by a Spanish policy of violence or cruelty. The island's economy was being systematically wrecked by the rebellion, and the Army was totally incapable of dealing with the problem.[24]

At the other extreme of the empire, a Philippine rebellion had broken out during the late summer of 1896. It was organized by a native Masonic-type nationalist society composed of whites and Filipinos who wanted to overthrow the existing quasi-theocratic administration and install an autonomous government that would recognize the equality of races and religions. Most native Filipinos enrolled in the Spanish forces went over to the rebels. The Captain General of Manila, Ramón Blanco, pleaded unavailingly with Madrid for more troops, and attempted unsuccessfully to negotiate with the insurgents.[25] At the end of the year Lt. Gen. Camilo Polavieja, who had resigned the Captain Generalcy of Cuba in 1892, was sent to take charge of field operations in the Philippines. Though Blanco remained titular Captain General, he not unnaturally considered the arrival of Polavieja a reflection upon his own reputation, and he re-

---

* After enduring vociferous North American denunciation of his policy, Weyler was able to note with some satisfaction in his memoirs: "No one who is even partially informed about contemporary military history will be unaware that the English later copied [my policy] in the Transvaal and the North Americans [used it] in the Philippines." Weyler, *Mi mando en Cuba,* I, 11. The term developed by United States Army advisers for a roughly similar formation they encouraged in South Vietnam in 1963–64 was "fortified villages."

signed, leaving Polavieja in complete command. After his return to Spain, Blanco was severely criticized for incompetence, though the Spanish difficulties in the Philippines were scarcely attributable to one general.[26]

Polavieja had a reputation for severity and honesty. Of an aristocratic but impoverished family, he had entered the Army as an enlisted man and worked his way up. He had strong views on public affairs and definite political ambitions. He was known both as an advocate of reform and as proclerical, which had won him the sobriquet of "the Christian general." Polavieja's Christianity was perhaps nearer to that of Torquemada than to that of St. Francis, for he initiated a stern repression and frequently held public executions of captured rebels. The severity of his command, climaxed by the judicial murder of the Philippine patriot José Rizal, provoked loud anti-Spanish propaganda in parts of eastern Asia. Spanish troops captured by the rebels were tortured and mutilated in retaliation. Soon the rigorous Polavieja was drawing almost as much criticism from the Spanish press as the lax Blanco had. The Cánovas government was not pleased with Polavieja's policy, and in the spring of 1897, after only a few months in the Philippines, he was recalled to Madrid.

Polavieja was replaced by Lt. Gen. Fernando Primo de Rivera, whose disloyalty as Captain General of Madrid had assured the triumph of Martínez Campos' restoration pronunciamiento 22 years earlier. Primo de Rivera arrived in an optimistic mood, bringing further reinforcements. It was soon evident that the new leader was gifted with a certain amount of inventiveness. He strengthened the Spanish forces by incorporating native volunteers into new Army battalions at the ratio of two Filipinos to one Spaniard. The Philippine rebel chiefs were more venal than the Cubans: lacking any immediate chance of military victory, they accepted a large bribe from the Captain General to disband their men and quit the archipelago. Lt. Col. Miguel Primo de Rivera, the commander's own nephew, served as temporary hostage of the rebels until the "indemnity" was paid. By midsummer of 1897, the revolt in the Philippines seemed to be under control.[27]

Weyler's policy in Cuba was also showing results. The entire island had been divided into districts, and Weyler planned to clear out one section at a time, keeping the rebel forces separated and off balance by sending flying columns across the countryside. Soon many of the insurgents decided to lay down their arms, and by the spring of 1897 most of western Cuba had been cleared of rebels and part of the central area was being flushed out as well.

The Spanish Army's main problem still was hygiene. Many soldiers sent to the island never had a chance to see action. Fever and dysentery struck tens of thousands each month. According to one set of statistics, the Army suffered 49,000 hospital cases from non-combat illnesses during the last ten months of 1895, 232,000 during the year 1896, and then, as the size of the Spanish forces reached its peak, 231,000 during the first six months of 1897.[28] This meant a yearly average per soldier of two illnesses requiring hospitalization. Such figures were not made public during the war, but the grotesquely high mortality rate in the Spanish Army during peacetime was a matter of common knowledge to many.[29] It eventually became impossible to disguise the realities of the Cuban campaign.

In Spain, the general attitude toward the colonial wars was a mixture of resentment, chauvinism, applause, and apathy, with apathy predominating. There was noise and flag-waving as the long lines of recruits were methodically sent off to die of yellow fever, but very little was done to organize the country's resources on their behalf. It was later remarked, "What could not be said of the way those overseas expeditions were organized! Herds of men [were sent off] without the slightest ideal, without the least coordination, without adequate armament and equipment!"[30]

Although "non-patriotic" talk was largely proscribed in all quarters save in the organized portion of the working class, constant criticism was directed against the policies and qualifications of the Spanish commanders.[31] Moreover, in the large cities there were demonstrations by the poorer classes during the summer of 1896 protesting the conscription. Republican conspirators hatched a plot with sergeants in several peninsular garrisons to provoke an anti-government mutiny, but this was discovered, and more than twenty sergeants were expelled from the Army.[32]

The real problem at home was how to sustain morale and give the troops a sense of purpose. This task was beyond the limited imagination of both politicians and generals. With thousands of supernumerary officers hanging around the home garrisons, it was still necessary to promote sergeants in order to staff the Cuban forces. In 1897 teenage cadets in the military academy were offered commissions, after only eleven months of classes, in return for service overseas, and second lieutenants of sixteen were not unknown. A military effort of this sort could not be taken seriously.

The Cánovas government had no solution for the Cuban problem save to persevere until military victory had been won, hoping all the while that the United States would not intervene. A feeble gesture to extend local political autonomy on the island appeased no one, and, in view of wartime conditions, was almost meaningless. Had he made genuine concessions, the Prime Minister would probably have been overthrown by the chauvinist factions in the Cortes. As it was, the opposition threatened to overthrow him anyway.[33]

By the winter and spring of 1897 most of the liberal newspapers in Spain had become vehement in their denunciation of Weyler's direction of the repression. The best and most widely read newspaper in Spain, with a circulation of more than 100,000, was the liberal *El Imparcial,* published in Madrid by the Gasset family. Together with the influential *Heraldo de Madrid,* it launched a major anti-Weyler campaign, emphasizing that the Spanish forces still did not have effective control of Cuba. Part of the Spanish press thus paralleled the activities of the Cuban junta and the "yellow press" in the United States, leading Spanish ultras to complain that the newspapers were becoming pro-Cuban.

While Liberals grew restive, the Conservative elements were also casting about for a new leader. On his return to Spain in May 1897 "the Christian general," Polavieja, began a triumphal march from Barcelona in which most opposition factions participated. He was assiduously courted by the most extreme sector of Spanish Catholicism, the Integrists, who presented him with a sword inscribed, "From the national Catholic party to the avenger of the insult inflicted on Spain in the Philippines—General Polavieja, a model gentleman and Christian soldier. You conquered because you trusted more in the cross than in the blade of your sword!"[34] The most politically active member of the Spanish hierarchy, Cardinal Cascajares, Archbishop of Valladolid and a former Army captain, was developing a scheme to reform the Conservative party by replacing Cánovas with Polavieja, who enjoyed the queen regent's favor.

Cánovas had been opposed to Polavieja's appointment in the first place, and directed that he be ordered to keep secret the itinerary of his return trip. Crowds continued to greet the general, nevertheless. On his arrival in Madrid, he paid a courtesy call to the queen regent. This led to the so-called "balcony crisis," when María Cristina, together with Prince Alfonso and one of the princesses, stepped out onto a balcony, to the cheers of a throng of onlookers, and waved farewell to Polavieja. Cánovas was infuriated, and quickly arranged for the queen regent to publish a note denouncing rumors that he had lost her confidence.[35] On May 21 he struck back in the Cortes against all his critics, observing that it was not professional soldiers but politicians and newspapermen who criticized Weyler's operations.[36] A few weeks later the Prime Minister managed to win a vote of confidence, and the Cortes recessed for the summer.

The Spanish regime's senior statesman never faced another assembly, for an Italian anarchist shot him down in a resort hotel near San Sebastián in August 1897.* The assassination was a profound blow to the government. No other leader had the experience, determination, or support to continue a firm course. To save the Cánovas policy, some Conservatives tried to regroup about the discredited Martínez Campos. Others wished to support Polavieja or the ablest of the civilian leaders, the conscientious Francisco Silvela. No consensus was possible because of the extreme factional division, so a temporary two-month government was formed under the former Minister of War Azcárraga, a colorless, honest general who could be counted on not to attempt anything radically new. Easygoing, malleable, and without great personal ambition, he was also a favorite of the queen regent, but his political ineptness and lack of personality made it impossible for him to hold the government together.[37] No faction of the Conservatives was able to muster effective support, although the situation was grave —a ministry composed of Sagasta Liberals would mean an end to Cánovas' policy, and possibly provoke a blowup by the ultras and the military as well. But leading political generals such as Polavieja and Martínez Campos were not eager to see the government dominated by Cánovas' heirs, and they made it clear to the queen regent and to several other leaders that no Army rebellion need be feared if a Cabinet of Sagasta Liberals were appointed.[38]

Sagasta, "the old shepherd," took office once more on October 4, 1897. His had been a career based on concession and compromise, and it was only natural that his return to power was predicated on the need to alter the policy of the preceding ministry. Five days later Weyler was recalled from Cuba. The order left the *españolista* faction and many Army officers in Havana in a state of utter outrage. In later years Weyler emphasized that a continuation of his policy would have brought Spain victory, but consideration of the achievements of his two-year command does not altogether support this contention. As

---

* The assassination does not seem to have been in protest against the Cuban policy; according to its author, it was an act of revenge for the torture of Spanish anarchists by Barcelona police.

Weyler himself admitted, he had not yet succeeded in clearing all of western Cuba of insurgents, and they still roamed the eastern part of the island almost at will.[39] Weyler's recall was not prompted by military problems in Cuba or domestic criticism in Spain so much as by mounting concern over possible intervention by the United States unless a more conciliatory approach were tried. Weyler was replaced by Ramón Blanco, earlier vilified by certain Spanish patriots for the apparent laxity with which he had dealt with the Philippine rebellion. Whereas Weyler had been chosen because he was "hard," Blanco was now chosen because he was "soft." The new offensive against the rebels was called off, and a full amnesty for political prisoners was proclaimed. This change in policy was as ineffective in persuading insurgents to lay down their arms as its critics had predicted it would be.

In Spain, the public was slowly becoming aware of the cost of the repression. At the end of November, the Compañía Transatlántica, which handled shipping to Cuba, published figures on the quantity of troops and arms sent abroad since the beginning of 1895. According to this source, 185,227 men had been sent to Cuba, 28,774 to the Philippines, and 5,848 to Puerto Rico. The Army had supplied these troops with almost two hundred thousand rifles, ten thousand carbines, and seventy million cartridges. Despite the relative inadequacy of the equipment, this was an exhausting effort for the Spanish economy. Rifle ammunition alone was estimated to have cost in excess of 36 million pesetas.[40] The Cuban correspondent for *El Imparcial* wrote on November 30:

Of the 200,000 men who have come [to Cuba], there remain, according to the last statistics for November, 114,961. Of these, 35,682 have been detached and 26,249 are sick, leaving 53,030 ready to fight; but from this figure one must subtract those who are assigned to other duties and many who, though not hospitalized, are ailing. The enormous difference between those who came and those who remain constitutes the casualties of the campaign. How many men has the war cost Spain? No one knows: we do not know if those represented by the difference between 200,000 and 114,961 are dead, have disappeared, or are not counted. Among them are those who have returned to the peninsula—but of these, how many have gone back to their homes? How many have survived the anemia with which the island infected them?

In the autumn of 1897, frequent public demands were made for investigation of the widespread administrative corruption, but there was little or no demand for an end to the struggle, for political opinion would not admit discussion of the loss of Cuba. The great majority of the draftees from the lower classes bore up stoically. During 1897 only about 4 per cent of the young men eligible to serve evaded the draft.

Weyler was lionized on his return to Spain. The chauvinist elements hailed him enthusiastically, and he gained support from both extremes of the political spectrum. The uncertainty of the new government, which held the prospect of a national or international crisis, lifted the hopes of the Republicans. Two generals of Republican background, Augustín Luque and Páez Jaramillo, were engaged in a conspiracy of sorts to overthrow the regency, and they hoped that Weyler would be willing to capitalize on resentment within the Officer Corps and chauvinist groups to take the lead. However, Weyler was nothing if not a disciplinarian. He detested insubordination, and used his considerable influence to discourage talk of a pronunciamiento.[41]

The Carlists also sought out the general. Don Carlos "VII"* had publicly criticized the recall of Weyler, and the leading Carlist ideologist of those years, Vázquez de Mella, stated in an article in *El Correo Español*† that the Carlists and General Weyler were "in substantial agreement." This was true with respect to Cuba, but not with regard to any other issue. However, the Carlists were taking advantage of the Cuban conflict to reactivate their latent conspiracy, and by the close of 1897 the four main sections of the conspiracy—in Madrid, Catalonia, Valencia, and Aragon—were under the direction of four retired Carlist generals. Negotiations were conducted with Weyler, who weakened momentarily and agreed to meet with Don Carlos himself, provided that complete secrecy be maintained. It was arranged that Don Carlos would sail from Ostend in the private yacht of an English aristocrat to Weyler's family home at Mallorca, where the general would slip out for an offshore chat. According to Don Carlos' personal secretary, this plan fell through because Weyler insisted that no outsider save the secretary be present. Don Carlos' domineering French wife, Marie Berthe de Rohan, insisted on accompanying her spouse, and this caused the crusty general to cancel the meeting entirely.[42]

Martínez Campos and Polavieja were correct in their assurance that the Army would not rebel against the Sagasta government. The only insubordination occurred in Havana, where the government's new Cuban autonomy bill went into effect on January 1, 1898. Twelve days later, a number of officers from the Havana garrison, followed by an españolista mob, broke into the offices of three pro-autonomist

---

* Duke of Madrid and pretender to the throne.
† "Weyler and Carlism," *El Correo Español*, December 14, 1897.

newspapers, shouting, "Death to Blanco! Long live Weyler! No more autonomy!"[43] The main consequence of this incident was that it provided the excuse for the United States consul in Havana, General Fitzhugh Lee, to demand protection from Washington for American interests in the capital. This led to the visit of the battleship *Maine*, whose mysterious destruction in Havana harbor on February 15 provided the *casus belli* for the Spanish-American conflict.

American pressure had been building steadily for nearly two years and was, of course, motivated by a variety of factors—financial interest, humanitarian ideals, anti-Spanish newspaper propaganda, and strong hopes for American expansion overseas. After the sinking of the *Maine* raised American pressure to the bursting point, war between the two countries could not have been avoided unless Spain had been willing to relinquish Cuba either by grant of independence or by transfer to American protection. This Spain would not do, and though its government went so far as to announce a unilateral truce on April 9, the United States declared war two days later.[44]

On April 20 the government in Madrid called up another 20,000 men for the Army, and the obsolete Spanish Navy was ordered into battle array. Weyler insisted that American attempts to blockade Cuba should be met by an amphibious assault of 50,000 Spanish troops on the Atlantic coast of the United States—a rash suggestion that completely overshot Spain's technological potential. The strongest words seemed to come from the Carlists, but there was a great deal of patriotic rhetoric and versifying in almost every group. Newspapers breathed courage and confidence, while virtually everyone joined in heaping curses on the American aggressors.

Al pelear con los yanquis,	When we fight the Yankees,
señores, tendrá que ver	gentlemen, you will see
cómo de dos ladrillazos	how we make them run
los haremos de correr.	with two blows of a brickbat.
Tienen muchos barcos,	They have many ships,
nosotros, razón.	but we have the right.
Ellos, armamento;	They are well armed,
nosotros, honor.[45]	but honor is ours.

The very terms of these verses indicated the hopelessness of the contest. A few farsighted Spaniards suggested that public speakers and editors cease vilifying the Americans so ferociously, since it would soon be necessary to make peace on their terms.

The brave front put up by civilian spokesmen deteriorated within a few months. Special excise taxes bore heavily on the lower classes, and by the middle of 1898 shipping shortages and economic disruption had resulted in a serious food scarcity in some provinces. News of the destruction of Spain's Far Eastern Fleet in Manila Bay at the beginning of May provoked widespread rioting and political protest. Twelve people were killed during the worst outburst, in the southern town of Linares, and it was necessary to impose martial law on Madrid.

On June 20 the American expeditionary force made a virtually unopposed landing on the southeastern coast of Cuba. Blanco had at this time approximately 100,000 troops in Cuba, but many were sick or unequipped. At the town of Santiago, near the American beachhead, General Linares commanded nearly 20,000 troops, but the majority were not fit for hard combat. Linares managed to concentrate only 1,700 of them on the high ground of El Caney and San Juan, in the path of the American advance. His supporting artillery in Santiago consisted of some twenty ancient bronze cannon of Spanish manufacture. The artillery of the Americans, though much better, newer, and more plentiful, was rather poorly coordinated, but it managed to knock down the crude Spanish fortifications. The Spanish Infantry at El Caney fought steadily, inflicting greater losses on the somewhat ill-organized American attackers than they themselves suffered, yet they could not long stand the weight of superior numbers and firepower.[46] Early in July the Spanish fleet in Santiago steamed out to destruction, and not long afterward the city surrendered.[47] Meanwhile, the Spanish land forces at Manila, after one pitched battle, withdrew from combat. Peace negotiations began in Paris on July 22, and a cease-fire was agreed upon by August 12. In the subsequent treaty, the Spanish government was forced to relinquish Cuba, Puerto Rico, and all Spain's possessions in the Pacific.

The equipment, leadership, and organization of the Spanish forces had been utterly abysmal. Three years of warfare had impoverished the government and stripped the country of the remains of its historic empire. The loss of life was staggering. Although the final casualty report listed only 2,159 deaths in combat, more than 53,000 men had died of disease by the end of the Cuban campaign.[48]

CHAPTER SIX

The Aftermath

S PAIN's military disasters in Cuba and the Philippines were a greater humiliation than the Abyssinian defeat had been for the Italians two years earlier. Lord Salisbury pronounced the Spanish a mori-
bund people; others suggested that Spain was "the sick man of the
West." The essential causes of the disaster—inefficiency, irresponsibility, and apathy—indicated that sudden national regeneration was
scarcely to be expected. The problem was well stated by the Conservative leader Francisco Silvela in a newspaper article published on
August 16, 1898, soon after the fighting ended. Entitled "Without
Pulse," it drew considerable attention:

The war with the ungrateful sons of Cuba did not move a single fiber of
popular feeling. Orators spoke eloquently in the Chambers of sacrificing
the last peseta and shedding the last drop of blood—the blood of others.
The municipalities honored their soldiers, who saluted and marched away
submissively, bringing to mind the "Hail Caesar" of Roman gladiators;
the "March of Cádiz" was played and the press applauded, while the country, inert, let things take their course. We used to say that this was because
the people could not become interested in a civil struggle—a war against
nature and the climate, a war without triumphs or defeats.

But as Silvela noted, the national war with the United States had
brought no change in this attitude:

One only notes a general cloud of silent sadness that lends a gray background to the canvas, without changing lives, or habits, or entertainments,
or the people's willingness to submit to whoever controls the government.
No one in Spain thinks about anything save personal benefit. Some say that
this is because we are dominated by materialism. Others say that egoism is
slaying us: that ideas of duty, glory, and national honor have passed, and
that the warlike passions have died.
    This is a profound error. The aggregate of good and bad passions consti-

tutes the soul of a people and lives as long as a man lives, because it is the expression of his basic nature. When peoples grow weak, and when their passions die, there is no transformation of their instincts, ideas, affections, or modes of feeling, but rather a much graver result: the extinction of life.

Thus we have seen that the very passivity shown by the country in the face of civil war, in its struggle with a foreign power, and, finally, in its acceptance of a defeat without glory, has prepared it to allow its sons to be taken away and its treasures lost. Such cruel amputations as payment in pesetas for Cuba and the other islands have been suffered without complaint by the middle classes, who are usually the first and best equipped for resistance and noise.

In vain has the mass circulation press, encouraged by minor successes, tried to stir up opinion by boldly knocking at the door of popular passion and calling attention to the errors and deficiencies of the political leadership. Everything has been useless, and much of the country looks with evident sympathy toward the censorship of a previous generation . . . which might serve now to make more palatable the daily fare served by the newspapers and thus preserve the readers' indifference and laxity. . . .

There is no need to pretend there are arsenals and shipyards where there are only buildings manned by small detachments who guard nothing and build nothing. There is no need to boast of fleets that neither maneuver nor fire; nor to classify as armies mere agglomerations of boys chosen by lot; nor to struggle to retain, for the sake of disastrous illusions, more than we can administer; nor to lavish rewards merely in order to create the impression that we appreciate heroism.[1]

Tales of military corruption and incompetence by troops returning from Cuba created a strong impression in Spain, and a few politicians arose to denounce the military as authors of national dishonor. On September 7, the loudest of these critics, the Conde de Almenas, declared in the Senate:

As a representative of the nation, I salute these victims of the war, these soldiers who return to the Fatherland worn down by sickness and bullets, conquered and humiliated. But I cannot extend this salute to their chiefs, who have not known how or have not been able to lead them to victory or even to an honorable defeat.[2]

A number of the generals with seats in the Senate—Chinchilla, Dabán, Primo de Rivera—rose in furious response. They demanded that the critics show proof of such charges or else be prosecuted. Weyler, who blamed the defeat on the weakness of the politicians, pressed for an inquiry into the responsibilities of the military, adding that if the Army's rights and its honor were not fully protected the generals would "take justice by the hand."[3]

In January 1899, after the final treaty had been signed, the Conde de Almenas returned to the attack: "Proofs, charges! Honorable Senators, do you not find these words extremely laughable . . . ? Who asks more proof than the bloody corpse of the Fatherland?" He later demanded: "Why have these incompetent generals not been shot?"[4] In the Senate debate of January 27, Martínez Campos confessed: "I went to conquer but I could not. I am, therefore, a military failure—but my own sense of dignity tells me that I will be able to justify myself before the parliamentary commission."[5] However, there was to be no such commission. Most political leaders did not support Almenas; they were aware that the failures of the Spanish regime went far beyond the responsibility of the military. Political generals like Martínez Campos had been their partners, not their agents. Francisco Silvela, who eventually succeeded Cánovas as head of the Conservative party, disclaimed any party responsibility for the more extreme charges.

The only leading commander who seems to have escaped the general opprobrium was Polavieja, who had been recalled for political reasons even though his policy was achieving moderate success. With the open support of part of the clerical ultra-right and the good will of the royal family, "the Christian general" seized his opportunity to capitalize on the mounting political discontent. He issued a manifesto in Barcelona on September 1, 1898, and called for a variety of reforms: universal military service without special exceptions, reduction of excise taxes in favor of the poor, a special tax on unearned income from capital, and administrative concessions to the Catalan regionalists.[6] Though Polavieja's entry into politics earned him the enmity of other rivals in the Army hierarchy, the Conservative leaders found it prudent to deal with him. When a new Silvela ministry replaced Sagasta in 1899, Polavieja entered the Cabinet as Minister of War.

The flurry of threats and charges aroused by the defeat had not yet subsided. On March 27, 1899, the Madrid daily *El Nacional* began an exposé of incompetence and corruption in the former Philippine command that featured a series of articles by an ex-captain of volunteers.[7] At the beginning of April, several honor tribunals were set up in the Army to deal with these and other accusations.[8] On May 12 and May 13 there were bloody brawls between university students at Valladolid and cadets of the Cavalry Academy.

The Conde de Almenas returned to his denunciations in the Senate on June 16. After another blast, General Blanco publicly lamented that he had not rebelled against the government when he held the Cuban command, and Weyler spoke out in plain terms:

Unlike General Blanco, I do not regret not having rebelled in Cuba, though I was in much worse circumstances than he. . . . Today it is much harder than it was in the past to get soldiers to rebel for a political cause. On the other hand, because of the manner of recruitment and the short period of service, it is easier for them to make common cause with the lower classes.

I have been contacted by some who have this aim [rebellion], although I endeavor to do no more than shoulder patriotic responsibilities. Do not forget, however, that not long ago the Fatherland was regenerated by military rebellion, and that if there had not been generals like O'Donnell, the Duque de la Torre [Serrano], Prim, and even Martínez Campos, who placed their valor and persons at the service of the Fatherland, the consequences would have been grave. I ask the government to keep this in mind so that greater ills may be avoided.[9]

Eduardo Dato, the Minister of the Interior, replied sharply that Weyler, "who did not know how to conquer in Cuba," lacked the authority to make threats. Dato asserted that the Army was no one's "instrument," and that the era of pronunciamientos had passed.[10]

A special commission was eventually sent from the palace to hear the generals' grievances. By the autumn of 1899, the furore created by the charges was blowing over, and it was becoming clear that the rights, privileges, and organizational status of the Army would not be interfered with, since that would upset the existing institutional balance. As it turned out, no investigation of Army leadership was made save by the Army itself. When the military honor tribunals rendered their verdict in August 1899, two generals and one admiral were retired prematurely, but that was all. The fate of Cervera, former commander of the Atlantic fleet, remained in doubt, but he was later officially cleared of blame by the margin of a single vote. Though the Conde de Almenas continued his antimilitary campaign the following year, few political leaders paid any attention.

Throughout the next decade the cornerstone of the government's domestic policy was financial restriction and reduction of the national debt. All that the Conservative ministry of 1899 demanded of the Army was that it spend less.[11] As usual, this was much more easily said than done, for the membership of the Officer Corps had ballooned during the Cuban war. The General Staff's *Escalafón* (officer list) of September 1, 1898, listed 499 generals, 578 colonels, and approximately 23,000 officers of lower rank. A high proportion of these were Reservists—former NCO's promoted to officer rank as a reward for service in Cuba and the Philippines. It seemed that even a crushing military defeat could not put an end to promotions and decorations. General Correa, Minister of War in the outgoing Sagasta Cabinet, had noted early in 1899 that there were eight thousand officers left without assignment after the forces in the lost colonies were dissolved and repatriated. "Such a considerable number of generals," said Correa, "is due to the prodigality with which campaign promotions have been granted. It has been a veritable flood, and I do not know if the ill can be remedied."[12]

The political leaders were determined to slash costs one way or another. On July 15, 1899, Liberal deputies voted for a Cortes bill to reduce the Army to a force of 60,000—a cutback of 75 per cent from the wartime maximum.[13] This measure failed to carry, but the Conservative Finance Minister Villaverde was almost as demanding. He not only wished to eliminate the extraordinary military budget but also insisted that the regular appropriation be sliced by at least 40 million pesetas, or more than 20 per cent. Implementation of the reduction was the responsibility of the new War Minister, Polavieja. Finding that he could cut no more than 8 million pesetas from the military budget without provoking strong resistance from Army leaders, he resigned on September 28. Polavieja was replaced by Azcárraga, the "teddy bear" of the monarchy's generals, who could be depended on to do as he was told.

The government also proposed to reduce the naval budget. In the Cortes debate of December 6, it was pointed out that Spain's naval expenses remained almost as great as those of Italy, though the Italian fleet was now many times larger. Intra-service squabbling tended to strengthen the government's position. *La Correspondencia Militar* criticized the ineffectiveness of naval support during the war and sarcastically dwelt on the fact that, though the Navy had only two major warships left, it was still paying the salaries of 142 admirals.

In the end, nearly all of Villaverde's demands were granted. The reduction was accomplished, not by lowering salaries or shrinking the Officer Corps but by spending less on equipment and training and by cutting back the number of recruits almost as far as the Liberals proposed. Under the 1900 military budget, 80 million pesetas, out of a total of 138 million, went into officers' salaries; 45 million went for troops and maintenance, and only 13 million was spent on matériel.

The structure of the Spanish Army had reached a new low of absurdity. After the final rounds of wartime "merit" promotions had been made in 1900, the Officer Corps numbered 24,705. Since the budget provided for no more than 80,000 troops, the ratio of men to officers was less than four to one.[14] There was scarcely any money for training or maneuvers. In some garrisons half the officers had absolutely no assignments at all, and many others had no precise duties in their nominal assignments. Consequently many officers preferred to be left without any specific post so that they might take another full-time job on the side.

Though the proportion of the budget devoted to officers' salaries later diminished, it was still much higher than in other European armies. Italy spent only one-sixth, and France less than one-seventh, of their total Army funds on officers' salaries, while the ratio was even less in Germany.[15] Though the 471 Spanish generals were, in terms of age, the oldest set of generals in any European Army, no particularly energetic efforts were made to encourage earlier retirement.[16] Moreover, despite the fact that the Corps took the lion's share of the budget, individual officers found their economic status sinking. Prices rose persistently in the early twentieth century, but no one dared to think of raising the salary level without reducing the enormous superfluity of officers.[17]

There was occasional discussion of Army reform, but little action.[18] Drastic shrinkage of the Army would logically dictate sweeping reorganization of the whole unit structure, but although the old system of Corps organization had been dissolved by royal decree during the war, scant effort was made to fuse and reorganize the individual units.[19] Most of the regiments formed in the years from 1896 to 1898 remained in being, though most had less than 400 members. Another attempt at systematization was belatedly made in 1904, when the Army structure was reorganized into seven territorial districts, each containing two Infantry divisions. Heterogeneous units were then coordinated into regular divisional form, and the transition from regimental structure that had begun early in the nineteenth century was finally completed. It had taken the better part of a hundred years.

No more than a fourth of the eligible draftees could be called up in 1900, and some of them had to be released after only a few months because of lack of funds for their maintenance. It has been said that at one point during the next few years, before the annual quota was recruited, the enlisted manpower fell as low as 30,000.[20] That would have made the officer-soldier ratio almost one to one. At no time during the postwar decade (1899–1908) could the Army draft more than half the available recruits, or about 40,000 men each year. The average soldier seems to have been retained no more than two years, so that at no given time were there many more than 50,000 trained troops available. Through 1906, the budget provided for the annual maintenance and training of 80,000 to 83,000 men.[21] This figure went up briefly to 100,000 in 1906–7, then dropped to 80,000 once more under the Conservative ministry of 1907–8. During all these years, the Reserve system remained a paper organization.

The number of healthy young Spaniards who emigrated to escape the draft apparently increased after 1900. Conditions of ordinary Army life had not improved: the food was still notoriously wretched and the barracks frequently full of lice. Because of the lack of proper food and medical care, many of the troops were in poor physical condition.[22] From time to time, there was parliamentary debate over the problem of the backward supply system, but any real improvement would have cost money, and consequently nothing was done.[23]

The ruinous state of the Army in the first decade of the twentieth century did not, however, result in its fading into the background of national life, for after 1900 its role in civic affairs began to expand. The main reasons for this were the growing social and economic tensions between classes and the rebellion of the progressive northeast against the political stagnation of central and southern Spain. As Spain turned in upon herself without achieving fundamental reorganization or revitalization, domestic conflicts gathered momentum. Since the cities and provinces lacked adequate police forces, the Army remained the guarantor of public order. Troops had to be called out periodically to repress disturbances, and every year or so martial law was declared in parts of Catalonia, Vizcaya, the Levant, or Andalusia.

For all its ridiculous ineptness, the Army held its place as the country's principal secular institution. Its officers were hypersensitive to the scorn often poured upon them, made their own calculation of their importance to the Fatherland, and could not help but respond in their own way to Spain's civic predicament. Nearly all the officers were bitterly opposed to Basque and Catalan nationalism, regarding it as an attempt to destroy the national unity for which they and their predecessors had bled. Ranking generals tended more and more to make common cause with wealthy elements in Spanish society. Special perquisites were usually available to the outstanding generals, though some of the more common sources of graft were being eliminated. Moreover, during the past generation there had been a tendency for high-ranking officers to marry into aristocratic families and wealthy upper-middle-class clans. These factors made the senior officers all the more apprehensive about threats to the social and economic order, particularly in the form of the working-class movements and anarchist cells, which the Army hierarchy feared would undermine all the allegiances to which the military were dedicated.

Though it may have seemed that the Army was becoming the sword-arm of reaction, this was not the case; most officers did not share the attitudes of the military hierarchy, although they rejected rebellion. The typical officer was middle-class in background, but a large minority had been promoted from the ranks and found it difficult to identify with the wealthy in the class struggle. The military overwhelmingly opposed regionalism and proletarian revolution, not in the name of the Spanish bourgeoisie or the existing political leadership but because they felt that such forces disrupted national order. Many officers fiercely resented being periodically used by politicians to prop up the status quo. Convinced of the significance of their calling and the purity of their patriotism, they fostered a mood of antipolitical scorn, and viewed ordinary political attitudes and tactics as cowardly and parasitical. *La Correspondencia Militar* expressed a common military sentiment when it editorialized on April 29, 1904: "Politics, like coal, cannot be touched without soiling oneself; politics is a most active, explosive, and terrible poison." Anarchists, to be sure, were regarded as enemies because they subverted national order and discipline, but bourgeois politicians were accused of exploiting the confusion created by social rebellion. Officers sometimes felt that the politicians looked on them as just one more minority group to be victimized. The criticism and supposed exploitation of the Army encouraged the tendency toward a more solid institutional spirit among the junior and intermediate officers. A significant minority were groping toward a corporate philosophy that would stress the role of the Army as the backbone of the nation while denigrating civilian politics and the ordinary governing system.

The emerging credo of Spanish militarism had little in common with the aggressive bellicosity infecting much of Europe at that time. It was not aimed at war or external action but rather toward enhancing the position of the Army within the national structure. There was no official leadership for this trend and no organized group supporting it; rather it was nourished by thousands of conversations at officers' tables, by growing numbers of articles in military newspapers expressing the general unrest, and most of all by the country's basic political malaise.

Although it could not be denied that other sectors of national life considered the Army discredited and in a state of decadence, some Army speakers replied only in terms of counterattack.[24] A few of them, at any rate, talked and wrote of the Army's special civic mission and held that, in view of the failure of the established political groups, the Army must strive to achieve "the progress of the Fatherland and the guarantees for development of that progress, destroying every opposition, every foreign interference and obstacle that might be presented." Its policy was to be "deeply social and therefore . . . profoundly revolutionary."[25] In opposition to revolutionary demands from the left, a handful of military publicists insisted that the Army was the proper institution to shepherd the common people and to provide mass instruction and social discipline. There were occasional suggestions for a system of Army schools and even "Army farms" to teach agrarian techniques to peasant recruits.[26]

Militant officers were usually in favor of the elimination of revolutionary demagogues, but felt that the Army must not permit itself to be used as a mere instrument in the class struggle. An interesting volume published by a General Staff captain in 1907 claimed:

As presently constituted, the Army represents the highest form of the modern political system, and it will be even more exemplary after the recruitment law has been reformed in the manner demanded by democratic sentiment. The Army cannot represent capital, but has its roots in today's proletariat; it does not represent the owner, but is related to the worker. When intervening in strikes, as in any other social problem, it must lean toward the side of the weak and oppressed, toward those in need, *toward itself, the worker.*[27]

The author went on to assert that only the Army could provide the mass civic education and discipline needed to unify and revitalize the country. Such explicit statements went beyond the conscious goals of most officers in those years, but they were indications of a special mystique of the military that was taking form among a significant minority.

Military problems were, in one way or another, directly associated with most of the Cabinet crises during the decade from 1899 to 1909. The civil-military problem was worsened in May 1902, when Don Alfonso XIII ascended the throne at the age of sixteen. He had been brought up by priests and Army officers, and as a child had formed play battalions with the sons of grandees and ranking generals.[28] While it would be an exaggeration to say that the young Alfonso "identified" with the Army, he certainly felt closer to the military than to any other element in the country save the high aristocracy. On the day of his coronation, Alfonso's general proclamation to the people of Spain was accompanied by a special one addressed "to soldiers and sailors," which said in part:

Happy is the sovereign who sees in you the strongest support of the social order, the surest cement of public peace, the most resolute defender of institutions, and the firmest base of the well-being and felicity of the Fatherland.

As for myself, I shall live close to you, like the great Alfonso XII. For you shall I keep my vigils, as did my noble mother. With you shall I be found in your moments of danger, and whenever history speaks of me, it shall speak of you.[29]

Though very young, Alfonso was intelligent and had a quick if lamentably superficial mind. Nevertheless, it is not clear that he himself was responsible for this proclamation. Even if the government ministers did not prepare or suggest it, they did not discourage it. This indicates that a special appeal to the military was not considered unreasonable by the nominally Liberal Cabinet, which was headed by Sagasta and included such figures as Romanones, Canalejas, and Moret.

Don Alfonso wished to rule as well as to reign, and he showed great stubbornness at his initial Cabinet meeting, berating the War Minister, Weyler, for having closed down several military schools.[30] With the political demise of Martínez Campos and Polavieja, Weyler had become perhaps the most important general in the Army, and he was little inclined to bow to the whim of a sixteen-year-old. Don Alfonso drew the Cabinet's attention to the article in the 1876 Constitution which stated that it was the king's prerogative to appoint to all government posts, including the military hierarchy. The boy-king was then reminded of another paragraph which specified that any and all appointments must bear the accompanying signature of a Cabinet minister. A subsequent law of 1889 had made it clear that the king could take direct command of the Army only on the approval of the Cabinet. On the original issue, however, Don Alfonso had his way. The weak and aged Sagasta sided against Weyler, and at the very outset of the new reign it was made clear that the king intended to follow his own personal policy with the Army.[31]

However, Don Alfonso, no matter what his age, was never a real soldier or a militarist but always remained something of a playboy. The sports-happy young king viewed most of life as a game. To him, the Army meant uniforms, parades, maneuvers, horseback riding, banquets, and target-shooting, but certainly not bloodletting or intolerable expense; the military life was merely a mode of sportsmanship to which personal power attached.

Though eager for power, Don Alfonso lacked the constancy, seriousness, and determination necessary to upset the established constitutional order. He merely subverted it by usurping or frustrating parts of its mechanism, especially in the matter of military and ministerial appointments. In the years that followed, Don Alfonso cultivated the habit of writing and talking directly to his favorites in the Army, rather than communicating through the Minister of War as the Constitution provided. Few of the king's ministers had the courage to resist such personal actions. After he grew older, Don Alfonso arranged special *audiencias militares,* to which were invited only Army and Navy officers. More and more frequently, he inspected barracks, made speeches at military banquets, and attended the occasional military maneuvers.

Although the king had a special appeal for certain elements, other generals felt slighted by his conduct. His blocking of further nominations by Weyler occasioned much gossip.[32] The War Minister resigned at the close of 1902, and the entire ministry was brought down in December after a parliamentary fight concerning a new naval expansion bill. The Conservative government that followed collapsed in the spring of 1903 because of a bitter struggle over the same issue. In the following year, Antonio Maura's Conservative ministry resigned after a quarrel with the king regarding the appointment of the new Chief of the General Staff. The War Minister decided that the best qualified candidate was a certain General Loño. Alfonso demanded the appointment of Polavieja, whom he had apparently held in high esteem since the events of 1898. Maura and his colleagues felt obliged to support their fellow minister, and the entire Cabinet resigned.[33] Immediately after the closing of the Cortes, the young king made Polavieja Minister of War. There was so much talk about the machinations of Alfonso and his military favorites that on May 23, 1904, *La Correspondencia Militar* felt obliged to comment:

It is said that contact is maintained between the Crown and the Army so
that a coup d'état may open the way to personal government by the king.
. . . There is no truth in this; neither the king nor the Army has fallen so
low. . . . Absolutism is not the medicine that will cleanse us of the putres-
cence that envelops everything; the very origin of our ills lies in the impunity of governments, and now that "official responsibility" has become a
hollow term, who would want to legalize the irresponsible despotism of
those who use political maneuvering as an excuse for infringing the Constitution, trampling on morality, and scorning law?

During the first years of Don Alfonso's reign, the irascibility of the
military was provoked especially by Basque and Catalan nationalists.
The more outspoken regionalists actively baited the Army, deriding it
as an instrument of centralist oppression, a gluttonous parasite, and
a retrograde influence. Reaction to this criticism was even sharper
than to that from working-class groups, because to some degree it was
felt that the workers were contesting the economic structure, which
was not the Army's concern, whereas the regionalists were questioning the integrity of the Fatherland itself. Since the military were professionally inactive and without matériel or training facilities, they
were forced to substitute pride for accomplishment. When their vanity was pricked, the response was sometimes violent. During one patriotic parade in Bilbao at the beginning of the century, a group of officers deserted the procession to assault Basque Nationalist headquarters and tear down the Basque flag.[34] In Barcelona, anti-Catalan feeling among the military was further inflamed by the Radical Republicans, the principal foes of the Catalanists. The Radicals assiduously
cultivated political contacts with the Army, hoping for military support in some future Republican pronunciamiento.

On November 23, 1905, the Catalanist weekly *Cu-cut* ran a cartoon
that showed some local Army officers expressing surprise at a Catalan
celebration of an electoral victory, then ruefully admitting that in
Spain only civilians had triumphs of which to boast. For months, the
officers of the Barcelona garrison (which was dubbed "the army of occupation" by the Catalan citizenry) had been growing more and more
agitated, and for several weeks *La Correspondencia Militar* and *El
Ejército Español* had been campaigning in Madrid for decisive action
against Catalan nationalism. Finally, on November 25 a gang of 200
officers invaded the offices of *Cu-cut* and the main Catalanist paper,
La Veu de Catalunya, where they destroyed furniture, smashed some
of the presses, and wounded several employees with their sabers.[35]

This act was enormously popular with officers all over Spain, who showered the Barcelona garrison with messages of support.[36] Even the commanders of the garrison, who had made some effort to preserve formal discipline, began to second demands for repression of the Catalanists. The Captain General of Barcelona went to Madrid to confer with superiors. He was given such a rousing sendoff by Army leaders in the capital that it was feared his return to Barcelona would prompt a coup to drive Catalanists out of the provincial government there.[37]

Vociferous demands were made by the military that the government take drastic steps to muzzle the Catalan and leftist papers in their attacks on the Army and on Spanish unity. Various cliques of officers demanded that all military men in the Cortes or Senate who did not support this policy be officially declared unworthy of wearing a uniform, that the king close the present Cortes, that regionalist deputies be banned from the Cortes in future, and that the present Cabinet members not be permitted to exercise their functions until these matters had been settled. In short, they demanded partial revision or suspension of the Constitution.

General Weyler had returned to his post as Minister of War, and the Cabinet members now insisted that he take energetic measures to restore discipline. Further, they wished him to replace the Captain Generals of Madrid, Barcelona, and Seville, who had been outspoken supporters of military intervention. Weyler was not in an easy situation; he had held more aloof from politics than any other Spanish general of his eminence during the past century, yet he shared the common military disgust with regionalists and revolutionaries. Therefore he took no part in the matter, and refused to punish those responsible.[38] A committee of captains, majors, and colonels from the Madrid garrison made clear, in a brisk visit to Weyler's headquarters, that they were not satisfied with his neutral stance, and they demanded that he openly support the Army's position.[39] The apprehension of government leaders mounted on November 27 and 28. The President of the Cortes asked the head of the Civil Guard detachment protecting the chambers whether or not his men would defend the assembly, should Army forces break in. The response was negative.[40]

The crisis was eventually decided by the personal influence of the king, who was counted on by the military to support them. On November 29, *La Correspondencia Militar* reported:

At three P.M. [yesterday] the barracks were informed, through members of the committee present in the Army-Navy Center, that His Majesty had summoned his ministers to a meeting to inform them that he had waited forty-eight hours in the belief that the government and the Parliament would defend the cause of the Army and the Fatherland; and that since they had not done so, he had decided to compel their cooperation, by virtue of the powers that the Constitution confers.

Don Alfonso wrote privately to Antonio Maura that same day that the officers blamed the civilian politicians for having brought Spain to its present state of "pettiness, anarchy, and lack of prestige in the concert of peoples."[41] He seemed to share this view, and the government had little choice but to resign. On November 30, *La Correspondencia Militar* announced that a close union between the king and Army would achieve the Fatherland's salvation.

The new ministry was headed by a leader of one of the factions of the former Liberal Party, Montero Ríos. Its mission was to give the military satisfaction. The new Minister of War was Agustín Luque, who, as Captain General of Andalusia, had been vehement in support of the Army's action. Luque's political antecedents were Republican, and he had been a key figure in the vague machinations to depose the queen regent in 1898 and 1899. However, Luque was a political general first and a Republican second. The threat of class and regional separatism, together with the encouragement given certain military leaders by the new king, was bringing Luque and some other pseudo-Republican officers into line behind a new kind of militaristic monarchism.[42] This was precisely the sort of reaction among the active generals for which young Alfonso was hoping.

The new ministry quickly prepared a "Law of Jurisdictions" to give the Army a voice in punishing "treason." However, it would have been too humiliating, not to say cowardly, for the Cortes and the civilian government to openly subvert the Constitution by handing over all treatment of "crimes against the Fatherland and the Army" to the military courts, and so a plan was set up whereby the proposed bill would simply streamline the regular civil procedure for prosecuting such crimes. According to this scheme, the bill would first be discussed and voted on by the Cortes, but would then be transferred to the Senate, where an amendment would be added remanding all crimes of "treason" to the military courts. Should the Army leaders question Luque about the original moderate proposal before it was amended, he would express violent disapproval of it.[43]

This complicated maneuver took some time to set in motion, and meanwhile pressure from the military mounted. *La Correspondencia Militar* counseled on January 11, 1906: "Those who think that a political stratagem can deceive General Luque ought to forget such an idea. We therefore advise the officers of the Army that no matter what they see or hear they ought not to lose complete confidence and calm, for it has been agreed that the crimes in question will be tried by military courts." Six days later there occurred an incident similar to the *Cu-cut* affair, but this time perpetrated against a newspaper in Alcoy. Accusations of the strongest sort were flung back and forth. When the Republican deputy Soriano leveled charges against the aging General Primo de Rivera, he was challenged to a duel, and subsequently wounded, by the general's nephew Miguel. Military leaders seemed determined to curb verbal criticism. When the writer Unamuno was invited to address a public audience on the question of legal jurisdiction, Luque announced that three officers and two stenographers would attend to take down what he said.[44]

Many of the Conservatives supported the military, and the government capitulated before the threat.[45] On March 13, members of various opposition groups began to walk out of the Cortes. The Catalans and Republicans left first, and were followed by the Carlist deputies, who resented the authoritarian centralizing pressures of the military. Within a few days, all newspaper reporters save one had left or had been evicted from the Cortes, and on March 20, 1906, the "Law of Jurisdictions" was passed by a nearly unanimous vote, giving the military courts the right to try all "crimes against the Fatherland and the Army." The special judicial power of the military, in abeyance since 1873, had been restored, and the first step taken toward the acceptance of direct military influence in civic affairs. The Army's power continued to grow steadily, save during the temporary liberal regime of 1931–33.

In 1906, there were still 497 generals on the active list, and a total of 18,000 officers for 80,000 troops. Officers' salaries still cost the government about 60 million pesetas yearly. This sum, together with officer retirement pay, accounted for nearly half the military budget. The separate units were still ridiculously small; the average regiment was made up of less than 500 men.[46] Luque, as War Minister, proposed to make yet another effort to cut part of the bloat. The age limit for mandatory retirement was to be lowered from 68 to 64 for major generals, and from 65 to 62 for brigadiers, while the rank of captain general was to be granted only to commanders who had triumphed in field campaigns (a rule that would virtually have eliminated the possibility of captain generals in the Spanish Army, had it been carried out).

Luque further proposed to increase the number of battalions in each regiment from two to three, and to develop paramilitary training among all the nation's youth.

It was presumed that these proposals would have to be approved by the Parliament, since the king and government had rarely been courageous enough to bring about military reforms by themselves. The only supporters of the Luque reforms were some of the Republicans and extreme liberals, since the proposals seemed to be a step in the direction of universal military service. In general, however, Republicans were becoming antimilitary because of the less progressive political attitude now taken by most officers. There was a general desire among ultra-progressives to have as little as possible to do with military matters, and the ardent Republican *España Nueva* was beginning to campaign for an expanded professional Army of 200,000 simply because this standing force would relieve ordinary citizens of any obligation to military service.

Most of the big political generals were opposed to Luque's proposed changes. This was especially true of Weyler and Polavieja, next in line to become regular, as distinct from territorial, captain generals. According to the *Anuario Militar 1906*, only 10,000 of the Army's 18,000 officers had regular assignments; furthermore, these 10,000 commanded only 80,000 men, whereas the officer-soldier ratio was about one to twenty in the German and Italian armies, and one to twenty-three in the French. When taxed with these figures Weyler would reply that there was not a surplus of officers, but a lack of troops.[47] The old general even began to talk of an Army of 500,000 for Spain—no more illusory a notion than many to be found in Spanish public circles.[48] As a result of this opposition, most of Luque's proposals could not be carried out, and he was soon replaced as Minister of War.

The tight-money policy followed by the Spanish government in the early twentieth century probably discouraged rapid social and economic development, but it balanced the budget and reduced the national debt. By 1907 the annual government surplus amounted to 23,500,000 pesetas, and it increased the following year. Military expenditures were augmented slightly, but Antonio Maura, Prime Minister in 1907–9, proposed to use most of this surplus on naval expansion, a pet project of his, which would stimulate the domestic steel industry but do little to solve the many social problems crying for attention. Army leaders were furious, for they wanted the bulk of the money spent on their interests. *La Correspondencia Militar* attacked the government repeatedly in 1907 and 1908, terming the decision not to spend the money on the Army a radical departure from historic policy.

However, the new budget did permit a 25 per cent increase in Army manpower, which in turn increased the number of officers who could be appointed to active duty.[49] Extensions of the military budget were used by the command simply to increase the size of the Army, without any concern for improving the quality of its training or facilities. The limit was taken off the Officers' Reserve, and promotions from the ranks were permitted once more. Since Reservists were paid as much as regular officers, this raised expenses further and revived old problems of jealousy, incompetence, and superfluity, and the measure was temporarily revoked in 1912. In 1908–9 the budget made provision for the fact that the enrollment of Infantry regiments varied from as few as 500 men to as many as 3,026, and that battalions contained anywhere from 80 to 1,024 men.[50] It was calculated that the same amount of money that was being spent for a Spanish Army of 80,000 would have provided for 146,000 men in the German Army or 127,000 in the French—and that in both the French and the German forces the men would have been better trained, better equipped, and better cared for.[51]

Clearly, the state of the Army was not improving. During 1908, the state artillery factory at Trubia (Asturias) produced only 117 cannon of all sizes, and even these were quite poor in performance. By 1909, the Spanish forces had the lowest proportion of artillery per 1,000 troops of any army in Europe, not excepting Montenegro and Portugal.[52] To cite another comparison, one analyst found that in 1914 the Rumanian Army (which was roughly equivalent in manpower to that of Spain) employed only a third as many officers, had a somewhat higher ratio of artillery, and required only about a third as large a budget.[53] The conclusion drawn was that the Rumanian Army, though not renowned for martial prowess, was a considerably more efficient military machine than the Spanish.

The only noteworthy effort to shake up Spanish Army organization and recruitment on the eve of the First World War was the limited reform carried out by General Luque during his third tour as War Minister in 1911 and 1912. One of its principal features was a partially successful effort to reduce social injustice in recruitment.[54] The 1912 draft law did not eliminate *redención a metálica,* but instead provided that henceforth everyone drafted would be liable to at least five months' service, after which he might be released on payment of 2,000 pesetas, providing that the commanding officer judged that he had received sufficient training. On a similar basis, those who had served ten months might be released in return for a fee of 1,500 pesetas.[55]

Another innovation in the 1912 law was the creation of a special new Reserve Officers' group, the *oficialidad de complemento*. Only recruits with a certain amount of previous education were admitted. After payment of an initial fee, they took a special examination in order to qualify for the rank of sergeant; then, after six months of special training, they were entitled to appointment as second lieutenants. Further training and advancement depended on the individual, who might eventually be promoted as high as captain. The aim was both to ease the terms of service for young men of the middle classes and to better utilize the abilities of educated draftees. In effect, the oficialidad de complemento was open only to young men with financial resources, for its members had to pay for all their own equipment save weapons, and, after leaving regular service, were obliged to spend a few weeks each year in retraining.

The 1912 draft quota would have provided the Army with approximately 64,000 recruits, but financial limitations permitted only 42,000 to be called. This increased the total membership of the Army in 1913–14 to 135,000—the largest it had been since the end of the Cuban war. Between 1909 and 1913, the Army budget varied between approximately 200 million and 220 million pesetas. This was about 50 per cent greater than it had been during the trough of 1900–1902, but inflation robbed the increase of much of its purchasing power. In 1913, a special budgetary allowance of 110 million pesetas was opened for Moroccan expenditures. Much of the total allowance went toward the maintenance of the Army, and very little was spent on any other aspect of government in the Moroccan Protectorate. This made it possible in 1914 to reduce the regular Army budget to 177 million pesetas though Spain's cost-of-living average was steadily rising. Even so, nearly 300 million pesetas were being spent annually on the Army, while the education budget received only about 20 million pesetas per year. At the start of World War I, Spain was spending more per capita on its Army than Russia and not much less than Austria-Hungary.

Military service became more unpopular with each passing year. This is understandable when one considers that the non-combat death rate of the Spanish Army (5.7 per 1,000) was the highest in Europe.[56]

Spain's draft evasion rate was correspondingly high—by 1914, a fantastic 22 per cent.[57]

Liberal exemptions were still granted after 1912, for the upper classes insisted that it was uncivilized to expect young men from decent homes to enter the foul, unsanitary barracks. The only sons of poor families were exempted as well. The budget for 1912–13 included a special appropriation for construction of new, more healthful quarters, but most of this money disappeared before anything was accomplished. So many middle- and upper-class youths endeavored to spend their five or ten months in the relatively pleasant supply and medical services that entry into those sections had to be limited to 20 per cent of the redemption quota. Increasing prosperity during the war years raised the number of those eligible to use the modified redemption system from 6,559 in 1912 to 16,242 in 1919.[58] However, few young men from any class served their full terms in the ranks, for budgetary restrictions made it necessary to increase the number of recruits dismissed after a token 30- or 60-day training period to nearly half the annual total of draftees.

So long as the total budget did not get completely out of hand, the political leadership paid little attention to details of military expenditures. During the fifteen years from 1906 to 1920 an average of only three and a half days per year was spent debating Army finances in the Cortes, though this was the largest single budgetary item with which the government dealt.[59] Politicians could not be bothered with problems of Army structure and organization; their interest rarely went beyond the appointees who might occupy the Ministry of War during successive Cabinet reorganizations. Altogether this office changed hands sixty-two times during the forty-nine years of the restored constitutional monarchy (1875–1923). Politicians took little interest in institutional problems, largely because few Spaniards took any interest in politics. The gulf between the *pays officiel* and the *pays réel* remained as broad as ever. *El Heraldo Militar* editorialized on November 23, 1908, under the banner "Worse Than Anywhere": "Wherever we look, we find more virility than we do in the people here. . . . Turkey, Persia, China, the Balkan states—everywhere we find life and energy . . . even in Russia! In Spain there is nothing but apathy and submission. . . . How sad it is to think of the plight of Spain!"

CHAPTER SEVEN

The Moroccan Protectorate, 1908–18

THE SPANISH military were distracted from domestic problems by the flare-up of fighting in Morocco in 1908 and 1909. During the years immediately after the Cuban disaster, Spain's political spokesmen had shown little interest in extending the government's influence in northwest Africa. France was almost alone in pursuing colonial expansion there; when the Quai d'Orsay settled most of France's Mediterranean differences with Italy in 1902, it also endeavored to make an agreement with Spain on Morocco. The proposed Franco-Spanish treaty of 1902 would have placed within the Spanish sphere of interest all of the ancient kingdom of Fez in northern Morocco and most of the southern region bordering Río de Oro. The Silvela government had refrained from signing this accord for fear of alienating Britain, but after the Anglo-French Entente of 1904 a secret Franco-Spanish agreement was negotiated that reduced the sphere of Spanish influence both in the north and in the south. The international conference at Algeciras in 1906 confirmed most aspects of the European status quo in Morocco.[1]

Since the close of the nineteenth century, internal affairs in Morocco had steadily disintegrated. In 1902 the Sultan's authority was challenged by the Roghi, a pretender who claimed to be the lost son of a previous ruler and held control of the region around Taza in the northeast. The Roghi's claim seems to have been fraudulent, but he was politically astute and succeeded in establishing independent relations with French financial interests. The Maura government, which took office in Madrid in 1907, stood on strict legality and refused any recognition of the Roghi. However, some Spanish businessmen, following the example of their French and German counterparts, took advantage of Morocco's political anarchy to win favorable bargains. The Roghi had already sold mining rights in the district south of Melilla to a French company, and in July 1907 he signed a contract with the newly formed Compañía Española de las Minas del Rif for the exploitation of mining resources in the hills southwest of the Spanish town. Both contracts included the right to build railroads.

From the Sultan's point of view, these agreements were completely illegal. The Marrakesh government, such as it was, had already sent a *mehalla* (military detachment) from the royal forces to Restinga, an outpost on the northeast coast near Melilla, in a vain effort to assert its authority. Unable even to hold his own position, the commander of the Sultan's mehalla managed to obtain Spanish protection for a safe withdrawal from Restinga, which was then occupied on the Sultan's behalf by a small Spanish detachment.[2]

In reality, the government of Morocco had not exercised effective control over the turbulent Riff region south and southwest of Melilla for many years. The Roghi, who held sway over a part of this area and the territory below it in the manner of a feudal tyrant, was able to maintain a degree of order. Partly because of this, relations between the Roghi and General Marina, the Spanish commander at Melilla, were comparatively amicable. During the summer of 1908, the Roghi tried to consolidate his control over nearly all the northeastern corner of Morocco. In September, one of his bands was dispatched to chastise the Beni Ourriagli kabyle in the central Riff southwest of Melilla. This tribe, which had never paid tribute to the Roghi, and had paid it only rarely to the Sultan, appealed to the Spanish authorities for protection. Marina was reluctant to become involved, but the Prime Minister, Antonio Maura, felt that Spain should not acquiesce in the extension of the Roghi's power, since he was in rebellion against the Sultan, whose authority Spain was bound by international treaty to respect.[3] Meanwhile, the Beni Ourriagli led all the neighboring tribes in an uprising against the Roghi. Before the year was concluded, he had been driven from his northern capital of Zeluan, just below Melilla, and during the following year he was captured by a mehalla of the Sultan's troops. Carried back to Marrakesh, he was, according to somewhat improbable reports, fed alive to the palace lions.[4]

Under the Maura government, Spain followed a somewhat contradictory policy, permitting extralegal economic bargains on the one hand and attempting to uphold the political and military sovereignty of the Sultan on the other. Anarchy and disorder were clearly a serious problem for European interests in Morocco. The Algeciras Conven-

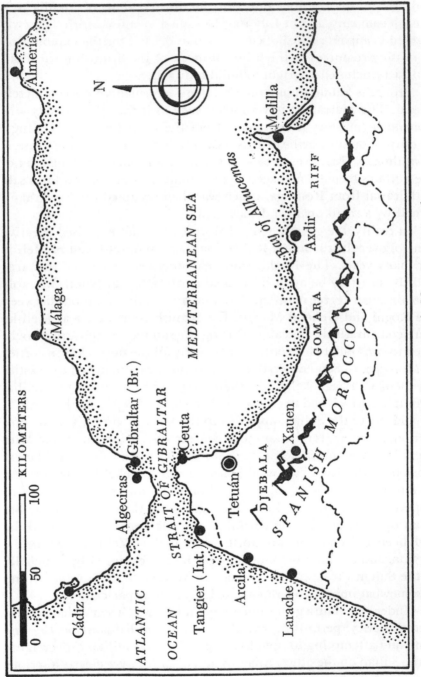

The Spanish Protectorate in Morocco, 1913–56

tion had provided for the organization of a police force in the major coastal towns. Placed under the nominal sovereignty of the Sultan, the force was, in fact, supervised by French and Spanish officers. Spain was to administer Tetuán and Larache in the north, and to share with France the supervision of Tangier and Casablanca, while France was to oversee the central zone of the country by herself. Following the disorders at Casablanca in 1907, French and Spanish troops were landed there. In the following year, command of the Spanish forces, together with supervision of the Moorish companies policing the district outside the city, was given to an experienced Cavalry officer, Lt. Col. Manuel Fernández Silvestre.[5]

With the fall of the Roghi, the last element of internal stability in northeastern Morocco was removed, and the area was plunged into virtual anarchy. Neighboring kabyles obstructed work in the Spanish-controlled mines outside Melilla, and in June 1909 Maura gave General Marina orders to take all necessary measures to protect the mine workers. When six miners were killed by the natives on July 9, Marina's troops scattered the aggressors, then occupied and began to fortify several positions well outside the Spanish zone, so that the mining operations might be effectively shielded from further attack. Marina had almost 6,000 officers and men under his command, but the territory to be covered was fairly extensive and the local tribesmen were excellent skirmishers who showed every sign of continuing their harassment.

For several years deeper Spanish involvement in Morocco had seemed almost inevitable, but the Army had done little or nothing to prepare for this contingency.[6] General Fernando Primo de Rivera, who was War Minister in 1908, later declared to the Parisian *Le Journal* that during his tenure he had kept a brigade of reinforcements on hand at Gibraltar, and that a special new division had been planned for Moroccan service.[7] However, General Linares, who succeeded Primo de Rivera in 1909, shared the conviction of other officials that very few of the approximately 85,000 troops then stationed in the peninsula could be released to go to Africa. Instead, the government sent the Third Chasseurs Brigade, which was only partially composed of battalions on active duty. Even these few were greatly undermanned, so that in order to bring the brigade up to its full complement, entire Reserve units, mostly from the urban areas, had to be recalled to active service. The so-called "First Reserve" did not receive regular training, and the men on its lists did not dream that they might be called upon

to fulfill any serious military obligation. Moreover, it was soon discovered that the Reserve units, too, were lacking in manpower, and
that although 850 men were needed to complete the Chasseurs battalion, only 330, including the members of the First Reserve, were available. For this reason, the bulk had to be drawn from the Second Reserve lists, dating back to 1903. None of these men had had any training for at least four years. Moreover, most of them had family responsibilities and were reluctant to serve in an army so poorly provided for
that a call to duty seemed tantamount to a death sentence. The Reservists might have accepted their lot with the apathetic stoicism of the
previous decade, had not the urban environment changed radically
since that time, especially in Barcelona. The economic pressure on the
working classes was still mounting, and their discontent was growing
more apparent day by day. Nevertheless, a disproportionate number
of Reservists were called up from the urban areas, apparently because
it was easier to mobilize troops there. The idea was becoming widespread among city dwellers that the whole Moroccan campaign was
designed merely to promote the interests of the mining companies and
bring cheap rewards for Army officers. On July 10, the day after the
first Berber assault, Madrid's *El Liberal* editorialized:

The loss of those poor soldiers and civilians, whose lives were sacrificed
not on the altar of the Fatherland but in defense of dubious industrial interests, has caused great pain. . . . The only matters at stake are the concerns
of certain French and Spanish profiteers who expect armed protection for
their operations.[8]

Popular disenchantment with the national enterprise in Morocco
and with Spain's bungling oligarchical leadership was perhaps best
expressed, not by any leftist or progressive publication, but by the
staunchly monarchist Madrid newspaper *La Correspondencia de España*, which declared on July 12:

It is impossible to conduct a war if the people do not wish it—and the
Spanish people do not want to hear any talk of fighting in Morocco. With
the exception of a half dozen political gentlemen, a few stock-market
speculators, and certain other fishers in troubled waters, no one wants adventures, or provocations, or unnecessary occupations, or any sort of ill-
timed or uncalled-for enterprise. If Spain had accomplished something in
Fernando Po and Muñi, and if the country knew that we were going to resolve some problem in Morocco, it would tolerate an imperialist policy.
But since it sees that we are going to Morocco without knowing how or
why, it does not support the venture.
Let us suppose that our troops move out from Melilla and occupy 10, 20,

30, or 100 kilometers. So—they are occupied. And for what purpose? None whatsoever. Absolutely none whatsoever, unless it be to spend a hundred million or more pesetas that are badly needed at home and would serve no purpose in Morocco at all. Several hundred soldiers would die, as many others would be promoted, we would once more exhibit our lack of organization, and would make ourselves look ridiculous for the hundredth time by calling a few stray shots a skirmish, a skirmish a military engagement, a scouting contact a combat, and a combat a field battle. We would send more generals than colonels, more senior officers than lieutenants, more lieutenants than soldiers, more promises than realities, and more projects than deeds. What is more, for all our striving we would only accomplish one thing: we would waste the soldiers' blood and the taxpayers' money.

Why go on lying, if this is the truth? Why propagate ridiculous illusions, if things are what they are, not what one wants them to be? . . .

Let it not be forgotten by the government and the king: going to Morocco will be a thousand times more perilous than not going there.

Maura once said that the Project of Associations [López Domínguez' bill to restrict clerical orders to their proper constitutional limitations] would mean civil war. I say to him that going to Morocco will mean revolution— and by saying so, I serve Fatherland and king much better than I would by pretending that going to Morocco serves the interests of the nation and the monarchy.

As it developed, these were prophetic words, for fourteen years of frustration and disorder in Morocco, capped by military disaster, were to eventually precipitate the collapse of constitutional monarchy in Spain.

The Reservists who were to serve in the Third Chasseurs had been collected at Barcelona by July 11, and they began to reach Melilla five days later. This was only the beginning, however, for thousands of other Reservists were being recalled. Since allowances for dependents were not paid by the Spanish Army, wives and children were, in many cases, left without support. In Madrid, the Socialists held an anti-war rally on July 11, and during the next few days several small antimilitarist demonstrations broke out spontaneously at the Barcelona port of embarkation. A set of Reservists was scheduled to leave Madrid on July 20, but their departure was delayed by numerous demonstrators, mostly women, who filled the railroad station and sat down on the tracks. The resentment of the group was not directed against the military but rather against government policy. Cries of "Down with the government!" were mingled with shouts of "Long live the Army!"[9]

The reaction was even more extreme in Barcelona, Spain's most modern and industrialized city, which was a hotbed of radicalism and resentment of every sort—social, political, economic, ideological, and esthetic. The city had seen a recent revival of trade unionism and anarchist agitation. As the civil governor Ossorio Gallardo put it: "In Barcelona the revolution is always ready; it appears in the street every day. If the environment is unfavorable, it withdraws; if favorable, it begins to spread."[10]

The environment was most favorable in the last week of July. Summer heat had severely taxed the tempers of the citizens, and the lower classes were in no mood to be led like lambs to the slaughter. When new Reserve notices were posted, a committee of anarchists and other leftist elements was hastily formed to prepare for a general strike in protest. Though none of the organized leftist groups officially sponsored the strike, feeling was so high that the work stoppage in Barcelona on July 26 became almost complete. After an altercation with his immediate superior, the Minister of the Interior, Ossorio resigned.

This left the Captain General, Santiago, in charge of Barcelona. His garrison had been depleted by transfers to Morocco and numbered only 1,400 men. When the strikers and their sympathizers began to fire on the police from improvised barricades in the streets, Santiago proved irresolute. The military had no fondness for serving as strikebreakers. Moreover, the insurgents did not threaten government institutions, and whenever troops appeared, the strikers applauded them and urged them not to fire on brother Spaniards. Discipline began to break down among the troops, and most of the garrison was confined to barracks. Public order was largely left in the hands of the 700 Civil Guards, who proved unable to cope with the situation. That night, the rebels set fire to some of the largest churches and religious institutions in Barcelona, and during the next three days more than half of the city's convents, churches, and Catholic schools were destroyed. Fearing the absolute collapse of discipline, the military command did not intervene, save to escort a number of priests and nuns to safety. It was obvious that the rebel leaders were using violent anticlericalism as a temporary channel for the people's rage, and as a non-treasonous revolutionary gesture. Many middle-class people applauded anticlerical activities, and there is evidence that a minority of army officers, some of whom were in contact with the anticlerical, anti-Catalanist Radical Party, also approved of the burnings. The forces of public order were so helpless—or indecisive—that at one point the Italian consul offered Santiago the assistance of units of the Italian Navy. After several days reinforcements arrived, and the greater Barcelona area was slowly cleared of barricades. When the revolt was over, approximately 104 civilians had been killed, and one officer and three soldiers were dead. The police and Civil Guards, who bore the brunt of the fighting, lost 28 men. Some 2,000 rioters were arrested, but only about 150 were convicted and only five were executed.[11]

The "Tragic Week," as it was called, was the greatest outburst of popular resentment in Spain since the end of the Carlist Wars. Though the riots had been diverted almost entirely toward anticlericalism, they were frequently labeled as efforts either at leftist revolution or at Catalan separatism. Despite the complacent attitude taken by some of the military in Barcelona, many officers felt stabbed in the back. In their opinion the whole affair simply reemphasized how vital they were to national security and how little the country appreciated them. About 90 per cent of the Reservists who were summoned had joined up without delay,[12] but the riots and protests had their effect even on those who appeared without complaint.* The confusion at home added greatly to the Army's already overwhelming deficiencies. As one general noted, the Melilla campaign was in the hands of "units composed, for the most part, of Reservists who had forgotten their previous instruction, whose morale had been shattered by the spectacles which occurred at embarkation points and during their transfer across the country, and who lacked the support of those auxiliary services indispensable to their transferral and entrance into action."[13]

While disorder was brewing at home, advance positions outside Melilla were being sharply harassed. An urgent call for reinforcements went out, and the first units to arrive in Morocco had little time to dwell on their grievances, for they were pressed into action immediately. General Marina's immediate objective was to occupy the approaches to Mount Gurugú, the peak that dominates the Melilla plain and the site of the mines. Several convergent columns were sent out on July 23, but the first day's action was chaotic. Movement of the separate units was not synchronized, and one of the flanking columns that started ahead of time, before sunrise, went astray. Daylight did not alleviate the confusion entirely, for there were no precise maps of the area. The lost battalion was ambushed by the Berbers and all the reserves of the main force had to be used to extricate it, which held up the advance.

* It should be pointed out that draft riots in opposition to colonial service were not limited to Spain. There were serious disturbances in Italy in 1896, 1911, and 1914.

By July 25, 17,000 troops had been concentrated at Melilla, but little progress was made. Another minor disaster of incompetence occurred on July 27, when the newly arrived First Madrid Chasseurs were sent under General Pintos to occupy the slope adjacent to a gully appropriately called "Barranco del Lobo" (Wolf Ravine). Ignoring his instructions, Pintos pushed on to the other side of the gulch with his advance battalion, and was caught in an ambush. Panic-stricken, the troops could be made to advance only after their officers had done so. Fifty-six officers were wounded that day, and Pintos, two lieutenant colonels, and dozens of troops and junior officers were killed. When news of the Barranco del Lobo "massacre" got back to the peninsula, there was another great outcry from the public and the political opposition. The Minister of War admitted that by July 27 total Spanish casualties in the Melilla operations had reached nearly a thousand. Unofficial sources put the figure considerably higher.[14]

By the end of July, Marina had received a full division of Chasseurs, plus a second reinforced division from the peninsula, which gave him a total force of 22,000. Most of August was spent preparing defensive fortifications and drilling the soldiers in the use of firearms. Because of the poor preparation and inadequate equipment of his troops Marina asked for even more reinforcements, and by the latter part of September his command had been expanded to approximately 40,000 men.[15]

The first significant Spanish gain was made in the last weeks of the summer, after the Quebdana kabyle east of Melilla had taken up arms against the Europeans. Several mobile Spanish columns were organized under the more experienced officers. These units ravaged the entire Quebdana area, living off the land, destroying the tribesmen's supplies, and forcing them into a corner where they had to surrender, give up most of their guns, and turn over several hostages as a pledge of peace.[16]

As the summer waned, popular resistance to the Moroccan operations began to subside in the larger Spanish cities. Signs of patriotic enthusiasm were more frequent, though still conspicuously absent among the urban workers. The activist minority in the Officer Corps insisted on full support for the Melilla campaign until it had been properly concluded. On August 21, *La Correspondencia Militar* warned that if the Army did not achieve its goals in Melilla it would be "morally annihilated," and would pull Spain down with it into "the abyss of dishonor." Nevertheless, when the provincial government of Vizcaya tried to show its support by organizing a Basque battalion, it was forced to abandon the plan for lack of volunteers.[17]

Because of the attitude of the Spanish public, Marina received orders from the government to proceed cautiously and to spare his troops as much as possible. No effort toward a general advance against the main resistance in the west was made until September 20. On that date, a large Spanish force supported by numerous artillery scattered the Berber irregulars at Taxdir, west of Melilla, enabling the Spanish to seal off the peninsula to the north, move beyond Gurugú and encircle it from the south, and dominate the surrounding countryside. On September 28, a surprise attack on an outlying battalion by a band of Moors produced the principal Spanish hero of this campaign, Corporal Luis Noval. Noval was a member of a small patrol captured by the tribesmen. They demanded that he lead them into the middle of his battalion's bivouac. When Noval and his captors had walked within firing range, he shouted, "Fire on us! They're Moors!" thus sacrificing his life but saving the battalion.

Though the most exposed units had to be moved back, the Spanish completed the occupation of Mount Gurugú on September 29. According to the official version of this action, a small detachment led by Col. Miguel Primo de Rivera scaled the peak and planted the Spanish flag. By that time, the Spanish forces had occupied a loose defense perimeter stretching from twenty to thirty kilometers south and west of Melilla. The units engaged had been quite clumsy in advancing against the ill-equipped, totally unorganized Berber irregulars. Infantry tactics were extremely old-fashioned. The command tried to compensate for this by moving a sizable amount of artillery to the battle zone. Cannon fire was often used indiscriminately, heavy barrages being laid down every few hundred yards against ill-defined targets. Though this tactic has been compared to killing flies with pistol fire, it did enable the Spanish to occupy small pieces of ground with minimal combat.

A handicap that could not be so easily overcome was the lack of maps and accurate intelligence regarding the enemy. This led to exaggerated use of "offensive reconnaissance"—scouting in force to find out where the Berbers were hiding and where the Spanish were going. On September 30, an offensive reconnaissance overshot its mark and pushed so far southwest that it entered the territory of an uninvolved and hitherto peaceful kabyle. The result was a needless clash that left 32 Spaniards dead.

With Melilla and the mining region made secure, operations came to a halt. Most of October and November were spent in negotiations with leaders of the hostile kabyles. The Spanish authorities in general were quite willing to spend a certain amount of money on bribes if by this means they could avoid further combat, but Linares, the outgoing War Minister, preferred a strictly military solution. He proposed a special amphibious landing at the Bay of Alhucemas, well to the west of Melilla at the coastal base of the Riff. It was hoped that such an operation might take the hostile tribesmen by surprise from the rear and permit the Spanish to cut through the heart of the difficult Riff terrain. However, the government vetoed this plan because of the inadequacy of the Spanish forces and the absence of any geographical study of the field of operations.[18]

Military action was not resumed until November 25, when the heights immediately south of Gurugú were occupied. This action initiated a general advance supported by artillery, cavalry, and a few machine guns. The operation was somewhat better planned than the preceding ones; its object was to broaden the center of the occupation zone, which at some points extended only ten kilometers inland. The resources of the tribesmen were severely limited, and hostilities came to an end in January 1910. The local chiefs made peace with the Spanish authorities, who theoretically still acted in the name of the Sultan. The Spanish General Staff was never able to compile precise casualty statistics for the campaign of 1909–10. Its best guess was that there had been 2,517 "battle casualties," including more than 500 deaths from wounds received in combat. According to this source, an additional 211 men had died of sickness.[19] Other contemporary estimates ranged up to 4,131 casualties.[20] Scattered information from the kabyles reported the burial of approximately 1,800 Moorish dead.[21]

The Melilla command was raised to the level of a Captaincy General, but the Cortes, which reopened in June 1910, was not impressed, and Marina was attacked by various speakers for his uncertain leadership. Though he was a responsible commander, his military talents were not remarkable, and in August he was replaced by the military governor of Ceuta, General García Aldave. By that time the forces in the Melilla zone had been cut back to approximately 20,000 men.[22]

The two-year ministry of the Liberal leader José Canalejas, which ran from 1910 until Canalejas' assassination in 1912, enjoyed more harmonious relations with the military than did any other government of that period. Leading political generals such as López Domínguez, Luque, and Weyler identified themselves with the Liberals rather than with the anti-expansionist, budget-minded Conservatives. These generals had played a significant role in breaking the Maura government, and they lent Canalejas valuable backing.[23] The Prime Minister did not hesitate to call on the Army to preserve civil order. In 1912, the Army Reservists among railway employees were mobilized to prevent a threatened general rail strike.[24] The new recruitment law of that year provided that workers employed in strategic industries might, in case of national emergency, be militarized under Army discipline without actually being incorporated into military units. When progressives criticized the severity with which military courts enforced the Law of Jurisdictions, Canalejas made a speech at the Madrid Círculo Militar reaffirming the unity of Army and government in the face of leftist demands.[25]

Not surprisingly, the Canalejas government was much more positive in its Moroccan policy than the last two ministries had been. A new treaty was negotiated with the Sultan in November 1910, which provided for Spanish administration of the expanded zone beyond Melilla and for the payment of an indemnity to compensate Spain for the kabyle attacks.[26] The Moroccan situation broke wide open again the following year, when anti-European riots at Fez and elsewhere provided French forces with an opportunity to occupy the central Moroccan cities. In the middle of 1911, French forces began to encroach on the Alcazarquivir district, on the Atlantic coast south of Larache, which formed part of the Spanish sphere of influence. Since the area had been in turmoil for over five years, the Spanish government dispatched troops to take formal occupation of the entire Larache district for Spain, though it was still under the nominal sovereignty of the Sultan. A larger sector of territory inland from Ceuta was also occupied. Efforts were made to reach an understanding with local leaders, and these initial moves were completed without bloodshed.[27] However, the French and Spanish operations served as the excuse for the German naval intervention at Agadir that led to the international confrontation known to diplomatic historians as the Second Moroccan Crisis. Spanish interests escaped from that episode relatively unscathed.

During the summer of 1911, Spanish columns reconnoitered part of the region adjacent to the Melilla zone, collecting information on topography. On August 24, a detachment of the Geographical Section of the General Staff was attacked by tribesmen, and that night signal fires blazed on the hills of the eastern Riff, for a local sheikh, El Mizzian, had begun to preach a *jihad,* or holy war, against the Spanish. Within a few weeks hostilities became widespread. Luque, who was now Minister of War, visited Melilla early in October and gave the order to expand the zone of occupation still further. The Spanish advance crossed the river Kert, which flows northward to the Mediterranean about 20 miles west of Melilla. This operation resulted in numerous casualties, thus provoking another outcry at home.

The Moroccan difficulties aroused general bewilderment. A writer for *ABC,* an influential, ultra-conservative daily published in Madrid and Seville, stated on October 11, 1911, that he was at a loss to understand how Moorish irregulars utterly without modern organization and lacking proper equipment or leadership could halt supposedly well-trained, well-disciplined, and adequately equipped European troops. Military leaders had difficulty in explaining why, after more than two years of desultory campaigning, the Army's forces in Morocco were still unequal to their task. The General Staff had prepared a sort of manual dealing with the techniques of irregular warfare, but many field officers in Morocco failed to make systematic efforts to adapt their units to this kind of combat.[28]

El Mizzian's *harca* (band of fighters) grew in strength during the autumn of 1911, adding to its members many tribesmen from central Morocco who had fled the French, as well as many from the Riff. The Spanish authorities endeavored to suspend operations, fearing that further advances might lead to complications with the French forces operating in the northern part of central Morocco. El Mizzian pressed the struggle, attacking exposed Spanish outposts and recrossing the Kert. Most advance positions were cut off, and at one point the Spanish command found itself virtually besieged in the city of Melilla. Reconcentrating their units, the Spanish managed to push El Mizzian's harca back across the Kert at the end of December, after an intermittent five-day combat. Nevertheless, the Spanish position around Melilla at the beginning of 1912 was more perilous than it had been six months earlier. Lines were overextended and great difficulty was encountered in moving supply columns across hostile territory to succor the advance posts.

Since 1909, efforts had been made to organize native Moroccan police and military units to help pacify the region, and in June 1911 the first group of volunteer *Regulares*—Moorish soldiers in the service of Spain—was formed.[29] Because of the bellicose tradition of the Berbers and the ancient rivalries between the various kabyles, it was not difficult to obtain recruits. All commissioned and noncommissioned officers in the Regulares were Spanish; one of the first second lieutenants to volunteer for this duty was the nineteen-year-old Francisco Franco, who had served in Morocco since December 1910. The Regulares immediately proved their usefulness as small shock units in the disorderly, intermittent engagements of the Melilla district.

More troops were sent from Spain to Morocco during the winter and spring of 1912. In May, El Mizzian was killed in a minor skirmish. His death deprived hostile tribesmen of their only effective leader, and the fighting soon died down. A new peace agreement was made with the kabyle chieftains of the eastern Riff in mid-1912. By that time, the extent of the Spanish-occupied zone around Melilla was about twice what it had been during the previous year.[30]

Meanwhile, France was attempting to regularize its intervention by establishing an official protectorate. Spanish authorities did not participate directly in the negotiations, but dealt only at second hand with the French. France's protectorate over nearly all Morocco—a territory of 193,000 square miles, with more than five million inhabitants—was formally created on March 30, 1912. Spain was left with five per cent of the total area of Morocco. Her holdings comprised 10,400 square miles in the north inhabited by three-quarters of a million people. An agreement with the Sultan giving Spain the right to supervise and "protect" this northern territory was arranged in November 1912, and was officially signed by the Sultan in Marrakesh in May 1913.

Had it not been for the vigor of French imperialism, Spain would probably never have become deeply involved in Morocco. It cannot be said that creation of the Spanish Protectorate was produced by a groundswell of expansionist sentiment in Spain. Rather, this decision was an act of the Romanones minority ministry then in power, and was encouraged, it would appear, by the king. Public reaction was scant, with dissenting voices more numerous than signs of approbation, though the most active elements in the Officer Corps were strongly in favor of expansion, as were a number of commercial interests.

The government of the Spanish Protectorate was to be administered by a deputy of the Sultan, called a caliph, with the customary Muslim hierarchy of local lieutenants, mayors, and judges. Spanish authorities were to be allowed to nominate the appointee for caliph and to intervene freely in the workings of the government. Spain's administration for the Protectorate was set up by a royal decree of February 27, 1913. The supreme Spanish authority was to be a High Commissioner residing in Ceuta, near the center of the zone. Three administrative departments were to assist him in governing: the Delegation for Native Affairs, the Delegation for Economic Development and Public Works, and the Delegation for Financial Affairs. The problem of keeping order was to be handled by an expanded force of Regulares and native police.[31]

No central Army command was established in the Protectorate. The three military districts of Ceuta, Melilla, and Larache were to function as virtually autonomous units.* The High Commissioner's general authority did not hold sway over local administrative problems, nor did it extend to military command.[32] In practice, each military governor was responsible to the Ministry of War in Madrid for military matters and to the Foreign Ministry for civil affairs. This arrangement was probably made to ensure a high degree of central authority in Madrid, but the long-range result was a kind of anarchy in the command structure.

The February decree did not stipulate that the High Commissioner be a military commander, but Madrid saw the Protectorate as primarily a military problem, and the usual practice of placing overseas territories under Army commanders was followed. The first High Commissioner, appointed (and simultaneously promoted to lieutenant general) on April 13, 1913, was Alfau, the former military governor of Ceuta.

Difficulties had already appeared in the Djebala, the mountainous northern peninsula of Morocco that formed the western part of the Spanish zone. The principal Muslim authority in the Djebala was the Sherif Muley Ahmed el Raisuli, a descendant of the prophet Mohammed, and a member of one of the leading families of the district. Originally something of a poet and intellectual, well versed in the Koran and in Muslim lore, he had long been an adversary of the Sultan, and earlier in life had spent some years as a political prisoner. Experience had made El Raisuli a clever politician, wise in the violent, superstitious ways of the kabyles of northern Morocco. By guile and force he had become the feudal lord of the western Djebala. He never

---

* Melilla's brief day as a Captaincy General came to an end in 1912.

hesitated to employ extortion or murder to keep his coffers full and to sustain his power. In 1908, he had forced the Sultan to name him *caid* (military commander) of the western Djebala and mayor of the coastal city of Arcila. El Raisuli hoped for the eventual independence of northern Morocco, but realized that the country was far from possessing the requisite unity. In the meantime, he preferred to work with the Spanish rather than the French. As he later put it to an English visitor: "I thought, 'The Spaniards are strong enough to help us, but not so strong that they will oppress us.' "[33] He hoped to be made caliph of the Spanish zone in return for his cooperation.

El Raisuli was a man of intense personal magnetism—a natural leader held in superstitious awe by his followers. He seems to have won over the Spanish commander of his district at their first interview. The commander in question, Colonel Fernández Silvestre, was the impetuous Cavalry officer who had earlier served as Commissioner at Casablanca. As a gesture of amity, El Raisuli permitted Silvestre to station a small garrison at his headquarters in Arcila. But soon relations became strained, as persistent protests from kabyles victimized by El Raisuli's forces caused Silvestre to change his original opinion of the Sherif. When Silvestre made inquiries into these complaints, El Raisuli refused him any satisfaction. The colonel's hands were tied, for only the Foreign Ministry, whose nearest agent was the consul at Tangier, had authority to interfere directly in civil matters. After further complaints, the impatient Silvestre ignored formal limitations and sent a column into the interior to break up one of the Sherif's armed units, which had been chastising a rebellious kabyle.

Early in 1913, Silvestre ordered his troops at Arcila to secure the release of 98 criminals and hostages who were being held in El Raisuli's dungeon. This lowered the Sherif's authority in the eyes of local tribesmen. Enraged, El Raisuli went off to complain to the Spanish civil authority at Tangier, instructing his lieutenants to stir up anti-Spanish feeling among the kabyles. Silvestre countered by seizing El Raisuli's private arsenal in Arcila and placing the Sherif's family under house arrest. El Raisuli set up a new residence at Tazarut, amid the hills of the central Djebala, and began to talk of an anti-Spanish holy war. At this juncture, the Spanish government intervened.

Silvestre understood little or nothing of politics and diplomacy; faithful to his own concept of justice, and appalled by what he had seen of the Arcila dungeon, he had simply plunged ahead. But it was clear that he had not acted within the letter of the law, for El Raisuli was at least nominally an appointee of the Sultan and the function of the Protectorate was theoretically to assist the Moroccan administration. The mehalla that had been dispersed by Silvestre's column the preceding year was an adjunct of the Sultan's forces, and Spanish military authorities were not authorized to intervene in kabyle disputes so long as outside interests were not endangered. Consequently Luque felt obliged to send a telegram from Madrid specifically disavowing Silvestre's latest action, while the consul at Tangier made an agreement with El Raisuli that recognized his authority to handle local affairs in his Djebala bailiwick.

Feeling betrayed by the government, Silvestre submitted his resignation. The Ministry refused to accept it, realizing that Spain would lose face if Silvestre were forced out of command by El Raisuli's complaints. Instead, Madrid determined to make Silvestre live up to the consul's arrangement with the Sherif.

This did not satisfy El Raisuli, who wanted to have Silvestre recalled from Morocco altogether. He refused to return with his family to Arcila, and asked for a final interview with the Spanish commander at Tangier near the close of the month. El Raisuli knew that the Foreign Ministry was under pressure from home to limit the country's commitment of men and money in Morocco, and he was confident that he would be able to withstand any demands that the Spanish authorities might make. He is supposed to have told Silvestre:

You and I form the tempest: you are the violent wind; I, the tranquil sea. You come and blow furiously; I become stirred up, am dashed about, and burst into foam. There you have the storm; and we, its two parts, differ greatly, for I, like the sea, am always in my place, while you, like the wind, are never at rest.[34]

Meanwhile, on the eastern side of the peninsula, the Protectorate's rudimentary administration was taking shape. Even before his appointment as High Commissioner, General Alfau had begun to move the seat of authority from the coastal Spanish town of Ceuta to the traditional Djebalan capital of Tetuán, which was to become the residence of the new caliph. This city held a certain degree of religious significance for the local population, and its occupation provoked considerable restlessness, especially after rumors spread that the Spanish military had been molesting native women. There was some apprehension that the whole Protectorate agreement might simply be a ruse to enable the Spanish to destroy Moorish custom, law, and religion.

A member of a branch of the Sultan's family was selected by the

Spanish authorities as caliph of their zone, even though the appointee lacked personal authority of his own in the district. After the installation of the new caliph in May, El Raisuli saw his hopes for increased influence under the Spanish dashed. He broke off his last conference with Spanish authorities and sounded a call to arms at Tazarut. Skirmishing broke out around Tetuán and Larache in June. So many travelers fell prey to banditry and raids by El Raisuli's followers that Europeans scarcely dared venture outside the main towns. Heavy guards had to be posted everywhere, and Spanish authorities began to build a network of fortified blockhouses in the small districts under their immediate control. On July 7, several hundred mounted tribesmen made a bold attack on the historic site of Alcazarquivir, at the southwestern end of the Spanish zone. They were driven off by a Cavalry squadron of 73 men led by Lt. Col. Gonzalo Queipo de Llano, who was later to play a leading role in Army affairs.[35] There were sharp encounters around Tetuán as Alfau sent out detachments to clear the main roads and occupy the surrounding hilltops. The High Commissioner soon attempted to suspend operations, hoping that the kabyles would be willing to negotiate and lay down their arms. Such was not the case, for Alfau's moderate approach was taken as a sign of weakness. The government demanded more active direction, and Alfau resigned in August, having served only four months as High Commissioner.[36] He was replaced by General Marina, the undistinguished commander of the forces at Melilla in 1909–10.

These difficulties fanned the fires of civilian criticism always smoldering within Spain. After four years of intermittent hostilities, there was some doubt that the Spanish would be able to hold and pacify their small slice of Morocco. Just at this point, a most unusual bid was made by the principal German entrepreneurs in the area, the Mannesmann brothers. According to *El Imparcial,* December 9, 1913, they offered, in return for all rights of exploitation in the interior, to use their talents in helping the Spanish to come to a profitable deal with El Raisuli in northwest Morocco. After such an agreement had been reached, the Spanish were to retire their troops to the coastal towns they had occupied prior to 1913; El Raisuli would become caliph, and order would be kept by a native constabulary responsible to him. These terms may have been an exaggeration of the original Mannesmann proposal, but their publication provoked infuriated cries of protest from Spanish patriots. Nothing more was heard of the matter.

Operations in Morocco were slow-paced during 1914, and the out-

break of the First World War made the Spanish even more cautious
than usual. There was extensive controversy within Spain over whether
the country should involve itself in the international conflict. However, it soon became clear that Spanish interests were not endangered
by the war; in fact, wartime exports proved a great boon to the economy. The excitement of the first months dwindled into the customary
apathy, and until the resumption of unlimited submarine warfare by
Germany at the beginning of 1917, there was comparatively little pressure within Spain for the government to take sides. On the eve of the
war a few super-patriots clamored for involvement, but their exhortations stood little chance of being heeded.[37] The Army's organizational
problems and its difficulties in Morocco made it almost impossible for
Spanish officers to copy the brand of militarism found in most other
large European countries.

In general, it was believed that most Army officers had pro-German sentiments, as did most Conservative political leaders. Many patriots had a long-standing feeling of animosity against France, which a
century earlier had twice invaded their country and, more recently,
had occupied nearly all of northwest Africa under Spain's very nose.
Almost the only war plans that Army leaders found worth drawing up
dealt with a hypothetical war against France.[38] Within the Army there
was great admiration for the German military machine. Pro-German
feelings were encouraged by an expensive German propaganda effort
in Madrid and Barcelona, where several newspaper editors took German bribes and at least two journals were purchased outright by German agents. Otiose Spanish generals might sometimes be found in
military casinos talking lazily about an attack on France, made in conjunction with German forces, which might open the way for appropriation of all Morocco. Yet in view of the severe frustrations already suffered in the Riff and Djebala, such ambitious speculations could not
be taken seriously.

The World War did lessen French competition in Morocco, but
its past experiences discouraged the Spanish government from accepting deeper military involvement in the Protectorate.[39] The High Commissioner, General Marina, was not a dynamic soldier. Moreover,
he realized that he was under obligation to avoid unnecessary risks and
losses. Silvestre vigorously opposed the go-slow policy, insisting that
El Raisuli must be crushed by force. In May 1914 a Cavalry strike had
almost captured the Sherif; his horse was killed under him, but he
managed to escape. While the High Commissioner endeavored to

avoid combat, Silvestre did his best to discourage compromise. The conflict in the decentralized Spanish command resulted in a serious scandal on May 8, 1915, when El Raisuli's Tangier agent, who had just returned from a conference with Spanish officials, was found strangled.[40] Apparently Silvestre himself was not responsible, but an investigation indicated that the murder had been arranged by the anti-Raisuli Muslim mayor of Arcila and several subordinate Spanish officers. Fearing repercussions, Madrid recalled Marina and Silvestre. Two of the junior officers involved in the killing were imprisoned, but the two generals received high military honors on their return to Spain.

The most capable senior commander in Morocco was General Gómez Jordana, the military governor of Melilla. He had expanded the small zone of occupation in the eastern Riff, bargaining with the kabyles when it was possible to do so and employing the Regulares to reduce Spanish losses when combat was unavoidable. Gómez Jordana seemed a good successor to the ineffective Marina. He was named High Commissioner on July 9, 1915, and was given instructions to reach a new compromise with El Raisuli. By September he had concluded an agreement which granted the Sherif complete authority over the domestic affairs of most of the Djebalan kabyles, provided he did not interfere with the remainder of the Protectorate. El Raisuli's harca ceased its efforts to stir up the tribesmen, and Spanish military operations in Morocco virtually came to an end.

Though this truce had been concluded thanks to Jordana's adroit efforts, the terms were not of his choosing. He felt that Madrid had forced him into military capitulation, and he later wrote bitterly of his "captivity."[41] The conscientious High Commissioner found his dealings with El Raisuli to be a veritable *via crucis,* for once the pact was signed the Sherif reverted to his customary ways, running his feudal domain with an iron hand and often persecuting or imprisoning those favorably disposed toward the Spanish administration. Jordana protested repeatedly, but to no avail. El Raisuli now had the authority he wanted, and, though careful not to interfere with the limited prerogatives of the High Commissioner, would accept no advice or restraint from him in exercising his own jurisdiction. After a year or so, Jordana became convinced that the local tyranny of El Raisuli made a mockery of the Protectorate, yet the Madrid government insisted on preserving amicable relations with the Sherif, even to the extent of providing him with new rifles to rearm his harca. Had the Spanish authorities possessed a greater knowledge of Moroccan affairs and some expertise in dealing with local leaders, they might have used the widespread resentment against El Raisuli's tyranny to break his power and to create a regular administration. But the Foreign Ministry had no such abilities, and the military commander at Cadiz, General Miguel Primo de Rivera, drew a not illogical conclusion when he suggested, in a speech of May 25, 1917, that Spain endeavor instead to transfer most of its Protectorate to Britain in exchange for Gibraltar. This caused something of a sensation, and prompted the outspoken general's temporary dismissal from command.

During the winter and spring of 1917, attention was diverted from Morocco by Germany's resumption of unrestricted submarine warfare, which aroused a flurry of interventionist sentiment. The naval campaign outraged pro-Entente Liberals as well as apolitical businessmen whose principal dealings were with the western allies. Upper-class and Conservative opinion reaffirmed Spain's need for neutrality, while pro-German military writers published assurances that the Spanish Army would refuse to fight Germany. Certainly the great majority of officers would have been unenthusiastic about a conflict with Germany, though a liberal minority may have felt otherwise.[42]

Amid such uncertainties, Spanish activity in Morocco was virtually frozen for the remainder of the World War.[43] Luque, in his last tour as War Minister, wrote to Jordana on January 3, 1917: "The present Raisuli policy ... ought, in my opinion, to be continued until the world situation clears up."[44] On January 19, Luque stated clearly: "It will be necessary to temporize."[45] These instructions were often repeated during the two years that followed. On November 11, 1918, the unfortunate Jordana was composing yet another of his frequent pleas to the government for effective action when he fell dead of a heart attack at his writing table in the Tetuán headquarters, a pathetic symbol of duty frustrated by ignorance and incompetence.[46]

CHAPTER EIGHT

The Military Defense Juntas

I N THE YEARS after the establishment of the Moroccan Protectorate and the outbreak of the First World War, resentment among Spanish officers of junior and middle rank increased greatly. This was fed more by reaction against inadequate incomes and slow promotions than by determination to overcome the disorganization and inefficiency from which the Army had suffered for so long.

Discontent was further nurtured by the favoritism that reigned unchecked in the senior command. The broadest single source of complaint was General Luque's reintroduction, in 1910, of promotion by *méritos de guerra* (combat merits). Accelerated advancement through combat merits had been discontinued eleven years earlier, after gross abuses during the Cuban campaign. However, the activists who volunteered for service in Morocco expected special recognition, and political generals like Luque were eager to circumvent the rule of promotion by seniority. It was easy for Luque to win the king's approval for restoration of accelerated promotion by méritos, for this offered Don Alfonso a way in which to reward his favorites and at the same time develop a special palace clique within the Army. After the first Melilla campaign was over, promotions by méritos were lavishly awarded.

Only a small proportion of the officers on active duty were willing to volunteer for combat service in Africa. The swollen military bureaucracy showed no more taste for adventure than might have been expected among any group of idle government employees. In the past, a young man of the middle class might choose to follow an officer's career because it offered security and moderate status without requiring special effort or ability, but after 1910 an Army career no longer fulfilled these expectations. As early as 1902 Weyler, the Minister of

War, had prepared a ruling forbidding lieutenants to marry unless they had either an independent income or a fiancée with a sizable dowry, since a lieutenant's salary was simply not large enough to support a family. Mounting inflation after 1914, uncompensated for by any salary increase, made the situation much worse. The possibility of improving status came very slowly, since the average officer's snail-like progress to seniority could be accelerated only if he were willing to risk his life in Morocco. Yet in spite of the social and economic misery it imposed upon them, the ruling system expected the military to defend it against political and economic agitation. In consequence, thousands of officers felt cheated and betrayed. Their animosity was directed not merely against politicians, regionalists, and revolutionaries, but also against those elements of the Army command who seemed in league with a corrupt and unjust government.

The military newspaper *La Correspondencia Militar*, subsidized by anti-Luque elements, had championed opposition to the méritos system of special promotion. A large demonstration by officers of various ranks was arranged in front of the newspaper's Madrid office on January 12, 1912, to protest this practice, and, indirectly, to support the political opposition in the Cortes. No generals took part, but *La Correspondencia Militar* insisted that it was a popular protest:

There are 2,300 senior officers of Infantry and Cavalry who do not want to be politicians, and who reject any government policy that tries, by means of favoritism, to introduce hated rivalries into the Army. They regard any reward for service that is opposed to their vehement desire to ascend by seniority alone as a menace to their only safeguard, the scales of seniority.

The language of this statement indicates how strong was the sense of bureaucratic property status among many officers, and consequently how threatened they felt by special requirements or incentives, or interference with their routine. Their position was, in part, supported by the 1878 Military Ordinance, which defined an officer's *empleo*, or commission, as his personal property, in defense of which he was presumably entitled to legal protection. However, the same law made it clear that the *destino*, or assignment of each officer in the scale of his Corps, was dependent on the judgment of the command. The officers' demonstration was fundamentally insubordinate, and Luque responded by closing the Círculo Militar (the main Officers' Club) temporarily, replacing the Captain General of Madrid, and arresting a number of officers, including the director of *La Correspondencia Militar*.

Officers in the peninsula not only resented the veterans of Africa, with their special promotions, but also the manipulations of the Army hierarchy and the palace military clique fostered by the king. As Don Alfonso grew older, he became bolder and more direct in his fundamentally unconstitutional contacts with the Army. In addition to visiting barracks, attending banquets, and making speeches to officers, he held personal audiences for favored officers and officially encouraged generals to communicate with him directly, rather than through the constitutional channel of the Ministry of War. A royal order of January 15, 1914, read:

His Majesty the King (may God protect him), motivated by his love for the Army of which he is the Supreme Chief, directly and constantly intervenes in everything related to the troops—just as, in the granting of commands and promotions, he shows special concern to encourage whoever demonstrates relevant merits and contributes to the greatness and prosperity of the Fatherland. On certain occasions, our August Sovereign has honored generals and officers by communicating with them directly through letter or telegram. In order that those favored with this high distinction may respond adequately in similar fashion, it is the will of His Majesty that in this specific instance such generals and officers be authorized to answer him directly, without the intervention of anyone else.[1]

Other injustices suffered by the junior officers were more tangible and oppressive. No members of Spanish society were harder hit by the accelerating price inflation of the World War years than they. The tens of thousands of new workers flocking to the export industries in the cities won several rounds of wage increases, and many joined syndicates that pressed for more, but the military had no such resort. By 1916, there were demonstrations among government employees to dramatize the economic plight of the bureaucrat; officers, however, were not free to stage such protests. Military salaries remained frozen, and a civilian engineer could make two or three times as much as an Army Engineers officer. All attempts to reform Army structure during 1915 and 1916 were blocked, and in 1916 the Army budget was lowered slightly and 272 officer posts were eliminated.[2] The gold braid of the uniform could not camouflage the sad fact that a junior officer's salary was insufficient to maintain even a modest lower-middle-class household.

The way out for some was service in Morocco, where pay was higher on every level and promotions were still given generously.[3] The best example of a young officer who took advantage of this opportunity is the Galician Francisco Franco, who established a wide reputation during five years of irregular combat in the Protectorate. In 1916, when only 23, he was promoted to the rank of major, thus becoming one of the youngest senior officers in any European Army. But the Moroccan encounters were part of a "dirty war," and the *africanistas* who fought in them were considered a rough, irresponsible, corrupt lot. Rather than join them, the great majority of officers dragged out their boring and unremarkable careers amid the sloth of peninsular garrisons, carping about low pay, slow promotion, and favoritism.

The promotion problem was compounded by the fact that scales of seniority in the Spanish Army had been jumbled for almost a hundred years. There was concern not only over the incidence of méritos, but also over promotion of men from the ranks to the Reserve officer list and promotion of Reserve officers beyond the rank of lieutenant. Dissatisfaction among regular officers was increased by a War Ministry ruling of 1915 that Reserve lieutenants might be promoted to the rank of captain if they had thirteen years seniority or sufficient méritos.[4]

Most of these complications were avoided by the Engineers and Artillerists, whose officers all had to undergo five years of "facultative" study in their respective academies. Both Corps had defended themselves against favoritism and political interference by strict insistence on a "closed" scale, or promotion by seniority alone. This gave their members a certain sense of superiority over other parts of the Army, a feeling not unmixed with chagrin that greater preparation did not bring higher economic rewards. Unified standards within the Artillery were made somewhat easier by the fact that many Artillery officers were still drawn from aristocratic families long after most sections of the Officer Corps had become thoroughly democratized. In 1888, the Artillery Corps had formed an unofficial "Junta Central" of senior officers to defend the strict seniority scale, and after 1891 all cadets graduating from the Artillery Academy had been required to sign an agreement renouncing any sort of special promotion.[5] Any Artillery officer accepting an accelerated promotion was removed to the list of the Infantry or Cavalry. These two Corps, more heterogeneous in background than the Artillery, had no particular spirit of unity or organization. Most home garrison Infantry officers thought of themselves as ignored and abused, and felt that they had less means for protecting their interests than did the most miserable proletarian syndicate member.

Discontent increased in 1916, when the Minister of War, General Serrallo, tried to establish a system of aptitude measurements to test the physical and professional capacity of officers. A royal order of January 4, 1916, set up certain standards for generals, and others were later specified for lower ranks. These rulings occasioned the customary protests that greeted any effort to change anything in the Spanish Army. Since an officer's rank was viewed as his permanent bureaucratic status, unrelated to merit, ability, activity, or competition, many garrison officers feared that yet another attempt was being made to rob them of their rights.[6] The new standards were to be applied first in Barcelona. There, as elsewhere, some of the senior garrison officers in their fifties and sixties literally did nothing; they were in wretched physical condition, and could not even mount a horse. They found it unbearably humiliating to engage in physical tasks and field exercises before an audience composed, for the most part, of their juniors, and one aging general asked to be allowed to pass to the Reserve rather than be forced to take the tests. After a sharp protest, all generals were exempted, but lesser officers remained subject. Artillery and Engineers officers stuck together and announced that they would not recognize the new standards. In view of the widespread resistance, Serrallo's plans were quietly shelved.[7]

The special focus of discontent was the Barcelona garrison, always conscious of its special role as guarantor of national unity and order in a hotbed of political and social rebellion. During 1916, Infantry officers formed the habit of meeting regularly in Barcelona's central Plaza de Cataluña to discuss grievances. When the onset of cold weather made this uncomfortable, they decided to create a special Junta of their own, with a number of colonels and captains as their representatives.[8] Junta delegates spoke with officers in other Corps and traveled to garrisons in many parts of the peninsula, urging that officers' Juntas be set up in every district. By January 1917, ex-officio committees had been formed by Infantry and Cavalry officers in most of the larger garrisons throughout Spain.[9]

The goals of the Juntas were somewhat vague. In broad terms, the Juntas were opposed to africanistas, the méritos system, the palace clique, and the generals. The junteros wanted greater equality of reward, higher salaries, and ease of access to the king. They were hostile to the parliamentary politicians, who, they felt, were responsible for a large measure of the Army's and the government's ills. They believed that both the government and the people ought to have greater respect for the military, whose mission was to serve as the backbone of the country—the arbiter of national responsibility. Professional problems such as the inadequacy of training and equipment came further down the list of Junta grievances and were sometimes given no mention.

The Captain General of Barcelona, Alfau, received a copy of the first statutes of the local Infantry Junta and took a comparatively benevolent attitude toward the new formation. Luque was serving what proved to be his final term as Minister of War; he did not deign to take notice of the Juntas until the spring of 1917 was well advanced. When Don Alfonso was finally informed, he reacted with considerable apprehension, fearful that he himself might become a target for the officers. The king wanted to have the Juntas dissolved, but Luque, with his customary guile, suggested that they might be manipulated: some of the king's personal adherents among the officers could be persuaded to join, and then the Juntas, under the direction of "safe" elements, could replace the Army's Honor Tribunal in its advisory role at Madrid. Romanones, the Prime Minister, agreed to support this stratagem. Although one of the main causes for the formation of the "Juntas Militares de Defensa" had been disgust with Don Alfonso's "military party," leaders of the Infantry Junta at Barcelona were told at the beginning of May 1917 that the king had their interests at heart and was working to straighten out injustices in the scale of promotion.[10]

By that time, a Junta Superior representing a majority of the Infantry officers in peninsular garrisons had been organized at Barcelona. The Cavalry officers had followed the Infantry's lead, and were setting up their own network of Juntas. Even the Artillery fell into line, dissolving their old Junta Central and establishing a regional system under a Barcelona Junta Superior. Little by little, Barcelona, the focus of regionalism and proletarian revolution, was becoming the location of a military shadow-command of officers of middle rank.[11]

On May 10, 1917, Romanones' second ministry resigned, mainly because of the pressure generated by the problem of Spanish neutrality in the World War, but to a lesser degree because Romanones saw in the Juntas a serious political problem that he had no wish to deal with. He was succeeded by a rival Liberal chief, García Prieto, who appointed one of the senior lieutenant generals, Aguilera, to replace Luque as Minister of War. One of those influential "Madrid generals" about whom the Juntas were complaining, Aguilera was a stern disciplinarian who detested anything that smacked of disloyalty or insubordination. He sent word to Alfau at Barcelona to dissolve the Juntas as quickly as possible.[12]

For reasons that are not altogether clear, Alfau temporized. Meanwhile, the Juntas Superiores of the three Corps prepared to affiliate in a general "Union of Juntas."[13] With Luque's maneuver apparently thwarted, Don Alfonso was doubly anxious to see the Juntas eliminated, and the new government supported Aguilera's attempt to restore discipline. On May 26, the Minister of War telephoned Alfau and told him that further delay could not be tolerated: either the Juntas disbanded immediately or the leaders would be arrested. On May 28, after their refusal to obey this command, the members of the Barcelona Junta Superior of Infantry were arrested and conducted to Montjuich prison, which was usually reserved for anarchists.[14]

In Madrid there was much dissatisfaction with Alfau's failure to act, and after the arrest he was replaced by Marina, one of the leading opponents of the Juntas. Garrison committees all over Spain reacted heatedly to this appointment, and special meetings of delegates from the various local Juntas were held in Barcelona.[15] The Zaragoza Infantry Junta even asked other leaders of the movement whether they ought to seize Marina as his train passed through town en route to Barcelona.

A second committee of junteros was ready to take over in Barcelona as soon as the Infantry Junta leaders were arrested. It broadcast a long manifesto to other garrisons reaffirming the Juntas' grievances:

Since the colonial disasters (which might have been a source of regeneration), the general government, including that of the Army, has been exercised for the benefit of the oligarchs, with constant contempt for the true interests of the country. . . .

Though we ourselves are alien to politics, we cannot fail to see that the administration conducts its affairs without goal or plan—subject to constant vacillation and to the interests of large-scale boss rule, drowning every significant initiative and rejecting every proposal for the reform of the old, pernicious, established system, and bringing everyone into contact with the repellent malady of favoritism.[16]

The manifesto went on to state that the Juntas had absolutely no political aspirations and did not propose to transform themselves into official organizations, but wanted only to defend the "rights" of the Army and to set a moral and professional "example" to the country. If the petitions of the Juntas did not suffice to win recognition of these rights, the manifesto concluded, the junteros would have to seek "other means of defense."[17]

The government meanwhile sent orders to the district Captain Generals to take action against the regional Juntas, and members were arrested at Vitoria, La Coruña, and elsewhere. But on his arrival at Barcelona, Marina found himself helpless to crush the Junta there, for the only forces willing to obey his orders were the Civil Guards and part of the Engineers, and even the leaders of these units declared that in a showdown they would not fire on fellow officers. When Marina tried to bring the leaders of the Junta Superior to trial before the Barcelona military tribunal, the chief judge resigned the case, feigning illness. On the morning of June 1, the new Infantry Junta Superior sent out word to the regional committees that if the leaders were not released by the following afternoon the Juntas would seize power in Barcelona.[18]

This menace was doubly dangerous in view of the highly disturbed political and social situation. The political opposition was eager to make use of the Junta movement, and Alejandro Lerroux, head of the Republican Radicals at Barcelona, talked about organizing 800 young volunteers to free the imprisoned junteros from Montjuich fortress.[19] The regime was in no position to face a coordinated mutiny; within a matter of hours the government gave in and ordered release of the Junta leaders. One of Don Alfonso's personal favorites was sent as an emissary to the rebels, but Colonel Benito Márquez, chairman of the Infantry's Junta Superior, declared, as he and his companions were released on June 1: "The king is not placing us at liberty; we do so ourselves. He can thank God that we are allowing him to stay in Madrid."[20]

A formal letter dated that same day assured the king of the Juntas' loyalty but warned: "The Infantry Corps, which garrisons every region of the peninsula, . . . obeys the Junta Superior of the Corps exclusively."[21] Moreover, it was stated that the Artillery and Cavalry stood with the Infantry Junta in its endeavors. The letter asked for the personal intervention of the king to assure complete rehabilitation of the prisoners, and requested official recognition of the Juntas within twelve hours. Though the deadline was not met, the government capitulated to the major demands. The Juntas received de facto recognition, and by June 3 all imprisoned junteros had been released.

The military rebels had shown their power, but what use they could or would make of it was not clear. Their organization was extremely loose—simply a pyramid of confederated committees. No firm central command had been established. The principal leader, Benito Márquez, was a middle-aged regimental commander without previous distinction and lacking both combat and staff experience. Though Márquez has frequently been described as lazy and swaggering, one of the best-informed critics of the Juntas called him "a man of good intentions, though easygoing and lacking in disciplined intelligence."[22] However that may be, Spain's ruling clique was so discredited that the junteros' open letter of June 1 was applauded by much of the press. Márquez received hundreds of letters and telegrams hailing him as "savior," "redeemer," "the nation's hope," and so on.

Nearly all the generals were outraged by the growth of the Juntas. Aguilera threatened repeatedly to resign if they were not quashed, and Brig. Gen. Miguel Primo de Rivera spoke for many when he publicly denounced the whole Junta movement as an "illegal and unrighteous separatist expedient."[23] Nevertheless, faced with organized and uncontrolled insubordination, the military hierarchy had little choice but to await a political solution of the crisis.

Don Alfonso was being encouraged by some to resume the ploy earlier suggested by Luque—that of persuading the Juntas to rely on him as the one who would solve the Army's problems—thus strengthening his personal influence and turning the entire conflict to his advantage. General Marina arranged further negotiations with Junta leaders in Barcelona. Márquez and his colleagues insisted on better treatment and more money for the officers and presented three concrete policy demands: the replacement of Jordana as High Commissioner in Morocco (he was seen by the junteros as an oligarch and a promoter of favoritism), the retirement of a number of influential lieutenant generals who were hated by their subordinates as political manipulators, and the reorganization of the king's personal military staff. It was hoped that this last move might bring Don Alfonso into contact with a broader cross section of the Army, thus breaking the power of the palace clique.

On June 8, the Cabinet agreed to give the Juntas legal recognition within the Army structure and also promised to work toward fulfillment of the demands for increased pay, an end to favoritism, greater regularity in promotions, and so on. This did not satisfy Márquez' group, who wanted immediate action on these matters as well as on the specific personnel changes requested earlier. The king, who had no stomach for a showdown, seemed willing to grant greater concessions, but this was too much for Aguilera, who resigned in protest. The rest of the Cabinet followed suit on June 9.

Two days later a new government was formed by the Conservative Eduardo Dato. One of its major problems was to find a Minister of War who could cope with the Junta situation. (In Barcelona, General

Marina, who was virtually without authority, had made his peace with the Juntas, and he now acted as their spokesman to Madrid, transmitting their criticism of any member of Don Alfonso's military faction who displeased them.) The Prime Minister finally appointed Fernando Primo de Rivera—at eighty-six, the oldest general in the Army —as War Minister, in the hope that his age might place him beyond partisan strife. The junteros sneeringly referred to the old general as "the mummy."

The Junta movement was quickly spreading downward through the ranks. On June 12, a committee of noncommissioned officers sent a statement to the Junta Superior of Infantry, saying that the lower ranks had been entirely ignored in the officers' demands, and adding that "before all else, above all else, and beyond all else" they wanted maximum social dignity. They insisted on "all the independence, prestige, and authority" possible within the bounds of military order, and authority to overcome "the stormy situation" in which they found themselves.

It is absurd for us to continue to accept such intolerable treatment. . . . If, contrary to our expectations, our hopes are frustrated, then the hour of retribution will surely bring with it the bitter thought that our officers are the first barrier we must destroy.[24]

This was strong talk, and showed how dangerous the game of insubordination could be when less disciplined players joined it.

Almost immediately, the Republican groups and other progressives showed their interest in using the Junta revolt to promote sweeping institutional changes. As in the nineteenth century, they were willing to incite revolt among the lower ranks. In his Barcelona organ *La Lucha,* one of the best-known Republican leaders, Marcelino Domingo, published this manifesto:

Soldiers: You have already seen discipline in your barracks shattered when it suited the whims of your leaders. You have already seen how, not in the name of the law but in that of justice, your leaders have been ready to battle the constituted authorities. . . . Remember, then, that because of the petitions made, not by your officers but by your brothers, discipline will soon be broken in the street. Be forewarned that, in the name of justice, not your officers but your brothers, fathers, and mothers will rise up. . . . Will you fire against the humble to protect the upper classes? Will you fire against the hungry to protect the glutted?[25]

Pamphlets distributed by Domingo's followers emphasized the combination of military insubordination and civil insurrection responsible for the fall of the Russian Tsar, which had taken place only four months earlier and had made an unforgettable impression on Spanish rebels.

Some Socialist and liberal writers took a different approach. Rather than using the example of the Juntas to incite insubordination, they tried to encourage the junteros to join forces with liberal reformers.[26] The Junta leaders were in a delicate position. Their attitude was perhaps best expressed by an editorial in *La Correspondencia Militar* entitled "Legitimate Rebellion," which stressed that this was a protest movement operating within a professional institutional structure, and not a subversive revolutionary movement like that of the proletarian left. The junteros had no wish to be identified with leftists or to encourage further insubordination in the ranks, but the government was slow to respond to their main demands, and after a fortnight they were sure that "the mummy"—Primo de Rivera—was merely playing for time by appealing to their patriotic feelings.

Some junteros thought they needed a political champion who, as Prime Minister, would have the power to carry out the changes they demanded. The only politician whom the majority trusted was Antonio Maura. Consequently Márquez and another Junta chief called on Maura's principal lieutenant in Barcelona and broached their plans: if Maura would agree to form the next government, the Juntas would guarantee him the support of the Army. After learning of this by letter on June 20, Maura replied that he must reject any bid to power that came from outside the regular constitutional system.[27]

By June 25 the Infantry Junta had drawn up a long manifesto insisting that the Juntas were neither politically oriented nor insubordinate but were simply trying to achieve national reforms neglected by the political leadership.[28] The Dato government suspended constitutional guarantees and imposed censorship to prevent the circulation of this manifesto. There was some talk among Junta leaders of taking direct action against the government, but most realized that this was not feasible while the Army remained divided by ranks against itself. Márquez himself was opposed to any Junta effort to seize political control, and the idea was soon dropped. By the end of June, it was clear to most Junta leaders that they must endeavor to achieve their goals within the established governmental system or a slightly reformed version of it.[29]

The government was under such heavy fire from all sides that it decided to compromise with the Junta leaders. Republican, progressive, and Catalan deputies were pressing demands for a constituent Cortes to revise the constitution—a proposal that would break up the existing oligarchical domination. To the left, the trade syndicates were threatening mass strikes, so it was imperative that the government regain the support of the military. The king was extremely uneasy, and seemed eager to win the junteros' favor; a royal decree of July 2 granted a special appropriation of almost two million pesetas to increase certain military benefits and, incidentally, to provide better care for the troops. It further specified that henceforth no member of the king's personal military staff would be permitted to remain in that privileged circle for more than four years.[30]

These concessions did not fulfill the junteros' expectations, but they encouraged hope, and negotiations with the government continued during the first week of July. The Ministry of War distributed questionnaires among the Juntas of certain garrisons to gain a clearer idea of just what would be needed to satisfy the bulk of the dissidents. Reference was made in the questionnaire to the problem of superannuated generals, and one of the Junta committees took this occasion to comment that the government knew full well which generals ought to be passed to the Reserve.[31] On August 9, a meeting of the Infantry Junta Superior recommended that eight generals, including the Minister of War, be retired or removed from command.[32]

Meanwhile, dissident Cortes deputies were preparing to hold an opposition assembly at Barcelona in mid-July. The Catalan regionalists, who had heard a copy of the Juntas' June 25 manifesto read in the Barcelona City Hall on July 5, were hoping for encouragement from the officers. However, there was little likelihood of that, for the Juntas were neither democratic nor revolutionary, and their basic goal was not national reform or political justice but simply recognition of the Officer Corps as a corporate entity deserving of special perquisites, equitable rewards, and public recognition as the country's leading institution. Such limited and selfish aims were not directed toward the overthrow of the dominant oligarchy but rather toward the establishment of the military as the oligarchic elite. A genuinely democratic constitution or a social revolution would thwart this goal. It was not for nothing that Don Alfonso had begun, by the end of June, to refer to the "patriotism" of the Juntas: in a showdown, they would support the political and social status quo. A week before the assembly opened, Junta leaders in Barcelona had already given evidence of strong opposition, making it clear that they did not extend the right of peace-

ful insubordination to others,[33] and their antipathy was heightened
by the role played by Francesc Cambó and other Catalan deputies in
calling the conference. In general, the junteros were just as opposed
to Catalanists as they were to Madrid generals and africanistas.

The Juntas agreed with the Barcelona assembly that the political
cliques of the recent past should be eliminated, but they were scarcely
eager to see this done through a changeover to mass democracy. On
July 15, four days before the assembly convened, the Junta Superior
issued a statement saying that the Juntas refused to become involved
in party politics. However, since the Juntas had been trying to pose
as patriotic reformers, and since at least some Junta leaders felt that
they should encourage political change, it did not seem fully consistent
to ignore the initiative of the dissident deputies in calling their own
assembly. On July 17, Cambó received a letter from Márquez asking
him to define the assembly's goals. Cambó replied at length, and in
order to soothe military antagonism he stated: "Catalonia is not and
cannot be separatist." By way of encouragement he added: "Catalonia's
present situation bears great similarity to that of the Army since June 1.
Neither the Army nor Catalonia is free to use its strength for selfish
goals. Both must work to liberate Spain completely from the present
political system, which, if it continues, will lead all of Spain to perdi-
tion."[34]

The Junta Superior would not endorse the assembly, but Márquez
did sign a letter to Don Alfonso requesting that the king summon an
official constituent assembly to work on constitutional revision. That,
of course, was one of the last things the king would have considered
doing. Such an inappropriate suggestion was indicative of the political
naïveté of the Junta movement.

The reform-minded deputies who attended the Barcelona assembly
represented only a small minority of the Cortes members, and their
meeting was closed by government order before it could accomplish
anything. Having disposed of the assembly threat so easily, the government felt less need to make itself agreeable to the Juntas. Early in
August an Army chaplain was sent to the king's summer court to present yet another Junta proposal to him. This message called for a government of national concentration and elections for a constituent
Cortes to reform the constitution. Don Alfonso was directly appealed
to:

If you step forward to carry out the revolution, you will have conquered
the hearts of the people, and the Army will applaud you. Do not forget,

Sire, that when a king opposes an oligarchy and bases himself on his Army and his people he strengthens his crown. The hour of the monarchy has not yet passed.[35]

The king is said to have scornfully torn up the message. According to Márquez, the chaplain who had acted as the Juntas' messenger was "paid no heed and not even listened to" during his "humiliating pilgrimage through the royal palace at Santander."[36]

Convinced that it held the upper hand, the Dato government refused further compromise with either the Juntas or the trade unions. A bitter labor dispute on the northern railways had been settled by agreement between the management and the union, but the railway would not take back the employees fired during the strike. The government supported the railway against the workers, perhaps in order to force a test of strength. The military Juntas' representative sent to Santander had warned against an intransigent, provocative attitude in the labor dispute, but the government ignored the warning, believing that it could count on the Army's help in a showdown with the left.

The two main branches of the working-class movement agreed to collaborate in support of the railway employees, and on August 10 the only general strike in Spanish history was begun. Many trade union leaders had been reluctant to take this step, but it was felt that the government's attitude left scant alternative. *Libertad,* the CNT strike organ in Barcelona, exhorted the military on August 10:

May the Army officers remember that the slogan of the [Junta] movement was "Morality! Justice! Equality!" What morality, what justice, what equality is there in stabbing an unarmed multitude that only wishes to defend morality, justice, and equality? The Army has created this dilemma, and the result may prove either mild or devastating.[37]

In those cities of northern Spain where the workers were organized and the strike was more or less effective, troops were called out by the second or third day. Because of the Army's practice of granting 90-day summer leaves, some Infantry companies at Barcelona were down to forty men, so reinforcements were moved in, and the Navy sent a cruiser to Barcelona harbor. Many officers, still distracted by the problems within the Corps, were reluctant to turn their attention to civil matters, and the junteros, for their part, murmured that the Army was once again being used to do the politicians' dirty work. According to Márquez, the Captain General of Barcelona called out the troops to patrol the streets of the city and its suburbs in irregular formation, thus breaking up the normal relationship between officers and men.

However that may be, the enforcement of martial law provided an enemy on whom to focus resentment, and soon both officers and troops were reacting brutally against the strikers. Márquez himself has written that the first demonstrators met by the troops at Sabadell on August 11 conducted themselves in a nonaggressive manner. They approached the military to explain their grievances, but were met with a volley and a charge.[38] Harsh treatment of the strikers by the Army was the rule all over Spain. General Burguete, the military governor of Oviedo, made himself notorious by declaring that he was going to deal with the rebels in the mountains by "hunting them down like wild beasts."[39] The general strike gave Major Francisco Franco, commander of the Infantry battalion at Oviedo, his first experience in repressing civil disorder. The strikers found themselves isolated and without resources of their own to continue the stoppage. By the time the strike was broken, several score workers had been killed.

Having badly compromised themselves in the eyes of the lower classes by their part in the suppression of the strike, the Juntas tried to rationalize their pro-regime, antirevolutionary posture by stressing the "subversive" aspect of such a disturbance. On August 28, they demanded that all those who had been arrested as a consequence of the strike be brought to trial by military courts under the Law of Jurisdictions.

However, patriotic feelings were soon impinged upon by bitterness and disillusion, as evidence mounted that the Army had merely been used as an element of social control in the class struggle. The officers' image of themselves as representatives of the "true, patriotic" Spanish people (as distinct from Spain's politicians, profiteers, regionalists, and subversives) did not fit in with the role they had recently played against the workers. When the Infantry Junta Superior met at Barcelona on September 7, it issued a new circular, in which it tried to excuse the Army's role in the repression: the whole affair was blamed on the government's tactics, which were criticized for having provoked the strike. The circular reiterated the Juntas' belief that the officers had a "sacred obligation" to intervene in matters of national concern, and warned that the Juntas might have to impose "procedures of morality, justice, and foresight" on the politicians.[40]

The apex of Junta activity came in the late summer and autumn of 1917. At that time Márquez claimed that the Juntas represented 9,000 officers, or well over half of those on the active list.[41] In some garrisons, 90 per cent of the officers belonged to the Juntas, and there was support among a number of the officers in Morocco as well. Even a few generals were endeavoring to make common cause with them. Despite the enmity that the junteros bore his uncle "the mummy," Miguel Primo de Rivera reversed his earlier stand: possibly deciding that the Juntas were having an important political effect, he offered Márquez his support.[42]

During the summer, many new groups sprang up in imitation of the original Juntas. Not only were juntas of noncommissioned officers formed, but also juntas of white-collar workers in the various civilian branches of government service. In June, juntas were set up by workers in the mail and telegraph services. Others were formed by employees of the Finance Ministry and members of the municipal police force. For middle-class people not employed by the government, a junta called "the Union of Taxpayers" was set up. The Officer Corps, the most powerful of the nation's petty bourgeois strata, had opened a Pandora's box of organized resentment. It has been suggested that the real Spanish social crisis of 1917 was not the proletarian revolt, but the emergence of radicalism among the petty bourgeois bureaucrats. Economically this was understandable, for the salaried employees often suffered proportionately more from wartime inflation than most sections of the proletariat did. Comparisons with the formation of the soviets in revolutionary Russia or with the Independent Socialist agitation for a *Räterepublik* in Germany were not very accurate, but they were made—adding to the nervousness of the upper classes.

The Juntas of the three Corps held sessions in Barcelona almost continuously throughout September and October, and filled the air with circulars, letters, and manifestos. These appeals were addressed by the junteros to each other and to the nation; to the king, the Prime Minister, and the Cortes; to anti-Junta generals, various politicians, newspaper editors, and so on. The junteros reiterated their complaints against the merit system, for even some officers in Morocco were beginning to resent the fact that méritos were distributed with little regard for qualities other than physical presence and daring. Demands were also made for abolition of the separate status of the General Staff, and its division into units serving the various Corps. There was still strong concern among the junteros lest the people be led by government propaganda to blame the Army for the repression of the strikes and the continuance of martial law, and one of the inter-Junta circulars warned: "The Army must not allow political maneuverers to burden it with exclusive blame for the repression [of the strikes] and its consequences, for this would result in the Army's being placed in opposition to the people . . . and would lead to the calumny . . . that the Army alone sustains the present state of war and demands cruel reprisals."[43]

To avoid this, and to achieve its major goals, the Infantry Junta Superior decided on "direct intervention" in politics.[44] It was agreed however, that for the time being negotiations with the government would be carried out through the mediation of General Marina, who had served as chief contact earlier in the summer.[45] The Juntas were now demanding the resignation of the Dato government and the formation of a new ministry that would be more "honest," "patriotic," and responsive to their demands. On the one hand the government faced the hatred of the leftist and progressive elements; on the other, the mounting ire of the military. To counter leftist and progressive charges that the Army was abusing its authority in the repression, Dato issued a statement on September 27 saying that the military courts were simply doing their duty and proceeding by the rules.[46] However, his implication that the Army was acting in support of the government raised the hackles of some junteros. The way they preferred to describe it, the Army, on its own initiative and in order to defend the Fatherland, was prosecuting subversives because this duty had been shirked by the government. *La Correspondencia Militar,* which had become the principal journalistic organ of the Juntas, prepared a statement saying that the Juntas did not support the present government, that the rules they obeyed were of their own choosing, and that they would like to see martial law lifted as soon as possible. This statement was suppressed by the government censor before the papers reached the street.[47]

Pressure increased in mid-October, when another general assembly of the Juntas Superiores of the three Corps was called in Barcelona. By this time the king had to a certain extent overcome his fear of the Juntas. Now he hoped to use them to enhance his personal authority, even if it meant the resignation of the present government. On October 18, the junteros had their way in the Ministry of War. The ancient Primo de Rivera resigned and was replaced by Marina, who had become public mediator for the Juntas. The rest of the ministers insisted that all Junta messages to the king should pass through the Cabinet as a whole and not just through the hands of the Minister of War. Meanwhile, the Junta Superior of Infantry drafted a new message to Don Alfonso demanding that the remainder of the Dato ministry resign, and requesting the election of a new constituent Cortes (which the

Junta promised to dissolve if it should get out of hand). The more conservative Cavalry and Artillery representatives did not sign this demand, but the king was quite willing to use the message against his own ministers, and he sent the statement back to Barcelona in the hope that all the Junta groups would endorse the use of the royal initiative. In the meantime, a Junta ultimatum demanding the Cabinet's resignation within 72 hours was delivered on October 24.[48] It was made public in Madrid on the following day, and a major crisis ensued; the Cabinet saw that Don Alfonso had no intention of abiding by his agreement to use constitutional channels, and the entire government resigned, as he had foreseen.[49]

The Juntas had succeeded in overturning Dato's ministry, but their second goal—the calling of a constituent Cortes—proved to be much harder to attain, for neither the king nor any other influential political leader in Madrid was willing to go that far. Instead, on November 1 the king and the major political bosses attempted to outflank the Juntas by establishing, under García Prieto, a multiparty "government of concentration," in which nearly all the important cliques were represented.

The choice for Minister of War fell on Juan de la Cierva, *cacique* (political boss) of Murcia and head of one of the principal factions of the former Conservative party. He was the first civilian to hold this office under the constitutional monarchy. La Cierva had gained notoriety as Minister of the Interior, election fixer, and patronage boss for the Conservatives during the ministries of Antonio Maura. His control of Murcian affairs had been so complete for the previous decade that a famous phrase had been coined—*Mata al rey y vete a Murcia* ("Kill the king and run away to Murcia")—to indicate that anything could be "fixed" in that district. La Cierva was of authoritarian leanings, and had always posed as a friend of the Army. He was one of the few established leaders who had offered his support to the Juntas, and he now became the center of their aspirations. Since the ostracism of Maura eight years earlier, La Cierva had been excluded from national politics. He thought that the pressure of the Juntas might catapult him into dominance. When he took office, *La Correspondencia Militar* expressed complete confidence that he would promote Army interests.

Henceforth there was little talk about a constituent Cortes, for apparently most Junta leaders felt that the issue was not particularly important now that a pro-Junta Minister of War had been appointed. One reason why most junteros were willing to accept La Cierva was that the tendency toward syndicalization was spreading further downward in the Army, and even ordinary privates, following the example of officers and NCO's, were beginning to join an informal "Unión de las Clases de Tropas" ("union of the ranks") which might become the seedbed for wholesale insubordination. Some sort of political solution to Junta demands had to be sought before things got completely out of hand.

La Cierva later admitted in his memoirs that he had had no particular knowledge of military problems when he took office.[50] However, he did not lack shrewdness. He began his term by asking the district Juntas for their suggestions concerning desirable reforms and by requesting the Juntas Superiores to suggest deserving officers in each Corps who might serve as his aides.[51] Then he turned his attention to the task of drafting an Army reform bill, the central feature of which was a substantial salary increase much larger than the token perquisites granted during the past summer. Meanwhile, he endeavored to build his personal influence with key junteros.

Another of La Cierva's tactics was to encourage Reserve officers to form Juntas of their own, apparently so that he might have a lever to use against the regular Juntas. Reserve officers had never been welcome in the Juntas. One of the junteros' principal aims was to tighten and regularize the order of seniority and promotion in the Officer Corps. This meant that the number of future Reservists would be reduced. Moreover, the regular officers were determined to keep those of the Reserve in a distinctly inferior position. Among themselves, Reserve officers had a stronger sense of group unity than regular officers did. In earlier years, the king had encouraged the Reservists to rely on him for special favors, but they lacked the political ambition of some of the regular officers. For the most part, the Reservists were a practical lot who tried to avoid political quarrels and to work for tangible, limited improvements in their professional situation.[52]

Yet another stratagem pursued by La Cierva was to encourage the NCO Juntas to strengthen their Unión de las Clases de Tropas, ostensibly so that he might represent their interests. On the face of it this was absurd, for if syndicalization went much further the structure of the Army would be completely destroyed, but in fact this was simply another gambit to help keep the regular officers' Juntas in line.

La Cierva's first major opponent was Colonel Benito Márquez, chief of the Infantry's Junta Superior. According to Márquez, La Cierva tried to bribe him into becoming a lackey of the War Ministry. According to La Cierva, Márquez had expected to be made the Director General of Infantry, and turned against the War Minister when he did not receive the appointment. The bulk of the evidence seems to support Márquez' side of the story. He was not unaware of the dangers of insubordination, and in his clumsy fashion he had endeavored to keep the Juntas from directly supplanting regular authority.[53] Other Junta leaders were less scrupulous and more clever than Márquez, and on occasion he had been talked into signing documents whose import he did not fully understand or whose argument he did not fully agree with. Moreover, not all Junta leaders kept faith with him, and secret communications sometimes found their way into the hands of the Ministry of War.

Fernández Almagro, the principal political historian of this period, has described Márquez thus:

A man of few gifts: ill-prepared, doubtless, to seize control of events, and hence used and manipulated by others toward goals which he personally repudiated. A liberal in his own way, Col. Márquez wanted to remain faithful to the [original] intentions of the Juntas, and declared, in the middle of a meeting of the Junta Superior, that La Cierva's reform plan, which consisted of salary increases, was nothing but a bribe.[54]

It was not difficult for La Cierva to undercut the chairman's power in the Junta Superior. He dealt directly with Márquez' colleagues, some of whom had never thought of the colonel as much more than a figurehead. A "Junta Central de Defensa" containing representatives of the various Juntas Superiores was set up on December 17, making it easier for the War Ministry to deal with the Junta directors. When Márquez urged the Juntas to unite behind him in opposition to La Cierva's ambitions, he was forced to retire, and another colonel was chosen by the Junta Superior of Infantry to replace him.[55]

By the end of the year the War Minister was making fair progress in establishing his influence over the Juntas. In return, he had to accede to the officers' insistence that the Unión de las Clases de Tropas be eliminated. It was said that sergeants were traveling from garrison to garrison organizing the lower ranks. According to the gossip, some NCO's even took their rifles to bed with them in the barracks, in case the officers should try to reimpose strict discipline; there was even talk of contacts between the sergeants and Pablo Iglesias, the head of the Socialist party. La Cierva ordered the dissolution of the Unión, which was carried out without bloodshed. Some two hundred sergeants and enlisted men who had been members were expelled from the Army during the first week of 1918.[56]

Martial law had been lifted in October, and in an effort to form a more workable Parliament new elections were held in January 1918. However, the country was now too politically conscious for old-style electoral fixing to obtain the results of an earlier day. Though 36 million pesetas were said to have been spent on campaign expenses and bribery,[57] the result was a new Cortes even more divided and discordant than the preceding one.[58] By 1918 the Spanish parliamentary system was well on its way to becoming totally unworkable.

The same multiparty government remained in power, and La Cierva continued to develop his military reform bill, which was first enacted by royal decree on March 7, though it was not formally presented to Parliament at that time. The War Minister seemed to be bringing the Juntas into line; his proposed changes would have given them at least part of what they wanted, and he had already identified many juntero leaders with his own political activities. Moreover, the character and composition of the Juntas was changing: Márquez was forced to retire on March 8, and some of the more conscientious officers who had earlier supported the Juntas were drifting out.[59] Whatever altruism had once existed within the movement was being submerged by the remaining members' narrower concern to use the Juntas merely as a vehicle for self-advancement. As a result, a new military faction not unlike the court clique which the Juntas had been trying to eliminate was being created. The example of the Unión had alarmed senior Junta officers, and some of the Artillerists wanted to abandon the whole business. At a general meeting of Artillery delegates, the Artillery Junta of Madrid voted on March 23 to dissolve all the military Juntas. However, when the measure was voted on by the Artillery delegates as a whole, almost two-thirds of them agreed to a continuation of the Junta system.[60]

Informed opinion now held that La Cierva was using the Ministry of War and the Juntas as stepping-stones to power, and that his bid to lead the government would be based on a platform of order, discipline, and patriotism. Certainly La Cierva was already the central figure in the Cabinet. He helped to squeeze out the two Catalan ministers, then seized the offensive against the burgeoning juntas of government employees. In the late winter of 1918, these same employees decided to engage in a work slowdown until they obtained a wage raise similar to the one that La Cierva was preparing for the Army. The military Juntas had made it clear that they had little intention of helping other professions win rights such as the Army bureaucracy claimed for itself, and on March 14 La Cierva took the initiative for the government by mobilizing the employees of the postal and tele-graph services. This was supposed to give the government authority to end their slowdown and break up their juntas. At the same time, a spokesman for the military Junta Central rejected any identification of the officers' groups with the various civilian juntas, and insisted that the main difference between them was the fact that the military groups strove to defend rather than to cripple the Fatherland.[61] To regularize the military Juntas and deprive the bureaucrats of part of their rationale, La Cierva announced on March 16 that the officers' Juntas were henceforth to be transformed into advisory commissions. There was to be but one Junta for each Corps—regional juntas being dissolved—and none of these would have anything to say about "any matter not the particular concern of their Arm or Corps."[62]

La Cierva felt that this cleared the decks for all-out action against the bureaucratic juntas, which could now be crushed by force if need be. Most of his colleagues in the Cabinet took a more cautious attitude. Though in decrees of March 15 and 16 the government ordered the outright dissolution of all the bureaucratic juntas, most of the min-isters were confident that this could be accomplished through concilia-tion—or, at the very least, without bloodshed. However, after publi-cation of the decrees, employees of the mail and telegraph services, the Ministries of Finance and Education, and several other departments walked out en masse. Public sympathy seemed to be on their side and to have deserted the military Juntas. Realizing that his insistence on a hard line was not going to be supported by the rest of the Cabinet, La Cierva resigned on March 19, thus provoking another political crisis. Rumor had it that La Cierva had been intriguing for leadership of a new ministry staffed by Junta colonels and endowed with decree powers. Had this been true, La Cierva stood little chance of bringing such a scheme to fruition: though he had the support of the Junta leaders, the officers as a whole were not strongly behind him, and his backing in civilian circles was scant.

The crisis was temporarily solved by the formation of a new min-istry of multiparty "concentration" under Antonio Maura. La Cierva was retained as War Minister, and soon he was sending out another round of questionnaires to senior officers and members of the Com-missions (as the Juntas were now technically known) concerning ad-ditions to the new Army bill that was under consideration by the Cortes. The bill was attacked by Julián Besteiro, the most intellectual of the Socialist leaders, who delivered a lengthy criticism of La Cierva's

relations with the Army in a speech of June 19.[63] At approximately
the same time, the Independent Conservative Sánchez de Toca published a pamphlet denouncing the fraudulence of Army organization
and the officers' persistent use of pressure tactics to gain their ends.
This prompted another outcry from the military, together with the
now customary threats against politicians.[64]

In spite of its opponents, the Army bill was approved by the Cortes
on June 29. It provided for a domestic military budget of 317 million
pesetas, plus 112 million pesetas for expenditure in Morocco, and made
provision for a force of 180,000 men. These figures were new records
for peacetime. The main cause of the budgetary increase was a pay
hike that benefited all ranks and ranged from an annual increase of
approximately 5,000 pesetas for generals to one of 385 pesetas for second lieutenants. Sergeants received a flat 30 per cent increase in pay
and privates a proportionately greater one (25 *céntimos* per day).
Larger bonuses were to be paid in the lower ranks according to length
of service.

The new law endeavored to meet the Juntas' criticism of promotion by méritos. Section 9 stated: "In time of peace, promotions by
election up to the rank of colonel are prohibited, except in extraordinary circumstances when special authorization has been given." It
established a Classifying Junta of five generals, whose function it was
to pass on the promotions and seniority of officers at the various ranks
of general and thus reduce the likelihood of favoritism in the higher
ranks.[65] A few structural reforms were also made, and Army units
were reorganized into sixteen divisions of three brigades each. Theoretically, the budget increase would provide for the extra manpower in
the divisions. But the bill had nothing to say about the Army's main
problems—the grotesque surplus of officers, the sloth, ignorance, and
irresponsibility of military personnel, and the absence of modern
equipment.

As it developed, La Cierva's attempt to make a deal with the junteros was not successful, for they would not be fully satisfied until they
were able to make Army policy themselves and hold a sort of veto
power over the government. The Prime Minister, Maura, took a much
less indulgent attitude toward the Juntas than La Cierva did. After
the new military law was passed, he instructed the Minister of War
that no further concessions need be made to the Junta Commissions.
Within a few months the juntero chiefs were restive again. During
the latter part of 1918 demands were made that the Commissions be

granted the legal right to supervise the sections of the Army from which they were chosen. Commission members wanted to be placed on permanent assignment in Madrid with no duties other than those connected with Junta affairs. After nearly a year and a half of threats, blackmail, negotiation, and compromise, discipline still had not been restored in the Army.

Domestic conflict deepened in the winter of 1918, owing to the economic dislocation caused by the termination of World War I. The angry, uncertain reaction of the military to domestic problems in 1919 showed that none of the contradictions in their aspirations had yet been resolved. After two years of Junta agitation, there was more talk than ever about the Army's special role in unifying and educating the nation.[66] Yet despite their protestations that they were above class and political prejudice, the officers felt that whenever conflict arose they must come down decisively on the side of order and repression.[67] This resulted in a wide gap between Army pretensions and the realities of Army interest and action, which only encouraged the officers' tendency to blame all their problems on the politicians.

In December 1918, while much of Spain's wartime export trade was collapsing, the syndicalist CNT (Confederación Nacional del Trabajo, or National Labor Federation) decided on an all-out campaign of organization, propaganda, and economic pressure. The third Romanones ministry, formed in Madrid at the end of the year, fought back by suspending constitutional guarantees and calling out the troops in some areas. The center of conflict was Barcelona, where an "Employers' Federation" was set up at the beginning of 1919 to defend layoffs and to coordinate resistance to worker demands. Its goal was destruction of the CNT. In February 1919, the conflict culminated in a city-wide strike of workers in the gas and electrical industries. Catalan employers demanded government action, and the Captain General of Barcelona, Milans del Bosch, was ordered to occupy the plants affected. The strikers were mobilized into the Army Reserve. Although some officers looked on these measures with disapproval, the military authorities at Barcelona, with their circumscribed understanding of social and political problems, were outraged that the government saw fit to limit their use of power in any way. They insisted that if the Army were to handle the conflict it must have untrammeled authority to do a complete job. Milans del Bosch invoked the Law of Jurisdictions, imprisoning a number of CNT leaders in the military fortress of Montjuich. After six weeks, a strike settlement was negotiated by civilian officials. One of the terms was that all CNT representatives held in military custody were to be released. When the government so instructed Milans del Bosch, he refused to comply, insisting that the Army would be no party to deals and compromises. Further, the Captain General threatened to resign his command unless the eleven CNT chiefs in question were tried before military courts.

Like most of the Spanish ministries of those years, the Romanones Cabinet was a minority government. It had been consented to by the Cortes so that the problems of transition caused by the close of the World War might be dealt with, but its members did not feel strong enough to cope with widespread social rebellion and renewed military insubordination. Faced with Bosch's ultimatum, the Cabinet resigned, but on March 24, just before its resignation became effective, the deadline agreed upon with the CNT passed and a general strike was declared in Barcelona. The city was completely closed down. Faced with the new crisis, the ministers agreed to withdraw their resignations temporarily. Reinforcements were hurried to the Barcelona garrison, warships were sent to anchor in the harbor, and cannon were placed at the intersections of the city's major streets.

The Barcelona commanders and the Junta leaders were disgusted with both the syndicalists and the government. Milans del Bosch insisted that only the Army had authority to solve a dispute into which it had been brought, and the Juntas sent a message to the Cabinet with the old complaint that the government's attempt to use the military for its own purposes was calling down upon the Army the "implicit hostility" of much of the public. Though admitting that the Army must be ready to intervene in social disputes if the good of the nation required it, the Juntas rejected "all assignments of politicking, compromising, or temporizing," and warned: "Orders must be clear, concrete, and explicit [or] the Army will not be responsible for what may happen if the troops are put into the streets."[68] They "invited" the government to take positive measures to solve social conflicts without their intervention, but claimed free jurisdiction for the military courts in situations where military aid had been invoked in the form of martial law.

The strike was broken by the second week of April. Several hundred syndicalists were arrested, and perhaps ten times as many were driven into exile. The most sinister agent of repression was not the Army but the so-called "employers' police" directed by the gunman

Bravo Portillo. It was mainly financed by Barcelona industrialists, but the original incentive seems to have been provided by German agents, who had spent large sums in 1917 and 1918 promoting the assassination of syndicalist chiefs and arranging counter-threats against employers in an effort to disrupt Catalan war production. By 1919, Bravo Portillo's gang was murdering with impunity on the streets of Barcelona in broad daylight. Milans del Bosch and the commander of the Barcelona Infantry garrison, General Severiano Martínez Anido, chose to overlook the crimes of the employers' police, claiming that their activities were necessary to prevent the CNT from getting completely out of hand. The civil governor of Barcelona protested, but to no avail. On April 13 the military authorities decided to take over completely so that they could impose their own solution on the struggle in Barcelona without any opposition from the government. Announcing that they would not tolerate deceitful politicians, they ousted the civil governor and the Barcelona police chief and sent them on the night train back to Madrid. A representative was dispatched to the king to complain of the way in which the Romanones government had handled the Barcelona situation. Martínez Anido temporarily took over the functions of civil governor, and another officer, Arlegui, was placed in charge of the Barcelona police. He gave free rein to the hooliganism and counter-terrorism already commonplace in the district.[69]

The danger of military dictatorship seemed a great deal closer than at any time since the restoration of the monarchy. Sympathy strikes brought the imposition of martial law in Madrid, Valencia, and other labor centers. The Romanones Cabinet resigned, and Don Alfonso summoned another Maura government. This ministry did not pretend to be a government of "national concentration," but was composed entirely of members of Maura's faction, and had few supporters in the Cortes. At any rate, Maura's return to power helped mollify the military, and most of the CNT leaders were released.

With national tensions decreasing, elections were held in the hope of obtaining a workable Maurist or Conservative majority, but the new Cortes was almost as divided as the old, and in July the independent Conservative Joaquín Sánchez de Toca formed a new ministry. Sánchez de Toca and a small band of his independent colleagues were highly critical of the administrative irregularities of recent years, and they were determined to try to make the constitutional system work. The new Minister of War, General Muñoz Cobo, ordered Milans del Bosch to have Bravo Portillo arrested. By this time Milans had become opposed to the continuation of martial law, but he refused to intervene against the employers' police. Feeling that the Army's authority was compromised by the conflict over strike repression, he offered his resignation as Captain General. The real military leader in Barcelona was not Milans, however, but the garrison commander Martínez Anido. He and Arlegui were mainly responsible for the freedom granted the employers' police. Moreover, Martínez Anido was a personal friend of Muñoz Cobo, whom he advised not to interfere in the highly complicated Barcelona situation. From its own investigations, the Cabinet concluded that nearly 15,000 anarchists and trade unionists had been imprisoned or run out of the Catalan industrial towns by midsummer of 1919.[70] Several score had been shot. But eager as it was to restore civil authority, the Cabinet was also aware of its political weakness in the Cortes, and no changes were made at Barcelona other than the appointment of a new civil governor.

The next Junta scandal developed in the autumn of 1919, provoked by the junteros' animosity toward the General Staff. The Junta members were still anxious to establish closed seniority scales for each of the Army Corps and to eliminate exceptional promotions. Officers from the Commissions were urging captains currently studying in the Escuela Superior de Guerra (Staff college) to join the Juntas and pledge to remain on the regular scale in their respective Corps or forfeit all right to seniority. This conflict drew public attention when the newspaper *El Sol* reported on October 22, 1919, that some of the captains studying in the Staff college had renounced Junta affiliation in protest against such pressures. The junteros replied by dragging 25 captains before an ad hoc honor tribunal, which ordered 16 of them expelled from the Officer Corps. The Supreme Council of the Army courts, supported by the Ministry of War, ruled this order invalid. Junta leaders began to mutter once more about the need for some sort of pronunciamiento.

The Sánchez de Toca government prepared two separate decrees for the outright dissolution of the Juntas but did not have the strength —or the determination—to promulgate either. Junta spokesmen reasserted that if the validity of their honor tribunals were not recognized, Junta members would no longer fulfill their responsibilities. At the end of October, the Cabinet decided that the case of the 25 captains should be heard by a regular military court subject to the review of the Supreme War Council. Nevertheless, the new Minister of War, General Tovar, ended by capitulating to the Juntas: a new Junta-dominated honor tribunal was constituted, and 23 captains (including the original 16) were expelled. At that point the Sánchez de Toca government, harassed throughout its tenure by Catalan employers' lockouts, mass strikes, terrorism, Andalusian peasant riots, and military insubordination, collapsed.[71]

As soon as the king returned from his latest hunting trip, another hodgepodge ministry was formed. Its leader, Manuel Allendesalazar, was an upper-middle-class politician with three brothers in the Officer Corps. His personal following was slight, but he broke with precedent and appointed another civilian, the independent-minded Vizconde de Eza, to the Ministry of War. For a Spanish cabinet of those years, the Allendesalazar government acquitted itself fairly well. On April 21, 1920, the Cortes, under administrative pressure, approved the first regular budget in six years.[72]

The year 1920 opened on a radical note, with an anarchist plot to take over the Infantry barracks at Zaragoza. At least one corporal and several recruits participated in the conspiracy, and there were even rumors that a few officers were involved. At any rate, a handful of armed anarchists entered the barracks to join the rebels, and killed a lieutenant and an NCO who resisted them. Prompt intervention by Civil Guards occupying an adjacent building quelled the revolt before it became serious, and seven mutineers were subsequently court-martialed and shot. The Republican agitator Lerroux took this occasion to proclaim dramatically: "The Soviet has knocked at the barracks door."[73]

The abnormal state of affairs in Barcelona continued. Bravo Portillo was himself murdered by anarchist gunmen, and after another labor blowup, Milans del Bosch was forced to resign as Captain General. The Cabinet replaced him with Valeriano Weyler, now in his dotage but still physically active and as critical as ever of the insubordination that marked Army affairs. Yet the aged Weyler was not the same vigorous leader who had cut such a swath in the 1890's, nor was it likely that the mess in Barcelona could be cleaned up simply by a change of command. Though Madrid garrison officers were ordered to see Weyler off at the railroad station, the majority boycotted the ceremonies. Few were on hand to greet him in Barcelona, and local shop owners closed their stores for two hours to protest the government's capitulation to "the forces of subversion." Officers in Madrid demanded restitution of Milans del Bosch, and only a small delegation of NCO's from the Barcelona garrison pledged their support to Weyler in restoring discipline.[74]

The Allendesalazar government was soon driven from office, to be succeeded by a Conservative cabinet under Dato which reverted to a hard line against the worker movement. Weyler was replaced by a new Captain General more acceptable to the Juntas, and Martínez Anido was made civil governor of Barcelona.

In this complex struggle between military pressure groups, working-class revolutionaries, industrialists, and political factions, none of the major antagonists was in a position to push the conflict to a climax. Each was divided internally and not a little confused. Their disputes sputtered and flared for three years more, amid mounting terrorism by syndicalist gunmen and their adversaries within and without the police, until the dilemma raised by the military problem in Morocco finally precipitated the overthrow of Spain's constitutional system.

CHAPTER NINE

The Riff War

THE MOROCCAN PROTECTORATE was comparatively quiet between 1915 and 1918, but it cast its shadow over Spanish politics.[1] When the third Romanones government took office after the death of Jordana in December 1918, Spain's policy in Africa was reexamined. With the conclusion of the great European conflict, France would be much more active in Morocco, and Spain could scarcely continue to mark time as it had been doing during the past three years. The feudal tyranny exercised by El Raisuli over the northwestern corner of the Protectorate was stronger than ever, while the scope and efficiency of Spanish authority had in no way increased. Unless its forces were able to control the Protectorate, Spain might as well give in to national opinion and withdraw.

The Army, the king, and key political leaders were opposed to this policy of "abandonment." It was decided that more forceful measures must be taken to expand Spanish colonial power. Early in 1919, the government began its program to bring the entire Protectorate under direct or indirect Spanish control. The military governor of Larache, General Emilio Barrera, was already working to extend Spanish authority in the western Djebala,[2] and his counterpart in Ceuta was directed to suffer no more insults from El Raisuli. Soon the Sherif was writing to complain of "crude interference" by Spanish officers.[3]

The death of Jordana had left vacant the office of High Commissioner, and the Romanones government, hoping to regularize Spanish policy, sought a capable civilian to fill the post. But the africanistas and the officers of the court circle had come to regard Morocco as their special preserve, and they appealed to the king and the leading generals to prevent the appointment of a civilian.[4] Consequently Major General Dámaso Berenguer, Undersecretary of War in the preceding Maura government, was named High Commissioner.

Though a royal favorite, Berenguer was no mere court fop. Born in Cuba in 1878 while his father was stationed there, he came from an old Army family; his four brothers were Army officers as well. Berenguer was more cautious, observant, and cerebral than was customary among the Spanish military. He had read considerably in the history of Muslim Spain, had served in the earlier Moroccan campaigns, had studied modern colonial operations, knew at least a little about the Berber kabyles, and, not long before his appointment, had brought out a small book on the problem of military tactics in Morocco.[5] He stressed short, well-planned advances based on knowledge of the terrain, and favored the use of native Regulares to cut down losses to European troops. Berenguer also emphasized diplomatic preparation among the tribes and urged that Spanish administration interfere as little as possible with the local sheikhs and *cadis* (Muslim judges).[6] In the Army he was considered a model officer and gentleman, and was credited with considerable appreciation of the importance of civilian authority.

When Berenguer arrived at Tetuán in February 1919, he had already decided on what his policy would be. He wrote a pro forma letter to El Raisuli, inviting him to visit Tetuán and discuss their problems. As Berenguer had anticipated, the Sherif, who stubbornly refused to come to the residence of the caliph, withdrew into the hills and broke off relations with the Spanish authorities. As in 1913, he intended to stir up the Djebalan kabyles and, by cutting off the roads from Tetuán to Ceuta, Tangier, and Larache, isolate the Spanish administration and its caliph. Berenguer endeavored to avoid widespread fighting, and pursued a policy of bribery and "attraction" toward local leaders. Yet it was impossible to sidestep clashes with El Raisuli's bands, and several columns were sent out that spring to drive hostile forces from the hills surrounding Tetuán.

When news of these skirmishes was reported in Spain, the political opposition once more decried the contradictions in recent Spanish policy. Each day Spanish recruits were being killed by the very forces that El Raisuli had been allowed to build up under the Protectorate. A Republican newspaper wrote:

Contrary to government promises, we continue to fight in Morocco. The Moors have killed many of our soldiers, and the war continues. The people do not wish to go to Morocco; they do not wish to spend another céntimo there. Spain is tired of sacrificing her sons in the conquest of a territory that brings her nothing but troubles.

Should Spain confront the perils of the conquest of a zone to which she can export neither her civilization nor her ideals of living?[7]

The extremist sectors of Catalan nationalism expressed their sympathy with Moorish resistance to "Castilian" imperialism.

The flareup of fighting in Morocco, as well as continued pressure from the Juntas in Spain, forced further expansion of the Army and its budget. For reasons of politics and bookkeeping, the official military budget was maintained at the approximate figure of 317 million pesetas yearly from 1918 through 1920, but a supplementary appropriation of 150 million (and 112 million more on the special Moroccan budget) was made for 1920, bringing total Army expenditures for that year to 581 million pesetas—a new high.[8] The statutory size of the Army was expanded from 190,000 men in 1918 to 216,000 in 1920.[9]

Yet no great strides had been made in Army organization or ordnance, save for the salary increases and improved mess conditions specified in the La Cierva bill. Equipment remained grossly inadequate, most officers still did nothing, most recruits received little or no training, and most soldiers sent to Morocco were quite unprepared for tough counter-insurgency combat. Since the Spanish lower classes were still basically illiterate, much of the recruit's first year was spent in learning to read. Though at that time the term of service was set at three years, most recruits were released after eighteen months or less because there were not sufficient funds to maintain them for further training.

Since adequate field maps of the Protectorate were still lacking, "offensive reconnaissance," sharply criticized by foreign observers in 1909, was still standard practice. Column commanders sometimes moved almost blindly, relying on instinct or dead reckoning. Even when qualified Staff officers were available their advice was usually ignored by the combat officers, who liked to boast of their reliance on *cojones* ("guts" or, literally, testicles) alone. The Spanish advantage of superior firepower over the Berber irregulars was customarily wasted. Spanish Artillery officers admitted in later years that cannon were frequently employed without adequate targets, or, conversely, were unavailable when targets presented themselves.[10]

Virtually the entire Protectorate was maladministered. Fraud and favoritism reigned in most sectors of the military hierarchy, and pilfering was common at almost every level. In those regions of the Protectorate where the Spanish administration controlled civilian affairs, standards of justice were often far from impartial. Many officers were guilty of misconduct toward the native population. In particular, stories about the molestation of Moorish women aroused bitter hatred of the Spanish.[11]

Life in the principal garrison posts seems to have been about as dissolute as a depraved imagination might conceive. The brothels of Tetuán, Melilla, Ceuta, and Larache were plentifully stocked with Spanish, Moroccan, Moroccan-Jewish, and even French whores. Gambling was a pervasive vice, and many a commissary budget was milked to pay off gambling debts. Drunkenness was much more common than in Spain itself. Officers apparently ignored their administrative duties as much as possible, leaving the supervision of their units to the NCO's. Most Army quarters were abominably dirty and lacking in proper sanitary facilities. The greatest suffering was undergone by the small garrisons of the sandbagged *blocaos* established at regular intervals throughout much of the zone. Many of these lacked any sort of toilet, and the soldier who ventured out of the filthy bunker risked exposure to the fire of lurking tribesmen. Morale among the conscripts was very low. They sometimes spent the nights before scheduled marches in frantic debauches, hoping to be placed on the venereal disease list and so escape combat.[12]

Since regular Army forces were generally not competent to do serious fighting, efforts were made in 1919 and 1920 to form a new elite group to carry much of the burden. One such organization, the Moroccan Regulares, was created in 1911 when the first company of Moorish Army volunteers was organized by Berenguer. At first, the Moorish troops were regarded with distrust. The Spanish officers in charge of them suffered from uncertainty and inexperience, though they tried hard to follow the French example of command. The ranks of the Regulares began to fill out after a revolt in the French zone in 1912. Moorish rebels fleeing into the Spanish area were more than willing to serve against "foreign" kabyles and fought well during the 1912 Melilla campaign, in which they suffered heavy losses. By 1919 there were four *tabores,* or companies, and when fighting recommenced in the Djebala they proved extremely useful.

The casualty rate among the Regulares' officers was higher than in any other part of the Army, but those who survived became the elite of the africanistas. Chief among them were such commanders as the convivial, popular José Sanjurjo, and the young Francisco

Franco, still under thirty, whose cold professionalism and rigid self-control made him seem abnormal among the loose-living africanistas. Perhaps the most outstanding was Lieutenant Colonel Manuel González Tablas, described as "tall, energetic, an authority to the Moors . . . whom he commanded. . . . [He seemed] very much like an aristocrat among the high officers, who mostly looked like wealthy chicken farmers, and who hated him cordially."[13]

A proposal was made in 1919 to organize parallel battalions of volunteer shock troops from Spain and other countries into a sort of Spanish Foreign Legion. The main proponent of such a force was a forty-year-old major, José Millán Astray, who had first won fame as a teen-aged second lieutenant in the Philippine campaign of 1896–97. Millán Astray had studied four and a half years in the Staff college, had taught a year at Toledo, and was the author of two small training manuals. He had been a commander of Regulares in Morocco, held an impressive series of decorations, and was eventually to become the subject of a legend of military fanaticism. After making a brief inspection of the French Foreign Legion in 1919–20, he carried his plea for a Spanish Legion to the Cabinet. With the king's support, he managed to overcome opposition within the War Ministry, and early in 1920 the order was given to begin recruiting volunteers for the first *Tercio de Extranjeros,* so called in memory of the invincible Tercios of the sixteenth century. Francisco Franco became commander of the first battalion, and recruiting was begun among soldiers willing to remain in Morocco. In the long run, the Tercio organization proved to be less a "foreign" legion than a volunteer Spanish force, for only a minority of the recruits had been born outside the peninsula (most of these came from Cuba).

Millán Astray had undeniable qualities of leadership. He was an extraordinary talker, quick and emotional, with a pronounced histrionic flair. His somewhat morbid cast of mind seemed to give him an understanding of the feelings of those dregs of Spanish society who volunteered for the Tercio. He did not flatter the recruits, but spoke to groups of newcomers about their wretched and vicious lives. Further, he offered them a path of redemption through duty. He suggested that his volunteers might purge themselves of past errors through their new vocation of military service and suffering. As an expression of the fanaticism with which he tried to imbue his charges, Millán Astray gave them the motto "¡Viva la muerte!" (Long live death!). According to their anthem, each Legionnaire became "El Novio de la muerte"

(The Betrothed of Death). Discipline in the Tercio was rigid, even brutal, and corporal punishment a matter of course. Millán Astray did everything possible to improve the public image of his legion, even to arranging carefully posed battle scenes for the first Spanish news-reels. By early 1922, five *Banderas* or Tercio battalions had been consti-tuted, and made up what was officially known as the Legion. The new force soon proved that it was indeed the elite of the Spanish Army, but it formed so small a fraction of the total forces that the Army's general tone of incompetence, irresponsibility, and low morale was scarcely affected by its presence.[14]

Military efficiency was undermined not merely by the gross tech-nical inadequacy of most units but also by the confusion over areas of responsibility in the command structure. This problem reached major proportions in Morocco after 1919. Berenguer had little senior-ity in the rank of general, and his appointment as Inspector General of the forces in Morocco brought the abrupt resignation of the military governor of Ceuta, General Arraiz, whose seniority was greater. This was scant loss, but a graver dilemma was posed for Berenguer when Arraiz was replaced in June 1919 by Major General Fernández Sil-vestre, the bitter foe of El Raisuli. Silvestre and Berenguer were old friends, having been commissioned from the same class of cadets. Silvestre, however, had greater seniority in the rank of general and had once served as Berenguer's commanding officer. After his earlier recall from Morocco, Silvestre had been chosen by the king himself as a personal aide, whereas Berenguer had gained entrée to the court circle only as a protégé of Luque. Informed sources had it that Beren-guer owed his appointment as Undersecretary of War in the last Maura government as well as his present position in Morocco to Silvestre's influence with the king.[15] At any rate, for these or other reasons Beren-guer found it difficult to impose his authority on Silvestre.

In 1920, another civilian, the Vizconde de Eza, was chosen as Minis-ter of War. During the summer Eza made an inspection trip to Moroc-co and was shocked by the degree of waste and confusion there. In an effort to coordinate the command structure, he obtained approval for a royal decree on September 1, 1920, which declared: "The High Com-missioner, so long as he is a general, will be Commander in Chief of all forces composing the Army of Spain in Africa."[16] Yet Berenguer remained reluctant to impose direct authority on Silvestre or on sev-eral other ranking generals, apparently feeling that interested parties were looking over his shoulder from Madrid.

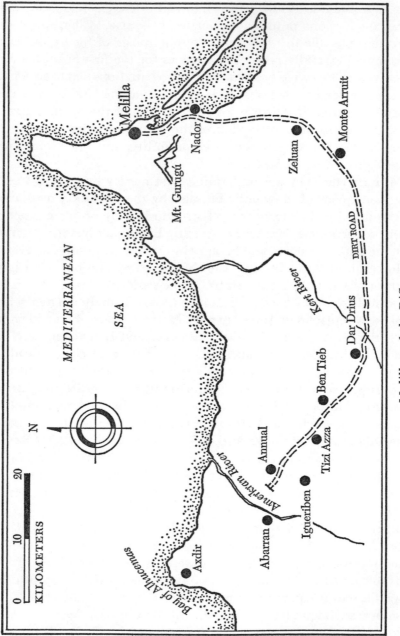

Melilla and the Riff, 1909–23

One of the main reasons for Silvestre's return to Morocco was that he was the major proponent of the hard line. He had become a favorite of Don Alfonso because he was a comparatively simpleminded fighting man, interested only in action and not concerned with the political ambitions of the military cliques in Madrid and Barcelona. Brought up in the rough-and-tumble of the last Cuban war, he had little sense of strategy but much boldness and vigor. As a commander he often gambled on blind operations, not because he was insensitive to losses or to the needs of his men but because that was the only way he had learned to operate.

Knowing that it could rely on Silvestre for action, the government determined to tighten its hold on Morocco. El Raisuli was declared an outlaw by the Sultan in order to provide legal justification for the Spanish campaign of repression, and during the summer there were bloody encounters in the northern and central Djebala. Despite heavy losses, the Spanish managed to seize the Fondak fortress, key to the road across the Djebala from Tetuán to Tangier, by the end of September. Some of the high land around Tetuán was occupied and several rebellious kabyles were subdued, but El Raisuli still held control of much of the western Djebala.[17] In the southwest, Barrera moved slowly inland, constructing groups of sandbagged blocaos in a crude attempt to imitate the French triangle system of armed outposts.

Heretofore, the mountainous Riff zone that formed the central part of the Spanish Protectorate had remained unpenetrated by European forces. Through a policy of compromise and bribery, the Spanish had been able since 1912 to keep the fierce Riff kabyles under control. At the beginning of 1920, however, Madrid decided that it was time to make the Spanish presence felt in the Riff area, and consequently Silvestre, the man of action, was transferred from the military governorship of Ceuta to that of Melilla. Plans went forward for a series of advances whose point of convergence was to be the east-central sector of the zone. Silvestre was to move westward from Melilla, Berenguer would press southward from Tetuán, and Barrera's forces would move in an easterly direction. However, the execution of the plan proved more difficult than its conception, and only limited gains were made against the tribesmen. In describing these operations ten years later, General Mola wrote:

Because of the way in which the expeditionary units were organized, the troops and the command cadres were unacquainted with each other. The soldiers had had little target practice, much less any combat training, and their rifles, for the most part, were of uneven calibers: the Colt machine guns jammed at the first shots, and so did the Campo-Giro pistols. The ammunition reserve was inadequate . . . the freight animals were not properly broken in, and their handlers lacked experience. . . . The Corps equipment was inadequate for mountain terrain.[18]

Berenguer could not ignore the grotesque technical deficiencies of the Spanish effort. Watching a sloppy, ill-supplied operation being carried out in the hills around Tetuán in 1920, he is said to have remarked despairingly, "This is a Protectorate of ragpickers!"[19] However, Berenguer was no boat-rocker but rather a cautious, politically minded general who thought it prudent to allow royal favorites and senior generals to carry on as they pleased.

The only significant success of 1920 was achieved by Colonel Alberto Castro Girona, who has been described thus: "very affable, but outlandish with his deep tan, his clean-shaven head, and his genuine interest in the Moors."[20] Such interest was rare among Spanish officers. Castro Girona spoke several Moroccan dialects and was held in esteem by a number of kabyles. In October, he negotiated the surrender of the holy city of Xauen, key to the operations southeast of Tetuán. He entered the city disguised as a Berber charcoal-seller. Once there, he approached the town elders and attempted to persuade them, by means of threats, bribes, and promises, to submit to Spanish occupation. He succeeded, and a regiment of troops was moved into the city before hostile tribesmen had time to react. This was a considerable triumph, for Xauen lies hidden among a group of hills and would have been costly to take by force.

Yet such clever negotiation did not set well with the other, less imaginative Spanish commanders. It was said that even Berenguer was jealous because Castro Girona's diplomacy was more effective than his own. However that may be, the resourceful colonel was not given a significant role in the campaigns of 1921. Moreover, the Spanish command, with its usual inefficiency, failed to take advantage of his achievement. The supply system was inadequate to cover the forty miles from Tetuán to Xauen, and the new garrison almost immediately found itself cut off and besieged by tribesmen from the surrounding hills.[21]

Meanwhile, in the closing months of 1920, Silvestre was eager to press on with his operations westward from Melilla. Berenguer suggested to the Minister of War that, during the winter and spring, operations be extended into the Riff from east and west. In letters of November 13 and 20, the Vizconde de Eza tentatively agreed to support this plan if the other members of the Cabinet raised no objections.[22] Silvestre's goal was the occupation of the hitherto untouched heartland of the Riff and the establishment of a chain of outposts and blocaos through the hills and down to the Bay of Alhucemas, which lay in the center of the Spanish zone. There had been little fighting in the Melilla area since 1912, but the farther Spanish troops advanced into the Riff the greater would be the possibility of a violent native reaction.

The Vizconde de Eza did not intend to give the commanders carte blanche to march all the way across the Riff. On the contrary, he understood that a major operation directed toward the Bay of Alhucemas would not begin before the troops had been adequately prepared. He wrote to the High Commissioner on January 16, 1921:

I am determined that no operation at all be begun unless you previously tell me, through the reports of the commanding generals, that all pecuniary contingencies arising from these operations have been foreseen, and that consequently nothing undesirable will occur through a lack of matériel. I do not want anything lacking that may be judged necessary, whether in Supply, Health, or Engineering, and I have made it clear to the Council of Ministers that I shall not authorize the movement of a single soldier if I do not have prior assurance that, so far as I am concerned as Army administrator, all is adequately cared for.
The demands and criticisms showered on me because of the taking of Xauen, and the charge that in the battle of the 21st [of October 1920] I was to blame for the lack of sandbags that caused the reverses and casualties suffered there, are things that a man like myself, who serves in good faith, cannot endure more than once. Therefore I told the Council of Ministers yesterday that next spring either there will be sufficient funds or there will be no military operations.[23]

One of Eza's problems was that the War Ministry could not trust the commissary reports; there was so much pilfering and peculation that honest statements were the exception. In a long letter to the Minister of War on February 4, Berenguer described the poor condition of his equipment and admitted that the level of training was extremely low. He also observed that a new military law had cut the recruits' term of service from three to two years, and that the Protectorate would be forced to rely more and more on the elite volunteer units.[24] But though the Minister of War and the High Commissioner both felt that the Spanish forces in Morocco were severely wanting in training, equipment, organization, and morale, no order was given to suspend Silvestre's advance.

The chief obstacle to Spanish ambitions in the Riff was the caid of the Beni Ourriagli kabyle, Abd el-Krim. Krim's father (who was caid until his death in 1920) had struggled to avoid direct occupation of the Riff by European forces; yet he was not unfriendly to the Spanish, and, recognizing the superiority of Western technical knowledge, had sent his two sons to Spanish schools. After completing his education, Abd el-Krim became the secretary for Arabic in the newly established Bureau of Native Affairs at Melilla. Since he was qualified to serve as a *cadi,* or judge, Krim was subsequently made an adviser to the Bureau, and in 1914 was appointed Moorish chief justice for the Melilla area. During the following year he became the first professor of Chilha (the chief Berber dialect) at the new Arab Academy founded by Gómez Jordana at Melilla.

For years, Abd el-Krim seemed willing to cooperate with the Spanish so long as they left the interior of the Riff in peace. He had preferred them to the French for much the same reason that had motivated El Raisuli: the belief that the Spaniards' military flaccidity and lack of driving ambition would keep them from ever becoming a real menace. In earlier years, Krim had concentrated his political hatred on the French, whom he blamed for having brought all of northwest Africa under European occupation. During the early part of World War I, he edited the Arabic columns of the Spanish newspaper in Melilla, *El Telegrama del Rif,* and succeeded in turning that section into a virulent anti-French propaganda sheet. Like El Raisuli, he was very possibly accepting funds from German intelligence. By 1917, French protests had become so insistent that the column was suppressed and Krim thrown into jail. Rumors later circulated that an equally likely cause of Krim's arrest was a personal quarrel with an overbearing Spanish commander. At any rate, at his trial on August 12, 1917, Krim made a strong declaration of his opposition to all European imperialism. He made it clear that he would oppose any Spanish attempt to occupy the Beni Ourriagli territory, and indicated that his father was already trying to create a spirit of unity and resistance to outside influence among the Riff kabyles.[25] Convicted of subversive agitation, Krim was imprisoned; an unsuccessful attempt to escape by leaping from a jail window left him with a broken leg and a permanent limp. After his release in 1918, Abd el-Krim turned completely against the Spanish. Fearing that he might share the fate of a group of rebels from the French Protectorate who had recently fled into the Spanish zone, only to be handed back to the French authorities, Krim sent word to his younger brother, Si Mohammed, who was studying at the School of Mines in Madrid, to return to Melilla as soon as possible and help him. In January 1919, Krim left Melilla for his father's village of Axdir in the central Riff, near the Bay of Alhucemas.[26]

For years the old caid had been smuggling in rifles through the Bay of Alhucemas. He and his sons were aware that after the end of the European war French and Spanish interests would expand their drive to exploit Moroccan resources. The mines of Melilla were proving profitable: Spanish authorities later released statistics showing that exports from the port of Melilla in 1920 were of greater value than those from Casablanca.[27] Krim's brother Si Mohammed was, if anything, even more intelligent than Krim, and he turned his talents to the technical problems involved in developing the mineral resources of the Riff. The Beni Ourriagli leaders were not opposed to the sale of mining leases and apparently dickered with several European groups, but they were determined to prevent military occupation of their land. In the summer of 1920, Spanish columns probed deeper. The old caid organized a sizable harca and took up a position to the east to resist military penetration. However, death took him suddenly while on guard there. He was succeeded as caid by Abd el-Krim in September 1920.

Despite signs of resistance from the Beni Ourriagli, neither Silvestre nor Berenguer saw any need to postpone operations in the Riff. The High Commissioner only hoped that the advance would be carried out carefully, with adequate military and political preparation. During the winter and spring of 1921, the bulk of the Spanish forces were engaged in small, slow, halting operations designed to expand the occupied zone of the Djebala and pacify the area around Xauen.[28] Berenguer hoped to be able to surround El Raisuli in his stronghold at Tazarut southwest of Tetuán. The High Commissioner's main concern seems to have been that no complications occur in the Riff to draw off forces before the campaign in the western sector was completed.

Berenguer visited Melilla in March. Silvestre did not specifically request reinforcements, and Berenguer thought it best to leave matters to the discretion of his old comrade and former commander. The two met on a ship in the Bay of Alhucemas to look over the area where Silvestre intended to advance. In a letter written soon after this meeting, Silvestre assured Berenguer that things were under control and that more reinforcements and equipment would not be necessary.[29]

The Spanish leaders hoped that the occupation of the Riff would meet with little resistance, but a commander who disliked Moors and lacked the arts of diplomacy could hardly be counted on to reach a peaceful agreement with such proud and independent people as the Riffi. Though Silvestre was said to be quite a ladies' man, adept at the social graces, his social finesse did not carry over into military affairs. According to one account, he had been wounded sixteen times in the Cuban war,[30] and his experience with El Raisuli showed that he reacted to strong opposition like a bull to a red flag. He and Abd el-Krim soon formed the worst possible opinion of one another. Silvestre believed that the tribal leaders would be unable to organize concerted resistance to his advance, but it would appear that, to facilitate matters, sizable amounts of Spanish money were spent on bribes to tribal chieftains during the early part of 1921.

By the end of April, there were nearly 20,000 troops in the Melilla zone, but half of them were ignorant recruits who had been called up in February and shipped directly to Africa. Because of the ammunition shortage, these men were given scarcely any target practice.[31] The condition of their equipment was such that it in no way compensated for their lack of training; several years earlier, inspection had revealed that 75 per cent of the rifles in the Melilla arsenal were not in proper condition, and there is no evidence that anything had been done in the meantime to correct this.[32] Silvestre could hardly have been oblivious to these problems, but he was even more conscious that the eyes of Madrid were on him, and he apparently felt that the king was expecting a straightforward campaign without any fuss over men or supplies. Though a favorite of Don Alfonso, Silvestre had no love for the courtiers, politicians, and financial oligarchs who held power in Madrid. He had earlier complained that nothing had yet been accomplished in Morocco because "in every operation, politics leaves the European forces in third place, stations the native auxiliaries second, and assign the vanguard to the Bank of Spain."[33] Moreover, Berenguer was proceeding successfully with his operations in the western zone, whereas Silvestre had never yet achieved a major triumph and therefore was eager to show the Madrid cliques what a courageous Spanish general could do by relying on "guts" alone.

In the last days of May, Silvestre's supply columns were harassed by growing numbers of armed Berbers. This was serious, for there had been little effort to provision and fortify the long chain of undermanned blocaos and outposts that stretched from Melilla into the Riff. The general had been hoping that a display of strength by the advance forces would discourage rebellion among the kabyles in the rear, but the harca organized by Abd el-Krim was making it dangerous for the Spanish to move any deeper into the hills. On May 29, Silvestre wrote the High Commissioner that heavier support would be necessary and that further advances would have to be "carefully thought out beforehand."[34] Two days later, an unexpected reverse occurred at the forward post of Abarran, when 200 men—an entire tabor of Moorish Regulares—mutinied and murdered the company's command. Most of the Spanish troops in the accompanying Artillery unit managed to escape, but the mutineers joined the nearby Temsamani kabyle, which was also taking up arms, and Spanish hopes of localizing resistance were shattered. On June 2, the small northern coastal outpost of Sidi Dris was attacked.[35]

These developments alarmed Berenguer, but in a telegram of June 4 Silvestre assured him that he would take steps to see that the Abarran incident was not repeated, and that he would proceed cautiously.[36] Nevertheless, Berenguer came by boat the following day to Melilla in order to confer with Silvestre. They held a conference in the harbor, during which Berenguer suggested that it might be better to suspend the advance toward Alhucemas until greater force was available; after completing operations against El Raisuli in the west, Berenguer could send a strong column east from Xauen and press the Riffi harca from the other side. Silvestre told the High Commissioner that he still did not think this necessary, and that he could advance through the Riff to Alhucemas that summer with no forces other than the troops currently under his command.[37] Just as Silvestre was eager for a triumph to gratify the king and confound the Madrid oligarchs, so the High Commissioner was reluctant to exercise close authority over an old comrade and benefactor who held military seniority and had come back to Morocco with the king's personal encouragement. He merely urged Silvestre (by letter and telegram, on June 7 and 8) to do nothing rash and not to resume operations until he was sure he could carry them through successfully.[38]

On June 8, Silvestre sent a detachment to occupy a site called Igueriben, a few kilometers northwest of the exposed camp at Annual in the heart of the Riff. The occupation forces met stiff resistance, and in a telegram the next day Silvestre admitted to Berenguer that the situation had become "somewhat delicate" but asserted that the reverse nine days earlier had been due to "isolated circumstances" that would not reoccur.[39]

Little more was done during June. In the middle of the month, a supply column was ambushed outside Annual and suffered 60 casualties. Silvestre became more concerned, and suggested to Berenguer that they ought to request further reinforcements. The High Commissioner apparently deemed this politically imprudent, especially in view of the commander's recent assurances. Moreover, Silvestre had agreed that no further advances should be made until the situation improved, and the official records indicated that there were already 25,790 troops (including 5,000 natives) in the Melilla zone.[40] Since it was doubtful that Abd el-Krim's harca numbered more than two or three thousand riflemen, it was thought that Silvestre could easily protect his present position. In a report to the Minister of War on July 8, Berenguer said that it appeared the Melilla area was adequately provided for.[41]

During the second week in July, Riffi harassment increased, and it became extremely difficult to supply the forward posts. Almost nothing had been done to fortify or stock most of the blocaos, and some of the main positions, such as that at Annual, were poorly laid out and dominated by surrounding heights. In a similar situation, the post of Akba el-Kola, near Alcazarquivir in the southwest, had been overrun eleven months earlier and its entire garrison massacred.[42] At long last, Silvestre grew worried. By mid-July the usually sanguine, carefree general had become so apprehensive that he had difficulty sleeping or digesting his food.[43] But he had recently received a telegram from the king saying, "Hurrah for real men! I expect you on the 25th" (Don Alfonso's birthday).[44] Knowing that he would be expected to have everything under control before his return to Madrid, Silvestre tried to conceal his worries in his communications with Berenguer.[45]

On July 16, a supply column from Annual was unable to fight its way to Igueriben. It managed to break through on the following day, but then could not get back because Igueriben had been surrounded by Abd el-Krim's harca—though at this time his band probably did not number much more than 3,000 men.[46] A new reinforced column was sent from Annual on the 19th, but was unable to reach the beleaguered outpost. The troops penned up at Igueriben had exhausted their supplies and, lacking any water, were licking the damp sides of rocks and drinking urine sweetened with sugar.[47] On the morning of the 21st, Silvestre arose early and drove by car from Melilla to Annual. Because there was no decent road, the trip lasted half the day. In the late afternoon, he attempted to lead a cavalry charge through the pass to Igueriben, but was stopped by Moors armed with a few machine guns and cannon that either had been captured from the Spanish or smuggled in through Alhucemas. The commander at Igueriben, Major Benítez, signaled for help by heliograph to Silvestre's column, saying that he could not believe his men would be left to die within sight of other Spanish troops. At the end of the day, all the surviving troops at Igueriben, with the exception of a few officers, made a desperate attempt to break out of their death trap. Only eleven managed to reach Silvestre's column, and of these only two survived their ordeal.[48]

Before dark Silvestre's troops returned to Annual, where the 4,000 Spanish defenders were barely able to hold off the Moors, who were firing into the camp from the surrounding heights. Berenguer has written that Silvestre sent him three radiograms in succession on June 21, the second requesting major reinforcements immediately.[49] Ammunition and supplies were running so low that Silvestre, beside himself with grief and frustration, was no longer certain that the main Spanish base in the Riff could be held. A council of officers, hastily called on the night of July 21, voted for general retreat. The prospect was a bitter humiliation that Silvestre almost refused to accept. He spent a sleepless night of agonized procrastination and finally gave the order to retreat at about 10 the next morning. No plans were made for an organized withdrawal; the Spanish forces were to pull out "by surprise." Within an hour or two, the retreat fell into chaos. Officers largely abdicated their responsibilities and the withdrawal degenerated into a frantic *sauve-qui-peut*—a stampede of thousands of defenseless troops.[50] Silvestre died at Annual. His campaign and career both hopelessly shattered, he apparently committed suicide with his own revolver.

As news of the retreat spread, tribesmen by the hundreds hastened to join Krim's harca. Soon the whole Riff was up in arms against the invaders, and most of the Regulares in the area began to desert. The rout was all the more disastrous because of the absence of prepared Spanish positions in the rear. The only barriers between Annual and Melilla were occasional blocaos of sandbags and wood, whose roofs could be blown off by hand grenades, and three or four larger semifortified camps. Because of supply difficulties, none of these flimsy sites were defensible for any length of time.[51] As it turned out, little effort was made to hold them, and the whole line of outposts collapsed like a row of dominoes. The Spanish troops, whose officers had sometimes treated the Berbers harshly in the past, were familiar with authenticated stories of native atrocities, and were consequently panic-stricken at the prospect of falling into the warriors' hands. In many positions there was no attempt at resistance; and at the last, the Berber triumph over the wildly fleeing Spaniards became pure butchery. Several hundred soldiers were taken prisoner, but many more were beheaded, hacked to death, or simply shot. Altogether, more than 8,000 troops were killed at Annual and Igueriben and in the rout that followed.[52]

The disaster was due more to Spanish demoralization than to Berber prowess. Those few units that preserved discipline, such as the Cavalry battalion of Alcántara, completed the retreat to Melilla with few losses. But in most sections the panic was so extreme that the few officers who did attempt to rally their troops were powerless. Silvestre's second-in-command, General Navarro, tried for seven days to halt the rout, but whenever one unit was shored up, it was deluged, then dissolved, by a new flood of crazed refugees from defeated battalions. Finally, on July 29, Navarro rallied three thousand fugitives for a stand at Monte Arruit, about seventy kilometers east of Annual and scarcely thirty kilometers from Melilla. Like the other posts, Monte Arruit had supplies sufficient for only a few days.

After receiving Silvestre's despairing messages on July 21, Berenguer gave orders to pull the two banderas of the Tercio, plus two of the best tabores of the Regulares, out of the Djebala and ship them as fast as possible to Melilla. The High Commissioner arrived on the night of July 23, and the first reinforcements from Ceuta appeared the following day. A sizable minority of the 20,500 Spanish troops supposedly serving in the Melilla zone were actually away on leave in Spain or did not exist except on paper. Berenguer could find only 1,800 military personnel in the town, most of them clerks and supply personnel. There were few fortifications around Melilla itself, and most of the field equipment in the eastern half of the Protectorate was in the hands of Abd el-Krim.[53]

Melilla was saved by the 4,500 troops from Ceuta, who were commanded by the tough, hard-fighting, popular little brigadier José Sanjurjo. As lieutenants, Sanjurjo had the two best battalion commanders from the western zone: González Tablas of the Regulares and Francisco Franco, who led the First Bandera of the Tercio. With the assistance of these officers Berenguer was able by August 1 to assemble some 14,000 men in Melilla, though many of them were not regular troops.[54] For the time being, the best this force could do was to fortify the environs of the town along much the same line that had existed prior to 1909.

It proved impossible to relieve Monte Arruit, though several officers volunteered to lead a relief column. Berenguer declined all offers because he believed that any such force would be cut off and destroyed; moreover, he had to conserve his 4,500 trained men for the defense of Melilla. The few minor outposts that were still resisting succumbed soon after August 1, leaving only General Navarro's redoubt. Abd el-Krim attempted to negotiate with the defenders of Monte Arruit on August 5, but because of a misunderstanding his emissaries were fired upon. Monte Arruit was tightly besieged and raked with rifle and cannon fire. On August 9, when the defenders' supplies were completely exhausted, Berenguer signaled to Navarro his permission to surrender. After the capitulation, many of the Spanish defenders were slaughtered by the triumphant Moors. The Army had lost control of the entire hinterland beyond Melilla; all the efforts of the past twelve years had gone for naught.

The response in Spain was stupefaction. At first the press had difficulty following events; even the Army newspapers could not grasp the situation, but wondered how "so many" Berber riflemen could have been gotten together. It was not until July 25 that the government imposed temporary censorship in a vain effort to head off the inevitable political storm. The brief resistance of the troops at Monte Arruit was acclaimed with banner headlines and there was talk of a "second Numantia,"* but after August 9 the extent of the collapse could not be disguised. The government resigned and was replaced by another Maura cabinet of "national concentration" in which La Cierva once again occupied the post of War Minister.

Protest swelled into a deafening chorus. After four years of insufferable pressure, interference, and pretensions on the part of the military hierarchy, it appeared that the Army was scarcely worthy of its name. In the months that followed, innumerable damning facts were brought to light. For example, it was shown that though the Moorish

---

* Numantia, an ancient Spanish settlement near modern Soria, at the mouth of the Duero, heroically resisted the attempts of the Romans to take it. It was first attacked during the campaigns of Cato the Elder in 195 B.C. Scipio Aemilianus finally captured it after an eight-month blockade in 133 B.C.

Regulares had been relied on as much as possible in the three preceding years to cut Spanish losses, those in the Melilla area had been grossly mishandled. Owing to carelessness on the part of the command, many Moorish recruits had been sent to fight against the tribes of their own regions. The few who remained loyal after the rout began were disarmed and discharged, and so had little choice other than to go over to Abd el-Krim. The General Staff had played no role in Silvestre's campaign, for the late commander of Melilla had never understood staff work, was uneasy with technical planning, and had not asked for serious advice. A few Air Force planes had been stationed at a field near the village of Zeluan. They might have been useful in communication and reconaissance, save that their pilots were billeted at Melilla and were not often available for duty at the airfield. Story after story of waste, corruption, vice, and laziness was passed around. It was reported that during 1920 eleven captains who had served as bursars for their Corps had resigned to avoid being detected in embezzlement, and one had committed suicide.

Just as in 1909, however, the explosion of rage and denunciation was followed by a moderate resurgence of patriotic feeling. During the summer and autumn a number of special donations were made to the Ministry of War by wealthy financiers and industrialists who had hitherto been quite reluctant to pay taxes. There was particular interest in contributing to the expansion of the Air Force; by the end of 1921, the Spanish could claim nearly 200 operational aircraft, though many of these were obsolescent.[55]

Berenguer tendered his resignation as High Commissioner soon after the Moroccan catastrophe. On August 4, before his own resignation as War Minister, Eza established a commission under the upright, independent (and Protestant) General Picasso, the purpose of which was to make a full and official investigation of the causes of the disaster and of those responsible for it. After the change of government, Don Alfonso and La Cierva refused to accept Berenguer's resignation. Since Berenguer had shown himself fully discreet in political matters, the king believed that it was better to leave him in charge. Berenguer agreed to stay on only if he were granted full immunity from all investigations, including those of the Picasso Commission. La Cierva assured him that he would be immune, and the Picasso Commission evidently received instructions not to pry into the High Commissioner's personal papers or to criticize the way in which he had exercised his command.[56]

The Cortes reopened on October 20, and for days was the scene of heated denunciations of Spain's military and political leaders. Army administration in both Morocco and the peninsula was condemned by deputies from almost every political faction, with certain conservative monarchists proving almost as energetic as the leftists in their accusations. It was observed that the *Anuario Militar* of 1921 still listed 466 generals in service, and that the 1922 military budget was scheduled to consume over 51 per cent of the government's funds. In spite of these figures, there was no evidence of either intelligent leadership or adequate equipment. The special appropriation for Morocco had increased three and a half times between 1913 and 1921, from 63 million pesetas to over 211 million, and seemingly it had all been wasted. It was remarked that no tanks had yet seen service in Morocco, though they had been available on the European market for two years, and that a sadly conspicuous minority of officers had shown cowardice or had hidden themselves to avoid combat duty. On October 21, the Marqués de Viesca observed in the Cortes that according to the Artillery's own figures it had lost 117 cannon to Abd el-Krim in the Melilla retreat, though only one senior Artillery officer was missing.[57] The Vizconde de Eza, who had in some ways been a victim of circumstances, defended his administration in a lengthy Cortes address on October 25 and eventually published much of his correspondence with Army commanders in an effort to show that he had asked for cooperation in anticipating all necessary requirements but had failed to receive it.

The entire administration of the Protectorate was laid open to criticism. The fact that the caliph in Tetuán had a budget of eight and a half million pesetas, or only half a million less than that of the Spanish royal family, drew unfavorable comment. Various critics pointed out that France dominated a region with five times the population and nineteen times the area of the Spanish zone through a mixed force of 70,000, only 26,000 of whom were Europeans.[58] Spanish-speaking Moroccans had their own refrain about the differing policies of the colonial powers:

Inglaterra pega y paga; England hits but pays;
Francia pega pero no paga; France hits but doesn't pay;
España ni pega ni paga. Spain neither hits nor pays.

During the first week of Cortes debate, however, no mention was made of two of the most delicate issues—the personal relations between Silvestre and the king, and the manifest reluctance of Berenguer to restrain his subordinate. The first clear reference to Silvestre's court connections was made by the Socialist leader Indalecio Prieto in a speech given on October 27. The story began to circulate among many critics that the king, Berenguer, and Silvestre had agreed between them in 1920 that Silvestre should push on to the Bay of Alhucemas, and that the High Commissioner had deemed it politically unwise to restrain Silvestre.[59] No proof of the king's complicity other than his brief telegram to Silvestre was ever presented, but nevertheless it was widely assumed that his involvement went far byond the simple act of sending a message of encouragement. The relative guilt of Berenguer and Silvestre was discussed at length in informed circles and in the newspapers, with the dead commander drawing the greater share of criticism.

Despite the enormous controversy surrounding Berenguer, on October 29 Don Alfonso pushed through his promotion to lieutenant general, and a new promotion bill submitted to the Cortes in November would have made him the king's own military aide. This was all the more surprising since criticism persisted about the slowness of Spanish operations to regain control of the eastern Riff, and since Berenguer was accused of having done nothing to rescue the hundreds of Spaniards held prisoner by the Moors. The king's bestowal of favor on the unpopular general was perhaps due to a combination of his sense of personal chivalry and the frivolous attitude he took toward nearly all political problems. There had been strong clashes since the beginning of his reign, but every storm had been ridden out thanks to the country's civic disunity, which could always be exacerbated by a certain amount of manipulation. However, Don Alfonso's recommendation of Berenguer for the post of royal aide was not approved, and Berenguer was greatly embarrassed by the entire situation. Once more he tendered his resignation to the government, but Maura and La Cierva rarely retreated under pressure. This time they not only rejected his resignation, but also explicitly reaffirmed the range of Berenguer's powers as Commander in Chief of all forces in the Protectorate, and gave him orders to proceed with a new counteroffensive.

In the meantime, Abd el-Krim was making extraordinary progress in the formation of a rebel government in the Riff. The Spanish collapse had given the Beni Ourriagli caid control of much of the eastern half of the Protectorate, and had raised his prestige among the kabyles to phenomenal heights. His ambitions began to soar. Not merely did he plan to resist Spanish reconquest but he began also to prepare for an independent Moorish state in the Riff—something that had never before existed in the history of Morocco. The rudiments of a western-style administration were crudely sketched out; the seat of government was to be located at his father's primitive village of Axdir. Volunteers continued to pour into the caid's camp, many of them armed with Spanish weapons. It was very hard to inculcate genuine discipline among the tribesmen, but in September an effort was begun to create the nucleus of a regular Riffian army. Krim's ablest lieutenants were given official rank, while a handful of contacts abroad searched for mercenaries who might be hired to train the Berbers in the use of more complex weapons. Captured cannon were placed on the slopes of Mount Gurugú, whence they fired down upon the environs of Melilla. Meanwhile, Krim's warriors were set to work digging trenches in anticipation of Spanish advances inland.[60]

By September 12, 30,000 Spanish troops had been concentrated at Melilla, and Berenguer launched a limited counteroffensive spearheaded by his elite units, the Tercio and Regulares from Ceuta. Within a fortnight, they had reoccupied most of the district southwest of Melilla that had first been seized in the campaign of 1909–10, including Monte Arruit, which was thus retaken only six weeks after its fall. According to witnesses, the ruins of the fortifications at Monte Arruit resembled an abattoir, covered as they were with dried blood and littered with rotting, mutilated corpses—the remains of the prisoners slaughtered after their surrender by the Berbers. Equally sickening sights were encountered at other posts that had been overrun.

By the end of September, the reinforced Melilla command was able to move its lines some thirty kilometers inland. Beyond that point, however, advances could be made only with the greatest difficulty. To invade the central Riff and strike at the base of Abd el-Krim's power was, for the time being, out of the question. So, it seemed, was the rescue of the untold hundreds of prisoners held by the Berbers.[61] Krim raised their ransom to such a high figure—four million pesetas—that negotiations came to a standstill. Army leaders in Morocco said that the very honor of the military institution required that these captives be liberated by conquest, not by ransom—though how and when the Army would acquire the means for conquest was highly uncertain.

The consequences of the Moroccan disaster did not lead to greater unity among the officers, but to renewed factionalism and recrimination, especially among that significant minority who continued to support the military Juntas, or "Advisory Commissions." With the intensification of the fighting in Morocco, the africanistas felt increasingly alienated from the juntero intriguers at home. By 1921, the Juntas had so obviously become mere self-promotion societies that 300 officers on active duty in Morocco had resigned from the Juntas in protest just two months before the catastrophe occurred at Annual.[62] The officers of the Artillery had been less enthusiastic over the course taken by the Juntas than had many of those in the other Corps, and in August, sobered by the military collapse, the Artillery Advisory Commission (Junta Superior) decided to abstain from further intervention of its own and leave Artillery affairs to the supervision of the proper legal agency, the Section of Artillery in the Ministry of War.

On September 29, a supply column moving toward the forward units southwest of Melilla wandered from its route and fell into a Berber ambush. Though the column managed to fight its way out, there was strong evidence of negligence on the part of the commanders. In this case, the military courts acted with surprising—even abrupt—speed in bringing the three senior officers involved before a court-martial. They were found guilty of irresponsible behavior and relieved of all command. The Infantry and Cavalry Juntas, eager to protect the "rights" of officers and contest the conduct of affairs in Morocco, leaped to the defense of those convicted, insisting that they had been unjustly prosecuted. They also protested the appointment of Sanjurjo as military governor of Melilla and the government's willingness to ratify the powers of Berenguer, since both these generals were enemies of the Juntas.

The anti-junteros retaliated with equal vigor. General Miguel Cabanellas, a leading africanista, sent a widely publicized open letter to the Infantry Junta, which said in part:

We have just buried the corpses of 500 officers and men. These are the ones at [Monte] Arruit who defended themselves so well that they deserved to have been saved. Instead, they were lost because the nation did not have even a few thousand organized soldiers. Before these scenes of horror I can only send you my most rigorous censure. I regard you as primarily responsible, for you are interested only in effeminate trifles, in bringing disrespect on the leadership, and in pumping the budget for increases in rank and salary—never worrying about inefficiency or the lack of proper matériel. You have been able to stay alive thanks to the cowardice of certain elements—a cowardice which I have never shared.[63]

The junteros no longer enjoyed the support of public opinion or of the active sections of the Army; but, as their influence declined,

Junta leaders responded harshly. They had already turned against La Cierva, realizing that he was not their ally but their manipulator and fearing that he was in league with the africanistas. *La Correspondencia Militar,* still the junteros' principal mouthpiece, began to publish strong criticism of the Minister of War in late December. At the same time, the Junta leaders sent a note to General Feijóo, head of the Infantry Section of the Ministry, saying that La Cierva must resign forthwith or they would come and throw him bodily out of his residence in the Ministry of War.[64]

Maura was not easily intimidated. After several days' reflection, he and La Cierva decided to implement the proposal made by Berenguer five years earlier.[65] The Juntas, under the name of "Advisory Commissions," would henceforth "form an integral part of the respective Sections [of their Corps] of the Ministry of War."[66] Integrated into the regular administrative structure, their functions would be brought under the strict discipline of the Code of Military Justice. Before this decree could become law, however, it had to be countersigned by the king. Though he had recently spoken of the desirability of throttling the Juntas, Don Alfonso could not overcome the notion that they were still a valuable piece to maneuver on the political chessboard. Maura made it a question of confidence, and from January 11 to 16 there was literally no government. Maura was cheered when he appeared in the streets, while jeers were heard for the king and the Junta leaders. Don Alfonso gave in and signed the decree, and the Maura Cabinet remained in power.

Members of the Advisory Commissions were henceforth to be appointed by the Minister of War on the recommendation of the heads of the various Sections. This was supposed to shake up the membership of the Commissions, but since the heads of the Sections were by no means immune to juntero influence in their recommendations, the device was not very effective. The Advisory Commissions remained a thorn in the flesh of the Army administration, and members of the earlier Junta groups continued their agitation. For example, in March 1922, Junta leaders called a special meeting to decree "obligatory syndicalization" for all officers stationed in peninsular garrisons. This was loud talk which the junteros were no longer in any position to enforce, but on March 17 Colonel Nouvilas, head of the Infantry Junta, stated that the junteros would use all necessary means to win their demands, including "guile" and "pressures." He added that "thirty per cent" of the officer corps should be cashiered,[67] apparently referring to africanistas and outspoken anti-Junta officers in the peninsula. On April 12 the junteros made another of their persistent demands that all vestiges of the méritos system be abolished. They were anxious that the Picasso investigation be carried out swiftly and implacably—since it was probing africanistas and not junteros.

In addition to the africanista-juntero conflict, there was a great deal of criticism and jockeying for position among the senior generals. Some, such as Luque and Aguilera, were demanding full investigation of the causes of the collapse, though others suspected that this was as much to discredit the current leadership as for any other reason. General Miguel Primo de Rivera was busily endeavoring to build a political reputation, and declared in the Senate on November 25, 1921: "From a strategic viewpoint, a single soldier on the other side of the straits is detrimental to Spain's well-being."[68] In turn, Primo was labeled, not inaccurately, an *abandonista*.

The seventy-nine-year-old Weyler, oldest active general in the Army, had been ignored during the collapse, although he was still Chief of the General Staff. Weyler was certain that he could have prevented the disaster and in December told newspaper reporters that he was going to resign his post because no one "paid any attention" to him.[69] His remarks were so critical that the War Ministry encouraged him to follow through on his gesture, and he did in fact resign on January 3, 1922. But the old general still had considerable energy and did not give up the hope of gaining a more active command. He remained President of the Supreme Court of Military Justice, and it seems that he wished this tribunal to examine the malfeasance of the africanista commanders, which he strongly condemned.[70]

The Spanish Army made what was, by its standards, a major effort to move reinforcements into Morocco during the autumn and winter of 1921–22, though tens of thousands of garrison troops were needed in Spain to safeguard public order. Troops of all different levels of training, background, privilege, and deferral were hurried to Africa. Hundreds of youths from the middle and upper classes volunteered in a surge of patriotic feeling after the disaster; and many volunteer *oficiales de complemento* were also transferred, since most juntero officers in the peninsula still shunned Morocco like the plague. Redemption recruits, scheduled to serve for very brief periods, were also sent across the straits for short tours of duty. The presence of a number of upper-class youths in the ranks, if it did not increase military efficiency, did encourage improvement of barracks conditions. These personnel changes also seem to have bolstered morale, and the Spanish Army began to acquire more of the characteristics of a national force.

The military problem had nonetheless become compounded by the extension of hostilities in the western part of the Protectorate. The ring that Berenguer had been drawing around El Raisuli in the summer of 1921 disintegrated with the transfer of the best units to Melilla. As news of the Annual disaster spread, several previously quiescent kabyles in the west joined the rebellion, and in mid-October Abd el-Krim's brother led a portion of the greatly expanded Beni Ourriagli harca into the territory of the restive kabyles in the Gomara district southeast of Xauen. This made it necessary to send some of the reinforcements to the western sector, where columns were organized during December 1921 to restore the interrupted blockade of El Raisuli in the Djebala.[71]

As Prime Minister, Maura tried not to interfere in the conduct of military operations, but he had little faith in an all-out offensive against the Berber kabyles. Aware of the obstacles and political difficulties that would be involved, he seems to have preferred that the Army merely protect the main cities near the coast and leave most of the interior to its native inhabitants, as in former times. But the High Commissioner, supported by the Minister of War, planned to continue the counteroffensive in the Melilla region during 1922, press the Djebala campaign against El Raisuli to a conclusion, then occupy the Riff itself, thereby breaking Abd el-Krim's revolt and completing the occupation of the Protectorate. The final phase of these operations would be the most difficult and would probably involve an amphibious assault on the Bay of Alhucemas, near Krim's capital, to catch the rebels from the rear.

The Foreign Minister, González Hontoria, was more emphatically opposed to this program than Maura was, and he questioned the feasibility of the Spanish Army's undertaking such a relatively complicated maneuver as would be involved in the final phase. Since it was felt that a visit by Berenguer to Madrid would touch off an uproar, the Cabinet ministers held a special conference with the High Commissioner near Málaga on February 4. Despite misgivings, they gave tentative agreement to Berenguer's plan, largely because he promised to carry it out with a somewhat reduced number of troops, which would mean that some of the new recruits could return to Spain.[72] Details of this decision quickly leaked out, and many newspapers expressed great displeasure over the prospect of expanded military operations. In return,

Berenguer complained to the government that Abd el-Krim had been able to learn details of the forthcoming operations simply by reading the Spanish press.[73]

Before a month had passed some of the Cabinet ministers sorely repented their approval of the military plan, and parliamentary pressures caused Maura's fifth and last government to break up. The subsequent Cabinet, formed on March 7, was led by the Conservative José Sánchez Guerra. Since the new ministers were known to be strong supporters of the supremacy of civilian power and highly critical of Berenguer's campaign plans, the High Commissioner sent in his resignation for the third time. Once more it was rejected. Berenguer traveled to Madrid for another conference at the end of March; there his authority was reaffirmed, with the understanding that no effort would be made in the near future to carry out the third and most difficult phase of his military offensive, and that all major decisions on Moroccan policy, whether political or military, would be made in Madrid. Another problem to be faced was the return of some 20,000 recruits to the peninsula in June 1922, after the completion of their second year of service. For political reasons the government could not afford to prolong their tour of duty.[74]

On February 1, 1922, Abd el-Krim officially proclaimed "the Emirate of the Riff." His harca, which he now called an army, had expanded to more than 10,000 men. Arms remained scarce, for much of the equipment captured from the Spanish was of scant use even to irregulars.[75] On March 19, Berber cannon placed on the coastal hills above Alhucemas sank a Spanish mail boat that made the mistake of not staying well out to sea, and the Peñón de Vélez de Gomara, the Spanish coastal fortress nearest Krim's capital, was sharply harassed by cannon and rifle fire.[76]

On April 18, 1922, the Picasso Commission completed its military investigation. This had been restricted to a technical study of the military operations involved in the Moroccan disaster and had purposely avoided the political aspects of the problem. The main conclusion drawn was that the officers of the Spanish Army simply had not been capable of meeting the challenges presented by the Moroccan campaign. In its summary of the causes of the disaster, the report listed

an extension of military lines . . . clearly disproportionate to the "official strength" of the command on July 22 [calculated at 19,923 men available], revealing an absurd lack of density at every point; with armed kabyles already in the rear, advancing recklessly into the center of the rebel region without military means or political preparation, simply trusting to luck ... ; entrusting the security of the rear positions to a jumble of dispersed outposts, deficiently organized, poorly supplied and garrisoned ... ; lacking secondary lines in case of retreat ... ; and once the final events began, hasty concentration on the front ... with the weakening of the rear areas, making irreparable ... the consequences of the calamity and the disastrous retreat.[77]

The Commission, perhaps with the encouragement of the new government, disregarded the previous ministry's promise of immunity for the High Commissioner, and listed thirty-nine officers for trial, twenty of them over the rank of captain, including Berenguer himself. The Commission's findings, however, were not published but were revealed only to the government. Nothing whatever was done about bringing the accused parties to trial by court-martial.

At the end of April Gen. Emilio Barrera, military governor of Larache for the past six years, was named Undersecretary of War. Barrera had at least committed no major blunders during his Moroccan career, which made him appear to be an outstanding officer. He was replaced at Larache by Sanjurjo, for Berenguer wanted to concentrate the major effort in the spring of 1922 on strangling El Raisuli's redoubt in the Djebala. Part of the elite forces in the Melilla area were transferred with Sanjurjo, and on May 12 El Raisuli's stronghold of Tazarut was taken by storm. Lt. Col. González Tablas was slain in this attack. El Raisuli managed to escape, but his position was becoming indefensible; he would soon be forced either to flee to Abd el-Krim or to surrender. Meanwhile, the return to Spain of thousands of short-term recruits was begun.

Berenguer was under a steady barrage of criticism from the newspapers. On June 27, the influential *El Imparcial* published an interview with Weyler in which the general was quoted as stating: "So long as General Berenguer remains High Commissioner, there is no real possibility of making an effort to rescue our prisoners." This was perhaps the principal censure levied against Berenguer during the winter and spring of 1922. It was indeed true that no direct military effort had been made to extract the survivors of the Annual disaster from the clutches of Abd el-Krim, and Berenguer's critics were quick to point out his earlier claim that a well-organized column of 4,000 European troops could move wherever it pleased in Morocco.[78] The apologists for the High Commissioner, however, stressed the political limitations under which he was forced to exercise his command.

On July 9, the Supreme Military Council approved the preliminary report of the Picasso Commission and adopted its recommendations that the Council prosecute Berenguer, Silvestre (if ever found alive), and Navarro (if rescued or ransomed). Berenguer was informed immediately and resigned forthwith. Exercising his rights as a lifetime Senate appointee, he defended himself in a speech in the upper chamber of the Spanish Parliament on July 14.[79] At the same time, he waived senatorial immunity so that the Council might be free to prosecute him. Until that time the current Minister of War, General Olaguer-Feliú, had not even informed the Prime Minister of the Council's decision.[80] Infuriated, the strong-minded Sánchez Guerra forced Olaguer-Feliú out of the Cabinet and temporarily took over the War Ministry himself, so as to be able to find out what was really going on in the Army. On July 21, a special parliamentary commission of eleven Conservatives and ten Liberals was named to hear the Picasso report and to undertake investigation of the political responsibilities involved in the Moroccan collapse.

Berenguer's replacement as High Commissioner and Commander in Chief in Morocco was the former Captain General of Madrid, Ricardo Burguete, who had played a major role in preparing the Picasso report. The two generals had a good deal in common. Like Berenguer, Burguete had a reputation as a minor military essayist, and in earlier years had made a respectable record as field commander in Morocco. He, too, was a *politique,* given to calculation rather than audacity. Yet Burguete was identified with quite a different part of the Army. Whereas Berenguer had become the leader of the king's africanistas, Burguete had long remained in the peninsula and had tended recently to be associated with the anti-africanista junteros. At the time of the last Junta crisis in January, it was Burguete who, in the name of the Juntas, had asked the Liberal Santiago Alba to form a new government.[81] Alba was popular among the junteros because he was a sharp critic of the Moroccan administration, and as Foreign Minister in the new Sánchez Guerra government he repaid the compliment with his nomination of Burguete.

Burguete fully understood that he was to pursue a political, not a military, policy in the Protectorate. The government charged him to utilize the caliph and the native authorities as much as possible; to stress civil administration; to keep all military activity under central control; to make a negotiated settlement with El Raisuli; to restrict military forces and expenditure; to do whatever was reasonable to pacify the Riff; to obtain the exchange of the prisoners; and to encourage such civic endeavors as educational projects and public works.[82]

Spanish military commentators have been almost unanimous in denouncing the political decision to negotiate with, rather than to crush, El Raisuli, for it seemed that the Sherif was clearly near the end of his rope. In the military sense this was true, yet El Raisuli, despite his penchant for kidnapping, extortion, and occasional murder, was no fanatic but a practical-minded politician.[83] Given complete autonomy within his feudal barony, he was unlikely to cause trouble for the rest of the Protectorate. Under the circumstances, the Spanish government felt that it could not hope for more. El Raisuli was delighted with the Spanish capitulation, and after two months of negotiation, largely conducted by the resourceful Castro Girona, an agreement was made in September 1922. Peace returned to the western part of the Protectorate, making it possible to close a few of the outposts in the Djebala and reduce the garrison appreciably. El Raisuli's apparent triumph raised his prestige among the western kabyles, and he took advantage of the situation by robbing, imprisoning, or killing Berbers who had opposed him and supported the Spanish administration.

It was much more difficult to make a deal in the Riff. In accordance with the new policy, liberal bribes were offered to Adb el-Krim; Burguete was even ready to decentralize administration of the kabyles in the eastern zone and provide the Beni Ourriagli sheikh with an autonomous "Emirate of the Riff." Fifteen months earlier, this would have been more than enough to win Abd el-Krim's collaboration, but by 1922 his ambition was greater. He sought complete independence.

During the summer of 1922, the sizable Spanish forces in the Melilla zone succeeded in pushing Krim's irregulars farther back toward the central part of the Riff. In September and October, Burguete rearranged the combat units in an effort to make them more maneuverable and logistically self-sufficient. At the same time, he continued negotiations for the return of the Spanish prisoners and tried unsuccessfully to lure some of the kabyles away from the wily sheikh. In late October, Burguete resumed military operations, pushing an advance column to Tizi Azza, well within Krim's home territory. The column was subjected to a heavy Berber attack on November 1; though the position held firm, there were numerous Spanish casualties. After the customary outcry from the Spanish press, a government order to the High Commissioner suspended any further advance. The Spanish position in the Riff was left unbalanced by the halting of Burguete's campaign. Because of its exposed location, Tizi Azza was not easy to defend, and it had been occupied only to cover future advances.[84]

Burguete was making a serious effort to introduce real spit-and-polish into Moroccan military administration, but it was a herculean task. One of the numerous discoveries made in the reorganization was the "Larache Million"—a massive embezzlement of nearly a million pesetas by the Army supply officers in the Larache district during the years preceding the defeat.[85] Since various forms of peculation had been fairly standard practice in Spanish Army supply during the past century, it was not unnaturally believed that thorough investigation would uncover quite a number of scandals.

The investigation of military negligence was carried out by the Supreme Council. By October 3, 1922, charges had been brought against 77 officers—only nine of whom were in senior command positions—for failing to discharge their responsibilities properly.[86] This did not satisfy public criticism. Political groups were also asking for a full investigation of government relations and royal interference in the events leading to Annual.

Don Alfonso excited further apprehension with his remarks at a military banquet on June 7, 1922, when he urged the officers present to emulate the unity of the German Army, which had maintained its cohesion after disastrous defeat. He asked the military to remember their vows of loyalty to their sovereign, and said that so long as they all remained united around the throne, they had nothing to fear. Don Alfonso's remarks were reported to have brought enthusiastic applause from the banqueters, but in many political circles they were interpreted as an extraconstitutional appeal to the Army and a pledge to avoid the prosecution of "responsibles."[87] The Prime Minister tried to explain away his sovereign's remarks, but the long summer vacation taken by Don Alfonso that year added to his reputation for frivolity, and the publicity given a number of dubious financial affairs in which the king was involved served to tarnish his image still more.

The attitude of most juntero officers toward the king remained equivocal at best. They felt that his promises remained unfulfilled and that he had continued to pamper and protect a special clique in particular and africanistas in general. When Don Alfonso and his wife attended military ceremonies at Seville in mid-October 1922 to decorate Sanjurjo and Lt. Col. González Carrasco and to honor the latter's unit of Moorish Regulares, the Infantry officers of the Seville garrison, who were mostly junteros, created something of a scandal by boycotting the proceedings. Leading africanista officers were outraged, and demanded that the junteros be punished. Millán Astray, one of the leading targets of the Juntas, struck back in an open letter to the king on November 7. With an eye to public opinion, he tendered his resignation, declaring that he could not serve in an Army commanded by two different hierarchies. Major Francisco Franco sent a telegram from Morocco expressing the complete solidarity of Tercio officers with their commander and adding that Artillery officers were also demanding immediate dissolution of the Juntas.[88] Millán Astray's resignation was not immediately accepted, but the Juntas were more vigorous than ever in demanding his removal. They were supported by some of the political liberals, who had always tended to favor the Juntas because the latter contested the power of the central oligarchy and were opposed to the fraud in Morocco. The government was also worried about the insubordinate quality of Millán Astray's public pronouncements. After six days had passed, a royal order of November 13 relieved him of command of the Tercio, ostensibly because his manifold wounds made it impossible for him to continue in so active a post. Disaffected africanistas regarded this as a concession to the junteros.

Fifteen months after the disaster of Annual, and five and a half years after the first Junta crisis, the Officer Corps was still divided by conflicting loyalties and ambitious rivalry. *ABC* mourned on November 10:

Spain has an Army budget that is greatly superior to her resources ... yet there is no Army. From the 157 million pesetas of 1906, the Army budget has advanced continually, without pause, to the 581 million of 1920, which represents, in such a brief period, an increase of 267 per cent. And yet there is no Army. The Juntas have made frightful ravages in the virtues and the ideals of the Army. The work of the Juntas culminated in the ignominious disaster of Annual.

By November 14, leaders of several factions of the former Liberal Party were preparing a parliamentary motion to abolish all the Juntas or "Advisory Commissions," but the Prime Minister beat them to the punch with a government motion that was passed without difficulty. This bill completely dissolved all Juntas and Advisory Commissions within the Army, left their leaders without regular assignment, and prohibited any such organizations in any form in the future. In order to satisfy one of the junteros' main complaints, it also contained provisions for careful scrutiny of all future merit promotions. Repercussions were anticipated, but the officers of the peninsular garrisons were now so confused and divided that there was no notable resistance.[89]

Meanwhile, the Sánchez Guerra government was also working to regularize the situation in Barcelona. The Martínez Anido–Arlegui terror had led to the reprisal assassination of a prime minister, Dato, in the preceding year. When the Sánchez Guerra Cabinet took office, it restored constitutional guarantees in the Catalan capital, but this did not end the bloodshed. Syndicalists blamed Arlegui's use of the *ley de fugas*—the killing of prisoners "attempting to escape." That such killings occurred was undoubtedly true, but this was not the whole story. Nor was it easy to assess the precise role of Martínez Anido in this grisly drama. He was a large, thick, red-faced man who wore glasses and had a jolly, friendly appearance. In 1910 he had been the king's military aide, and he was a ranking member of the palace clique. To friends he was a good-natured companion who did not seem particularly domineering. To syndicalists he was a fiendish sadist, a decadent sexagenarian who spent his leisure hours viewing pornographic movies at military headquarters. Wherever the truth lies, it is clear that he did little to check the excesses of Arlegui's gunmen, who drew little distinction between honest trade union leaders and anarchist assassins. Even Catalan businessmen began to agree that military rule was doing more harm than good, and the Sánchez Guerra government finally forced Martínez Anido's resignation on October 24, 1922.[90] Arlegui was also removed, bringing a change in police tactics that curtailed the "white terror." Altogether, in eight months the Sánchez Guerra ministry had accomplished more than any of its predecessors in bringing discipline to civilian-military relations, but it was a minority cabinet whose days were numbered. Defeated in the Cortes shortly before the end of 1922, it was replaced by another makeshift government under the Liberal García Prieto.

The new ministry endeavored to continue the same Moroccan policy. Arrangements were finally made at the beginning of 1923 for the ransom of the prisoners taken by Abd el-Krim eighteen months earlier. The forward party among africanistas had always insisted that the prisoners must be rescued, not bought, but private intermediaries arranged for the transfer of three million pesetas in exchange for the prisoners in January 1923. They accepted Krim's stipulation that no Spanish officer should participate in the arrangement.[91] This was an extreme humiliation for the africanistas and polarized them in opposition to the new government.

Ten days earlier, on January 17, a royal decree issued by the government had reversed all the orders of recent years that had tended to concentrate central military authority in the Protectorate in the hands of the High Commissioner. On February 17, Burguete was replaced by Luis Silvela, son of the former Conservative leader and the first civilian High Commissioner in the ten-year history of the Protectorate. This was another blow to military prestige, and Burguete complained bitterly to the press that it made little difference: "It seems absurd to me to be called commander in chief of an army whose efforts are frustrated at every turn."[92]

Within the next few months the unsatisfactory nature of the recent pact with El Raisuli in the Djebala became evident. In addition to persecuting old enemies, the Sherif meddled in the affairs of neighboring kabyles over whom he had no jurisdiction. Yet after ten years of frustration the civilian High Commissioner, Silvela, and the commander of Ceuta, Castro Girona, still felt that they could not afford further conflict, and continued the policy of bribery and coddling. The situation was so maddening that the civilian Minister of War in Madrid, Niceto Alcalá Zamora, who had originally been opposed to further expenditure of blood and money, came to support a forward policy as the only means of overcoming the gross contradictions of Spanish policy. The Foreign Minister, Santiago Alba, was strongly opposed to this, as was most of the Cabinet, so Alcalá Zamora resigned. He was replaced by General Aizpuru, whose political affiliations were unclear.

In the Riff, Abd el-Krim had in no way been intimidated by Burguete's flying columns and mobile artillery bombardments. He proceeded with his plans to create a modern state organization, and had the local kabyles send representatives to an assembly in his stronghold at Axdir. Since the theoretical justification for the establishment of a European protectorate had been the argument that Moroccans were unable to govern themselves, Krim tried to show that this was not true. He even attempted to create an "Air Force of the Riff," a plan based on foreign mercenaries and doomed to frustration. Krim's "army" still numbered only a few thousand troops equipped in European style, but he hoped to procure arms for all the tribesmen of the Riff, which would enable him to field a native militia of up to 60,000 men.[93]

In the spring of 1923 he stepped up harassment of Spanish outposts, and nearly succeeded in sealing off the route to Tizi Azza, the most exposed position. A determined attack by the Tercio on June 5 broke the blockade, but it cost the life of the Legion's new commander, Lt. Col. Valenzuela. This opened the way for the promotion of Franco, commander of the First Bandera, to the rank of lieutenant colonel and Commander in Chief of the Tercio, which, within two years, had become the combat elite of the Spanish Army.*

The government then refused to permit General Vives, the current commander at Melilla, to carry out further operations to remove the danger to Tizi Azza. Though the civilian High Commissioner had come to agree with the former civilian Minister of War that some sort of military offensive was the only way to resolve the problem, the government believed that it could not risk the political consequences. In protest against this decision, General Vives resigned.

No satisfactory solution for the humiliating Spanish position in Morocco was in sight. Heretofore, only one colonel had been sentenced for dereliction of duty. Political opinion demanded the placing of responsibility for the 1921 disaster, while vetoing any serious attempt to face its consequences. The fact that *abandonistas* were becoming more and more numerous led some Army leaders to believe that the civilian officials would never be able to resolve the Moroccan problem and restore national honor, and that it was up to the Army to provide a political and military alternative.

* See Appendix A, p. 455, for a biographical sketch of Francisco Franco.

CHAPTER TEN

The Primo de Rivera Pronunciamiento

B ETWEEN 1919 and 1923, approximately 12,000 Spanish soldiers were killed in Morocco. Cumulative government deficits for the five-year period amounted to approximately three and a half billion pesetas, or almost as much as the regular government income. During 1923, domestic opposition to the Riff War seemed to be increasing: Spain's leading cultural center, the Madrid Ateneo, held a public lecture series on the question of responsibility for Annual, and the Socialist labor organization UGT (Unión General de Trabajadores) staged demonstrations to protest further military operations. A "commission of fathers" called on the government and insisted that their sons not be sent to die in Morocco. Most insulting of all to the Army were the actions of two Catalan extremist groups, Acció Catalana and Estat Catalá, who whistled and jeered at the Spanish flag in Barcelona, cheered the mention of the "Republic of the Riff," and sent an official expression of solidarity to Abd el-Krim.

Such incidents heated the feelings of africanista officers to the boiling point. Even among those disgusted with the incompetence of their commanders there was resentment at the way in which punishment of those guilty of misconduct in Morocco was demanded by political groups and sometimes used to discredit the entire Army. It seemed to them that the politicians wanted to close down most of the Protectorate and write off the investment of blood and toil, while at the same time holding the Army responsible for all the grief involved and denying it any opportunity to fulfill its "mission." Furthermore, the new Minister of Finance, Bergamín, was saying in effect that the government simply could not afford the expense of continued military operations.

Though some of the older officers in Morocco may have been willing to let well enough alone and forget future ambitions in favor of a return to the quiet stagnation and petty corruption of the past, the younger or more vigorous officers—the ones who were conducting the halting efforts at a counteroffensive—had a strongly militant attitude. They demanded protection of the nation's and the Army's "honor" by the direct reconquest of the entire Protectorate. Furious with junteros and politicians alike, some of them expressed sympathy with the Italian Fascist "March on Rome" in October 1922. Early in 1923, the military governor of Melilla wrote the Minister of War that feeling among his officers about the political investigation of "responsibilities" was strong, and that he knew some of them were contemplating extreme measures. His recommendation was that no further inquiry into the Moroccan disaster be made.[1]

Perhaps the only thing that both africanistas and junteros could agree upon was their mutual opposition to the successive governments that were formed in Madrid. After the Sánchez Guerra law dissolving the Juntas, diehard junteros continued to meet privately, and still wielded great influence in some garrisons. They, too, were forgetting their earlier concern for "responsibilities," and were concentrating their animosity on the politicians who had eliminated their official power rather than on rival sectors of the Army. But neither Junta colonels nor battalion commanders in Africa had much influence over the sprawling, fragmented Officer Corps as a whole. A leader with prestige and support was needed if the Army were ever to do anything direct to "save its honor" or to "save" Spain.

By 1923, the country had gone through six years of continuous social, political, economic, and military turmoil. Persistent demands for constitutional revision and broad reform had been ignored. The workers' trade unions had been attacked, the politicians manipulated and frustrated, and the votes of the provincial rural population systematically controlled or falsified by caciques. The king refused to take responsibility for national problems, and the Cortes was perpetually deadlocked. Though the economic situation had recently improved, political and diplomatic affairs had become more tangled. It was not surprising that most politically conscious Spaniards were hoping for some new upheaval that might bring order in its wake.

Since 1900, some of the country's most prominant intellectuals and pundits had been calling for the emergence of a new elite to regenerate Spain, and not all of them demurred at the use of authoritarian means. Joaquín Costa, the most forceful of the reformist voices at the turn of the century, had once called for a national dictator, a man of iron, to perform the drastic surgery needed to amputate the gangrenous elements of the existing system. In *España invertebrada* (1922), Ortega y Gasset had written: "Force of arms is not brute force but spiritual force. . . . A people ought to feel its honor tied to its Army. . . . The important thing is that the people be aware that the degree of perfection of its Army measures with astonishing precision the degree of its national morality and vitality."

One politically ambitious lieutenant general who deemed himself able to provide leadership for officers and civilians alike was Miguel Primo de Rivera. Primo came from an upper-class landowning family in Andalusia and had graduated from the Infantry Academy at the age of eighteen. He had fought in Cuba, the Philippines, and in Morocco, winning several combat decorations (his rights to which were questioned by his detractors). More important than his combat record, however, was the fact that his uncle Fernando had been one of the most influential political generals in the Army. Primo's promotions were acquired by méritos or "election"; by 1919, at the age of 49, he had reached the rank of lieutenant general.[2]

Primo considered himself something of a liberal. A disciple of Costa, he liked to be thought of as a reformist even though his own career had been based on the favoritism of the established system. The reform Primo envisioned was authoritarian, nationalist, and nonpolitical, for he had been brought up on tales of the nineteenth-century caudillos and moved among those who spoke with scorn of ordinary politicians. Primo had a bluff, hearty, friendly personality, but was not overly popular among his colleagues, who regarded him as pushy or associated him with favoritism and the palace clique. Since 1917, he had traveled about the country giving occasional speeches on Army problems, and had fought at least one duel in defense of his aged uncle.[3] Allendesalazar considered offering Primo the Ministry of War in the 1920 Cabinet, but finally rejected him as "too dangerous."[4] He was not afraid to speak his mind on controversial issues, as his frank remarks in 1917 and 1921 on the feasibility of the Moroccan Protectorate indicated. These statements, like his recommendations on the Army budget, were temperate and revealed a certain amount of common sense, but the 1917 speech cost him the military command at Cádiz and his discourse four years later brought to an end his brief tour as Captain General of Madrid. These outspoken declarations won him the reputation of an abandonista and might well have served to eliminate him as a potential leader of the forward faction in the Army. However, Primo's intermittent frankness was mixed with a great deal of that slyness Spaniards like to associate with the Andalusian temperament. The contradictory association of such qualities in his makeup helps account for the ambiguities in his political career. Well before 1922, he had shown an ability to change sides in the face of political opportunities; his switch in favor of the Juntas in 1917 gave ample proof of this.

Primo's fortunes sharply improved in the autumn of 1922 when the government named him Captain General of Barcelona. The political and social struggle in Catalonia made this the most important assignment in Spain, and Primo was careful to exploit his opportunity. More discreet and flexible than Martínez Anido, he made a good impression on the Catalan middle-class leaders. They had need of allies, for recent efforts to extend the sphere of Catalan autonomy had been blocked, and after the removal of Martínez Anido and Arlegui there had been a resurgence of anarchist terrorism. The Catalan leaders were eager for the establishment of firm authority. Primo, like Polavieja a quarter of a century earlier, let them know that he favored granting regional autonomy within an effective national administration, and from the winter of 1923 on, some of the most important Catalan moderates and conservatives began to look to Primo for a solution to their dilemma.

Rumors of these talks drifted through Barcelona circles. At the beginning of March 1923, Salvador Seguí, the most influential leader in the syndicalist CNT, called a private meeting of syndicalist leaders to outline a plan for a general strike in Barcelona should the Captain General try to take complete power into his own hands in conjunction with the Catalanists.[5] On March 8, Seguí discussed further efforts to curb anarchist terrorism so that the CNT might devote itself to constructive labor union activity. Two days later, he was arrested by the police and murdered "while attempting to escape."

There is no indication that at this point Primo de Rivera was contemplating any kind of rebellion. In the spring of 1923 he lacked the support for such ambitions. He was, however, hoping to win a Senate seat, and to move from the Senate into the Ministry of War. Since the Conservatives had excluded him from their lists after his outburst in 1921, Primo asked to be placed on the Liberal ticket in his native Cádiz province for the elections of May 1923. The Prime Minister and certain other influential politicians were willing, but the Liberal cacique in Cádiz vetoed the idea, complaining that heretofore Primo de Rivera had been too thick with the opposing Maurist cacique.[6]

Temporarily, at least, this blighted his prospects for advancement through ordinary political channels.

The general most in the political limelight in the spring of 1923 was the aging Francisco Aguilera, President of the Supreme Council of Military Justice and, since the death of the elder Primo de Rivera, senior lieutenant general of the Spanish Army. Aguilera held a lifetime seat in the Senate and was considered a very honest man and something of a liberal. He had won attention during 1922 by demanding that the full investigation of responsibilities for the Moroccan collapse be given priority "above all else."[7] To avoid making the issue a political football, he insisted that it be investigated only by the relevant military authorities. Aguilera thus had the advantage of being able to appeal to officers resentful of pressures and accusations by civilians as well as to civilian critics who wanted the investigation of the Moroccan fiasco completed and made public. His seniority and experience had made Aguilera widely known and respected in the Army, and the idea was circulated that the military might gladly close ranks behind him if he forced the government to bring matters to a fair conclusion. The Conde de Romanones, a politician close to the king, was quoted as saying in private conversation that a government led by Aguilera would be the best solution to the nation's problems.[8]

With many rumors in the air, Primo de Rivera made a trip to Madrid in June 1923 to see how things stood. The ostensible excuse for this visit was that he wished to confer with the government about the situation in Barcelona, where terrorist incidents were reaching an all-time high. Supported by his Catalanist followers, the Captain General asked the government to grant him full powers, including the authority of martial law, to deal with the disorder. This was refused, for the government feared a return to the days of Martínez Anido. Meanwhile, Primo de Rivera talked with Aguilera, who assured him that he had no intention of organizing military pressure to seize power.[9] When he returned to Barcelona on June 23, Primo was greeted at the station with an enthusiastic demonstration by members of the Catalan middle-class militia, the Somatén. There he made a ringing endorsement of the Somatén as a patriotic security organization and announced that if need be he would restore tranquillity to Catalonia by mobilizing the civilian militia.

Soon afterward, the speculation regarding Aguilera reached its climax, then vanished altogether. On June 30, Aguilera, as President of the Supreme Military Council, wrote a letter to the Minister of

Justice, Sánchez de Toca, accusing him of having lied when he declared to the Senate that the Ministry had not received adequate files on the Berenguer case from the military courts, and ending with a threat: "A repetition of this case, or another such case will force me to proceed against you with the rigor and energy that men of your ilk deserve."[10] The indignant Sánchez read this letter to the Senate, calling it an example of military coercion. A few minutes later, he and Aguilera chanced to meet in the Senate corridor. It is said that, after a quick exchange of words, Sánchez de Toca struck the general with his fist. Though no damage was done, there was considerable excitement, and at least one senator thundered: "Long live the supremacy of the civil power!"[11]

Aguilera became involved in a complicated series of charges and countercharges with Sánchez de Toca and the Prime Minister. It was rumored that at the time of the scuffle in the Senate Aguilera had threatened a military coup, and on the night of July 3 large crowds milled through the streets of Madrid in a mood of excitement and expectation. There is no evidence, however, that Aguilera was involved in any concrete conspiracy. A denunciation in the Cortes soon afterward forced him to take a public stand disavowing any intention of a pronunciamiento. He abstained from direct political activity, and those elements that had earlier seemed anxious for an Aguilera government soon lost interest.

The active center of military conspiracy in Spain during the summer of 1923 was not the residence of Aguilera or the Captain General's headquarters in Barcelona, but a downtown hotel suite in Madrid occupied by the Cavalry general José Cavalcanti. Cavalcanti was an africanista, valiant on the battlefield and royalist and hierarchical in his political attitudes. Like many Cavalry officers, he was a descendant of the provincial hidalgo class; he was also a favored member of the king's Army clique. Utterly fed up with the governmental situation, he drew to himself three like-minded figures in Madrid military circles, Generals Federico Berenguer (younger brother of the onetime High Commissioner), Leopoldo Saro, and Antonio Dabán.* All three had

---

* Antonio Dabán was the son of General Luis Dabán, one of Martínez Campos' key associates in the 1874 pronunciamiento and a leading political general of the Restoration era. Also, as noted earlier, Miguel Primo de Rivera's uncle had played an important role in that revolt. (See pp. 41–42.) These examples of family continuity in the active military elite illustrate the tendency toward formation of a special caste in the Army hierarchy under the restored monarchy (in contrast to the situation that prevailed during much of the nineteenth century).

recently held commands at Madrid, which gave them broad contacts, while Cavalcanti was also widely known and esteemed for his character and bravery. This quartet—popularly known as "the Quadrilateral"—had earlier received the king's attention and become part of his military circle. The members now hoped to obtain royal backing for their design, which was to line up support for a forward policy in Morocco that would carry the flag on till the job was done. Whether this were achieved by a military or civilian government was not important in itself; the Quadrilateral was mainly concerned with uniting the Army behind strong leadership that could force a positive decision. They began to sound out officers at the more important provincial garrisons concerning their willingness to support direct action. The officers contacted proved lukewarm or indecisive, and the Quadrilateral decided that the only solution was to bring about the appointment of a resolute senior general as Prime Minister with emergency powers. Weyler was certainly forceful, but he was too old, too liberal, and too respectful of legal processes for an operation of this sort. Aguilera was the second candidate in point of seniority, but he had taken a strong public stand in favor of prosecuting the "responsibles" and had renounced all political ambitions. Lack of a real caudillo was the conspirators' major handicap.[12]

Meanwhile, the struggle over policy in Morocco went on. The latest military commander of Melilla, Martínez Anido, made a report to the government recommending that a further advance be made beyond Tizi Azza in the Riff in conjunction with the long-projected amphibious operation in the Bay of Alhucemas. The major part of this plan, and especially the amphibious operation, was rejected by the government, and Martínez Anido promptly resigned in protest.

The government insisted that the General Staff play a major role in the planning of any new operations. After an absence of more than a year, Weyler had again been appointed Chief of Staff, and the eighty-one-year-old general headed the commission that arrived at Melilla on August 16 to trace out an adequate line of defense behind which the Spanish forces might retire. Just a few days later, the forward Spanish positions were strongly attacked by a hostile harca thought to be 9,000 strong, some members of which had been recruited in the French zone.

Despite the renewal of hard fighting, the government wanted to avoid sending large numbers of new recruits to Morocco, for fear of the political consequences. The supposedly secret recommendation for a landing in the Bay of Alhucemas had already become a matter of discussion in the press. The Catalan leader Cambó published a series of articles in *La Veu de Catalunya* condemning the project and insisting that the government abandon part of the Protectorate. In this atmosphere, a group of new conscripts refused to leave the dock at Málaga on August 23, mutinied, and shot their sergeant. The leader of this little revolt, a corporal, was quickly sentenced to death, but was reprieved by the government a few days later after a strong newspaper campaign in his behalf. Further movement of reinforcements to Morocco was temporarily canceled.

The sense of outrage felt by africanistas and many other officers could scarcely be contained.[13] So little priority was given to Army requirements that during 1922 and 1923 troop trains on the Spanish railroads often had to wait until all civilian traffic had passed before receiving the right of way. Thus, several carloads of recruits might need as much as four days to traverse the three hundred miles or so from Lérida to Málaga. There were usually further delays at the port of embarkation until shipping was available, during which time the troops were placed on leave. The alternation of enforced inactivity and liberty created tensions that gave rise to situations such as that which had just drawn national attention,[14] and it appeared to the military that the government was condoning mutiny.

It is not possible to determine the exact nature of the relationship between Primo de Rivera and the Cavalcanti committee during July and August. Primo de Rivera employed his own staff in Barcelona to send feelers out to a number of key garrisons, only to find that the Cavalcanti group had already been active in organizing support for a move by the Army. The main obstacle between Primo de Rivera and other conspirators was the Captain General's reputation as an abandonista, which contradicted what seems to have been the Cavalcanti group's only precise political goal—completion of the Morocco campaign. This difference would have been fatal had not Primo made strenuous efforts to take another tack.[15] He had reversed himself 180 degrees before and did so again, explaining privately that he had never advocated "abandoning" Morocco but only avoiding unnecessary losses and expense: certainly the goal of any patriotic government must be an "honorable" solution, one that would restore the dignity of the Spanish Army. Such assurances to fellow officers did not prevent Primo from promising Catalan leaders greater regional autonomy and tariff protection in return for Catalan support of a patriotic, Army-led government. In fact, Brigadier General Eduardo López de Ochoa, who commanded the Infantry brigade stationed at Barcelona, understood that Primo had even signed a written document to this effect. Primo explained that it had been necessary to promise contradictory things to different groups in order to win their support.[16]

The precise role played by Alfonso XIII in the military conspiracy of 1923 may never be fully known. López de Ochoa has written that Primo de Rivera made a secret visit to the king's summer palace at San Sebastián before the end of August to gain royal support for a military government and to discuss details of the coming pronunciamiento.[17] However, no direct proof of such a visit has been produced. On the other hand, there is little doubt that Don Alfonso was well informed about the progress of conspiratorial talks and pressures among the military. The Cavalcanti group were all ultra-royalists and would hardly have gone so far as they did had they not felt assured of the king's support. It has been commonly supposed that the efforts of the Cortes committee to investigate royal advice and intervention in the Moroccan affair, together with their plans for full parliamentary debate on the expanded Picasso report in September, prompted Don Alfonso to agree to a military government that would head off royal implication in the "responsibilities." Circumstantial evidence makes this appear logical, but documentary proof has never been obtained.

At any rate, in the last days of August the king consulted one of his most respected subjects, Antonio Maura, about the advisability of appointing a military government, or at least of naming a general as Prime Minister with full decree powers. The venerable old Conservative told Don Alfonso that such a course would eventually bring about the death of the monarchy: if the present constitutional monarchy chose to transform itself into a military government, it would be next to impossible to reverse the process, and the future of the Bourbon dynasty would be tied to a military regime. Maura counseled that if worst came to worst and the military could not be restrained, it would be better to let the Army take over on its own authority, without royal ratification, so that the monarchy might not be compromised.[18]

Don Alfonso chose not to heed this advice. He seems to have felt that a temporary decree-administration might be installed to straighten out the present situation, after which the government might once more return to the old system. After all, constitutional guarantees had been suspended in various parts of Spain for much of the past four and a half years. Parliament was barely functioning, and there was a serious question whether the constitution held authority any longer. Leftists and progressives were demanding that it be broadly reformed, while the Army, conservatives, the clergy, and the vested interests were anxious for order and stability.

The plotting that was going on in military circles was not completely unknown to the government, but such abnormal pressures had become a normal way of life in Spanish politics, so no special measures had been taken. One opportunity came soon after the Málaga mutiny, when Primo de Rivera wrote a letter to the Prime Minister protesting the negative government policy toward Morocco and decrying its lenient treatment of the mutineers. This was a part of Primo's effort to overcome his reputation for *abandonismo*. Santiago Alba, the strong-minded Foreign Minister, felt that it was dangerous to leave Primo in his Barcelona command and recommended to the other Cabinet members that he be dismissed, but the government, fearful of further enraging its multitudinous critics at both extremes, decided to take no action.

At this point the government was dealt a heavy blow by the preliminary version of the General Staff's recommendation on Morocco, which was ready by August 29. For months the africanistas had been condemning the government's efforts to create an autonomous native administration under an "Emirate of the Riff" before having reached a military decision with Krim. Even the civilian High Commissioner, Silvela, had sent a number of letters to Alba endorsing the Army's claim that further offensive operations were absolutely indispensable, and that no withdrawals should be considered.[19] The government, expecting the support of the General Staff, had spurned all such appeals. The report of Weyler and his colleagues, which paralleled the recommendations of the activists, had the effect of a bombshell. Weyler's commission said that it would be necessary after all to pursue further advances into the Riff to achieve a stable defensive line. Since no political compromise with Krim could be struck, the difficult landing in the Bay of Alhucemas should be made: it was the only way to break the center of Krim's power and achieve lasting security for the Protectorate.[20]

The plan was not officially released until September 3, but its major conclusions had been leaked to the politicians and the press by the last days of August, precipitating another furore. Alba was willing to reverse his position and accept the recommendations of the report, but other Cabinet ministers refused to give in. Three of them resigned, and the government was temporarily dissolved on September 1; however, it was immediately reconstituted with much the same membership as before.

The military conspirators may have been hoping that increasing pressure of this sort would bring about the total collapse of the government, after which they might persuade the king to appoint a general with emergency powers. But the constitutional system, lame and ineffective though it was, continued to limp along, and might have done so indefinitely. Outright force was required to topple it. Therefore, after the government had been reconstituted on September 2, the Cavalcanti group offered the leadership of the military movement to Primo de Rivera. He accepted immediately and made a quick trip to Madrid, where the generals evidently came to an agreement during conversations held on September 7 and 8. Primo provided an official excuse for this visit by first issuing a public statement that severe measures should be taken to deal with the class struggle in Catalonia, then meeting with Cabinet members to discuss the situation.

Subsequent events made it clear that the Cavalcanti group had achieved no firm and clear consensus among Army leaders concerning what course to follow. The senior officers, like most Spaniards, believed that something should be done to resolve the Moroccan problem, and many were not averse to having the Army do it, but there were few serious advocates of military dictatorship. It is said that when Primo de Rivera sent a number of agents to visit the major garrisons after his last trip to Madrid, they found little outright resistance to a move by the Army against the government, but also little concrete agreement on what action might be taken and scant enthusiasm for a proto-fascist effort or a genuine dictatorship.[21] The prevailing idea among those officers who were informed and gave their tentative approval was that a brief Army-led government was to be established to solve the Moroccan problem and end terrorism within Spain, after which there would be a swift return to an ordinary civilian regime.

The second parliamentary investigating committee planned to render its report on September 18, after the Cortes reopened. The military movement was therefore scheduled to begin early on Sunday, September 13. The conspirators did not have many categorical pledges of support, but they counted on the other Captain Generals' falling into line once the standard had been raised. The strongest encouragement came from Zaragoza, where General Sanjurjo had been made second-in-command after his removal from Melilla the preceding year. Burning for revenge against the government, this influential africanista busily mobilized support in the Zaragoza district, even though by so doing he attracted the suspicion of civil authorities.

During his annual extended vacation, the king relaxed in his summer palace at cool, rainy San Sebastián on the northern coast. One Cabinet member was always present as Minister-in-Residence, and during September 1923 it was the turn of the Foreign Minister, Santiago Alba. Though he had once been a favorite of the Juntas, Alba's strongly anti-militarist Moroccan policy had earned him the hatred of the conspirators. On the afternoon of the 12th he received, from a government official in Barcelona, a letter dated September 10 but mistakenly sent to Madrid before being rerouted to San Sebastián. It read:

Yesterday, the 9th, General Primo de Rivera arrived. He immediately got in touch with other Captain Generals by coded telegrams. This morning Primo de Rivera called a meeting of the senior officers at military headquarters. The object of this meeting was to tell those present that the Captain Generals had agreed to overthrow Alba and the government during this very week.[22]

Primo urged them to be prepared. He told them that he feared being betrayed to the government and arrested on his way back from Madrid.[23]

Later that afternoon, García Prieto sent Alba a telegram from Madrid saying that the government would back him all the way. Nevertheless, a communication from the Minister of War, General Aizpuru, indicated that he was not willing to relieve Primo of command. The rest of the Cabinet assembled in emergency session in Madrid about six in the evening. García Prieto informed his colleagues that he had learned Primo de Rivera was already in contact with Milans del Bosch, at this time head of the king's Military Household. Furthermore, said García Prieto, he had been given to understand that the government could not count on the support of the Captain General of Madrid, Muñoz Cobo. The ministers consequently commissioned Aizpuru, who was still unwilling to relieve Primo of command, to talk with him by telephone and try to restore discipline. A proposal that the government arrest the Cavalcanti group was rejected because its members were known to be close to the king. It has also been said that the Cabinet received a personal telegram from Don Alfonso to the effect that the government should try to negotiate some sort of understanding with the conspirators. There is no direct evidence of such a message, however.

At midnight, Primo de Rivera declared martial law in Barcelona and ordered troops into the streets. At two in the morning, he called newspaper reporters to his headquarters and distributed copies of his opening manifesto. It grandiloquently announced:

The thick net of grasping politics has caught even the royal will in its meshes. . . . This is a movement of men; let whoever does not feel sufficiently virile sit in a corner. . . . In virtue of the confidence and mandate given me, I announce that a Military Directory of provisional character will be constituted in Madrid, charged with maintaining public order.

We do not want to be ministers nor do we feel any ambition other than that of serving Spain. The country does not want to hear any more talk of "responsibilities," but wants to see justice carried out swiftly . . . against the political parties at fault.[24]

The proclamation went on to detail the problems crying for solution: terrorism, inflation, financial mismanagement, "Communist propaganda," impiety, the agitation of separatist extremists, the Moroccan dilemma, political immobility, and attempts to derive special advantage from the investigation of "responsibilities."

One of the excited Barcelona journalists asked if the military movement had been inspired by the Italian Fascist march on Rome eleven months earlier. Primo is quoted as replying: "It has not been necessary to imitate the Fascists or the great figure of Mussolini, though their deeds have been a useful example for everyone. But in Spain we have the Somatén and we have had Prim, an admirable military and political figure."[25] He promised to restore unity, honesty, and a sense of purpose to the country. He pledged the establishment of a general militia, on the order of the Somatén, to ensure national security. Of Morocco, Primo declared, "Neither are we imperialists nor do we think that the honor of the Army hangs on a stubborn policy in Morocco,"[26] but added that the commanders in the Protectorate would be allowed to complete their current operations. He promised to provide a solution that would be *"pronta, digna, y sensata"* (swift, worthy, and sensible).

The government was informed of the proclamation by telephone, and called another hasty Cabinet meeting very early on Sunday morning. Neither the Minister of War nor the Madrid garrison could be counted on. When Civil Guard commanders were queried, they replied that they would not take up arms against their military comrades. The only general to whom the ministers felt they could turn was the aged Weyler, currently resting at his home on Mallorca. In desperation, García Prieto sent Weyler a telegram later that morning asking if he would be willing to try to restore order in Barcelona. Primo de

Rivera had twice approached Weyler in recent weeks in a vain effort to win the old warrior's support, intimating that he already had an agreement with the king.[27] But Weyler never wavered in his insistence on discipline; moreover, he particularly detested the garrulous, ambitious Primo. He therefore told the Prime Minister he would do everything possible to help the government.[28] On receipt of this reply, García Prieto appointed Weyler Captain General of Barcelona, and immediately dispatched a warship to carry him to the Catalan capital.

The Navy apparently played no role in the conspiracy. Compared with the Army, it had always been relatively apolitical, and the Naval Minister, Admiral Aznar, told his colleagues that he was certain the Navy would remain fully loyal. Had details of the plot been discovered in time, said Aznar, naval forces might have been used to help break the Barcelona revolt, but now that support for Primo seemed to be spreading into the interior, it would be imprudent for the Navy to risk civil war.[29]

Meanwhile, Primo had dispatched telegrams to the seven other Captain Generals requesting their support. The only commander to send a clear assurance of support was General Palanca at Zaragoza, where Sanjurjo had rallied most of the officers. In Madrid, Muñoz Cobo was officially neutral until the king expressed his wishes. The Captain General of Seville was the king's uncle, Carlos de Borbón, a convinced constitutional liberal. He had been one of the few generals to recommend pardon for the Málaga mutineers. After receiving Primo's telegram, he called the senior officers of the Seville garrison together for discussion. Most of them were opposed to the government, but since their commander recommended supporting the Cabinet, they agreed that the Seville garrison would remain neutral, at least temporarily. So did three of the other Captain Generals. General Zabalza at Valencia replied in the negative and sent a message of support to the government.[30] Thus, only the forces in Morocco and in two of the eight Captain Generalcies came out squarely for the pronunciamiento. By the late hours of the 13th, Primo de Rivera began to show signs of anxiety. He had not planned a violent coup and had never expected serious resistance. According to López de Ochoa, he remarked: "If they come to fight us, we are lost."[31]

The decision was up to the king, who had not yet taken a formal stand. The government urged him to return to Madrid immediately. He sent Milans del Bosch instead, saying that he would follow the next morning (September 14). That night, Milans conferred with Muñoz Cobo and the Cavalcanti group in Madrid. They urged that the king ask for the government's resignation.[32] When Don Alfonso arrived in Madrid at 9 the following morning, two groups were waiting on the platform—the Cabinet at one end and the Cavalcanti group at the other. Shortly afterward, the king received García Prieto at the palace, and the Prime Minister asked for approval of the recall of the Captain Generals of Barcelona and Zaragoza as well as for the reopening of the Cortes on the date scheduled (September 17). When the king refused both requests, García Prieto submitted the resignation of the entire Cabinet.

Don Alfonso was not at all displeased to see the politicians under pressure from the Army, but neither did he appear overly anxious to appoint a military dictator as the conspirators wished him to do. The new situation offered him room to maneuver, and he informed the Captain General of Madrid that he was willing to listen to proposals from Primo de Rivera in order to make a decision about formation of a stable government. This alarmed the Cavalcanti Quadrilateral, because it sounded like more of the king's cat-and-mouse routine. Together with Muñoz Cobo, they insisted on seeing him before the morning was out. After much discussion, they finally succeeded in convincing him that he had little alternative save to give power to the military.[33] On leaving the audience with Don Alfonso, Muñoz Cobo announced that Primo de Rivera had been invited to form the new government and would arrive the next day. Meanwhile, the king had granted interim administrative powers to a military directory composed of Muñoz Cobo and the four members of the Quadrilateral. In Barcelona, Primo, who had managed to stop the departure of the vessel that was to have brought Weyler to arrest him, declared: "The monarch has accepted the facts."[34] In protest against Primo's takeover, the CNT attempted to call a general strike in Barcelona and several other cities; but martial law had been extended throughout Spain, and the strike efforts were quickly suppressed.

Primo de Rivera arrived in Madrid on the morning of September 15 to assume full power to govern by decree. In lieu of a cabinet he established a Military Directory of eight generals and an admiral. In his first statement to the press he declared:

I am aware that some have alleged we intend to destroy the Constitution. The mere suggestion of this is an insult to us. Circumstances may perhaps force upon us the necessity of lengthening certain terms insofar as the calling of elections is concerned, but I declare that in no way will we modify any essential point of the basic Code of the Spanish State.

Fully convinced of the ineffectiveness of the present Cortes, we propose to give the country a new parliament, where public opinion, until now falsified by professional politicians, will be represented without subterfuge or intrigue.

The root of the evil from which Spain suffers is very deep. It is located in rural *caciquismo,* and we shall direct our efforts toward extirpating it. Before holding new elections, we will attempt to destroy all the sham and trickery perpetrated by the political organizations.

This does not imply the suppression of ideas. The ideological structure of Spain is for us untouchable, and we feel that modern peoples cannot live without a lively contrast of opinions. We only intend that these be freely and spontaneously expressed . . . and therefore we shall work to see that those whose disastrous action has led us to the state of debility which we now suffer do not return to their benches. . . .

I am not a dictator. No one can, with justice, apply that term to me. I am a man whose comrades in arms, perhaps mistakenly, have honored him with the difficult mission of directing the reconstruction of the Fatherland.

On the following day the new dictator published, by royal decree, the text of a letter he had sent to Don Alfonso at the beginning of his pronunciamiento. It said in part:

Your Majesty well knows that neither I nor the persons who have prepared the new regime with me think ourselves capable of concretely fulfilling ministerial responsibilities, and that our aim was and continues to be to form but a brief parenthesis in the constitutional government of Spain, in order to restore it to power as soon as the country offers us men who are not infected by the vices with which we charge the political parties; we will in turn present these men to Your Majesty [as agents of] the swift reestablishment of normality.[35]

Primo received the editors of most of the Madrid newspapers on September 17 and told them: "We are going to see what nine men of good will, working intensively nine or ten hours daily, can do in the space of ninety days."[36]

Modern commentators have generally agreed that by 1923, the constitutional monarchy in Spain had reached an impasse and badly needed more forceful and unified leadership. Almost everyone with a civic conscience was looking for change of some sort, and it was this which had encouraged Cavalcanti, Primo, and the other conspirators to believe in their chance for success. Even those groups most strongly represented in the Cortes seemed to have little faith in an ordinary political solution to the governmental crisis.

Initially, establishment of the Military Directory was greeted with general approval by Spanish citizens of widely varying social backgrounds. Even outstanding Madrid liberals such as Ortega y Gasset felt that there was no future for the Spanish parliamentary system in its present state. Ortega wrote:

If the military movement wanted to be identified with public opinion and be fully popular, it has certainly achieved its aims. . . . Consider the gratitude that the great bulk of the nation must feel toward these magnanimous generals, who, generously and in a disinterested manner, have carried out the aspirations of half a century felt by twenty million Spaniards, and have done so without asking the people to expend any effort at all.[37]

Yet to say that the constitutional system had reached an impasse does not mean that it was in a state of collapse. As Salvador de Madariaga has written, the constitutional system was overthrown, not because it had become more fraudulent than in earlier years but, paradoxically, because it was becoming more responsive to public opinion and more amenable to the pressures of representatives. During the preceding decade, the Spanish people had shown greater interest in public affairs and had participated more directly in politics than ever before in their history. But they were seriously divided among themselves, and genuine representative government inevitably reflected this fractionalization, making coherent parliamentary administration very difficult. Civic demands were not directed against political representation but the obstacles against its effective expression that thwarted the appointive membership in the Senate, the powers of the king, provincial boss rule, and so on. Left to its own devices, the parliamentary system might very well have struggled along for another decade until a constitutional resolution of the conflicting pressures had been achieved. At any rate, the contention of one of the military conspirators, prior to the pronunciamiento, that if Primo's group did not take over the government, others would,[38] is not borne out by the evidence. The parliamentary system was not overthrown by the weight of national protest at all, but rather by a limited conspiracy sustained by the king and certain business interests.

The jubilation with which some middle-class Liberals greeted the pronunciamiento was an expression of their belief in Primo's assurances that he was merely heading an interim 90-day reform committee that would make ready the reorganization for which there had been such heavy demand. They thought that Primo, who was constantly mouthing precepts from Joaquín Costa, was leading a pronunciamiento in the style of Riego or Prim. In the provinces, peasants and lower-middle-class people welcomed the idea of a strong hand in Madrid that would free them from the petty tyranny of local caciquismo.

General acceptance of Primo de Rivera as Spain's savior, who would solve the frustrations of two decades of monarchy and boss rule, was nonetheless surprising, for, as his entire career attested, the dictator was himself a typical product of the old system of privilege. But this drawback was counterbalanced by many of the man's personal qualities. Primo's simplicity, emotionality, and apparent frankness appealed to ordinary people. The rudimentary nature of his political ideas, and his tendency to speak from emotion rather than reason were easily compatible with the average citizen's notion of political "honesty." If he had no formal ideology or doctrine, neither did most Spaniards, and his very lack of preconceptions gave his intuitive opportunism greater range.

There was considerable confusion in the Army on the morrow of the pronunciamiento. It is undoubtedly correct to say that the majority of the officers were opposed to the García Prieto government, but there is no evidence of a great groundswell of sentiment in the Army for a dictatorship led by Primo de Rivera. The conspiracy had been the work of no more than a few dozen generals and colonels. Most officers seemed to have felt as late as September that if the Army were to enter the government, the leader of a reform Cabinet would probably be Aguilera. Primo had neither the seniority, the popularity, nor the reputation. Even in Morocco, where agitation was keener than in the peninsula, most officers were not eager for a government run by the palace clique. According to one story, when Brigadier General Queipo de Llano learned in Ceuta on the 14th that the king was allowing Primo to take over the government, he exclaimed: "They're giving power to Miguel Primo! He'll lead us into anarchy!"[39]

Primo de Rivera was careful not to appoint any influential senior generals to his nine-man Directory. With the exception of the naval representative, all appointees were brigadiers—in other words, men inferior in rank to the dictator. In accordance with the Army's professed horror of politics, members were not called "ministers," but "advisers." Most had little administrative experience and almost no acquaintance with the problems of government, so the work of the various departments had to be left under the direction of the chief civilian bureaucrats in each branch, who were given the rank of undersecretary.[40] The only person with direct ministerial powers was the dictator himself. In order to get things done, it became necessary to organize multitudinous technical committees of bureaucrats, and the number of these increased with time.

Terrorist acts reached an all-time high in the summer of 1923, but the new government applied effective repression by means of martial law. Martínez Anido was made Undersecretary of the Ministry of the Interior and so became the only general with personal administrative authority. His brutal lieutenant Arlegui was appointed Director General of Security, or national police chief. Police and military units now had full jurisdiction to act as they pleased against suspected terrorists, and the rate of disorder dropped precipitously. By 1924, domestic tranquillity reigned within Spain.

The Cortes was prorogued indefinitely, which meant that the second parliamentary committee investigating "responsibilities" for Annual was unable to make a report. In fact, its records were confiscated by a platoon of troops the very night that the Military Directory was formed, and all further investigation was placed under the exclusive jurisdiction of the Supreme Council of Military Justice. Under the constitution, the king had the right to prorogue the Cortes for as long as three months, and Primo insisted that the Directory would complete its work in 90 days. Therefore, moderates and liberals were not at first overly alarmed by the postponement of parliamentary sessions, for there was considerable hope that elections would be held for an entirely new constituent Cortes.

However, on October 3, after the incumbent Cortes had been completely dissolved—leaving its members stripped of parliamentary immunity—a special military judicial Junta was appointed to inspect court procedures and acts of irregularity among deputies and senators over the past five years. No action at all was taken on the scores of reports of corruption and maladministration within the Army.

Primo's appetite increased with eating. A royal decree of September 30 dismissed all incumbent municipal councillors throughout Spain. They were temporarily replaced by "associate members" who were supposedly less closely identified with the old political groups. In the future, new mayors and provincial governors were to be appointed from Madrid. The probity of local administration was to be supervised by military *delegados,* who were soon to be dispatched to every provincial capital and every city of any importance. Though the position of delegado was only open to officers holding the rank of captain or above, nearly 600 were appointed during October and November. The delegados were to receive three salaries: their regular Army pay, a salary from the local government to which they were attached, and a special perquisite from the national government. The appointment of these military commissars for local government strongly reemphasized the military tone of Primo's dictatorship.

One policy on which the dictator's military colleagues quickly forced him to change his attitude was Catalan autonomy. Primo had enjoyed the support of conservative Catalan leaders, and in his first manifesto of September 13 had said that "administrative decentralization and a reasonable degree of municipal autonomy" were "ineluctable necessities to purify the suffrage, to mortally wound caciquismo, to awaken civic spirit, and to develop cordiality between regions and between governors and the governed." It would seem that at first Primo planned to maintain the present authority of the Catalan Mancomunitat (interprovincial government) and possibly even to extend it. But this ran contrary to the convictions of most politically minded officers. Exactly what took place among members of the Directory and their associates in the last months of 1923 has not come to light, but evidence indicates that there was heavy pressure on Primo for a hard line against the Catalanists.

When Primo visited Barcelona on January 9, 1924, he invited approximately thirty of the more moderate Catalan leaders to meet with him at local military headquarters. He explained that it would be necessary to alter the existing structure of the Mancomunitat and asked for suggestions about how regional government could be made more responsive to the broader problems of the country. No consensus could be reached with the Catalans, who strongly opposed the reimposition of central power. Three days later, a decree dissolved all provincial assemblies save those of the Basque provinces. This eliminated the entrenched strength of the Catalanists in local government. They were replaced by conservative pro-centralists appointed by Madrid. A subsequent decree, "Against Separatism," stated that anyone displaying a flag other than that of Spain would be liable to prosecution by the military courts.[41]

In this way Primo kept peace with the ultra faction in the Army. There is no evidence that his betrayal of the Catalanists bothered him overmuch. At the beginning of 1924, affairs were going smoothly in Spain and the economy was expanding. The experience of power exhilarated the dictator. The more decrees he signed, the more impressed he became with his work and the stronger became his desire to "carry it out thoroughly"—that is, to stay in power longer. He had even enjoyed one opportunity to play the potentate abroad, when he accompanied the king on a state visit to Mussolini's Italy in November 1923. The meetings had been very cordial, and the Duce had offered some advice: take firm control of the Army or expect trouble in the future.[42]

CHAPTER ELEVEN

Primo de Rivera and Morocco

W HEN HE TOOK over the government, Primo promised to find a "swift, worthy, and sensible" solution to the Moroccan problem. The main fault of previous policies, he later declared, was not so much the inadequacy of the differing interpretations as the failure to follow any one course consistently. Every year or two the policy had changed, bringing six different High Commissioners within a decade. But this criticism did not stop the dictator from appointing a seventh —General Aizpuru, the outgoing Minister of War, who replaced Luis Silvela, the only civilian to have held the office.[1] Aizpuru had a reputation for discretion. He had prudently refrained from supporting his colleagues in the last constitutional government when the chips were down. Now he received his reward.

After the end of his regime, Primo admitted that at first he had hoped for some sort of compromise settlement in Morocco. The Spanish authorities were empowered to negotiate a partial withdrawal toward the coast if Abd el-Krim proved willing to accept a status of peaceful autonomy for the Riff.[2] Consequently General Aizpuru arranged a personal conference with the sheikh on October 12, 1923, to discuss Primo's terms. He soon found that Krim had no intention of settling for less than full independence.

Characteristically enough, the old Sherif of the Djebala, El Raisuli, showed more willingness to compromise. A few days after Primo's pronunciamiento, El Raisuli sent him a formal message of congratulations. He promised full cooperation with the new Spanish government and suggested that it would now be possible for Spain to withdraw most of the troops still stationed in the western part of the Protectorate and concentrate its forces against Abd el-Krim.[3] This suggestion was very attractive to Primo, for one of his major goals was to lessen military involvement and thus reduce both the size of the Army and the military expenditure. These were not opportunistic whims on Primo's part, but long-standing convictions, which he had been voicing for nearly a decade. The 1921–22 budget for Army and Moroccan expenses had reached 534 million pesetas, not including an extraordinary credit of five per cent more, and Primo hoped to cut this figure drastically. On October 7, 1923, the Directory announced that only 78,000 recruits would be drafted during the coming year, in place of the 90,000 to 92,000 recruited during the previous term.[4] Primo realized that he was faced with a threefold problem: that of reducing the number of draftees, dealing with the enormous officer surplus, and raising the living standards of the lower ranks. In an effort to right one imbalance, the Directory instituted a pay raise of 25 pesetas per month for NCO's, and three days later it formally requested each department of the civil government to see what economies could be effected.[5]

By the establishment of a broad national militia system, the Somatén, Primo hoped to increase the security of the Spanish cities and, at the same time, to reduce formal military requirements. It was expected that such a force would attract many volunteers. On September 17, only two days after the Directory was formed, Primo decreed that preparations for such a militia should begin.[6] Meanwhile, still hoping for a negotiated settlement, the government continued to withdraw troops from the inactive areas of Morocco. By the end of 1923, 29,000 recruits had been released before their term expired, and 26,000 more were sent home during the first three months of 1924. They were, in part, replaced by recent draftees, but the total size of the force in Morocco was considerably reduced. Primo tried to compensate for the withdrawals by the creation, on November 1, 1923, of a reserve section of the Army of Africa. This consisted of a number of brigades of indeterminate strength stationed in the coastal cities of Alicante and Almería, whence they could be transferred to the Protectorate on a few days' notice.

These developments were extremely disquieting for africanistas and for the palace generals who had arranged the pronunciamiento. By the beginning of 1924, Krim's forces had resumed the offensive in the Riff, once more blockading the advanced position of Tizi Azza. Though they were dislodged by a Spanish assault on January 7, the

Riff chieftain was making plans for a broad extension of hostilities.[7] A guerrilla leader from the western zone, Ahmed el-Kheriro, who had fled to Krim's camp with a story of having been cheated by El Raisuli, led several raids westward into the Xauen area in the spring of 1924, thus extending Krim's influence among the Gomara kabyles. During the first days of May, Krim resumed heavy attacks on Spanish convoys in the eastern Riff; he was now launching assaults on two fronts.[8]

In general, Primo continued to procrastinate throughout the spring of 1924. He had gone far beyond his original "ninety days," but business was good in Spain and the domestic scene was quiet, and he still hoped for some sort of settlement in Morocco. A few administrative reforms had been initiated during the autumn and winter months. A royal decree of January 18, 1924, gave the High Commissioner full military and civil power in Morocco, subject only to the authority of Primo himself, while at the same time a separate "Moroccan Office" was established at Madrid to consolidate the various branches of administration in the Protectorate.[9] However, there was still no organization of offensive operations against Krim; while the Berber attacks mounted in intensity during the summer months, the dictator apparently began to plan a general withdrawal toward Melilla.[10]

Uneasiness and resentment among africanistas increased. At the beginning of 1924, a journal called *La Revista de las Tropas Coloniales* was founded by Brigadier General Gonzalo Queipo de Llano and a number of other officers in Ceuta. This was not a periodical devoted to technical problems, but rather served as the political organ of the africanistas. Several spokesmen for ultra-nationalistic groups in Spain also wrote for the *Revista*. A lead article by Queipo in the first number, January 1, 1924, eulogized Primo de Rivera; but another piece, written by Antonio Goicoechea of the Maurist Youth, called for an all-out offensive in the Riff and a landing in the Bay of Alhucemas. A subsequent edition carried a widely discussed article by Lt. Col. Francisco Franco entitled "Passivity and Inaction," which criticized the fundamentally defensive Spanish policy that allowed Abd el-Krim to retain the initiative. The dictatorship put an end to such barbs by having the *Revista* closed down after only a few numbers.

By early July, the Berber offensive in the Xauen district had reached sizable proportions, and nearly all the Spanish outposts in the hills surrounding the town were under siege. The European forces were completely unable to regain the initiative, though the Spanish

Air Force retaliated by bombing and strafing a number of villages in rebel-dominated territory, killing Moorish women and children.[11]

The dictator crossed over to Melilla with his entourage in mid-July for a visit of inspection. On the 19th, he was invited to a banquet given by officers of the Legion and the Regulares at their forward headquarters of Ben Tieb, in the eastern zone. Thus far, Primo had given no sign of discarding his plan for withdrawal to the coast at Melilla. The Tercio officers feared the worst and decided to give vent to their displeasure. When Primo arrived at Ben Tieb, he found the walls of the dining room arrayed with Tercio slogans such as "The Legion's spirit is blindly and fiercely aggressive." The banquet menu was composed almost entirely of different kinds of egg dishes. This was a bold piece of insubordinate vulgarity, for in Spain, the word "eggs" is slang parlance for testicles, and signifies courage and virility. With his customary slyness and informal, joking manner, Primo at first affected not to notice what was going on. He finally asked why so many egg dishes had been prepared, and was told that "eggs" were not needed by those who wished to abandon Morocco, but that the officers of the Tercio had "eggs" aplenty, and were determined to stay and fight.[12]

The first after-dinner toast, blunt and provocative, was offered by Lt. Col. Franco, who has been paraphrased thus: "We should be filled with joy by your visit, General, but unfortunately this is not the case, for distrust grips our hearts."[13] He went on to say that the Army's policy must be the avoidance of "further disaster" and that the only course proper to the shock units was "to go forward."[14]

It has been said that amid the shouts of "¡Viva la Legión!" there was even heard a cry of "Down with the dictator!" Nevertheless, Primo took the floor, and, gesturing at the Tercio slogans plastered across the walls, declared sternly that the Legion's mottoes ought to include a promise of blind obedience to the command.[15] Then, in a display of the frankness and personal courage not untypical of him, Primo went on to give the assembled officers a detailed explanation of his views. He asked why there was any need to go on to the Bay of Alhucemas, saying that this was not necessary either for military security or for national honor. At this point, he was interrupted by whistles and catcalls. To be treated thus must have been an insufferable humiliation for the dictator, but he had the wisdom to demand silence so that he could explain what he had in mind. He assured the officers that the Moroccan campaign would be fought to a successful conclusion, but that it was not up to them to question matters of grand strategy or strategic withdrawals. He promised the combat veterans that they would be asked to give up very little territory, but that it was sometimes necessary to step back in order to make a longer leap forward. He also rebuked the Legion officers for their doctrinaire intolerance and told them they had no right to think they possessed a monopoly on patriotism.[16] Primo could not possibly sack all the officers for insubordination—the elite units were far too important to his plans—so he indicated that he was granting dispensation for this affair but warned them not to repeat it in the future. "Now I talk to you in an informal way," he said, "but on the day when your orders are given to you, you will have no choice but to obey them, whatever they may be."[17]

Primo had made the best of a difficult situation, for his frank, courageous reply won the respect of many of the officers present (though it did little to reassure them with regard to his future intentions). Franco felt either that he had gone too far in speaking up to Primo or that the dictator's policy was still too mild, for he sent in his resignation soon after the banquet.[18] This put the dictator on the spot, for Franco was one of the most celebrated officers in the Army. All the other Legion officers declared their solidarity with him, as did many africanista officers outside the Legion. Even the sergeants of the Engineering Corps in Morocco sent Madrid a declaration of their loyalty to Franco.

Primo de Rivera refused to accept the resignation. Moreover, in view of the increased hostility of the africanistas, he decided against any general withdrawal in the Melilla area.[19] This satisfied them—at least for the time being—and Franco withdrew his resignation. Primo made a public statement on July 23, four days after the banquet incident, implying that those guilty of fomenting division among the military would be punished.[20] It does not appear, however, that any of the instigators of the Ben Tieb affair actually suffered for it.

During August, Krim's warriors grew even bolder, both in the eastern Riff and in the western area around Xauen. Pressure in the latter district had become extreme, with Xauen and dozens of smaller outposts cut off from contact with Tetuán. Franco and most of the Legionnaires were concentrated in this area as reinforcements. The situation grew so critical that on September 5 Primo de Rivera returned to Morocco, accompanied by three generals from his Directory. On the 9th he initiated a program of retrenchment in the western and central districts that was to include the evacuation of the Xauen area and the pulling back of the equivalent of four or five divisions to a line farther north based on Tetuán and Larache.

In a review of troops at Tetuán early in September, Primo indulged in one of his customary platitudinous exhortations. "Don't let the wearisome military life bore you," he told the untrained, poorly equipped troops. "Stay neat; wash your uniform, and wear it proudly."[21] But words were powerless to raise morale or to overcome the disarray evident in the military operations. By the autumn of 1924, it was plain to the meanest recruit that the majority of the senior commanders in Morocco were professionally incompetent. A severe crisis of confidence among ordinary officers and troops seemed unavoidable.

At this time, the general in the Tetuán command most outspoken in his condemnation of Army shortcomings was Queipo de Llano, who had been involved in a series of incidents since his work with *La Revista de las Tropas Coloniales* early in the year. Queipo had a reputation for being violent and impulsive, but was known as a courageous critic and as a good field commander, unafraid either of the enemy or of the displeasure of the ranking generals. He had written to Primo of the disastrous consequences that might result from the granting of promotions and decorations to undeserving officers (Franco also brought this problem to the dictator's attention). In consequence, Queipo found himself relegated to garrison duty at Tetuán, without active command. As a result, regimental and battalion officers grew increasingly restive over Primo's leadership, which they feared was leading to a sellout, or to a disaster in the Xauen district.[22]

On September 21, two lieutenant colonels talked with Queipo about the urgent necessity of resolving the crisis of confidence among the officers. They were followed by a third caller, Francisco Franco. Queipo described his visit in these words:

The latter [Franco], after expressing to me the disgust that reigned among the officers, spoke without mincing words, and told me that the commanders of the shock forces [Tercios and Regulares] and those of several battalions of peninsular troops currently stationed at Tetuán had met and agreed to imprison General Primo de Rivera and the other generals with him in the Hacho [a military prison]. He was coming to ask me, as a commander of high rank who could unify the movement, to accept leadership in carrying out the plan. He added that he already had a battalion of the Tercio ready and waiting, and that he would arrest the generals as soon as I gave the order.[23]

It was not surprising that the more active commanders were thinking of a coup against the Directory. The situation was indeed critical,
and there were few reasons for them to have confidence in the military
hierarchy. Moreover, most of the effective units of the Army were now
in Morocco. There were already a few signs of disillusionment with
the dictatorship among officers in the peninsula, and a successful stroke
by the forces in Morocco might have made them at least briefly arbiters
of the destinies of Spain. But field officers like Queipo and Franco were
hardly in a position to snatch control from the dictatorship all by themselves. Neither had any political experience or the slightest political
following in Spain. Failure in the enterprise would cost them their
lives; furthermore, the military consequences of even a successful coup
were uncertain, and might lead to more serious disorientation and uncertainty than now existed. Queipo quickly dissuaded Franco, saying
that a revolt within the command would, under the prevailing circumstances, further imperil the already grave military situation. Franco
was apparently not hard to discourage, and the idea was soon dropped.[24]
Meanwhile, Queipo sent a letter to the dictator asking to be relieved
of command in Morocco if his services were not to be utilized in a combat post or in a position of responsibility. On September 24, Primo
acceded to this request but at the same time sentenced Queipo to a
month's imprisonment in Spain for "creating obstacles for the command." If the dictator was aware of Franco's plotting, he gave no
public notice of it.

With the aid of new reinforcements from Spain, Primo was able
temporarily to clear some of the hills around Xauen, and on September 30, he broke the blockade. But he found that his plans for a general
withdrawal had to be delayed because of the anarchy in the command
and the supply system. He was eventually forced to court-martial several of the senior officers who had been criticized by Queipo, Franco,
and others. Unfortunately, Primo made little effort to disguise his
general strategy, and Abd el-Krim began to concentrate the great bulk
of his forces around Xauen in preparation for another rout of the
Spanish.[25]

The dictator was obviously running the Protectorate himself, and
he officially took over the High Commissioner's office on October 16.
With a major retreat in the offing, he sent out an order on November 3
that officially decreed summary court-martial for any officer or soldier
who criticized commands. Outlying posts in the western zone were
abandoned, one after the other, throughout the autumn. The weather

was very bad all fall, complicating the task of withdrawal. When possible, the local kabyles were bribed not to interfere with the evacuation. On other occasions, as many lives were lost in the relief columns protecting certain withdrawals as were saved among the soldiers abandoning the posts. The major phase of the retreat, the evacuation of Xauen, began on November 17. By the middle of December, when it had been completed, a total of 180 Spanish outposts had been closed down. The very pronouncements of the Spanish command made it clear to neighboring kabyles that the forces of Abd el-Krim were about to replace the Europeans in the district. Eventually, as in the rout from Annual, almost every Berber in the area seemed to take up arms in order to harass the Spanish retreat and win easy booty.

The road from Xauen northwest to Tetuán is only about forty miles long, but the valley in which it lies is traversed by sharp ravines and gullies, and there are hills on either side. It is the perfect setting for guerrilla ambush. During the retreat, the main route was held open, but the smaller flanking columns trying to bring back the garrisons of lonely outposts were sometimes cut off and in many instances suffered severely. The withdrawal was all but complete by December 10, after which the Spanish forces held a line across the northern and western sectors of the peninsula from Ceuta to Tetuán to Tangier to Larache. Precise statistics of the casualties in the retreat were never made public, but it has been estimated that 2,000 lives were lost in the withdrawal from Xauen alone.[26]

Reviewing the remnants of his forces in Tetuán on December 13, the dictator put up a brave front. Making full use of his oratorical powers, he harangued the weary units just back from the hills: "You are entering Tetuán in triumph. . . . Bravo!"[27] Before such a mockery of reality some soldiers scarcely knew whether to laugh or cry. The feelings of the rank and file are perhaps best illustrated by the anecdote about a recruit who was finally shipped back to Spain at the end of 1924.[28] As he stepped off the boat in Málaga harbor, the recruit cried, "Hurrah for the sea!" When asked why he was cheering the sea, he replied, "Because if it weren't for the sea, the Moors would already be in San Sebastián."*

In the final withdrawal from Xauen there had been scenes of panic and incompetence similar to those in the rout at Annual. The example of the earlier disaster, and three years of tension and criticism,

---

* San Sebastián is a town on the Bay of Biscay, in the northernmost portion of Spain.

had had little effect. The events at Xauen led to a surprising announcement by General Ignacio Despujol, Chief of the General Staff:

I am every day more convinced that the surprise attacks on the part of the
enemy are much less due to his competence than to our own incapacity and
negligence. Often the soldiers march in close order, half asleep, with their
ears covered by the collars of their cloaks, and their rifles unprepared.... It
is indispensable and urgent that once again, and immediately, the commanders should summon all officers, and they in turn the noncommissioned officers and men, and instruct them, explaining how to mount guard,
how to carry out their duties, and how to march on the paths or tracks.

No patrols should proceed in groups; they should advance in open
order, with their flanks covered and protected and with their arms ready to
reply to the first shot fired at them.... It is incredible that after the long
experience of this war it should be necessary to add these lessons to the
unhappy lessons that this campaign has already taught us, and above all
that it is needful to repeat the recommendation to train and to instruct on
all occasions our soldiers, who are so obedient, so patient, so disciplined, so
honest, but so trustful and inexperienced.... From the date of the issue
of this order, every aggression of the enemy will be followed by an inquiry
and judges will establish whether the troop that has suffered attack was
properly instructed, accustomed to mounting guard, daily inspected by the
commanders, and properly supported.[29]

To raise the spirits of officers and troops alike, Primo insisted from
the beginning that the whole operation was simply a *reculer pour
mieux sauter* affair. He had concluded his speech of December 13
by saying: "Within a short while we will be able to go to Xauen without any precaution or danger, guarded by the same Moors who today
have fought us."[30] Such a drastic transformation could only be wrought
by an extraordinary effort on the part of the Spanish or an abrupt
change in the entire Moroccan situation. The dictator seems to have
had three objectives in mind: to revitalize the Army, to negotiate a
settlement with Abd el-Krim, and to obtain from the French a promise
of help in quelling any further trouble in the Riff.

Nothing could be done in Morocco unless the Army was whipped
into better shape. Conditions among the ordinary units were as dreadful as ever. As many as 80 per cent of the recruits from certain regions
were illiterate and could hardly be considered desirable military material. Customarily, they would have received four or five months of
training in Spain before being exposed to combat, but this was not
always the case during the difficult period of 1924: after only a few
weeks' drill, draftees were sent across to the Protectorate. Even worse
than the lack of preparation of the troops was the incompetence of the
officers, many of whom still could not read maps. As Barea notes, "a

mass of illiterate peasants commanded by irresponsible officers was the backbone of Spain's Moroccan field armies."[31] It was no wonder that general morale was low; on the other hand, cases of insubordination were rare, for most soldiers exhibited a listless acquiescence.

During the winter of 1924–25 the Staff laid emphasis on drill and training, in an attempt to raise the tone of the Moroccan forces. However, since little could be accomplished within a few months, Primo came to rely more and more on a small minority of the best combat officers and on the shock units they commanded. Major attention was given to the Tercio, for whom 800 German volunteers had been recruited in Hamburg during the German social crisis of 1923.[32] The Tercio was expanded to include seven battalions, and was given better equipment. In February 1925, Franco was promoted to full colonel and ratified in the post of Tercio commander in chief.[33] The salaries of both officers and men, always comparatively high, were raised even higher. When not in the field, the men of the Tercio ate the best food the Army could provide. Discipline and conduct remained brutal, but *esprit de corps* was improving and executions for insubordination were becoming rarer. Early scandals, such as instances of Tercio officers being shot in the back by their own troops, had all but been forgotten. On the other hand, the rest of the Army, still inadequately cared for, looked on the shock troops with envy and dislike.

At the beginning of 1925, Primo de Rivera could take some comfort in the fact that his new defensive line was proving to be strong and well chosen. The opportunity for cheap Berber victories against the Spanish was over, and by early spring Spanish forces were once again undertaking a few limited offensive operations.

Abd el-Krim appeared to be at the height of his power, but the situation of the Riff forces was not so strong as it appeared to pessimists within Spain. Sources of supply had been greatly reduced, and the food supplies of the Riff kabyles, at no time abundant, were running low. Smuggling was being curtailed by Spanish pressure, and because of the retreat it was no longer possible to replenish military stores with captured equipment. Early in 1925, one of Krim's lieutenants stormed El Raisuli's stronghold at Tazarut (which remained outside Primo de Rivera's defense line), and took the Sherif prisoner.[34] His capture, however, was of little more than symbolic importance, for the real problem lay in the fact that the Emirate of the Riff could not possibly hope to become self-sufficient unless new sources of supply and support were found.

This may have been the major reason behind Abd el-Krim's decision to attack the northern sector of the French zone. A year earlier, in the spring of 1924, he had tried to gain control over the kabyles in the Ouergha River valley but had met with armed resistance. Lyautey had always viewed the Riffi successes with misgiving, but the French authorities had never been willing to cooperate directly with the Spanish, owing to a sense of rivalry and the idea that identification with an unsuccessful power held in low esteem by the Moors would lessen their own prestige. In 1924, Lyautey had sent small French detachments to occupy positions in the Ouergha region, thus forming a fragile barrier against further attempts by Krim to expand southward. Throughout the great expanse of the French Protectorate there were only about 60,000 troops, of whom less than half were European—in other words, a mere fraction of the Spanish manpower concentrated in a small region to the north. If the Riffi attacked in force and a significant number of France's African troops were induced to desert, the entire French position would be in danger. Lyautey had petitioned Paris for reinforcements, but the heavy financial obligations of the French government in 1923–24 dissuaded it from sending more than a few token contingents.

Primo de Rivera's withdrawal of troops in late 1924 created alarm in both Rabat and Paris. Despite its general scorn of the Spanish, the French command could no longer permit itself the luxury of detachment. In the winter of 1925, Lyautey began to speak of common measures that France and Spain might take to cut off the arms trade between the Riffi and European merchants.

Abd el-Krim had had little time for anti-French agitation since 1917, but he had scarcely more respect for the French than for the Spanish. He doubted that France and Spain would ever be able to cooperate effectively. Some of his lieutenants and tribal leaders were eager to strike southward and appropriate the supplies of the Ouergha-Taza region. Through contacts abroad, Krim learned that several powers, notably the Soviet Union, would encourage such an effort, and that the French Communist Party was doing all it could do to obstruct the French colonial budget and hamper imperialist interests. Krim was well aware of the small number of European troops in the French Protectorate and was beginning to think that only a slight push might be needed to bring down the whole French regime, or at the least to drive it into a corner, as had been done with the Spanish. Negotiations in March 1925 made it clear, however, that the French authorities would not peacefully relinquish the Ouergha region to Krim's control. Consequently the Beni Ourriagli leader decided on the boldest venture of his career: invasion of the French Protectorate.

The attack on the border outposts began in April 1925. For four months, the French were hard put to stay the Berber onslaught, and numerous posts were lost. Some of the kabyles in the border territory rallied to the rebels, and at one point the city of Taza was in danger of falling. Sizable reinforcements were hurried from France. Lyautey, who had been in wretched health for several years, resigned, and Marshal Pétain was sent to direct operations. It was now clearly in the French interest to make common cause with the Spanish government. During June and July 1925, lengthy discussions were held in Madrid by representatives of the two powers. Joint military measures and the precise delimitation of the boundaries of the two Protectorates were agreed upon, and a formal accord was signed on July 21.[35]

During May and June, Berber detachments in the eastern Riff sharply harassed a number of Spanish convoys and outposts, but Sanjurjo's troops repulsed these efforts in good order. When Pétain came to Tetuán on July 28 to consult with the Spanish dictator about details of the counter-offensive, Primo de Rivera was able to display Spanish forces in better condition than at any time in the past generation. The new military plan called for diversionary tactics: the French were to exert steady pressure from the south, thus pinning down a considerable proportion of Krim's manpower while the Spanish carried out their long-debated landing in the Bay of Alhucemas, near Krim's primitive capital. Though for four years the Beni Ourriagli caid had kept several batteries of captured Spanish cannon on the hills overlooking the coastline above Axdir, he apparently had never seriously believed that the Spanish would attempt an amphibious operation. However, by way of a strategic diversion the caid disengaged some of his men on the southern front, and on September 3 opened a major assault against the Spanish positions below Tetuán. Some outlying terrain was lost, but the main Spanish line had been well dug in along high ground at Ben Karikh, and was successfully defended by a comparatively small force.[36]

Primo de Rivera was determined not to be dissuaded from the Alhucemas operation, which was scheduled to be carried out on September 7 by a squadron of 32 vessels, including one French battleship.[37] The general field commander was Sanjurjo, the main column was to be led by Saro, and the landing was to be spearheaded by a

Bandera of the Tercio under Franco. As it turned out, the winds on September 7 were unfavorable and there was some thought of delaying the operation, but Primo insisted on going ahead. During a last-minute conference held at sea, it was decided to delay the landing for a day and switch its site from the original target to the beach of Ixdain farther down the coast, which might be easier to navigate and would probably be unfortified.[38]

Though Krim had installed a few cannon in the vicinity, the Berbers were taken by surprise and initial resistance was slight. This was fortunate for the Spanish, since adequate landing craft were not available and the first troops had to wade ashore in four feet of water. By noon on September 8, several low coastal hills had been occupied, with the Spanish suffering only some 50 casualties. However, no immediate effort was made to exploit this initial triumph. Though within a few days 10,000 men had been landed, the expeditionary force entrenched itself after advancing only about a mile inland.

As soon as the landing had been made secure, Primo de Rivera returned his attention to Tetuán, even switching some of the shock troops back to the west. On September 11, three columns set out to dislodge the Moorish forces south of the Protectorate's capital. Within two days the warriors who had pinned down the advance post at Ben Karikh were scattered, and the pressure greatly lessened. Afterward, in a review of one of the Tercio units, the dictator was rather shocked to see severed Moorish heads impaled on the ends of bayonets. This was not uncommon practice among the shock troops, but it did not coincide with the dictator's sense of civilized warfare. He issued a stern reproof, and in subsequent campaigns mutilation of the enemy dead was much rarer.

The advance inland from Alhucemas finally began on September 22, with two Banderas of the Tercio leading the way and several companies of Regulares covering the left flank. The Spanish were somewhat disconcerted to find that Krim had gotten hold of several relatively modern French 75 mm. cannon, which outranged the Spanish guns. However, the Berbers had few such guns and scarcely knew how to use them against the much greater volume of Spanish artillery. Krim had never been able to organize his forces into regular units, and now they began to desert in large numbers. The Berber leader did his best to entrench them in the coastal hills; dead Moorish artillerists were later found chained to their guns.[39] But the most desperate measures did not avail against the well-supported, reasonably well-organized

Spanish advance. Though heavy Spanish casualties were suffered in the first week of the breakout, the town of Axdir was seized on October 2. With their arms trade strangled and ammunition running low, the rebels gave ground rapidly. By the end of October, the French had rewon all the territory lost in the south, while within the Riff itself Krim's forces had dwindled to only a few thousand poorly armed irregulars.[40]

Early in November, Primo de Rivera held a victory celebration in Tetuán. In a grandiloquent address, he likened the landing at Alhucemas to Trafalgar and to the capture of Tunis in 1535, then awarded himself the Gran Cruz de San Fernando. An extensive round of new promotions ensued.

On February 6, 1926, a new Franco-Spanish accord was signed to coordinate efforts in the coming year. By that time, most of the Djebalan kabyles had submitted to Spanish rule; Primo's prophecy seemed to be coming true. However, Krim's forces in the Riff and Gomara were not yet fully subdued. His lieutenant in the Xauen area, el-Kheriro, made new attacks on the Spanish positions south of Tetuán in February, despite the shortage of ammunition. This was to some extent a strategic diversion, for Krim had learned of the new Franco-Spanish talks and hoped, by throwing his main weight against the Spanish, to encourage dissension or a relaxation of French efforts. In April, he met French and Spanish representatives at Uxda, in the northeast corner of Morocco, but he still refused to surrender.

During the following month a Spanish advance toward Xauen scattered most of el-Kheriro's followers, while a large column under the veteran Castro Girona moved southeast from Axdir to break up what remained of Krim's harca.[41] Soon Krim found the Riff too small a zone in which to elude the European forces. He vented his rage by murdering several dozen Spanish prisoners who had been held in the hills; then, before the month was out, he surrendered to French forces some distance to the south. The French authorities subsequently decided to exile him to the island of Réunion.

The surrender of Abd el-Krim did not mean the disbanding of all hostile forces in the Protectorate, and Spanish operations continued on a reduced scale there for another year. A column under Major Capaz traversed the Gomara district west of the Riff, while another force from Larache completed occupation of the southern Djebala.[42] By 1927, the only remaining pocket of resistance lay in the northeastern Riff. In March, the Temsamani kabyle attacked a column under

Colonel Emilio Mola that had been moving in to disarm the northern tribesmen. The Spanish detachment was pinned down, and a sudden late snowfall made it difficult to send relief through the roadless surrounding territory. Nevertheless, Mola's troops withstood the assault, and in April two new columns moving from east and west broke the last remaining resistance. Sanjurjo, who had been appointed High Commissioner soon after the Alhucemas triumph, was able to report on July 10, 1927, that the pacification of the Protectorate was complete.[43] By the end of 1927, most of the soldiers who had participated in the campaigns of 1925–26 had been returned to Spain. In the following year, the total armed forces in Spanish Morocco were reduced to 61,000; nearly half of these were Moorish recruits.

On December 15, 1925, Primo de Rivera had consolidated the government of both civil and military affairs in Spanish Africa under one directory (Dirección General de Marruecos y Colonias). Throughout the crucial operations of 1924–25, he had been aware of the possible political and financial consequences of renewing the Moroccan offensive, and had hoped to avoid the waste and confusion that had attended past campaigns. Never enthusiastic about colonial enterprise, he had no illusions about making a showplace of the Protectorate. In letters to Sanjurjo, he emphasized the importance of holding down expenses and made it clear that the Spanish administration would not be able to do much for social and economic development.[44] During the next years, a few good roads and a handful of schools were built. The sanitary commission vaccinated many natives against smallpox, and was able to reduce the incidence of syphilis. A new system was established whereby officers acting as military *interventores* were assigned to almost every kabyle as observers and instructors. This brought the Spanish administration into closer contact with the ordinary Moroccan and enabled the High Commissioner's office to collect a certain amount of information. In general, however, Spanish administration was less direct than in the French zone. Scarcely extending beyond military occupation, its net effect on the local population was negligible. On the other hand, after 1927 the officers proved generally correct and well-behaved, and did not try to interfere with local mores, so the Spanish administration was in some ways easier for the Moors to tolerate than the more rigorous French system to the south.

It might be argued that, in the long run, affairs in the Moroccan Protectorate had a greater effect upon Spain than Spain had on the Moorish tribesmen. The political imbroglio arising from Annual was the main cause of the overthrow of constitutional government in Spain. Later, the shock troops that were maintained for the security of the Protectorate formed the spearhead of the forces that attempted to overthrow the Second Republic in 1936. Without the special conditioning provided by the Moroccan experience, it is hard to see how events could have taken the shape they did in Spain in 1923 and 1936.

It should be stressed that the Spanish Army performed better in the campaigns of 1925–27 than at any time since 1860. Part of the credit was due to Primo de Rivera, who made a serious effort to reorganize the forces in the Protectorate. Moreover, he hastened the emergence of a group of regimental and brigade officers, men who began to assume a dominant position in Army command and provided leadership distinctly superior to that of their predecessors. Chief among them was the veteran Sanjurjo, only about five feet two inches tall and not impressive to look at, but a man of tremendous physical endurance and bravery. Good-natured, talkative, and generous, he was extremely fond of cards and women, and—it was said—of wine. At any rate, his warm, human qualities endeared him to officers and troops alike. Though no military genius, Sanjurjo was a sound field commander, especially in the handling of units at the brigade level. He deserves a good share of credit for the Spanish successes of 1925–26, since he pressed for complete victory even when the dictator himself wanted to hold back and avoid losses.

Perhaps second in importance was Franco, who in February 1926 was promoted to the rank of brigadier, thus becoming, at the age of 33, one of the youngest generals in postwar Europe. Also noteworthy was the irritable, ambitious, but intelligent Colonel Manuel Goded, who did much of Sanjurjo's staff work. A number of officers had shone in the Regulares: the clever, literary Colonel Emilio Mola, not at all flashy but a good organizer and something of an anomaly among africanistas because he was six feet tall; the five-foot-two-inch Major José Enrique Varela ("Varelita"), lacking in technical education but a shrewdly intuitive field commander; and Major Agustín Muñoz Grandes, a stoical, competent officer who knew how to handle Moorish troops and enjoyed a reputation for complete devotion to duty. These africanista veterans constituted an active, determined nucleus that would in large measure dominate the Spanish military during the decades that followed.

CHAPTER TWELVE

Primo de Rivera and the Army

THE PACIFICATION of the Moroccan Protectorate constituted the Spanish Army's first major success in fifty years. Yet, while leading the military to this triumph, Primo de Rivera experienced anxious moments in maintaining his personal control over a restive Officer Corps. Soon after establishing the dictatorship, he made a number of appointments and changes to guarantee command of the Army and its organizational structure. By naming only brigadiers to the Directory, he kept the senior, more influential generals out of direct participation in government. He also drastically reorganized the Classifying Junta for generals so that it would control all promotions to and within that rank. Heretofore, the Classifying Junta had been composed of the only full captain general, Weyler, and four lieutenant generals selected from among retirees—a setup designed to keep it free from special interests. But Primo replaced the four incumbent lieutenant generals with two new ones of his own choice and one major general who was to serve as secretary. All these new appointees—who happened to be, respectively, head of the king's Military Household, head of the Supreme War Council, and the second in command of the General Staff—were on the active list, and were not immune to what might be termed professional conflicts of interest. Contrary to custom, Primo himself attended the first sessions of the new Junta, and arranged for the Minister of War—a purely political appointee—to attend also and, when present, assume the presidency of the Junta.[1]

The way in which promotions were to be handled under Primo was shown two months later when two vacancies occurred at the rank of major general. In most cases, such vacancies were filled on the basis of seniority, but at the beginning of 1924 the Army's two senior brigadiers, López de Ochoa and Sosa, both happened to be officers of moderately liberal political views. López de Ochoa had been commander of the Barcelona Infantry garrison while Primo de Rivera was Captain General there, and, like a good many other liberals, had supported the pronunciamiento as the only means of cutting through the political tangle. According to Ochoa, Primo personally promised him, before the state visit to Italy, that he would not be passed over when the next regular vacancy occurred at the rank of major general. However, as the dictatorship became entrenched, Primo grew concerned about the danger of independent attitudes among the generals, and the dictator's principal supporters in the Army were scarcely eager to see officers of liberal views promoted to senior rank. Consequently, the Classifying Junta passed over both López de Ochoa and Sosa in filling the new vacancies in January 1924. Ochoa, who in earlier years had occasionally spoken out directly for liberal ideals, was informed that, although there was no question regarding his professional competence, he could not be promoted because of his record of "indiscipline."[2] Moreover, his name was taken completely off the seniority list, which effectively ended his career.

A subsequent decree gave the Classifying Junta special powers to collect and employ personal and political information about candidates, to draw up new lists of officers for promotion by special selection, and to eliminate others who might be deemed undesirable.[3] The Junta's senior member, Weyler, was eliminated at the end of 1925 because of his personal opposition to the dictator. The powers of the Junta were further extended by a royal decree of July 4, 1926, which ruled that those passed over in seniority by promotion need not be told the reasons for such action, and declared that no appeals would be heard.[4]

It was not, however, liberal officers alone who were restricted by Primo; he also kept independent-minded conservatives and royalists on short rein as well. For example, only a few months after the pronunciamiento, Cavalcanti and several other generals in Madrid began to grow disillusioned with the dictator. Fearing that he had only pretended to renounce abandonismo, they resumed secret conversations. They were arrested and court-martialed at the beginning of 1924. Cavalcanti was absolved, perhaps because of his favor with the king, but three other generals were sentenced to brief terms of confinement.

The dictator was attempting to strike a balance between africanistas and junteros, but africanistas were made nervous by the fact that the secretary of the Military Directory, Brigadier General Godofredo Nouvilas, had been the last head of the Infantry Junta. On December 31, 1923, the Directory denounced a foreign news article, picked up by a Pamplona newspaper, which stated that the "Juntas de Defensa" were "pressuring" the government to speed up the prosecution of those responsible for the Moroccan disasters. No such pressuring was possible, said the Directory, because the Juntas had ceased to exist.[5] Formally this was correct, but a large minority of the Officer Corps in the peninsula was still under juntero influence—a factor that continued to complicate Army politics.

A number of cases involving dereliction of duty in Morocco were handled during the first months of 1924,[6] but the dictator did not intend to let the work of the Supreme Council go too far. Two new generals were introduced to membership without the prior consent of the president, General Aguilera. This violated customary procedure and led to Aguilera's resignation. The Army's senior lieutenant general was a strong legalist, as his posture in 1923 had shown, and he had never approved of the establishment of a Military Directory. The dictator patched things up temporarily by replacing Aguilera with Weyler, the only general of higher rank and seniority. But another step to reorganize the military hierarchy was taken a few weeks later, on March 27, when Primo dissolved the advisory security council, the "Junta for the Defense of the Kingdom," and transferred its functions to the Military Directory.

The trial of Berenguer, Navarro, and other officers implicated in the Annual disaster was formally begun by the Supreme War Council on June 19. After four days of deliberation, Navarro was absolved, and relatively light penalties were given to several other officers, but Berenguer was sentenced to separation from active service.

The trial coincided with the first period of major unrest in the Army during the dictatorship. This discontent was due not merely to the apprehensions of the africanistas over the dictator's Moroccan policy, but also to the qualms of senior generals like Weyler and Aguilera about the besmirching of military honor by the establishment of a military dictatorship. That this uneasiness was shared by at least a few of the junior officers was indicated in a letter sent to the dictator on April 20, 1924, by Engineers Captain José Martínez de Aragón of the Vitoria garrison. It read as follows:

The most distinguished president of the Military Directory.

My Dear Sir:

When, on September 13 of last year, you rebelled against the government, I sent telephone messages to the Prime Minister and the Minister of War, telling them that I was not rebelling but was at the orders of the legally constituted government.

My understanding of the [function of the] Army is totally different from your own.

I continually read in the newspapers your statements that public opinion and the entire Army support what you have done. It may be that public opinion and the immense majority of the Army are supporters of your acts, but I request that, when you make further statements to this effect, you specify that all the Army supports you save the Captain of Engineers Don José Martínez de Aragón.[7]

When this missive received no reply, its author mailed a copy of the original in a second letter on May 12. The dictator had, in fact, ordered a court-martial of the writer after receiving the first letter, but the military courts were very slow to take up the case. After receiving the second letter, Primo personally ordered that Martínez be confined for two months in a castle at Mahón in the Balearics. The preliminary deposition made by the accused before his court-martial said in part:

That he understands and affirms that the Officer Corps can never, under any interpretation, use the soldiers and their weapons to coerce the nation.

That in order to require discipline and obedience of the troops, and to apply to them with all necessary moral authority the penalties established by the Code of Military Justice, it is necessary, in fact indispensable, that the Officer Corps absolutely respect and fulfill and never in the slightest diverge from what is specified in the Code, which applies to everyone, from the highest officer to the last soldier—transgression or negligence being the graver the higher the rank of whoever may be guilty of it. . . .

That the Army must always remain subordinate to the nation. It would be well to recall that when Daoiz and Velarde [heroes of the anti-French rising in 1808] rebelled, it was after being insistently urged to do so by the people of Madrid, who had already raised the flag of Spanish independence by themselves.

And finally, to complete his reply . . . , he wants to make clear that there can be no crime or military fault at all in the fact of not wanting to rebel, and that to make this known is not only not a crime, but is instead an obligation.[8]

Faced with this logic, the court-martial ruled that Martínez de Aragón was guilty of no crime but rather of an error in comportment that could be corrected through disciplinary measures by the Captain General of his district. The prosecution appealed this verdict, and the Supreme Council finally sentenced Martínez to a year's imprisonment. But Primo, shortly before his first visit to Morocco, made a gesture toward the incipient opposition by declaring a general amnesty for all those convicted of political or military misbehavior since the establishment of the Directory. This amnesty brought freedom to Martínez, as well as remission of the mild penalties imposed on Berenguer and others implicated in the Annual affair.

None of this impressed Cavalcanti, who had been appointed head of Don Alfonso's Military Household and was holding secret conversations with military and civilian enemies of the dictator. Cavalcanti was himself mainly concerned with forcing Primo's hand in Morocco, but his negotiations with certain liberal politicians—the very men against whom Cavalcanti had been conspiring only a year earlier— may have been encouraged by the king as means of reestablishing royal contact with the civilian liberals who had been so abruptly ejected from public affairs. It was rumored that Cavalcanti was even talking with Republicans and leftists. Primo de Rivera called him into his office in September, shortly before the dictator was to leave Madrid to assume full command of the operations in Morocco. Soon afterward, Cavalcanti issued a statement denying all the gossip about his conversations with enemies of the dictatorship. He then was sent on a military inspection tour of the Balkans.[9]

A few weeks later, a banquet held in Madrid to honor a minor literary figure was attended by a number of liberal politicians. General Dámaso Berenguer was also invited. When the toasts were offered, the gathering began to take on the character of a protest meeting against the dictatorship. The presence of Berenguer in such a group so soon after Cavalcanti's negotiations aroused Primo's ire. Berenguer was arrested, and on October 31 was sentenced to six months' enforced residence for "inciting to rebellion."[10]

Tension between the dictator and the military in 1924 was not due solely to Primo's plans for withdrawal and retrenchment, but also to growing dissatisfaction among the home garrisons over the use of the Army to sustain a political dictatorship. Resentment focused on the hundreds of *delegados militares gubernativos* appointed to oversee local government, and also on the fact that local commanders of military districts were sometimes given the additional post of provincial civil governor. The original justification for the creation of the post of delegado was the need to clean up local corruption and end the cacique system. It was true that in some provinces the power structure had been overturned by the coming of the delegados; but in a good many others, the delegados found it easier to ratify the old local hierarchy. In many communities, the old interests and coteries continued to dominate after a few minor compromises and outward changes had been made.

A case in point was Murcia, the seat of La Cierva's political organization. The delegado for the coastal city of Cartagena was Lt. Col. Joaquín Tirado, who played a key role in recruiting support for the 1923 pronunciamiento among the garrisons of Castellón and Valencia. Tirado believed that the principal mission of the dictatorship must be the dismantling of the cacique system. He removed the previous municipal officials and made arrangements for their judicial prosecution. The colonel was infuriated to learn that his colleagues at Murcia, the capital city of the province, were doing no more than shift around and ratify the old La Cierva politicians. His complaints to Madrid accomplished nothing, and, as the months passed, Tirado began to drift away from the dictatorship.[11]

A similar but more important case was that of Granada. The chief delegado for this province was a senior brigadier, listless and without political acumen, who left the old cliques undisturbed. Conversely, the delegado for the Granada city of Baza, an Artillery major named Claudín, rooted out the old politicians and attempted to shake up the local oligarchy. This caused such strong protest that Claudín was removed.[12]

It was becoming clear that the appointment of military men to political positions accomplished little and merely compromised officers with the corruption that the Army had previously taken such pleasure in denouncing. After Claudín's dismissal, many of the Infantry officers in the Granada garrison protested to the Directory against using the military in political administration. A representative was sent to Madrid, where the Chief of the Section of Artillery insisted to Primo that Claudín, a ranking Artillery officer, could not be treated in such fashion.[13] The dictator partially backed down, and sent Claudín to a suitable command in Morocco.

The Director General of Local Administration under the Directory was a young Maurist lawyer, José Calvo Sotelo. He received a steady stream of complaints from civilians in the provinces about the delegados' inexperience, arbitrariness, or simple lack of finesse. He was also aware that the bulk of the Officer Corps resented the reputation that such appointments were giving the Army. On October 19, 1924, Calvo wrote a letter to the dictator emphasizing that the delegados ought gradually to be replaced by civilian officials, until military personnel had been entirely withdrawn from local administration.[14] The combination of complaint and suggestion had its effect: by the following year, Primo had begun to replace delegados with civilian appointees in certain provinces.

Another aspect of the Army's involvement in government under conditions of martial law was its use of the military courts in the prosecution of those accused of perpetrating "armed rebellion." This procedure, under which many anarchists were sentenced, was not discontinued until May 1925. The first major scandal occurred late in 1924, after a bloody affray near the border crossing of Vera del Bidasoa, at the foot of the western Pyrenees. On November 7 of that year, some thirty émigré Spanish workers who had been distributing leftist literature on the Spanish side of the frontier became involved in a skirmish with the Carabineros (border guards). Two of the guards were killed, but the remainder, with the aid of French police, captured most of the workers involved. More than thirty former émigrés were tried before a military court for "armed rebellion," but since it was not at all clear that the authors of the gunplay had been captured, some of the defendants were absolved and the remainder were given light sentences. This infuriated the Carabineros, who demanded punishment for the murderers of their comrades. In response, the dictator dismissed the Army's legal prosecutor in the case, imprisoned for thirty days the three officers who composed the tribunal, and sent the case before the Supreme Council. The Army's highest court quickly sentenced three of the defendants to death, though it seemed more than likely that they were merely being used as scapegoats. The full facts of this case have never been brought to light, but evidence suggests the presence of agents provocateurs as well as the participation of some Carabineros in smuggling operations.[15]

Despite several similar scandals, opposition to the dictatorship was restricted to very small groups. The CNT and certain other leftists had been actively working against the regime from its inception, but were powerless alone and easily controlled by force. Though the professional politicians were alienated, the middle classes, who benefited from prosperity and public order, seemed content. Government censorship quickly earned the ire of many intellectuals, but there was no widespread resentment of the fact that the dictator had forgotten his pledge of a 90-day government.

The first Moroccan successes of 1925 raised Primo de Rivera's stock in the Army. However, they also magnified the importance of the africanistas, and reawakened the jealousy of rival officers. In the spring of 1925, the juntero element centered its hostility on the one-armed Millán Astray, who was especially hated because he had won so much publicity. He was scheduled to give a lecture on Spanish military organization in the Madrid Army-Navy Center on May 4, and it was rumored that afterward he was to be named Director of the Infantry Academy. The junteros raised such a protest that the lecture had to be canceled, and no more was heard about the proposed appointment.[16] The virulent criticism to which he was subjected was perhaps what influenced Millán Astray to ask for reassignment to Morocco in 1926. There he suffered his last mutilation—the loss of his right eye—in one of the concluding operations. His enemies in the Officer Corps then circulated the rumor that this wound, and most of the previous ones, had been self-inflicted in an effort to gain prestige. (In addition to blocking the career of Millán Astray, the same elements struggled to prevent Franco's promotion to brigadier at the beginning of 1926.[17] But by this time the junteros had no more than a negative nuisance value, and, lacking the organization they had enjoyed in their heyday, could no longer attempt to control Army policy.)

Though several of the senior generals, especially Weyler and Aguilera, were bitterly opposed to the dictator, the only officer who tried to organize opposition within the Army itself in 1925 was Segundo García, a colonel on the Reserve list. Like most of the Reservists, García had worked his way up from the ranks, winning a commission for his service as a sergeant in the Philippine campaign of 1895–97. He had a reputation for high integrity, had earned several decorations, and had educated himself as a lawyer in order to be licensed for the Army's juridical corps. The Reservists had taken little part in the political machinations that had rent the Army in the past decade, but García held strongly liberal and constitutionalist convictions and believed that the time had come to organize opinion against the dictatorship's distortion of the Army's role. On the pretext of raising funds for the families of soldiers killed in Morocco, he invited nearly 300 officers to a meeting in Madrid on the night of January 6, 1925, and broached his plans. During the next few months, he received scattered messages of support, including some from NCO's, and

established contact with avowed opponents of the dictator such as
López de Ochoa. The police were aware of these activities almost from
the beginning, and finally cracked down in May 1925, arresting García, Ochoa, several other officers, and eleven NCO's. The terms of imprisonment subsequently imposed were commuted, in one of the dictator's characteristic gestures of leniency. García's experience did not
daunt him, and by the closing months of the year he was conspiring
more actively than ever.

For the time being, the relatively obscure García was ignored, but
the dictator did move to unburden himself of his bitterest critic in the
Army hierarchy, Valeriano Weyler. Though he was by this time
eighty-three years old and growing feeble, Weyler's spirit still flamed
on occasion—especially when he thought of Primo de Rivera's usurpa-
tion of authority. Heretofore the dictator had responded by ignoring
him or by prodding him with minor vexations,[18] but when in October
1925 he learned that Weyler had been criticizing him in public conversation, he removed the aged general from his last major post, that
of Chief of the General Staff. Two months later, on December 15,
Primo gratified the animosity felt by most other Corps toward the General Staff when he dissolved its organization as a separate unit and
divided it into a series of planning sections, one of which was assigned
to each of the Corps composing the Army.[19]

The closing months of 1925 brought the pinnacle of Primo de
Rivera's success. The Moroccan nightmare was coming to an end, civil
order had been restored in Spain itself, and the economy had achieved
a new height of prosperity. Had he opened the year 1926 with elections to a constituent assembly that would draft the structure of a
genuinely democratic and orderly constitutional monarchy, Primo de
Rivera would undoubtedly live in Spanish history as one of the peninsula's greatest modern benefactors. The dictator had probably been
sincere in his original statements that the regime was a transitory arrangement, but during the course of two years he had become intoxi-
cated by his own apparent success: what he had done with so little
logic and calculation might be continued indefinitely, until even
greater laurels were won. Therefore, rather than resigning, Primo
proposed to reorganize the dictatorship for a lengthened tenure of
power. The king may not have been entirely pleased, but he had identified himself with the dictator in almost all his own public statements,
and could scarcely have relished the alternatives to a continuation of

Primo's regime—a difficult transition to the old system or, worse, the establishment of a constituent Cortes.

But if the dictatorship were to continue, its crudely military structure would have to be modified. In the autumn months of 1925, basking in the glow of the victories in Morocco, Primo became convinced of this fact. Some military leaders expressed their agreement. The Marqués de Magaz, speaking for the Navy, strongly urged political change, and indicated the desirability of a new arrangement that entailed less direct political responsibility for the military. Most members of the Directory made no political contribution of their own to the government, for, with the exceptions of Magaz, Martínez Anido, and Jordana (son of the former High Commissioner), they were political nonentities who had never made any impression on the public.

Under the influence of these ideas, Primo dissolved the Military Directory on December 3, 1925, after his return from Morocco, and inaugurated the "civilian" phase of the dictatorship. His first regular Cabinet, however, contained only five civilians among its nine ministers. Four generals assumed regular Cabinet responsibilities—chief among them Martínez Anido, who, as Minister of the Interior, was to continue the police repression. Anido was elevated in rank above the other Cabinet members to the post of vice-premier of the Council of Ministers. Shortly afterward, the number and functions of the delegados were greatly reduced. A royal decree of March 20, 1926, limited their number to no more than three in any province, and placed them under the direct orders of the civil governors. The four district garrison commanders who had also held the post of civil governor were relieved of that office.

This reorganization was designed to permit continuation of the dictatorship for an indefinite period, yet Primo de Rivera still denied that he had any wish to supplant the constitution, and repeated that its enforcement would remain suspended only temporarily, "without any intention of changing or departing from its spirit."[20] To a considerable degree, the regime was coasting on the economic prosperity of the mid-1920's, which was bringing the Spanish people the highest standard of living in their history—a standard that would not be equaled for the next three decades. The government undertook a public works program, extended certain credit facilities at a lower rate of interest, and established *comités paritarios* (labor arbitration committees) representing both capital and labor. These were organized into twenty-seven different corporations, and were to some extent inspired by Mussolini's Corporate State, but the ethos of the Spanish economic administration was distinct.[21] In many regions, an agreement was made with the Socialist UGT that Socialist trade union representatives might be elected to the *comités,* thus enabling the UGT to retain much of its independence, increase its membership, and gain substantial improvements in wages and working conditions. Until the end of 1929, at least, the regime continued to enjoy the acquiescence, if not the genuine support, of most of the public.

But whereas in the first months of the dictatorship Primo had frequently listened to the advice of others, by 1926 he was talking incessantly himself, and was often unwilling to give others a chance to speak. On certain days he worked unrelentingly—up to twelve hours or more—but on others he ignored his responsibilities or assigned them to his subordinates, some of whom were badly chosen. Moreover, the fact that the demilitarization of the political structure of the dictatorship was not going to lead to greater freedom was made clear in the first months of 1926 by new decrees that extended some of the government's legislative and administrative powers.

If the regime had few organized opponents, there was widespread resentment of it among the elite. Intellectuals and writers continued to chafe under government censorship. Among the military, the lieutenant generals had never reconciled themselves to the arbitrariness of the regime and its tampering with the legal hierarchy, either in the Army (which was most important to them) or, to a lesser degree, in the government.

By the time Primo effected his transition from Military Directory to cabinet government, Colonel García had broadened his plans. Since his arrest, García had come to feel that the simple overthrow of the dictator would not be enough. Too much had happened for the country simply to go back to the pre-1923 system. He foresaw the need to call the long-demanded constituent Cortes, which many had thought Primo was about to convoke in 1923. But García also recognized that most of the opponents of the regime in the Army were not strongly anti-monarchist.[22] Meanwhile, another conspiratorial committee was being organized in Madrid and had managed to attract the interest of the Army's two senior generals, Weyler and Aguilera. Early in 1926, contact was established between these elements, which were strongest at Madrid, Valencia, and the Cartagena naval base.

The small group of "respectable" civilian opponents of the dictatorship, composed mainly of certain politicians prominent under the old regime, was not slow to get in touch with the military conspirators, and by the spring of 1926 plans for a revolt began to take shape. It would nominally be led by Aguilera and Weyler, but most of the political planning would be done by a handful of veteran liberal politicians such as Melquiades Alvarez, Alejandro Lerroux, and the Conde de Romanones. The Captain General of Valladolid was said to have offered his support, and portions of the CNT were willing to collaborate. Backing came from such varied sources—ranging from Republicans to monarchist oligarchs to young Reserve officers to an octogenarian captain general—that afterward Primo de Rivera not inaccurately described the conspiracy as a "mosaic." The plan was to center the revolt in Valencia, which was easily accessible to exiles and equidistant from the three key cities of Madrid, Zaragoza, and Barcelona. The military rebels in Madrid were to try to seize control of all the barracks in the capital, installing one of their number, the ultraliberal but erratic Riquelme, as nominal Captain General. Romanones and Melquiades Alvarez would call upon the king, urging him, in order to spare bloodshed, to withdraw authority from the dictator and appoint Aguilera as Prime Minister.

On the evening of June 24, 1926, the "Night of San Juan," the rebels' manifesto was read to a small group in the Madrid Military Casino. It declared that Primo had not consulted the Army before launching the 1923 pronunciamiento, but had used the military institution for his own purposes.

Taking advantage of censorship, it [the dictatorship] makes people believe that public opinion sustains it and that it is the Army which most encourages it to continue. . . .

The Army cannot tolerate the use of its flag and its name to maintain a regime that despoils the people of their rights. . . . Without liberty, no people can live, nor easily attain prosperity and greatness. Believing this to be so, the Army has always shown itself, in the most brilliant periods of its history, a resolute and enthusiastic supporter of public liberties. It fought for them unceasingly against absolutism during the past century, and with its energy and blood both embraced and installed constitutional and parliamentary ways. To pretend that it could not forget its glorious tradition and lend itself as an instrument to enslave the citizenry would be equivalent to dishonoring it.[23]

There was much coming and going at the various Madrid barracks, with noisy movement of trucks and motorcycles. Yet the expected support was not forthcoming, and on the following day Aguilera and

García drove to Valencia, where sympathy was supposed to be much stronger. However, after learning of the situation in Madrid, the Valencian officers also began to withdraw their support. By the night of June 25 the situation was desperate, for the police were closing in. Aguilera was nonetheless determined to carry out the gesture of rebellion, even if it were with only 20 or 30 men. As a last chance, he went north up the coast road from Valencia to Tarragona, where the military commander was his good friend General Domingo Batet, a man of wealthy upper-middle-class background and liberal sympathies. Soon after he arrived, both he and Batet were arrested by the police. The "Conspiracy of San Juan" failed before it had even begun.[24]

Though five weeks later he was the object of an isolated assassination attempt in Barcelona, the dictator pretended to be undisturbed by opposition and resentment. He personally administered his own kind of subjective Andalusian justice, taking great relish in scaling the fines according to each conspirator's ability to pay. Romanones, by far the wealthiest, was fined 500,000 pesetas, Aguilera 200,000, Weyler—who said that he had never actually signed the manifesto but agreed with it completely—100,000, and a certain member of the CNT, only 1,000. Formal sentences for the military conspirators were announced in April 1927. García was expelled from the Army and had his prison term lengthened by eight years. Four other officers were sentenced to six years each, but Aguilera, in deference to his rank, received a term of only six months.[25]

Support among the Officer Corps for the San Juan conspiracy had been minimal, but the dictator's worst conflict with his fellow officers was just beginning. This had to do with that old bone of contention, promotion by méritos, and with the special customs of the Artillery Corps. It was only natural that Primo de Rivera should be opposed to the closed scale, for his entire career had been based on special promotion. The dissolution of the original Classifying Junta had been carried out so that the dictator would be able to control at will promotions in the senior ranks, and with new successes in Morocco Primo planned to extend these powers across a very broad range. By 1926, there were rumors that the dictator was preparing a new decree that would open promotion scales in all sections of the Officer Corps. Such rumors roused deep apprehension among the Artillery officers, who were determined to maintain their separate scale. They were gravely offended by a gesture made early in 1926 by General Correa, head of the Artillery Section in the Ministry of War. To feed the dictator's vanity, Correa endeavored to award Primo the special rank of colonel in the Artillery Corps (commissions within the Artillery *per se* never extending beyond that rank). The Artillerists raised such a protest that Correa had to desist, to the dictator's manifest annoyance.

A royal decree of June 9 had declared that an open scale of promotion would henceforth exist in all sections of the Army. This ruling was made retroactive to the beginning of 1925 for officers who had been awarded promotion by méritos but had refused owing to the oaths sworn in their particular Corps.[26] Article Two of this decree relieved officers from such obligations, and Article Three declared that anyone who refused special promotion would be appointed to that rank anyway or receive seniority commensurate with it. Resistance in the Artillery was almost unanimous. The Engineers and Sanitary Corps officers, who also had a closed scale, joined in the protest, though less openly. Thirty senior Artillery officers in the Madrid district met on June 12 to consider means of defense.[27] In his first interview with their representatives two days later, Primo hinted that if a single officer asked to pass to the Reserve because of this conflict, the government would resign, Spain would return to political chaos, and the nation would then see where the blame lay.[28] At the time, Primo was not in a good position to crack down because of the imminence of the San Juan conspiracy, about which the government was well informed. Therefore, a compromise was negotiated verbally with General Correa on June 17. According to the report given by Correa to the assembly of Artillery officers on the following day, Primo agreed that méritos would be awarded in only a few of the most extraordinary cases, that officers so promoted would not be placed in command of colleagues who had greater seniority, and that new regulations would be worked out before October 1, after which further méritos would be abolished and all complaints would be heard by the Third Chamber of the Supreme Council.[29] The king was said to have intervened in the settlement, for he was eager to avoid conflict with the Army and as desirous as ever of exercising more personal influence on national events.

A month after the conspiracy, the dictatorship felt strong enough to bend the facultative Corps to its will. On July 26, a decree was issued which declared that after October 1 all promotion by *méritos de guerra* would cease, but that a certain number of vacancies at each rank—

a quarter of those to general, a fifth of those to colonel, a sixth of those to major, and a tenth of those to captain—would be filled by special selection. A separate classifying junta would make proposals for such promotions within the Artillery Corps, but final decisions would be made by the War Minister after receiving reports on the "social attitudes" of each candidate—a veiled form of political investigation.[30]

This outraged Artillery officers, who not unnaturally felt that the dictator had broken his promise once the threat of the *sanjuanada* had been overcome. There was special resentment because nothing was said about referring conflicts to the Third Chamber of the Supreme Council of Military Justice. A few days later, when the Ministers of War and of the Navy made an inspection visit to Minorca, the Artillery officers in the local garrison refused to attend the ceremonies. This brought the dismissal of the local commander, General Miguel Cabanellas, and of his second in command, though Cabanellas had been a leader in organizing support in Morocco for the 1923 pronunciamiento.

On July 31, in Barcelona, Primo de Rivera denied that he had ever made a binding agreement with the Artillery. "Undeniably," he affirmed, "there has never been any such pact."[31] During the week following, General Correa, Chief of the Artillery Section in the War Ministry, retired and was replaced by General Fabriciano Haro, who sought to formalize the agreement as the Artillery understood it by sending the dictator a written memorandum. In a letter of August 10, Primo replied that all this was incorrect, and went into great detail about the errors he said were involved in the Artillerists' version of the problem.[32]

There was a second meeting of Artillery officers in Madrid on August 20, in which it was decided to resist the new regulations to the absolute limit, either under Haro or, if he were arrested, under his successor. On the 21st, Haro wrote again to the dictator, asking if he would be willing to make a binding compromise to protect the Artillery's interests. Primo's reply four days later indicated that he regarded further opposition as intolerable and intended to go ahead with the open scale.[33]

The esprit de corps of the Artillery officers remained high, and Haro was instructed by their representatives to present the requests for retirement of all those Artillery officers who would have been promoted under the July 26 decree. As soon as he did so, the government placed him under arrest. On September 4, the *Diario Oficial del Min-*

isterio de la Guerra published an order to apply the full measures specified in the original decree. When this was read, Artillery officers throughout the peninsula ordered their troops to retire to barracks. The following day, the government declared martial law and suspended from active duty all Artillery officers save those serving in Morocco.[34] For a time, the Spanish Artillery almost ceased to exist.

Don Alfonso, vacationing in the north, was taken by surprise. He would apparently have preferred another compromise, and yet things had gone so far that he had little recourse save to back the dictator. In this whole affair, Primo had been too clever for his own good. He had thought to soothe and manipulate Artillery opinion while carrying out his original plan, but his compromising, procrastinating tactics had made it easier for the Artillery to organize resistance. The king did hope to offer some way out, and on his way back to Madrid he stopped for a private audience with Artillery representatives. According to the Artillerists, Don Alfonso told them that he disapproved of Primo's policy, that it had been made without consulting him (which was more or less true), and that he was going to ask for the dictator's resignation.[35]

Meanwhile, the government had speedily arrested scores of senior Artillery officers and ordered that all Artillery barracks be taken over by the Infantry. The only resistance came in the Artillery unit at Pamplona, where a young officer and a soldier were killed. On the same day that the Corps was dissolved (September 5), the dictator made an appeal for the support of public opinion in suppressing military rebellion, and by the late afternoon of September 6 the government was in control of all Artillery barracks.[36]

In the measures that followed, a direct effort was made to break the unity of the Corps. Only a minority of the officers were actually punished. Many were sent to provincial exile rather than to military prisons, while the *Diario Oficial* and the civilian press periodically published lists of those who were to be excepted. Some sixty-three were eventually condemned to terms of imprisonment, none particularly lengthy, but in the meantime only enough Artillery officers were retained on active duty to operate basic facilities. In late September, a royal decree stated that those senior officers whom it was judged impossible to restore to active duty would be allowed to pass to the Reserve. A series of newspaper reports indicating that the government hoped to carry out the Artillery reorganization as gently as possible added to the climate of uncertainty. A subsequent decree of November 17 reduced the size of the Corps from 37 to 31 regiments, arguing that it was vital to lower military expenses.[37] Moreover, a new commission, the Dirección Superior de la Industria Militar, was established under the Ministry of War to replace the near-monopoly previously enjoyed by the Artillery in directing Spanish military industry. Finally, a deadline was set in mid-December by which time all officers who desired reinstatement must petition the government. Hundreds had already done so, but approximately 800 officers (about half the Corps) waited until the last possible day. On December 13, the *Diario Oficial* began to publish lists of officers who had been reinstated. These were ordered in hierarchical fashion, according to the dictatorship's new standards of promotion and seniority, and provoked further grinding of teeth among Artillery traditionalists. A final decree of December 31 canceled any further prosecution of the rebels, and unofficial promises were given that no further reprisals would be made against the Corps as a whole.[38] Though opponents of the dictatorship had hailed the Artillery revolt, it had not enjoyed widespread support among the public. Political apathy still prevailed amid the economic prosperity of 1926; moreover, the Artillery Corps had always been considered something of a snobbish clan. Since the interests they were defending had been so narrowly personal, lacking any direct appeal to national sentiment, there was little popular response.

It has been suggested that Primo de Rivera's dictatorship was like a bicycle, that it had to move constantly to new triumphs because if affairs ever reached a standstill the regime would fall over from lack of natural balance. By 1927, the dictatorship had settled the war in Morocco, which had been to a great extent its original *raison d'être*. It could remain in power only so long as it had something to offer a significant number of Spaniards. Since prosperity was a major factor in stilling political unrest, the new semi-civilian government had been conceived in part to encourage continued economic well-being. One of the major problems it had to face in this regard was the question of public expenditure. Inability to balance finances had been one of the principal weaknesses of the parliamentary regime, but since Army expenses and the Moroccan operations ate up nearly 30 per cent of the budget, the dictatorship had done no better.[39]

By 1927, the Riff war had swelled the Army to a new high for the twentieth century. The *Anuario Militar* of 1927 listed 219 generals and 19,906 officers for 207,000 troops, with approximately 5,000 other officers on the Reserve list. The officer-soldier ratio was at least twice as great as in the French Army. Moreover, 1,192 new cadets had entered the military academies in 1922, and the figures for 1923–25 averaged about 550 annually. Because of the great expense of salaries and maintenance, the government had never been able to afford genuine modernization of equipment.

Since 1918, Primo de Rivera had been proposing modest reductions in the military budget, and had made some effort to provide better equipment. In 1924, the dictator had decreed that 25 per cent of all future vacancies in the Officer Corps should remain unfilled until the Corps had been reduced by at least 5,000 members. After the fighting ended in Morocco, new openings in the military academies were sharply curbed, being restricted to 250 in 1928, 200 in 1929, and 100 in 1930. At the height of the Moroccan war, in 1925, annual military expenditures were reduced 20 per cent; they dropped 10 per cent more in the following year. Primo de Rivera, who saw no need for Spain to fight any further foreign wars in the foreseeable future, later talked of a permanent army of no more than four divisions, supplemented by complete premilitary training for all able-bodied males. This was a repetition of Primo's pet proposal of a national militia, but he was never able to realize this project because of opposition among the vested interests in the Army and lack of response from the citizenry. However, by the time the dictatorship came to an end in 1930, the Officer Corps, including Reservists, numbered 22,208, a decrease of nearly 10 per cent in three years, while the manpower had been cut to 130,000, a nominal reduction of about a third.[40]

The financial scandals in the Moroccan commands were finally recognized by a royal decree of August 8, 1926, which set up a judicial commission to investigate irregularities in the supply centers at Ceuta and Larache. The investigation scarcely touched the surface, but was apparently intended as a symbolic prosecution of some of the worst examples. Only officers of the Supply Corps were investigated, and this not unnaturally led to the feeling that they were being used as scapegoats to placate critics of the Moroccan leadership in general. In fact, there was no direct prosecution for any sort of embezzlement, doubtless for fear of the complications involved. During 1927, thirty-one Supply officers between the ranks of captain and colonel were forced into retirement without benefit of a formal hearing or defense plea. Beyond this the investigative commission did not go, alleging insufficient information.[41]

While making some effort to tighten Army organization, the regime did permit increases in the budget for new equipment.[42] The obsolete foreign matériel and poorly built domestic products used during the early years of the Moroccan campaigns had become a national scandal, with reports of rifles and cannon that sometimes blew up in the soldiers' faces. In 1926, the government announced a ten-year state investment program of which the Army was to receive 26 per cent, mainly to improve equipment and training. The Navy was granted a new building program that was to include three cruisers. Thus, although total military expenditures were kept somewhat below the high point of 1924–25, the Army's budget rose in the later 1920's. This, together with the sizable state spending program in internal improvements, placed continued pressure on the national budget and contributed to the strains that began to weigh against the dictatorship by 1929.

One former opponent of the dictator who became completely satisfied with his administration of military affairs was Brigadier General Francisco Franco. At the beginning of 1928, Franco was appointed the first director of the General Military Academy being organized in Zaragoza. Such a general academy for Army cadets had been frequently suggested during the past century. One had existed from 1824 to 1850, and then had been revived for ten years in 1882, but there had been no general academy in the twentieth century. Aspiring officer trainees for each of the various Corps had been trained in separate academies, which was one reason for the strong insular feeling within the Army's different sections. The Zaragoza Academy was planned to train all officer candidates for two years before they went on for specialized study in the separate academies of their own Corps. Franco was chosen as the first director because the government wanted to have the Academy led by officers with combat experience, who were alien to the persistent intrigues of the peninsula garrisons and able to train young officers in the tough-minded professional mystique of the africanistas.

Franco had little theoretical or technological education in military affairs, and apparently had to rely on his staff to prepare the details of the organization of the Academy, which opened its doors in the autumn of 1928.[43] The plan of studies avoided technical specialization, but was devoted to providing a rounded military education and strong professional feeling. Much time was allotted to physical and psychological training, in the hope of producing tough, caste-conscious officers. Franco soon became respected as an efficient director, though among the cadets this feeling was apparently tinged with apprehension.*

These and other minor military reforms were carried out during the Indian summer of the dictatorship. Primo de Rivera was still groping for some way to give institutional coherence to an improvised regime that had begun as a 90-day military directory. In 1927, Primo established a consultative National Assembly in Madrid, its members appointed mainly from the ranks of the Unión Patriótica, the pious, conservative political front ("Religion, Fatherland, Monarchy") that had been set up nearly three years earlier.[44] The inspiration for this had been drawn in part from the observations made in Italy by Labor Minister Eduardo Aunós, who found that a consultative corporate chamber was useful in the public relations façade of Mussolini's regime.[45]

In a speech before the Assembly on March 6, 1928, Primo publicly gave up the pretense he had long maintained of intending to return to the Constitution of 1876, saying: "Today, new problems, such as Communism and divisive nationalism, make the constitutional work of Cánovas unserviceable."[46] In a speech at La Coruña on August 14, 1928, he promised that the Unión Patriótica would give Spain an absolutely original constitution, which would owe nothing to imitation, but how and when this would be accomplished was not explained.[47]

During 1927 and most of 1928 there was little agitation within the Army, save for the smoldering discontent of the Artillerists. The ranking officers in the Infantry and Cavalry settled down to enjoy Primo's promotions, while the junior officers were encouraged by the salary increases of June 1, 1926, which provided significant raises for all officers under the rank of brigadier.[48] Ordinary recruits still received less than one peseta per day, but living standards in the barracks were at least somewhat better than they had been a decade earlier.

Given the apathetic response to the *sanjuanada* and the effective repression of the Artillery revolt, the dictator did not expect any more serious difficulties with the Army. He delivered periodic homilies on

---

* Some of the Academy's graduates later recounted that Franco sometimes tried to trap strolling cadets on the streets of Zaragoza by pretending to look in shop windows while actually watching the reflections in the glass to see if his students would try to walk past his back without saluting. They claimed that he was greatly concerned about hygienic conditions and especially proud of having reduced the incidence of gonorrhea among officer candidates. He is said to have insisted that every cadet going out on leave for an evening carry at least one condom with him, and once or twice to have stopped cadets in the streets and ordered them to produce theirs, according to regulations. Kemp, p. 115.

the need for discipline, a subject that always evoked the uneasy memory that his own regime was based on military rebellion. In a speech of October 26, 1927, he stressed the Army's duty to set an example of discipline and subordination, though with the theoretical concession that when the government was verging on subversion or collapse (as he implied had been the case in 1923), the military had an obligation to intervene.[49]

Nevertheless, if the great majority of the Officer Corps gave no sign of overt opposition, neither was there much positive enthusiasm. Throughout the years of the dictatorship, there was a vague feeling that the dictator and his inner circle did not so much represent the Army as use it for their own purposes. During the spring of 1928, Martínez Anido carried out a private inquiry among a list of selected commanders and found that, in one way or another, the majority of them were opposed to continuation of the dictatorship.[50]

During most of 1928, however, the Artillerists represented the only active nucleus of conspirators. Officers at the Carabanchel Artillery base a few miles west of Madrid hatched a scheme to open long-range fire against the government court buildings on the west side of the city in order to force the dictator's resignation, but abandoned the project for fear of harming innocent people. There were also conspiratorial whisperings among the cadets at the Artillery Academy, and later talk of a two-pronged rebellion based in Madrid and Barcelona. For the time being, however, nothing came of these plans.[51]

By the close of 1928, another committee of military conspirators had been secretly organized in the capital, and was in close touch with leading civilian opponents of the regime. This committee was nominally led by Aguilera and several other senior officers, for the old general apparently could not rest until the dictator's power had been broken. The chief civilian leader among the plotters was José Sánchez Guerra, onetime Prime Minister and Minister of War under the constitutional regime. Like many of the pre-1923 parliamentarians, Sánchez Guerra had owed his seat to the cacique system and had never been a progressive; nevertheless he had always been devoted to the constitutional regime as he understood it. He loathed everything connected with Primo de Rivera. The experience of the dictatorship moved his own political thinking somewhat further left, for by the end of 1928 the regime's opponents were more and more frequently coming to take an anti-monarchist as well as an anti-dictatorial attitude. There was slowly increasing support for the calling of a constituent Cortes to reconsider the entire question of political institutions. The means to this would be a pronunciamiento, not dissimilar in structure to that which had been planned for the *sanjuanada,* but more elaborate and hopefully more effective.

The conspirators counted on the bulk of the Artillery, plus other units in the south and east of Spain. The pronunciamiento was supposed to be supported also by pro-Republican volunteers and by the CNT. It would begin in provincial garrisons. While loyal troops were occupied with these revolts, military rebels in Madrid would take over the capital.[52]

Though the coup was to be consummated in Madrid, its base, as three years earlier, was Valencia. This was because of that city's location and even more because of its political climate—highly liberal, strongly opposed to the dictatorship, and increasingly pro-Republican. Yet another reason for emphasizing Valencia was the need for the support of a reliable and influential captain general. Castro Girona, the Captain General of Valencia, had been one of the five or six most capable Spanish leaders in Morocco. Through his attitude and activities in Valencia, he was known to be a man of liberal convictions and a foe of the dictatorship. Yet, though Castro Girona did not rebuff overtures from the conspirators, no definite arrangement could be made with him.[53] He gave the impression that he would second any pronunciamiento, but he had scant faith in the enterprise, and it was not clear to the conspirators that he would shoulder any responsibility for initiating the movement.[54]

The government was by no means ignorant of the plotting, but had no desire to excite opposition by a premature or unnecessary crackdown. On January 25, 1929, the conspirators sent instructions to the various forces involved that the pronunciamiento would take place on the night of January 29. The police were evidently not aware of the exact timing of the plot, but in the interim the dictator himself made a trip to Valencia to ensure Castro Girona's loyalty; he is said to have overwhelmed the Captain General's impressionable wife with an invitation to visit the queen in Madrid.[55] It was also rumored afterward that Primo dangled before the Captain General the prospect of being named the next High Commissioner of Spanish Morocco, a post to which the Arabic-speaking Castro Girona had long aspired.[56]

Sánchez Guerra's son and other conspirators talked with Castro Girona on the 28th and 29th, but could not wring from him a definite promise to lead the rebellion. Plans were now fixed for the garrisons in nearby Alcoy, Murcia, and Cartagena to second the revolt, while both the Artillery units and the clandestine CNT group in Valencia were ready for action. The plotters could therefore only hope that Castro Girona had become so involved that the pressure of circumstances would finally bring him in on their side. Yet when Sánchez Guerra called at his residence on the morning of January 30, the Captain General feigned sickness and refused to receive him. His demurral paralyzed the conspiracy at Valencia, though Sánchez Guerra went to one of the main barracks in a vain effort to rally support. The other garrisons in eastern Spain waited forlornly for a sign from Valencia. This rebellion, like that two and a half years earlier, collapsed before it could begin, and the forces in the Levant never moved.[57]

The only place where the rebels actually seized control was in the provincial capital of Ciudad Real, some distance south of Madrid. By the morning of the 30th, the local Artillery forces dominated the town, but they were completely isolated from potential allies and in a hopeless situation.[58] A column of loyal troops was hastily dispatched from Madrid, commanded by two of Primo's unconditional supporters, Generals Sanjurjo* and Orgaz, who quickly forced the surrender of the rebels.

The situation in Valencia nevertheless remained uncertain for some seventy-two hours. Because the government was no more certain of Castro Girona than were the rebels, it hesitated to intervene until the situation became clearer, and the Captain General made no effort to arrest the conspirators who still hoped to foment rebellion in his district. While the Artillery revolt in Ciudad Real was being put down, the government received word that the Artillery garrison at Valencia planned to raise the banner of rebellion all by itself, if need be, on Sunday, February 3, when Valencia would be crowded with many visitors for a championship soccer match. An emergency Cabinet meeting was held at Madrid on the afternoon of the 3d, and security measures in the capital were increased. After no word of rebellion arrived from Valencia, the trusted Sanjurjo was dispatched before dawn on the 4th to relieve Castro Girona of command. He accomplished this mission without difficulty, ordering the Civil Guard to place Castro Girona under arrest and to round up most of the civilian and military conspirators, very few of whom had fled.[59]

Once more the Army had given only minimal support to an anti-Primo conspiracy, but this plot, the third attempted revolt in two and

* Since November 3, 1928, Sanjurjo had been Director of the Civil Guard.

a half years, was disillusioning to the dictator, despite his brave words to the National Assembly.[60] He seemed to have been somewhat shaken that none of the members of his Unión Patriótica in Ciudad Real had lifted a finger to oppose the Artillery.[61]

On February 1, a royal decree ordered that the Ministry of War establish a local commission in each garrison to study means of restoring vigorous discipline. It was specifically stated that the Ministry must eradicate the idea that the present regime was the product of a military rebellion: "Our rebellion was a response to a situation that had deteriorated to the point of mockery; it was acclaimed by the people and sanctioned by the king, and was motivated by wisdom and patriotism.[62]

It was obvious that the military backbone of the attempted revolt had once more been the Artillery. Primo de Rivera soon took his revenge, and on February 29, after overcoming Don Alfonso's persistent desire to arbitrate the matter personally, gave the order that dissolved the Artillery Corps for the fourth time in a little over a century.[63] There was a brief rebellion in one Artillery regiment at Madrid, but it was smothered without difficulty.[64]

The failure of the pronunciamiento temporarily deflated the opposition, but Sánchez Guerra and the Ciudad Real rebels were regarded by many as heroes. Sánchez Guerra was held on a prison boat in Valencia harbor, because, it was rumored, the government could not rely on the security of a military prison. Nine of the Artillery officers from Ciudad Real were sentenced to death by court-martial, and Castro Girona was transferred to the Reserve list, then sentenced in June to a year's imprisonment for having dallied with the conspirators. This sentence was roundly criticized as too severe. Meanwhile, Sánchez Guerra won further sympathy and prestige by taking full blame for the conspiracy on himself and absolving all his colleagues. The head of the special military court that tried him for rebellion was General Federico Berenguer, Captain General of Madrid and one of the men who had placed Primo in power. Like his brother Dámaso and his colleague Cavalcanti, Berenguer had grown disillusioned with the dictatorship. As a result (and to the surprise of most people), his court chose to absolve Sánchez Guerra. This constituted a direct affront to the furious dictator. He ordered the case referred to the Supreme Council of Military Justice, where the absolution was upheld. In the process, his reputation was further damaged by rumors that he had attempted to coerce the generals deliberating the case.

Primo eventually tried to make the best of a bad situation, as he had done five years earlier at the Ben Tieb banquet in Morocco. Sánchez Guerra could not be convicted, so the dictator tried to allay further discontent by pardoning everyone else implicated at Valencia save the unfortunate Castro Girona. The nine Artillery officers had their terms commuted to life imprisonment, then further shortened by a decree of December 18, 1929.

Despite such signs of uneasiness within the Army, the government never ceased to meddle with the armed forces, changing commands and promotion scales. A decree of April 2, 1928, further altered the membership of the Classifying Junta, so that in future all the appointees were to be generals chosen by the Minister of War.[65] It seemed that the dictatorship simply could not resist rearranging the standards and systems of appointment. Some of the changes were in themselves desirable, and many were no more than the normal prerogative of a legitimate government, but Primo's Directory rested on insecure loyalties, and its changes in the Army's structure and command aroused a resentment that might not have been directed against a stronger, more representative regime.

During 1929, the dictatorship turned its attention to the naval command as well. A decree of January 9 lowered the retirement ages for naval captains to 58, eliminating five captains who were in line for seniority promotions to the rank of counter-admiral.[66] Another decree five days later made promotion to the ranks of admiral, counter-admiral, captain, and corvette captain by election, whereas they had formerly been made on the basis of seniority. Moreover, the decisions of the Navy's Supreme Classifying Junta were now made subject to Cabinet approval.[67] On March 11, a royal decree was issued reorganizing certain branches of the Navy and arbitrarily retiring 24 elderly officers.[68] Many of these changes may have been desirable from the viewpoint of increased efficiency, but they won the enmity of a great many senior naval officers, and this the regime could no longer afford. Naval critics questioned the government's concern for economy when, contrary to the terms of the constitution, 76,000 pesetas could be officially spent in converting part of the Ministry building into luxurious living quarters for the Navy Minister and his family.[69]

There was greater surveillance of military activity and conversation during 1929 than in preceding years. Officers were removed from command or switched to other garrisons, and a number of fines were levied for infractions against what Primo called "good military spirit." Such measures, however, only encouraged the psychological dissociation of the majority of the officers from the dictatorship.

The regime had still not built any permanent structure or achieved ideological consistency.[70] Worst of all, the dictator himself was declining in vigor. A victim of diabetes, the undisciplined Primo found it almost impossible to control his harmful excesses. His speeches and public messages became more and more incoherent; a few were even composed while he was drunk. As his personal control and prestige declined, he could no longer ignore the need for some kind of change or liberalization. The trade slump that began in the autumn of 1929 increased the restiveness of influential upper-middle-class elements, and the king had long since come to repent his concession of power to the dictator. Don Alfonso was impatient to be rid of a regime that was becoming a liability, and feared that Primo's efforts to retain control might so exacerbate political antagonism as to imperil the very future of the monarchist state.

In the autumn of 1929, the three leading civilian ministers in the government—Aunós, Calvo Sotelo, and the Conde de los Andes—informed Primo in writing that the regime must soon prepare for some sort of change.[71] The vice-premier, Martínez Anido, whose behind-the-scenes advice sometimes belied his public image as a mail-fisted tyrant, echoed this opinion.[72] On November 4, the government released a note announcing that, "desirous of smoothly preparing the transfer of power to a normal situation that can guarantee and consolidate its work," the regime had been "planning the measures necessary for setting up a new government."[73] According to Calvo Sotelo, the main opposition to change within the regime came neither from the Cabinet nor from the Army command, but from the civilian leaders of the Unión Patriótica, who had important interests vested in the status quo.[74]

After comparing opinions, Primo sent a long letter to the king on December 30 outlining a plan to hold national elections on three successive levels, from towns to provinces to the National Assembly. Half the representatives would be chosen by universal male suffrage, but the other half were to be selected by the corporate vote of special groups. No later than September 13, 1930, the present National Assembly would be replaced by a new body of 500 members, and within two more years the transition to government under a new constitution was to be completed. However, neither the king nor all the Cabinet members were fully satisfied with this proposal, which they feared would prove too slow and perhaps too authoritarian.[75]

Primo de Rivera wrote his young Finance Minister on January 2, 1930, that the king had agreed to beginning the transition with successive elections on separate levels, but had suggested that the selection of the National Assembly might be somewhat liberalized.[76] The dictator spent the next few weeks in an agony of indecision. Primo was aware that both his health and prestige were failing, but to relinquish power was almost more than he could bear. He could not bring himself to schedule municipal elections, yet spoke vaguely of resigning leadership to some sort of Junta that would preside over the transition.

In such circumstances, organized opposition quickly came to the fore. Middle-class liberals, many of whom were Republicans, had set up a secret committee in Madrid during 1929. They considered the Army the most effective means of ending the regime. There were many elements that might provide assistance: most of the Artillery; officers cashiered by the dictatorship; the genuinely liberal minority; the senior generals who had always wanted to put Primo in his place; the professionally frustrated; and even some of the General Staff officers, who resented the dictator's rough treatment of their Corps. The spirit of rebellion was especially strong in the Air Force, the newest and most radical branch of the armed forces.

By the beginning of 1930, military conspiracy was centered around the commander at Cádiz, General Manuel Goded, who had served so competently as Sanjurjo's chief of staff during the closing campaigns in Morocco. He was a highly capable and intelligent officer who clearly perceived the artificial nature of Primo's dictatorship and the dishonor it brought upon the Army. An efficient organizer, Goded won extensive support among leaders of units in southern Spain. Though three officers from the Seville garrison were arrested in the last days of 1929 for political conspiracy, the regime did not yet seem aware of the extent of the organized opposition in the south.[77]

Goded had difficulty charting a final course of action. Support in the garrisons at Granada and Málaga had developed only slowly, and there was the further problem that a revolt, even if it achieved success, might get out of hand and lead to political excesses. Goded felt no particular fervor for democracy, and his political ideas were vague. Like so many officers, he was attracted toward a sort of patriotic progressivism only partially defined in terms of concrete goals. The civilian committee that established relations with him stood for moderate constitutionalism, and its only aim after driving Primo de Rivera from power was to call a constituent Cortes to decide on a new government.[78] Goded was not a monarchist, and he seemed to agree. Yet there was some concern about what he would do when the chips were down, for he feared that in the event of a revolt the dictator would quickly call over loyal elite forces from Morocco. He hoped to avoid this by persuading naval commanders to join the plot and blockade the straits. Most of the naval leaders in the bases on the south coast of Spain no longer felt much loyalty to the dictator, but they refused to promise the Army conspirators more than neutrality in case of conflict.[79]

On January 25, 1930, the dictator held a press conference in Madrid in an effort to bolster confidence after the drastic decline of the peseta in the international exchange market. One of the questions brought up by reporters dealt with the loyalty of General Goded. Newspapers reported the ensuing exchange approximately as follows:

Primo: I don't understand the question.
Reporter: There is talk of a conspiracy led by that general.
Primo: Nothing more absurd! Goded is one of the most respected generals in our Army, with a bright future because he is one of the youngest and has more discipline and more sense of fulfilling his duty than some suppose.

Should I find a man of absolutely good faith who wanted to assume this task [of head of the government], I would resign it to him. But I would assure you that no mere *coup de main* can separate me from this responsibility. Not at all!

But the dictator was quite worried, and took an unprecedented step to elicit an expression of support from the military hierarchy. The next morning, January 26, Madrid newspapers carried a long announcement from Primo—a fine example of his cavalier approach to syntax:

Since the dictatorship was inaugurated by the proclamation of the military, in my opinion interpreting the healthy wishes of the people, who were not slow in demonstrating their enthusiastic support, which it believes it still enjoys in broader form, since the latter cannot be easily determined with speed and numerical exactitude while the former can be, the ten Captain Generals, the commander of the forces in Morocco, the three Captain Generals of the Maritime Department and the directors of the Guardia Civil, Carabineros, and Inválidos, are authorized and encouraged, after a brief, discreet, and private exploration, which ought not to extend beyond the commanding officers of units, to communicate to the government by writing, and, if they prefer, to meet in Madrid, under the presidency of the one most appropriate to make agreements, to inform it if it continues to enjoy the confidence of the Army and Navy. If this is lacking, the powers of chief of government and of the dictatorship will be returned within five minutes of learning it to the king, since it received them from the latter as the interpreter of the will of the aforementioned. . . .

And now I only ask of my companions in arms in the hierarchy that they consider this note directly intended for themselves, and without wasting a minute, since they must understand the delicacy of the situation which this step—whose gravity I cannot determine—creates for the regime over which I must preside, decide, and communicate their attitude. The Army and Navy set me up as dictator in the first place—some with their support, others with their tacit consent; the Army and Navy are the first to be called to declare, in conscience, if I ought to continue as such or resign my powers.

This extraordinary public statement may have been the frankest political statement ever made by a twentieth-century dictator. Its frankness, indeed its naïveté, was representative of Primo de Rivera and his entire regime. The dictator may have been a blowhard, but he was incapable of the sophisticated, calculated hypocrisy of most authoritarian rulers. It has been said that the king was particularly offended by this note, because its frankness made no effort to disguise the ultimate military, rather than monarchical, basis of existing political sovereignty in Spain. According to one version, he immediately summoned Primo to the palace and denounced the action, while the dictator defended himself by saying that he had sent the request, not merely as head of government, but also as a general of the Army who must assure himself of the support of his comrades.[80]

The replies from the Army hierarchy were much less than Primo hoped for, since nearly all the messages carried some kind of reservation about indefinite continuation of the dictatorship. Primo felt, not unnaturally, that he had been let down by his colleagues, though his initial reaction seems to have been to carry on as though the replies had met the terms he had set. But after talking with his vice-premier, Martínez Anido—who was fully aware of the malaise in the Army— Primo came to realize that the loss of confidence could not be glossed over. He informed the king that he would shortly resign, though no date was set.[81]

The most radical elements in the armed forces were pressuring the leaders of the conspiracy to get on with their work. The plotters formed a strange hodgepodge of military men. One of the most sensible civilian liberals of this period has written of them: "A minority were Republicans—others, simply soldiers—the rest, merely crazy."[82] Among the chief activists were a handful of aggressive young Air Force officers, some of whom might be termed Republicans, but others of whom were judged as among the crazy. Their nominal leader was Major Ramón Franco, daredevil brother of the general, from whom he differed almost completely in personality. Whereas Francisco gave the impression of coldness and absolute self-control, Ramón was reckless, impulsive, and almost entirely lacking in reflection. He had become a national hero less than four years earlier when he piloted a crew of three on the first transatlantic flight to Buenos Aires. More recently, however, his personal and professional affairs had been plagued with frustration.[83] By 1930, the younger Franco was an innovative rebel determined to help open Spain to broad new currents of twentieth-century life, whatever these might bring. Because of his lack of self-control and of political understanding, he was heavily influenced by radical colleagues who tried to use his reputation to further their schemes. On January 27, 1930, he and fellow Air Force officers talked with Goded in Cádiz in an effort to convince the general of the need to act swiftly and to broaden the base of the pronunciamiento by wholesale inclusion of civilian progressives, perhaps with the added support of a strike among the scattered followers of the CNT. Ramón Franco later wrote:

Goded tells us that he wants to make a military movement, with military forces; that he fears popular demonstrations, for he does not know where they will lead. . . . He cannot make up his mind. He says that his forces are still not prepared [for a pronunciamiento], that in Cádiz the Infantry regiment is opposed to it. . . . He prefers to give up rather than unleash a popular revolution. He tells us that he is not a Republican; that he will accept the Republic by evolution, but not by revolution; and that he swears to us that he has not a drop of Alfonsine blood in his veins, and that he does not support this king.[84]

In 1930, the Captain General of Seville, under whose jurisdiction Cádiz lay, was Don Carlos de Borbón, the king's uncle, who had held the same post seven years before. This elderly legalist had long been opposed to the dictatorship, and feared that its prolongation might endanger the future of the monarchy itself. But he also was opposed to military rebellion; after learning of the extent of the conspiracy in the southern garrisons, he sent a personal letter to his nephew on the 26th. Don Carlos believed that another attempt at military revolt was imminent, and he hoped that if warned in time the king could head it off. On the morning of the 28th, he sent his son to Madrid by private airplane with a second, stronger message stressing the seriousness of the situation. He said that the conspiracy was not necessarily anti-monarchist but that it was being subjected to strong pressure from leftist elements.[85]

This apparently convinced the king that Primo must be removed without delay. He sent the Public Works Minister, the Conde de los Andes, to persuade the dictator to resign immediately. Under such direct pressure, lacking positive support from the Army, feeling the disrespect and impatience of the country's leading elements, and urged to step down by his closest collaborator, the dictator agreed within a few hours. His resignation was announced on January 29, and on the same day he took the train to Paris. On the ride to the border he had to overcome one last desire to summon loyal regiments and try to re-impose personal control. In his final statement on leaving Spain, he insisted that he firmly believed that the country should be governed by a dictatorship "for many years to come," but added that some kind of representative body was also needed.[86] Bitter and lonely, he took up residence in Paris, where he died three months later.

The Primo de Rivera dictatorship was over. It had been one of the most curious authoritarian regimes of the century. Though in practice he flouted the Constitution, in rhetorical utterance Primo often invoked it. The ideological milieu of the country in the 1920's had been far too liberal for the installation of a ruthlessly coercive dicta-torship, nor did Primo have the temperament for that. The class strug-gle had not yet developed to the point where an intense antiliberal movement could gain mass adherence, and once the first crisis had passed, support for the dictatorship was only lukewarm. Primo's pur-pose was not really to clean up Spain, as he avowed, but to stabilize the political situation, preserve the throne, and put a lid on the Moroccan problem. Only the last of these difficulties was really solved, and that through a combination of good luck and Spanish fortitude. The na-tion's prosperity under Primo was due largely to the economic mo-mentum developed during the preceding quarter century and to fa-vorable international conditions, though the regime contributed a few constructive ideas of its own. It built a road system, managed to stabilize the national debt (though at a rather high rate of interest), created several new economic agencies such as the national oil mo-nopoly, and established the *comités paritarios,* which helped secure honest labor arbitration, at least for the Socialists.

On the other hand, the dictatorship wrecked the constitutional monarchy. Despite its inadequacies, this system of monarchy had been the most creative government modern Spain had known. It had provided room for development while curbing excess. Once the constitutional monarchy was relinquished, it proved increasingly difficult to find a middle ground between leftist revolution and rightist dictatorship.

Most of the dictator's enemies, however, soon forgave or forgot their personal ire against him, for Primo's regime had truly been a *dictablanda,* not a *dictadura.* The remarks of the opposition give perhaps the best measure of the affable authoritarian who ruled Spain for seven years. Socialists were soon congratulating themselves for having put over a good one on the impulsive Primo with the expansion of UGT membership during this period. The extremist Socialist Luis Araquistáin opined in mid-1931: "Such cautious, effective revolutionary agitation was never before carried out anywhere. Poor Primo de Rivera never realized what was happening. His political naïveté prevented him from noticing the storm that was developing before his eyes and beneath his feet."[87] Julián Zugazagoitia, the moderate Socialist Minister of the Interior during the Civil War, wrote: "That dictatorship which we berated in the press so strongly—a circumstance which proves well enough the liberal and somewhat paternal tone with which it was exercised by Primo de Rivera—committed outrages [*atropellos*] . . . , but at the same time accomplished things well worthy of praise."[88] Manuel Burgos y Mazo, one of the civilian leaders of the final conspiracy of 1929–30, concluded his account of Primo's downfall with the words: "In this way ended the dictatorship of Primo de Rivera, in which the best thing to be found was the dictator himself."[89]

CHAPTER THIRTEEN

The Collapse of the Monarchy

B Y 1930, many military men were badly disposed toward politics. The experience with Primo de Rivera had largely dissipated the activist potential of earlier years, leaving the Officer Corps disillusioned and embarrassed. Most of the Army preferred to dissociate itself from government entirely.

After Primo de Rivera's departure, Don Alfonso was faced with the problem of the political succession. At no time during his twenty-eight-year reign had such heavy responsibility devolved upon him. The palace circle felt that an abrupt reversion to the constitutional system was hardly feasible: the old political groups no longer existed, and feeling against the king was strong among the veteran politicians who had been forced out of public life in 1923. On the other hand, an attempt at royal despotism after Primo's failure was unthinkable, for it was likely to provoke the fall of the monarchy. The most prudent course seemed to be a gradual liberalization of the political structure, under which constitutional government would be restored by degrees. Primo would be succeeded by another general exercising royal decree power, but the rigors of dictatorship would be progressively relaxed.

There were few reliable candidates for Primo's position. Despite his many efforts to meddle and mediate in Army affairs, Don Alfonso had no more than a handful of trusted contacts in the military hierarchy. Before departing, Primo de Rivera had suggested three potential successors: Martínez Anido, the expert in "public order"; General Emilio Barrera, a staunch monarchist and africanista who had served as Captain General of Barcelona under the dictatorship; and General Dámaso Berenguer, who had been named head of Don Alfonso's Military Household in 1927.[1]

It was not surprising that the choice fell on Berenguer, who had kept the king's personal favor during five years of political ostracism and had recently been ennobled as the Conde de Xauen. Impassive and calculating, Berenguer was in many ways the opposite of Primo de Rivera. He had won a degree of popularity within the Army because of the numerous political attacks on him after 1921, and his brief imprisonment by the dictator in 1925 had drawn the sympathy of some civilian liberals (a regard later increased by the fact that his brother Federico was head of the tribunal that absolved Sánchez Guerra). Berenguer had cultivated friendships among people of varying social backgrounds. He was considered one of the more broad-minded generals—even something of a liberal—but he had no genuine political experience and no clear idea of what to do in his new role. When newsmen asked him, on January 28, 1930, if he had a precise program in mind, Berenguer replied candidly: "Nothing; I have none. The only thing I can tell you is that I will do my duty. I come as a soldier, but I wish to act as a citizen."[2] In the new Cabinet there were only two other military men (the Ministers of the Navy and the Interior), and most of the civilian ministers were of proven parliamentary background. Primo de Rivera's National Assembly was dismissed and new municipal and provincial councils were named on February 5, under the regulations established by the late dictatorship.

The new Minister of the Interior, Lieutenant General Enrique Marzo, had served under Berenguer's command in Morocco a decade earlier. He was politically unknown and, as it turned out, lacking in administrative energy. An attempt was made to neutralize Goded by naming him Undersecretary for War; however, he assured his fellow conspirators that he was entering the government only in order to work for their goals more effectively.[3] Another military appointment was that of Brigadier General Emilio Mola as Director General of Security, or national police chief. Mola's was the delicate task of maintaining order during the coming period of transition without reimposing dictatorial methods.

Mola had been born in Cuba of an old military family. His father had served as an officer in the government forces during the Carlist wars, and his grandfather, also an officer, had participated in a liberal pronunciamiento against Narváez in 1849. Mola had always been a rigid professional, and his stern habits as a cadet won him the nickname of "The Prussian." A capable field officer, he had won his major promotions by méritos in Morocco, where his performance impressed

Berenguer. Like Marzo, Mola was politically unknown and heretofore had not revealed strong convictions. His political inclinations seem to have been oriented toward a moderate "patriotic progressivism," the closest approximation to a political philosophy likely to be found in most parts of the Officer Corps. Like many of his comrades, Mola apparently had no particular love for the monarchy.[4]

The new government was informed by agents of the Dirección General that leaders of the conspiracy in the southern garrisons had temporarily canceled their activities, waiting to see what the Berenguer ministry was going to do.[5] One of the first things it did was to reverse many of the changes in military structure and appointments that had turned so many officers against Primo de Rivera. A decree of February 6 restored to active service the 29 senior naval commanders arbitrarily retired by Primo in the preceding year, and granted them the rank they would otherwise have held by seniority. The same decree also gave a general amnesty to all military men charged with crimes of political rebellion. Yet, as Berenguer later admitted, these measures came about a year too late, for by 1930 most of the officers had been alienated from the existing political structure.[6]

The most radical opponents, such as Ramón Franco, were busy during the first weeks of the Berenguer government organizing the Republican Military Association (AMR), whose opening manifesto was widely distributed among the garrisons. Strongest support for the clandestine AMR came from the young Artillery officers; there were also a significant number of adherents in the Supply Corps and the Air Force.[7] Not surprisingly, the Cavalry Corps was the least responsive. Most of its officers were drawn from the upper classes, and its commanders had been especially favored by the king; consequently it remained staunchly loyal to the monarchy.

The government acted swiftly to pacify the rebellious Artillery. Don Alfonso made a speech to Artillery officers in Madrid, saying that he had taken steps to see that the irregularities suffered by the Artillery were rectified and that justice returned to Spanish affairs. A royal decree of February 15 restored the cherished "closed scale" that had existed prior to 1926; and during the months that followed, most of the other changes made by Primo were reversed.[8] This almost ruined the careers of newly appointed Artillery commanders who owed their advancement to Primo. From the government's viewpoint, however, it had the far more important result of quelling discontent and undermining Artillery support for the AMR conspirators.[9] As civilian liberals had suspected, the Artillerists' opposition to the regime had not been founded primarily on love for constitutional liberty but rather on concern for professional privilege.

The new government tried to attract dissidents from both the Army and civilian society with a policy of concession and compromise. Mola followed a cautious course as Director General of Security, for he had no experience in police administration. He found the police a poorly trained lot and unfit for strenuous activity, and the facilities for investigation and surveillance were hardly in better shape than the men. Month by month, demonstrations by workers and students became more frequent and intense, sometimes developing into riots. Mola's methods of dealing with these crises made him an object of hatred among Republicans and leftists, but in fact he used the rod rather sparingly. Police repression under the Spanish "dictablanda" could hardly be likened to that of any other authoritarian regime in Europe. Mola had little personal faith in a sharp crackdown, feeling, as he later wrote, that the monarchy was doomed.

Though Mola may not have succeeded in putting together an effective police organization, he did manage to keep fairly well informed about conspiracy in the Army, and was even criticized for wasting too much of his time dashing about the peninsula to check up on disgruntled officers. Chief among the plotters in 1930 was Major General Gonzalo Queipo de Llano, the colorful, talkative, and rather daring officer who was soon to take credit for having talked Franco out of rebelling against Primo six years earlier (pp. 213–14). Though he was a middle-aged man, Queipo was a chronic malcontent whose patience had not increased with the passage of time. After being arrested by Primo and forced into the Reserve, he had developed an undying animus against the regime, and he insisted that Spain's salvation lay in a republic.[10] Six years later, he was to play a major role in the fateful rebellion against the same republic that he had labored to establish. In 1930, his seniority gave him nominal leadership of the AMR.[11] Yet the police, reluctant to arouse greater resistance by suppression, did little to curb his activities.

Faced with mounting opposition, the Berenguer government could not find an "appropriate" time to initiate local elections. Month after month slipped past. Apprehension over the attitude of the Army grew, and on September 5 General Berenguer sent a circular to all the territorial Captain Generals, exhorting them to stand fast.[12] All the while, progressives and malcontents intrigued actively. Alejandro Lerroux, a longtime leader of Republican radicalism, had always stressed the importance of the military. For years he had kept a file of *militares aptos*—discontented or liberal officers who might be induced to join a Republican pronunciamiento.[13] On October 11, the Chief of the Artillery Section in the War Ministry ordered Artillery commanders throughout the peninsula to remove the firing pins on cannon and machine guns and to store their arms in secure depots where they might not be easily commandeered by rebels.[14] On November 24, Ramón Franco, under arrest for conspiracy, managed to escape from prison,[15] and General Marzo resigned the Ministry of the Interior on the following day.

The Republicans were profiting greatly from the long delay in scheduling elections, for large segments of the respectable middle classes now looked to a change of regime as the only solution to the country's unrest. Ever more fearful of facing the electorate, the government appealed to the Army's loyalty in the only way it knew. A general salary increase was authorized for January 1, 1931.[16] The military remained politically confused and listless. They were neither for the monarchy nor for the Republicans. By the beginning of December, however, two small nuclei of conspirators had been organized for action. One was grouped around Queipo and Ramón Franco in Madrid, the other around Captain Fermín Galán in the Pyrenean garrison town of Jaca.

Galán came from a military family; three of his brothers were also officers. He was a veteran africanista who had held commissions in both the Regulares and the Tercios. He was well-read, and an independent thinker. It was rumored afterward by his enemies that he had become embittered about his career because he had not been decorated or rapidly advanced. Four years earlier, at the time of the Artillery trouble, he had planned a rebellion in Tarragona, where he was then stationed, which was to have moved concentrically through the provincial garrisons toward Madrid. This scheme had come to nothing for lack of support.[17] By 1930 he had developed a highly individualistic revolutionary attitude, which has been labeled "humanistic communism" and had little or nothing to do with Marxism. Galán was much more than a Republican, for he believed that rebellion should be the prelude to sweeping social and ideological revolution. He outlined these ideas in a lengthy manuscript entitled "Nueva creación." He had no use for the commanders of the Spanish Army, and in his last writings spoke of the eventual replacement of the Army by a revolutionary National Guard, from which would be excluded anyone holding the rank of colonel or above.[18]

In collaboration with civilian Republicans, the leading Army conspirators had prepared plans for a pronunciamiento in the middle of December 1930. Because of its small size, the Jaca garrison did not figure very prominently in the plot. It was intended that the troops merely be used to stir up support among other provincial garrisons in northeastern Spain. But a few days before the target date, December 15, it was decided by leaders in Madrid and elsewhere to postpone the revolt because of lack of support. Captain Galán, however, sent coded telegrams to his civilian contacts to come up to Jaca so as to be ready to support his pronunciamiento on Saturday, December 13. Realizing that Galán might precipitate the action all by himself, two of the Republican conspirators left Madrid on the 11th so as to arrive in Jaca in time to talk Galán out of his plan. They reached the garrison town at 1 o'clock on the morning of the 12th and went to bed at the local hotel, intending to contact Galán at breakfast time.

Meanwhile, Galán had advanced his timetable by another 24 hours. He calculated that the moral standing of the authoritarian monarchist state was thoroughly corroded. Though he realized that the other Republicans might not be prepared to second him immediately, he thought, in rather typical pronunciamiento fashion, that all the situation required was a push in the right direction, after which most other garrison commanders would begin to fall into line. Moreover, as he explained on the 12th, he believed that if leadership were left entirely to the civilian Republicans, they would never have the audacity to attempt a direct political revolution. Several reliable officers in his garrison were scheduled to go on leave on December 15, and syndicalist contacts in Zaragoza had promised a general strike there. Galán had also sent word to sympathetic elements in the garrisons at Madrid, Seville, and Valencia. Before dawn on the 12th, while his civilian collaborators still slept at the Jaca hotel, Galán arrested his superiors, declared martial law in the little Aragonese town, and pronounced for the second Spanish Republic.[19]

His garrison forces numbered scarcely 800 troops, and he was hard put to find enough trucks in Jaca to carry 500 of them (including a few civilian volunteers) on a march to Huesca, where he hoped to rally the next garrison and move on to Zaragoza. The column was unable to leave Jaca before 1 P.M., and spent all afternoon and the following night traveling the 87 kilometers to the outskirts of Huesca. Rain had fallen throughout the morning, a cold wind blew steadily the rest of the day, and the troops had hardly any food or sleep that night. A large detachment of loyal forces, dispatched by the government from Zaragoza about 7:30 P.M., moved much more quickly, arriving at Huesca around 1 A.M. on the 13th.[20] Galán had never intended to engage in major combat, and his soldiers were dispirited. Finding its way blocked, the rebel column broke up early on the morning of December 13. Galán and his second-in-command, Captain García Hernández, escaped by automobile, but soon surrendered to the authorities. They were tried and executed on the 14th, thus becoming the martyrs of the Republican movement. The members of the Republican coordinating committee, who represented most of the ultra-liberal political groups in Spain, were arrested by the police.

On December 15, the AMR leaders tried to launch a revolt in Madrid. While Queipo de Llano attempted to rally troops in one of the suburban barracks, Ramón Franco and fellow Air Force conspirators commandeered a number of planes at the Cuatro Vientos airfield. Their idea was the usual one: by starting a rebellious demonstration, they hoped to draw all the other military units around Madrid to their side. After buzzing the palace for a while, Franco and his comrades saw no sign of support and flew away into exile.[21] Queipo was similarly unable to rouse a following. A column of loyal troops under Orgaz occupied the airfield and quelled the last of the disorder. Three weeks later, the Air Force cadres were dissolved by royal decree, and a special classifying committee was named to reorganize their officer list and to decide who had been disloyal and who was reliable enough to be retained.

The government no longer had any confidence in the Army, yet only the merest handful of officers had any intention of sticking their necks out politically. Mola later wrote of their attitude:

A nucleus of ranking officers [*jefes*] and a more important group of junior officers found themselves compromised, for some of them had offered to cooperate at the head of their forces; but the rapid and exemplary conclusion of the Jaca rebellion dampened a great deal of enthusiasm. There were even those who, fearing possible reprisals, beat their breasts in repentance; however, this did not prevent them from boasting of their revolutionary merit once the Republic had triumphed.[22]

Obviously, the eventual break in the situation would not be made by the Army, but by either the government or its civilian opponents.

Nevertheless, with its own moral authority corroded, the monarchist regime felt that it could not rely on ordinary military units to maintain order. After a minor anarchist outbreak in the east in February, a Bandera of the Tercio was moved from Morocco to garrison the district, and there were reports of a unit of Regulares being transferred as well. Some of these shock troops got out of hand and mistreated civilians, which provoked an outcry from civilian liberals and condemnation from some Army personnel.[23]

Berenguer's government inspired no confidence at all, and the general's health, which had been poor for some time, grew steadily worse. Berenguer could not see his way clear to hold free elections that might pacify the opposition, so a new Cabinet was organized under the influence of those old-guard monarchists of the parliamentary regime, Romanones and García Prieto. Berenguer was replaced as Prime Minister by Admiral Juan Aznar, one of the Navy's most respected commanders, who, as Navy Minister in 1923, had opposed the dictatorship. Aznar enjoyed a reputation for honesty and was not compromised by earlier associations, but, like his predecessor, he lacked experience and public support. Despite his health, Berenguer remained as Minister of War and Mola stayed on as Director General of Security.

The new Cabinet projected an image of weakness and uncertainty. The trial of the members of the Republican committee, held in late winter, was turned into a virtual pro-Republican demonstration. It was conducted by the Army's high court, the Supreme Council, because of the category of the offense and because one or two of the Republican leaders held official positions within the state system. The President of the Council, General Burguete, wrote for newspapers and magazines and was considered a man of advanced ideas. For years he had been a personal enemy of both the king and Berenguer. Moreover, his son Ricardo, a major, had been involved in the conspiracy and was frequently referred to in the court record. Against the opposition of the civil judiciary, Burguete insisted that the trial be held in the largest public courtroom in Madrid, thus assuring maximum publicity. No police were permitted in the building, and defense statements were allowed to degenerate into Republican harangues. It was repeatedly stressed that none of the accused could have committed a political crime, since there had been no legal government since the constitution was overturned in 1923. Burguete "not only permitted this, but appeared more than pleased, even delighted, throughout the whole bacchanal."[24] On March 23, the Council rendered its verdict, imposing on the defendants the minimum sentence of six months and one day. At a press conference four days later, Burguete announced, with some fanfare, that he and two other judges had voted for outright absolution, and that he hoped the country would soon return to constitutional law under parliamentary government. This was the final straw for the regime, whose leaders had writhed in frustration throughout the affair but had not dared interfere in the due processes of Army institutions. After Burguete's public statement, Berenguer removed him from the Council's presidency and sentenced him to two month's military detention for insubordination. The same penalty was levied against his son.

In this state of grave weakness, the government decided to begin the return to parliamentary rule by holding municipal elections on April 12. These elections were expected to show that the Republicans lacked general support. As anticipated, most of the rural districts returned heavily monarchist lists. The surprise came from the larger cities, which voted overwhelmingly Republican. What made this such a stunning psychological blow was the government's tacit acceptance of the idea that the urban electorate constituted the free, responsible, civic-minded, at least semi-educated sector of the population. In the towns, voting was fair and honest; urban opinion represented the wave of the future. These results, coming on top of the cumulative display of the indifference of most of the population toward the existing regime, left the handful of remaining monarchist leaders in a mood of apathetic depression. Berenguer, the closest thing they had to a strong man, was tired, sick, and despairing. His telegram to the district Captain Generals after the tallying of the major results was a logical extension of the "soft" policy that he and Mola had been following for fifteen months. It advised the Captain Generals to keep their patience and take things as they came, and concluded: "The destiny of the Fatherland will follow, without disturbances that might seriously damage it, the logical course imposed by the national will."[25]

The old cacique Juan de la Cierva, one of the few political leaders who stood by the king, was astounded by the attitude of the military. He was especially anxious to gauge the attitude of Sanjurjo, who, as Director of the Civil Guard, commanded the only effective armed police in Spain, and who probably had more influence among the active sections of the Officer Corps than anyone else formally connected with the government. Sanjurjo was neither a liberal nor a Republican, but simply a hardy soldier without elaborate or precise political ideas.

Like most officers, he had little sympathy for the king and was reluctant to see the Army involved in another dictatorship. Moreover, as pressure from the electoral returns mounted, influential conservatives encouraged him to cooperate with the Republicans to avoid violence, whereas the Republicans were letting it be known that a change of regime would not involve radical alterations in nonpolitical institutions.[26] When La Cierva asked if he would fight to preserve the monarchy, Sanjurjo replied, "Until last night you could have counted on it," and added that he could not contest national opinion as expressed in the elections.[27]

During the Cabinet meeting on April 13, La Cierva asked Berenguer for the last time whether or not the government could count on the Army's loyalty. The Minister of War said that Sanjurjo had assured him the regime was not supported by a majority of the military. When the Minister of the Interior asked Berenguer if he himself had made a careful check to determine the accuracy of this assessment, or had taken special measures to guarantee order and discipline, Berenguer repeated his earlier statements that it would be "dangerous" and also "useless" to intervene in the flow of events. The Minister of the Navy echoed these sentiments.[28] It was obvious that the situation was hopeless.

A number of district Army commanders pledged their active support to Don Alfonso by telegram on April 14, but they represented only a small minority. A handful of loyal generals, led by Cavalcanti, who had replaced Burguete as president of the Supreme Council, offered to lead a counterrevolutionary repression, but the prospects for such an effort were not encouraging,[29] and Don Alfonso had no desire to provoke civil war with such limited support. He accepted the counsel of the Conde de Romanones, who "doubted the loyalty of the Army" and advised him to leave the country to avoid bloodshed.[30] In his farewell message to the military, the king said with irony: "Thank you for the loyalty that you have always shown to me, and for the certainty I feel that you will at all times continue to be a model of discipline."[31] While the liberals rejoiced, the lower classes demonstrated, and the vast majority of Army officers stood by impassively, the second Spanish Republic was proclaimed.

CHAPTER FOURTEEN

The Azaña Reforms

THE ATTITUDE of most of the military toward the new Republic was passive and expectant. The general feeling seems to have been that the onus of semi-military government would be eased, leaving the Army free to lead its own independent existence. Like most middle-class Spaniards, military officers accepted the Republic not because it was expected to bring great changes, but because it was thought to guarantee a free and autonomous society in which individual institutions would be unhindered by coercive authority.

At first there was little idea of what Republican military policy might be, for the Republican leaders did not represent a cohesive, organized political movement and were still in the process of developing their program. The Minister of War in the provisional Cabinet of April 1931 was Manuel Azaña, a writer and intellectual of limited accomplishment, most recently president of the Madrid Ateneo, who had become prominent during the past few years as spokesman for Madrid ultra-liberals. Azaña had passed most of his life in the library and writing room. His liberal principles were based on firm intellectual and moral convictions, but his practical experience was nil and his prominence was due in part to the very lack of strong Republican leaders. Solitary and physically unattractive, he was an ardent foe of whatever he deemed reactionary or obscurantist. He looked toward a regime of constitutional law that would guarantee individual freedom and do away with the obstacles of the past. Within a few months he became the key figure in the left Republican coalition because of his rhetorical eloquence, the vigor of his convictions, and his driving determination to brush aside every obstacle to the realization of his ideals.[1]

The two institutions in Spain that he considered primarily responsible for the nation's civic backwardness were the Church and the Army. A majority of the Republican left were agreed on the need to separate Church and State, end the financial subsidy, and abolish Catholic schools (save for seminaries). By the close of 1931, such provisions had been written into the new constitution, solidifying Catholic antagonism toward the regime and creating one of the major stumbling blocks to the kind of civic response that Azaña hoped to create.

While anticlericalism served as an indispensable political cement to hold the new government coalition together, Azaña's military policy was more personal. Despite his quiet existence, Azaña had taken great interest in the Army, which he despised as inefficient, vulgar, and pretentious. He felt that military ambition and interference were major institutional obstacles to the development of a civic spirit, and held that drastic changes were necessary in the military system. Over a period of years, he had made a careful study of French military policy, for the Third French Republic was his model of enlightened constitutionalism.[2] As early as 1919, he had come to the conclusion that "the abolition of the existing [Spanish] military system" was "a question of life or death."[3] He had subsequently observed with acerbity that the Spanish were "not gifted with military spirit: that is, with talent or capacity for the organization of armed forces."[4] He quoted Angel Ganivet's observation: "To cite a military figure of outstanding rank, we must hearken back to one who was no more than a captain—the 'Grand Captain' himself [Gonzalo Fernández de Córdova, Spanish commander of the early sixteenth century]."[5]

When he took over the Ministry of War in April 1931, Azaña had a fairly clear idea of what he wanted: to reduce radically the great bloat in the Officer Corps, to cut expenses, and to "democratize" the military institution. He was not interested in directly copying the French system, for he recognized that Spain's position in the world was in no way comparable to that of France. The Spanish Republic was to be a staunch supporter of the League of Nations and an upholder of the peace. It would maintain no more than a small defensive force as a minimal deterrent to aggression. Obviously, the 566 generals and 21,996 officers listed in the *Anuario Militar* for 1930, and the welter of confused units and departments they staffed, were not needed to realize these modest aims.

Between 1918 and 1930, there had been three different projects for reforming the Army and reducing the size of the Officer Corps.

There had been plans to induce several thousand officers to accept early retirement by offering them bonuses or special privileges. Such schemes had been thwarted by a combination of political and economic factors, while the practice of appointing officers to multiple commands in order to increase their income had actually been extended. Under Primo de Rivera, the size of both the Artillery and Cavalry Corps had been slightly reduced, and the equipment of the Army as a whole had been improved slightly in quality, but such measures had been no more than stopgaps.[6]

Azaña wasted no time. On April 25, eleven days after the inception of the Republic, he signed a decree permitting all generals and most officers, whether on Reserve or on the active list, to pass into the Second Reserve—that is, to accept complete retirement from all regular duties —with full pay, provided they asked to do so within a specified thirty-day period.[7] This seemed the least painful way of excising super-numeraries, and no policy could have been more generous financially. It had an immediate effect, for within the year approximately half the Officer Corps took advantage of the offer.

In the weeks that followed, the organic structure of the Army was reduced in proportion to its actual manpower. Since the sixteen nominal Infantry divisions were at scarcely half their regular strength, a decree of May 25 ordered them reorganized into only eight divisions. The Artillery was to be further compressed into eight brigades (one for each of the new divisions), plus twelve separate regiments and a number of special groups.[8]

The structure of the Ministry itself was streamlined. Separate subsections for the various Corps were eliminated, and administration was channeled through one centralized hierarchy. For planning, the Central General Staff was once more reorganized. The special judicial facilities of the Army were progressively dissolved, and the Supreme Judicial Council was abolished outright. In its place, a special judicial chamber for military trials was set up within the regular civil judiciary.[9]

Azaña abolished the ranks of Captain General and Lieutenant General. The former was an archaic residue from the empire, and had no meaning in the twentieth century; whereas the latter was deemed superfluous for an Army so relatively modest in size and function as the new Spanish force. The office of military governor was also eliminated.[10]

The military administration in Morocco was replaced by a civilian one, and Gómez Jordana was forced to resign as High Commissioner. Henceforth, the military Commander in Chief was to deal only with the technical problems of the local garrison, which was to be reduced in size. General Miguel Cabanellas, one of the leading foes of the Primo de Rivera regime, was the first appointee to that post. Colonel Capaz, who had demonstrated considerable understanding of Moroccan problems as Delegate for Native Affairs in Tetuán, resigned because he could not get along with the new civilian High Commissioner.[11]

In addition to reducing the size and influence of the Officer Corps, Azaña also moved directly toward the "democratization" of its structure. On May 6 he ruled that NCO's could be promoted directly into the Officer Reserve (*oficialidad de complemento*) after passing a series of examinations. The General Academy at Zaragoza, one of the few military creations of the dictatorship, was closed by Azaña on June 29; it had been judged inimical to the spirit of a Republican Army, since it was heavily staffed with africanistas and devoted to cultivating a rigid and exclusive esprit de corps among its officer candidates. The closing of the Academy was a bitter blow to its director, Francisco Franco, but he was not a man to waste energy in futile opposition. Franco did allow himself to express resentment in his farewell speech to the cadets on July 14; but he nonetheless exhorted them to maintain discipline and unity even when faced with an order that might seem unjust.[12] Only the day before, the War Ministry had further diminished the special status of academy-trained professionals by fusing the list of Reserve officers with that of the regulars.[13] Heretofore, rankers promoted into the Officer Corps had automatically been placed on the First Reserve list, but the two separate hierarchies were now merged.

Later, on December 4, the Ministry created a special Corps of Sub-Officers, which was composed of four ranks: first sergeant, brigade sergeant, sub-aide, and sub-lieutenant.[14] Any qualified sergeant might be commissioned in the Corps after passing a qualifying exam and undergoing a six-month training course.[15] The purpose in establishing these cadres was twofold: to create a new group of second-echelon leaders, hopefully democratic in spirit because of its basis of social recruitment, from which regular officers might be commissioned after further training; and to raise the technical quality of the infrastructure of Army leadership. For generations, the real administration of military units had been conducted by the sergeants, who were ill-equipped for such responsibility. The traditional Spanish non-com was a poorly trained, semi-illiterate peasant recruit who simply decided to stay on after his original term of service ended; he received little or no specialized instruction for his new "career."

It was decided that 60 per cent of the enrollment in the regular academies was to be reserved for outstanding NCO's. A law of September 12, 1932, required all officer candidates to serve at least six months on active duty in the ranks before commencing academic work. To cure the incompetency long characteristic of so many officers, Azaña further stipulated that all officer candidates must complete at least one year of regular university study before concentrating on military courses.

At the time, some of these changes seemed to pass almost unnoticed by the general public, whose attention was largely absorbed by the anticlerical issue. The constituent Cortes was completely dominated by the Republican groups and the Socialists, with the small conservative representation making up scarcely an eighth of the total. The more moderate Republicans were not altogether enthusiastic about the military reforms, but very few spoke out against them, and Azaña moved blithely on. At a banquet held on July 17, 1931, he declared that Spain already had "a Republican Army ready to give its life in defense of the popular Republic."[16] A fortnight later, José Ortega y Gasset felt it necessary to draw the attention of the Cortes to the "marvelous, incredible, fabulous, and legendary radical reform of the Army."

This reform, currently the dream of all the peoples of the world, has been realized by the Spanish Republic and has been achieved without grave difficulties—with consideration both on the part of the Minister of War and on that of the military, who have facilitated accomplishment of this magnificent project. Such a reform should not go without proper praise. One can expect little of a people who do not applaud, and neither can one expect much from a Chamber that still has not rendered its tribute of applause to the Minister of War, to the Army that has passed, and to the Army that remains.[17]

Most of the deputies then stood up and applauded, but only with momentary interest. Just as before 1923, technical details of military organization attracted few of them. The major features of the reform were ratified with scant discussion when presented for Cortes approval during the last months of 1931.

Azaña made his most lengthy speech regarding military affairs on

December 2, just as he was about to become Prime Minister of the first regular Cabinet under the new constitution. Routine approval of his latest military proposals came as something of a disappointment: Azaña had hoped for a debate, which would have afforded him the chance to further propound his new program. He explained that he had tried "to provide the Republic with a military policy," something the country "had been without since the end of the eighteenth century." While enumerating the ills of the military structure, he made it clear that these had, in the past, been due at least as much to legislative neglect as to any other factor. Azaña said that he had begun his reforms by "suppressing everything irrelevant in the military institution, that is, all the residues of its extravagance, inherited from past centuries or created and maintained by the monarchy."

In Morocco, the national Army has nothing further to accomplish, and one of the things that the government of the Republic proposes to do is to have those interests that must be defended there defended by a force that is not part of the metropolitan Army.

In the interest of efficiency, it has been necessary to reduce the units of the Spanish Army by at least half in a cruel, radical way. There used to be 21,000 officers on the list; there remain 8,000. There used to be eight or ten Captain Generals; now there are none. There used to be seventeen Lieutenant Generals; now there are none. There used to be some fifty Major Generals; there remain twenty-one. There used to be more than a hundred Brigadier Generals; now there are only forty or so. There used to be a budget for the Cavalry stables; there used to be special military services, and also a special budget for the bureaucracy. It was necessary to destroy all this, and I have done so with a completely tranquil mind.[18]

During the debates of January 27–28, 1932, Azaña spoke extensively on the perennial problem of the arms industries. He contended that their potential capacity was already in excess of current needs; and he announced that he would introduce a bill decentralizing their operation, in order to encourage competition and individual responsibility.[19] In February the Cortes approved the establishment of a new consortium designed to take the arms industries out of the hands of the largely military committees that had previously controlled them. The new directorate would be composed mainly of businessmen and technical experts, but would also contain spokesmen for plant employees; most of the engineers employed in the future would be civilians. Passage of this measure drew protest from the conservative minority.

On March 3 yet another group of proposals was submitted to the

Cortes. These included provisions for the enforced retirement of generals and Staff officers who had been without specific assignment for more than six months. It was also provided that the salaries of recently retired officers be ended if they engaged in any of the acts of insubordination or conspiracy proscribed by a law approved four months earlier. Another article forbade the publication of all military "journals of opinion" save those dealing with purely technical matters, and thus eliminated the Army newspapers that had flourished during previous decades. It was brought out in discussion of this measure that, during the dictatorship, *La Correspondencia Militar* had received large subsidies from the multi-millionaire smuggler, monopolist, and business fixer Juan March.[20] With conservatives and moderates largely abstaining, these latest reforms were approved by a vote of 170 to 32.

Azaña outlined further changes during the budget discussion on March 10, 1932. He proposed a general reorganization of the oficialidad de complemento. Over 3,000 officers had been produced by this program since its inauguration by Luque twenty years earlier, but Azaña was thinking of expanding it into a sort of Republican militia, or general reserve, under civilian control. Its purpose would be to provide military or premilitary training for all Spanish males.[21]

He declared with assurance on March 11:

I am very satisfied with my work in the Ministry of War. Do you know why? Because no one talks about the Army in Spain. No one! What a singular thing! For a whole century, the greater share of Spain's political worries centered around the military! This situation has cleared up, and so has the converse one, for not only is it certain that no one talks about the Army, but the Army does not speak out either. Everyone quietly keeps his place.[22]

The drastic changes he had made were not the product of personal caprice, Azaña said, but merely a technical exercise in adjusting the Army to the needs of the government and the people: "What kind of Army do you want? An Army that costs a lot of money and is incapable of fighting a war, or an Army that is capable of fighting under the only conditions in which Spain could be involved in a war? You shall have whatever you want."[23]

A series of laws enacted during the spring, summer, and autumn of 1932 served to complete Azaña's reorganization. Military training had become compulsory for all healthy adult males; the period of liability was to last eighteen years and include at least one year in active service. The annual contingent of recruits was divided into two categories, according to the draftees' qualifications. Recruits in the first group, with the highest educational background or skills, would serve only four weeks; those in the second, or regular, category would serve a full year. Those in the regular group might be released after six months upon payment of a special fee, and during 1932 more than 15,000 of the 80,000 young men called up bought their way out in this manner. Furthermore, recruits who showed special aptitude were sometimes released after only eight months, according to the judgment of their superiors. Thus the system was by no means so egalitarian as Azaña and others sometimes pretended. The redemption program had not been entirely discarded, though it was now based more on technical qualification than on financial resources. The Ministry stopped short of organizing a compulsory Reserve, and by 1933 the Army had undergone an overall manpower reduction of approximately 20 per cent.[24]

The Azaña reforms did not come cheaply. In 1929, the main section of the Army budget had cost 367 million pesetas; by 1933, in a deflationary economy, it had risen to over 400 million. Azaña had admitted that, in the short run, the mass retirements were costing a great deal of money, but he pointed hopefully to the day when all these officers would have died, by which time, he calculated, the budget would have realized a great saving.[25] In 1933, however, the new Sub-Officer Corps was costing 7 million pesetas per year, as the number of sub-officers and sergeants rose from approximately 7,400 to more than 9,200. Moreover, sorely needed salary increases had been granted to nearly all civilian employees serving the Army.

The 1931 Army budget had cost approximately 422 million pesetas, to which must be added much of the 181 million spent for Morocco. Azaña had reduced this figure to approximately 384 million for 1932, though the new civil development program in Morocco, such as it was, raised expenses there to more than 218 million.[26] When the Cortes debate on the 1933 military budget began on December 18, 1932, Azaña announced a total increase in Army expenditures both in the peninsula and in Morocco of nearly 16 million, which brought combined military costs to nearly 563 million. This increase, Azaña explained, was the result of the extensive efforts made to improve the food, clothing, and living conditions of the troops. Reenlistments were being discouraged because they cost more than did provision for first-year draftees. Moreover, according to Azaña's figures, 7 million pesetas had been lopped off military administration during the past year, while 79 million had been saved by eliminating superfluous services. Over a period of two years, special military expenses in Morocco had been lowered by nearly 53 million pesetas.[27] This budget was approved with only minor changes.

Azaña was much more interested in the political and moral aspects of Army affairs than he was in technical military matters. The elimination of supernumeraries, the marked improvement in barracks conditions, and the creation of new cadres of second-echelon leaders were calculated to revitalize military institutions, but it cannot be demonstrated that Azaña did much to improve the combat equipment or the general technical competence of the Army. The Navy was granted a new building program, which was to include the construction of two powerful modern cruisers, but Azaña had scant interest in tanks or artillery, for he was convinced that Spain would never be called upon to fight a major war. A new Transportation Corps was organized for the Army; and the Air Force budget was raised to 7 per cent of the total armed forces expenditure, though Azaña implied that the country really did not need an air force at all.[28]

The situation was worst in the Infantry and Artillery. Mola wrote that at the end of 1931 the Army had only 300 machine guns that did not date back to the Moroccan campaigns.[29] The Artillery was inadequate from every point of view, and the troops were for the most part still using rifles designed in 1893. Several tank regiments had been projected, but had not been fully organized.[30]

The brief Army debates of 1931–32 showed that most of the deputies and Cabinet ministers knew little and cared less about military matters. The small conservative minority opposed most of the reforms, but was helpless to block their passage. The only vigorous criticism from within Republican ranks was made by a Radical deputy, Tomás Peire, who took a special interest in military questions and had spent six months in a subordinate post in the War Ministry during 1931. After quarreling with the Azaña program and leaving (or being forced from) the Ministry, he made a number of Cortes speeches in 1932–33 denouncing the reforms and suggesting alternatives. He criticized Azaña for rejecting the classical Republican goal—the creation of a volunteer force—and condemned retention of a modified redemption system as undemocratic. Peire found relatively little concern for military efficiency in the reforms. Expenditures remained high, the overall size of the Army was not drastically reduced, and the quality of equipment and training was not being significantly improved. He agreed that the preparation of noncommissioned officers needed up-grading, but criticized the formation of the special Sub-Officer Corps as another instance of the sort of bureaucratic boondoggling that created new systems rather than correcting the defects in those that already existed. Peire also condemned Azaña's invalidation of the full seniority granted by méritos de guerra as a refusal to recognize talent and leadership in an institution that badly needed both.[81]

Some aspects of the reorganization were applauded by the military, but Azaña's radical reconstitution of the Officer Corps seems to have left many in a state of shock. The officers had not expected favoritism, but neither had they expected such rough treatment. On the other hand, the fact that half the Officer Corps had accepted Azaña's lenient terms of full-pay retirement indicated that morale had not been high in the spring of 1931. The retirees seem to have been of several dif-ferent types: the ultra-monarchists, who did not wish to serve a Repub-lican regime and feared persecution; some of the more intelligent and sensitive officers, who had not found a military career congenial or rewarding; and many ordinary officers who were simply disgruntled, wanted out, and were happy to have full pay for doing nothing.

Thus, the post-1931 Officer Corps was composed, for the most part, of bedrock professionals who stayed on by choice and narrow-minded incompetents who would have had difficulty adjusting to another pro-fession or style of life. These men were not political reactionaries, but they were in a difficult position vis-à-vis Republican progressivism. It was not so much what Azaña had done to the Officer Corps, but the way in which he had done it. The Republican leader completely lacked a politician's tact, and gloried in being able, as he put it, to "pulverize" (*triturar*) the Army. The supercilious tone of his speeches, in which he gloated over the discomfiture of the old military hierarchy, raised the hackles of hundreds of military men. To them, the reform had soon ceased to be a "reform," but was rather a revolutionary attack— an attempt to weaken, humiliate, and degrade the old Army spirit. And so, in a sense, it was.

Mola spoke for many of his fellows when he wrote in 1933:

The real pulverizing of the Army comes from the anarchy and indiscipline that has been created within it; from the scorn for the moral values of its institutions and the regard shown extraneous factors; from having elevated individuals whose life has been spent in sorting through the articles of the

Code of Justice (though miraculously never falling into them); from tolerating with complacency, and even favoring, the most denigrating attacks against the Officer Corps; from the partiality and favoritism that have ruled in the selection of people for certain posts; from the belligerence permitted the inferior whenever he spoke ill of his superiors; from the stimulation of inadequate or unspeakable activities; from the publicity given the penalties imposed on certain generals and officers because they did not enjoy the favor of or refused to consent to the requirements of the Minister or his henchmen; from the vexations suffered by officers of every rank at the hands of janissaries and thugs serving that political group which public opinion today [1933], with rare unanimity, rejects; from placing party ideals above national ideals. . . .[32]

There had been little or no consultation with the existing military hierarchy. Instead, Azaña worked out the reforms with his Undersecretary, General Ruiz Fornells, a former military academy professor, and with his so-called "Black Cabinet" of liberal intellectual officers, led by Lt. Col. Hernández Sarabia. The in-group at the Ministry forced their changes on the hierarchy in such a high-handed fashion that exaggerated diatribes like Mola's were inevitable.

Within the Army, Azaña's bitterest foes were the africanistas. They may not have been troubled by some orders, such as that of March 9, 1932, which ordered all major generals to prohibit official religious services in barracks, for that sort of thing primarily aroused the civilian conservatives and clericals, but the ruling of November 12, 1932, eliminating merit promotions below the rank of general was much resented. They were still rankling over the fact that most of the merit promotions of the dictatorship had been thrown open to question. Moreover, these veterans felt that the reduction of the Moroccan garrison and the elite units struck at the security of the Protectorate, and therefore at their very reason for existing.[33] Nevertheless, Azaña was close to the truth in his rather condescending remarks about the good discipline of the military. During the first year of the reform, the thought of rebellion found serious expression among only a tiny handful of the officers on active duty. Humiliated and infuriated though they were, the military were not anxious to involve themselves in politics again.

CHAPTER FIFTEEN

The Sanjurjada

F ROM THE VERY BEGINNING of the Republic, the Army was required to fill its familiar role of guarantor of public order. The initial disturbances did not occur in metropolitan Spain, but in the larger towns of the Protectorate. The urban population of Spanish Morocco had been remarkably quiet during the bloody years 1909–27, but by 1931 the agitation of Spanish leftists and Moorish nationalists had created a tense situation. The outgoing High Commissioner was forced to leave Tetuán suddenly for fear that his official residence might be assaulted, and leftist activity was discovered in several of the main Army bases. On April 25, General Sanjurjo, whose cooperation as Director of the Civil Guard had expedited the transition to the Republic, was hurried across the straits to restore order. On May 3, there was a major strike in Tetuán, in which demonstrating workmen were joined by a large crowd of Moroccans. When a company of Regulares was called out, one of them was killed by the mob. Sanjurjo declared martial law and occupied the Moorish district with troops. This show of force had a calming effect. Sanjurjo toured the Protectorate during the next two weeks, tightening discipline at the military camps. By mid-May, all signs of rebellion had vanished and life in Spanish Morocco seemed to have returned to its customary somnolence.[1]

Meanwhile, most of the senior generals who had played openly political roles between 1923 and 1931 had had to flee the country or submit to arrest, for the Republican government was determined to bring to trial the leaders of the dictatorship. Outstanding military figures in the transition governments of 1930 were also sought. After evading arrest for several days, both Berenguer and Mola gave themselves up and were temporarily sent to military prisons. The hapless

Berenguer now found himself facing prosecution for the third time in a decade. Because of Franco's prestige, Berenguer requested his services as legal defender, but this petition was denied. Both Berenguer and Mola were brought to trial in the summer. After the court review of the mild, equivocal course they had followed in the preceding year they were released, but their names were removed from the active list and thus their careers were brought to an end.

On the other hand, leading anti-Primo military conspirators such as Goded, Queipo de Llano, and Cabanellas were rewarded with important positions. Goded was made Chief of the General Staff, a position for which he was well qualified; Cabanellas became Commander in Chief of the armed forces in Morocco; and Queipo was appointed head of the First Division, stationed in Madrid, one of the choicest commands in the Republican Army. (Yet another reason for Queipo's prominence was the fact that one of his daughters was married to the son of Alcalá Zamora, head of the provisional government.)

Units of the First Division had to be called into action on May 11, less than a month after the advent of the new regime, when anticlericals set fire to a large number of churches and monasteries in Madrid. Troops also had to be used in other cities of southern and eastern Spain. In Seville, one of the few areas where Spanish Communism had enough strength to be active, declaration of a general strike gave rise to a small but violent civil disturbance two months later. On July 23 troops were called out in force, but it was only after cannons had been used against the rebel quarter that the insurrection subsided.

The Minister of the Interior in the provisional government, Miguel Maura, was one of the few responsible, farsighted leaders produced by the Republic. He realized that the problem of public order was fundamental to the future of the new regime. Urban violence had plagued the country intermittently for years, in part because of the absence of an effective police force. When such a disturbance became really alarming, the Army was usually called on to restore peace in the towns, while the Civil Guard kept order in the countryside. Neither institution was properly equipped or trained for urban police duties. To invoke military assistance in these crises was to risk the same civil-military difficulties that had plagued Barcelona before 1923. On the other hand, the Civil Guard was a paramilitary force whose brutal tactics had earned them the hatred of the leftist groups. Untrained in effective methods of crowd dispersal, the Guards often resorted to bloodshed, thus exciting more violence and resentment.

To avoid recourse either to the Army or to the Civil Guard, Maura created a national Republican police force, armed only with pistols and clubs; these "assault guards" were to be used for the suppression of demonstrations in the larger towns. As chief of the Assault Guards, the Director General of Security selected Colonel Agustín Muñoz Grandes, who had won an impressive reputation as a leader and organizer for his work with the Regulares. A man of strong professional discipline, he was thought to be pro-liberal. In his new task, "he gave proof of his great capacity for organization, creating, in less than three months, a perfect corps of trained, selected, and disciplined troops in impeccable form."[2]

However that may be, the rash of disorder that marked the first months of the Republic was unsettling for the military temperament. Even more disturbing were events in Barcelona, where the Catalanist movement made gigantic strides after the proclamation of the Republic. Catalan nationalists had seized control in Barcelona even before the official inauguration of the new regime, and passage of some kind of autonomy statute seemed inevitable. Moreover, on his triumphal return to Barcelona, the Catalan leader Maciá had promised his followers that "the sons of Catalonia" would no longer be subject to military service, nor would they "fight outside their own frontiers."[3] Such talk turned ultra-patriotic, unity-minded Army officers livid. These general political developments, together with the vast changes in the structure of the Army itself, caused the prestige of the liberal Republican leaders to drop steadily among the officers.

On the other hand, the bourgeois conservatives and ultra-clericals did not have much standing with the military, either. The latter group was interested only in economic and religious issues and did not show much concern for the professional and patriotic dilemmas of the Army. By and large, the conservatives were no more anti-Republican than the military. They merely wanted their own kind of Catholic, conservative republic.

The only directly anti-Republican activity on the right was being carried on by a tiny clique of monarchists, whose conspiracy began in émigré circles in Paris during the spring and summer of 1931. Don Alfonso gave tentative support to the preparation of a monarchist coup by the Army. This plan involved considerable proselytizing among the remaining senior officers, as well as the publication of a special political journal devoted to monarchist ideology and the theory of justifiable rebellion.[4]

Leadership among the military was provided by a small group of monarchist generals who had retired under the Azaña laws, including Barrera, Cavalcanti, Ponte, and Orgaz. They were seconded by younger officers of lower rank still on active duty such as Varela and Major Heli-Rolando Tella, a fiery, unstable young Tercio officer. On June 1, three of the senior officers met with civilian leaders of the conspiracy in Madrid to concert activities. The free lifetime railroad passes given all officers on retirement made it easy for Orgaz and others to travel about the country drumming up financial support for the monarchist cause. Their efforts met with success; by July, one aristocratic family had placed 100,000 pesetas at Orgaz's disposal to cover the initial costs of the conspiracy.[5]

Nevertheless, despite their increasing disenchantment with the Republic, very few officers in 1931 would listen seriously to monarchist plots. They wanted no return to the political vexations of the preceding decade, and for several months the conspirators had little need of their expense funds. A small amount was spent to subsidize *La Correspondencia Militar,* which remained strongly hostile to the new government until its suppression under Azaña's law against military "journals of opinion."[6] The new monarchist journal, started at the end of 1931, was called *Acción Española* in emulation of the *Action Française,* whence it drew a portion of its rationale.

The traditional extreme right, the Carlists, reacted sharply to the coming of the Republic. Heretofore the Carlists had been steadily losing adherents, but the advent of a rigorously anticlerical regime was the strongest tonic they had received since the First Republic of 1873. They immediately began to reorganize their peasant militia, the Requetés, in Navarre. This did not mean, however, that they were willing to support the restoration of the semiliberal dynasty of Don Alfonso. Approached by Orgaz in mid-1931, Navarrese leaders of the Requetés refused to second an *alfonsino* pronunciamiento.[7] Though representatives of Don Alfonso and the current Carlist pretender developed a temporary working agreement during the autumn and winter of 1931, it was never acted on.[8]

Yet another possibility for the conspirators was the second strong socially conservative movement in the Basque provinces, Basque nationalism, which had its origins in Carlism. Though evolving in a liberal direction, the Basque movement's pro-clericalism placed it on the far right of the constituent Cortes. In the summer of 1931, Orgaz attempted to obtain the cooperation of Basque leaders in a movement to overthrow the Republic, evidently by promising recognition for local Basque fueros. Orgaz was anxious to attempt a coup before September, when the first new recruits under the Republic would be entering the Army. But no agreement could be made with the Basques, and the regular Army was apathetic, so plans for any immediate pronunciamiento had to be dropped.[9]

Resentment against the government over religious and regional policies, rather than any upsurge of monarchism, was the cause of disturbances in the Basque provinces during the summer and autumn. In response, Azaña ordered special controls placed on the arms factories at Guernica and Eibar, and field maneuvers were held in the region during the autumn. Prosecution of Primo de Rivera's deputies went on undeterred. In September, nine more generals who had held positions under the dictatorship were arrested. Meanwhile, evidence of the monarchist activities was being uncovered. In December, Orgaz was exiled to the Canary Islands and several of his associates were arrested.

The africanistas were those who suffered most from Azaña's decree of January 28, 1932, annulling the seniority rights earned by méritos de guerra awarded under Primo de Rivera. A certain amount of confusion arose over the precise rank of outstanding young generals like Franco, who had originally been promoted to brigadier by méritos, but who might, by 1932, have expected the same promotion by virtue of seniority. Before this decree, Franco had stood near the top of the seniority scale of brigadier generals on active duty; deprived of his original seniority at that rank, he now was relegated to the bottom of the brigadier list.[10] Franco had been extremely circumspect since the advent of the new regime, despite his resentment over the closing of the Zaragoza Academy. He was rewarded for his patience when Azaña, early in 1932, gave him command of the Infantry garrison at La Coruña, near his home town. Encouraged, both he and Mola later petitioned the Ministry of War that any doubt concerning the validity of their original promotions to general be removed. This, however, amounted to asking for nullification of the decree, and an announcement in the Ministry's *Diario Oficial* on July 18, 1932, refused recognition of such seniority.

More important than either Franco or Mola was José Sanjurjo, whose honeymoon with the Republic ended at the close of 1931. A Socialist peasant outbreak at Castilblanco in Estremadura brought the death of several Civil Guards. Soon afterward, a small Civil Guard detachment fired on a group of demonstrators at Arnedo (Santander), killing six. Strikes and violence by anarcho-syndicalists in the Llobregat Valley near Barcelona required extensive use of the Civil Guard and of Army detachments as well. All leftist groups vigorously protested what they called police brutality, and demanded the removal of Sanjurjo as director of the Guard.

Disturbed, Sanjurjo went to talk with the pragmatic, opportunistic leader of the Radicals, Lerroux. Throughout his long experience as a Republican conspirator, Lerroux had cultivated good relations with military leaders. He was one of the most moderate, if also one of the most corrupt, figures in the new regime, and had watched the progress of anticlerical laws and Army reorganization with apprehension. He tried to reassure Sanjurjo that things were not getting out of hand, saying that the Republic was a system of order and freedom, but that its present leaders were radical, unrealistic, and inexperienced. According to Lerroux, all problems could be solved by a change of Cabinet; if power were given to people like himself, the reign of demagogy and disorder would soon be over.[11]

Azaña, however, agreed with Sanjurjo's critics. He thought the methods of the Civil Guard heavy-handed and outmoded, and on February 5, 1932, replaced Sanjurjo with Cabanellas, an elderly Masonic liberal, who was recalled from Morocco to take over his new duties. Sanjurjo was given the post of chief of the Carabineros, a far less prestigious position. Lerroux talked him into accepting the new post, however, evidently intimating that the fall of the Azaña government was only a matter of time.[12]

These meetings had not gone undetected, though they were vigorously denied by Lerroux. On January 7, the Socialist Minister of Labor, Largo Caballero, had warned frustrated generals against rebellion, saying that any new pronunciamiento was clearly doomed to failure. In the Army debate on March 11, Azaña declared that most of the thousands of newly retired officers were loyal to the Republic, but admitted: "There are some—I don't know the exact number—fifty, a hundred, two hundred—who apparently are not satisfied, or regret having retired, or who expected catastrophes that did not occur, and who are now involved in constant or intermittent action against the Republic."[13]

A few weeks later, Sanjurjo made his attitude clear in an interview given a French journalist: "We will loyally serve the existing government; but if, by chance, the trend to the left should lead Spain to anarchy, we will rapidly assume full responsibility for the reestablishment of order. Our first duty is the maintenance of public order, and we shall perform it at all costs. No revolutionary government will be established in Madrid."[14] In other words, Army leaders would continue to accept bourgeois liberals, but a Socialist regime would be intolerable. By the spring of 1932, Sanjurjo was in intermittent contact with the monarchist conspirators as well as with the right-wing Republican elements determined to drive Azaña from power.

Their prospects having thus improved a trifle, the retired monarchist generals spread their net. In April, Ponte arranged to fly to Rome with a monarchist politician to talk with the Italian Air Marshal Balbo. An unofficial agreement was concluded, which did not formally commit the Italian government but promised arms and financial aid through indirect channels for the restoration of an "authoritarian" monarchy.[15] It was not clear how such assistance was to be effected, however, and the monarchist generals later decided that Italian assistance might prove undesirable.

The dissidents gained further strength from the alarm generated among the military by the progress of the Catalan autonomy statute in the Cortes. One of the bill's most ardent opponents was General Juan Fanjul, a conservative nationalist who had won a seat in the rightist Agrarian Party. Long obsessed with the danger from the left, Fanjul read a series of Catalanist diatribes into the Cortes record in an effort to prove that the ultimate goal of the Catalan movement was outright separatism. These and other alarms prompted Sanjurjo to a third consultation with Lerroux, evidently in early June. Once more the wily old politician counseled patience, saying that he was working hard to arrange matters, but was not certain that the Catalan Statute could be headed off.[16]

The monarchist conspiracy meanwhile assumed more definite form. A clandestine junta was set up, and Barrera, highest in seniority among the participating generals, was asked to assume its direction, primarily because it was thought that his presence would give an appearance of authority and discipline to the movement. Though not overly enthusiastic, Barrera accepted chairmanship of the junta, for which an expense fund of 300,000 pesetas was collected.[17]

Non-monarchist generals in Madrid such as Goded, the Chief of Staff, and the africanista General Villegas, head of the First Division, were also conspiring.[18] They, in turn, were approached by a small group of ultraconservative Republicans led by Melquiades Alvarez and Manuel Burgos y Mazo. Leaders of the struggle against Primo de Rivera, these conservatives believed that the Republic had gotten off the track, and they hoped to provoke a moderate Republican coup before the lines became too clearly drawn. They had considerable difficulty obtaining support from wealthy people, however, and had to compete with the monarchists for the favor of disgruntled generals.[19]

By June, the conspirators were so active that their maneuvers could not be kept secret. The anarchist FAI published a leaflet denouncing such intrigues, and in a speech given at Avila in June the Radical Socialist Alvaro de Albornoz sneered: "The generals think the regime is going to quake just because they sneeze."[20] At first, however, the only dissident to draw punishment was Cavalcanti, who was sentenced to a month's imprisonment for outspoken public criticism of government measures.

A more serious incident occurred on June 27, when a military review was held at the Carabanchel airdrome outside Madrid. Most of the local military hierarchy was on hand as General Goded addressed the assembled troops and urged them to maintain discipline, "nerve and essence of military institutions," and emphasized that soldiers "should abstain from political quarrels, which demean the mission of the military." Nonetheless, he could not resist giving vent to his feelings against the regime, and ended his speech with the words, "Now, a *viva* to Spain, and nothing more, will suffice," thus ignoring any salute to the Republic.[21] Most of the assembled officers echoed his cry. The conspicuous exception was Lt. Col. Julio Mangada, also an africanista but an ultraliberal and professional nonconformist. When Goded reprimanded him for not joining in the patriotic shout, Mangada began an argument. Villegas, the commander of his division, ordered Mangada arrested. Mangada had played an active role in the pro-Republican plots of 1930–31, and his incarceration provoked loud protests in the press of the liberal left, which demanded the dismissal of Goded and Villegas.

Azaña had no illusions regarding Mangada's good sense, noting in his diary "Mangada is crazy," describing him as a "vegetarian, an Esperanto faddist, and a spiritualist." He finally observed: "He [Mangada] is the type of officer who is a nonconformist because of mental imbalance; such men flourished under the monarchy."[22] Yet Azaña was convinced that he must complete the republicanization of the Army, and hence was not free to ignore either Goded's words and attitude or the demands of the liberal left. Pressure was therefore exerted to obtain the resignation of Goded, and Villegas and the commander of the First Infantry Brigade were also removed.[23] All three were replaced by generals of proven Republican sympathies.

The official Socialist organ, *El Socialista,* made a strong attack on the military on June 30 in an article entitled "Military Psychiatry," which brought a sharp reaction from the generals. Meanwhile, the Catalan Statute proceeded apace in the Cortes. Sanjurjo made his fourth and final visit to Lerroux in mid-July. He said that he now despaired of conservative politicians, and could rely only on his fellow officers to make the necessary changes.[24] These fellow officers were not, however, of one mind about what to do. Goded was thirsting for revenge against Azaña, but he was not a monarchist and did not see eye to eye with the Barrera junta, which was eager not only to gain full control of Sanjurjo but to obtain support from the Carlists as well.

The right-wing Republican plotters hoped to keep Sanjurjo on the side of Republicanism. They were also trying to win the support of the moderately liberal Cabanellas, new head of the Civil Guard.[25] The jovial Sanjurjo was an emotional, nonintellectual man who had built his reputation mainly as a combat leader. He had few clear ideas about politics, and could not be depended on to chart a straight course. According to Burgos y Mazo:

Sanjurjo was brave and chivalrous in the extreme; yet, though he had a great heart, his [political] understanding was scant. Because it seemed that he might vacillate for emotional reasons, we worked directly and constantly to influence him. For this purpose we placed General Goded at his side, though with sufficient tact so that he would not feel under supervision. The two generals complemented each other: Goded possessed the intellect to conceive plans and organize them, while Sanjurjo had the heroic arm of iron to carry them out.[26]

During the month of July, Sanjurjo traveled widely throughout the country, ostensibly on an inspection tour of the Carabineros. His actual purpose was to talk with a wide variety of military leaders and try to achieve some consensus about what to do. Literally hundreds of officers were directly or indirectly urging him on,[27] but complete confusion reigned as to what form intervention should take. At this time there existed the monarchist conspiracy of Barrera, the right-wing Republican plot linked with Goded, and the machinations of various cells of officers who wanted to do something but distrusted almost all the politicians.

The Carlists refused to participate officially with either Sanjurjo or the Barrera junta, though individual Carlists were left free to take part purely on their own responsibility. The commander of the Cádiz garrison, Colonel José Enrique Varela, one of the very few active officers with Carlist sympathies, told Sanjurjo that he would support him in a revolt, but added that fundamental political differences between himself and most of the other participants prevented his taking the initiative in any such action.[28]

The great majority of the officers on active duty refused to commit themselves, but the Barrera junta eventually obtained promises of cooperation from a handful of officers willing to lead a revolt in a number of key garrisons. Even to obtain this much, the monarchist plotters had to promise some of the other conspirators that there would be no immediate effort to restore the king, and that elections for a new constituent Cortes would be held. Thus, many officers understood the movement to be directed, not against the Republic, but simply against the present leadership, in nineteenth-century pronunciamiento style. Through such maneuvering, and the urging of old comrades, the Barrera junta outdistanced the right-wing Republican plotters in winning the cooperation of Sanjurjo.

The final meeting of the conspirators was held on August 8, just outside Madrid. There was considerable apprehension over the flimsy organization of the plot, but the monarchist generals feared that further delay might be fatal to its success. Barrera would assume principal direction in Madrid, while Sanjurjo seized command in Seville. Uprisings were also scheduled for four other centers. Non-monarchist rebels, such as General Goded, were not even informed of the exact timing of the pronunciamiento,[29] because the monarchists were hoping to bypass the moderates and proceed directly to a restoration. Barrera had already established a secret headquarters with the ultra-monarchist generals Cavalcanti and Fernández Pérez.[30] It appears that only a few hundred officers pledged themselves to action, though many more promised to do nothing to oppose a coup. It was foreseen that it might not be possible to seize government headquarters in Madrid by assault; but the rebels were hoping that the Cabinet, faced with revolt, would collapse. As Sanjurjo's aide later wrote, with only slight exaggeration: "No one thought that it would come to the point of fighting."[31]

Meanwhile, the government was well informed about the plot. Numerous confidential conversations had been nonchalantly conducted over the telephone, and some "secrets" had become common knowledge.[32] The *sanjurjada* was to begin in the early morning of

August 10. In Madrid, the plan was to capture Azaña in his residence at the Ministry of War. The rebels hoped to win over the commanders of the Civil Guard, though Barrera was by no means certain that this would be possible.[33]

As it turned out, only one undermanned Cavalry battalion supported the rebellion in the capital, and all the Guards units remained loyal. While Azaña watched part of the skirmishing from a window in the War Ministry, the revolt was easily broken. A score of insurgents were killed, and most of the leaders in Madrid were captured, though the skeptical Barrera succeeded in making a prearranged getaway by private airplane.[34] The other revolts, planned for northern Spain, never occurred, for local conspirators were awaiting signs of success in Madrid before acting. When none appeared, they scattered.[35]

The only centers won by the insurgents were Seville and Jerez, where Sanjurjo easily gained control. The rebels declared that their coup was aimed against the Cabinet, not the regime. Sanjurjo's manifesto stated that a provisional junta would be installed prior to the convocation of some undefined kind of constituent Cortes, and, in an effort to reassure non-monarchists, ended with the slogan "Long live national sovereignty!"[36] Though resistance was offered only at the Seville airdrome, lack of response from other parts of the country made Sanjurjo's position desperate. Officers of the local garrison had never been especially enthusiastic, and after word spread that the rebellion was aimed at restoration of the king, some units refused further support.[37] On August 11, with a column of loyal troops moving rapidly toward Seville, the general saw no alternative save to free his associates from obligation and flee. He set out in a touring car for the Portuguese border. He had never been eager to participate in the revolt; now, no longer knowing where to turn, he first fled, then surrendered to the Civil Guard at Huelva.[38]

Some two hundred rebels were brought to trial over a period of seventeen months. Sanjurjo, the most important of those arrested, did not even try to put up a defense. He was condemned to death, but his sentence was commuted to life imprisonment. Eventually 144 convicted conspirators, mostly Army officers, were sent into penal exile at Río de Oro, in the Spanish Sahara.[39] A small-scale purge was carried out among the military, and approximately 300 other officers who were found to be implicated were deprived of command and left without assignment. Three monarchist generals who had escaped the country —Barrera, Ponte, and Manso de Zúñiga—were expelled in absentia

from the Officer Corps. To conclude the cycle, the official trial of the
generals who had sat in Primo de Rivera's Military Directory was also
held, and sentence was passed on December 8, 1932, decreeing terms
of from six to eight years in military prison or provincial exile for
those unlucky enough not to have fled the country.

Republican leaders congratulated themselves on how easily they
had smothered the revolt, and laughed at the futile efforts of the conspirators.[40] That only five per cent of the Officer Corps had directly
backed the plot seemed to prove that the Spanish military had finally
been tamed; lacking the support of public opinion, how could they
pose a threat to the established authorities?[41] Nevertheless, just to be
on the safe side, the government increased the Assault Guard to double
its size, or 10,000 men.

The rebellion provided justification for the only measure of direct
agrarian reform carried out by the Azaña administration: the confisca-
tion of the land of the grandees of Spain. Most of the high aristocracy
had directly or indirectly encouraged the conspiracy, and the government used this excuse, on September 8, to expropriate the territories
of 382 titled families. Coinciding with final approval of the Catalan
autonomy statute, this was the last of the Azaña reforms.

The Republican regime seemed more secure than ever, but there
was less cause for satisfaction than the Republican left supposed. Lack
of inherent unity, brought out more clearly by the apparent absence
of danger from the right, made it increasingly difficult for the several
liberal and leftist groups supporting the government coalition to work
together. The Azaña regime had already passed its zenith, and early
in 1933 began to founder.

Moreover, satisfaction regarding the failure of the *sanjurjada* was
somewhat exaggerated. So poorly conceived and executed a plot never
enjoyed much chance of success, but its failure did not prove that the
Republic had won over or neutralized the Army; it simply indicated
that the climate of opinion in mid-1932 discouraged rebellion. Should
that climate change and the military remain disaffected, the regime
would be less secure than its leaders believed. Although only a few
hundred officers had actually supported the rebellion, a great many
more had listened with varying degrees of sympathy to the entreaties
of the conspirators. Sanjurjo's prestige did not suffer greatly from his
failure; rather, the sight of one of the bravest of the African generals, a
soldier who held Spain's highest military decoration, the *Gran cruz
laureada,* condemned to a Republican jail for the rest of his days won

many sympathizers among the Officer Corps.[42] As was later pointed out, the Republican leaders might have done better to shoot him.

Scarcely a month passed before the monarchist conspirators resumed their activities. The young ideologue Vegas Latapié proposed that there be a special commando-type assault on the government centers in Madrid rather than any more attempts to coordinate rebellion among the military garrisons. This notion was quickly discarded as inadequate, and the Staff captain Jorge Vigón, who joined the conspirators in southwestern France, convinced them that their best chance still lay in a well-articulated plot among the active Army commanders.[43] However, careful planning and guarantees were needed, and especially a sort of insurance fund from which to provide pensions for the families of generals who might lose their lives in a revolt: some such assurance was necessary to overcome the wait-and-see attitude that had been fatal to the plot of August 10. It was hoped to collect no less than twenty million pesetas for the pension fund. The wealthiest monarchist families were asked to make a minimum contribution of 50,000 pesetas each.[44] A number did so, for the agrarian confiscations levied against the grandees made ultraconservatives more willing to contribute to a conspiracy in the autumn of 1932 than they had been during the preceding spring. Though the ultimate goal was never achieved, within a few weeks' time at least one and a half million pesetas had been collected.[45]

During the last months of 1932, the technical direction of the conspiracy among the military was assumed by Lt. Col. Valentín Galarza of the General Staff, who adopted the code name "El Técnico."[46] He had covered his tracks carefully and, though involved in the *sanjurjada*, had not compromised himself so badly that any charges could be proved. The only penalty he had suffered was dismissal from active duty. Azaña had noted on August 29:

I have left without command another lieutenant colonel of the General Staff, Galarza, an intimate of Sanjurjo and of Goded, who was, until the coming of the Republic, one of the most conspicuous loiterers in the Ministry of War. Galarza is very intelligent, capable, accommodating, slippery, and obedient. But he is definitely on the other side. In the legal report there is nothing against him, but he is nonetheless one of the most dangerous.[47]

Galarza built up a rather extensive espionage ring among the police and other government agencies that was said to cost the monarchists 5,000 pesetas a month to operate. One of his major goals was to win over the most important generals on the active list. Franco was an object of particular attention. "Thorough and addicted to detail, he [Galarza] professed great affection for General Franco, to whom he was drawn by a certain similarity . . . of character." However, it was impossible to ascertain how close Franco actually was to the monarchists. Ansaldo remarks:

Franco is a man who declares himself, and then retracts; draws near, and then steps back; vanishes or slides away; always vague, never clear and categorical. He had seemed to be the most monarchist of the young Spanish generals, and presented himself as such before the king, who firmly believed in him. He was the king's *gentilhombre de cámara* [lord of the bedchamber] when that was a special favor bespeaking signal loyalty. On the other hand, in spite of the fact that his participation in the coup had for some time been considered certain, shortly before the day appointed for its execution he excused himself from all obligations and counseled various other officers to do likewise.

His constant declarations of loyalty to the Republican regime, and the celebrated speech given by him in the General Academy, . . . in which he defined, as the absolute and unquestionable duty of every officer, blind discipline to the established power, "even more when the heart bleeds than when our natural impulses prompt us to it," won him the confidence of successive Republican cabinets.[48]

The government handled the commanding generals with a carrot-and-stick policy. So long as they remained politically loyal, they were left to enjoy comfortable posts. On March 16, 1933, Franco was promoted to the military command of the Balearic Islands. Galarza and his colleagues enjoyed scant success with generals holding such positions.

A leader of senior rank and prestige was needed by the conspirators. With Sanjurjo in prison and Barrera somewhat discredited, their choice eventually fell on the ogre of Montjuich, Severiano Martínez Anido, who was living in exile at Nice. At the end of 1932, he received a written invitation from Don Alfonso to move to Rome and assume direction of the monarchist conspiracy, but he remained unconvinced and declined the request.[49] At the other extreme, the monarchists carried on "limited contacts" with the CNT, encouraging leftist extremism against the Republic.[50] This naturally fell in with the plans of the anarchist FAI, which, in January 1933, carried out a kind of commando raid on the Army barracks at Lérida in which four soldiers were wounded.

The terms of the offer to Martínez Anido indicated that the monarchists hoped to make Rome their base of operations. Don Alfonso was moving there himself, for the Fascist regime might provide special assistance. Early in 1933, another conference was held with Air Marshal Balbo. This time the chief monarchist representative was José Calvo Sotelo, who had been spending the greater part of his exile in Paris. There he had come under the influence of the Action Française, and his thinking had evolved beyond somewhat parochial notions of Maurist Youth reformism to a more contemporary European creed of corporative monarchism under some form of dictatorship.[51] In his conversations with Balbo, the possibility of concrete Italian assistance was discussed, and during the course of 1933 other leading monarchist exiles, such as Cardinal Segura, General Barrera, and Antonio Goicoechea (head of the new monarchist political organization Renovación Española), participated in talks at Rome.[52]

These peripheral maneuvers could accomplish little, however, unless they received the support of important elements within Spain. In the summer of 1933, Azaña's tenuous liberal coalition finally broke up, and new elections were scheduled for the autumn. The reaction of pro-clerical conservatism was taking organized shape in the political confederation known as the CEDA (Spanish Confederation of Autonomous Rightist Groups). It was preparing the best-financed, best-organized electoral campaign in Spanish history, and had won the support of most anti-leftist elements. With the forces of moderate conservatism predicting imminent victory at the polls, neither military nor civilian opponents of Republican liberalism showed much interest in armed conspiracy.

CHAPTER SIXTEEN

The Army and the Bienio Negro

THE ELECTIONS of November 19, 1933, were a disaster for the Republican left. The conservative coalition won 192 seats and the center returned 163 deputies, while the Socialists held only 60 places and Azaña's group was reduced to a mere 5 seats. Stronger unity, organization, and finance among those on the right, a general reaction against the Azaña regime by much of the middle class, and an increased vote resulting from the introduction of female suffrage had all contributed to the left's defeat. However, the CEDA itself held only 115 seats, and the clerical leader Gil Robles was unable to form a Cabinet without the support of part of the center. This he could not obtain. The President, Alcalá Zamora, feared and distrusted the CEDA, and intended to keep the Republic on an even keel. Consequently, during the next two years the government was composed of fragile center-right coalitions dominatd by the opportunistic Radicals of Lerroux.

As he had told Sanjurjo, Lerroux thought that the Republic had moved too far too fast. Though the CEDA was frustrated in its efforts to achieve reform of the religious laws, the government neglected the implementation of those articles and refused to speed up agrarian reform. The two years 1934–35 thus constituted for the left a *bienio negro*—a "black biennium" of governmental immobility, which effectively blocked, if it did not altogether reverse, the policies of the preceding administration. If this was a period of frustration for the left, it also offered little encouragement for the radical right, since political leadership anchored on dead center tended to soothe a large portion of the frightened middle classes and discourage recourse to violence.

Yet leftist disorder was not lessening, and several incidents during the winter of 1933–34 directly affected the Army. In mid-December, an anarchist peasant group led by a disaffected Army sergeant occupied the military recruitment center at the village of Villanueva de la Serena in Badajoz, and several companies of troops and guards had to be called to drive them out. Nine men were killed in this disturbance. At about the same time, four Civil Guards were slain near Valencia while attempting to control a demonstration. In March, a Socialist plot was uncovered within the Nineteenth Infantry Regiment, stationed at Aranjuez, southeast of Madrid. A captain, a lieutenant, and a sergeant were cashiered, and some two hundred troops disciplined.[1]

By the end of 1933, a certain number of officers—though apparently only a small minority—believed that the Republican system in its present form was not likely to work, no matter what the outcome of one or two elections. The result was a mild recrudescence of juntero feeling. During the winter, a new clandestine officers' association, the Unión Militar Española (UME), was organized. It had only a small fraction of the support enjoyed by the Juntas in 1917. The UME's structure, like that of the Juntas, was decentralized, even anarchic, and its membership was drawn almost entirely from junior and middle-rank officers. There was no precise agreement on aims, which seem to have varied from cell to cell. Some UME groups were concerned about professional perquisites and others mainly about protecting the Fatherland from leftist revolution, while a few established close contact with monarchist conspirators.

The first director of the organization was the retired colonel Emilio Tarduchy, a former partisan of the Primo de Rivera regime. Tarduchy was also a leading member of the small fascistic movement Falange Española, which had been organized in October 1933 by the late dictator's eldest son, José Antonio Primo de Rivera. Partly as a consequence of these connections, military associates soon came to regard Tarduchy as too sectarian, and after the beginning of 1934 he played a less active role in the UME's development. He was replaced by the General Staff captain Bartolomé Barba Hernández, a relatively young and well-to-do officer with an almost paranoid hatred of the left and of Azaña.

Leaders of the Madrid UME group drew up a sort of political program in the spring of 1934 that emphasized the need to "save order and authority" in Spain. It stated that the organization's goal was not to overthrow the legally established regime but rather to defend it against revolution or departures from "legality." It was stressed that the Army should not seek to impose itself on the nation, but instead should strive to protect order and justice, and, if forced to intervene, should resign power as soon as possible in favor of the "responsible" portion of the citizenry. During 1934, a right-wing Republican lawyer and *capitán de complemento* named Eduardo Pardo Reina, who served as a kind of judicial secretary to the Junta Central, was active in the Madrid UME and helped develop a "constitutionalist" policy. But this program did not represent the political feeling of all UME members, for some officers could not agree with Pardo Reina's emphasis on moderation.[2]

A major weakness of the UME was its lack of influence among the generals. Its leaders were especially interested in the younger, more active and politically oriented generals who had not tied themselves to monarchist reaction—men such as Goded, Mola, and Franco. Mola approved the program drawn up by the Madrid Junta Central, but said that because of political pressures he felt that he must reject the committee's request to serve as its leader. Goded in turn emphasized the importance of winning Franco's support, while Franco himself refused to join, though promising vaguely to do his duty.[3]

The organization of the UME was regularized in May 1934, when the Junta Central, though itself a committee without any official head, assumed supervisory powers. Goded indicated he would accept the Junta's authority, though he was not actually a member of it. He is said to have asked Pardo Reina to prepare a draft of any legislation that might be needed to avert subversion, together with the juridical logic for such statutes. Apparently such an outline was discussed and approved by both Goded and Mola.[4]

Meanwhile, the Ministry of War had been taken over at the beginning of 1934 by one of the Radicals, Diego Hidalgo, a middle-class politician from southern Spain with literary pretensions but no experience in military matters. In general, he tried to implement the Radicals' policy of conciliating the pressure groups that had suffered under Azaña. On February 2, ten days after assuming office, he softened the terms imposed by Azaña for the total elimination of vacancies occurring in certain branches of the Officer Corps. In those branches where maximum reductions had been decreed, Hidalgo ruled that only three out of every four positions left vacant would be done away with, and that one would be left open for promotions. Except for introducing this relaxation of Azaña's rule, Hidalgo accomplished little as Minister of War, disclaiming the right to make "basic changes" at that time. He raised sergeants' pay slightly but lowered the total budget, for the government was still trying to balance its finances. The War Minister early formed a very favorable impression of Franco, whom he promoted to major general in March 1934, thus settling once and for all the question of whether or not Franco's campaign méritos would be recognized.[5]

In the spring of 1934 the last territorial expansion in recent Spanish history took place. Amid a welter of domestic frustration and negative legislative proposals, the government decided to go ahead with the long-delayed occupation of the coastal slice of western Morocco known as Ifni, which had originally been awarded to Spain in the 1860 treaty. This action was feasible because the French authorities had recently pacified the tribes in that area. An expedition to establish Spanish control was placed under Colonel Capaz, an expert in native affairs. Capaz was a moderate liberal, and was associated with the Radicals. These factors made him the logical choice to direct the force of 935 men that landed on April 6 to guarantee Spanish sovereignty. The troops encountered no resistance in this barren region of 2,000 square kilometers and 20,000 nomadic inhabitants,[6] and soon Capaz was being hailed by spokesmen in Madrid as "the last of the Conquistadores."

Meanwhile, the monarchist conspirators realized that the lack of response among Army officers, combined with the electoral victory of civilian moderates and conservatives, made it necessary for them to seek help abroad. Their ideology was developing into a theory of corporate dictatorship; should their plot ever succeed, they would be the natural allies of Fascist Italy. At the beginning of spring, yet another delegation was sent to Rome. This one was received by Mussolini himself, for the Duce had come to regard the apparent success of a democratic republic in Spain as a reef in *mare nostrum*. On March 31, 1934, he signed an agreement with Spanish monarchists, both alfonsino and Carlist, pledging the Italian government to supply a limited amount of arms and money for a monarchist restoration in Spain.[7] It soon became plain that the Carlists and alfonsinos would not be able to agree on a division of the equipment, even if any were sent; however, the Carlists did obtain facilities in Libya and Sardinia to train Requeté squads in modern warfare. During the year following, three Requeté units of 40 volunteers each, together with the units' chaplains, left Spain for military instruction.[8] Yet the broader terms of the pact would remain a dead letter unless the monarchist conspirators within Spain could generate positive support—and there was no indication that they could during 1934.

It was the extreme left, not the extreme right, that was ready for violent rebellion. Claiming that "the triumph of reaction" must be stopped at all costs, fearing loss of support to the anarchists, and seeing an opportunity to carry out a real revolution, the main group of Socialist leaders dropped their allegiance to the Republic. On March 11, 1934, *El Socialista* declared: "We were only circumstantially Republican. . . . The cataclysm can and must be the rebirth of the great Spain of which we have dreamed, and whose restoration we have planned." Like the monarchists, they imported arms: in June, a large cache of pistols was found in the home of one Socialist Cortes deputy.[9] In several parts of the country efforts were made to form "workers' alliances" of Socialists, Communists, and anarcho-syndicalists. Moreover, the Supreme Court's veto of a Catalan law to protect the land tenure of poor peasants left many Catalanists disillusioned with their supposedly autonomous status and alienated from the Madrid government. Catalan extremists were ripe for a revolt that would give them the opportunity to proclaim their "independence."

At the beginning of October, the minority Radical Cabinet collapsed. Lerroux was authorized to form a new government, but could not gather enough voting support to do so until he accepted three CEDA members as Cabinet members. To the extreme left, the proclerical CEDA was "objectively" fascist and stood for total reaction and the end of any democratic republic. Formation of the new Cabinet became the signal for a general strike by the Socialist UGT, and armed revolt in Barcelona and Asturias. Both the attempted general strike and the Catalan rebellion quickly failed for lack of planning and organized support. The Army commander at Barcelona, General Domingo Batet, was a wealthy liberal who had been involved in the conspiracies against Primo de Rivera. The Minister of War had recalled him to Madrid in mid-September and had assured himself that the general was thoroughly reliable. Batet was able to stifle the Barcelona revolt with little bloodshed.

The insurrection in Asturias was an entirely different matter. With Socialists, Communists, and anarcho-syndicalists all cooperating (at least to a certain degree), it became the first organized attempt at proletarian revolution in Spanish history. Workers and peasants from the mining districts proved tough and determined. Police barracks all over the province were stormed by sheer force or blown up with lighted sticks of dynamite tossed like hand grenades by the miners. Within a few days, the insurgents controlled all the mining district save the center of Oviedo itself, where the Army garrison of less than a thousand men was dug in firmly.

Although the government had foreseen its coming, the Asturian revolt was soon completely out of hand. The War Minister seems to have lacked confidence in the Chief of the General Staff, Masquelet, who had replaced Goded in 1932. This may have been because Masquelet, a Mason and an appointee of the Azaña group, was rumored to be a liberal Republican. At any rate, in mid-September Hidalgo had called Franco to Madrid to serve as technical adviser to the General Staff during field maneuvers, then encouraged him to remain a few weeks longer in case trouble broke out.[10] Despite his nominally marginal position, Franco played a leading role in coordinating forces for the Asturian repression. He has been given credit for the decision to call elite units from Morocco to suppress the miners. In view of the speed with which these forces were dispatched, it seems likely that they had been placed on alert before the rebellion began.

In hurried consultation with the new Cabinet, Masquelet obtained approval for a plan of combined operations under the overall command of General López de Ochoa, Army inspector for the northwest region. Few generals were more genuinely Republican than Ochoa; because he was identified with the moderates rather than the ultraliberals, he was the choice of Lerroux and the other ministers.[11] Three columns of garrison units were hastily organized on October 6 to converge on Asturias. The largest, composed of two Infantry battalions and a few Artillery units from the garrisons southeast of the battle zone, was blocked by miners in the mountain passes leading from León and could not break through until the 16th. Another battalion, shipped from La Coruña, was unable to move inland from Gijón. The third column, under López de Ochoa, consisted of a single battalion; this force marched eastward from Lugo and fought its way into Oviedo on the afternoon of the 11th, but was too weak to break the siege, and served only to reinforce the beleaguered garrison.

The tide was turned by several battalions of veterans from the Tercio and Regulares in Morocco that arrived at Gijón on the 10th. Commanded by Lt. Col. Juan Yagüe, an africanista and former comrade of Franco, they incorporated the battalion from La Coruña and, 3,000 strong, fought their way through to the relief of the Asturian capital on the afternoon of the 12th. By the morning of April 14 the units from Morocco had completely cleared the district around Oviedo, and the arms works at Trubia were re-won three days later.

On April 19, López de Ochoa was able to report that the revolt had been completely subdued.[12]

Lacking artillery and military organization, the rebels surrendered unconditionally, asking only that the Moorish Regulares not lead the occupation of the workers' districts. Atrocities were committed by both sides. It is possible that the revolutionaries shot as many as forty people, but an equal number of rebels may have been killed out of hand by the men of the Regulares and the Tercio, and there were numerous charges of attacks on women.[13] After the surrender, the Civil Guard took over the task of repression. Headed by the notorious Captain Doval, who had won his spurs under Martínez Anido at Barcelona, they employed a variety of tortures to obtain confessions of guilt, and a number of prisoners vanished altogether during their incarceration.[14] The well-known journalist Luis Sirval, who had published several articles about the repression, was shot down by a Legionnaire who took umbrage at the writer's "insults."

López de Ochoa was eager to dissociate the Army from the repression.[15] He ordered that there be no reprisals against captured revolutionaries; moreover, he tried to keep the African units under control, and apparently ordered the execution of several Moroccans guilty of misconduct. This brought a sharp clash with Yagüe, who charged that the commanding officers were being too soft with the rebels. Yagüe and several other africanista critics, such as Colonel José Solchaga, were soon ordered out of Asturias and back to regular commands.[16] After public debate over Doval's police tactics, the government removed him from his post.

The revolt was a strong stimulus to rightist conspirators. In Madrid, Galarza and Vigón said that the moment had come for a monarchist coup. They calculated that the revolt had caused such revulsion among the middle classes that even conservative Republican authorities might be tempted to support a rightist takeover, and the attitude of certain generals at the Ministry of War seemed encouraging. Since 1932, most discontented officers had looked to Sanjurjo as their symbolic leader. Pardoned by the Radical government, he was currently living in exile at Lisbon. It was suggested that, if properly encouraged, Army commanders might join his banner in revolt, and plans were made to fly him to Oviedo. This notion was soon dropped, however, when Franco and other leading generals at Madrid declared the moment inopportune for action.[17]

Thereafter, nearly all the groups in the center and on the right competed directly for the favor of the military. The monarchist leader in the Cortes was Calvo Sotelo, who before the last election had obtained cancellation of the charges against him for having been a minister of the dictatorship. Calvo was now groping toward some kind of radical, dynamic rightist ideology that would attract nonmonarchist elements as well. High on his list of priorities was the need to win over the Army. On November 6, two and a half weeks after the fighting ended in Asturias, he stood up in the Cortes to denounce the antimilitarist character of the Republican Constitution, two articles of which, he said, amounted to "a defeatist's catechism." One was Article 70, which declared military personnel ineligible for the office of President of the Republic unless they had been retired for ten years.

> The other is Article 6, which says: "Spain renounces war as an instrument of national policy." I say to you that this Article is largely responsible for the recent disaster that we now lament.
> The spirit and letter, the tone and wording of this precept—an absurd nuisance got up in a few hours of madness by a Chamber factiously raised up against the Spanish national spirit—must be completely rectified. It is necessary to infuse a new spirit in Spanish youth. It is necessary to organize premilitary education—today more necessary than ever—and to erase from the heart of youth the monstrous hatred of this sacred institution that for years has been freely implanted by leaders . . . who flee when the movement fails, while their poor, deceived comrades are taken to jail or the cemetery. It is necessary to affirm Spain's need for a powerful Army and to restore moral satisfaction and spiritual dignity to the leaders of that Army. It is necessary, in a word, that the honor of the Army be the very honor of Spain. Senor Azaña said that the Army is no more than the arm of the Fatherland. False, absurd, sophistical! It is now obvious that the Army is much more than the arm of the Fatherland. I shall not say that it is its head, for it ought not to be that; but it is much more than the arm. It is the spinal column—and if it breaks, bends, or cracks, it is Spain that is bent or broken.[18]

Calvo Sotelo led a political assault on Hidalgo for inefficiency and discrimination, and denounced the War Minister for not having taken sufficient precautions to prevent the initial success of the revolt. Moreover, he wanted to know why certain "senior leftist officers" had not been removed from their posts. Hidalgo insisted that none of these charges could be substantiated, but feeling against him was so strong that he resigned on November 16. To avoid worse complications, Lerroux, the Prime Minister, assumed the duties of Minister of War as well.[19]

While the right demanded the death penalty for leading revolutionaries, leftist propagandists mounted a large-scale campaign against the police atrocities in Asturias and the use of African mercenaries against Spaniards. Several thousand leftists were in jail, and the Lerroux government realized that it would be best to make as few martyrs as possible. Only three rebel leaders were condemned to death, and their sentences were commuted by the Prime Minister, following the precedent set in the case of Sanjurjo two years earlier. The only rebels legally executed were a Sergeant Vázquez, who had deserted his Army detachment to join the revolutionaries, and an Asturian worker convicted of having personally directed the murder of eight Civil Guards. Rightist leaders were not satisfied with this, and continued to demand the execution of all the top revolutionaries. They were not slow to denounce the partiality of justice that could shoot a mutinous NCO but spare the leaders of the mutiny, including a former Army officer, Major Pérez Farras, who had commanded the Catalan militia.[20] Rightist opposition on this issue led to another Cabinet reorganization in March.

While avoiding harshness in dealing with most of the leftists, Lerroux pacified the military by arranging promotions or new assignments for ambitious generals. The old Radical *jefe* did not think there was any great problem in dealing with the military. As a Republican in the Ruiz Zorrilla tradition, he had always been aware of the importance of good relations with the officers:[21] "The Spanish Army has a frankly liberal spirit. A majority of the officers are indifferent to the form of government, and a minority are Republican, or, more frequently, monarchist."[22] This was a roughly correct evaluation, and Lerroux believed that reasonable treatment of the military would suffice to keep them manageable. In February 1935, Franco was rewarded for his prudent abstention from political involvement by being given the coveted post of Commander in Chief of the forces in Morocco. Goded, without assignment for nearly three years, was brought back to serve in the War Ministry. The ultra-nationalist Fanjul, who was considered a "dangerous" brigadier, was promoted to major general because he stood at the top of the seniority list and Lerroux deemed it impolitic to delay him any longer. The Prime Minister was especially proud of giving a regular assignment to the mutilated Millán Astray, whom some had wanted to place on the inactive list.

Such appointments and maneuvering did not, however, satisfy a minority of the most radical and activist officers, especially in the lower ranks. Reaction to the leftist revolt brought a surge of new members into the UME, and by the beginning of 1935 the organization had begun to attract a genuine following.[23] During and after the fighting in Asturias, UME leaders held conversations with the heads of the recently formed fascist party, Falange Española. On the morrow of the miners' revolt, the more radical Falangist leaders, like the monarchists, had been eager to use the declaration of martial law to arrange a coup.[24] However, the Falange's *Jefe Nacional,* José Antonio Primo de Rivera, could not forget that the officers had given his father very uncertain support, and he professed scant regard for the political talents of the military. At the beginning of 1935, a long conversation was finally held between José Antonio and several UME leaders, among them Barba Hernández and Pardo Reina. Like all radical anti-Republicans, José Antonio recognized that only the Army could provide the force to overthrow the Republic in the near future. The most that UME leaders would concede the Falangists was a place of priority for their propaganda under the temporary military junta that would result from a rebellion.[25] Beyond that, José Antonio and the UME chiefs agreed on a program of limited economic reform that would preserve the capitalist order, affirmed the principle of republicanism (or at least nonmonarchism), and supported the separation of Church and State (though they rejected some of the existing anticlerical legislation).[26]

At the end of February, the UME also established contact with Carlist and alfonsino conspirators.[27] The main link was Galarza. After consultation with Don Alfonso in Rome, Galarza told the UME leaders that the monarchists would be willing to subsidize UME activities, just as they were currently underwriting part of the Falange's expenses.[28]

By the spring of 1935, the political complexion of the UME's Junta Central was changing. There was less concern about defending the government from revolution and more talk about taking the lead in a pronunciamiento. Membership was eclectic: the six principal figures were Barba Hernández, who might simply be termed a militarist; the retired Infantry lieutenant colonel Tarduchy, formerly Falangist, now pro-Carlist; the retired Infantry major Luis Arrendondo, the first chief of the Falangist militia and currently one of the UME's most active organizers; the retired Infantry colonel Ricardo Rada, a strong Carlist; and finally, the Engineers captain Sánchez Sacristán and the Infantry captain Gándara, whose political views were less easily labeled.[29]

The most active and influential were Barba Hernández and Goded. Barba served as chairman, and Goded, though not technically a mem-

ber, lobbied with great effectiveness after Lerroux appointed him to
a new inspectorate in the Ministry of War. Prompted by Barba Hernández and Goded, the Junta Central sent Pardo Reina to Paris in
May to try to obtain a million-dollar loan from the Standard Oil Company, presumably in return for a favored position in the Spanish
petroleum market after a coup. Pardo later declared that he talked
with a M. Janet, the chief European representative of the company,
but accomplished nothing.[30]

Despite growing numbers and a more militant posture, the UME
found that its influence was still circumscribed. This was presumably
due to its lack of contact with most commanding generals, as well as
to the fact that during 1935 the CEDA-Radical coalition had things
under fairly tight control.

The man in a position to profit most from the abortive Asturian
revolt was Gil Robles. As head of the most powerful political group
in the country, he could capitalize on national reaction by establishing a CEDA government that would promote basic constitutional reform. But if Gil Robles was dedicated to constitutional reform, he was
also more or less committed to constitutionalism. After the defeat of
the Asturian miners, his relations with Army leaders were not particularly close, for he assumed that the CEDA was strong enough to
achieve its aims by constitutional means.

Though the CEDA urged restoration of some of the military prerogatives eliminated by Azaña, and the increase of Spain's armed
strength, Gil Robles would not endorse the militarism of Calvo Sotelo.
He replied to Calvo's speech of November 6, 1934, by saying that he
did not share the other's vision of an authoritarian regime. Constitutional reform to correct the excesses of anticlerical liberalism would
suffice, said Gil Robles, for statism was itself a menace. Later, on February 15, 1935, a rightist deputy introduced a motion to outlaw the
affiliation of any Army officer with Masonry, just as the constitution
forbade those on active duty to belong to political parties.[31] Gil Robles
helped to amend the motion so that it became little more than an ex-
hortation to military discipline.

As the months passed, however, the impatience of the CEDA
mounted, for the winter of 1934–35 brought no major achievements.
Lerroux was forced to reorganize his government for the fourth time,
in May 1935, when Gil Robles took over the Ministry of War. It was
widely rumored that the CEDA leader had entered the Cabinet "to

prepare for something"—the implication being that the "something" was a coup d'état. Gil Robles naturally denied all such rumors, and there is no direct evidence to support them. Such ambitions would have contradicted his previous policy, for the CEDA chief had announced in the preceding year:

> While I have any influence among the Spanish right, I will never consent to use catastrophe as a tactic. They [the monarchist extreme right] think to save their ideals by the reaction resulting from a hecatomb, but that cannot be. After the dictatorship [of Primo de Rivera] ... came the political revolution. A new dictatorship could produce, after a period of tranquillity, the social revolution—the Communist Republic.[32]

If Gil Robles did not intend to organize a coup, he did plan to promote military reorganization, to restore hierarchy, and to increase the Army's fighting strength. In addition to undoing the Azaña reforms, he sought to augment combat efficiency and create solid political connections with the military elite, thus broadening the base of support for a more conservative Republic. Immediately after taking office, Gil Robles called a meeting of ranking generals in order to receive their report on the state of the military and hear proposals for improvement. The consensus seemed to be that the Army was, as usual, in disarray. Munition dumps contained enough shells and cartridges for only about twenty-four hours of modern battle, and new equipment was still lacking in every branch.[33] The Air Force was obsolete: its only bombing planes dated from 1919, and the largest bombs in its supply weighed about eleven pounds.

Gil Robles began with a series of key personnel changes. On May 17, Franco was recalled from his new post as Commander in Chief in Morocco and appointed Chief of the General Staff and also of the Superior War Council, thus placing the man whom *ABC* had recently hailed as "the young caudillo"[34] in charge of the technical reorganization of the Army. Gil Robles made this choice for a number of reasons. Franco probably had more professional prestige than did any other general at that time. His excellent Moroccan record, his direction of the General Academy, his clean slate under the Republic, his avoidance of political compromise—all this made him the logical nominee. Moreover, Franco's brother-in-law, Ramón Serrano Súñer, was the leader of the "Juventudes de Acción Popular" (JAP), the main CEDA youth movement, and there seemed to be definite political rapport between these two ambitious men of early middle age. Franco was made Chief of Staff, not merely because Gil Robles thought that he would be good for the Army but above all because he was judged to be good for the CEDA.

Mola was reassigned to Morocco, thus receiving his first major command since the beginning of the Republic,[35] and Goded was further upgraded. In addition to being head of special Army inspection under the War Ministry, he was also appointed Director General of Carabineros, Inspector General of Military Aviation, and Judge of the Sixth (or Military) Chamber of the Supreme Court. For his Undersecretary in the Ministry, Gil Robles chose the ultra-nationalist, UME-affiliated Fanjul, who was a member of the Agrarian Party, the CEDA's chief conservative ally.

The Franco–Gil Robles leadership carried out a purge of the command positions, removing a number of known liberals such as General José Miaja and Lt. Col. Hernández Sarabia, as well as some conspicuously leftist sympathizers like Riquelme, Mangada, and the Air Force leaders Sandino and Hidalgo de Cisneros. They were replaced by africanistas or staunchly nationalistic senior officers. Promotions by merit on intermediate levels were authorized once more: the Carlist Col. Varela was promoted to brigadier, and men such as Martínez Anido were recalled to active service. The Code of Military Justice was revised, and the Honor Tribunals (a regular feature of the pre-1931 system, with the power to expel from the Officer Corps those accused of "dishonorable" acts) were restored. Official religious services and officers' meetings were also authorized once more.

Some officers estimated that by mid-1935, 25 per cent of all Army recruits (most of whom were drawn from the lower classes) were members of leftist organizations. If this figure was an exaggeration, it did not entirely misrepresent the state of things. Draftees from urban proletarian districts usually brought left-wing opinions into the Army with them, and revolutionary groups from outside sometimes attempted to proselytize in the barracks. Of all the subversive organizations, none had proportionately directed so much attention to the Army as had the small Spanish Communist Party. Close tabs were kept on all Party members drafted into the Army, and cells were established in as many garrisons as possible. A regular intra-Party bulletin was prepared, and for several years a clandestine military newspaper, *La Voz del Cuartel* (Voice of the Barracks), intermittently published by the Communists, demanded the establishment of military soviets and the election of officers. A special "Antimilitarist Office" in the Spanish

Communist organization was busily engaged in collecting information on armament, Army structure, planning, and so on. These data were passed on to the "Antimilitarist Secretary" in the Spanish Communist Central Committee. Spanish Morocco received particular attention. Communist agitators had been active among the native population, the Moorish Regulares, and a few sections of the Tercio. These agitators had, in large measure, been responsible for the riots of May 1931.[36]

Franco was determined to break up existing political cells in the barracks and eliminate leftist propaganda. During the second half of 1935, the General Staff created a rudimentary spy system whose duty it was to track down subversive elements. Revolutionary literature was confiscated, a number of agitators were arrested, and some of the most dangerous individuals were expelled from the Army.[37]

A definite effort was made to improve the quality of the Army's fighting equipment. It was decreed that all Spanish soldiers must be provided with steel helmets; bids were solicited for the construction of 24 new batteries of artillery and the refitting of all old cannon; three hundred and fifty new workers were hired by the Toledo cartridge factory in the hope of increasing its potential output to 800,000 bullets a day. For the first time, a study of poison gas was made by the Army, and a limited campaign was carried on to try to educate the public about chemical warfare.

General maneuvers were held in northwestern Spain during the summer and autumn. At the end of July, there were special exercises around Oviedo. The military command there had been given to Col. Antonio Aranda, who had helped prepare the Alhucemas operation ten years earlier and was thought of as one of the brightest Staff officers in the Army. His political views were moderately liberal. Associated with Lerroux's Radicals, he was said to be a Mason, but his discretion and talent were undisputed. The object of the July maneuvers was to gain experience in conducting relief operations in the Asturian-Leonese mountains, and to study ways of quelling any future rebellion there.

A general aerial exercise provided further proof that over half the existing military aircraft either were unserviceable or would quickly break down under stress. Consequently, contracts were drawn up in December for new bombers and pursuit planes to be assembled at the national aeronautical factory in Guadalajara. This factory was a creation of the 1920's that had heretofore existed in name only. Workers in the small-arms and aviation industries were mobilized in an effort to ensure better work performance.

Lerroux's Cabinet broke up in September 1935, when the ultra-conservative Agrarians withdrew their support. The new Prime Minister was the politically independent lawyer and economist Joaquín Chapaprieta. Gil Robles remained Minister of War, but he had already lost hope of becoming Prime Minister under this Cortes. Instead, the CEDA was concentrating on the passage of constitutional amendments, with emphasis on changes in the religious laws. This proved a hard path to follow, for moderates, as well as liberals, objected to such legislation. The President, Alcalá Zamora, remained apprehensive of Gil Robles, and was heard to complain that most of the new military appointees were "enemies of the Republic."

On October 1, the War Minister spoke in the Cortes to still the worry some had voiced: "I assure you of this: while I am in the Ministry of War, the Army will be nothing other than the faithful servant of the nation, under the laws which constitute its honor, never marching down the road which would lead to anarchy and the ruin of the very Fatherland it has the obligation to defend."[38] On the following day he stated: "Neither military coups nor displays of force are necessary for us to win power."[39]

These words were nonetheless spoken with private reservations, as Gil Robles later demonstrated. He was well aware that some of the new appointees were "enemies of the Republic," but he found them a useful counterweight. His Undersecretary, Fanjul, who had been named to please ultra-conservatives, was closely connected with the UME's Junta Central and had completely renounced Republicanism. Earlier, as an Agrarian deputy, Fanjul had proudly declared in the Cortes: "All the parliaments of the world are not worth one Spanish soldier."[40] Now in his early sixties, he had become perhaps the most rabid militarist among the senior generals, and was telling other UME leaders that a coup d'état was absolutely imperative.[41]

Yet Fanjul spoke for a very small minority on this point; none of the other top generals save Goded would have anything to do with the UME. The group's organization, always incoherent, became even more so during the last months of 1935. An indifferent administrator at best, Fanjul was now senile and in poor health. He remained incommunicado for days at a time, and UME groups in other garrisons had difficulty making any contact at all with the Junta Central. Because of this disarray, and because of the increasingly radical tone of the

Junta, senior officers of the First Division in Madrid set up a more moderate junta of their own to communicate with UME groups in other garrisons.[42] The various divisional juntas organized for each section of the Army functioned autonomously, and the Junta Central ceased to be a reflection of the attitudes of the officers or of UME members. With the monarchists providing small subsidies, and CEDA intriguers also trying to win over officers, the remnants of liberal sentiment in the Junta Central were eliminated.[43] This did not mean, however, that the UME was becoming more dangerous, for the Junta Central had lost most of its influence.

More calculating than either Goded or Fanjul was Mola, now military commander of Melilla, whose political attitude had largely been determined by his experiences in 1930 and 1931. The failure of Berenguer's soft-line tactics, personal humiliation at the hands of the liberals, and his experience with the Azaña administration had soured Mola on liberal constitutionalism. During the autumn, Lerroux wrote a worried letter to Mola concerning rumors of a military conspiracy in Morocco; Mola replied that no such plot existed.[44] In November, Gil Robles raised Mola to the post of Commander in Chief of all the armed forces in the Protectorate.

The Gil Robles–Franco leadership had the Army pretty well under control, and hard-core monarchist conspirators were bitter and depressed. As one later wrote:

The Officer Corps, tranquilized, ... resisted enticement, since its immediate desires were apparently going to be satisfied by the Minister and the Chief of the General Staff. ... The scales of seniority are rather like the earthly incarnation of paradise for the "military type." Franco was a master at enlarging, broadening, and bending them, and, by many devious maneuvers, captivating gallant officers with the hope of rapid promotions and brilliant careers.[45]

However, to carry out their plans, Franco and Gil Robles needed more money. During the bienio negro, the amounts spent yearly on the Army had decreased: from 433,600,000 pesetas in the last Azaña budget, the figure had sunk to 378,300,000 by 1934. This was raised only slightly to 404,400,000 in 1935.[46] The manpower level remained the same as at the end of Azaña's term—there were, theoretically, about 110,000 troops led by an Officer Corps of less than 8,000. The only notable increase was in the number of second lieutenants commissioned. Steps were being taken to encourage a greater proportion of long-term volunteers, so that the number of politically unreliable draftees might be decreased, but this changeover required money also.

The final months of 1935 were marked by increased Anglo-Italian tension in the Mediterranean. Since the possibility of war was no longer completely remote, Mola had been placed in charge of drawing up a general mobilization plan before returning to Morocco. By the beginning of December, the General Staff had prepared a three-year program of national rearmament based on an extraordinary budget of 1,100,000,000 pesetas.[47]

This project was submitted to the Cabinet by Gil Robles at the moment when the Prime Minister was about to present a special economy budget project for 1936. Because of the drastic decline in receipts since the worsening of the depression, the governmental deficit had risen steadily, from 199 million in 1931 to 594 million in 1934, and this made it all the more difficult to accept the General Staff's request. Finally, the Cortes agreed to increase the Army budget by approximately 40 per cent in 1936. The only other budget section to be raised was that of Public Works, for total expenditures were to be reduced to only a little more than four and a half billion pesetas, the lowest figure since 1931.[48] Even so, new income would be necessary to attain an even approximately balanced budget. Chapaprieta therefore proposed to increase inheritance taxes from one per cent to three and a half per cent, and to levy a land tax on the larger holdings. The Radicals had already been involved in a series of financial scandals, but, to the conservatives, this proposal by an independent prime minister to make the tax scale slightly more progressive was far more odious. The CEDA deputies, like the Agrarians, withdrew their support, and in December the Chapaprieta government collapsed.

Gil Robles may have believed that there was now no alternative to a genuinely rightist government under himself or some other *cedista* or Agrarian. Alcalá Zamora refused to give way, however. If the CEDA would no longer support a centrist government, then a caretaker administration would be appointed to prepare for new elections.

Constitutional dissolution of the Cortes only twenty-five months after the last elections was more than the Minister of War had bargained for. Though he seems to have believed that the CEDA stood some chance of increasing its support in new elections, political reactions in Spain are always uncertain. The CEDA had gone into the bienio negro in a strong parliamentary position, but had achieved next to nothing. To wager the future on new elections was, after all, a great hazard. The President's refusal to allow the party with a plurality to form a government was not fair play; therefore, the Minister of War felt he no longer need be bound by the letter of the law. Such seems to have been Gil Robles' reasoning when he requested Franco, Goded, and Fanjul to sound out support among the Army for a declaration of martial law to force the President's hand. The response was not encouraging. Most senior officers were reluctant to act against the constitutional government so long as it remained in the hands of moderates.[49]

The caretaker government of Manuel Portela Valladares was installed on December 15, and there was much concern about Gil Robles' reaction. Civil Guards and Assault Guards were concentrated near the Army barracks in Madrid, and their machine guns were trained on the Ministry of War while the CEDA chief packed up his papers. Yet there was little that Gil Robles could have done. Franco had been very careful not to become politically compromised with the CEDA, and had kept his distance from the War Minister. Concentrating on professional matters, he refused to support a declaration of martial law.[50] Fanjul demanded action; so did Goded, insisting that Gil Robles had promised to call out the Army rather than permit the moderates to expel him from the War Ministry. Whether or not he had privately said such a thing, Gil Robles realized now how narrow a clique these two generals represented; moreover, he was not encouraged by Goded's communications with Calvo Sotelo and other extremists. Several days later, he told a CEDA group that if he had called out the Army the CEDA's position would not have been strengthened, and he himself would have become the prisoner of a small faction of militarists and reactionaries.[51]

The elections were later scheduled for February 16, 1936. In the intervening period, Portela Valladares was charged by the President with the creation of a center bloc, whose object was to build a fulcrum of power between the Popular Front, which was being formed by the ultra-liberals and most of the left, and the National Front, which included the conservatives and most of the extreme right. Alcalá Zamora was decidedly apprehensive about many of the changes, particularly in personnel, that had taken place in the Army during 1935, but he and Portela apparently felt that they must try to win the support of at least part of the Army hierarchy for the proposed bloc. The sympathies of Franco lay with the conservatives, and those of Goded with the extremists; but Mola, the Commander in Chief in Morocco, had heretofore avoided explicit identification. He was recalled to Madrid by the Prime Minister to discuss whether or not he would lend personal support to a center coalition slate. Mola seems to have felt that he was being primed as the new Berenguer. He had salvaged his career and made important professional advances during the bienio negro, and he refused to risk any further involvement in politics.[52] The negative attitude of the key commanders and the frequent rumors of military conspiracy were not reassuring to the government. Though most of the ministers apparently did not take the gossip about Army plots seriously, early in January Alcalá Zamora sent notes to district military commanders warning that the military must not think of interfering in the electoral process or its results. The note stressed that conditions in 1936 were not analogous to those in 1923: "Today, a coup d'état, rather than being carried out without contest, would begin with the most serious kind of struggle."[53]

It seemed to many officers that the Popular Front was trying to carry through an antimilitary plebiscite. It was rumored that the left front aimed at the dissolution of the Army's general cadres and the elimination of the Civil Guard. Available evidence indicates that this was probably not true, but it was accepted at the time as gospel by worried Army men, since a good deal of space in the Socialist and anarchist press was devoted to antimilitary propaganda. Now that recent changes had undermined the political unity and effectiveness of the Army, leftists felt that they could disparage the military with impunity. Luis Araquistáin had written in *Foreign Affairs* in April 1934: "There are few regiments whose officers can count unconditionally on the non-commissioned officers and men." This conclusion was reiterated by Socialist spokesmen during the next two years.

There was considerable apprehension in both the center and rightist groups as to what would happen if the Popular Front actually won the elections. The CEDA, the Agrarians, and the monarchist groups were not so firmly united as in the preceding contest, and their working understanding with the Radicals had largely broken down. Nevertheless, Gil Robles seemed to be staking the entire future of the government on the outcome of the balloting. Trusting in the CEDA's financial and organizational resources, he still hoped that power and constitutional reform could be achieved by ordinary political means. Calvo Sotelo, his chief rival on the right, had no such expectations. José Antonio Primo de Rivera, whose Falangists were completely excluded from the National Front, publicly served notice that his movement might not respect a Popular Front victory at all. UME cells in certain provincial garrisons were making secret arrangements to declare martial law should the Popular Front win.[54] This possibility was also in the mind of Franco, who as Chief of Staff would have to bear a major share of the responsibility for any military action that might be decided on. Gil Robles' successor as War Minister, General Molero, was a colorless moderate who had been appointed precisely because of his tepidity and reluctance to act boldly. Franco realized that if matters were to get completely out of hand, the weak military forces in the peninsula might have difficulty controlling the situation. He therefore sent secret instructions to Mola to be ready to move units from Morocco to the peninsula on short notice.[55]

Under the constitutional regulations, the electoral list with the highest number of ballots in each district won a majority of the seats, even though it might have only a minority of the total votes. On February 16, the Popular Front garnered a fraction more than 50 per cent of the ballots—as compared with about 43 per cent for the right and around 7 per cent for the center—but gained a heavy Cortes majority of nearly two to one over the right, while the center forces were nearly eliminated.[56]

That night, Fanjul sent word in the name of the UME Junta Central that all troops in Madrid were to be assembled in their barracks ready for action. By this time, however, UME members in Madrid were no longer paying much attention to Fanjul or to the phantom Junta Central. The *Junta de enlaces* (divisional junta) of the First Division provided the real UME leadership in the Madrid garrison, and it decided not to act unless the victorious left were to launch a successful attack on government centers. Before dawn on the 17th, Goded was in the main Infantry barracks, the Montaña, trying to rouse officers to action, but without success.[57]

In the early hours of the morning, Gil Robles called on the Prime Minister, presumably urging him to have martial law declared in order to prevent a leftist takeover.[58] Obtaining no satisfaction from Portela, Gil Robles asked Franco to use his influence with the Army. The Chief of Staff rejected direct intervention, saying that the situation was not favorable for such an initiative.[59] According to Franco himself, he did go so far as to telephone General Pozas, head of the Civil Guard, in the early morning hours, and ask him whether the Civil Guard would support the Army in a declaration of martial law. When Pozas said they would not, Franco went to the office of General Molero, the moderate Minister of War, who had still not gone to bed. He suggested that the Minister, by means of legal channels, place a request for a declaration of martial law before the Cabinet meeting later that morning. According to Franco, the Cabinet approved the text of a declaration of martial law, and Army units were placed on the alert in Madrid and Zaragoza, where leftist disturbances were already reported.[60] There are no direct sources to corroborate this account. The only thing that is certain is that the government decree issued by Alcalá Zamora and Portela on February 17 did not declare martial law (a "state of war," in Spanish juridical parlance), but the much milder "state of alarm." Under the Republican constitution, this merely meant that security forces were to be placed on the alert.[61]

Though reports of radical leftist demonstrations, mass jailbreaks, and other excitement reached Madrid in mounting volume on February 17 and 18, it was clear that the government had no intention of annulling or even of restricting the electoral results. If a Popular Front victory were to be averted, the Army would have to take action by itself. Commanders of the Madrid garrison refused to move without the support of the regimental leaders, and further soundings indicated that most senior officers did not believe anything could be done unless the cooperation of the Civil Guard and Assault Guards was assured.[62] Though Goded continued to dash about trying to rally followers, this reaction was quite sufficient to deter Franco and more than enough to discourage Molero. Franco himself called on the Prime Minister early in the afternoon of February 19. According to Portela, Franco asked him to declare martial law and cancel the election results before it was too late. According to his own account, Franco insisted that the initiative lay with the government and that the Army could take no responsibility alone because it lacked "moral unity."[63] The formal press release that followed simply stated that Franco had come to inform the Prime Minister of his "complete removal from all political activity."[64]

If the press reports of those days are to be believed, Portela was much more concerned about the possibility of incendiary leftist outbursts than he was about military rebellion. To newspaper reporters he stoutly defended Franco's loyalty, but he grew more and more uncertain about the ability of the minority caretaker Cabinet to control the political situation while the results of the balloting were being officially registered. According to the Constitution, the government under whom elections were held was to validate the results four days after the voting—in this case, on February 20—and to preside over any run-off elections that might be necessary. Yet Portela feared that the impatience of the left could not be controlled more than a day or two longer. Minutes before talking to Franco, he had left a special Cabinet meeting at the presidential palace during which Alcalá Zamora had agreed to begin arrangements immediately for the formation of a new Cabinet by leaders of the Popular Front. Portela's Ministry resigned a few hours later, and a new leftist government, led by Azaña, was hastily sworn in on the evening of February 19.

CHAPTER SEVENTEEN

The Military Conspiracy of 1936

T HERE HAD LONG been talk of irrepressible conflict between left and right, and after the formation of the new Azaña government a few voices spoke of civil war by April. But the CEDA and the center groups by no means threw up their hands in despair. Cardinal Gomá, Primate of the Catholic Church in Spain, analyzed the causes of the electoral defeat in his report to the Vatican, and added that "a series of contacts has been initiated to form a center-rightist group that could further coexistence and collaboration with the government in that which touches the common good. This permits one to harbor some hope for moderation."[1] For his part, Gil Robles had said that the CEDA would "submit itself to the country's verdict." His recent experience with the military encouraged him to seek moderation, at least for the time being.[2]

The change of government was immediately felt in the Army. Molero was replaced as Minister of War by the liberal Masquelet, Franco's predecessor as Chief of Staff. On February 21, Franco was relegated to the obscure post of military commander of Tenerife in the Canary Islands, some five hundred miles distant in the Atlantic. Mola was recalled from Morocco and named garrison commander at Pamplona. Fanjul was removed as Undersecretary and retired from active service. Goded lost his posts in the War Ministry and was sent to command the garrison of the Balearic Islands. So it went, down the line. In wholesale changes on February 22 and 28 all the top positions were given to generals considered more or less friendly to the liberal Republic.

After meeting on the evening of the 17th, the outgoing generals held another conference, on the 20th, then met in smaller groups several times during the three weeks that followed. Franco talked briefly with the new Prime Minister, engaged in a long conference with the President, and also had a short conversation with the leader of the Falange.[3] Before taking his family on the long trip to Tenerife, he met with Mola and some africanistas in Madrid during March. This meeting was attended by Goded, Saliquet, González Carrasco, Varela, Galarza, Villegas (one of the few generals in the UME), Rodríguez del Barrio (the new National Inspector of the Army), the ultra-monarchists Orgaz and Ponte, and other officers of lesser note. Ever since the elections, Goded had been urging a direct coup by the Madrid garrison against the government; but Mola was reported to be very pessimistic, fearing that it was already too late for the Army to do anything. It was generally agreed that any effort at an immediate coup in Madrid had little chance of success;[4] and there is some evidence that Franco still did not regard either the political or the professional situation as desperate, and counseled that they give Azaña a chance to work things out before attempting anything rash. Nonetheless, it was agreed at this meeting that if worst came to worst garrisons all over the country would be alerted for rebellion. No precise plans were made, because those present differed considerably in political criteria and personal attitudes. The most that could be agreed upon was a pledge that all would take direct action should any one of the following occur: dissolution of the Civil Guard, dismissal of Army recruits, disbanding of the Officer Corps, armed rebellion by the left, or a premature coup by a single garrison due to confusion or misunderstanding. How concerted action might be achieved was not decided, and the generals went their separate ways after promising to keep in touch with each other.[5]

In the spring of 1936, there were but 84 generals on the active list in the Spanish Army, for most of the 425 names in the *Anuario* belonged to generals in various stages of retirement. Of the 84 men in command positions, the majority held moderate views on politics, and after the sifting and shifting of recent years few were monarchists or outright reactionaries. Almost all the major territorial commands and posts in the Ministry of War were by March in the hands of generals known either for their pro-Republicanism or for their sense of duty to the Constitution. Only a minority of the ranking generals were clearly anti-Republican or radically nationalist or militarist. The authoritarian minority was mostly, if not exclusively, composed of africanistas, though there were also a few africanistas among the liberal hierarchy in command. In 1936 the bulk of the Officer Corps was as petty bourgeois as ever. The democratizing influences of the last five years had encouraged the entrance of youths from marginal social environments. As Lerroux had noted, if few of the military were rabidly liberal, not many more were monarchist. The strife of the Republican Cortes had scarcely encouraged officers to identify with particular political groups or ideologies. Most officers still identified patriotism with a vague sort of progressivism, but they scorned more than ever the political labels of progressive groups. The bulk of them had no civic goal more specific than a hazy wish to see the country prosper in an orderly fashion, avoiding extremes and disturbances. But the spring of 1936 was full of strikes and shootings by radicals of right and left, and though the officers may not have been pro-rightist, almost all were anti-left and anti-Catalan. To most, proletarian revolution seemed a special menace to the established order, and, therefore, to their own careers and status.

Before many weeks passed, Azaña's inability to cope with the situation was demonstrated. The Prime Minister lacked the will to throttle extremists, perhaps because he was not certain that the Army would prove a reliable instrument of suppression. Azaña's reluctance or incapacity to use the forces of order to maintain order aroused great discontent among the military, the Civil Guard, and even the Assault Guards. Young activists in the Officer Corps more nearly agreed with the disgruntled minority of ranking generals than they did with the majority of senior Republican generals who tried to smile benignly at the dissolution of civic discipline.

The Falange, responsible for much of the swelling tide of violence, was officially dissolved on March 16, but became even more active underground. By the first days of March, the group had established its own military committee, composed of pro-Falangist officers (almost all of whom were UME members), which maintained contact with officers of middle rank in all the major garrisons.[6] The aftermath of the elections brought a great revival of UME groups throughout the Officer Corps, and the Falangists worked to influence the restless toward a fascistic solution of Spain's problems.

Military moderates could hardly be encouraged by such spectacles as the arrest of General López de Ochoa, who was charged by the government on March 11 with committing atrocities against the Asturian revolutionaries. This was leftist vengeance of the most narrow sort, since the revolutionaries had all been amnestied, and a serious effort to get at the facts would have shown that López de Ochoa bore little, if any, responsibility for the violence dealt the miners. But as commanding general, López de Ochoa was a symbol, and the Socialists demanded that he be offered up. For his defense attorney, López de Ochoa chose the lawyer and onetime Army captain Pardo Reina, formerly an organizer in the Madrid UME. Needless to say, the majority of the military regarded López de Ochoa as guiltless of any excess; indeed, most felt that he had been too lenient.

On March 13, two days after Ochoa's detention, the new Minister of War, Masquelet, issued a public statement denying rumors of indiscipline and conspiracy in the Army. Nevertheless, arraignment of one of the most liberal generals for "atrocities" only increased the feeling among the officers that they could expect nothing but persecution from the new Republican leadership. As it turned out, the evidence brought against López de Ochoa was insufficient to sustain the charges made, and he was later released. Freed from prosecution, Ochoa finally joined the UME in Madrid, a step he had earlier rejected. His presence exerted significant influence over the UME Junta of the First Division, for he had become a symbolic figure not merely for the left but among moderates in the Army as well. He had not, however, joined the UME so that he might wreak political vengeance on the leftist administration, but rather so that he might be in a position to direct military influence toward moderation and warn his colleagues of the schemes of rightist civilian politicians.[7]

The UME grew rapidly during the early spring. A circular distributed toward the end of March claimed that the various UME committees had enrolled 3,436 officers on active duty, 2,131 NCO's and troops, and 1,843 officers either on Reserve or retired.[8] If these statistics are trustworthy (and they are probably not too far out of line), the UME held the support of nearly half the officers on active duty, together with that of a considerable number of NCO's.[9]

While the UME became more militant and the Falangists turned to outright terrorism, the Carlists and other ultra-right groups also rejected ordinary political activity. Soon after the elections, the Carlists established their own "Supreme Carlist Military Junta" just across the French border in St. Jean de Luz. It was composed of certain retired officers, members of the Carlist political organization Comunión Tradicionalista, and was nominally led by General Mario Muslera, who had been a member of Primo de Rivera's Directory. By mid-March, the members had completed a plan of their own for armed rebellion.[10]

Even as Gil Robles and the more moderate CEDA leaders were trying to work out some kind of *modus vivendi* with the leftist government, the CEDA itself had begun to disintegrate. The first section to renounce constitutionalism in favor of armed conspiracy was the CEDA affiliate in eastern Spain, the Derecha Regional Valenciana (DRV). Its official leader, Luis Lucia, had been the CEDA's vice-president, and was one of the more moderate figures in the organization, but he lost much of his influence after the election. By the end of February, proponents of direct action had taken over the DRV. They began to organize a clandestine militia made up of small cells, and briefly published a weekly newspaper that stressed corporative political and economic organization. This group encountered great difficulty in gaining funds and allies, especially in the Army.[11]

The moderates suffered another blow on April 7 when the Popular Front Cortes voted to depose Alcalá Zamora as President of the Republic. The Constitution specified that if Parliament were dissolved twice during a single presidential term, such action on the part of the chief executive would be subject to review after the second general election. Alcalá Zamora not illogically contended that there had been only one dissolution, because the original body of 1931–33 had been a constituent assembly and not a regular Cortes. The real problem was that in trying to maintain a balance between extremes of right and left Alcalá Zamora had antagonized most of the major forces only to see his own centrists submerged during the recent balloting. With their heavy parliamentary majority, the Popular Front parties promptly deposed the President for having taken the only measure that could have brought the Popular Front to power—a measure that they themselves had vigorously demanded.

The only figure with enough prestige among the Republican left to succeed Alcalá Zamora was Azaña, but the military opposed his ascent to power, for they feared that it might be the prelude to a Popular Front dictatorship, or might lead to implementation of the Communists' and Socialists' demand that the regular Army be dissolved and replaced with a worker-peasant "red army" with officers elected by soldier soviets. Though Azaña did not support such goals, he seemed completely unable to control the forces that had voted the Popular Front coalition into power. As usual, the anarcho-syndicalists ignored the government altogether, while the revolutionary Socialists under Largo Caballero, who had broken with the moderate minority in their own party, made it clear that their support of the middle-class left-Republican government was temporary and limited. They persistently denounced the "illusion of reformism" and advocated direct revolution.[12] The Socialist Youth had just been fused with the expanded Communist Youth organization, and Communist propaganda in Spain was reaching unprecedented proportions. All the extreme left groups were gaining members, and labor disturbances were increasing. The revolutionaries believed that the moderates were already defeated and on the run, and that after a violent death struggle the extreme right minority would expire as well. On April 15, the Secretary of the Spanish Communist Party insinuated in the Cortes that Gil Robles might meet the fate of Sergeant Vázquez and others killed in the Asturian repression.[13]

The only focus of military conspiracy in the capital was a vague "Junta of Generals," organized by Fanjul after his retirement, which was supposed to represent the dissident senior officers. Through the medium of Galarza, such generals as Franco, Goded, and Mola maintained some kind of contact with it, but the active members of the committee were a number of older generals who had retired in 1931 and 1932. Efforts to dominate the UME having proved ineffective, Fanjul was trying to set up a direct coup of his own. Yet unless some sort of rapport could be established with the Madrid garrison commanders, or at least with the UME Junta Central, such an effort would come to naught, for the members of Fanjul's clique had no troops under their control. At the beginning of April, however, General Rodríguez del Barrio, a nominal moderate who had recently been appointed Inspector General of the Army, agreed to try to use his influence to bring about a pronunciamiento. Fanjul and his associates seem to have hoped to present the garrisons in Madrid and nearby provincial capitals with a *fait accompli* that would compel their support.

The date of the coup was arbitrarily set for April 20. On the 18th, Fanjul set out for Burgos to rally the headquarters of the Fifth Division.[14] Word was sent on the following day to the heads of the UME Junta Central in Madrid, asking them to assemble the troops in their barracks and await Rodríguez del Barrio's order for a coup early on the 20th. The UME leaders had scant desire to follow a Fanjul-organized pronunciamiento; moreover, they had just heard that Rodríguez del Barrio was too sick to get out of bed. Nevertheless, they used this opportunity to test the speed of barracks mobilization, and put the Madrid troops on the alert for several hours.[15]

Just as the UME leaders had suspected, Rodríguez del Barrio was seriously ill. His nerve gone, he pled poor health and withdrew from the plot the day before the action was to begin. The government soon learned of his involvement, however, and he was removed from his post as Inspector General. Fanjul and Galarza somehow managed to escape arrest, but the other two principal conspirators, Varela and Orgaz, were seized. As in 1931, Orgaz was exiled to the Canaries, and Varela was sent to military prison in Cádiz.[16]

The police seized certain papers in Varela's possession, including the Cabinet list for a projected military government. Sanjurjo was the suggested Junta president, and six other members were listed: Martínez Anido, Franco, Mola, Goded, Queipo de Llano (currently in command of the Carabineros), and Cabanellas, now the most senior active general. Fanjul was to be the new head of the Army's tribunal, and the retired General González Carrasco, Inspector General.[17] This did not mean that all the generals listed were directly associated with the plot, for it was only a tentative sketch reflecting the preferences of Fanjul's junta, which, as already shown, had little support in the Army as a whole. The significance of all this activity was not entirely lost on the government, but it was felt that the agitation would subside more easily if no drastic punitive measures were taken. Several dozen officers were again switched to new assignments or relieved from active duty, but otherwise the government preferred to ignore the discontent in the Army, in the optimistic hope that it would come to nothing.

The multitude of reassignments since February 22 made it difficult for UME activists to organize a unified network. After being reconstituted in March, the UME's nominal Junta Central was largely composed of members of the Junta of the First Division in Madrid, who rejected the manipulations of Fanjul. An important new affiliate in the capital was the head of the First Infantry Brigade, José Miaja. He had been promoted to brigadier by Azaña in 1932 because of his reputation as a liberal and had been named commander of the Madrid brigade the following year.[18] Gil Robles removed him in 1935, but he was reassigned to the post after the Popular Front victory. However, though a Mason and a moderate liberal, Miaja was also an africanista who had been heard by fellow officers to speak rather nostalgically of the old days under the monarchy.[19] A cautious, fatherly figure often called "Papa Miaja," he stood nearer to the center than to either extreme.[20] Generals such as Miaja and López de Ochoa kept the Junta Central from plunging into irresponsible conspiracy, even though UME groups in other garrisons were becoming quite radical.

At the end of April, the Junta Central placed itself under Ochoa's orders. Ochoa no longer discounted the possibility of a pronunciamiento, but emphasized that it must come at the proper time and after careful preparation. The moment seemed to arrive on May 8, when the leftist parliamentary majority was about to elect Azaña to the presidency of the Republic. Even a good many of the more moderate officers feared that this would be the prelude to dissolution of the Army or the complete breakdown of public order. Ochoa talked with commanders of most units stationed in Madrid and won their agreement for military action to avert the installation of Azaña as President. His plan was to ask Alcalá Zamora to declare the government dissolved and to appoint a general, probably Sanjurjo, as temporary Prime Minister. Having already been deposed, Alcalá Zamora lacked authority for such a step, but the military needed at least a façade of legal authorization, and most conservatives still considered Alcalá Zamora the legitimate chief executive. The proposal was transmitted by Rafael Sánchez Guerra, son of the prominent politician of the old regime and a family friend of the former President. Alcalá Zamora did not reply until the following day, after Azaña's election. He said that it was not up to him to issue a decree of dissolution or to install a military Cabinet, but hinted that he would not discourage the officers from acting on their own initiative. Urged a second time, he still refused. Alcalá Zamora's reluctance to take the law into his own hands frustrated the UME plan, for Ochoa could not bring himself to act without some sort of constitutional mandate.[21]

Meanwhile, the small ultra-liberal minority in the armed forces organized a group of their own, the "Unión Militar de Republicanos Anti-fascistas" (UMRA), to combat the UME and rally leftist support.[22] It was originated by Captain Eleuterio Díaz Tendero, a pro-left officer appointed to active duty on the General Staff after the Popular Front victory. The UMRA was open to membership from the ranks, and supplied a number of military instructors to the Socialist militia. One of these, the Engineers captain Carlos Faraudo, was shot down in a Madrid street by rightist gunmen on May 7.[23] Five days later, UMRA leaders decided on a policy of counter-assassination if any more of their members should be killed.

Though there was a great deal of rightist violence, there was as yet no coordinated conspiracy against the liberal regime. A dozen plots had been laid, but for lack of planning, coordination, and support none had come to fruition. No leader had emerged to evoke a broad allegiance. Whenever the need for such a chief was discussed, military dissidents always came back to Sanjurjo. The exiled martyr of Estoril was the only general who seemed to arouse the confidence of a majority of the conspirators.

Sanjurjo received a steady stream of messages from Spanish groups emphasizing, in flattering terms, the idea that his stand in 1932 marked him as the natural leader of patriotic reaction to leftist extremism. Nevertheless, the general was wary of committing himself. He felt that he had been deserted four years earlier, and now he paid attention to few communications other than those from a trusted handful of senior officers.

As the bitterness of recent years focused his thoughts on the more distant past, the aging general was increasingly given to nostalgia and outbursts of tearful emotion. Both his father and grandfather had served in Carlist units, and early in 1936 his elder son, an Army captain, became associated with the Carlist militia in northern Spain. This reawakened old memories, and in Estoril a snapshot was taken of his infant son—the child of his recent marriage—decked out in miniature Requeté garb.[24]

Such sentimental gestures encouraged Carlist leaders to think that Sanjurjo might at least let them use his name if he saw that they meant business. At the beginning of May, Don Javier of Bourbon-Parma, nephew and executive secretary of the current Carlist pretender, the aged Don Alfonso Carlos, visited the general in Estoril, and in a subsequent conversation with Manuel Fal Conde, Secretary of the Comunión Tradicionalista, Sanjurjo explained that, though he felt his primary obligation in any revolt would be to his fellow generals, he was willing to make a "statement" on behalf of the Carlists.[25] Fal Conde proposed that Sanjurjo become head of the "Provisional Government of Monarchist Restoration" that was to be established after the overthrow of the Popular Front regime. This proposition was agreeable to Sanjurjo,[26] but he had no clear idea of how a successful rebellion could be brought off. One plan confected by the Supreme Carlist Military Junta in France called for two Carlist militia groups to begin hostilities in the west and southwest near the Portuguese border; when government troops marched to put down this rising, the main body of Requetés in the northeast would fall upon Madrid, where other squads in the capital would already have seized key points.[27] Sanjurjo seems to have been understandably skeptical about the project's chances, and it was later dropped. In a personal note of May 15, Sanjurjo gloomily observed that the "Generals' Junta" led by Fanjul and Villegas in Madrid had a membership of five at most, while almost all the commanding officers, including even Mola, who had become an active conspirator at Pamplona, remained uncommitted. Nevertheless, he concluded, the best prospect of success was a rebellion led by Mola, which might be brought off with the aid of the Carlists.[28]

This was a correct evaluation, for it was Emilio Mola who eventually put together the conspiracy of 1936. Born in a garrison town in Cuba, Mola had been an officer all his life. He was one of the very few literary generals in the Army, having written three volumes of memoirs on the Moroccan campaigns, the Berenguer-Aznar government, and the military problem. (During the lean years 1931–34, he had helped support his family by turning out a manual on chess.) After becoming Commander in Chief in Morocco, he had, as Lerroux suspected, endeavored to purge ultra-liberals under his command, as well as to increase the combat efficiency of the elite units in Morocco.

Mola was six feet tall, but he was homely, wore thick glasses, and held no illusions about cutting a dashing military figure. He had relatively few personal friends and lacked the human touch of Sanjurjo. When he first came to the Pamplona command in mid-March, he made no effort to hold political discussions with his subordinates, even though he must have learned that as early as February 8, ten or twelve members of the local UME Junta had signed a pact to rebel if the Popular Front won the elections.[29] Like almost all the generals, Mola preferred to wait and see.

In the past, Mola had been considered a moderate conservative, but he had come to despise Gil Robles and other conservative leaders for having let power slip through their fingers. He scorned the center as compromising and ineffectual, but most of all he hated the liberals and the left, all of whom were antimilitarist, and many of whom were, by his definition, unpatriotic and subversive as well. Like many people, Mola believed that the world was dominated by plots and conspiracies. He seems to have been genuinely convinced that many of the difficulties of the Republic were caused by an international conspiracy of Jewish financiers.[30]

After a month in Pamplona, he came to the conclusion that the military radicals were right: the political situation was hopeless, and the Army must redeem it. As to how this could be done, Mola was at first no more certain than Sanjurjo was. Communication between commanders was not easy, because of surveillance by both the government and leftist groups. Mola, however, was in a more favorable location than most, for Pamplona is the capital of Navarre, an ultra-conservative Carlist region. On April 19, a meeting was arranged with UME representatives from the garrisons of Pamplona, Burgos, and Logroño. The younger officers were more than willing to accept the leadership of a brigadier, and from that day on Mola was the director of the military conspiracy in Navarre and upper Castile.[31]

The Pamplona meeting coincided with the abortive effort of Fanjul's Junta in Madrid, and may have been inspired by it. After the collapse of that effort, Mola apparently realized that nothing more was to be expected from the handful of retired generals in the capital: to succeed, any pronunciamiento must be much more thoroughly organized, and must project clear political goals. By the end of April, Mola had begun to sketch out plans for a new military directory. Each garrison of any size should form its local military junta, and district Army leaders should supervise the establishment of local juntas of trustworthy conservatives and nationalists for civil administration. In his first outline Mola stressed: "It should be understood that the blow must be violent in the extreme, in order to subdue the enemy—who is strong and well-organized—as soon as possible. All the directors of political parties, societies, or syndicates not in favor of the movement will be arrested, and exemplary punishments applied, so as to stifle strikes or rebellions."[32]

The unsuccessful efforts of December, February, and April had shown how difficult it would be to bring off a successful coup in Madrid. The capital was the stronghold of the left Socialists, backed by tens of thousands of organized, excitable workers who might be called out as revolutionary militia on twenty-four hours' notice. Early in May "the Director," as Mola was now known in intraconspiratorial correspondence, wrote another memorandum for his colleagues. It said in part: "In Madrid, the assistance that one would logically expect is not to be found. . . . We do not know if the leader or the followers are lacking. Perhaps both. The capital city . . . exercises a decisive influence on our politics . . . to such an extent that we may be sure any deed carried out there will be accepted as an accomplished fact by the immense majority of Spaniards."[33]

Mola went on to say that there were two undeniable facts governing the enterprise: (1) Madrid, the center of power, had to be conquered; (2) the greater the distance from which the coup was made, the harder it would be to carry out. He then outlined a plan whereby the Fifth, Sixth, and Seventh Divisions, stationed in the north, would march upon Madrid and seize it from the outside a few days after the start of the rebellion. By the end of May, Mola had drawn up a detailed plan for the northern divisions, complete with timetable.[34]

The problem was that even in the conservative north only a minority of the officers were strongly in favor of a rebellion. Save for Mola himself, scarcely a single general in those districts seemed willing to place his authority behind it. Moreover, Mola was only a brigadier and did not command widespread personal devotion. What was needed was the prestige of someone like Sanjurjo. After talking with Don Javier early in May, Sanjurjo had given the Carlist leader a note to transmit to Mola: "I need your decision; if you are decided, I should like to have you represent me."[35] But this message was apparently some time in reaching Pamplona.

Thus far, most of the hundreds of officers implicated in the conspiracy had no idea who, if anyone, was taking central responsibility, or what the precise goal of the revolt would be. Most of the UME groups functioned in semi-isolation, and there was always the chance that a self-appointed committee of lieutenants and captains might try to declare martial law in some provincial capital. On May 29, Mola and his chief of staff spent an anxious night after word arrived that the Valencia garrison intended to rebel immediately without waiting for other units.[36]

An organized network to coordinate the revolt was lacking, for despite their large membership the UME groups lacked unity and consistency. Without central direction of some sort, no rebellion would be possible; and only Sanjurjo seemed to have the prestige to keep the conspiracy together. On May 30, Mola sent a messenger to Estoril requesting that Sanjurjo grant him official recognition as coordinator of the revolt. Being assured that Mola was working only for a military dictatorship headed by Sanjurjo himself, and that he was not averse to including Carlists in the rebellion, the General agreed that Mola might use his name and authority in acting as the effective director of the plot.[37] This greatly strengthened Mola's hand in trying to form a unified conspiracy among the garrisons throughout Spain.

Limited efforts were also made to ascertain the attitude of the leading European powers regarding a military coup. For several years, the main Nazi propaganda agency for the Spanish-speaking world had published a journal entitled *Ejército, Marina, Aviación,* whose function was to extend the Nazi influence among the military in Spanish-speaking countries.[38] Many officers had long tended to be pro-German, and the rearmament of Germany under a strong nationalist regime made the Teutonic example appear even more attractive. Early in February, just before the elections, Sanjurjo had made a brief trip to Berlin, where he was attended by the Spanish military attaché, Colonel Juan Beigbeder. Sanjurjo visited German arms factories and probably talked with a number of officials. Reliable details of these contacts are lacking, but he apparently made it clear that elements in the Spanish Army would be ready to rebel if the Popular Front came to power, and he seems to have received some indication of German support for such a move.[39] In the months that followed the elections, several different monarchist agents had made private arrangements in Germany and elsewhere for small shipments of arms.[40]

Meanwhile, Mola's plotting could scarcely pass unobserved, even though the current opinion among Madrid leftists was that the general had been "shut up" in Pamplona. He resorted to an elaborate series of dodges to hold secret conferences with fellow conspirators, meeting them on lonely Navarrese hilltops or conspicuously entering the local movie house only to dash out the side door for another session as soon as the house lights dimmed. He tried to display himself daily in the main window of the Café Kutz, Pamplona's leading coffeehouse, in order to show passersby that he had nothing serious on his mind.

One of Mola's most valuable collaborators was Santiago Báguenas, chief of police in Madrid, who gave him important information on government security activities. On June 3, when the Director General of Security made a flying trip to Pamplona with two or three police cars to catch the general red-handed, Mola was warned just in time to sweep all the evidence under the carpet. The police returned to Madrid in frustration.[41] Mola mopped his brow in relief, and wondered at the incredible leniency and torpidity of the Republican police; surely such a regime could not endure.

Incidents of violence between leftists and military men were becoming more frequent. It was no longer rare for an officer to be pelted with rocks or jeered at. In Alcalá de Henares, leftist demonstrators hooted at a section of Cavalry riding through the streets. The commanding officers lost their tempers and ordered their troops to charge the hecklers. This outburst brought a purge of the Alcalá garrison and a new round of transfers throughout the peninsula. Since the end of April, a clandestine sheet called *El Soldado Rojo* (The Red Soldier) had been appearing, with lists of officers to be purged and demands for dissolution of the regular Army. This was echoed by the Socialist, Communist, and anarchist press. Officers were also being jeered at from the other side. Middle-class women invited to a dance at the Madrid Army-Navy Center threw corn and chicken feed on the floor to indicate that the officers thus far had shown themselves too cowardly to defend Spanish honor![42] How about the unified Socialist-Communist youth movement, which was marching every Sunday to cries of "¡Viva Rusia!" and even occasional shouts of "Down with Spain"? What was the Army going to do about that?

To Mola's intense frustration, most officers still were vacillating. Even some UME members seemed reluctant to commit themselves to outright rebellion. There was a dim awareness that the historical accomplishment of Spanish military pronunciamientos had been slight. There was no surety that Largo Caballero would necessarily overcome Azaña, no guarantee that a coherent rebellion could be planned, no clear understanding of who would gain what from a coup, and only limited trust in the men behind the machinations. Most officers were still uncommitted, while almost all the generals in command avoided any serious discussion of rebellion.

The one region in which nearly all the officers could be relied on was Morocco. The pugnacious temperament, elitist mystique, and closed caste attitude of the africanistas, especially the Tercio officers, made them the rebellion's strongest backers. They were infuriated by treasonous literature occasionally found in the barracks. Moreover, they had not forgotten that mutiny had briefly flared up in one small unit of the Tercio in 1931, or that in December 1931 the FAI of Melilla had made a raid on an Engineers barracks.

In Ceuta, one of the three main Moroccan centers, the head of the conspiracy was Lieutenant Colonel Juan Yagüe, known to leftists as the "hyena of Asturias." Since February 4, he had been commander of the Second Bandera of the Tercio. With his jutting jaw, broad, rugged face, and bristling head of prematurely white hair, Yagüe fitted the stereotype of the tough Legionnaire officer. He was one of the best field commanders in the Army, both popular and respected. In addition, he was a good organizer and—rare among africanistas—scrupulously honest in money matters. His professional ambitions had been partly frustrated, and in early middle age he was still no more than a lieutenant colonel. It was perhaps because of this that he began to develop an insatiable passion for politics. The son of a modest Castilian rural doctor, Yagüe burned with patriotic feeling and a desire for social justice under a nationalist regime. Many of the officers in the Protectorate, including at least one brigadier, had joined the Moroccan section of the Falange, and Yagüe also affiliated in the spring of 1936, finding in Falangism a program for national reintegration that pleased his martial spirit.[43]

In addition to solid support in Morocco, Mola had apparently found a leader for the rebellion in Seville, the capital of Andalusia— Gonzalo Queipo de Llano, Director General of the Carabineros. At first, the two generals eyed each other warily, and it was not until after a second visit by Queipo to Navarre that they could speak frankly. This was not surprising, for in 1930 they had been on opposite sides of the political fence. Queipo had been honored by the Republic—he was appointed commander of the First Division, then later was made head of the President's military staff—but he had expected much more recognition. In the beginning, he had hoped to become Minister of War in place of Azaña, and more recently he had been outraged by the deposition of Alcalá Zamora, to whom he was related by marriage. These disappointments, plus the rising tide of leftism, threw the grizzled old intriguer on the side of the rebels.[44]

In early June, Mola felt that the coup might be brought off with about thirty days' further preparation, and therefore attempted to clarify the political goals of the rebellion. The movement was to be entirely controlled by the military, and no political faction was to be allowed to interfere. Mola made it clear that the revolt was not aimed at restoration of the monarchy; it was hard enough to enlist officers for the conspiracy without frightening away hundreds of moderates and liberals by waving the monarchist banner. One of Mola's circulars stressed that "the monarchy ought not to be spoken of."[45] Instead, the military directory would seek to construct a corporative, technocratic, quasi-authoritarian Republic in which executive power would eventually be transferred to an elected civilian president. Special veto powers would be held by the Army, which would retain permanent control of the Ministries of the Interior and of Communications. In a memorandum of June 5, Mola proposed recognition of all the gains "legally achieved" by the working classes, and also the continuation of land reform. He affirmed "separation of Church and State" and "freedom and respect for all religions," though with the implicit understanding that discriminatory left-Republican legislation prohibiting

Catholic education and the work of the religious orders would be repealed. The future electorate would be controlled by creating "an electoral card excluding illiterates and those guilty of social crimes." The armed forces would be reformed and expanded, a national militia organized, and paramilitary instruction arranged for in the schools.[46]

The time had come, Mola believed, to inform rightist political leaders that the military reaction was under way. The only political group other than the Carlists to work actively among the military for rebellion had been the Falangists. From his prison cell in Madrid, José Antonio Primo de Rivera had addressed an open letter to the "Militares de España" on May 4 urging them to strike to save the Fatherland. Direct contact between José Antonio and Mola had been established on May 29, and the two discussed the possibility of Falangist collaboration in the rebellion, though Mola was not sure that such cooperation was either feasible or desirable. Early in June, Mola also sent word to Calvo Sotelo that a military revolt was being prepared, saying that its goal was to save Spanish institutions without regard for political parties. Though no concessions were made to monarchism, he received a reply on June 13: "Tell General Mola that I do not at all disagree with his message; that I only expect to be told the day and hour in order to be one more person at the orders of the Army."[47]

Three days later, in the Cortes, Calvo declared that he did not believe there was "a single person in the Army ready to rebel against the Republic in favor of the monarchy." "If there were, he would be crazy. I say this clearly, though I also consider crazy any member of the Army who, facing his destiny, would not be willing to rise up for Spain against anarchy, should such a situation arise."[48] The monarchists were willing to support a military rebellion on any terms, and to put off worrying about manipulating it for their own purposes until after the Azaña government had been overthrown.

The assistance they were best able to lend was financial. Captain Justo Sanjurjo, the general's son, was heard to say in Barcelona early in June that certain intriguers wanted to involve his father in another fiasco without providing adequate support. The main monarchist clique in Madrid, therefore, made ready to place a special fund of 300,000 pesetas at Sanjurjo's personal disposal, to guarantee that this time he would be cared for, no matter what.[49]

Gil Robles and the CEDA leaders were not left entirely ignorant of the conspiracy. By the end of May, Gil Robles was heard to remark that he expected the military to act before autumn.[50] He had completely given up hope of any political compromise, for the same reasons enumerated by Miguel Maura in an article in *El Sol* on June 18. Maura had reported that the latest membership figures compiled by the Director General of Security showed that the Socialist unions had 1,447,000 members enrolled, the CNT 1,577,000, and the Spanish Communist Party 133,000, while all the right-wing groups combined had only 549,000 registered affiliates. Even if these statistics were somewhat distorted, it was obvious that in the present state of things the Popular Front's victory could not easily be reversed at the polls. Therefore, during June the treasurer of Acción Popular, the main CEDA group, transferred 500,000 pesetas from his party's propaganda fund into a private account for the use of Mola.[51] Even the more moderate UME Junta Central in Madrid had established contact with Mola by mid-June.[52]

A few of the most strongly Republican officers and the more outspoken supporters of the government urged it to take action against the conspirators. However, Azaña and the new Prime Minister, Santiago Casares Quiroga, feared this would cause more harm than it would prevent. Both the pro-government leaders and the anti-administration left Socialists regarded the Popular Front's electoral victory as definitive, and could scarcely imagine that what they conceived of as an operetta Army was capable of rising against the will of the people. Whenever some spoke of this danger, Sanjurjo's fiasco was laughingly mentioned. In June, one of Madrid's favorite jokes, started by a friend of Casares Quiroga, told of certain conspiratorial officers whose leader insisted on postponing the planned revolt until a certain debt owed him came due; after collecting his money, the fictional plotter decided that they might as well forget about it, for with so much to spend on drinking and whoring, it was foolish to risk political adventures.[53] The leftist politicians guffawed, slapped their knees, and refused to take the *opéra bouffe* Spanish Army very seriously. For his part, Mola went along with the image, writing to acquaintances in Madrid that Navarre contained only hills, priests, and peasants, and that he would prefer to exchange this boredom for the seaside command of La Coruña.[54]

Azaña and Casares Quiroga still deemed it impolitic, or even self-defeating, to crack down on the dissidents so long as the commanding generals remained loyal. The most that the government would do after receiving detailed reports of an intrigue in some garrison was to transfer a number of officers to another post. It hesitated to do even this much with generals such as Mola and Goded, though lesser lights in the UME were rotated two or three times during the spring of 1936. A handful of liberal officers suggested that an elite Republican Guard be formed to protect the regime, since some units of the Assault Guards, originally formed for this purpose, had been placed under more conservative commanders during the bienio negro, and were so enraged by leftist demonstrators that certain of their officers were talking with the Army plotters. All such proposals were waved aside. Azaña and Casares seem to have believed, just as the rightists did, that the main threat would come from Azaña's own allies of the revolutionary left.

By the latter part of June, Mola could scarcely disagree with the government's assessment of the Army's reluctance to rebel. Though the degree of disorder in Spanish cities had not diminished, the conspiracy was not going well. In a "Confidential Report" of June 13, Mola had warned that there was not yet sufficient enthusiasm among the conspirators.[55] In a circular of June 20 he threatened: "The timid and vacillating must be warned that he who is not with us is against us, and will be treated as an enemy. With *compañeros* who are not *compañeros,* the triumphant movement will be inexorable."[56] The military conspirators were making common cause with Falangists and rightist provocateurs in encouraging new terrorism, in the hope of stretching the tension to the breaking point. In one memorandum, Mola noted: "An effort has been made to provoke a state of violence between the two opposing political sectors in order that, from such a base, the work may go forward [*para, apoyados en ella, proceder*]."[57] Fictitious revolutionary plots were drafted by rightist agents, then published or distributed among middle-class groups to frighten them with the prospect of an imminent leftist coup.[58]

Mola lamented that even toward the end of June many moderates still thought it would be possible to work with the government. The response from certain garrison commanders infuriated him. Colonel Villalba Rubio, commander of the force at Barbastro (not far from Pamplona), was supposed to have demanded 100,000 pesetas as his price for bringing his troops into the conspiracy.[59]

The biggest individual question mark was posed by Franco. Mola felt that the rebellion could scarcely succeed without active support from the former Chief of Staff, yet for three months Franco had been sitting in the sun, enjoying the balmy spring climate of Tenerife and refusing to commit himself definitely one way or the other. Such reluctance had been a decisive factor in quashing plans for rebellion in October 1934, December 1935, and February 1936. Until recently, the Republic had done well by Franco, and he had no intention of ruining his career through some rash political stroke.

After arriving in Tenerife, the cautious general had maintained political contact with CEDA elements through his brother-in-law, Serrano Súñer. How little confidence Franco had in the argument that the political situation was absolutely hopeless had been shown by his willingness to have Serrano enter his name on the conservative list in the run-off elections held at Cuenca on May 10. During April, Franco had apparently felt that a Cortes seat might provide him with either protection or influence in facing the political uncertainties of the future. The Cuenca candidacy aroused more opposition than either Franco or Serrano had counted on, however. In an election speech in that province, the shrewd Socialist moderate Indalecio Prieto pointed out the potential consequences of a mandate for Franco, saying that "because of his youth, his talents, and his circle of friendships in the Army,"[60] he might emerge as the military caudillo whom the rightists were seeking. Objections from the other side of the political spectrum were equally sharp. José Antonio Primo de Rivera, the Falangist chief, had been enraged when word reached his prison cell that Franco's name appeared on the CEDA list at Cuenca. He was disgusted with all the generals who refused to take action against the regime, and regarded Franco as one of the most compromising of the Army leaders. According to acquaintances, he had been saying: "All the generals are chickens and Franco is the biggest chicken of all [*la gallina mayor*]."[61] He finally sent his brother Miguel to tell the CEDA leaders that unless Franco's name were withdrawn, the Falange would also issue a propaganda circular denouncing him.[62] Fire from such different angles forced Franco to retire his name before the balloting began.

He received visits in Tenerife from Serrano and from the monarchist intriguer Galarza.[63] Franco encouraged Galarza to think that he would support a rebellion, saying that he always knew how to do his duty; but he refused active involvement in any specific plan. He was also in contact with former Tercio subordinates in Morocco and, by June, with Mola. His vagueness, uncertainty, and political coquetry so infuriated Mola that the Pamplona clique privately dubbed him "Miss Canary Islands of 1936."[64] Nor were they encouraged by the attitude of Franco's old comrade Muñoz Grandes. In 1935, Muñoz Grandes had been relieved as Director of the Assault Guards, after which he returned to a command in the Regulares to escape political involvement. He was uninterested in joining the conspiracy in Morocco, and so firm was his refusal that the rebels finally asked him to resign his command to avoid conflict with them. The government then offered to reappoint him as Director of the Assault Guards, but he preferred to remain on the inactive list.[65]

On June 23, Franco wrote Casares Quiroga a personal letter. It has since been cited by the general's official biographers to show that Franco was trying to warn the government of the consequences if it did not change its policy. Franco insisted that the Army was perfectly loyal, but that the subversive antimilitary campaign of the left was sapping its spirit and turning it against the government. "Those who represent the Army as being alienated from the Republic are not telling the truth," he said. "The degree of worry that the latest military measures [of the government] seem to produce in the spirit of the officers is . . . grave." He urged that the officers be treated with greater respect and generosity.[66]

The story has been told among dissident military elements in Madrid that Franco, in return for his aid in the rebellion, requested a financial arrangement similar to that being made for Sanjurjo. According to this tale, his old Galician comrade Col. Camilo Alonso Vega was sent to Pamplona with a personal letter from Franco asking that sufficient funds be deposited in a foreign bank to guarantee his major general's salary for his family.[67] Visitors to Estoril brought back word that Sanjurjo was saying: "With little Franco [*Franquito*] or without little Franco, we will save Spain."[68]

Mola had originally wanted to set the target date for rebellion at June 30. Instructions were dispatched on June 24, according to which the conspirators in the north would seize control of the units stationed there, declare martial law, seal off Catalonia, and march on Madrid. Elite units from Morocco would vault the straits, occupy Andalusia, and settle the fate of Madrid by taking the city from the south.[69] But the nearer the date approached, the greater were the doubts and hesitations; there seemed no end to the backing and filling. Garrisons that seemed certain one week were very much in doubt the next. It was no wonder that Franco, hundreds of miles out in the Atlantic, refused to commit himself; he knew the Spanish Army very well. Before June 30 arrived, Mola decided to postpone the date of the coup.

With so much of the Army undecided, Mola had to consider the possibility of using anti-Republican civilian volunteers as auxiliaries in the coup. In the neighboring province of Alava, the Traditionalist leader José María Oriol had been connected with a vague conspiracy that drew in Carlists, clergy, Falangists, and local conservatives.[70] Mola had met with Oriol on June 3 to discuss civilian support. The reply was so encouraging that the general arranged to meet the Carlist Secretary, Fal Conde, a fortnight later, on June 16. At the meeting, Fal took a stronger line: the Traditionalists demanded, at the very least, dissolution of all political parties, adoption of the old monarchist flag, and two seats in the new Cabinet.[71]

This justified Mola's worst apprehensions about the rightist groups, and his spirits began to sink, for even negotiations with the Falangists were not going well. There was a slight improvement, however, on June 29, when José Antonio Primo de Rivera issued his first orders for limited Falangist collaboration in a coup. That same day, after the Madrid government had decided to replace the special provincial commission of Navarre with a new committee of its own, three Navarrese Carlist leaders offered Mola the support of 7,000 Requetés if he would promise to preserve the present commission. Mola had no intention of precipitating a coup to protect the privileges of Navarre and replied that the Army would act because of a national, not a provincial, emergency. He added, however, that he hoped the Requetés would volunteer when the time came.[72]

The demands for special consideration were so many, and the genuine commitment in the Army so problematical, that on July 1 Mola considered dropping out of the conspiracy. He prepared another "Confidential Report," which dwelt pessimistically on the usefulness of the Falangists and Carlists: "Collaboration is offered in exchange for inadmissible concessions that would make us prisoners of a certain political sector."[73] Secrets were being leaked to the authorities, and the presence of a single active "loyalist" had been enough to discourage plotters in one provincial capital. Mola had already drawn up an official petition for retirement from the Army, but his aides prevailed on him to wait until the following day and see if prospects had improved. During the afternoon, Mola received several new reports more favorable in tone, and once more screwed up his courage to see the rebellion through.[74]

It was apparently just about this time—the first days of July—that Mola finally received Franco's categorical pledge. In return, Franco had to be promised the command of the forces in Morocco—that is, of all the militarily significant units in the Spanish Army.[75] Franco was favorably located for such a task, and arrangements were made to have him flown from Tenerife to Tetuán. Most of the Tercio officers had deep respect for their old chief, and Mola doubted that the revolt could succeed without Franco's active collaboration.

Days were becoming precious, for Yagüe had already been called once to Madrid for questioning, and Mola feared that he himself might soon be arrested. Summer maneuvers were planned in Morocco for the week of July 5–12, and would provide opportunity for co-ordinating final details of the revolt among the unit commanders. On July 5, a Tercio captain arrived in Pamplona bearing Yagüe's message that all was ready and waiting. Meanwhile, José Antonio Primo de Rivera, ever suspicious of military conspirators, insisted from his prison cell that an immediate firm date be set. Fearing that further delay might invite disaster, Mola sent word throughout the peninsula for the rebels to be ready to act by July 10. Soon after these instructions had been dispatched, the Falangist leader in Toledo was arrested while carrying part of the message. Mola was not sure how much information had fallen into the hands of the police, so he canceled these latest instructions within two or three days. New signals were given, and the network was alerted to be ready for instantaneous action any time after July 15.[76]

The Falangists still promised support, but Mola had little faith in them, while relations with the Carlists were at an impasse. On July 6, Fal Conde had sent an angry letter to Mola, declaring that the day before he had been visited by Gil Robles and another CEDA leader, who claimed to be "emissaries" of the military conspirators. They had told Fal that the rebellion was also being led by moderate liberals like Queipo de Llano and Cabanellas, and that the aim of the coup was to hand back the government to the conservative parties, while in Lisbon it was rumored that Cabanellas was working for a centrist Republican dictatorship under Miguel Maura.[77] Mola replied on the 7th that this was incorrect; that the movement was being led by the Army alone, which would not restore power directly to the conservatives (whom the Carlists so bitterly opposed). But he added that the military dictatorship would have to prepare some sort of representative civilian assembly.[78] This was countered by a vehement missive sent across the border by Fal Conde on July 8, in which he demanded that Mola guarantee that all the parties would be dissolved, that he explain just what sort of "assembly" he had in mind, and that he tell the Carlists what would happen after a military government was installed.[79] Not illogically, Fal Conde wanted to know precisely how a military rebellion without concrete political plans could be so purely "patriotic" as Mola had insisted. It looked as though the military would either hand power over to Gil Robles & Co., or else try to hog it themselves, as Primo had done. Either way, Fal Conde wanted none of it. He insisted on guarantees for a corporative, Catholic monarchy.

Angry and despondent, Mola wrote his final letter to Fal Conde on July 9:

After receiving your letter yesterday, I am convinced we are wasting our time. The price you ask for your collaboration cannot be accepted by us. The Army is only interested in the salvation of Spain; it has nothing to do with party ambition.

We turn to you because in our barracks we have only uniformed men who cannot be called soldiers; were it otherwise, we should have acted alone.

With its intransigence, Traditionalism is going to contribute as effectively as the Popular Front to Spain's disaster. There you rest, with your historical responsibility.

Of those who have participated in this adventure, the only victim is going to be me. It will be the recompense for my good faith.

You may some day have cause to repent your present attitude.[80]

Mola sounded as though he were ready to give up once more. In this moment of darkness, a new gleam of light appeared. Not all Carlists were so stalwart as Fal Conde, and in Pamplona itself the Navarrese Junta Regional opposed Fal's direction. The Junta was dominated by the Conde de Rodezno, a wealthy nobleman with literary aspirations who owned extensive domains in Estremadura and was head of the Carlist Cortes delegation. He was a rather tolerant and skeptical man whose affiliation with Traditionalism was based more on family legacy than on faith in the principles of Carlism, which he believed doomed by the modern world. After the Popular Front's victory, Rodezno had decided that the Army was the last remaining instrument of the Spanish right. He considered it inevitable that the Carlists make broad concessions to the military. Furthermore, the youths in the Navarrese militia were spoiling for a fight. Rodezno had already asked Don Javier, Prince delegate of the Pretender, to reconsider the Carlist position. The same day that Mola sent his letter to Fal Conde, a meeting was arranged between himself and Rodezno. The Count suggested that the Army make arrangements for the rising directly with the Navarrese Junta, thus bypassing the Carlist high command.[81] This was the best news Mola had had in several days.

The only loyal supporter of Fal Conde in the Navarrese leadership was Antonio Lizarza, the regional Requeté chief. Lizarza had already been sent to Lisbon to see if Sanjurjo could resolve the differences between Mola and the Carlist leadership. Sanjurjo wrote identical letters to Mola and to Don Javier suggesting that the Carlists be allowed to use the old monarchist flag, while the regular Army kept its present Republican banner; no concrete political concessions could be made, but Sanjurjo and the Army would guarantee the eventual establishment of a political regime in full accordance with Traditionalist principles.[82]

This note reached Mola on July 12, and aroused his suspicions. He immediately sent an adjutant across the border to inform Lizarza that although the signature on the letter resembled that of Sanjurjo, the content did not sound as though it had been written by him. Lizarza was shocked, and Fal Conde declared all relations with Mola were definitely at an end.[83]

That very afternoon, Rodezno and the Navarrese Junta suddenly appeared in St. Jean de Luz. They had come to ask permission of Fal and Don Javier to mobilize their local "red berets" (*boinas rojas*) for the rising about to be launched by Mola. Asked what conditions the General had granted, they said that he had conceded them use of the bicolor flag and control of local government in Navarre. Fal was aghast, but Rodezno and other Navarrese leaders insisted. Faced with virtual insubordination and the impossibility of holding back Navarre's Requetés, Don Javier declared that he must refer the matter to his uncle the Pretender in Vienna. He consented to the participation of the Navarrese in the revolt should it begin before a reply had been received,[84] but an order was sent to Pamplona that no boina roja be mobilized without the express permission of Lizarza.[85]

The reluctance, not merely of Carlist leaders but also of many Army officers, was such that the conspiracy might never have come off had not the political and social situation continued to deteriorate during the first two weeks of July. The revolt of landless peasants in southwestern Spain was completely out of hand, and the government seemed helpless to maintain economic order. The general incidence of violence was, if anything, even higher than in earlier months.

What finally brought the situation to a climax were the dramatic events in Madrid on the night of July 12. About 10 that evening, one of the most active young leftists among the Assault Guard officers, Lt. José Castillo, was shot down on his way to work. An enthusiastic UMRA militant, Castillo had helped train the Socialist-Communist youth militia on weekends, and while involved in the repression of street affrays had killed at least one rightist. His comrades in the UMRA demanded immediate vengeance, and no ordinary officer or Falangist would do. Several hours after the Castillo killing, an Assault Guard troop carrier pulled up before the apartment house where Calvo Sotelo lived, and hauled him off. The next morning his corpse was found in the morgue of a small cemetery outside the city limits.

Security forces of the Republican government had murdered the chief political leader of the Spanish right,[86] and to conservatives this symbolized the death of their last hope of compromise or survival under the Popular Front regime. At the funeral, Calvo's lieutenant, Antonio Goicoechea, declared: "Before this flag, placed like a shroud over your chest, before God who sees us and hears us, we pledge a solemn oath to consecrate our lives to this triple task: to imitate your example, to avenge your death, and to save Spain."[87] Conservative deputies soon quit the Cortes completely. When an elderly monarchist leader, the Conde de Vallellano, was asked to help work out some kind of understanding, he shook his head: "It is already late; no agreement can be attempted."[88] The effect of all the violence in recent months was cumulative. Many civilians and Army officers who would earlier have been lukewarm to a revolt were ready to respond with enthusiasm and ferocity by mid-July. The Socialist moderate Indalecio Prieto observed dourly: "Only one thing is clear—that we deserve a catastrophe because of our stupidity."[89]

On July 14, Mola's assistants met with Lizarza to coordinate final plans. The Requeté chief still refused to proceed without some sort of political guarantee. The General was equally determined to make no concrete concessions to political parties, but because of his need for auxiliaries he finally made a grudging verbal compromise. That afternoon a brief handwritten note was sent to Lizarza: "I am in accord with the orientations indicated by General Sanjurjo in his letter of the ninth, and with those he may determine on the morrow as head of the government."[90] It was not much, but it was all the Carlists were going to get. The next day, Don Javier and Fal Conde dispatched a written accord to Mola authorizing Carlist participation in the rebellion on condition that its directors accept the political standards indicated in the Sanjurjo letter.[91]

In the Alicante prison where he had been moved weeks earlier, José Antonio Primo de Rivera could not contain his impatience, for he felt that the wave of indignation currently sweeping the middle classes might give an anti-government coup the support it needed, and that if Mola did not act immediately, the chance would be lost. When the morning of July 15 dawned with no sign of activity, José Antonio sent a courier to Pamplona to announce that unless Mola gave the signal within three days, the Falangists would precipitate the revolt with whatever allies they could find.[92]

Mola was under severe pressure. A civilian representative had been delegated to meet in Madrid with Gil Robles, Calvo Sotelo, and Rodezno on the 14th to coordinate civilian support, but Calvo's murder had disrupted the meeting.[93] There were signs that some of the junior officers were deserting UME committees to join the Falangists, who promised direct action.[94] Meanwhile, Mola's own divisional commander in Burgos, the scrupulous Major General Domingo Batet, was trying to force him to renounce the conspiracy altogether.

After the assassination of Calvo Sotelo, Mola had apparently intended to set the date for the rising at July 21.[95] However Batet, who had already talked with Mola three times during the past fortnight, requested that the general meet him at a certain spot along the Burgos-Pamplona highway on the afternoon of the 16th.[96] General Mola feared a trap and considered stepping up the timetable.[97] José Antonio Primo de Rivera and the Carlists continued to insist on action, and Franco, now that he had agreed to help lead the revolt, was urging Galarza in Madrid to get things moving.[98] The regional Falangist chief in Burgos was making extensive promises of Falangist militia support, and Mola realized that success would be possible only by means of a quick coup. On July 15, at about the same time that José Antonio dispatched his last angry note, Mola sent a new message to Yagüe in Ceuta with word that the rebellion was to begin in Morocco on the 17th.[99] The peninsular garrisons were to follow suit on the 18th and 19th.[100] Mola then met with Batet on the Burgos highway during the afternoon of July 16 and, fearing arrest, gave his word of honor that he would not rebel.[101] Thus reassured, Batet returned to divisional headquarters in Burgos, evidently unaware that his own chief of staff, Lt. Col. Fernando Moreno Calderón, was a leading conspirator and ready to snatch his whole command away from him.

The next morning, July 17, Mola's younger brother, a captain in the Barcelona garrison, slipped into Pamplona to report on behalf of some of his comrades that a rising in Catalonia would be suicidal.[102] The working-class groups in Barcelona were militant and organized, enjoyed mass support, and were already partly armed. Moreover, the recently appointed leader of the rebellion in Barcelona, Goded, apparently had grave misgivings about the political affiliation and goals of the conspiracy, and was in turn distrusted by other plotters.[103]

Nevertheless, not all the rebel officers in Catalonia shared the younger Mola's pessimism. Some UME leaders held that though they might not be able to seize all Catalonia in a single blow, they could at least pin down leftist forces there until Madrid itself had been taken and the main nucleus of Popular Front strength had been destroyed.[104] Others felt that a quick, determined blow might at least win them the center of Barcelona, and that this could be a vital factor. Mola could not ignore his brother's report of the lack of response among the top Barcelona commanders, but it was too late to delay any longer. On the 17th, Mola's brother took the night train back to Barcelona, fearing the worst.[105] Many in Spain slept fitfully while he traveled.

CHAPTER EIGHTEEN

The Rebellion

IN MOROCCO the timetable for revolt remained somewhat confused throughout. Apparently a last-minute effort was made to delay the rising until July 18,[1] but events at Melilla were precipitated by betrayal, forcing the rebels to act early on the afternoon of Friday the 17th. Yagüe seized control of Ceuta late that evening, and the officers in Larache moved at about 2 the following morning. General Romerales, military commander of Melilla, was arrested at pistol point in his office. The Assault Guards and trade unionists at Larache attempted to resist, but were soon quelled. More serious opposition came from the Air Force. Units of the hydroplane base at Ceuta, and those at the Tetuán airfield commanded by Major Lapuente Bahamonde, Franco's first cousin, refused to join the rising. At dawn on Saturday the 18th, light artillery bombarded the airfield, and its defenders surrendered after a brief skirmish. The rebellion in Morocco achieved complete success in little more than twenty-four hours.[2] All officers and men who resisted the rising, as well as most of the leaders of trade unions and Popular Front parties in the Protectorate, were quickly placed under arrest.

Franco, who was to take command in Morocco, had moved his family from Tenerife to Las Palmas, capital of the Canary Islands, on the morning of the 17th. A valid excuse for the journey was at hand in the impending funeral of General Balmes, military commander of the islands, who had just been killed by accident during target practice. One of Franco's old africanista comrades, Balmes had been under heavy pressure to join the rebellion. He had apparently refused to do so, and there were widespread rumors that his death was no accident, but suicide or murder.[3] At any rate, the elimination of Balmes made the work of the conspirators in the Canaries somewhat easier. During the early hours of July 18, Franco received word from Morocco that the rebellion had begun, and the leaders of the conspiracy in Las Palmas declared martial law at dawn, quickly smashing an attempted general strike by the unions.[4]

Shortly after 5 A.M., Franco issued the rebels' first manifesto to the Spanish people. There was not a word of militarism, clericalism, monarchism, fascism, or even anti-Republicanism in it. Rather the proclamation dwelt on the current state of disorder in Spain and the growth of subversive, anti-patriotic activity. It appealed to all loyal Spaniards to rally behind a movement whose leaders had determined "to make real, for the first time in Spanish history, and in this order, the triad Fraternity, Liberty, and Equality."[5]

Franco estimated that the whole venture was risky in the extreme. For safety's sake, before leaving Las Palmas Franco placed his wife and daughter on board a German passenger ship bound for Le Havre.[6] Arrangements had earlier been made to hire a private British airplane that would fly Franco to Tetuán,[7] where he was scheduled to arrive on the evening of the 18th.[8] However, his plane stopped to refuel in Casablanca, and the general managed to get a few hours' sleep. Before continuing the journey, he put through a long-distance telephone call to the Spanish zone, and was assured by Yagüe and other rebel leaders that the revolt was a complete success. Thus encouraged, he left at once for Tetuán, and arrived on the morning of the 19th.

In Spain itself, the conspirators moved with considerable uncertainty. It appears that Mola expected the garrisons in the southern part of the peninsula to rebel on the 18th, and all the rest to follow suit by dawn of the following day. The leader of the revolt in Seville was Queipo de Llano. Though sixty years of age, the tall, grizzled Queipo was still a rather striking figure. If he had always had a reputation for being impulsive, violent, and egotistical, he had also shown strong leadership on the battlefield and resolution when the chips were down. Now he took decisive action. On the 18th, clad inconspicuously in civilian clothing and attended only by a few aides, he arrested the commanding general of the Seville district, then locked up those Infantry officers who had not been able to decide whether to join the revolt or not. At first Queipo was supported by no more than a handful of trusted officers, and the entire Army garrison at Seville numbered little more than 400. By the end of the day, however, both the Civil Guards and Assault Guards had been won over and the center of

Seville occupied by the insurgents. Military rebels had also taken over the local government in Córdoba, Cádiz, Jerez, and Algeciras, though the airfield at Seville remained loyal to the regime. The anarchists and Communists in the working-class districts of the city were attempting to arm and organize tens of thousands of followers, but guns were lacking.[9]

Mola was on the telephone half the night of July 18, trying to make sure that military leaders in the northeast would act together. Martial law was declared in Pamplona early on the 19th.[10] The Carlists began to assemble en masse, for their leaders chose to ignore an order sent by the Pretender the day before forbidding them to participate in a military coup unless they were given full and precise political guarantees.[11]

The rebellion also seized control of Zaragoza, headquarters of the neighboring Seventh Division, without difficulty. Major General Miguel Cabanellas, the division's commander, was the highest in seniority among the generals on active duty. Together with Aranda, Capaz, and López de Ochoa, he was a leader of the small group of moderate liberals within the military who supported Lerroux, and he had won a Cortes seat on the Radical list in 1933. Cabanellas had participated in the conspiracies against Primo de Rivera and at first hesitated to take part in an anti-Republican revolt. The story that he did not make up his mind until a subordinate put a pistol against his head may well be true.[12] At any rate, he was the only divisional commander to join the rebellion. Martial law was declared in Zaragoza at dawn on the 19th, and the threatened CNT strike was smashed, leaving the Army in control. Victory at Zaragoza was doubly important because Mola had only 1,200 rifles in the Pamplona arsenal; Cabanellas was able to send 10,000 more to complete the armament of the Navarrese Carlists.[13]

On the night of the 18th, General Batet, the divisional commander at Burgos, and General Molero, commander at Valladolid, were both arrested, though not until after a bloody fray at the Valladolid headquarters.[14] The Burgos garrison had, in fact, been in a state of rebellion since the preceding afternoon, for a day earlier the Director General of Security had come up from Madrid and arrested a brigadier and five other conspirators. The garrisons in Salamanca, Zamora, Avila, Segovia, and Cáceres were more reluctant, but the rebels managed to swing them into line on the 19th.[15]

To the far northwest, in Galicia, everything remained quiet. The conspiracy was somewhat weaker there and the divisional commander, Salcedo, disinclined to join the revolt, while the garrison chief at La

Coruña, General Caridad Pita, was a leftist sympathizer. The leader of the conspiracy in Galicia was Major Pablo Martín Alonso, earlier exiled for his participation in the *sanjurjada*. The rebels were somewhat indecisive, and it was not until Monday, July 20, that they arrested the ranking generals and declared martial law. The small military garrison at the key naval base of El Ferrol had not even been brought into the conspiracy,[16] and two full days of skirmishing were needed to win control of Vigo, La Coruña, and El Ferrol.[17]

In the crucial northwestern province of Asturias, the fate of the rebellion depended largely on the military governor of Oviedo, Col. Antonio Aranda. A large, heavyset man with a thick face and glasses, Aranda was a corporal's son. As a staff officer and field unit commander in Morocco he had been responsible for much of the technical planning behind the Alhucemas landing, and had built up an excellent professional reputation. A Mason and nominal liberal, he was nonetheless involuntarily taken off the active list for some time after the advent of the Republic. The victory of the moderates in 1933 and the accession of Lerroux, with whom Aranda was politically identified, enabled him to resume his career. In December 1934, he had replaced López de Ochoa as commander in Asturias, and it was said that Lerroux wanted to make him Minister of War. Yet, though near the top of the promotion list for several years, he had never been made general. His attitude toward the Republican liberals was such that there had been no strong pressure to remove him from his command after the 1936 elections.

On July 18, Aranda gave no sign of having changed his political attitude, and the leftists felt safe that night in sending 3,000 semi-armed miners away from Oviedo to reinforce the defenders of Madrid. Nevertheless, Aranda had remained in close contact with the conspiracy, and for a year and a half had been carefully planning the military defense of Oviedo against any further attacks by the Asturian miners. He felt that if the military did rebel, he would have no recourse but to go along with them. On the 19th, he stalled all day long to avoid fulfilling government instructions to arm the lower classes, and then, at 9 P.M., when he could no longer delay, threw off the mask. Declaring martial law, he put into action his plan to hold Oviedo against the leftists. Counting some 856 civilian volunteers, most of whom were Falangists, he had about 2,300 men at his disposal to defend a perimeter of 19 kilometers around the city. Fortunately for Aranda, the garrison was one of the best equipped in Spain, with at least two hundred machine guns and two million cartridges. Under his expert direction, a well-knit defensive position was built up and the machine guns placed to command intersecting lines of fire. If all went well, the defenders would be able to withstand mass assaults by the miners until reinforcements came up from Galicia and the south. In the neighboring province of León, the revolt was almost completely successful. At the district's only airfield, the noncommissioned officers turned against the insurgent garrison commanders. Just as they were about to shoot their senior officers, the rebels were persuaded by them to return to discipline.[18] By the 21st, León was effectively under the control of the rebel leaders.

The paralysis of the Republican government during the first twenty-four hours of the revolt has been frequently commented on, but there were valid reasons for the government's inaction. Though the entire past century had been full of limited, uncoordinated pronunciamientos, not since 1868 had there been a successful, cohesive, nationwide military conspiracy. Government leaders were correct in judging the revolt ill-planned and poorly coordinated, and in believing that nearly all the ranking territorial commanders were loyal. Conversely, Azaña and Casares Quiroga were aware of the danger from the left. They did not want to provoke the right and loyal elements among the military unnecessarily by arming the working classes. If the rebellion of 1936 followed the pattern of those in 1926, 1929, 1930, and 1932, it would take form only in a few isolated areas; gunboats patrolling the straits would prevent the units in Morocco from crossing to the mainland, and the rebellion would fizzle out.

But the revolt slowly gathered momentum in the north as well as in the south, and during the afternoon and evening of July 18 the last trace of optimism at government headquarters in Madrid vanished. The Prime Minister resigned, and a new and more moderate Cabinet was formed. Republican leaders placed their hopes on some kind of compromise with the rebels, for they did not want to precipitate a class struggle or civil war. Mola had usually been considered a man of some discretion, and as late as July 14 Casares Quiroga had told a delegation of Basque leaders that to take measures against him would harm the the Republic.[19] In preceding weeks, a liberal Navarrese politician with reliable connections in the government had hinted to Mola that the general might become War Minister in a new Cabinet shake-up. Formation of the new moderate ministry under Diego Martínez Barrio was completed in the early hours of July 19. Soon afterward, both

Martínez Barrio and the new Minister of War, Miaja, got in touch with Mola by telephone. There is no reliable evidence to reveal exactly what was said, though sources from both sides agree that concessions were offered by the government in an attempt to bring about a peaceful compromise. Rebel sources claim it was suggested that Mola might take over the Ministry of War, but the general is supposed to have replied that even if the alternative were civil war he could not step back, for his obligations admitted no compromise—nothing less than the resignation of the entire Cabinet in favor of a military junta.[20]

Thus efforts to compromise quickly foundered. Later that same day a new ultra-liberal Republican ministry was formed under the leadership of José Giral. It saw no alternative but to grant the Socialist demand to arm the workers and crush the rebellion, which henceforth would be labeled "fascist." Miaja, who objected to the distribution of guns to the lower classes and feared disorder from the leftist militia, resigned as Minister of War.[21] Command was assumed by two UMRA leaders, General Sebastián Pozas (Director of the Civil Guard), who became Minister of the Interior with control of the police, and General Castelló (military commander of the Badajoz district), who was summoned to Madrid to become the new Minister of War.

Calculation of the strength of the opposing forces left the issue in doubt. The 1936 Army budget theoretically provided for a maximum of 145,000 officers and men, but since the February elections, recruitment and retention of men in the ranks had dropped off sharply. On July 19, there were approximately 8,000 officers on the active list, of whom 1,627 were stationed in Morocco. The NCO's totaled less than 8,000, approximately 1,600 of whom were currently assigned to the Protectorate. Nearly all Infantry battalions were 50 per cent or more under strength, averaging about 200 men each, so that all the units stationed in the peninsula scarcely totaled 60,000 men.

Two Infantry divisions—the Seventh, with headquarters in Valladolid, and the Eighth, in Galicia—were being taken over completely by the rebels, who were also winning over most units of the Second, Fifth, and Sixth Divisions, in the southern and northeastern provinces. This gave the rebels about 30,000 troops in the peninsula. More important was the Moroccan Army, composed of the 4,200-man Tercio, 17,000 Moorish Regulares, and 11,000 Spanish recruits from the ordinary units—a total of 32,239 of the best-trained, best-led, best-equipped, most sternly disciplined and combat-worthy troops in the Army.[22] This force would soon be launched against the government, together with whatever rightist militia auxiliaries could be mustered.

The Madrid authorities hoped that the Air Force and the Navy would remain loyal to the government. The Air Force numbered some 200 planes, most of which were obsolete or obsolescent, but if the Navy could maintain a firm blockade of the Moroccan coast, Franco's forces might be held off until the rebellion inside Spain had been crushed. Fortunately for the government, much of the country's military equipment had been taken over from the regular Army centers and deposited in the arsenals and mobilization centers created by the Azaña laws of 1931–32, and therefore was under the direct control of the Ministry of War. Consequently the Madrid government had more matériel at its disposal than did the rebels, though trained manpower was lacking. The only remaining organized units were the security forces. The regular police (Seguridad) officially numbered 17,500, the supposedly pro-Republican Assault Guard 18,000, and the Civil Guard more than 34,000, but these figures were probably inflated. Moreover, in some provinces the Civil and Assault Guards were going over to the rebels.

In an effort to shatter discipline among the forces in rebellion, an order was sent out about 10 P.M. on July 19 by the acting Minister of War dissolving all these units, discharging their officers, and releasing their enlisted men from all oaths of service and obedience.[23] This had no effect at all upon the rebels, who had imposed ruthless martial law in the districts under their control. The "Republican Army" was ceasing to exist, for even those units under officers still loyal to the government were looked askance at by the Madrid leaders and the Popular Front. The government was now forced to rely on loyal elements in the security forces and on the armed proletariat. The Socialist and anarchist militias, receiving guns by the tens of thousands in Madrid, Barcelona, Bilbao, Valencia, and other centers, were exultant. Contemptuous of the "fascist" military, they felt supremely confident of their ability to crush the rebellion with their bare hands, if need be, and to carry out a Spanish social revolution.

The security of Madrid was only briefly in doubt. There were 6,400 loyal Assault and Civil Guards in the vicinity of the capital, while the half dozen barracks in the area contained scarcely 7,250 troops, most of whom were inexperienced and poorly armed. The officers stationed in Madrid shared the political attitudes of their comrades elsewhere. The majority held moderate or conservative political opinions, but did not want to get mixed up in a rebellion unnecessarily. A small minority were pro-left or liberal, and a larger minority, especially among the junior officers, were eager to rebel. Because of these conflicts, and also because of the political pressures in the capital, it had been hard to organize an effective conspiracy among the Madrid garrison. As has been seen, the so-called Junta Central of the UME in Madrid was conservative and Republican in orientation, opposed to the monarchists, and suspicious of Mola. Hours before the revolt began in Morocco, it dispatched a special representative to Sanjurjo in Portugal with word of the Junta's willingness to accept his leadership if he agreed to reject any compromise with the monarchists.[24]

Though news of the rebellion had spread through the capital, there was still no organized plan for a revolt in Madrid.[25] Mola had earlier tried to establish a committee of four colonels there, but because of problems of rank and prestige these officers received scant recognition. The first act of rebellion by the Madrid garrison occurred almost by accident on the morning of July 19, at the Carabanchel barracks west of the city. When Socialist militiamen arrived before dawn to demand arms, one of the commanders, Lt. Col. Carratalá, head of the UMRA in the Cavalry Corps, made ready to hand over a supply of rifles. Other officers intervened; the colonel and two of his aides were killed, and the Socialists were driven off. The whole Carabanchel garrison then came out in revolt.

The leading conspirators in Madrid were by this time totally confused. The retired General Villegas, whom Mola had selected to occupy the Ministry of War, seems to have cracked under the pressure, leaving the somewhat unbalanced General Fanjul, who was slated to seize command of the First Infantry Division, as the only alternative leader. Fanjul had been about to flee north to Burgos when word came from conspirators in other barracks that he must try to take charge of the revolt in Madrid. Much was expected from the squat, personable, circumspect Miaja, who had talked with the conspirators two days earlier, and had given them the impression that they could count on him. Even after the first news from Morocco had come in, Miaja had ordered the release of several officers in his brigade who had been arrested for conspiracy. As far as can be seen, Miaja was trying to remain on good terms with both sides.[26] The slowness and disorganization of the rebellion, together with the government's offer of a ministerial appointment in the early hours of July 19, drew him into the loyalist camp, where his working-class origins would later enable him to be hailed as "a general of the people."

Miaja's position made it impossible for Fanjul to install himself at headquarters, so on the same Sunday morning he entered the Montaña barracks in the western district of the city to await the column of troops that would supposedly march from Carabanchel. But the column was pinned down by the security forces and leftist militia, and by the night of July 19 Fanjul found himself cut off in the Montaña barracks with some 2,000 troops and several hundred Falangist and monarchist auxiliaries. Because of confusion, lack of planning, and vigorous pressure from the armed militia, the barracks had been isolated from one another. The Montaña was overwhelmed by assault on the following morning and several hundred of its defenders were killed, including some 20 or 30 officers who either committed suicide or were butchered by the militia after their surrender. Carabanchel also fell on the 20th, and scattered resistance in the other barracks soon came to an end.[27] The First Division was then dissolved. In central Spain, armed power and political control passed into the hands of the workers' militia, who instituted a revolutionary reign of terror that the nominal government was helpless to control.

The revolt was also crushed in Barcelona, just as Mola's brother had foreseen. Goded declared martial law at Mallorca early on the morning of the 19th, then flew to the Catalan capital to take charge of the rising there. His precise plans at that point remain a matter of conjecture. In view of his misgivings during recent weeks, he may have hoped merely to use the rebel forces to maneuver the government into a compromise. The first message received from the Barcelona insurgents did not make clear how precarious the situation had become, and Goded may have overestimated the rebels' power. As it turned out, the onslaught of the security police and thousands of CNT militiamen made it difficult even to hold the rebel headquarters. By the afternoon of the 19th, Goded was asking Luis Companys, president of the Catalan administration, to inform Azaña that he would like to negotiate.[28] But it was much too late for compromise, and Goded's appeal was rejected; a few hours later, he was forced to surrender to the leftist forces. The last remaining nuclei of rebel resistance were overcome on July 20.[29]

The smaller garrisons in the vicinity of Barcelona and Madrid ran into similar difficulties. Army leaders temporarily seized power at Guadalajara, Alcalá de Henares, and Albacete, to the south and east of the Republican capital, but were overwhelmed within a few days. Toledo was the only place in the center of the peninsula where the rebels made a successful stand. In Catalonia, the failure was absolute. Officers of several units stationed in Lérida rebelled, but were easily maneuvered into submission after Goded's surrender. The garrison of Gerona, near the French border, joined the revolt, but then remained in its barracks while the Assault Guards rallied to the regime and anarchist militia took over the town. Within a week, all regular Army units had been disbanded in Catalonia, and power had passed into the hands of the anarchist militia, who numbered 50,000 or more. In the Balearics, the rebels dominated Mallorca and Ibiza, but on Menorca a group of NCO's affiliated with the UMRA led 700 undisciplined recruits in a successful mutiny against the Army command.[30]

The attempt to provoke a revolt in Valencia proved futile. The garrison in this city was comparatively large, consisting of five regiments, and since 1931 its commanders had been chosen from among the coterie of generals most loyal to the Republic. The present head, Brigadier General Fernando Martínez Monje, had been given an appointment superior to his rank because the government considered him especially reliable. However, like many other officers, Martínez Monje tried to play both sides, and in June made contact with the civilian conspirators of the DRV (see p. 318), who promised hundreds of rightist volunteers. Monje was also in contact with Mola and criticized him for indecisiveness.[31] Several times UME leaders among the junior officers in the Valencia garrison had threatened to precipitate rebellion on their own.[32] There were, however, signs that much of this was mere braggadocio. Despite his complaints, Monje could not be relied upon to seize the initiative, and the local UME leaders did not have full control of the Valencia barracks. The retired Major General González Carrasco was eventually named by Mola to head the rebellion there. Though he had shown considerable bravery during his years in Morocco, González Carrasco was now irresolute and confused. He first refused to go to Valencia, saying that it looked hopeless there anyway, then changed his mind. Monje would not, however, relinquish command to González Carrasco, insisting that the revolt would be futile unless they could count on help from within the Madrid government.[33] The regimental commanders, in turn, said that they would not lead their troops into the streets unless González Carrasco gave them the order from division headquarters. The unfortunate Carrasco was caught in a vise: he could not depose Monje without the support of the colonels, yet the colonels refused to support him unless he first took over Monje's command. By the morning of the 19th, Carrasco was ready to give up. The dilemma became worse when the government made public on the radio the contents of a message on its behalf from Luis Lucia, official head of the DRV. The workers were being armed in Valencia, and on the afternoon of the 20th Monje called the colonels together to determine their allegiance. With but two exceptions they agreed to remain loyal, and they were able to dominate the more junior UME officers.

Though they did not revolt, the Army units remained in their barracks. Only a very few officers accepted commissions in the workers' militia. At the end of the month, the NCO's and troops in several units rebelled and placed themselves under the command of the authorities, but the main Infantry barracks remained closed. It was surrounded by thousands of armed militiamen on the night of August 1, and surrendered at dawn the following morning.[34] Much the same sort of thing happened at Alcoy.[35] Virtually the only fighting in the east took place at Cartagena, where part of the military contingent rebelled but was put down rather easily.[36]

The insurgents suffered another fiasco at Málaga. The local military commander, General Patxot, a veteran africanista, was cultivated, correct, a devout Catholic, and something of a linguist. He was not a rightist and not very enthusiastic about the revolt. However, Málaga was a key point in communications with Africa and eastern Andalusia, and the conspirators persuaded Patxot to declare martial law. In order to avoid any association with fascism he refused the assistance of local Falangists, but the Assault Guards remained loyal to the government and the Civil Guards deserted the rebellion on the night of July 18. Several Army sergeants had come under the influence of local Communists and were said to be planning mutiny. Patxot could see no sign of the promised reinforcements from Morocco, and surrendered to the government at dawn.[37]

In the north, the rebellion failed in the provinces of Santander, Vizcaya, and Guipuzcoa. Only in San Sebastián did a general revolt occur. The commander, Major León Carrasco, was a conservative monarchist, but was also pro-Basque and apparently not trusted by Mola. He was only brought into the conspiracy on July 12, and even then was given no details. Consequently he was unprepared when the storm broke six days later. He ordered his troops to fortify themselves in their barracks, where they held out until July 28.[38]

The rebels suffered a major loss on a small airfield near Lisbon on July 19. Sanjurjo was to take over as head of the rebel junta, and planned to fly to Mola's headquarters in the two-seat plane of the aviator Juan Antonio Ansaldo, one of the principal troubleshooters among the rightist conspirators. However, because of diplomatic complications, the authorities would not let them use the main airfield. Ansaldo had been in a score of narrow scrapes, and anticipated no difficulty on this vital mission. The emotional Sanjurjo wept tears of joy while his luggage was being loaded into the small plane. As wealthy monarchist friends waved goodbye, the plane rolled down the airstrip. Just as it began to leave the ground it lost power, plowed into the earth, and burst into flames. Ansaldo, though badly hurt, survived; but Sanjurjo was killed almost instantly.[39] The rebellion was bereft of its symbol of leadership and unity.

A week after the revolt began in Morocco the military rebels held less than a third of the national territory: in the north, Navarre, León, Galicia, most of Old Castile and Aragon; in the south, only the areas immediately surrounding Cádiz, Seville, Córdoba, Granada, Huelva, and Cáceres. Since most of the Navy remained loyal, the generals were stymied in their efforts to transport the bulk of the Moroccan Army to the peninsula. The Popular Front forces controlled almost all the major urban and industrial areas, had a nucleus of trained manpower in the security units, and could exploit the credit resources of the central government. When the Socialist Indalecio Prieto, reputedly a pessimist, made a national radio speech on Friday, July 24, he declared that victory was a matter of days. The German Chargé d'Affaires was also dubious of the rebels' chances.[40] The Italian ambassador Pedrazzi had sent a report to Mussolini the week before the uprising, saying that the right was so hesitant and divided that the revolt could not possibly succeed. He had emphasized his conviction that the only fruitful policy for the Italian government was to reach an understanding with the Azaña regime. When he saw a diplomatic agent of General Mola in Biarritz a week after the revolt began, he congratulated the emissary on the effort the rebels had made, and added words of consolation for its "failure."[41]

The crisis facing the insurgents was due in large part to the breakdown of the attempted revolt in the Navy. Since the Navy ordinarily avoided political entanglement, the conspiracy had been almost entirely an Army affair. It was known that the great majority of naval officers were fed up with the Popular Front regime, and evidently Mola assumed that once the banner was raised the Navy would cooperate. Though maritime support was vital in transferring the Army of Morocco to the peninsula, it was not until early on July 17 that Mola dispatched Air Force Colonel Alfredo Kindelán to Cádiz to urge naval commanders to second the rebellion.[42] But during the previous evening, the Naval Ministry in Madrid had given orders that warships in southern waters were not to dock in Spanish ports but to stay on the alert and remain close to shore. Thirty-six hours later, on the morning of July 18, three destroyers were sent from the Cartagena naval base to bombard rebel units in Melilla. On the way, the officers commanding these vessels heard Franco's opening manifesto over the radio. Having earlier been contacted by Army conspirators, they decided to join the revolt. Instead of shelling Melilla, the first two ships to arrive asked permission to dock. However, the lower ranks of the Navy had been much more deeply penetrated by leftist influence than had those of the Army, and the crews aboard the three destroyers immediately reacted against their officers. They mutinied, seized control of the ships, and moved out to sea.

In rebel waters there remained only one destroyer, one torpedo-boat destroyer, and five small gunboats. Two of the gunboats deserted almost immediately. Late on July 18, two cruisers at the El Ferrol base, which had not yet rebelled, were hurriedly ordered south to intimidate the rebel garrison at Cádiz. When commanders of these two vessels tried to take their ships over to the rebels, their crewmen mutinied and held the cruisers for the Republic. Three days later, after the Army units in northwestern Spain had gained control of Vigo, the old battleship *Jaime I,* which had been in dock there, was sent south to provide naval cover for the Moroccan forces; but en route there was another successful mutiny, and its crew took the ship back to the Republican Navy. The torpedo destroyer that had joined the rebellion at Ceuta was used to ferry one company of Regulares across to Andalusia,[43] but its crew commandeered it on the return trip and steamed off for Cartagena. By July 21, the Republican Navy had concentrated a fleet of two cruisers, two destroyers, three gunboats, and seven submarines near Tangier, in an effort to blockade the coast of the Protectorate and prevent the transfer of the Army of Morocco to the peninsula.[44]

Time was of the essence in moving reliable troops to Spain for the assault against Madrid. With the passage by sea blocked, the alternative was to vault the straits with airborne transport, but the Army had only nine old planes in Morocco and would be hard put to find more. The nine craft were immediately pressed into service, and soon were making three flights daily to Jerez or to Seville.[45] Under optimum conditions, they could ferry a maximum of two hundred men per day; but breakdowns could be expected at any time, and there was insufficient equipment to keep the planes in good repair.

Franco never acted on impulse, but by the evening of the 19th he apparently realized that the situation was reaching a crucial stage. Air support would be necessary to move his forces across the straits, and this could only be provided by foreign sources. France, like Spain, was living under a Popular Front government, and the rebels could expect no help from her. Britain was also out of the question. Only Germany and Italy were potential sources of aid. Monarchist elements had been scheming with Rome since 1932; during the past ten days they had intensified efforts there and in Berlin. On July 20, an aide was dispatched to Biarritz via Lisbon in the British plane that had earlier carried Franco to Tetuán. In Biarritz it picked up the monarchist conspirator Marqués de Luca de Tena, who was flown on to Rome, where he talked with the Italian Foreign Minister, Count Ciano, on July 22. Franco requested twelve new transport planes to help bring the struggle to a swift conclusion, but the Italian government had no clear understanding of what was going on in Spain and for the moment would not grant the request.[46]

Meanwhile, Mola had been working feverishly at his Pamplona headquarters, wheedling and threatening reluctant territorial commanders by long-distance telephone in a desperate effort to marshal forces for a drive on Madrid. However, the failure of the rebellion in the Basque provinces and along most of the northern coast threatened the flank of the rebels in north central Spain, and meant that much of their meager manpower had to be used in sealing off the Basque country and stamping out pockets of resistance in isolated areas of Old Castile and Aragon. Falangist volunteers began to pour in by the hundreds, but it was the Carlists who shifted the balance. No less than 7,000 boinas rojas appeared for duty in Alava and Navarre within the first twenty-four hours. During the first week of fighting, eleven different battle columns were organized in Pamplona, ranging in size from 200 to 2,000 men. Seven columns were sent north into Guipuzcoa; the other four went south to hold Aragon and drive on Madrid.

Mola has sometimes been criticized for not adhering more faithfully to the original plan of concentrating all his forces for a direct blow at the capital. Yet the uncertainty of those days was so great and the pattern of support and resistance so confused that the rebel effort might have failed completely, had not Mola consolidated his position in the north center. The combined columns from Pamplona, Burgos, and Valladolid totaled scarcely 5,000 men, and when they reached the mountain passes north of Madrid, they found them already occupied by proletarian militia forces greatly superior in number.

Mola moved his headquarters southwest to Burgos on July 22. By that time it was becoming clear that the original plan had failed; the quick drive on Madrid could not be organized. In the old Castilian capital the first civilian politicians to meet Mola were the alfonsino monarchists, who counseled him to set up a military junta of some sort immediately, even if it had to be staffed with colonels.[47] That same day, Mola sent General Ponte to Lisbon to win over Salazar, who, on July 26, privately promised his support.

The fighting in the mountains above Madrid went slowly. The rebels could bring only light artillery on their forced march, but they had a fair complement of machine guns and enjoyed the advantage of superior training and leadership. They inched their way forward peak by peak, and if there was any reluctance on the part of the ordinary soldier, he found an officer at his back ready to drive him forward at pistol point. For their part, the militia pressed the fight with suicidal courage, and hundreds were slaughtered by the rebel machine guns.[48] By the 25th, the highest passes were in Army hands; but more and more militia were being moved up and resistance was stiffening, while the rebels' ammunition was running very low.

Mola, like Franco, soon realized that foreign aid would be necessary. Though he had never allowed the monarchists a central place in the Army rebellion, and in recent months had complained to intimates that he was badly informed on their maneuvers in Rome and Berlin,[49] they were now entirely at his disposal. On July 24, he dispatched Goicoechea and two others to Rome in one of the few usable aircraft under his command. There the monarchist envoys repeated Luca de Tena's request for aircraft, and also asked for ammunition, but Mussolini still could not make up his mind.[50]

Meanwhile, Franco had initiated direct contact with Berlin. He was encouraged to do so by the head of the Nazi party in Spanish Morocco, Johannes Bernhardt, son-in-law of one of the owners of a prosperous export firm. During the preceding spring, Bernhardt had been informed of the anti-Republican conspiracy by local Falangists. Before the revolt began, he had offered his services to Army leaders in obtaining transport planes from a private German firm to move troops to the peninsula in a lightning attack. The conspirators in Morocco

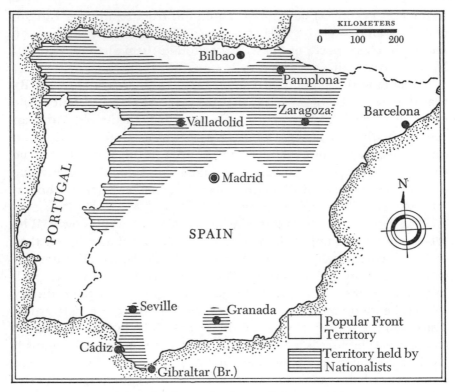

The Division of Spain, ca. July 25, 1936

had felt that this would not be necessary, but Bernhardt visited Berlin in June to convince Nazi officials that Germany should support the projected rebellion. Higher German authorities did not, however, wish to commit the government in advance.[51]

After Franco arrived in Tetuán, Bernhardt repeated the offer, even pledging private German credit to help obtain airplanes. Franco was probably also aware that monarchist agents in Madrid and Berlin had already been negotiating with representatives of the German aircraft industry.[52] With only three transport planes functioning in Spanish Morocco, the general probably felt that he had little choice.[53] On July 22, the German Air Attaché for Lisbon-Paris received a wire informing him that one of Franco's staff colonels, Juan Beigbeder (a former military attaché in Berlin), had requested the Germans to provide "through private firms . . . ten transport planes with maximum seating capacity."[54]

Since prompt action was imperative, Franco decided to send a personal delegation to Berlin. There was no Spanish plane in Morocco

fit for such a mission, but a Lufthansa transport was currently ground-
ed in Las Palmas (Canaries) between flights. Despite official German
protests, it was seized to carry Bernhardt, Air Force Captain Francisco
Arranz, and a subordinate Nazi official to Germany on July 24.[55] The
German Foreign Office was reluctant to have anything to do with this
delegation, but on July 26 the envoys were flown down to Bayreuth,
where Hitler was attending a Wagner festival. The Führer, along
with Field Marshal Göring, War Minister Werner von Blomberg,
and "an admiral who was present in Bayreuth," received them late
in the evening. It has been assumed that the admiral was Wilhelm
Canaris, soon to become Chief of German Naval Intelligence. Canaris
had served with German espionage in Spain and Morocco during the
First World War, had been sent to Spanish America, and had visited
Spain several times since the war. He knew a number of the Spanish
military leaders personally and strongly urged German support, emphasizing the danger of revolution and Bolshevism in Spain, which
might turn the western flank of Germany in collusion with the French
Popular Front.[56] The Spanish delegation stressed the same possibility
in melodramatic terms. Though German and Italian fear of Communism has usually been discounted as a mere propaganda ploy in
explaining the eventual decision to intervene in Spain, the importance
of such feeling in motivating both Hitler and Mussolini should not
be ignored: the central European fascist powers were concerned not
only with promoting a pro-fascist military takeover in Spain, but also
with blocking the victory of the Popular Front revolution that the failure of the military rebellion had provoked. Hitler agreed that same
night to aid the Spanish rebels, and it was soon learned that Mussolini,
after considerable hesitation, had made the same decision.[57] Though
the Italian and German governments seem to have arrived at the same
conclusion independently, their decisions to act coincided.

Meanwhile, on July 23 Mola had officially constituted in Burgos a
seven-member "Junta de Defensa Nacional" to serve as the executive
board of the military movement.[58] Nominal president was General
Miguel Cabanellas, highest in seniority among the rebel commanders
and one of the least enthusiastic. At Zaragoza, Cabanellas' district headquarters, the rebellion had been proclaimed against the Azaña government, but clearly not against the Republic. Luminaries of the Radical
Party, in whose ranks Cabanellas had earlier been a Cortes deputy,
had been given major posts in city and provincial government. Cabanellas had quickly made concessions to moderate civilian groups to
avoid antimilitary sentiment, and was considered by other rebel lead-

ers to be wavering and indecisive at best.[59] Within little more than
forty-eight hours, Mola had decided that Cabanellas must be replaced
at Zaragoza with a more ruthless commander, but because of his rank
he could only be kicked upstairs. A week earlier Cabanellas had feared
that he might have to shave off his beard and flee across the Pyrenees
disguised as a priest.[60] Instead, he soon found himself the puppet leader
of the rebellion, for it was hoped that the image of this elderly Mason
and well-known liberal as nominal Junta president would help to rally
the moderates and the undecided.

In addition to Cabanellas, the Junta was composed of Mola, the
retired Generals Ponte, Andrés Saliquet, and Fidel Dávila (who had
played key roles in the revolt in Old Castile), and two lieutenant-
colonels from the General Staff, Federico Montaner and Fernando
Moreno Calderón.[61] It was rumored in Burgos that the generals hoped
to include distinguished civilians as subordinate members,[62] but the
factionalism of Spanish politics made this seem inadvisable.[63] In accordance with Mola's plans, some kind of patriotic junta—usually with
civilian members or advisers in subordinate roles—was being set up
in almost every province dominated by the rebels,[64] but the real government in the rebel zone was obviously the new self-appointed military hierarchy. Theirs was the main responsibility, and when the Junta
members signed their first decree in Burgos, Moreno Calderón is said
to have murmured, "If Spain does not respond, this is our death sentence."[65] Despite the lack of seniority or official authority of some of
the new rebel commanders, very nearly 100 per cent of the officers in
the rebel-controlled areas rallied to the rebel cause. This attested a
considerable degree of unity, at least momentarily, among the military
in revolt.

The official statements of the rebel command sounded tough and
confident, but they concealed a deepening anxiety. Franco was mentioned as leading a mighty force from the south, but no one was sure
how soon the Moroccan Army would be able to cross the straits. Meanwhile, the shortage of men and munitions in the north was growing
critical. Mola was doubtful that it would be possible to break through
the mountains north of Madrid. He admitted that he did not see how
the Junta could organize more than 40,000 new recruits, even with a
month's grace. On July 26 he had his staff secretly draw up a plan for a
possible retreat northward to the Duero river.[66] García Escámez, commander of the main column in Somosierra pass, was ordered to conserve men and supplies as much as possible. Mola wired: "Impossible

to send ammunition; I have [only] 26,000 cartridges for the Army of the North."[67] Mola's secretary has written that by the 29th prospects were so bleak that the general was contemplating suicide.[68]

Later that same day, July 29, Mola received the first encouraging news in a week from the south. A telegram from Franco read: "We are the masters of the strait; we dominate the situation."[69] What had happened was this: on the 27th, the day that the first German Junkers 52 transport planes left Berlin en route to Tetuán,[70] the Italian government also began to send assistance;[71] within two days thirty German aircraft were ready for use in Morocco,[72] and the first tri-motored Savoia-Marchetti bombers were arriving from Italy.[73] This dispelled the clouds of gloom hanging over headquarters in Morocco and, through Portugal, Franco sent his jubilant wire to Mola. Six hundred thousand cartridges were then flown to the Burgos depot to enable the rebels to hold on in the north.[74]

On August 6, the German transport *Usaramo* docked in Cádiz harbor, carrying technicians and equipment for full-scale operation of the German planes. By the end of August, nearly 9,000 troops, together with part of their equipment, had been flown across the straits.[75] German and Italian bombers helped to scatter the blockade fleet temporarily on August 5, permitting passage of a large shipment of matériel and 2,500 more troops.[76] Though the Republican warships maintained a partial blockade of the straits until September 29, they eventually lost the numerical superiority they had held during the early weeks.[77] Never able to replace the officers slaughtered in the first days of the revolution,[78] they were usually incapable of coping with air attacks, and seldom ventured out of port during the remainder of the war.

By the first of August the insurgents dominated all of western Andalusia,[79] but their operations were greatly behind schedule. The drive northward had to be launched immediately, though the bulk of the Army of Morocco was still in Africa. Command of the assault forces was given to the brawny, bull-necked Yagüe. During the first week, his force of effectives was quite small; the original unit that set out from Seville on August 2 was composed of only one Bandera of the Tercio and three pieces of artillery.

The rebel columns did not move directly north over the Córdoba highway, but branched off northwest toward Badajoz and the Portuguese border. This detour was prompted by the unexpectedly stiff resistance they encountered, which made it important for the two main insurgent forces, north and south, to secure joint communications and

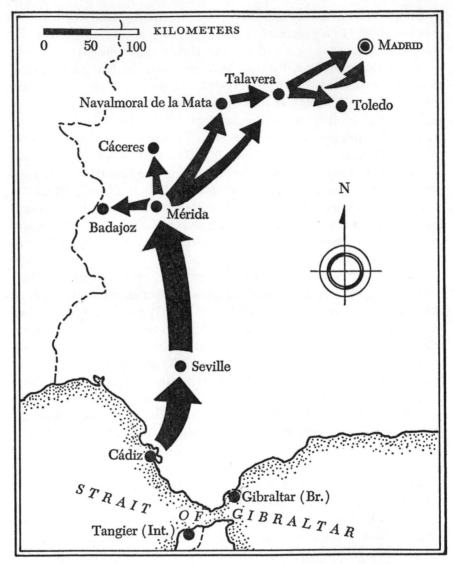

The Route of the Army of Africa toward Madrid, August–October 1936

supply lines across the Portuguese border before the final push on Madrid. The combat columns were divided into small, mobile groups that advanced indirectly, using tactics similar to those developed by their officers in the decisive Moroccan campaigns of 1925–27.[80] On August 10, the ancient city of Mérida was taken by a swift flank attack and the road to Badajoz lay open. By that time, Yagüe's units had been reinforced to total 4,500 men, and his order of the day on August 11 declared: "Technique rests in our hands. If we forget that, we place ourselves on the level of the enemy, lose the advantage, and become responsible for any casualties caused by lack of foresight or skill. We must be very jealous of spilling our own blood."[81]

The Defense Ministry in what was left of the Republican government at Madrid strove desperately to organize battalions of workers' militia to stay the onslaught. Nearly all regular Army units in Republican territory had been dissolved, and professional officers were considered politically unreliable. There was little or no time for training: as soon as a new group could be patched together, it was thrown pell-mell into the path of the advancing African forces. The ineffectiveness of these amateur formations was soon apparent. Moreover, stories of the ferocity of the Moorish Regulares proved unnerving, whether broadcast over Radio Seville by Queipo de Llano or passed by word of mouth among militiamen.[82]

Yagüe's column reached the Estremaduran capital of Badajoz on August 14. The local garrison of 800 had been held loyal to the Madrid regime by the determination of leftist-influenced NCO's, and was supported by a thousand or more militia volunteers. Moreover, the thick medieval walls of the town proved impervious to the light rebel artillery. One section of the attack column managed to penetrate the city through the southern suburbs and slowly fight its way toward the center of town. Communication between the rebel units broke down, and, hearing nothing from the section entering the other side of Badajoz, Yagüe eventually ordered that a narrow breach in the eastern wall be taken by storm. The subsequent charge of the 16th Company of the 4th Bandera of the Tercio into the muzzles of two sandbagged machine guns became one of the most celebrated feats of the war. Though the Company was almost annihilated, it carried the breach, and Badajoz was finally occupied after hours of savage hand-to-hand combat. Subsequently hundreds of captured Republicans and leftists were shot by the victors, and this mass killing gave rise to some of the most lurid atrocity stories of the entire conflict.[83]

By mid-August, Mola calculated that the rebels had at their command about 100,000 men in the north and 60,000 in the south,[84] but it is likely that regular soldiers comprised no more than 80 per cent of the total in the south and little more than 40 per cent in the north. Even among the Carlists, most volunteers lacked training and often had to be shown how to use guns while moving to the front.[85] Yet the spirit of the Requetés was excellent, and they showed their willingness to sustain heavy losses in the conquest of Guipuzcoa province, on the French border, during August and September. After August 20 or so, ammunition moved regularly through Portugal for the Army of the North, and Mola anticipated no difficulty in holding the high ground north of Madrid until Franco and Yagüe struck the main blow from the southwest.

By September, nearly all units of the Tercio and Regulares had been transported to the peninsula. There was not enough motor transport in the south of Spain to accommodate 20,000 men, so they were moved north in waves as space and vehicles became available.

The army would proceed in coaches looted from the villages, coloured rumbling Spanish country motor-buses. Eighty of them packed with legionnaires: forty of them with Moors: eight lorries of ammunition: a signal wagon: an ambulance: a petrol tank on wheels: a touring-car with machineguns. On the roofs was loot: on the radiators, religious emblems: on the men's faces, health and zest. They were in khaki drill, short sleeves, shirts open at the neck, and their dark faces were white with dust, though their dark eyes gleamed with that exhilaration which comes to men in battle. The Moors were quieter, more solemn, at times more curious; not much darker than the Spanish soldiers, but thinner and more primitive.

This mechanized army must fight light cavalrymen: they must reconnoitre swiftly: move suddenly: charge with élan, and overwhelm by their sheer audacity until the country felt them to be ten times more numerous than they really were.[86]

The junction of Talavera de la Reina, halfway between Badajoz and Madrid, was taken on September 3 and 4, and the connection with Mola's troops strengthened. Thousands of militiamen were killed, captured, or put to flight in the march from Badajoz, and the courage that had marked their counterattacks during the first days seemed to diminish. By mid-September, the rebel commanders believed the struggle would be over in six weeks or so.

The last major target before Madrid was the historic city of Toledo, where approximately 1,290 insurgents under Lt. Col. José Moscardó were holding out in the ancient Alcázar against half-hearted militia assaults. This great building, with its thick walls, deep foundation, and enormous cellars, was a natural fortress. Since the militia from Madrid had little artillery and could not handle the guns they did possess, the defenders had managed to resist for two months even though burdened with approximately a thousand civilians, including scores of hostages.[87]

During September, the semi-motorized columns of the Army of Africa, now doubled in size, moved up the Tajo valley at the rate of ten to twenty kilometers a day. Supported by a Cavalry brigade and by German and Italian planes, they easily turned each successive line of defense. A pro-rebel observer wrote:

Red trenches were clearly visible, but they never seemed adequately defended. The militia bunched in the redoubts near the main or side roads, while good positions on hill slopes were left unguarded. The . . . Legion and the Moors never failed to take advantage of such gaps to infiltrate the red lines and place their guns time after time to enfilade those positions still held. There would come the moment of hesitation when the rot would set in and one could see first two or three and then entire lines of men making for the rear. For that was the terrible error the red militia always made. They stuck to the roads, and then ran to the roads when defeated; whereas any man of experience would have known that the best line to fall back on was the open country, avoiding the roads like the plague.

The Nationalists, fully aware of this mistake on the part of the reds, never failed to have their machine guns placed to command both the road and all its lines of access; and time after time, the red mortalities were infinitely greater in the moment of panicky retreat than during the whole fight.[88]

Yagüe fell ill of a circulatory disorder, and on September 22d was replaced by Varela. The drive toward Toledo continued without pause. By September 24, the Alcázar defenders were driven back to the inner shell of their stronghold, which lay in ruins. Crouched in the cellars, they subsisted on moldy potatoes and rotting horseflesh. Filth and decay created an unbearable stench in the lower levels, while the late summer heat and the questionable condition of the water made an epidemic seem imminent. Two young women successfully gave birth in this inferno, but several of the older ones died from privation. A few defenders deserted each night, and three who could no longer bear it shot themselves.

The Alcázar temporarily occupied the focus of the whole struggle. It became a symbol for the rebels, who vowed that it would never fall to the "reds." By the afternoon of September 26, the defenders could glimpse flashes of gunfire on the hills to the west, marking the advance of the rebel columns. On the following morning, another mine smashed the ruins of the northeast tower of the Alcázar,[89] but the militia attack that followed was beaten off. At about 7 on the evening of the 27th, two small units of the Tercio and Regulares fought their way to the Alcázar, and the main insurgent force occupied Toledo on the morning of the 28th. The defense of the Alcázar was a signal tri-umph for the rebels,[90] but its glory was tarnished by the slaughter of scores—perhaps hundreds—of captured militiamen that followed.[91]

The occupation of Toledo placed Franco's advance column only forty miles from Madrid and completed the last major diversion be-fore the assault on the capital. Victory in this bloodiest of pronuncia-mientos seemed within sight.

CHAPTER NINETEEN

The Establishment of the Franco Dictatorship

T HE MILITARY REBELLION did not begin as a specifically "anti-Republican" movement. It had no precise program or ideology other than that of "saving Spain from anarchy." In at least two cities—Zaragoza and Mahón (on Menorca)—the first municipal governments set up by the Army rebels were not staffed by conservatives, but by the Radicals and other center elements.[1] On July 19, after declaring martial law in Pamplona, Mola had hastily reedited his earlier political sketch. The new draft suggested a corporative economic organization, a system of cooperatives, and the continuation of a moderate program of agrarian reform. Freedom of education was to be permitted generally; but the encouragement of "anarchy" and "pornography" was to be rigorously prohibited. Concerning religion, Mola's memorandum stated: "We are Catholic, but respect the religious beliefs of those who are not. We believe that the Church ought to be separate from the State, for this benefits both institutions."[2]

The Junta de Defensa Nacional was not dominated by Mola, but worked as a team. While Mola busied himself with military matters, the paper work was handled by the Junta's two staff colonels, and Cabanellas signed the decrees. On July 30, a representative of the Navy, Captain Francisco Moreno Hernández, who had earlier been placed in charge of that portion of the fleet under rebel command, was added to the Junta.[3] The fact that Franco was not a member had already been remarked upon by German authorities. Finally, as his Moroccan units began the drive north, Franco was invited to become the Junta's ninth member.[4]

No matter what its leaders may have intended, the rebel movement soon assumed the character of a holy war. The provincial clergy in most of Spain received the revolt with open arms, and Catholic laymen were among the most zealous volunteers. Though Franco had ignored the Catholic Church in his opening manifesto on July 18, religion afterward figured prominently in the public statements of the rebel generals, for they quickly found that the religious appeal provided strong assistance in mobilizing their forces. Ostentatious religious displays and celebration of the Mass in the town plazas attended the organization of Army units and civilian auxiliaries, and the Virgen del Pilar was officially proclaimed Captain General of Zaragoza. Though for political reasons the Spanish Catholic hierarchy had to remain officially aloof until the rebel movement became better established,[5] the revolt and Catholicism were understood to be intimately allied from the first days of the conflict. This fact cut through whatever personal ideas Mola or other officers may have had about maintaining the Republic's separation of Church and State.

At the outset, the generals had baptized their movement "Nationalist." Though the rebels tried to reassure the lower classes about their economic aims, the bulk of their support came from the middle classes and the conservative north, so that the term "Nationalist" was soon understood to denote an affirmation of religion, tradition, and Spanish patriotism, with little of the revolutionary connotation found in some other countries. Before many weeks had passed, official pronouncements declared all current land reform projects abolished,[6] and the workers were held to their positions by martial law. Falangist propagandists did talk loudly about radical social reform, but the Falange, despite its enormous growth in membership during the latter half of 1936, had lost most of its leaders and lacked any official standing.

Yet despite the increasingly reactionary character of the Nationalist movement, representatives of the monarchy were kept at a distance. When Don Juan, third son of Alfonso XIII, slipped across the French border to volunteer for the Nationalist Army, he was sent right back again by Mola without being permitted to see any of the Junta members.[7] Mola also declined to receive other members of the royal family, including Air Force General Don Alfonso de Orléans-Bourbon, a cousin of the former king.[8]

The Burgos Junta's only firm plan seems to have been to maintain an all-military government, at least until the war was won. Administration was loose, and the Junta made no effort to govern the southern zone directly. Most of this zone was under the personal rule of

Queipo de Llano, now official commander of the Army of the South, who administered western Andalusia and southern Estremadura from his headquarters in Seville. The main field units moving on Madrid were directed by Franco. Beyond this, there is no evidence that the Burgos Junta was especially concerned during August and early September with putting the Nationalist government on a more orderly foundation. The scope and complexities of the conflict had spread far beyond the Junta's control. Not even Mola had expected a full-scale civil war; now he was simply carried along on the tide of events.

The monarchist politicians and the German and Italian officials seemed more worried about the problem of government and leadership than were most of the rebel generals. Since the earliest diplomatic contacts with the two foreign allies had been made by monarchists, each element was to some extent influenced by the other's concern. Moreover, Carlists and alfonsinos alike were disturbed by the fact that Mola and other officers continued to fly the Republican flag. After a few weeks this practice was generally abandoned in the Nationalist zone, but the use of their banner was the only official concession made to the monarchists.

The first monarchist general to raise the question of the nature of the future Nationalist regime was Alfredo Kindelán, one of the creators of the Spanish Air Force under Alfonso XIII and a personal friend of the ex-king. He had talked to Franco by telephone from Algeciras on the afternoon of July 19, just a few hours after the latter's arrival in Tetuán. When he assumed command of the African forces, Franco had requested that Kindelán send a formal message to Don Alfonso, who was currently residing in Rome, as well as to Hitler and Mussolini. Franco pointedly addressed the missive to "His Royal Highness Don Alfonso de Borbón," not "His Majesty Alfonso XIII" as the monarchists would have preferred.[9]

After Kindelán arrived in Morocco, he asked if Franco intended to work for the restoration. The general replied that the return of the monarchy must be the eventual goal of the military movement, but that this could not be considered at the moment, for there were too many Republicans—or, at least, antimonarchists—in the ranks of the movement. Somewhat reassured, Kindelán insisted that a single, unified command must be created as soon as possible. Trusting Franco's discretion and knowing his qualities of leadership, he suggested that Franco be made commander in chief and also be named regent until it was possible to bring back the king. Kindelán appears to have felt that Franco could be relied on politically. General Franco, however, rejected the notion of a regency, saying that it would weaken the unity of the movement. Nor did he seem anxious to have personal supporters work to install him as commander in chief of the Nationalist Army. Perhaps, calling to mind the fate of Primo de Rivera, he felt that such a position was not a strong one. On the other hand, Franco's current position as commander of the Army of Africa gave him control of the most important sector of the rebel forces, and carried with it none of the compromising responsibility of political leadership.

Whatever reluctance Franco may have felt, he was persistently represented in German reports as the main leader of the military movement. This was due to a number of factors: the zeal of the Moroccan Nazis, the kind of information supplied by monarchist politicians and generals like Kindelán, and the Germans' practical assessment of Franco's reputation and the military strength at his disposal compared with that of the Army of the North.

On July 29, Langenheim, the Nazi party chief in Tetuán, sent a wire to Göring explaining that the rebel government functioned primarily as a directorate of Mola, Queipo, and Franco, but that Franco now was the dominant figure.[10] The German agent Seydel reported on August 16: "The Commander in Chief is definitely Franco. I stress the latter point since recurrent rumors of rivalry between the generals [Franco and Mola] are absurd, particularly since each of them, and everyone else, knows that everything is at stake."[11] Franco was, of course, senior in rank to Mola, if not to Cabanellas, and far outshone the other members of the Burgos Junta. Since most of the fighting was being done by the Army of Africa, the German officials naturally thought that it was advisable to deal directly with Franco. Eberhard Messerschmitt, head of the German war matériel export consortium, visited Spain between August 27 and September 8, but talked only with Franco and Kindelán among the generals. He too seemed convinced of Franco's relative superiority to the other Junta members.[12] The same impression was received by at least one of the foreign correspondents in the Nationalist zone, who contrasted the precision and strict security of Franco's headquarters with the informality and carelessness that prevailed at other rebel command centers.[13]

The month of August was occupied almost entirely with military problems. On August 20, when the juncture between the Army of Africa and the Army of the North was about to be established, Mola moved his military headquarters southwest to Valladolid so as to be closer to the main theater of action. On the 26th, the Burgos Junta reconfirmed Franco's position as commander in chief of the Army of Africa and of all field units engaged in the assault on Madrid.[14]

As August turned into September and the Nationalist troops gained control of the Tajo valley, military action entered its decisive phase. The time had come to broach the problem of more precise and coordinated leadership. A meeting of all the top rebel officers was finally organized at San Fernando airfield near Salamanca on September 21. Apparently it was again Kindelán who took the initiative. The officers invited were Cabanellas, Mola, Queipo, Orgaz, Gil Yuste, Saliquet, Dávila, and the two Staff colonels of the Burgos Junta, Montaner and Moreno Calderón. Franco had at first shown his usual reluctance to have the meeting arranged, but after thinking about it for two days had signed the proposed agenda.[15]

According to Kindelán,[16] during the morning session the rebel leaders discussed nearly everything except the business at hand, a not uncommon procedure among the Spanish military. The two generals most anxious to proceed with the establishment of a unified command were the two leading monarchists, Kindelán and Orgaz. During the afternoon session, Mola agreed that there was need of a single commander in chief for the rebel Army, and said that if a *mando único* (single command) were not established, he, for one, would wash his hands of the whole business. The only direct opponent of the mando único was, logically enough, Cabanellas, who stood to lose by any alteration of the present Junta arrangement. When the question was put to a vote, his was the only dissenting ballot.

Since everyone save Cabanellas was agreed on the need for a mando único, the next step was the choosing of a caudillo. Here the two colonels immediately excused themselves because of their junior rank. Once more the initiative was taken by Kindelán, who asked to be allowed to vote first, and advanced the name of Franco. The *Anuario Militar* for 1936 listed Franco only 23d in seniority among major generals, and he was outranked in years of service by Cabanellas, Queipo, and Saliquet, yet no one else had as much combat experience and military prestige, or as much political tact and influence abroad. Franco had apparently already made a compromise of sorts with Moroccan authorities in the Protectorate that secured the rebels' rearguard and thus provided Spain with a valuable staging area and many thousands of combative mercenaries.[17] Not only was Franco's name the best known among the rebel generals, but it had never been directly associated with political activity odious to moderate Spanish opinion. Mola was still remembered as the police chief of the dictablanda and was now becoming known as the "Carlist general" because of the tens of thousands of Requetés flocking to the Army of the North. His name had acquired a negative, even reactionary, political connotation, and the tall, bespectacled general was not unaware of this. Understanding that the issue at stake was simply that of a unified military command, Mola also voted for Franco, as did everyone save Cabanellas, who excused himself by saying that since he deemed the mando único unnecessary there was no point in his voting for anyone. The meeting adjourned with the understanding that Franco's appointment as commander in chief was to remain secret until formally announced by the Burgos Junta.[18]

Several days then passed without word from Burgos, where Cabanellas appeared to be in no hurry. Worried, Franco's promoters took counsel together. Kindelán talked with the General's brother Nicolás, a businessman then serving as rebel representative in Lisbon, which had proved to be an excellent listening post. The German and Italian ambassadors to Portugal had emphasized the importance of a clearly defined, unified Nationalist government, and Don Nicolás, eager to advance family interests, hoped to impress this point on the other generals. Another of Franco's ardent backers was his former commander in the Tercio, Millán Astray, now without active command but still prominent in Nationalist propaganda activities. The generals urged Franco to call another meeting of the rebel hierarchy, this time to make clear the powers of the Generalissimo and to define his position as that of Chief of State. Franco agreed to the new meeting, but seemed reluctant to seek the powers of leadership that his backers urged upon him.

On Sunday, September 27, Nicolás Franco crossed the Portuguese border to visit his brother's temporary headquarters at nearby Cáceres. He and Kindelán thought they might need more dynamic support for Franco, and for this purpose sought out the rebel field commander Yagüe, who had been relieved of the direction of the assault on Madrid just a few days earlier because of illness. Though Yagüe was very nearly the same age as Franco and had served in the Army almost as long, he had received no special méritos and had only recently attained the rank of full colonel, in the Nationalist Army's first significant wartime promotion. He had deep respect for Franco and, as a Falangist, hoped for the establishment of an effective Nationalist dictatorship to reform Spain.

Yagüe had never before met Nicolás Franco, and was displeased at being greeted by him effusively as "Juanito," but he immediately agreed to help when it was explained that officials in Lisbon were pressing for a mando único. In his brusque, direct fashion, Yagüe went to Franco's office and insisted that he become Commander in Chief immediately. Yagüe is supposed to have said that all the combat officers wanted a mando único, and that if Franco did not accept the post, they would find another candidate immediately. Later that evening came the news that the first relief column had broken through to Toledo. A great crowd assembled before the balcony outside Franco's headquarters and was joined by a reserve unit of the Tercio on its way to the front. Franco stepped out on the balcony to say a few words to the throng, with Yagüe at his side. After the general had finished speaking, there were demands from the crowd that Yagüe say something too. The popular Tercio leader took this opportunity to launch into an extempore speech on the need for a unified command. He said that the Tercio needed a man it could trust—a *jefe único* from its own ranks—and that the man for the post was Franco. His speech ended amid a chorus of cheers for Francisco Franco as the new Generalissimo.[19]

The second meeting of the rebel hierarchy was held the following morning, September 28, at the Salamanca airfield while the last Republican militia were being driven out of Toledo. As head of the Nationalist Air Force, Kindelán was in charge of the local arrangements, and took the precaution of posting a small detachment of Air Force guards and some Falangist militia in case of difficulty. Anxious to avoid protracted haggling, Kindelán pushed through the reading of his draft decree defining the scope and powers of the Generalissimo's role. Article Three of this document stated: "The office of Generalissimo will also carry the function of Chief of State so long as the war may last. For this reason, it has authority over all national activities: political, economic, social, cultural, etc."[20] This proposal came as something of a shock to most of the Junta members. Though the draft had been read to Mola privately before the meeting began, he joined all the other members in opposing it. The feeling of surprise and disorientation was such that even Orgaz was inhibited from supporting Kindelán as strongly as before. To end the discussion in time for lunch, Cabanellas promised that the decree would be studied in Burgos.

Yagüe had accompanied Franco and Kindelán to Salamanca, but had not attended the morning session, presumably because of his lesser rank. However, he joined the main group for lunch and insisted that the senior officers recognize Franco immediately, hinting that otherwise there might be insubordination. As the wine flowed, the atmosphere began to thaw. Knowing full well that the war could not be won by committees, they apparently decided to ratify Franco's appointment and get it over with. Afterward, Cabanellas promised that within forty-eight hours the Burgos Junta would promulgate a decree declaring Franco "Chief of the Government of the Spanish State."[21]

The decree was printed that very night. Several hundred copies had already been distributed when an order came to withhold it from circulation because the text was being revised.[22] Col. Martínez Fuset, a military jurist, had drafted a new version at the behest of Franco's promoters.[23] As officially published under Cabanellas' signature on September 29, this read: "In accordance with the resolution adopted by the Junta de Defensa Nacional, General Francisco Franco Bahamonde is named Chief of the Government of the Spanish State, and will assume all the powers of the new State."[24]

That day, as the decree was being promulgated, Franco was at Toledo visiting the ruins of the Alcázar and congratulating Moscardó. After the directive had been distributed on the 30th, there was some criticism among the senior officers of the clause stating that Franco would "assume all the powers of the new State." Martínez Fuset said that the terms might be a bit imprecise, but that it was now too late to change the decree.[25] There is some suggestion that Nicolás Franco and others immediately tried to publish another decree declaring Franco simply "Chief of the Spanish State."[26] At any rate, in his first government order Franco referred to himself as "Chief of State."[27]

In place of the Burgos Junta, Franco set up a "Junta Técnica" composed of seven commissions. He also created a General Secretariat of the Chief of State, a Secretariat for Foreign Relations, and a "General Government," or Ministry of the Interior.[28] All the principal posts save that of Foreign Secretary were occupied by generals, but each commission was directed by a civilian administrator. The basic idea differed little from Primo de Rivera's Military Directory of 1923. Cabanellas was given the largely honorary post of Inspector General of the Army, in an early example of what came to be a standard Franco tactic—kicking upstairs unwanted notables. General Fidel Dávila, a bureaucratic officer par excellence, was made President of the Junta Técnica and also Chief of the General Staff.[29] The veteran Orgaz was assigned the vital post of High Commissioner of Morocco, and was charged with keeping peace among the natives and encouraging the flow of mercenaries.

In this fashion, a determined minority took advantage of the great need for unity among the rebel military leaders to promote their most accomplished member to the position of Generalissimo and Chief of State. After the second meeting on the 28th, Franco had seen the green light and no longer showed the slightest reluctance about assuming supreme power, though he was careful to spare the feelings of his colleagues. Mola must have had some bitter thoughts about the course of events, in view of the great difficulty he had experienced in dragging Franco into the rebellion in the first place. But however that may have been, he outwardly gave way to Franco's elevation with good grace, conceding the many advantages that Franco's backers had enumerated.[30] The monarchist politicians had given their blessing; Gil Robles was in exile, his power broken; the Falangists were still without a leader; and Fal Conde had been called away to Vienna by the death of the aged Pretender on September 28. The decision had been almost exclusively a military affair.

For thirty years, Franco would protest that he had not sought power, but, answering the call to "save Spain," had found authority thrust upon him by his colleagues. As witness to the purity of his mandate he could cite his earlier hesitation. During his first months as Chief of State he showed his usual slowness in making decisions and commitments. Indeed, after being named Caudillo, he seemed to become more cautious and calculating than ever. This slowness and deliberation maddened his allies and subordinates and did much to prolong the civil war, but it steadied the Generalissimo's foot in every new step he took.

The propaganda resources of the new government inundated Nationalist Spain with photographs and eulogies of the Caudillo, but he did not fully look the part. Only forty-three, he was balding, plump, and about five feet, three inches tall. One of the best impressions of Franco at this time was penned by the American correspondent John Whitaker:

Personally I found Franco shrewd but disconcertingly unimpressive. I talk[ed] with him first when he was still slender, and later after he had gone to fat. A small man, he is muscular; but his hand is soft as a woman's, and in both instances I found it damp with perspiration. Excessively shy as he fences to understand a caller, his voice is shrill and pitched on a high note, which is slightly disturbing since he speaks quietly, almost in a whisper. Although effusively flattering, he gave me no frank answer to any question I put to him; I could see that he understood the implication of even the most subtle query. A less straightforward man I never met.[31]

After becoming Chief of State, Franco enjoyed an almost completely free hand, holding greater political power than any Spanish ruler since Fernando VII. Though the Nationalist regime had been created through military rebellion, the mounting pressure of an all-out civil war forced all potential rivals in the Army to hang together, and no serious effort was made to oppose the new command. Franco's original reluctance soon gave way to an exalted sense of pride and authority that eventually reached almost pharaonic proportions, but his relations with the senior military hierarchy—in 1936 and for thirty years afterward—were careful and tactful. Franco preferred to define his sovereignty as power resting on the "choice" of the military family and of all sane, patriotic elements. His role was to preside over the other senior generals as first among equals, and to serve as supreme arbiter of the political forces that rallied behind the rebel movement. He was careful to avoid the grotesque mistakes and corporate insults that had eventually ruined Primo de Rivera's relations with the military community.

Most of the Generalissimo's attention was necessarily devoted to military matters. The failure of the main assault on Madrid and the need to organize a mass army left scant alternative. Because of the uncertain, improvised character of the Nationalist war machine and the slowness of his own work habits, Franco preferred to ignore purely political affairs as much as possible. The Carlists were allowed to govern their own fief of Navarre, and the Falangists had some voice in other provinces. Ultimate authority over routine matters rested with the military governor of each district.

In the first months, Franco's main political adviser was his brother Nicolás.[32] Though he had a certain amount of guile and experience, together with great ambition, Don Nicolás lacked the imagination and finesse to create a political structure capable of transforming an ad hoc military directory into a viable twentieth-century dictatorship. His only solution was a short-lived effort to create a franquista party, when what the regime needed, even in the short run, was a well-organized program with ideological substance. The Caudillo seems to have understood that a franquista party might be a dangerous essay, for a party built solely on Franco would expose him too directly to political attack and identify him with the government's failures. Franco preferred to interpret his dictatorial function as that of an absolute arbiter between all the political, social, and economic forces supporting the rebel movement. Any new state political organization needed to be sufficiently eclectic to include most of them.

Such key Army leaders as Mola and Queipo did not want to create a new political movement. They had envisaged a purely military dictatorship that would hold sway for a certain period of time, then give way to a more conservative civilian regime. Nor did the monarchist generals believe that any intermediate phase was necessary between the current military directory and the restoration of the Bourbons. But it was not until the end of 1936 that any of them really faced up to the prospect of a long civil war. By that time, the political initiative lay entirely with Franco; he might consult his senior colleagues, but they were no longer in a position to check his decisions.

The appearance in Salamanca late in the winter of 1937 of Franco's brother-in-law Serrano Súñer was of great importance to the regime's development. The Generalissimo had been casting about for some sort of reliable political counsel, but had not been sure where to turn, for he did not fully trust any of the organized rightist groups. Because of his family ties with Franco, Serrano was trusted by him; since 1934 he had been Franco's chief civilian contact. Serrano was not especially well acquainted among the military. As CEDA youth leader, he had moved primarily among clerical politicians, maintaining distant contacts with the Falange. It was as Franco's representative to these groups that he had corresponded with the general in the crucial spring of 1936, but he had not been a party to the military conspiracy and apparently had not even been informed of the date of the revolt; consequently he had been trapped in Madrid. His two brothers were shot, and he himself was imprisoned for several months until an escape was arranged.

As he has explained in his memoirs, Serrano addressed himself to the problem of the political structure of his brother-in-law's regime as soon as he arrived in Salamanca.[33] He wanted to save Franco from the errors of Primo de Rivera, and urged him to avoid a purely military dictatorship. Meanwhile, strong encouragement was being offered Franco by his German and Italian advisers. Just as they had earlier urged a mando único, so now they stressed the importance of a modern political program and movement for the regime. The obvious solution was an organization built around the Falange and including the Carlists.

Most Army officers lacked strong enthusiasm for either the fascists or the Carlist traditionalists. The majority were strongly behind Franco and resentful of political parties. Only a minority—most of them young—were strongly pro-Falangist, while most of the senior officers regarded the fascist movement as little more than a necessary nuisance. The Falangists' only influential backer was Juan Yagüe, who was fast becoming known as "the Falangist colonel," but Yagüe's ideological orientation and political ambitions aroused the ire of some senior commanders. Mola felt that Yagüe had overstepped his rank, and he suspected that "the Falangist colonel" was attempting to inject fascist party politics into the military government. After Yagüe recovered from his heart ailment in the closing months of 1936, Mola blocked his reappointment to the Madrid front, and gossip had it that he was also threatening to have Yagüe court-martialed for engaging in political intrigue.[34]

The Carlists were respected mainly for their combative spirit, but few military men could be attracted by their ideology. In fact, there was resentment about the publicity accorded the Requetés' battlefield achievements;[35] and when Fal Conde, the Traditionalist secretary, announced on December 8, 1936, a plan to establish a Carlist military academy at Toledo, site of the former national Infantry Academy, the reaction was explosive. The Army hierarchy would never tolerate a separate, politically dominated military hierarchy; but conversely Franco could not afford to alienate Carlist support. The Generalissimo solved this dilemma by encouraging the Navarrese clique that had brought the Carlists into the rebellion to disavow this proposal, thus isolating Fal Conde and enabling Franco to exile him from Nationalist Spain while avoiding an internal crisis.[36]

The military disappointments suffered by the Nationalists in the winter of 1937 made it clear that the war would be a comparatively long one and so encouraged Serrano's efforts to build a regular political structure for the military dictatorship. By the beginning of spring, it was common gossip in Salamanca that the Generalissimo was planning to unify Falangists and Carlists under a single fascist-type political front similar to the "Fatherland Front" created by the corporative Catholic dictatorship in Austria about three years earlier.[37]

Yagüe talked with Franco in mid-April and learned that his chief was determined to carry out what Serrano later termed a "unilateral decree" merging Falangists, Carlists, and whoever else might choose to join them. Yagüe wanted to have the original national syndicalist and revolutionary Falange made the state party, but feared that the dictatorship would simply water down Falangism to another version of Primo de Rivera's "Unión Patriótica." There is some evidence that Yagüe had already begun to have second thoughts about the desirability of the dictatorship he had at first been so eager to help create.[38]

Franco's proclamation of April 19, 1937, established the Falange Española Tradicionalista y de las Juntas de Ofensiva Nacional Sindicalista (FET) as the official political organization of the Spanish Nationalist state. The Falangist program of national syndicalism became the doctrine of the new regime. The ideological transition was not especially difficult, because from the beginning military leaders had made vociferous announcements in the newspapers, over the radio, and to foreign correspondents of their intention to promote social justice for the lower classes[39] and build up a Nationalist spirit among all parts of the population.

There is no evidence that any of the leading generals raised serious objections to Franco's proclamation of a nominally national syndicalist state. The Generalissimo later told the German ambassador that Queipo de Llano had been urging him for weeks to come forward with an official "reform program,"[40] though it is doubtful that Queipo desired the organization of a new state Falangist party. In fact, both he and Mola would probably have preferred continuation of the regular military directory for the duration of the war, and the same was doubtless true of the monarchist generals. But no one thought of opposing the Generalissimo's decisions in wartime, and Mola, despite reservations, limited himself to grammatical editing of the party unification decree.[41]

One reason why there were no strenuous objections from the military or from the majority of civilian conservatives was that Franco moved so slowly and carefully that at first it seemed the establishment of a state party would change very little. The first step in the demilitarization of the political structure was the appointment of a Junta Política to serve as an advisory committee for the new FET. When the first fifty members of the party's National Council were appointed in October, however, five senior Army officers were included, which indicated that the military would be directly represented in major government institutions. A subsequent decree made all Army officers ipso facto members of the Falangist unity party. Though there was some grumbling against the Falangists within the Army, most officers had already disclaimed any desire to exercise direct political power, and asked only for a stable government that would protect the country's interests as well as their own. In the radical atmosphere of 1937–38, Franco's new regime seemed to promise this protection.

On July 17, 1937, in his speech on the first anniversary of the rebellion, Franco defined his regime as a kind of political caretaker for the Spanish people, who were eventually to "decide their own destiny." Meanwhile, the new Nationalist state must win the war, regenerate the country, and restore unity of purpose: "It will follow the structure of totalitarian regimes such as Italy and Germany. It will adopt corporative forms. . . . As in every empire, special prominence will be given the principle of hierarchy. . . . [The State] will, of course, draw inspiration from the forms of Italy and Germany, but will have specifically Spanish characteristics. It will be a suit cut to Spanish measurements."[42]

In an interview published in the *New York Times Magazine* on December 26, 1937, Franco insisted that Spanish totalitarianism would copy no one: "The majority of the modern formulae found in the totalitarian countries can already be discovered in our national past." Two years earlier Franco might have been shocked to hear himself saying such things, but the power configuration of the civil war had wrought mighty changes.

The first regular Cabinet in Franco's national syndicalist state was appointed on January 30, 1938. It completely superseded the Junta Técnica and realized Serrano's goal of regular government with a civic base. Franco was Chief of State, Generalissimo, and also Premier of the Council of Ministers. General Gómez Jordana, last head of the military Junta Técnica, was made Vice-Premier of the Council and also took over the Foreign Ministry. Jordana was a man of the old regime, having served as one of Primo's Military Directors. He was not, however, an extremist, but an intelligent and cultured general who gave the appearance of aristocratic refinement and made a good impression on associates. In addition, he was a more efficient administrator than the Spanish Army usually produced.[43]

Cabinet posts were divided between generals and civilian conservatives. Dávila, now director of the main field operations of the Nationalist forces, was also appointed Minister of National Defense.

For the post of Minister of Public Order—or police chief in charge of the repression—Franco resurrected the 75-year-old Martínez Anido, whose savage repression at Barcelona fifteen years earlier had won him enduring fame among the military. The Naval Engineers officer Juan Antonio Suances, a boyhood friend of Franco, became Minister of Industry and Commerce, charged with the revitalization of Spanish industry. The other seven Cabinet posts went to civilians; Serrano became Minister of the Interior. Only two of the civilian ministers were genuine Falangists, and there was accordingly no ground for the expression of antifascist sentiments by Franco's military colleagues and civilian collaborators. Thanks to the structure of this new group, the regime remained under Army influence while avoiding the onus of being a "military" regime.

Apparently the only dissatisfied Army leaders were Queipo de Llano and Yagüe. It was said that Queipo had expected to be given the War Ministry by the Republicans in 1931, and quite possibly he expected this plum from Franco seven years later. To be passed over in favor of a military bureaucrat like Dávila was especially galling. Hitherto he had supported Franco—if for no other reason than that he had no chance to be Generalissimo himself—and apparently he had not at first seriously opposed the creation of the new Falangist state party. However, as Primo de Rivera had observed in 1925, no one could ever be sure what Queipo would do next. Discontented by nature, he grew restive under this new slight, and began to react against the political structure.

For eighteen months, Queipo had been able to govern western Andalusia as an autonomous proconsulate. In many ways, he had behaved like a second—though infinitely more bloody—Primo de Rivera. He had shown considerable interest in social and economic relief. A series of committees and juntas had been organized to oversee the production of staple goods, and two million pesetas had been raised to build modest homes for poor families in Seville. A certain amount of free seed was distributed to small landowners between 1936 and 1938,[44] and a decree of November 2, 1937, set an absolute limit of 6 per cent interest on all agricultural loans.[45] A broad range of labor tribunals were also established.[46]

Queipo's nightly talks over Radio Seville were, in their chatty, vulgar, witty fashion, perhaps the most useful single item of Nationalist propaganda. Often crude and undignified, like some of the pronouncements of Primo de Rivera, they nevertheless went directly home to millions of ordinary Spaniards. Queipo had never been one to avoid engaging in personalities, and he did not balk at divulging details of marital infidelities that came to his attention, provided they would embarrass leaders on the other side. The gaudiness and paternalism of his style were almost irresistible as he loudly announced that he dispensed the same justice to rich and poor in Seville,[47] where indeed he did fine a number of merchants for raising prices and withholding goods. However, in February 1938 he abruptly brought his broadcasts to an end out of disgust with the new political structure in Salamanca.

Soon after the creation of the FET, Queipo had become outspokenly anti-Falangist. Falangist leaders in Seville had cooperated closely with him during the months of the war, but Queipo had been careful to exclude them from positions of major influence. He could never take their talk of national syndicalism too seriously, and seems at first to have thought that Franco was merely incorporating the Falange into a new political front under Army control. Consequently he was infuriated to see Falangists taking over much of the social and political administration in other parts of the Nationalist zone. When a female relative of his in the north was involved in a dispute with the Falangist social welfare agency, he complained in his broadcast of August 11, 1937: "Señores, can it be that those who are not Falangists cannot live in Spain?"[48] To Falangist propaganda proposals to restore Spain's imperial dimensions, Queipo was heard to reply that the present size of Spain was enough for him.[49] When he attended the graduation of officer candidates at the Seville naval school in May 1938, only the classic patriotic cheers were given; Falangist slogans were pointedly excluded, despite their dominance in public propaganda.[50]

During 1938, Serrano Súñer endeavored to end the many anomalies that had heretofore existed in provincial administration. The biggest single gap was in the Seville area, where Queipo had ignored some of the original regulations laid down by the Nationalist government. He had earlier appointed as mayor Ramón Carranza, a conservative and son of the former cacique of Cádiz; but in mid-1938, Serrano named one of the brightest young Falangist leaders to be civil governor, who in turn designated a new mayor and sought to draw local administration into the general political network. Queipo regarded these changes as grossly arbitrary,[51] but his civil and political power was gradually reduced until, by the end of 1938, his only real control was as military commander in chief of the southern front.[52] According to certain Falangists, one of their ardently pro-Franco comrades even proposed to Serrano that local Seville Falangists assassinate Queipo and blame it on the "Reds," thus getting rid of the Falangists' major foe in the Nationalist zone. Serrano quickly vetoed this plan, knowing that Franco did not deal with his senior military colleagues in such crude fashion.

Yagüe's discontent was expressed more bluntly than Queipo's. Yagüe had been given command of a section of the Madrid front during 1937, and had led an expanded Moroccan Corps in the recent breakthroughs in Aragon. On April 19, 1938, after the Nationalists had reached the Mediterranean and were pausing to regroup, he made a public address in his native Burgos. Yagüe was troubled by several matters. Whereas Queipo had wanted a free-wheeling military dictatorship that would permit him a maximum of personal influence, Yagüe wanted a Nationalist revolution. He had come to regard the Franco–Serrano Súñer FET as a fraud, for few genuine social reforms were in sight. Perhaps he had begun to repent the elevation of Franco to unquestioned power. He had thought that he was helping to provide Spain with dynamic new military leadership, but now it turned out that the most influential general in domestic affairs was the aged police chief Martínez Anido, who was not a reformer but a liquidator. Yagüe was tired of this long fraternal strife, and of the constant vilification of the Republicans. He was weary of the presence and influence of the Axis units and revolted by the heavy terrorist bombing raids carried out on Barcelona in March 1938.[53] Franco had not been directly responsible for ordering these attacks,[54] but neither had he been energetic in preventing them. Yagüe and at least one other of the recently promoted Corps commanders, Moscardó, had already protested.

The German ambassador reported:

The speech which General Yagüe, noted and able leader of the Moroccan Corps, made in Burgos on April 19 at the celebration of the establishment of the Unity Party threw an interesting light on ... conditions. In his speech, excellent in itself, which only a few newspapers were able to publish (apparently in a milder form), the General expressed his ideas concerning the comprehensive social reforms which he considered necessary, the need for an honest and incorruptible administration ... , with a frankness and a critical attitude which were at the very least inconvenient for the present Government. In particular, it was felt that the parts of his speech in which he gave free recognition to the bravery of the Red Spanish opponents, defended the political prisoners—both the Reds and the "Blues" (Falangists), who were arrested because of too much political zeal —and severely attacked the partiality of the administration of justice, went beyond his authority and represented a lack of discipline.[55]

Since, as the German ambassador had observed in the same dispatch, in Nationalist Spain, 40 per cent of the population were still "politically unreliable," Franco could not let such a "lack of discipline" go unpunished. Yagüe was relieved of command of the Moroccan Corps and confined to his residence in Burgos province for the next few months. On the day of Yagüe's speech, Franco had addressed a huge crowd at Zaragoza, just behind the main combat zone, and declared that the war was won.[56] On the 22d, after the Yagüe incident had been settled, a new decree was issued affirming that the Chief of State had assumed "all 'the absolute powers of the state' " in order to realize Spain's "totalitarian aspirations."[57] Neither Yagüe nor Queipo nor anyone else attempted to dispute this declaration.

The stiffening of Republican resistance on the battlefield increased the tension at Nationalist headquarters just when the dictatorship was consolidating its administrative control, but the ultimate effect of the Republican military successes of mid-1938 was to halt dissension in the Nationalist command before it became serious. The working relationship at headquarters was never in danger, and by the end of the year Yagüe was restored to his old command. Throughout the Civil War, the great strength of the Nationalist leadership was the military discipline maintained by its forces.

CHAPTER TWENTY

The Nationalist Army in the Civil War

M OST OF THE MILITARY calculations made by the conspirators of 1936 proved inaccurate. The plan to seize Madrid quickly was foiled not merely by the failure of the revolt in key areas and the partial blockade of the Moroccan coast, but also by the efforts of Popular Front militia forces, which, though technically incompetent, were brave and energetic. Even after German and Italian aircraft helped surmount the naval blockade, progress was much less rapid than had been hoped.[1] One of the most resourceful column commanders, Colonel (later Lt. Gen.) Carlos Asensio, ruefully observed twenty-five years afterward: "For lack of effectives, our advance turned out to be terribly slow."[2]

During the month of October 1936, Franco's troops fought their way the last forty miles from Toledo to Madrid. Meanwhile, the Popular Front defense command was reorganized.[3] Thanks in part to a shipment of Russian arms, the resistance stiffened. Despite heavy losses in men[4] and matériel, the militia volunteers still greatly outnumbered the small cadres of the Army of Africa. Several times Nationalist spearheads were in danger of being cut off by large-scale counterattacks.[5]

Franco's forces for the initial assault on the capital did not exceed 20,000 men,[6] but the Nationalist command feared that further delay might prove fatal. Mola had always seen conquest of Madrid as the key to the entire operation, and he was given field command of the attacking forces. Yagüe is said to have doubted that the small Nationalist Army could carry the city by direct assault, and to have recommended a flanking move from the north and northwest to confuse the

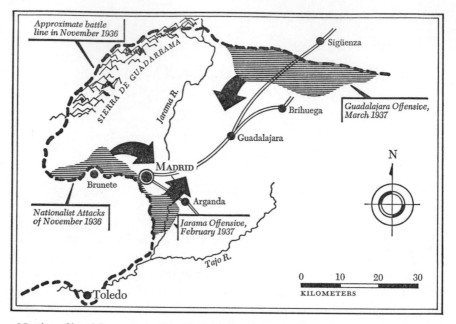

Approximate battle
line in November 1936

Sigüenza

SIERRA DE GUADARRAMA

Jarama R.

Brihuega

*Guadalajara Offensive,
March 1937*

Guadalajara

N

MADRID

Brunete

Arganda

*Nationalist Attacks
of November 1936*

*Jarama Offensive,
February 1937*

Tajo R.

0   10   20   30

KILOMETERS

Toledo

Nationalist Advances in the Madrid Region, November 1936–March 1937

Popular Front command and take Madrid from the rear. Mola and
Varela, however, doubted that the insurgents had the strength for an
extended maneuver, and Franco accepted their plan for a direct attack
due east as the most feasible.[7]

Pessimistic reports led to increased German and Italian aid. The
most important new element was a German air corps, the Condor Legion, made up of nearly 100 combat planes, which was assembled at
Seville during November.[8] Kindelán has written that, in a desperate
effort to swing the balance, "Franco ordered an experimental attempt
to demoralize the population [of Madrid] through aerial bombardment."[9] As it turned out, terrorist attacks by German aircraft only increased the will to resist.

Some 4,500 Nationalist troops were used in the first assault on Madrid on November 8.[10] Captured Republican records are said to indicate that at this time the armed militia in the capital numbered no
more than 18,000.[11] The arrival of the first Communist-organized International Brigades helped to tighten the defense. For a week small
Nationalist columns tried to ram their way across the Manzanares
River into western Madrid. A major effort by Asensio on November 15
with 18 light Italian tanks managed to place 1,500 troops on the other

side of the river near the University, where they were pinned down. After November 21, the Nationalists went over to the defensive in this sector.[12] The rebel command was shaken by this development. Major Castejón, a badly wounded column commander, remarked despairingly to the American journalist John Whitaker: "We who made this revolt are now beaten."[13]

Three efforts to outflank the Madrid defense line to the north, made in late November, mid-December,[14] and early January, ended in failure, for the terrain northwest of Madrid—uneven, sometimes wooded, dotted with low hills and occasional villages—is not well suited to mobile warfare. The last of these attacks employed 12,000 troops—the largest single Nationalist force yet committed—and was supported by German planes and artillery and Italian tanks, but had to be suspended on January 9.[15] Improved equipment and organization, revitalized morale, and the advantage of numbers and interior lines had enabled the Popular Front forces to create a successful defense. Indeed, the Nationalist line was stretched so thin by the middle of January 1937 that a determined counterattack by several strong Republican brigades might have disrupted the entire front.

Fortunately for Franco, the Italian government was being drawn ever deeper into the conflict. Its air support had helped the Nationalists hold the key island of Mallorca against Catalan assault,[16] and by the close of 1936 it had decided to send Franco much more matériel, along with a separate Italian artillery corps and several divisions of Italian troops and Fascist militia. These forces began to arrive in Spain during January and February.[17] Meanwhile on January 5 Franco had accepted the formation of a joint German-Italian staff of ten military advisers to coordinate operations. The Germans apparently wanted the new Italian units sent directly to the central front, where they might shift the balance in favor of the rebels, but the Italians insisted on first launching a separate offensive in the south.

At the beginning of 1937, the Popular Front forces still occupied over half of southern Spain, behind a line running from Madrid to the east of Córdoba, curving farther east around Granada, and then turning west of Málaga to the southern coast. Queipo de Llano held the Nationalist front with a motley force of second-class troops, Civil Guard units, and Falangist militia. He was willing enough to receive Italian assistance, and a convergent Italian-Spanish operation to seal off the Málaga sector from west and north began in January 1937. The Republican defense of this area was crippled by political rivalry and lack of equipment and leadership.[18] On February 8, the city fell to the advancing Italians.*

The Nationalist command prepared a new offensive on the central front to coincide with the Málaga operation, but it was delayed for two weeks by bad weather. Abandoning any effort to break through the Republican lines to the north, forces were to aim at the hilly ground along the Jarama River to the south, and attempt to outflank the capital's defenders from the southeast. The main assault was begun on February 6 by five reinforced brigades totaling 18,500 men,[19] and within 48 hours penetrated five miles, reaching the heights west of the Jarama, whence artillery batteries soon brought the vital Madrid–Valencia highway under fire. But Nationalist reserves were severely limited, and the momentum could not be sustained. After nine days the initiative passed to the more numerous Republican forces, who also began to win temporary control of the air, thanks to Russian assistance. By the time it was finally broken off near the close of February, the Jarama engagement had become the bloodiest battle thus far,[20] yet had resulted in no more than a minimal success for the Nationalists. A secondary attack northward from Córdoba was also stymied, and by the end of the month disillusionment was deepening among Franco's staff.[21]

Meanwhile the Italian contingents were being increased. By March 1, they amounted to almost 25,000 troops, organized as a "Corpo di Truppe Volontarie," (CTV) and well supplied with artillery and mobile equipment. An Italian plan for a coastal offensive beyond Málaga up the coast toward Valencia proved too difficult, so the Italian commanders agreed to transfer their corps to the central front, where they would occupy the extreme left flank of the forces ringing Madrid, in the Guadalajara region to the northeast. With the main Nationalist forces exhausted, the Italian corps would make the boldest of the encircling moves yet attempted, striking southward through Guadalajara to cut off Madrid from the east.

This operation began on March 8, as soon as three Italian divi-

---

* The Republican commander left behind him in a suitcase a repellent object said to be the petrified hand of Santa Teresa de Avila, which had been taken from a convent in nearby Ronda. Learning of this, Franco had the relic sent to headquarters. Becoming more religious as he grew in years and power, the Generalissimo adopted it as his chief personal relic, and after a time installed it on a nightstand in his bedroom. It is said that whenever he traveled a special military aide was given charge of the hand (Galinsoga, pp. 284–85). By the 1950's the hand was being accorded the honors of a Lieutenant General on certain public occasions.

sions, or some 20,000 men, could be moved into position. It achieved complete surprise and drove through a big hole in the vaguely defined Republican lines north of Guadalajara. During the first 36 hours, the semi-motorized Italian forces averaged nearly a kilometer an hour over broken terrain. However, it was nearly 100 kilometers from the starting point to Madrid and the weather soon turned very bad, bringing snow mixed with sleet and grounding the Nationalist aircraft. Only one of the roads south was in good condition, and by the evening of the second day the most experienced Popular Front units were being moved to a new defensive position across the highway north of Guadalajara. The attempted advance of a reinforced Nationalist division farther west was stopped by Russian tanks. For five days the Italians made fruitless efforts to move ahead on a frozen battlefield, but were met with stiff Republican counterattacks. Their commander, Mancini, finally broke off the struggle on March 14. The Guadalajara offensive had gained a certain amount of territory in the mountains, but had fallen far short of its main objective.* Thanks to the bitter weather and the inadequacy of training, maps, air support, and leadership among the Italians, as well as to the aggressiveness of the Popular Front elite units and the propaganda of their commissars, the Republicans had won a great psychological victory.[22]

The failure to seize Madrid during the winter of 1936–37 made it clear to the Nationalist command that a mass twentieth-century Army would have to be developed for a long war, just as the Popular Front regime, with Russian support, was laboring to construct its own regular military force. Since early autumn, German advisers had been urging Franco to declare mass conscription. Because of the political unreliability of much of the population in the Nationalist zone, the Generalissimo was not eager to do this. However, broad mobilization measures had been taken immediately in certain areas such as Mallorca[23] and western Andalusia, where, in one of his first decrees, Queipo had called up the draft quotas for the years 1931–35 inclu-

---

* The Guadalajara affair did not especially dishearten Spanish Nationalists, many of whom felt that the pushy, supercilious Fascists had been given their comeuppance. The Navarrese companies in Moscardó's division threw back the original Italian sneers about primitive Spanish transportation with the following ditty, set to the tune of a popular Italian song (Zugazagoitia, pp. 238–39):

Guadalajara no es Abisinia.	Guadalajara is not Abyssinia.
Los españoles, aunque rojos,	Spaniards, even if Red,
son valientes:	are brave:
Menos camiones y más cojones.	Fewer trucks and more guts.

sive.[24] By early August of 1936, the Burgos Junta had mobilized the draftees of 1935, but this had brought in little more than 20,000 recruits in the northern part of the insurgent zone;[25] therefore, on August 26 the Junta called up the quintas for the years 1931–34.[26] When this mobilization was completed early in 1937, some 270,000 recruits had been assembled.[27] On February 22, 1937, the first quarter of the 1937 draft was summoned as well.[28]

One of the major problems was the preparation of a large cadre of reliable officers. The first step was taken by the Burgos Junta on September 4, 1936, when Cabanellas signed a decree establishing a series of courses in Seville and Burgos for the training of *alféreces provisionales* (provisional second lieutenants).[29] The first classes were to last 15 days, and graduates would be eligible for promotion up to the rank of colonel. Young men between 20 and 30 years of age, of sound political background, and possessing a professional license or degree equivalent to the *bachillerato* (B.A.) were eligible. In effect, this meant university students or graduates from the middle classes. Two hundred fifty were admitted to the first term, of whom 183 were commissioned as alféreces on October 3.

After the establishment of Franco's government, the training of alféreces provisionales was greatly expanded. During October new training schools were set up in Xauen and Santa Cruz de Tenerife, and a fifth was created on Mallorca in November. German assistance was a crucial factor. During the autumn of 1936, the German High Command dispatched two Panzer companies and one transport company, plus a staff of advisers in armored warfare, to instruct Nationalist troops. In January 1937, Franco officially requested greatly expanded German aid, with special staffs to assist in new schools for alféreces, NCO's, and special technical trainees.[30] By the spring of 1937 this aid was being provided in large quantities.

On the morrow of the stalemate at Guadalajara, the training program of the Nationalist Army was brought under one chief, General Luis Orgaz. He had served as High Commissioner of the Protectorate during the autumn of 1936, and had replaced Mola as commander of the central front after the failure of the first assault on Madrid. A decree of March 25, 1937, named him "general in charge of mobilization services and the recuperation of personnel, matériel, cattle, and automobiles, and of the preparation and instruction of officers in rearguard academies."[31] The stubby little Orgaz was not a military genius, but he was spirited and possessed of both sound professional instinct and tested reactionary convictions. During the next two years his bureau, the MIR (Mobilization, Instruction, and Recuperation), expanded the number of training schools to 22, with at least a few German advisers in every one. In January 1937, the age requirement for officer candidates was lowered to 18 years, but the courses were extended to 24 days, and two months of front-line duty were required before entrance. During its first eight months of operation (to May 1937), the program commissioned 5,132 alféreces. By the end of the war the total had reached 22,936, not including approximately 19,700 NCO's trained in other sections.[32]

When the MIR began operating, the Nationalists had already drafted 350,000 recruits. That total was greatly expanded in March 1937, when the regime called up *reemplazos* from 1927 onward and mobilized all healthy males in the rebel zone between the ages of 21 and 31. During the remainder of 1937 the age limit was steadily lowered, until by August 9, 1938, the first trimester of 1941, made up of 18-year-olds, was drafted. This provided another 450,000 recruits and militiamen by the beginning of 1939.[33] Of these, 325,700 were used to form new divisions, 104,156 were assigned to existing units in place of casualties, and 65,348 were employed in the special services.[34] From start to finish, the Nationalist Army and the militia together mobilized approximately one million troops—by far the greatest concentration of military manpower in Spanish history.

Probably the major question facing the organizers of the new mass Army was the bugbear of political reliability. Ordinary conscript divisions were not used in major engagements until 1938. The greater share of the real fighting was done by a select group of elite units, which suffered high losses. During the first year the single most important source of reliable manpower was Morocco. By the spring of 1937, 35,089 Regulares and 27,872 European soldiers—a total of 62,-961 troops—had been moved across the straits.[35] Almost all of these were either professionals or volunteers, ready and eager for combat. The Carlist Banderas from northern Spain proved invaluable. Most of these were incorporated into the special Navarrese Brigades, which by 1937 were the size of divisions. Likewise, most of the more capable Falangist volunteers were directly organized into the shock units; only the inferior were left in the Falangist Banderas that formed part of the second-rate outfits patrolling quiet sectors.[36]

Even in the last year of the war, Franco relied upon picked divisions for the most serious fighting. Among the outstanding combat

groups were the First, Fourth, and Fifth Navarrese Divisions, commanded by García Valiño, Alonso Vega, and J. B. Sánchez; the
Twelfth, Thirteenth, and One-hundred-and-fifth Moroccan Divisions,
composite groups led by Asensio, Barrón, and López Bravo; and the
Eighty-second, Eighty-third, and Eighty-fourth Galician Divisions,
commanded by Delgado Serrano, Martín Alonso, and Galera. Some
of these suffered casualties two or three times as great as their original
enlistment, but replacements were constantly fed in from the best
new manpower so that their special quality as elite units would not
be lost.

Strong inducements to enlist were offered by the Tercio. Falangist
leaders and other officials told former leftists and trade unionists that
the best expression of their loyalty would be to volunteer for the strict
discipline of shock detachments.[37] Thousands of former leftist mili-
tants did so, and most of them fought well, eventually learning a new
pride in the achievements of the Nationalist Army. Yet there were
dangers in this practice, as was shown by a serious incident at Zaragoza early in 1937. Hundreds of CNT activists in that major anarchist
center had been induced to join new units of the Tercio as a kind of
insurance against the White Terror. The leftist volunteers in one
Bandera developed a scheme to rebel, seize the center of town, and
liberate several thousand political prisoners in the Zaragoza jails. A
successful revolt might have caused the entire Nationalist front in
Aragon to crumble, with potentially disastrous results for the whole
cause. The plot was apparently discovered just in time, and most of
the rebellious volunteers are said to have been machine-gunned on
the parade ground.[38]

By the latter part of 1937, large sections of the new conscript Army
were ready for service. The vital element was the alféreces provisionales. Though their military training was deficient, most of them were
university men with a level of intelligence at least as high as that of
the ordinary Nationalist officer. Above all, the new alféreces were enthusiasts of the rebel movement. What they lacked in technical preparation they made up by courage and personal example. Their losses
were among the highest of any sector of the Army, leading to the
phrase "alférez provisional, cadáver efectivo" ("Provisional lieutenant,
permanent corpse").[39]

For the ordinary recruits, basic training was brief, lasting only 30
days. By 1937, medical services were fairly well organized but living
conditions remained crude. The incidence of lice seems to have been

greater than in most western armies, and thievery among the rank and file reached excessive proportions.[40] Such barracks problems do not seem to have worried the officers, who were only interested in outward discipline. Relations between officers and men were formal at best, and order was ruthlessly maintained. Discipline was more severe than during the years of the monarchy; indeed, perhaps harsher than in any other western Army of the period.

Though the combat quality and armament of the Nationalist Army were enormously better than those of previous Spanish forces, its tactics and performance still followed a rigid pattern. Despite experiments in aspects of mobile warfare introduced by the Germans, large Nationalist units ordinarily advanced in a straight line, without special craft or strategy. The superiority of their officers enabled them to retain greater cohesion than the Republicans on both offense and defense, but this advantage was only relative. Even in the Fourth Navarrese Division, according to one of its alféreces, some of the old-line regular officers could not read complex field maps. The Nationalist Army never became a first-rate twentieth-century military machine; it won because it proved less ineffective than the motley contingents of the Popular Front.

In the Republican zone, a thorough program of mobilization was eventually carried out. By April 1, 1937, the Republican Army had approximately 301,000 men under arms, a figure roughly equivalent to the number being trained on the other side.[41] Shortages of equipment always handicapped the Popular Front forces more than they did the Nationalists. It has been said on good authority that the central Republican arms depot at Valencia dipped to a reserve of only 800 to 900 cannon shells and a million rounds of rifle ammunition during the winter of 1936.[42] The situation improved during the spring of 1937, then deteriorated badly in the last months of 1938.

During the first half of 1937, organizers of the Republican Army and their Russian advisers labored to create a new formation, the "mixed brigade." This was roughly similar to the mixed combat groups being essayed in several contemporary armies, and Republican staff officers claimed to have arrived at the idea independently of their Russian advisers.[43] Just as heterogeneous formations were organized on both sides, so both armies did their main fighting with special shock divisions, using ordinary units for passive sectors or the reserve. The International Brigades and the Communist-led units were almost always in the thick of the action, partly because of their superior discipline and combat potential, but also because of Russian pressure and the fact that these groups were always the best equipped.

One of the Republicans' greatest deficiencies was the lack of a large group of fairly competent junior officers like the alféreces provisionales. Starting without an adequate nucleus of professional military leaders, the Republican command was never able to improvise direction on the lower levels. This was no doubt due in part to the spontaneity and thoroughness of the anarchist-socialist revolution during the first six months of the war. After leveling the old leadership cadres, the revolution left no well-organized force on the Popular Front side save the Communist Party, which by itself was not strong enough in Spain to turn the tide. During the Russian civil war of 1918–21, the Bolshevist effort had been under central control throughout, and had made effective use of thousands of ex-Tsarist officers while building its own Red Army Officer Corps. The sweep and ferocity of the Spanish revolution were so great that they prevented such a policy, and this was a decisive factor in the outcome of the war.

The Communists and others did try to set up officer-training schools in the rear, and Spanish professionals of slightly suspect loyalty were often employed as instructors. But the Russian advisory staff was never large enough to provide the sort of supervision given by German instructors at the schools under Orgaz's bureau, and even had it been, the quality of such supervision would have proved inferior. Moreover, Republican recruitment and training centers were hotbeds of espionage.[44]

The extent and success of Nationalist intelligence were due to several factors: there were many sympathizers in the Republican zone, a significant number of those professional officers who remained in Republican service proved disloyal, and the Red Terror was less effective than the mass shootings of the Nationalists in shattering the will of the opposition.[45] Some of the foreign legations in Madrid, crammed with Nationalist refugees, were also useful. Generals Barbero and Méndez Queipo, who may not even have been members of the original conspiracy, had to flee for their lives into the Turkish embassy, and during prolonged residence carried out valuable espionage with a kind of diplomatic immunity.[46]

From time to time, parts of the espionage network were uncovered. In the spring of 1937, Communist-led counterintelligence revealed a spy ring whose central figure was the secretary of General

Miaja, at that time Republican commander on the Madrid front. All those implicated were shot, and the reliability of Miaja, an ex-UME officer, was called into question. During the past six months, however, propaganda had made "Papa" Miaja the main hero of the defense of Madrid. A useful symbol, he was ostensibly left alone, though it now appears that he was subject to blackmail by the Communists, who possessed evidence of his earlier UME affiliation.

After Guadalajara, the Nationalist command and its advisers temporarily gave up their efforts to seize Madrid directly. Instead it was decided to launch a major offensive to eliminate the northern zone of Republican territory—the provinces of Vizcaya, Santander, and Asturias—before it could be strongly fortified. For nine months, weak Nationalist forces had manned the irregular lines that held this northern area in isolation.[47] Containing most of Spain's heavy industry, it was a valuable prize, and a simpler target than the central Republican front around Madrid.

As commander of the Army of the North, Mola was given direction of the campaign. His removal as head of the assault on Madrid in late autumn had led to hard feelings, but in the spring of 1937 he returned to the center of action. For the first time, the Nationalists were able to muster a slight superiority in manpower. During the last days of March, 50,000 of their best troops were concentrated in a 90-degree arc south and east of the key Basque industrial province of Vizcaya. The core of this force consisted of the four strongly Carlist Navarrese brigades, each of which numbered 4,000 to 6,000 troops.[48] These brigades had been organized into the new Navarrese Army Corps under Colonel José Solchaga, and were supported by 50 batteries of artillery, most of which were Italian, and by the bulk of the German and Italian aircraft. By contrast, the Basques had little more than 30,000 men under arms, with few cannon and hardly any serviceable airplanes.[49] Nearly all their officers were amateurs, and the "Cinturón de Hierro" (Iron Belt), an inexpert system of fortifications intended to protect Bilbao, was scarcely 40 per cent complete on March 24, when the Army engineer in charge, a Major Goicoechea, deserted to his Nationalist comrades with most of the plans.[50]

After large-scale aerial bombardment, the offensive opened on March 31, but bad weather, stout resistance, the mountainous terrain, and logistical problems soon halted the advance. Progress was made during the last ten days of April, and it was during this surge, on April 26, that planes of the Condor Legion destroyed much of the town of Guernica, the symbolic home of Basque liberty.[51] The advance slowed again in May amid more bad weather, after the arrival of new equipment for the Basques. In the rugged countryside there was little room for maneuver, and in view of the relatively short distances involved the offensive was moving slowly.

On June 3, Mola left Burgos by plane for Franco's headquarters in Salamanca. Shortly after taking off, the plane crashed against the side of a hill, killing all aboard. Rumors immediately began to circulate that certain agents, working either for the Germans or for Franco, had sabotaged the plane to get rid of Mola. The German ambassador himself wrote that Franco was "undoubtedly relieved by the death of Mola."[52] Certainly the sudden demise of the principal architect of the Nationalist conspiracy, an influential general both anti-Falangist and antimonarchist, eased the Generalissimo's political problems, yet neither Mola's widow nor his personal secretary ever found verifiable evidence of sabotage of the flight,[53] and according to the best available knowledge, the crash was due to a mechanical or operational accident. However, the manuscript that Mola had been preparing about the conspiracy and the beginning of the civil war was quickly confiscated.[54] Mola was succeeded by General Fidel Dávila, a man more used to the desk than to the battlefield, who was unlikely to create friction among the high command.

The offensive was resumed when the weather cleared on June 11. After a week of hard fighting, Bilbao was occupied on June 19, which precipitated the collapse of the remainder of Vizcaya. Though lacking numbers, firepower, and organization, the Basques had displayed high morale and fighting spirit, and it had taken about twice as long to conquer them as the Nationalist generals had originally expected.[55]

Meanwhile, in the central zone the Popular Front command was working hard to create *unidades de maniobra*—organized combat groups capable of offensive maneuver. By June 1937 the Republican Army had been expanded to 360,000 men, and was supported by 750 pieces of artillery, 250 tanks and armored cars, and 200 planes.[56] Most of this power was concentrated near Madrid. Amid great political dissension, plans were made for the first major Republican offensive in that area. If successful, it would draw the main Nationalist forces back to the central front and save what was left of the northern zone. The spot selected for attack lay about 15 miles west of Madrid, just above the little town of Brunete.

The assault that began on July 6 was launched by the cream of the new Republican Army—six divisions and several reinforced brigades totaling 59,000 troops, which were supported by 128 Russian tanks manned by hastily trained Spanish crews. It achieved complete tactical surprise, punching a hole in the thinly held Nationalist line almost immediately. However, there was only one passable road through the battle zone, which made the movement of large amounts of men and matériel difficult. The weaknesses of the Republican military organization were soon revealed, for communications became snarled and lower-echelon commanders could not keep their units moving. The initial success was not exploited; instead, field officers let their forces be tied down in a series of frontal attacks around a handful of fixed positions where the heavily outnumbered Nationalist defenders had dug themselves in.[57]

The superior cohesion of the Nationalist Army was reflected in the speed with which reinforcements arrived. Six new battalions were thrown into the gap within the first 24 hours, twenty-nine had arrived after 48 hours, there were fifty after three days, and about eighty-five at the end of six days.[58] A bulge about 75 kilometers square had been made in the Nationalist line, but a genuine breakthrough was averted. By July 15, the Republican units were exhausted and had to go over to the defensive. Ideal flying conditions enabled the Nationalist-German-Italian aircraft to gain control of the skies,[59] and their strafing and bombing contributed heavily to the demoralization of the Republican troops. A week-long counteroffensive by the Nationalists regained most of the ground lost. By the end of July, even the best Popular Front units were exhausted and dispirited.[60] The Republican Chief of Staff, Rojo, has suggested that a major Nationalist assault against Madrid at that time might have brought the war to a speedy conclusion.[61]

To have seized the dramatic new opportunity on the central front would, however, have been contrary to Franco's cautious nature. Victory in the north was, if less decisive, more certain. The unity and enthusiasm of the Nationalist forces was, in good measure, based on their military superiority and all but uninterrupted string of victories. Triumph at Madrid was still problematical, and the Generalissimo probably felt that he could not afford the political and psychological consequences that a setback might produce. Having stabilized the central front, he withdrew the two Navarrese divisions brought down from Vizcaya and sent them back to resume the northern offensive that had been halted for three weeks.[62] After the fall of Bilbao, the bulk of the Basque battalions had escaped westward into Santander province, but the 50,000 men under arms there were even more poorly supplied, and morale was low.[63]

The second phase of the northern offensive began on August 14, and, despite the mountainous nature of the terrain, was over within a fortnight. It was led by Solchaga's Navarrese Corps and the three reorganized Italian divisions, with the Condor Legion providing devastating air support. Though the Italian units muffed a major opportunity on the fourth day of the campaign, they suffered a majority of the total Nationalist casualties[64] and regained a bit of the prestige they had lost at Guadalajara. The sudden collapse of Santander was another serious blow to the Popular Front cause.

By the end of August, all that remained of the northern Republican zone was the upper half of the province of Asturias. The district of Oviedo had been held for the Nationalists since the beginning of the conflict by a well-organized, determined defense under the local commander, Colonel Antonio Aranda. His troops, though heavily outnumbered, had given one of the best performances of any section of the Nationalist Army,[65] and Aranda had been the first colonel promoted to brigadier by Franco.[66] The Oviedo garrison was slowly reinforced during the spring and summer of 1937. After the fall of Santander, part of Solchaga's corps moved on to attack the Republican sector of Asturias from the east, while Aranda launched his first general offensive operation from the south on September 1. The terrain here was as difficult as that of Santander, and the Asturian militia fought harder. Though Nationalist casualties were light, organized resistance was not brought to an end until the last days of October 1937.[67] Hundreds of leftist guerrilleros remained in the hills, and some of them were not run down until ten years later.

Altogether, seven months were required to complete the Nationalists' northern offensive, which greatly increased the amount of territory and the human and industrial resources under Franco's control. Given the insurgents' superiority of leadership, equipment, and organization, the issue had at no time been in doubt. The victorious units had maneuvered reasonably well, and brigade commanders had sometimes showed more resourcefulness than was common in the Spanish Army.[68] In later years, this northern campaign would be remembered with nostalgia by some senior officers because of the respect felt for the Basques and the comparatively smooth relations between the commanders and within the detachments. Total Nationalist casualties were apparently in excess of 100,000, including approximately 10,000 dead,[69] but in this campaign the Popular Front forces lost 100,000 in prisoners alone.

Meanwhile, the Republican command tried another strategic diversion, this time not near Madrid but in the northeast, on the Aragon front. Commentators have criticized the Republican command for commencing a major operation in a mountainous area so near the main axis of Franco's strength in the north central part of Spain. However, for political and logistical reasons, Republican strategy was based on concentration near the major population centers. Furthermore, in the Zaragoza sector "many soldiers"[70] had deserted the Nationalists during the first months of war, and the Republican staff considered this area a weak point that might easily be penetrated.[71] By late August, the best units from the central front, badly clawed at Brunete, had been reorganized and re-equipped, while the former Catalan militia, now the Republican "Army of the East," was prepared for regular service. Altogether, nearly 80,000 troops and almost 100 tanks were readied for the assault.

On August 24, eight separate attack columns struck the irregular Nationalist line north and south of Zaragoza and on both sides of the Ebro River. Though the efforts in the north went awry, initial gains were made in the Belchite sector to the south. Although there were only three or four Nationalist battalions in reserve at Zaragoza, the battle of Belchite was in many ways a repetition of Brunete. At first the Popular Front forces seemed to be making a complete breakthrough; but they failed to penetrate decisively, stopping instead to concentrate against three small nuclei of defense,[72] the largest of which, the town of Belchite, was valiantly defended until September 5, when the Caudillo radioed permission to surrender. The Republicans were unable to advance further, and part of the rather small territory seized was rewon by a Nationalist counteroffensive at the end of the month. The Belchite operation interrupted the Nationalists' northern campaign even less than Brunete had, for only one unit was diverted. Most Nationalist reinforcements were drawn from the inactive central front, and Republican efforts to resume the attack in Aragon during October were easily repulsed. However, the lack of strong air and artillery support made a major Nationalist counteroffensive in that region impossible, and Franco's staff had no wish to commit the Nationalist Army to the Aragonese mountains as a major theater of operations.

After the end of the Asturian campaign, the war became easier for the Nationalist command, which could henceforth concentrate its striking power on a single front. November was a month of rest. Franco journeyed to Pamplona to preside over a massive welcome for the Navarrese divisions, which were enjoying a brief furlough. Thanks to German and Italian aid, Nationalist military superiority continued to grow. By the end of 1937, the shock units were being equipped with four new light Fiat machine-guns per rifle company, and in the main engagements each of these units could often count on a tank screen of eight vehicles—usually six of the light-machine-gun-bearing German or Italian models, and sometimes two of the larger captured Russian tanks with 37 or 45 mm. cannon.[73] Even the troops of the Tercio seldom learned to dig themselves in properly, but the Nationalist preponderance in firepower made this seem of small importance. Franco still relied primarily on his elite units, but more ordinary conscript divisions were being moved to the front, supplemented with smaller sections of trained and reliable soldiers. In secondary areas still manned by doubtful units, small groups of Moors or Civil Guards sometimes patrolled the lines.[74]

By November 1937, the Nationalist Army totaled approximately 600,000—about a third more than the Republican effectives at that time. It was supported by between 300 and 400 batteries of artillery, including the large artillery corps of the CTV, and the total number of aircraft was approximately 400.[75] Nationalist superiority in planes was nearly five to three; for the first time, Franco's army had more tanks than the Republicans, though the German and Italian models were less effective than the heavy Russian types. On the Republican side, casualties had been heavy. It has been estimated that by the close of 1937 nearly 800,000 men had been under arms in the Popular Front zone at some time; of these, 49,000 had been killed and approximately 200,000 wounded during 1937 alone.[76] In both quantity and quality of men and matériel, the Republicans were falling far behind.

Nevertheless, the Republican command believed that it could not afford to relinquish the initiative. Intelligence reports indicated that the Nationalists planned a major offensive in the Guadalajara region for December 1937. While extremely cold weather forced temporary postponement of the assault, the Republican command decided to forestall it with an anticipatory Republican offensive. The sector chosen was to the east of Guadalajara, where the front turned sharply north at right angles near the provincial mountain capital of Teruel, which had been in Nationalist hands since the beginning of the war.

Nearly 100,000 of the best prepared Republican troops were assembled, but only 40,000 were initially committed. Once more the first assault achieved surprise, and broke through to a depth of 10 kilometers in twelve hours, but the secondary attack to the north was less successful. Nationalist intelligence proved faulty in the extreme; the entire sector was manned by only 18,000 troops, and the town of Teruel was immediately cut off. German and Italian advisers urged Franco not to be dissuaded from his own plans, but to withdraw to a more easily defended line in Aragon so that the main Nationalist forces could proceed with their new Guadalajara offensive. The Generalissimo, however, remained acutely sensitive to political and psychological prestige factors. He felt it dangerous to concede the Republicans the smallest gain in territory. On December 23, after the Popular Front forces had pinched off the entire Teruel salient and were tightly besieging the city, Franco canceled his own operation and ordered preparations for a general counteroffensive, promising the commander of the beleaguered garrison that Teruel would soon be relieved. The newly organized Castilian and Galician Corps under Varela and Aranda moved in and began a two-pronged counterattack near Teruel on the 29th, as bitter sub-zero weather descended over the mountain country. A heavy freeze on New Year's Eve put hundreds of motor vehicles out of action; troops in exposed positions had to be relieved every fifteen minutes, and operations momentarily came to a halt. Despite Franco's order to the contrary, the Teruel garrison finally surrendered on January 7, after having suffered more than 75 per cent casualties. For the first time, the Republicans had managed to win back a significant position.

Matters had worked out badly for Franco, who was roundly criticized, especially by the Italians, for his "indecisiveness."[77] Always sensitive to the conditions under which he had become Generalissimo, Franco allowed the Corps commanders considerable latitude and sometimes left the overall coordination of military affairs incomplete. Operations proceeded slowly, for most field officers were wanting in initiative, and would not press matters to a quick conclusion unless they enjoyed overwhelming superiority or saw Popular Front morale collapsing.

Nevertheless, the Nationalists had moved 78,000 troops and 240 guns to the Teruel sector by the first days of January 1938. Weather prevented development of the counteroffensive until January 17, but

Nationalist Advances in the Northeast, 1938

after that it made steady progress, exhausting the last Republican reserves. With complete air control and great superiority in artillery,[78]
the Nationalists began the decisive phase of their advance on February 5, and Teruel was finally retaken on the 22d. The battle had
been perhaps the bloodiest of the war. Coming as it did after the heavy
losses of 1937, it seemed to weaken the Republican Army almost beyond repair.[79]

By the end of February, the corner of the Nationalist line southeast of Zaragoza lay less than 100 kilometers from the Mediterranean.
A hard blow might cut the Republican zone in two. With the main
Nationalist units already concentrated in this area, it was decided to
give up once and for all another encircling maneuver against Madrid

in favor of a two-pronged advance east and southeast of Zaragoza. The main blow would fall against some 34,000 Republican troops in the sector just south of the Ebro, where three times that number of Nationalists were poised to attack.[80] The offensive began on March 7. Exhausted, ill-equipped, half-organized Republican units collapsed, and major breakthroughs were made at every point of advance. German and Italian armor, supplemented by captured Russian vehicles, totaled nearly 200 tanks, and these were used as a screen for the infantry when the assault moved down from the mountains through the river valleys and toward the coastal plain. Yet this was no predecessor of the blitzkrieg, for armored units were only occasionally used independently, as compact units. Aranda later observed: "The advance was completely frontal, without any preconceived idea of maneuver."[81] The more sophisticated suggestions of German advisers were largely lost on generals like Franco and Dávila.[82] In March 1938 such ideas hardly seemed important, for at some points the Republicans were scarcely fighting back. Some of the best Nationalist divisions were semi-motorized, and in one area advanced nearly 100 kilometers in eight days. So faint was the resistance that by March 19, when they stopped to regroup, the main assault forces had suffered only one per cent casualties.[83] On March 22 the advance was resumed at the northern end of the front, where the defense had almost disintegrated. Lérida, the first Catalan provincial capital to fall, was taken early in April, and the Nationalist advance only came to a halt in the middle of the month, after outrunning its supply line.[84]

Parallel to this offensive from northern Aragon into Catalonia, an even more powerful attack was launched in the southern part of the Aragonese front. Its objective was the sea. Franco and Dávila selected the Italian-Spanish CTV, Aranda's tough Galician Corps, and a special new Corps under the most capable of the recently promoted brigadiers, Rafael García Valiño. Before this force could reach the coast, however, it would have to cross the northeastern extremities of the tortuous Maestrazgo, which had baffled government troops in the Carlist campaigns of the preceding century. The Maestrazgo is a desolate region with an irregular terrain. Shallow gorges, low hills, and desert stretches form a geographic maze well suited to defense.

The assault began southeast of Alcañiz on March 24. Hasty Republican fortifications had been thrown up behind natural barriers, and all available reserves were used in counterattacks, but many front-line Republican units were 30 per cent undermanned and some lacked as much as 40 per cent of their regular armament.[85] After three days, the CTV and Valiño's troops, who had been given the easier terrain, made several breakthroughs. By April 1, the Italians were near Gandesa, halfway to the sea, and one of Valiño's units was even closer. Unlike these two Corps, Aranda's Galicians farther to the south were not even partially motorized, and they found the going tough through the heart of the Maestrazgo. Aranda also had to peel off battalions to guard the right flank of the offensive, but Morella, the capital of the Maestrazgo, fell on April 4, and four days later the Nationalists were little more than 30 kilometers from the sea. At this point, Aranda's Corps was halted while García Valiño's troops were switched farther south to exploit the opening. The advance was resumed on April 12, and at 4 P.M. on the 15th, Camilo Alonso Vega's Fourth Navarrese Division occupied the seaside town of Vinaroz, thus slicing the Republican zone in two. Valiño's forces then wheeled northward to the right bank of the Ebro, where they joined hands with the CTV. The remaining Republican soldiers in the northeast Maestrazgo were penned up and forced to surrender. By April 19, Franco's Army held a wedge of coastline nearly 70 kilometers long.[86]

The Popular Front forces had fought more poorly than at any time since the first weeks of the war, and their morale seemed to be collapsing. The more optimistic Nationalist officers calculated that the struggle was nearly over. The defenses of Catalonia were known to be poorly organized, and much of the civilian population there was becoming dispirited, partly because of the terrorist bombing raids in recent weeks. Franco, however, chose not to strike for the swift capture of Barcelona, current seat of the Republican government, but turned his attention southward to Valencia. Valencia was the most centrally located of the three main Loyalist centers, and loss of the east would totally disrupt resistance, bringing the war to a swift conclusion. Further, the need to protect both Madrid and Catalonia would make it hard for the Republicans to defend the east.

Rather than attack due south along the narrow coastal road, Franco shifted the emphasis farther west to the trenches of the old battleground at Teruel. There Varela's Castilian Corps had remained on the defensive while other units advanced from the north to the sea. The attack that began southeast of Teruel on April 23 came as a complete surprise to the Republicans. A heavy artillery barrage churned up the opposing trenches and Varela's infantry tore big holes in the defense line. Later that day, however, the temperature dropped and the skies darkened as a storm of rain, sleet, and snow covered the front. Rain continued on the days following, submerging truck and artillery wheels in the mud and placing a damper on the combat enthusiasm of the Castilian troops, who sank in slime up to their knees. On April 27 the attack was called off, after an initial gain of more than 20 kilometers.[87]

Meanwhile, further attempts were made to breach the main Republican line 150 kilometers north of Valencia. Though local successes were achieved, there was no breakthrough. The Republicans had found the will, the matériel, and the leadership to reorganize their defenses, and by May 24 the Nationalists had been able to advance only a fourth of the distance from Morella to Valencia. Two days later the attack was renewed, and Castellón, the last major city before Valencia, was occupied on June 14, but a new defense line to the south brought the advance almost to a standstill during the remainder of June.[88]

The first days of July were spent in regrouping, for Franco intended to concentrate 20 divisions, the CTV, and nearly 900 cannon and 400 aircraft for a definitive breakthrough to Valencia.[89] Confidence in victory mounted among the Nationalists, whose newly organized tourist bureau announced motor tours to former battlefields beginning on July 1. Most of the Nationalist forces were readied for an indirect attack through the southern Maestrazgo, where Republican defenses were somewhat weaker, while Aranda still belabored the coastal route. The assault began on July 13 and got off to a rather good start. Within five days nearly all the Republican reserves in this sector were committed, yet the advance slowly continued. On July 25, however, the attack had to be broken off to enable the Nationalists to repel a sudden Republican counteroffensive in Catalonia.[90]

Nationalist commentators have claimed that the eastern campaign could have been quickly carried to a conclusion, had it not been for the sudden enemy counteroffensive across the Ebro. Conversely, they have argued that Franco never intended to seize Valencia before turning toward Barcelona.[91] These rationalizations are not convincing, for, though by July 25 the eastern offensive had carried two-thirds of the distance from the original coastal breakthrough to Valencia, resistance had steadily increased. It is possible that Franco was repeating the mistake of battering away against a central but strongly defended target.[92] Had the Generalissimo reconcentrated his forces to complete the occupation of Catalonia after the April breakthrough—thus emulating the successful northern strategy of 1937—the Republicans might never have had the opportunity to build up a counteroffensive in that area and Barcelona might have fallen six months earlier than it did, with much lighter losses for the Nationalists.

Yet it is not surprising that almost no one on Franco's staff believed that the scattered, ill-equipped, partially demoralized Republican divisions northeast of the Ebro could have been reformed for a major counteroffensive within three months. Though these units of the Army of the East and the Army of the Ebro had initially been among the more potent Popular Front forces, their reconstitution after the rout of early spring ranks as one of the two or three major accomplishments of the Republican Army. This feat had in part been made possible by the final large shipments of military supplies that reached the Republican zone.

The new Army of the Ebro, composed of three reorganized corps, attacked across the bend of the Ebro River about 20 kilometers north of Tortosa in the early hours of July 25. The main assault by pontoon crossing came as a partial surprise,[93] and within little more than 24 hours the Republicans had occupied a bulge southwest of the river about 20 kilometers long and 15 kilometers deep. As elsewhere, the initial Republican tactics were not unlike those of the Red Army offensives of World War II, possibly because of the influence of Russian advisers. Masses of infantry and matériel were piled up to smash a selected portion of the enemy's line. Once having flooded their first objective, however, the Popular Front units lacked the maneuverability to exploit the success with speed and imagination. The town of Gandesa, some 20 kilometers west of the Ebro, was almost seized in the initial assault. But the terrain west of the Ebro has a broken surface suited to defensive battle, and after the first attack, a comparatively small Nationalist detachment managed to hold on until a solid resistance could be organized. By the second day the attackers were already running out of steam, and within a short time the Nationalists had completely stabilized their line about 15 kilometers west of the bend in the Ebro. After the failure of a new attack on July 31, the Republicans suspended offensive operations.[94]

The Ebro assault did take pressure off the east, and in that sense was definitely more successful than the Brunete and Belchite engagements. As at Teruel, Franco decided to abandon his own objectives and switch to a battlefield chosen by the Republican command. Though some of the foreign advisers as well as a few of the Generalissimo's staff officers were reluctant to do this, and stressed that the goal ought not to be to regain open territory but rather to seize the core of the Republican zone, Franco had his way. Popular Front propagandists loudly proclaimed that the Ebro effort was an all-out offensive designed to break the enemy, and Franco apparently felt that for political and psychological reasons he could not afford to let the Republicans retain the ground they had won from the Nationalist Army. By the first days of August, hundreds of cannon and most of the German and Italian bomber squadrons were transferred to the Ebro, where the Nationalists gradually built up an enormous superiority in firepower. The Republican units had little opportunity to fortify their new line, but, in the words of a leading Nationalist general, tried to hold on from "newly improvised positions, which they defended primarily with hand grenades and antiquated machine guns."[95] During August, the Nationalists mounted three local counterattacks against limited sectors and won back a small amount of territory.[96]

Altogether, it took at least six weeks to complete the Nationalist buildup west of the Ebro, and even after that progress was slow. Kindelán has written that this sluggishness was due to the "depressive effect that the Red offensive had on our troops and some of their commanders, producing temperamental aberrations . . . , logistical errors, and exaggerated meticulousness in preparing the operations."[97] Moreover, the losses of two years of fighting and the problems of staffing a mass army had lowered the quality of Nationalist field officers. "In the battle of Gandesa, the deficient quality of officers at battalion and company level was evident. . . . Exaggerating a bit, it could be said that every intermediate-level [professional] Infantry officer with field experience had died by the end of the second year of the war."[98] The Artillery was affected in much the same way as the Infantry. Despite comparatively light Artillery losses, batteries that could once have been moved in four hours now required twelve hours to change positions.[99] The slowing down of Nationalist operations especially infuriated Mussolini, who on August 24 "used violent language" in blaming Franco for "letting the victory slip" when it was "already in his grasp."[100]

But the Republican forces along the Ebro suffered to a much greater extent. Morale sagged under intensive bombardment and slowly increasing Nationalist attacks. More and more troops tried to walk away from the fight. Field commanders often dispatched false reports, and the Republican General Staff had to send out special investigators of its own.[101] However, some Popular Front troops fought valiantly throughout, and shattered units were regrouped and sent back again and again to the battle.[102]

The bulk of the Nationalist forces were finally in position by September 3, when the main phase of the counteroffensive began. There was nothing subtle about it, for the object was the center of the Republican line on the heights just east of Gandesa. More than 300 cannon were concentrated along a distance of 10 kilometers, but there was no effort at an all-out assault. The Nationalist tactic was to zero in a great mass of artillery on a specific position, bombard it by land and air for four or five hours, then send a battalion or two in to occupy the ruins. From the main group of 336 guns employed at the Ebro, an average of 13,593 shells were fired daily for 114 days, making this the heaviest sustained barrage of the war.[103] German commanders of the Condor units complained that their squadrons were being worn down from constant ground support missions. A number of hills were re-won, but even Franco became uneasy at the slow pace. In the latter part of October he moved his headquarters uncommonly close to the front and began to demand more action from his Corps commanders.[104] García Valiño mounted the last major attack on October 30, against the Sierra de Caballs in the south central sector of the reduced enemy front. He drove his battalions relentlessly, and some Republican positions, deserted under bombardment, were seized before the defenders could recover. The attack was pressed during the early part of November until the entire line of hills had been occupied, thus enabling the Nationalists to dominate the valley of the Ebro. Lacking adequate air and artillery support, their equipment exhausted and their best troops knocked out of action, the Republicans could not hold on. By November 16, all the land west of the river had been reconquered.[105]

In the long struggle the Popular Front forces suffered severely.[106] Though the final withdrawal back across the river had been made in good order with few losses,[107] Republican attacks farther north during August and September failed completely. Most of the better Republican units had eventually broken down either militarily or psychologically. A comparison of the sources of manpower of the opposing armies was made by checking the age of the 11,831 prisoners taken by Yagüe's Moroccan Corps. Only 47 per cent of these came from the same age groups being drafted for the Nationalist forces; 10 per cent were younger and 43 per cent were older men.[108] By the late autumn of 1938, the Republicans were scraping the bottom of the barrel.

The Nationalists had suffered 57,000 casualties in the Ebro battle —about a quarter less than their adversaries—but only 4,007 men were listed as killed.[109] Their Army had suffered little structural damage, save perhaps among the Navarrese divisions and Barrón's Thirteenth Division, which incurred disproportionate losses. Franco had finally consummated his long-deferred mining agreements with the German government–sponsored consortium, and the flow of arms from Germany and Italy remained heavy. By contrast, the Republicans were completely unable to make good the heavy losses of four months of fighting along the Ebro. In that sense, Franco had correctly calculated that a battle of attrition would wear down the Republican Army to the breaking point. When the Nationalist offensive was resumed in Catalonia early in December, there was no chance of stopping it.[110] By February 1939, all of northeastern Spain was occupied, while a Republican diversion on the Andalusian front was being effectively contained.[111] Final victory for the Nationalists was in sight.

The war ended on an anticlimactic note in March 1939, after an anti-Communist revolt by professional officers and leaders of other Popular Front groups at Madrid. The government of Juan Negrín, which had ruled the Republican zone during the last two years of the war, had completely lost the confidence and respect of the Popular Front coalition. Most of the few professional officers who still held important commands in the Republican Army were fed up. After the evacuation of Catalonia, the Chief of Staff, Rojo, did not return to the war. He wrote a few months later of his disgust with the confusion and division in Popular Front ranks, and pointed with some envy to the military discipline of the Nationalists, stating: "In the social and human order, Franco has triumphed, . . . for he has achieved moral superiority at home and abroad."[112] Colonel Segismundo Casado, commander of the Madrid sector and key leader of the March 5 revolt, apparently believed that it would be easier for professional officers, unencumbered with any of the political excesses of the leftist groups, to make a reasonable peace with Franco. The Nationalist Caudillo had always insisted on unconditional surrender, and he did not modify this demand now. Negotiations with Casado's Junta were carried on at first by means of fifth-column agents in the Republican command; then, at the end of March, they were resumed with representa-

tives at Burgos. Faced with Franco's intransigence, which echoed
Mola's words of three years earlier—"With *compañeros* who are not
compañeros, the triumphant Movement will be inexorable"—Casado's Junta collapsed.[113] Franco's forces quickly occupied what remained of the Republican zone, and by April 1 the Generalissimo
could officially announce that the war had ended.

Exactly how many lives it cost will probably never be known. Nationalist Army losses were comparatively light.* One source with access
to official statistics has listed 70,000 killed and 300,000 wounded,[114]
though other informed estimates are higher. Fatalities among the ill-
trained, poorly equipped Republican forces were considerably greater, amounting to perhaps 125,000 or more. This was a military loss of
life at least twice as great as in any of the nineteenth-century Spanish
civil wars. Such bloody losses on the battlefield and so many thousands
of shootings behind the lines had scarcely been anticipated even by
the most radical when the irreparable breach was created in 1936.
Even so, had the killing ended with the close of the military engagements, it would have been much easier to create a new national consensus afterward. But the end of the war brought no amelioration of
the grim policy of government by violence.

* For losses among Falangist and Carlist battalions, see Appendix B, p. 458.

CHAPTER TWENTY-ONE

The Repression

AT THE BEGINNING of the Civil War, the rebel generals, conscious of their limited resources, realized they must take strong measures in order to remain in control of the situation. They made it clear before the revolt began that they would act ruthlessly to crush potential opposition before it appeared. Directives concerning police measures called for the arrest of Popular Front and syndicate leaders, and at least one undated plan made provision for the summary execution of anyone who opposed the movement.[1] The "White Terror," as this purge has been called, grew in relation to the extent of the "Red Terror," which prevailed in areas dominated by leftist groups. Initial incidents such as the shooting of rebel officers in the Montaña barracks at Madrid had a strong effect on military motivation. An American correspondent reported:

The memory of that shooting of the Madrid officers is one of the strongest motives in the hearts of the White Army. I have seen officers carrying pictures of the shootings, clipped from foreign publications. There were some remarkable pictures. One of the most vivid and terrible photographs I have ever seen was that of a Madrid officer coming out of barracks with his hands in the air and a wildly grinning Red militiaman holding an automatic revolver to the officer's head. Another shows the bodies of several score of officers in the court of the Montaña barracks, with weeping women looking for their dead.[2]

On July 28, 1936, the Burgos Junta declared total martial law throughout Spain.[3] All civil and military crimes were thus officially prosecuted under the Military Code. In Valladolid, for example, a "Consejo de guerra" was set up within twenty-four hours of the rebel takeover. Further Junta rulings on August 31 and September 8 di-

rected all Army and Navy courts to conduct their proceedings as swiftly as possible and to suspend jury trials even for civil cases.[4]

During the first weeks of fighting, the rebels took few prisoners, and
the Popular Front militia were perhaps equally bloodthirsty. Mola
himself was surprised by the rebels' ferocity. The account written
by his secretary reflects the attitude of the rebel command. For example, early in the conflict Mola had occasion to order that a truckload
of captured militiamen be executed at the side of the highway. When
he subsequently changed his mind and rescinded the order, a staff
colonel complained, "General, let us not have to repent afterwards
for mildness!"[5] Iribarren noted: "People [at Mola's headquarters] talk
of the purge that must be made in Madrid among streetcarmen, policemen, telegraphists, and doormen. Someone proposes that the signs
in doorways reading 'Do not pass without speaking to the *portero*'
should be changed to 'Do not pass without shooting the *portero*.' "[6]
Mola is said to have remarked: "A year ago I would have trembled
to sign a death sentence. Now I sign more than ten a day with an
easy conscience."[7] When visited by a representative of the International Red Cross, he showed little interest in the exchange of prisoners,[8] and on August 18 he declared: "In this state of affairs I have
decided on war without quarter. If I see my father in the opposing
ranks, I will shoot him."[9] At Seville, Queipo de Llano was even more
outspoken, at least during the first week of fighting. In his nightly
radio broadcasts he made direct references to the brutal reprisals
being carried out against the Popular Front forces, apparently in order
to terrify his listeners into submission.[10]

A lucid account of the White Terror was penned by the American
correspondent Edmond Taylor, who spent several months in the rebel
zone at the outbreak of the war.[11] On July 24, he cabled home one of
the more apt early definitions of the struggle: "This civil war or insurrection, or whatever you want to call it, is something like a crusade,
something like a Chinese bandit war, something like a family feud
in the Kentucky mountains, or an ax murder in a basement."[12] He
later wrote:

After the first few weeks, the original idea of killing prisoners as a military
necessity or as a joke evolved into . . . [a] higher moral feeling. . . . So far
as I could tell, the principle seemed to be this:
     The enemy was a complex molecule of a spiritual poison called com-
munism for convenience; but liberalism was the most deadly individual
element in it and the most hated. Introduced into the human organism,

this poison acted like a germ virus; not only incurable, but infectious. Certain men known as the Leaders had perversely inoculated themselves with the poison and, like Satan in Catholic mythology, were deliberately trying to spread the infection as widely as they could. As the incarnation of evil, these men deserved punishment. Their victims, who might have been good Spaniards if they had not had the bad luck to be infected by the Leaders, did not merit punishment properly speaking, but they had to be shot in a human way because they were incurable and might infect others. (Later, purgatory was discovered and the victims could be saved under certain conditions.)[13]

When the British journalist Denis Weaver and another correspondent were accidentally driven outside the shrinking Republican defense line south of Madrid in October 1936, their Republican driver and guard were summarily shot by the advancing Nationalists. The journalists were taken to General Varela's headquarters. Weaver describes his encounter with Varela thus: "The general, a thin-faced little man in a soft leather jacket and a black tie, took down our names and Christian names in a laborious scrawl and then heard our tale. He roared with laughter. 'I can't imagine how it is that you were not shot at once,' he said. 'Of course, there's time for that yet—if you do prove to be spies.' He laughed again. This was a tremendous joke."[14]

The American correspondent John T. Whitaker, who had received an Italian Fascist decoration while covering the Ethiopian campaign, was allowed extensive freedom of movement and observation during the first months of the conflict. He later wrote:

For two months I kept a room at Talavera de la Reina which served as a base camp for trips to the front. I slept there on an average of two nights a week. I never passed a night there without being awakened at dawn by the volleys of the firing squads in the yard of the *Cuartel*. There seemed no end to the killing. They were shooting as many at the end of the second month as in my first days in Talavera. They averaged perhaps thirty a day. I watched the men they took into the *Cuartel*. They were simple peasants and workers, Spanish Milquetoasts. It was sufficient to have carried a trade-union card, to have been a Freemason, to have voted for the Republic. If you were picked up or denounced for any one of these charges you were given a summary, two-minute hearing and capital punishment was formally pronounced. Any man who had held any office under the Republic was, of course, shot out of hand. And there were mopping-up operations along the roads. You would find four old peasant women heaped in a ditch; thirty and forty militiamen at a time, their hands roped behind them, shot down at the crossroads. I remember a bundle in a town square. Two youthful members of the Republican assault guards had been tied back to back with wire, covered with gasoline, and burned alive.

I can never forget the first time I saw the mass execution of prisoners. I stood in the main street of Santa Olalla as seven trucks brought in the militiamen. They were unloaded and herded together. They had that listless, exhausted, beaten look of troops who can no longer stand out against the steady pounding of German bombs. Most of them had a soiled towel or a shirt in their hands—the white flags with which they had signaled surrender. Two Franco officers passed out cigarettes among them and several Republicans laughed boyishly and self-consciously as they smoked.... Suddenly an officer took me by the arm and said, "It's time to get out of here." At the edge of this cluster of prisoners, six hundred-odd men, Moorish troops were setting up two machine guns. The prisoners saw them as I saw them. The men seemed to tremble in one convulsion, as those in front, speechless with fright, rocked back on their heels, the color draining from their faces, their eyes opening with terror.... The two guns suddenly roared in staccato, firing short, lazy bursts of ten or twelve rounds at a time, punctuated by the silences. Then, or later, I have never understood why the prisoners stood and took it. I always thought they might rush the machine guns or do something—anything. I suppose all volition is beaten out of them by the time they surrender....

Franco's fixed policy of shooting militiamen brought protests.... Strunk [the German attaché] told me that he had twice intervened with Franco on the ground that the reds had fought bravely and merited treatment as prisoners of war and also on the ground that it was stiffening Republican resistance. "Why, this sort of thing can't be right, Captain Strunk," said Franco. "You are not the sort of German to get the facts wrong."...

Such stories of these atrocities as leaked out were categorically denied abroad by the propaganda bureau and its apologists. The executions in the Badajoz bull ring were first reported by Jay Allen, in the Chicago *Tribune*. He had been the first correspondent to interview Franco and he had generally proved himself the best informed journalist in Spain. His story was denied and he was vilified by paid speakers from one end of the United States to the other.... Colonel Yagüe, who commanded the Franco forces at Badajoz, laughed at these denials.

"Of course we shot them," he said to me. "What do you expect? Was I supposed to take 4,000 reds with me as my column advanced, racing against time? Was I supposed to turn them loose in my rear and let them make Badajoz red again?"

The men who commanded them never denied that the Moors killed the wounded in the Republican hospital at Toledo. They boasted of how grenades were thrown in among two hundred screaming and helpless men. They never denied to me that they had promised the Moors white women when they reached Madrid. I sat with these officers in bivouac and heard them debate the expediency of such a promise. Some contended that a white woman was Spanish even if red. This practice was not denied by El Mizian, the only Moroccan officer in the Spanish army. I stood at the crossroads outside Navalcarnero with the Moorish major when two Spanish girls, not out of their teens, were brought before him. One had worked in a textile factory in Barcelona and they found a trade-union card in her leather jacket. The other came from Valencia and said she had no politics. After questioning them for military information, El Mizian had them taken into a small schoolhouse where some forty Moorish soldiers were resting. As they reached the doorway an ululating cry rose from the Moors within. I stood horrified in helpless anger. El Mizian smirked when I remonstrated with him. "Oh, they'll not live more than four hours," he said.[15]

It might be asked why such an innately cautious general as Franco was presiding over a program of mass horror. Part of the answer is that Franco was not responsible for initiating the killings: they had begun almost spontaneously all over Spain. Savagery was as widespread among Nationalists as among leftists. When in 1937 the Italian ambassador Roberto Cantalupo urged him to moderate the repression that followed the conquest of Málaga, Franco replied that feelings were so strong it was difficult for him to interfere and restrict them on the local level.[16] In his cold, calculating fashion, Franco apparently found it expedient not to thwart the blood lust of his followers, but to acknowledge it as one of the main unifying forces behind the rebel movement. It served to eliminate the enemies of the new regime, and it made large numbers of Nationalists participants in a common orgy so gruesome as to irrevocably bind them together. Though Franco did not begin the mass shootings, there is not the slightest evidence that he did anything to end them.

Franco had set an important precedent in Morocco when, shortly after arriving to assume command, he had approved the execution of his own first cousin, Major Lapuente Bahamonde, who had resisted the rebellion at the Tetuán airfield. Almost all the ranking commanders in the Nationalist zone who had refused to join the rising were shot during the first year of the Civil War, including Generals Romerales in Morocco, Villa Abrille in Seville, Campins[17] in Granada, Salcedo and Caridad Pita in La Coruña, and Batet in Burgos, as well as Admiral Azarolo at El Ferrol.[18]

Perhaps with more justification, the Popular Front authorities were equally severe toward rebel officers. At least a third of the Officer Corps had found itself in territory controlled by the Popular Front during the last days of July 1936. There is evidence to indicate that many of these officers, whether because of political loyalty or simply because they preferred to make a virtue of necessity, would still have been willing to serve as officers in the Republican Army for the rest of the war. But to all the leftist groups save the Communists, military men were suspect, and vague suspicion sufficed for execution. Not merely the rebel leaders such as Generals Goded, Fanjul, Barrera, Patxot, and Fernández Burriel were shot, but several hundred lesser officers as well. By August 11, 1936, 1,100 officers were said to be held in Madrid's Cárcel Modelo, 400 of them holding the rank of major or above.[19] Some were later released, but the slain included even moderate, Republican-minded officers such as the valiant López de Ochoa, and Capaz, "the last of the conquistadores."

Of the several thousand officers who were originally trapped in the Republican zone, only a small minority were allowed to serve in the wartime Republican Army. During the last months of 1936 the Republican government established a Classifying Junta whose purpose was to investigate and classify every member of the military stationed in the Republican zone. Four categories of loyalty were set up: completely loyal, apparently loyal but not completely reliable, unreliable, and pro-Nationalist. Officers in the last category were subjected to court-martial; those in the first category were admitted to active duty; those in the second were given positions behind the lines, in supply and training; and those in the third category were simply suspended from all functions. A scant 300 were admitted to the first category, and an equal or slightly greater number were employed in supply and training. The majority were excluded altogether. A few of those who did lead militia units during the first weeks were shot by insubordinate militiamen. Thus, less than 10 per cent of the regular Officer Corps served in the wartime Republican Army.[20] The almost complete lack of trained leadership, especially at the company and battalion levels, proved in the long run to be the most serious weakness of the Republican Army.

Because of their own personal loyalties and also because of the murderous hatred shown them by leftist groups,[21] the bulk of the regular officers in the Republican zone justified the leftists' suspicions. Most of those able to escape to the Nationalists did so, and during the first months there were many desertions from field commands. Proportionately, the greatest purge in the Republican zone was made among naval officers. The commissar of the wartime Republican fleet, Bruno Alonso, afterward calculated that 70 per cent of the naval officers who fell into the hands of the Loyalists were shot.[22] All this helps to explain, though in no way to justify, the ferocity of the repression in Nationalist Spain.

There is no way to measure exactly the number of executions in the Nationalist zone. Hugh Thomas seems to suggest that the leftists executed more people during the Civil War than the Nationalists did because they dominated the major population centers and had, so to speak, more people available to shoot.[23] On the basis of closer investigation, Gabriel Jackson advances a different logic, pointing out that many more people belonged to leftist organizations than to identifiably rightist groups, and that thus the Nationalists had many more identifiable enemies to eliminate.[24] The bulk of evidence seems to support Jackson's contention that even during the wartime period the number of Nationalist executions exceeded those carried out by the left.

The White Terror was at first episodic and disorganized. In the regions seized by the rebels, the most prominent liberals and leftists were usually shot, as an example to their comrades. In most cases they were not even brought before a court-martial. However, as the conflict lengthened into a full-scale civil war, the second phase of the Terror began. Needing to mobilize all politically reliable manpower, the military command had to pull troops out of every reserve area and send them to the front, leaving the rearguard dangerously short-handed. This left the Civil Guard and other auxiliary forces such as the various right-wing militia groups and the Falangists free to act almost at will as police and executioners. Some effort was made to regularize procedures, and sometimes conservative jurists were summarily deputized for subordinate status on the courts-martial, as the original decree had stipulated.[25] In this way the Army escaped direct identification with the repression, and was able to throw every trained man onto the battle line. During the first months, the Army commanders had not worried about the adverse publicity that might arise from the shootings,[26] but as the Civil War developed into an international ideological conflict, tight censorship was clamped down.

One region where the repression seemed especially fierce was the island of Mallorca, which was under heavy pressure from the Popular Front forces of Catalonia during the first months of the war. To discourage revolt by the lower classes, mass shootings were begun there during the second week of August 1936. The local Falangists were allowed no voice in government, but were widely used as a terrorist force. Arconovaldo Buonacorsi, the Italian Fascist chief sent to Mallorca by Mussolini, especially encouraged this use of local Falangists as the agents of a ruthless repression.[27]

Some commentators have recognized that the Falangists, often blamed as the main agents of the repression, did not bear primary responsibility for its horrors. Thousands of killings were their doing, but the ordinary conservatives and rightists often equaled or exceeded them in ferocity,[28] and ultimate authorization came from the military dictatorship, which allowed a sort of limited anarchy to prevail for the better part of a year. During this time the various elements on the Nationalist side were, in effect, free to kill almost whomever they chose, so long as it could be said that the victim had supported the Popular Front.

A common pattern in the early phase of the terror is well illustrated by the death of the famous poet Federico García Lorca at Granada. At the beginning of the Civil War, military command in Granada fell into the hands of the head of the commissary at the local garrison, Major José María Valdés Guzmán, who was also chief of the Falangist militia in the province. Valdés did not have any particular enthusiasm for the Falangist program, but amid the widespread confusion of the spring of 1936 he had stepped in to use the Falangists in support of the military revolt.[29] As head of the rebel junta in the Granada garrison, he forced the reluctant commander, General Campins, to declare martial law on July 20, 1936.[30] For several weeks the hilly region of Granada was cut off within Republican territory, hemmed in by Málaga to the south and Jaén to the north. After the deposition of Campins, a new military governor, Colonel González Espinosa, was flown in from Seville on July 29, but Valdés remained in charge of civil administration. In addition to fearing the imminent threat of attack from north or south, the rebel authorities were apprehensive lest the captive leftist population attempt to rise against them. A ruthless policy of terror was imposed. To support the rebel movement, an auxiliary middle-class militia called Españoles Patriotas (Patriotic Spaniards) was organized by Catholic Action leaders, and headed by Martín Ruiz Alonso, a former CEDA deputy in the Cortes. Within a few days this group signed up 5,175 volunteers, few of whom ever fought at the front.[31] Every night, detachments of the Civil Guard or the Españoles Patriotas or the Falangists took "dangerous" elements out to the edge of town for execution—first by the score, then almost by the hundred.

Though García Lorca took no part in politics, he was deemed a moral radical because of his homosexuality and his unsympathetic portrayal of religious traditionalists and the Civil Guard. Lorca's brother-in-law Montesinos, the Socialist mayor, was among the first to be shot, and the poet eventually took refuge in the home of a close friend and fellow-writer, Luis Rosales, whose brothers were among the principal leaders of the Granada Falange. Ruiz Alonso and the Españoles Patriotas added Lorca to their list. Many people had already been shot with much less reason, and Ruiz Alonso was not dissuaded by the fact that the poet was lodged in the home of parents of Falangist leaders, for he blamed the Rosales brothers for having blocked his electoral plans during the previous year. No one but the parents was home when Ruiz Alonso came with his militia on August 18 and took Lorca away "for questioning." When José Rosales, eldest of the Rosales brothers and one of the founders of the Falange in Granada, arrived home in the late afternoon, he feared the worst, and he went at once to talk with Valdés Guzmán at government headquarters. It does not appear that Valdés Guzmán himself had anything to do with the arrest, but he approved on principle of getting rid of all radicals, and therefore told José Rosales that Lorca would have to remain in prison for awhile. On the other hand, according to Rosales, Valdés distrusted Ruiz Alonso because of his ambition, and told Rosales that if he really thought that Ruiz Alonso had smeared the Rosales family name with the charge of sheltering subversives, the Falangists could seize Ruiz Alonso and shoot him "on the Granada highway."

After Rosales' visit, Alonso also came to see Valdés. He laid out the full case against Lorca, probably mentioning the poet's anticlericalism and homosexuality. He suggested that Falangist leaders were trying to assert independent power by harboring known enemies of the movement. Other rightist militia leaders also condemned Lorca.

Luis Rosales relates that he did not return home until quite late in the evening. After learning what had happened, he dashed out to round up other young Falangists and arrived with them at headquarters sometime after midnight. They were not allowed to see the civil governor, though Luis Rosales insisted on reading aloud a written indictment of Ruiz Alonso.

The efforts of his friends had no effect. Lorca and a number of other prisoners were shot at dawn on a hillside not far from town. Enraged by Luis Rosales' gesture, Valdés later used his authority as Falangist militia chief to expel him from the party. He also levied a stiff fine against the father of the Rosales brothers for having sheltered Lorca.[32]

There was little protest against the Terror from supporters of the rebel movement. Perhaps the only leaders who spoke out were a few Falangist chiefs who disliked seeing their erstwhile followers used as policemen by the military. At one point during the winter of 1936, Manuel Hedilla, interim head of the Falange, protested to Mola against the shooting of ordinary working people (*gente de alpargatas,* as Hedilla put it) in the north.[33] The military command was unmoved; it seemed more worried over the peril to sanitation created by the glut of unburied corpses.[34]

Gradually during the course of 1937 the dictatorship brought the repression under central control. On October 31 Martínez Anido was made Chief of Internal Security, Public Order, and Frontier Inspection. Under Martínez Anido, an execution could not take place unless an official court-martial had passed sentence on the accused. However, so many of these tribunals were functioning that the rate of killings was not greatly lessened by this restriction. The inflexible policies of the rebels broke the spirit of part of the opposition, but could hardly promote the moral and spiritual unification of Spain. Well might "Tebib Arrumi" (Dr. Víctor Ruiz Albéniz), the chronicler of military headquarters in Salamanca, write: "Let us not deceive ourselves—when this war ends we shall have conquered many but convinced no one."[35]

The end of the Civil War, which brought with it the occupation of the final third of Spain and hundreds of thousands of new prisoners, made possible a broad extension of the purge. A special Law of Political Responsibilities was promulgated on February 9, 1939, to cover what were termed "political" crimes. Its definition of such acts extended liability all the way back to October 1, 1934, some two years before the regime even came into existence, and also included the category of "grave passivity"—whatever that may have meant—by which certain people who had lived in the Republican zone might be prosecuted even though not directly connected with government or leftist groups. Three categories of punishment were set up for those guilty of ordinary "political responsibilities," and entailed from three to fifteen years' imprisonment. A series of "Courts of Political Responsibilities" were established throughout the country, composed in approximately equal parts of Army officers, civilian judges, and FET representatives.[36]

For those charged with implication in major crimes or activities during the Civil War, penalties were much stiffer, and such cases were

usually handled by military courts. Those connected, however remotely, with any killings, or with the Republican Army—that is, the
better part of a million people—were liable to execution as accessories
to murder or "armed rebellion." Enormous concentration camps were
hastily established at the end of March 1939 to intern what remained
of the Republican Army—well over 300,000 men—plus all other "politically responsible" individuals who could be apprehended. In most
cases, ordinary conscripts at the rank of private were soon released
from captivity, provided that there was no indication that they had
volunteered, had been promoted, or had been even remotely connected with any political or "criminal" activity. In this way, some
200,000 were set free.

At the time of the final surrender—that is, around April 1, 1939
—the prison population in Nationalist Spain was listed at 100,292,[37]
but during the months that followed twice that many were added
from the roundup of war prisoners and civilians in the newly occupied zone. The military courts moved quickly during the spring to
prosecute the tens of thousands of accused. In the larger prisons and
concentration camps, mass executions commenced at once. During his
visit to Spain that summer, Italian Foreign Minister Ciano noted
with some shock that the Franco regime was apparently shooting 200
to 250 men per day in Madrid, 150 in Barcelona, and *"80 in Seville,
a city that was never in the hands of the Reds"* (the emphasis is
Ciano's).[38] Originally, many of those shot were judged and condemned
en masse, then mowed down by the score before firing squads, usually
in the late evening or early morning hours. In many cases, little care
was taken to investigate the justice of the condemnation. Personal
denunciations of all sorts were accepted as binding evidence. This
gave infinite opportunity for private vengeance. In certain cases, the
relatives of victims of leftist gunmen were allowed to enter prisons
in order to beat and torture the suspected murderers of their kin. It
was considered nothing to execute ten, twenty, thirty, or more men
for a single murder, even though the identity of the actual killers
could not be accurately determined. Professional officers who had
served in the Republican Army were an object of special concern.
Death sentences were usual for those who had held positions of responsibility, though officers in subordinate roles or those who carried out
strictly technical functions were sometimes treated more leniently.[39]

From the beginning it was the practice to impose very heavy sentences and then attenuate them through partial remission of penal-

ties. Some of the very large number of death sentences passed in 1939 were commuted to varying terms of imprisonment, and a decree of June 9, 1939, gave prisoners a chance to shorten their sentences by volunteering for labor. On September 8, 1939, a number of "militarized penitentiary colonies" were established to build public works projects in Spain and Morocco. On September 23, 1939, the special military Undersecretariat of Public Order was abolished and all its functions transferred to the normal police agency, the Bureau of Security. This, however, was a purely formal change and brought no alteration in policy.

At the beginning of 1940 the prison population was still very large —270,719, according to the official figures.[40] The shootings did not end after the first year of peace, but went on in great volume throughout 1941 and part of 1942. After that they began to slacken, not only because of the lack of victims, but also because the heyday of the European fascist powers, which had seemed to provide a sort of sanction to mass murder, had been passed. Beginning in 1942, amnesty was granted to many surviving prisoners. This practice became more common year by year. The majority of those prisoners who survived the bloody years 1939–42 were released after serving only a portion of their nominal terms. But for tens of thousands, all chance of amnesty came too late. Opposition elements in Spain cite enormous figures—370,000 or more—for those shot after 1939, but there is no way of verifying such statistics. The only total obtained from any government source was an informal tabulation of 192,684 executions between 1939 and 1944 given to an American correspondent in 1944, and this is not trustworthy.[41]

However many people it may have liquidated, the goal of this mass purge was not merely to exact justice or even to wreak vengeance, but to carry out a thorough social and political prophylaxis. The repression achieved this goal. It strengthened the dictatorship by decimating the opposition and cowing those who survived, while binding the members of the rebel movement firmly together in a partnership of slaughter.

CHAPTER TWENTY-TWO

Franco's Army

THE END of the Spanish Civil War did not bring general demobilization of the victorious Nationalist Army. Social and political division within Spain, together with the intransigence of the regime, required that the Generalissimo maintain a very firm hand. Moreover, the Second World War broke out only a few months after the Civil War ended, and it seemed doubtful that this time Spain could remain aloof, as she had in 1914.

At the beginning of July 1939, Franco informed the Italian ambassador that he had decided to maintain the Army at approximately 600,000 men instead of reducing it to 300,000 or less as he had earlier contemplated.[1] It appears, however, that financial pressures restricted maximum military manpower during the following decade to at least 30 per cent less than the 600,000 total. The largest single item of expense was still the Officer Corps, which by 1939 had approximately 30,000 members, the majority of whom were alféreces provisionales with the technical rank of reservists. The 1939 soldier-officer ratio of 15 to 1 was a much healthier one than previous peacetime periods had seen, but this was due to the expansion of cadres as a whole rather than to any reduction in the Officer Corps. There were not nearly enough professionals for a permanent mass Army, so the most capable of the provisionales—perhaps 10 per cent—were given regular commissions on the active list. Some of the rest were retired to the inactive Reserve, but most were kept on duty to train and command troops, even though they were still listed as reservists.

On July 24, the basic units of the Army were reorganized into 24 fully manned, staffed, and equipped divisions and formed into ten Corps, one for each of the eight military districts in Spain and two for the Moroccan Protectorate.[2] This was the professional nucleus that Franco had originally planned.[3] In addition, the annual contingents of new recruits were to be trained in separate cadres, then incorporated or dismissed according to need. However, the flow of arms from Germany and Italy had virtually ceased when the fighting ended; the Spanish economy was prostrate from the war, and the problem of equipping and supplying the Army over a long period of time was obviously a grave one.

During the war Franco had been most sparing in promotions, for bitter memories recalled how much antagonism could be created by the hasty advancement of a chosen few.[4] Even until the end of the Civil War it had not been unusual for colonels to command divisions or for brigadier generals to direct entire Corps, but now the pressure was off and the Red menace could no longer be invoked to sustain discipline, so promotion was made fairly general. A decree of April 11, 1939, restored the ranks of lieutenant general and full admiral, achieving a fundamental goal of Sanjurjo and others that Franco had carefully avoided during the war. Further decrees in May and October provided for the promotion of officers on the Reserve and retired lists who were sufficiently senior in length of service or had performed with special merit during the war. A decree of August 25 reserved eighty per cent of all government bureaucratic posts for demobilized Nationalist veterans, thus ensuring that the government would be staffed and administered by the victorious forces.

The military leadership was on the whole content. Perhaps at no time since the sixteenth century had the Army enjoyed such prestige. Though salaries remained low,[5] special privileges were obtainable: for example, the well-stocked commissaries, the only places in Spain where decent food could be obtained cheaply, were opened to the NCO's. Pride in victory and hatred of the defeated enemy unified Army sentiment as never before.

Yet there were a number of important dissidents, including Yagüe, Queipo de Llano, Solchaga, Moscardó, and Aranda. None of these generals indulged in direct insubordination, but each in his own way made known his discontent. Aranda, for example, had always been as ambitious as he was talented, and there was talk of an early rivalry between him and Franco. Aranda found it hard to forgive the fact that his Corps had been left to fight its way through the Maestrazgo and the narrow coastal roads while other units had been semi-motorized for the more spectacular breakthroughs of 1938. He had never been friendly with the Falangists, and it was rumored that he had not wanted to include them in the defense of Oviedo and had been obliged to do so purely by military necessity.[6] On the other hand, it was no secret that many Falangists wanted to see Aranda relieved of command. As the main commander on the eastern front, Aranda was made military governor of the Valencia district. Soon he had brought down on himself the criticism of the ultra faction by releasing hundreds of Republican prisoners from the local jails.

It may have been Aranda's reputation as an anti-fascist, in addition to his great professional prestige, that led Franco to appoint him head of the large Spanish military mission invited to Germany in June 1939. During the months between the end of the Civil War and the beginning of the World War, Hitler's regime showed considerable interest in strengthening military and economic bonds with Spain.[7] Because of the possible complications that might develop, the Spanish government remained reluctant to become more closely tied to Germany. In Berlin, Aranda and other Spanish generals made the positive statements about German-Spanish friendship that were expected of them;[8] but, to the Germans' disappointment, they showed little interest in close military association save on terms of absolute equality, which was not precisely what Hitler had in mind.[9] On June 19, the London *Daily Express* published an interview in which Aranda stated that Spain would stay "benevolently neutral" should Germany become involved in war. On June 24, at the conclusion of the German visit, the Portuguese *O Diario de Norte* published another statement by Aranda, which stressed the importance of Spain's maintaining good relations with Britain: "[This must be done] without prejudicing the friendship that binds us to the totalitarian countries." He was also quoted as saying, "Even the Balearics, which are coveted by Italy, must remain completely ours." This last statement was somewhat embarrassing to the regime and was labeled by the official Spanish news agency as an error in reporting. Ten months later, after Germany had seized Denmark and Norway and was about to unleash its offensive in the west, Aranda was kicked upstairs to the directorship of the Superior War College, a newly created school for the advanced training of higher-ranking officers. This post utilized Aranda's recognized technical ability while removing him from active command of troops. Yet, in his aversion to ultra-fascism and his desire to avoid entanglement in German-Italian military designs, Aranda was not acting as a liberal maverick but rather was speaking for the majority of the military hierarchy. On June 24, 1939, at the time of the *Diario de Norte* article, the Italian ambassador reported that the Army leaders, together with conservative Spanish elements, opposed a more fascistic orientation.[10]

Franco and his closest associates were concerned about the intentions of certain of the monarchist generals. The Caudillo was being strongly urged by Mussolini not to restore the monarchy, and Franco needed little encouragement. It was becoming clear that he intended to postpone the restoration for a long time—perhaps for "twenty years," as Serrano had told the Italians during his visit in June.[11] During that visit, the Minister of the Interior had asked that Italian police keep a close watch on Kindelán during the Air Force chief's forthcoming trip to Italy, for the man who had done so much to make Franco dictator was now suspected of plotting with the monarchists to remove him.[12]

Meanwhile, Queipo de Llano had lashed out in a public speech at Seville on July 18, the third anniversary of his daring coup, stating that Seville and Andalusia had been the real key to the rebel movement. Miffed because Franco had not named him for the Gran Cruz Laureada, Queipo announced that he had never asked to be given this medal, even though he was sure he deserved it.[13] According to one version, he went on to declare that the Spanish state should be run by the fighting men who won the war, not by a gang of political *arrivistes*.[14]

This outburst drew an immediate reaction. Franco relieved the obstreperous Queipo of his command and replaced him with the walrus-moustached Saliquet, who was unconditionally loyal to the dictator. The Foreign Minister, Gen. Gómez Jordana, endeavored to serve as go-between with Queipo and other dissident generals, explaining to them that the international situation required Franco to maintain a pro-fascist line at this time and that circumstances prevented both an immediate restoration and the removal of political power from the hands of Falangist appointees. Queipo reluctantly made his peace with Franco[15] and accepted a post as head of a special Spanish military mission to Italy, which departed at the end of August. The assignment was a purely honorary one that left the grizzled old Cavalry general gnashing his teeth. He detested Rome, but had to endure nearly two and a half years of gilded exile before he was permitted to return to Spain in January 1942.[16]

Among other incidents in the spring and summer that followed the victory was a special banquet given for Yagüe in Madrid by his old africanista comrades. This took on the character of a protest against Franco's treatment of their leader: after the fighting had ended, Yagüe had once more been relieved of command of the Moroccan Corps, and it had been led by the Carlist Varela at the grand victory parade in Madrid. On July 18, a banquet was given in Pamplona to honor the Conde de Rodezno and several important officers, including Solchaga, García Valiño, Rada, García Escámez, and Orgaz, who either were of Navarrese descent or had commanded Navarrese units. These officers had been greeted with popular acclaim in the villages of Navarre. Largely to prevent such recognition of anti-Falangist generals, Serrano Súñer took the occasion of an incident of violence between some Pamplonese Carlists and local Falangists to arrange for the promulgation of a government decree forbidding that military banquets or special honors be arranged without official approval.

During the summer, before the government headquarters were moved to Madrid, the Cabinet was reorganized. Makeshift measures would no longer do, but Franco seemed uncertain about how to proceed. He had already said that a minimum of five years would be necessary to put Spain back on her feet economically.[17] In the meantime, he tried to avoid major changes. The military-civilian synthesis was continued in the new Cabinet. Four of the fourteen posts were given to Army men, three to Falangists, and seven to civilian conservatives.

Jordana was replaced as Foreign Minister by Colonel Juan Beigbeder, the capable staff officer who had served as High Commissioner of Spanish Morocco for the past two years. Jordana was considered a military conservative and an Anglophile, whereas Beigbeder had once been attaché in Berlin and had served as liaison officer with the Germans early in the war. Serrano wrote that throughout the Civil War Beigbeder had "distinguished himself by his Falangism," until the Falange in Africa, thanks to his protection, had become "one of the strongest sections of the party."[18] Yet Beigbeder's apparent pro-fascism was more a matter of temporary opportunism than of ideological conviction. To Franco and the Army hierarchy he was known as a dexterous, practical-minded staff officer. Though his appointment seemed to draw Spain closer to the Axis, it did not indicate a major shift in policy, for the differences between Beigbeder and Jordana were not so great as they seemed.

In the government shakeup, the Ministry of National Defense, which had coordinated all the armed forces under the preceding administration, was replaced by separate Ministries for the Army, Navy, and Air Force. Varela, now a major general, was named War Minister, the recently promoted Vice-Admiral Salvador Moreno Fernández became Minister of the Navy, and, in a surprising appointment, Yagüe was made Spain's first Air Minister.[19] This was but another instance of Franco's tactic of kicking dangerous subordinates upstairs and attempting to compromise them through bringing about their identification with the regime's policies. Yagüe's political ambition was in some measure assuaged by the opportunity to administer what would hopefully be the first significant Spanish Air Force.

At the same time, the FET was taken temporarily out of the hands of Falangists; its new Secretary General was Brigadier General Agustín Muñoz Grandes, whose appointment was in part intended to satisfy the anti-Falangism of many generals. Muñoz Grandes was an old africanista comrade of Franco. After his flight from the Republican zone, he had commanded a division in the decisive campaigns in the northeast during 1938, and he was promoted to brigadier at the end of the war. Though he was a strong nationalist, his experiences in the Republican zone during the first year of the war helped turn him against liberalism.[20] Though hardly a genuine fascist, he believed that the future belonged to the patriotic authoritarian movements, and had become known as one of the few "Falangist generals." The accent, however, was squarely on his role as general, rather than Falangist, and it was understood that his function was more to control the Falange than to promote it. Muñoz Grandes had no political experience whatever, and was little concerned with matters of ideology. The army leaders wanted to make sure that the Falangist volunteers, thousands of whom served throughout the war in all-Falangist battalions led by regular officers, would not be permitted to form an independent armed militia. Under Muñoz Grandes, the Falangists' *excombatiente* organization turned out to be no more than an unarmed fraternal organization.[21] Further emphasis was given to military tutelage of the political-administrative structure by the restoration, on April 5, 1940, of the pre-1931 system of captaincies general.

As the German ambassador noted, the Officer Corps was the only major group in Spain that demonstrated genuine solidarity behind the regime,[22] but it was not of one mind on the course Spain should follow regarding the continental struggle that had begun in September 1939. Generalissimo Franco well knew that his ravaged land was in no shape to face the challenge of a general international war. On the eve of Germany's attack on Poland, he had appealed to Mussolini to use his influence to restrain Hitler. Most of Franco's generals were pro-German, but not necessarily pro-Nazi, and some of the more influential, especially the monarchists, were Anglophiles. The words and deeds of the pro-Axis Serrano Súñer were resented by the military. Conservatives opposed his Falangism and ambition, while pro-Falangists such as Yagüe,[23] Muñoz Grandes, and Brigadier General Carlos Asensio regarded him as an intriguer who lacked a genuinely nationalist spirit.

The fall of France directly posed the question of the degree to which Spain might collaborate in what seemed to be the closing stages of a victorious struggle. Muñoz Grandes, who was not a political success as Secretary of the Falange, was removed from that post and named commander of the 22d Division, in the military district opposite Gibraltar. This placed one of the most ardently pro-German generals in charge of the troops who would move against the key British position in the western Mediterranean should negotiations with Germany prove fruitful. At this time, however, Hitler was not interested in buying Franco's aid, and on August 27 the German Chief of Staff, General Halder, noted that most of the Spanish generals were opposed to participation in the war.[24] Moreover, a careful German military report made that same month on the condition of the 340,000-man Spanish Army was not favorable.[25]

In September, Serrano Súñer traveled to Berlin and Rome to present Franco's price for Spanish entry into the war, which included, in addition to sizable shipments of food and arms, massive expansion of the Spanish holdings in northwest Africa. The German government found Franco's price high. To facilitate relations, Serrano took over the Foreign Ministry in October 1940 from Beigbeder. Though Beigbeder was not himself particularly influential, this change was not popular with the generals. Franco's dapper little brother-in-law was being dubbed, inside and outside Spain, "the Axis minister." His apparent eagerness to make a deal with Nazi Germany annoyed the military, who felt he was too concerned with fascism and not sufficiently concerned with the needs of Spain. The generals knew full well the weakness of Spain's military position, and many of them preferred to keep out of the war unless Spain could gain the economic assistance and territorial advantages that would make participation meaningful.

This feeling was encouraged by the pessimistic attitude of Admiral

Canaris, chief of German Naval Intelligence, who carried on some of
the negotiations. The anti-Nazi Canaris was on especially good terms
with influential monarchist staff generals such as Vigón and Martínez
Campos. He discouraged them from supporting Spanish entry into
the war, and painted a gloomy picture to German leaders in Berlin.
After talking with Canaris on November 2, General Halder wrote in
his diary: "Franco, who has nothing behind him and hence cannot
risk anything, is in a difficult position. This position will be weakened rather than strengthened through Serrano, who can be described
as the most hated man in Spain."[26] Stohrer, the German ambassador,
reported on December 9:

The opinions of several very influential generals have awakened in Franco
the fear that the personal and objective opposition between S. Súñer and
the military could lead the regime into acute danger, if the thoughts expressed by these generals against an early entrance into the war, especially
because of economic but also because of military problems, are not taken
into consideration. This attitude of the generals does not in any way mean
an unfriendly act toward us. The generals, for the most part, want war on
the side of Germany for the fulfillment of national aspirations. Their
criticism corresponds more with reality than does the notion which the
largely isolated Generalissimo and the Foreign Minister, struggling against
the military, seem previously to have had.[27]

The United States embassy reports during the same month also indicated deep division within the regime. Certain generals were said to
be intimating revolt, insisting that their forces were too weak for a
major war and would not fight under overall German command.[28]
    On February 6, 1941, Stohrer reported:

The scarcity of food [in Spain] will grow still more acute. Hunger revolts
are expected. As a consequence of this and because of simultaneously
rising unemployment, cases of highway robbery and banditry are increasing. Even the Army, too, is to some extent underfed and ill-clad. Because of that there is dissatisfaction in the barracks. It is feared that here
and there soldiers are making common cause with Communist bands and
others, and in this way are supplying them with weapons.
    The situation is today so tense that attempts to overthrow the govern-
ment are not out of the question. For the time being, however, a putsch
against Franco and the entire regime is less to be feared than an ultimatum
by the generals to Franco that he form a military government without
Serrano Súñer.[29]

After three and a half months, the tension had increased still
more. The German ambassador wrote on April 22, 1941:

In the conflict between Serrano Súñer and the generals, who are closing ranks more and more against him, the domestic political problem is now coming to a head.

Franco, isolated and undecided, can only with difficulty be moved to make decisions; he personally attends to many details, with respect to which he makes decisions that often contradict the policies approved by him in general. There is increasing criticism that Franco sees fewer and fewer people and does not allow himself to be advised even by old friends. Although he has found himself in opposition to the Foreign Minister, more than is known, through the postponement of unpleasant decisions and the failure to approve the plans and intentions of Serrano Súñer, he does, however, stubbornly stick by him since he cannot get along without the latter's keen mind. In this way, the antagonism between Franco and the military men, who are quite upset over the removal of deserving generals from their offices and are demanding the dismissal of Serrano Súñer, is assuming serious proportions. A coup d'état in the form of an ultimatum to Franco is possible at any time.

The generals are mostly friendly to the Germans (except, perhaps, for the present War Minister, Varela), mostly energetic, competent, aggressive, but not too well educated politically.

Too close relations with the military party have been avoided [by the German embassy], although indirect contact is being kept with it continuously.[30]

Stohrer's persistent references to the "military party" might be considered another example of the German penchant for abstractions, for no clear-cut "military party" actually existed. The only political motive uniting most of the generals was their common animosity against Serrano. Serrano may have favored Spanish entry into the war at a lower price than most of the generals were willing to settle for, and in the long run the generals were much more important to the regime than the Generalissimo's brother-in-law was. Though Franco was not so acutely aware of technical and economic problems as his staff officers were, he tended to agree with the generals' attitude. Hitler never found it feasible to pay the Generalissimo's price. By the spring of 1941, German planning concentrated on the forthcoming invasion of Russia, and a German-Spanish assault on Gibraltar began to seem remote and unimportant. Ironically enough, the swift, crushing Axis victory in the Balkans soon afterward raised Germany's stock in the eyes of the Spanish military, and they began to show more enthusiasm for Spain's participation in the war.[31]

The profound antipathy between Serrano and the Army hierarchy was perhaps not so much caused by the question of relations with Germany as by a basic resentment of his influence in and manipulation of the government. When the Generalissimo made his next Cabinet change in May 1941, he endeavored to mollify the military. Serrano's former post as Minister of the Interior, vacant for seven months, was filled by Colonel Valentín Galarza, who for nearly two years had served as Franco's personal Undersecretary for the Presidency in the Council of Ministers. Galarza was one of a number of monarchist officers who had often proved useful to Franco, and he had served as the latter's chief military liaison in Madrid during the conspiracy of 1936. He had recently been director of the Falangist militia, charged with the task of keeping it under military control, and his appointment to the Ministry of the Interior was very possibly calculated to reassure civilian and military conservatives. At the same time, the able pro-fascist Brigadier General Carlos Asensio was brought back from his post as High Commissioner of Morocco to replace Martínez Campos as Chief of the General Staff. Thus Franco maintained a balance between the pro-fascist and conservative elements in the Army.

The successful launching of the German invasion of Russia increased Madrid's desire to reach some kind of profitable understanding with Hitler. Serrano quickly announced the formation of a unit of Spanish volunteers to fight beside the Germans, a move which seemed to foreshadow Spain's official entry into the war. This was greeted with enthusiasm by some of the younger, more radical officers, but many of the senior generals were not convinced. On June 28, six days after the German attack against Russia began, Ambassador von Stohrer reported from Madrid that most Spanish generals wanted to enter the war, but only after the Spanish Army had been prepared militarily, which would be a laborious process. Because of this, General Juan Vigón, head of the Joint Chiefs of Staff (Alto Estado Mayor), had asked Stohrer to use his influence to help keep Spain out of the conflict for the time being.[32] Meanwhile, the "Blue Division," a Spanish unit of 20,000 men accompanied by aerial volunteers, was shipped to the eastern front. Almost all the members of the Blue Division were volunteers, and approximately 8,000 of them were Falangists. Their commander was Muñoz Grandes. In October, they were committed to a comparatively quiet sector of the front south of Leningrad.

When winter came, bringing the German failure before Moscow, the outlook changed once more. Franco was not so interested in entering the war as he had seemed to be during the excitement of July. The Army hierarchy's political uneasiness mounted. In another trip to Berlin during November 1941, Serrano Súñer complained once again about the influence of certain "seditious militarists" who were trying to thwart his pro-Axis policy.[33] The force of Russia's winter counteroffensive in 1942 only increased this influence. By the following spring, the monarchist generals had generated considerable support for a Bourbon restoration to regularize Spain's position. It was reported that they had even asked Muñoz Grandes to bring up the matter in Berlin and try to obtain German approval, or at least understanding.[34] The senior active monarchist general was Juan Vigón, Air Minister and head of the Joint Chiefs of Staff. He had always seemed fully loyal to Franco, but at this time the Generalissimo became so anxious about Vigón's possible activities vis-à-vis Berlin that he canceled an official visit to Germany that Vigón was to have made in June 1942.[35]

The special object of military enmity in internal politics was the Falange. Falangist attacks on Galarza in 1941 had been balanced by new Cabinet changes, and the generals resented what appeared to be the increased influence given the party. In December 1941, Falangist chiefs found it expedient to arrange several large demonstrations to exemplify what they called "the friendship which unites, for the good of the regime, the Army and the Party,"[36] but these had scant effect. In August 1942, while the German forces were driving to new victories in Russia, a serious incident occurred in the town of Begona in Vizcaya. The Minister of War, Varela, was attending an annual religious festivity in the local church when a bloody brawl erupted outside between Carlists and Falangists. Varela was one of the leading anti-Falangists in the government. Together with other generals, he demanded punishment of the Falangists involved, including national Falangist leaders accused of provoking the incident. One local Falangist was executed, but this did not satisfy the Army conservatives. Varela and Galarza seemed determined to use the incident to eliminate the remainder of Falangist influence. They sent a circular to the district Captain Generals throughout Spain, asking for their response to this "attack against the Army." In so doing, however, they overreached themselves. The Falange was still quite necessary to Franco's political balance. He was willing to give the Army guarantees against excessive Falangist influence, but he would not allow ultraconservative generals to eliminate the regime's fascistic political front altogether. Moreover, the sending of the circular was a political act for which Varela had not received approval from his commander in chief.

The result was Varela's political downfall. Heretofore he had seemed fully loyal to Franco, and it had even been rumored that he aspired to be the Caudillo's successor. In September both he and Galarza were dropped from the Cabinet. The strongly pro-fascist General Carlos Asensio was named as the new War Minister; it seemed that the Spanish government was drawing nearer the Axis.

However, Franco could not stop there: to have eliminated Varela and Galarza while bringing in a "Falange general" would have disrupted the domestic political equilibrium. In October, the generals won one of their main objectives: the dismissal of Serrano Súñer. He was replaced by the elderly and conservative Jordana. Blas Pérez, the new Minister of the Interior, was neither an officer nor a Falangist, but one of Franco's staunchest personal supporters. In this way, the political weight of the regime was once more balanced off.[37]

Coming when it did, at the time of the German stalemate at Stalingrad and only a few weeks before the Allied counteroffensive in Africa, this Cabinet shuffle was interpreted abroad as an opportunistic turn away from the Axis. In part that may have been true, but in general the changes were made to right the equilibrium of forces behind the regime. Though Varela and Galarza had made their own dismissal necessary, the military had still to be propitiated. Serrano's usefulness to Franco had, after five and a half years, come to an end. He had helped create a new civilian political synthesis behind the military dictatorship, but his ambitions and enthusiasms had come to have disruptive effects on this synthesis. The appointment of Jordana was certain to alter the direction of foreign policy somewhat, but even under Serrano the regime had always avoided the final step into the Axis camp. The change in the war after the end of 1942 made it inevitable that Franco would draw farther off, yet he was careful not to oppose Germany openly. To this end, it was Asensio, and not one of the conservative Anglophiles, who was entrusted with the War Ministry.

Excitement among monarchist elements was mounting. Rumors of an impending Anglo-American landing in northwest Africa encouraged some senior officers to think that the opportunity for restoration was near at hand. A few radicals, such as the Air Force colonel Juan Antonio Ansaldo, began to consider the feasibility of some kind of generals' coup against Franco, supported by the new Pretender Don Juan (third son of Alfonso XIII, who had eventually abdicated). After the Allied landing on November 8, Kindelán, currently Captain General of Catalonia, made a speech stressing the terms of corporate selection by which Franco had been named Generalissimo. To stop such speculation, Franco relieved Kindelán of command and sent him to temporary internal exile in the Canaries.[38]

During the winter and spring of 1943, Franco drew farther away from Germany. Muñoz Grandes, commander of the Blue Division in Russia, enjoyed very cordial relations with the Germans, who found him determined, hard-working, and cooperative, though he was said to have sent back rather pessimistic reports to Franco of German prospects on the eastern front. There were rumors in Madrid that the Caudillo was somewhat concerned about the closeness of relations between his old comrade and the German High Command. In December 1942, Muñoz Grandes was promoted to lieutenant general and ordered back to Spain, and his command was given to Major General Emilio Esteban Infantes, Sanjurjo's former aide. Several months later, Muñoz Grandes was appointed head of Franco's Military Household. During the first five months of 1943, he was used by the Generalissimo as unofficial contact with the German embassy to sound out the future course of German-Spanish relations should a change in the fortunes of war once more make closer cooperation advisable.[39]

Each passing month, however, made that alliance seem less likely, and reinforced a growing feeling that some sort of political change must come in Spain. In July, twenty-six prominent conservatives signed a petition asking Franco to restore the monarchy as soon as possible. Yet the only military leader who added his signature was Ponte, one of the least influential of the lieutenant generals.[40] By September, the situation seemed more serious, and after Italy had been knocked out of the war it appeared that the anticipated crisis could not be long delayed. Most of the lieutenant generals took counsel together, and on the 8th of September eight of them—Luis Orgaz, Fidel Dávila, José Enrique Varela, José Solchaga, Alfredo Kindelán, Andrés Saliquet, José Monasterio, and Miguel Ponte—signed a collective letter to the Caudillo, which was delivered personally by Varela a few days later. It read:

Excellency,
The high commanders of the Army are aware that it is the only organic reserve on which Spain can rely to subdue the grave crises that destiny may allot her in the near future. These authorities, wishing to give no excuse to enemies domestic or foreign by allowing them to think the Army's unity weakened or its discipline diminished, made certain that no subordinate ranks took part in the exchange of views to which patriotism obliged them. For that same reason, they employ the most discreet and respectful means to make known their concern to their only senior com-

mander in the Army, doing so with affectionate sincerity, in their own names, and without claiming the representation of the entire armed forces, which was neither requested nor granted.

They are companions in arms who come to share their worry and concern with him who has achieved by his toil and his own merit the highest rank in the Armies of Land, Sea, and Air, won in a difficult and victorious war; the same who . . . placed in your hands seven years ago in the Salamanca airdrome the supreme powers of military command and of the state.

On that occasion, the correctness of our decision was crowned with glory by complete and magnificent victory, and the exclusive act of will of certain generals was transformed into national agreement by the unanimous assent, tacit or enthusiastic, of the people, to such a degree that prolongation of the mandate beyond the term foreseen was legitimate.

We hope that the discretion which then accompanied us has not abandoned us today as we ask our Generalissimo, with all loyalty, respect, and affection, if he does not think, as do we, that the moment has arrived to give Spain back a regime as fondly remembered by himself as by us; one that can uphold the state with the bulwarks of unity, tradition, and prestige inherent in the monarchical formula. The hour seems propitious to delay no longer the restoration of this authentically Spanish form of government, which created the grandeur of Spain and from which she departed to imitate foreign models. The Army will unanimously support Your Excellency's decision and stand ready to repress any attempt at internal disturbance and opposition, either open or covert, without the slightest fear of the Communist menace . . . or of foreign interference.

This, Your Excellency, is the prayer that your old companions in arms and respectful subordinates address with the strictest discipline and most sincere loyalty to the Generalissimo of the Spanish armed forces and Chief of State.[41]

This made little impression on Franco, who knew that the lieutenant generals were in no position to act. He received each of the eight separately, and assured each in turn that he intended to restore the monarchy when the country's interests permitted him to do so, stressing that, were the king to be restored amid the uncertainties of war, the monarchy would be severely handicapped from the outset. Though it was not at all certain, Franco said, that Germany would lose the war (for he had been informed that Hitler had secret weapons in reserve), Spain was safe in any case, for he had obtained an official guarantee from the Allies that in the event of their victory, no action would be taken against the Spanish government. Flattered by his appeals to their caste pride and patriotism, and assured that Franco would respect the rights of the Army and keep its senior hierarchs informed of his major decisions, not one of the lieutenant generals had the courage to stand up to him. They ended by agreeing to abide by his judgment and, in effect, by ratifying his dictatorial powers.[42]

In the following month (October 1943), Franco found it expedient to dissolve the "Blue Division." As the 250th Division of the German forces, it had been located since October 10, 1941, in the Leningrad sector near the northern end of the Russian front. Counting reinforcements, a total of approximately 40,000 Spaniards served in Russia. The Blue Division casualties totaled more than 4,000 killed or captured and approximately 8,500 wounded. After the division was dissolved, some of its more ardent members volunteered for the international units of the Waffen SS, while others were reorganized into a battalion called the "Blue Legion." After further losses, this legion was dissolved in the spring of 1944, but some Spaniards continued to fight on the eastern front right down to the fall of Berlin.[43]

As German power crumbled, the future of the Franco regime looked ever more dim. Guerrilla bands from liberated France first crossed the Pyrenees in the autumn of 1944.[44] There was sometimes sharp fighting in these mountain clashes, which went on intermittently for two years and brought the concentration of the best units in the Spanish Army along the French border.[45]

The first efforts to introduce anti-fascist maquis in Spain had been encouraged by somewhat exaggerated reports that morale in the Spanish Army was disintegrating. It was true that morale was not of the best, owing to low salaries and the absence of genuine professional opportunity in the peacetime Spanish Army. The rank and file were still not well cared for, and the quality of equipment was deteriorating steadily. Just as in previous years, lack of funds and matériel made it impossible to train all units properly. Moreover, officers were being permitted, in fact almost encouraged, to take second and even third jobs in private business to supplement their income. This was feasible because the low level of professional activity left most officers with a great deal of free time. Such an irregular arrangement no doubt raised the standard of living of thousands of officers' families, but it underscored the fact that military leadership was only a part-time job in Spain. This tended to have a bad effect on professional spirit.

To a considerable degree, these drawbacks were counterbalanced by the special privileges provided the officers and, to some extent, the NCO's as well. The Officer Corps was exempt from a great many of the excise taxes paid by ordinary Spaniards. The commissaries provided abundant food and other goods at comparatively low prices at a time when many staple articles were nonexistent on the legal market. Many officers took advantage of this to resell large amounts of supplies at high prices on the black market. Moreover, further perquisites were available to the more influential generals in the form of lucrative posts on the boards of private firms; businessmen found that these appointments expedited their negotiations with government economic agencies. Furthermore, the leftist guerrilla action of 1944 and afterward had the effect of rallying most of the officers around the regime, and special benefits were made available to the units stationed in the northeast. A very few officers did establish clandestine contact with the leftist groups, but they were a tiny minority.

The military hierarchy was pleased by such measures as the dissolution of the Falangist militia in December 1943, but during 1944 there was a certain amount of murmuring and furtive talk about how the Spanish regime might be altered before the final defeat of Germany. It was not merely monarchists who were worried, for such figures as Serrano Súñer and Muñoz Grandes feared that their identification with Nazi Germany had badly compromised them, and toyed with the notion of trying to promote a political change in Spain before it was too late. This was idle speculation. None of the generals would act by himself, and an anti-Franco coalition was impossible. The winter and spring of 1945 came and went, leaving Franco the only signator of the Anti-Comintern Pact still in power in Europe.

Since the pro-monarchist generals had gotten nowhere in their attempt to bring about a restoration, some now thought that the easiest way out of the present regime might be to have Franco resign power to a junta of generals, since it was they who had named him in the first place. Kindelán, who had been rehabilitated in 1944 and made head of the Superior War School, openly suggested as much in the summer of 1945. It was at this juncture that Ernest Bevin, the Foreign Secretary of the new British Labor government, made a well-publicized speech stressing that the fate of the Spanish regime was up to the Spanish people. Its tenor was reassuring to Franco, for it indicated that, in accordance with Roosevelt's pledge of November 1942, the Western powers would not directly intervene in Spain.

The Generalissimo shuffled his Cabinet once more at the end of July 1945. Jordana had been killed in a hunting accident in August 1944, but he was not replaced by a general, for such appointments heightened the militarist or fascist image of the regime in the eyes of other countries. In the new Cabinet, military nominees were assigned to the three ministries of the armed forces only. Asensio was replaced as War Minister by the more conservative Dávila, and Major General Eduardo González Gallarza, the first Air Force officer to hold the post, took over as Air Minister from Vigón.

From 1944 to 1948, there was more active unrest in Spain than at any other time before or after in the history of the Franco regime. The defeat of European fascism gave temporary impetus to the domestic opposition. Other guerrilla bands, Communist[46] and non-Communist, tried to cross the Pyrenees, but much more numerous were the ordinary irregulars in Asturias and the mountains of Andalusia who had never been fully subdued. Groups even operated briefly in the Guadarramas, only thirty miles from Madrid. Some of the thousands of men involved were mere bandits, but the majority were political dissidents. Communists and others took to robbing banks in the larger towns to finance their operations.[47] At the height of the disorders, assassination of Civil Guards and Falangist leaders in the provinces was not uncommon. During the spring of 1946, reports indicated that two or more skirmishes a day were being fought with guerrillas in Andalusia.[48] The rate of action did not significantly diminish until 1949.[49]

Such pressures, together with the three years of diplomatic ostracism imposed on the Spanish government after 1945, tended to rally the Army round the Caudillo. Whenever it looked as though the Pretender, Don Juan, might be appealing to foreign opinion against Franco, the lieutenant generals moved away from monarchism and closer to their commander. Their hostility seems to have been an important factor in causing Don Juan to break off negotiations with the Spanish left in the autumn of 1947.[50]

Meanwhile, the outward liberalization of the regime was stepped up, bringing relaxation of the military court system. The new Penal Code of 1944 was a trifle more lenient than preceding regulations, while the promulgation of the *Fuero de los Españoles,* or Spanish Bill of Rights, and a subsequent decree of April 18, 1947, served technically to remove certain nonviolent "political crimes" from the purview of courts-martial, thus easing the restrictions of martial law under which Nationalist Spain had lived since 1936. Henceforth only political rebels theoretically connected with sabotage and guerrilla activities were to be subjected to the summary justice of Army judges.

After 1948, the situation of the regime improved markedly. A private loan was arranged with a New York bank, and with the intensification of the Cold War high hopes were entertained of the possibility of cutting Spain in on the American military and economic aid program. These developments were most pleasing to the Army hierarchy. The upswing in the regime's stock on the international market convinced the lieutenant generals that they had been right in backing

Franco all the way. Muñoz Grandes, who had been uncertain in 1943–44, staunchly agreed that there was no possible leader save Franco, who knew how to slide around every difficulty. The Generalissimo had already made it clear that the development of a set of "Fundamental Laws" to regularize the regime made no difference in the special status of the military. During a brief visit to Salazar in October 1949, Franco temporarily allowed the functions of Premier of the Council of Ministers to devolve upon the Army Minister, Dávila, thus making clear who was the most important Cabinet member.

From the point of view of organization and matériel, the Spanish Army was still in a deplorable state. As one general frankly confessed in later years, at the time the Second World War ended Spain found itself with "an antiquated Army."[51] Though the military had been receiving the lion's share of the budget since the close of the Civil War,[52] Spanish industry could produce little more than light artillery and submachine guns to chase guerrilla bands. There was no new heavy equipment to replace that which the Germans and Italians had sent prior to 1939. The equipment of the armored battalions,[53] the heavy artillery, and the Air Force was completely worn out or obsolete. The government voiced some hope that military expenditures might be increased in 1950, but significant expansion of the Army budget was not possible until two years later.[54]

By this time, the membership of the top military hierarchy was changing, for many of the senior generals of 1939 either were dead or had retired. Younger generals such as Juan Bautista Sánchez González and Rafael García Valiño were receiving more attention. Sánchez had ended the Civil War as a divisional commander, and in 1949 was made Captain General of Barcelona. He had always enjoyed a solid professional reputation and had never mixed much in politics. In Barcelona, however, he blossomed as a civic figure as well as a military leader, winning esteem as one of the few important generals sensitive and intelligent enough to gain insight into the Catalan problem. He showed considerable tolerance, and won the respect of business leaders and the civic and social elite in Catalonia. During the big strikes at Barcelona in the spring of 1951, he refused to employ armed intervention, and openly enjoyed the discomfiture of the regime's political appointees. This only increased his popularity in Catalonia, though it drew strong criticism from franquistas and Madrid bureaucrats.[55]

The most important of the generals, however, was no new figure. Muñoz Grandes had survived the vicissitudes of 1943–45 and had become one of Franco's most devoted and trusted supporters among the lieutenant generals. Unlike many of them, he was not involved in black market operations or other forms of financial corruption, and he held the respect of the lower ranks of the Army. When Franco reorganized his Cabinet in 1951, Muñoz Grandes replaced Dávila as Minister of War. Negotiations had already been broached for a military agreement with the United States, and to have held a command on the eastern front was now possibly more of an asset than a liability.

During 1952, the Army leaders were increasingly absorbed in the prospect of military renovation paid for and produced by the United States. As early as January 25, the Ministry of the Army was able to announce that Spanish small arms and artillery were being converted to accommodate American ammunition.[56] Reforms were planned to reduce the quantity and improve the quality of the Officer Corps, which was as bloated as it had been in the 1920's. There must have been at least 25,000 officers in service, most of them on the Reserve list but drawing regular salary. Since many officers were near the top of their age category, it was decided to lower the age limit for retirement by two years at every level. Another announcement on July 18 provided that Reserve officers might take full-time jobs in the civil service to make room for younger professionals.[57] It was hoped that these measures would affect nearly half the Officer Corps. They did not, however, achieve the desired results, and in June 1953 the Cabinet prepared another law on retirement, which was rubber-stamped by the Cortes on July 13. This affected the intermediate ranks of captain, major, and lieutenant colonel, and provided for the retirement with full pay and allowances of approximately 2,000 senior officers at these levels. It was rather like the Azaña bill of May 1931, save that it was not voluntary. By this process, the nominal size of the Army was reduced from 24 to 18 divisions, and the manpower to little more than 250,000. For actual military purposes, the regime scarcely needed this much.

In 1953, a ten-year military and economic treaty was signed between Spain and the United States that provided for the construction of several large SAC air bases in Spain and a new naval station at Rota in the south, all under joint Spanish and American command. The kind of economic terms that Hitler had refused in 1940–41 could now be more easily met by the United States, which undertook all the expenses involved and agreed to provide extensive assistance to the Spanish economy and armed forces. During the ten years of the original pact, the United States sent approximately one billion dollars in aid of all types to Spain. Military assistance amounted to some 350 million dollars during the five years it flowed most heavily, from 1954 to 1958. Of this, 40 per cent was devoted to the Air Force and 30 per cent each to the Army and Navy. The Spanish Air Force acquired its first jet fighters, and the acquisition of squadrons of heavy tanks made it possible to create an armored division. Nearly 5,000 young Spanish officers and NCO's received advance training in the United States during this period.[58]

During the mid-1950's, the major political concern of the military hierarchy was the dangerous situation developing in Morocco. For more than two decades following the final conquest in 1927, there had been no serious disturbances in the Spanish zone. During the Civil War, Franco and Beigbeder had distributed large bribes to venal native leaders and thus avoided political difficulties. During the Second World War and after, however, Franco showed greater ambitions in Africa. Temporarily ostracized by the Western powers, unable to exert any significant influence on Latin America, the Caudillo had leaned heavily on the "special relation" of Spain to the Arab world that he had once stressed to Moroccan volunteers during the Civil War. This eventually paid off in the form of Arab votes for Spain's entry into the United Nations, but its consequences in Spanish Morocco proved less felicitous.

The last High Commissioner, appointed in 1951, was Lieutenant General Rafael García Valiño, who had been Chief of Staff for eight years and was one of the most competent, hard-driving men in the Army. But Valiño was also known for his ambition and political adroitness, and this, together with gossip about his financial dealings, deprived him of the reputation enjoyed by Muñoz Grandes. In the Protectorate, he had the task of implementing a tricky policy aimed at encouraging the incipient Moroccan nationalist movement against the French, while bolstering the prestige of the Spanish regime as a friend of the Arab. For several years, García Valiño permitted refugees from the French zone to take refuge in the Riff and even organize forays on the other side of the boundary. It has been said on good authority that some of the preparations for the Moroccan outburst of October 1955 were made in the Spanish zone.[59] The Spanish regime's policy was predicated on the assumption that the position of the French empire in northwest Africa was strong and that of the nationalist forces weak, so that Spain might reap diplomatic profit without greatly endangering its own sovereignty in northern Morocco.

Some Army leaders were not so sure of this. To many senior officers the question of Spanish sovereignty in northern Morocco was a matter of personal honor, just as it had been to their predecessors three decades earlier. They could not forget what it had cost the Army to conquer the zone and were not eager to see their interests threatened by a deceitful political stratagem. The events of 1955 began to bear out these misgivings, for before the end of that year the French decided to reverse their own policy. They announced that the Sultan would be allowed to return to Rabat, and that political reforms would be inaugurated and a native Moroccan government formed. Until this time, there had been only occasional mutterings among the Spanish Army officers, who lacked the energy or presence of mind to contest Franco's political decisions. Now the old africanistas were alarmed, and so was Franco. He announced in December that Morocco was not yet ready for independence. But things had now gone too far to be easily repressed, and a wave of strikes, demonstrations, and terrorist acts broke out in the Spanish zone.

If France really intended to grant independence to its zone of Morocco, the Spanish regime would have no choice but to follow suit. On January 10, 1956, Valiño held a diplomatic conference with French representatives to try to convince them to delay further concessions to the Moroccans, but the French rather enjoyed seeing the Spanish beaten at their own game. Spain quickly expanded the powers of the local Moroccan government in Tetuán and tried to separate it even more completely from the Sultan's administration in Rabat, but the native leaders in the Spanish zone rejected this stratagem. On January 14, Franco officially recognized the impending independence of a united Morocco.[60]

The following day, 50 Moorish Regulares deserted their battalion in Larache. On January 16 and 18, Spanish troops had to fire to disperse demonstrations among the Beni Ourriagli and neighboring kabyles. The French government soon signed the formal agreement for Morocco's independence, and excitement in the Spanish zone mounted. Two days of rioting at Tetuán in early March required violent suppression, and Franco realized that he could not drag his feet much longer. The independence treaty for Morocco was signed at Madrid at the beginning of April.

Army dissatisfaction over the withdrawal from Morocco was compounded by recent domestic political developments, and there was more restlessness among senior officers in 1956 than at any time in the previous eleven years. Some of the generals said that the whole

Moroccan affair was a grave insult to national honor, while others merely resented the loss of special highly paid field assignments in Morocco. To assuage the injured pride of his officers, Franco tried to arrange for the incorporation of the Regulares and the employment of Spanish officers in the new Moroccan Army. Valiño offered five battalions of Regulares for the independence parade in Rabat on May 14, as well as a sizable number of Spanish technical advisers to provide future assistance. The Sultan and his counselors were not impressed by the offer; they rejected the military advisers, and only two battalions of Regulares were permitted to march in the parade. Valiño, accepting these snubs with the best grace he could muster, said after his return from Rabat that the parade had been "the high point" of his career as High Commissioner of Spanish Morocco.[61]

By the mid-1950's there were signs of renewed political discontent within Spain, and the military could not remain entirely passive amid mounting civic uncertainty. When the Conde de los Andes, personal representative of Don Juan, visited Barcelona on February 17, 1954, he was invited somewhat ostentatiously to a private conversation with Captain General Sánchez. Several months later, a private poll of the Madrid garrison showed a large majority in favor of the monarchist candidate in the limited municipal elections. During a meeting between Franco and Don Juan on December 29, 1954, the latter is reported to have said that he had recently received telegrams from four lieutenant generals who had never previously paid him homage.[62] Partly as a consequence, when the monarchist Chief of Staff Juan Vigón died in 1955, the anti-monarchist Asensio was named as his successor.

The next domestic crisis was touched off by events at the University of Madrid, where an incident among liberal, monarchist, and Falangist students on February 9, 1956, resulted in one Falangist militant's being gravely wounded.[63] Falangist fanatics wanted to seize this as an excuse to strike against the leading liberal intellectuals of Madrid, slaughtering them in a 1936-style night raid as revenge for the frustrations suffered by the Falange in recent years. The plot went so far that arms were distributed to a number of party activists. As word of this spread on the morning of February 10, and Franco did not intervene, the Army leadership reacted swiftly. Shortly after noon, the Caudillo was visited by Muñoz Grandes, Minister of the Army, Lt. Gen. Rodrigo, Captain General of Madrid, and Lt. Gen. Martínez Campos, official tutor of Prince Juan Carlos. In the name of the Army, they asked Franco what he planned to do. Showing his customary aversion to action, the dictator replied that he doubted that the Falangists would go through with their plans, and therefore he did not think it necessary to do anything. The generals declared that if any of the Falangists' intended victims were harmed, the Army would be forced to take over Madrid to restore order. This brought a prompt order from Franco for the arrest of the Falangist conspirators, which was carried out that very afternoon.[64]

The generals' initiative had not been directed against the regime at all, but against the threat posed by a handful of Falangist zealots. This affair forced a change in the leadership of the Falange, and Franco recalled the trusted José Luis de Arrese to the post of Secretary General. However, Arrese called a special national conference of Falangist leaders in the spring of 1956 to prepare a series of recommendations for the reorganization of both the party and the government. These were intended to block a "pure" monarchist restoration, slightly liberalize the regime, and establish a firm Falangist monopoly on political leadership.[65]

These developments coincided with the Spanish withdrawal from Morocco, and the Army's restlessness began to change from latent dissatisfaction and private murmuring to outspoken criticism. As a result, the independence of the Spanish Protectorate was accompanied by a new increase in military salaries. This increase became effective on the first of June,[66] but it was not enough to quiet the officers' resentment. Meanwhile, 149 conscript troops deserted the Spanish enclave of Ifni and took refuge with French authorities in Casablanca just before the French pulled out.[67]

All the while, concern over the proposed new Falangist statutes (*anteproyectos*) was mounting. A delegation of generals protested personally to Franco on July 1, 1956, even before the proposals had been formally completed. Versions of the finished statutes began to circulate in October and were denounced by civilian conservatives and church hierarchs as "totalitarian" and productive of a "politburo of pure oriental style." Moreover, Franco had apparently not yet abandoned his original Arab policy, for the official press followed a rabidly pro-Nasser line in opposition to the Anglo-French action at Suez. The generals feared that all this might eventually lead to the loss of the remaining Spanish enclaves in Morocco. Earlier in the year, a handful of officers had organized semi-clandestine "Juntas de Acción Patriótica" in the garrisons at Madrid, Barcelona, Seville, Valladolid, and

Valencia. They were plainly dissatisfied with the regime's handling of affairs in Africa, though it is not clear to what extent, if any, they opposed the arbitrary structure of the regime itself.[68] Since only a small fraction of the Officer Corps was involved in the Juntas, which seemed mainly to be grumbling societies, Franco took no formal note of them.[69] The diplomatic situation and the challenge of the anteproyectos, however, could no longer be allowed to drift. On December 16, 1956, Franco was visited by the American ambassador and Muñoz Grandes, in that order.[70] As a result, he changed course once more, and the press attacks on Britain and France ended two days later. Early in January 1957, both Muñoz Grandes and the Cardinal Primate informed Franco that the Falangist proposals were intolerable, and a few days later the Caudillo told Arrese to withdraw them.

Meanwhile, in mid-January, Barcelona was shut down for several days by strikes. During the repression that followed, the Archbishop of Tarragona and Barcelona's Captain General, Juan Bautista Sánchez, protested the police brutality. By this time, relations between the Caudillo and Sánchez were known to be bad. Sánchez had become one of the staunchest monarchists in the Army command, and made little secret of his disdain for Falangism and franquismo. When the first big strike wave had occurred in Barcelona six years earlier, Muñoz Grandes had warned Franco against adopting too complacent an attitude toward social disorder. It has been rumored that after receiving an earlier letter from Sánchez complaining about low Army pay, the Generalissimo had sent his Army Minister to Barcelona to inform Sánchez that he was being dismissed, but that the Captain General had threatened rebellion should Franco try to remove him. At this juncture, Sánchez died suddenly of a heart attack on his return from a long border inspection. There was great popular mourning at his funeral, and it was widely whispered that Franco had had him assassinated, but no proof of this has appeared.

Franco gave his ultimate answer to the malaise among the military with his Cabinet reorganization of February 1957. It was an almost complete victory for the Army, which obtained more direct influence in the government than at any time since 1939. Arrese was replaced as Secretary of the Falange, and an even tamer bureaucrat took his place. Muñoz Grandes stepped down as Army Minister, and was succeeded by Lt. Gen. Antonio Barroso, one of Franco's most trusted personal adherents.[71] Two new Cabinet posts, those of the Interior and Public Works, were given to generals. The former was occupied by Camilo Alonso Vega, another of the Caudillo's veteran colleagues, and the latter was given to the capable pro-monarchist Jorge Vigón,[72] while the post of Minister of Industry was filled by Joaquín Planell, a former officer. The Army now held nearly half the seats in the new Cabinet. Muñoz Grandes was raised to full Captain General, thus becoming the only military hierarch to hold the same rank as Franco.[73] This distinction made him a sort of watchdog over the Army as a whole.

The regime's previous Moroccan policy was revised. Military consultations were held with the French at Madrid in the spring of 1957, and the new Moroccan government was told that no concessions would be made on the remaining Spanish enclaves. In November 1957, Istiqlal activists crossed the border of Ifni to drive the Spanish out with a display of force. The garrison was, as usual, unprepared, and suffered unnecessary casualties, but reinforcements were rushed in. Fighting broke out in the Spanish Sahara in the middle of January 1958, and hostilities continued through the following month until new Spanish units, in cooperation with the French from Algeria, pacified both regions. The Ifni-Sahara buildup provided new colonial employment and higher pay for many of the officers retired from the Protectorate eighteen months earlier, and it may have hastened the dissolution of the Juntas de Acción Patriótica. The reassertion of Spain's military presence placated many, and the upgrading of Army influence in the Cabinet assuaged others.

Franco handled the military hierarchy with his customary prudence. The generals found that their interests were to be respected, and that was all they asked. For the majority of senior officers, the extensive economic perquisites—or outright corruption—inherent in the opportunities of their rank, combined with their prestige as members of the hierarchy and glorification as saviors of the Fatherland, sufficed. The main difficulty came from the *duros*—the super-patriots or super-professionals with specific ambitions—but the Caudillo also managed to manipulate these activists satisfactorily.

The great majority of officers of junior or middle rank were anxious to keep out of political disputes. By the late 1950's, they were becoming more and more professionally oriented. Given their low pay and marginal role in a middle-class society, they could be more easily aroused for negative than for positive issues, and especially to ward off anything that might be construed as a threat to their position. By and large, they accepted the nationalist propaganda of the regime

about the need for unity and strong control provided by a disciplined
Army.

Their problems were not political, but professional. After a quarter of a century of military-dominated dictatorship, Spain was still not
capable of supporting a fully modern, efficient, professional Army.
Below the rank of brigadier, officers' salaries were still not large
enough to enable them to support their families. Second jobs were
still more the rule than the exception for lieutenants and captains;
only thus could they stay afloat in the highly inflationary Spanish
economy of the 1950's. Graft flourished among the upper echelons as
it had in the past, and the Officer Corps continued to be a part-time
force with uncertain morale.

Technologically, the Spanish armed forces remained the better
part of one generation behind the armies of Russia and the rest of
the Western world. The resources of the most powerful government
that Spain had seen since the 1780's had been used to shore up an
oligarchic system rather than to reorient national energies to an efficient, productive, twentieth-century pattern. The improvements made
in the armed forces during the 1950's scarcely seem in any way to have
been due to the independent efforts of the Spanish government, but
rather were almost entirely the result of the massive shipments of
American aid and matériel.

It began to appear that it might not be possible for the regime to
rely upon the Army if corruption and inefficiency made it impossible
for the Officer Corps to find professional satisfaction. In 1958, the new
Minister of the Army, Lt. Gen. Barroso, proposed a drastic reform.
His plan was to reduce the manpower and organic size of the Army
by at least 25 per cent, but to upgrade sharply the quality and efficiency of what remained. The Officer Corps would be further pared
down and the total number of divisions cut from eighteen to twelve,
five of which would be thoroughly reorganized on the new "pentom-
ic" structure and might even be armed with tactical atomic weapons.
The catch was that by 1958 inflation, bolstered by the regime's expenditures, was bringing the government to the brink of bankruptcy.
Almost all the money for the proposed reorganization would have to
come from the United States, and to achieve this end Barroso made
a special trip to Washington in August 1958. He was only partially
successful, but altogether American military aid to Spain between
1953 and 1964 amounted to approximately $600 million and paid for
a high proportion of the Army's expenses during that period.

Much of the proposed reform was carried out between 1959 and 1961, and the unit structure was even further reduced in 1964. Atomic weapons were never obtained, however, and a great deal of the new equipment was lacking. The Officer Corps was not reduced proportionately, so that there still remained approximately 15,000 officers in service, as well as approximately the same number of full-time NCO's.[74] Yet total active manpower was reduced to less than 200,000, the smallest figure since 1936. In the 1960's, the average contingent of draftees varied between 100,000 and 150,000. The normal period of service was eighteen months, though volunteers served for two years.[75] There was still no effort to create a regular Reserve force aside from the sizable cadre of oficiales de complemento. Ordinary recruits were simply placed on a cadre list after being released, but there was no program for retraining them. Altogether, even the post-Barroso organizational structure represented an unsatisfactory compromise, and an even more drastic reform was announced at the beginning of 1966, which further reduced and reshaped the Spanish military organization to conform with contemporary technological requirements.

One of the paradoxes of the Franco regime was that a government which, in the final analysis, remained a military dictatorship had reduced the size and expense of the Army to a lower proportion of the national population and income than had many of the constitutional ministries of the past century.[76] It had drastically cut the imperialist commitments built up under the constitutional monarchy. The police forces were proportionately no larger, and were comparatively less expensive by 1958 than they had been under the Republic in 1936.[77]

The Barroso reforms and those that followed strongly encouraged the tendency of officers to concentrate on professional concerns and to avoid politics. More money was budgeted for maneuvers than formerly, and new barracks were built away from large cities to stress the military role of the Army and deemphasize the old function of urban garrison duty. Special attention was also paid to the NCO's. Since the beginning of the regime, a strong effort had been made to develop a unique sense of hierarchical identity among them. They enjoyed special housing and commissary privileges, so that they and their families might live together as a social and professional group, nearer the officers than the enlisted men.

The sense of corporate professional identity was strongly reinforced by the fact that the Officer Corps was becoming to a considerable degree a self-perpetuating elite. During the three years 1961–63, approximately 70 percent of the new officer candidates were sons of Army men. Of these, about two-thirds were the offspring of officers and approximately one-third the sons of NCO's and enlisted men. Though accurate statistics are not available for earlier generations, it would seem that a higher proportion of Army sons were entering the Officer Corps than ever before—certainly a greater percentage than in most other Western armies.

The constitutional governments of the liberal monarchy and the Republic had to call out the Army periodically to maintain order; the military dictatorship of Franco never resorted to such an extremity, for the latent threat sufficed.[78] Civil order was enforced by the police and the Civil Guard. The Guard's structure had been reorganized in 1940. All its officers were Army men, and the ordinary members enjoyed a status similar to that of the NCO's, with comparatively high wages and with housing privileges for their families.

By the early 1960's, the regime's only serious political problem stemmed from the sobering fact that the dictator had passed his seventieth birthday in 1962. This disquieting intimation of mortality induced even some of the more complacent to ponder the awesome legacy that might face the Generalissimo's successors. Franco made a minor concession to this problem in his next Cabinet shakeup in July 1962. For the first time since 1939, he appointed a vice-premier for the Council of Ministers—Muñoz Grandes. Since the beginning of the regime, 26 of the 67 Cabinet ministers appointed, or approximately 39 per cent, had been Army men.* The nomination of Muñoz Grandes was apparently intended to safeguard the special influence of the military.[79] On the other hand, Muñoz Grandes was only a year younger than the Caudillo, and had suffered intermittently from poor health for over a quarter of a century. Despite his moral ascendency within the Army, he was in no position to entertain further personal ambitions.

Occasional rumors of a "Military Directory" that might take

---

* Yet it should be noted that 15 of these 26 Army men have held the defense ministries. Only a comparatively small number of the non-defense ministries have been staffed by military men. Professor Juan J. Linz has classified the political identification of the various officers in Franco's Cabinets as follows: those with Falangist leanings, 3; those with Traditionalist leanings, 1; those with Acción Española or Opus Dei ties, 2; those with CEDA backgrounds, 2; those who were former office holders under Primo de Rivera, 2; those with no particular identification, 16. "An Authoritarian Regime: Spain," in Allardt and Littunen, pp. 291–341.

power from Franco to hasten the monarchy's restoration[80] held little substance, for only under circumstances of actual crisis could the lieutenant generals be expected to unite for independent political action. Franco took care to keep them divided by creating rivalries and counterbalancing appointments, or, in some cases, by permitting them to ruin by massive peculation whatever prestige they might otherwise have had. Though most of the senior generals claimed to be monarchists, the most active figures, such as Muñoz Grandes, García Valiño,* and Asensio, tended to be anti-monarchist. There was no central territorial command, for most of the existing manpower and matériel was divided among the district Captain Generalcies, which left central control the prerogative of the Army Ministry and the Generalissimo himself.

The prestige of the military in the country as a whole was not very high,[81] but the Army did serve to inculcate formal discipline in young Spanish men. During twenty-five years, more than two million recruits had passed through its ranks, imbibing at least a smattering of official ideology and some sense of hierarchy. Moreover, the Army also served to some extent in the education of peasant youth. As under the monarchy, illiterates often learned to read while in the Army,[82] and according to the Ministry a total of 46,561 troops received some kind of technical training, limited though it may have been, during 1962.[83]

That the Army continues to be the ultimate arbiter of public affairs in Spain was once more emphasized by both Franco and his Minister of Information in formal statements at the close of 1965. No matter how the dictatorship may eventually be terminated, Franco's Army has served him faithfully in this role. Created by the military in the first place, the dictatorship has relied upon the Army above all else in preserving its long life. No other military-based regime of the twentieth century has demonstrated such endurance.

---

* García Valiño was abruptly transferred to the Reserve in December 1964, apparently because of his political machinations.

The Basis of Military Power in Modern Spain

LITTLE SIMILARITY exists between the role played by the military in Spain's recent history and the functioning of the armies of most other European lands. The influence of the military leadership was extensive in a number of European countries, especially during the late nineteenth century, but such leadership was usually in the service of dynamic militarist goals. In Spain, on the other hand, there has been little European-style militarism. Its absence can be explained by a number of factors: scant concern for active nationalism, relative meagerness of imperial ambition, lack of involvement in the major strategic quarrels and economic interests of the continent, the failure of industrialization to take hold in Spain until the twentieth century was well advanced, and the somnolent, traditionalist state of Spanish culture. The only problems shared by Spain with some of the more militaristic countries were those of class struggle and internal disunity, which in Spain became so severe as to swallow up most other concerns.

In some ways, Spain's political-military experience can be fruit-fully compared with that of Latin America and a few of the emerging non-Western countries. These areas have in common the problem of building the foundations of national polity at a time when most Western states have already achieved consistency, and, secondarily, of representing the aspirations of new social groups not sufficiently organized or developed to do the job themselves. The fairly democratic sources of recruitment of the Spanish Army Officer Corps parallel those of the armed forces of some Latin American and Near Eastern lands but contrast with the situation in most European armies, at least during the nineteenth century.

Such comparisons, however, may be misleading. Spain is not a South American or Middle Eastern country, but a Western European land, albeit of a unique and marginal sort. Since 1812, Spanish leaders have attempted to build political structures similar to those of the more advanced Western countries. The same is true of Latin America, but perhaps the basic difference between the Spanish and Latin American experience in political-military affairs is that the Spanish Army, for all its inadequacies, has remained a fairly well disciplined, hierarchically organized force. It has never lapsed into the crude, uninstitutionalized, machete-wielding kind of caudillismo found in the armies of many Latin American countries during the early and middle nineteenth century. The institutional breakdown occurred in both regions at the same time and for largely the same reasons, but in the aftermath the mother country managed to regain at least minimal institutional cohesion based on the idea of monarchy and on a national army, though it had great difficulty achieving a viable new political structure. By contrast, in parts of Latin America there was little institutional cohesion of any kind during the first two or three generations after independence.

The institutional vacuum in both Spain and Spanish America—as in many non-Western lands later on—made it almost unavoidable that organized or unorganized force take the lead. During the "Era of Pronunciamientos" (1815–75), the Spanish Army to some extent played the role of what social scientists sometimes like to call a "modernizing elite." In this it went counter to the trend of military affairs in Europe during most of that period, yet its role was never so extensive as that of the military in some non-Western or even Spanish American lands in the twentieth century. Spanish social and economic groups were developed, if not to the point where they could successfully cope with the country's problems, at least to the extent that general institutional control did not of necessity devolve upon the military per se. The Spanish Era of Pronunciamientos coincided with the age of classical Western liberalism, which in most Western European countries was decidedly anti-militarist.

However, an Army that was usually considered politically "liberal" during the Era of Pronunciamientos has frequently been labeled "conservative," "reactionary," or "dictatorial" during the twentieth century. This loose categorization makes it appear that a profound change occurred in the political orientation of the Spanish Army. It may just as simply be contended, however, that the political orientation of the Spanish military changed comparatively little between the 1830's and the 1930's. What did change, incontestably, was the structure of Spanish society and the organizational forms and goals of the groups comprising a steadily expanding body politic. Insofar as one can generalize about the attitude of the officers as a whole, one can say that their concern has been directed toward patriotism, unity, and national progress, however vaguely or narrowly they may define such goals. The liberal cause—constitutional monarchy—was favored in the 1830's when the principal menace seemed to be a mixture of obscurantist authoritarianism and regionalist rebellion. To the military, the menace of the twentieth century has seemed to be national division, as represented by violent class struggle, liberal-oriented regional separatism, national impotence, dishonor in the face of new challenges that parliamentary politicians could not or would not face, and international leftist conspiracy.

It is natural and proper that a hierarchically organized national Army be concerned with sustaining discipline, order, and unity in the country which it serves, yet it is most unnatural that a military organization should presume to replace or control the structure of the state itself. At no time in the nineteenth century did Spanish Army leaders attempt to establish a military government. When finally the restored monarchy of 1875 began to develop a national polity of at least minimal viability, the activity of the military in political affairs was considerably reduced. The government's inability to cope with the Cuban problem precipitated the first step in the breakdown of the restoration arrangement. This breakdown was not completed until 1917. Had the country ever enjoyed a prolonged period of effective constitutional government, it would have been easier for Army leaders to have restrained themselves during the frustrations of 1917–23 and 1932–36. Since the early evolutionary period of constitutional government in Spain was so extraordinarily prolonged, difficult, and often ineffectual, it should not have been altogether unexpected that Army leaders would revert to past examples when faced with twentieth-century problems.

What was new about the Army revolts of 1923 and 1936 was their establishment of military dictatorships without parallel in the preceding century. This was a radical response to grave political and social pressures unknown in earlier generations. It was also encouraged by the emergence of modern totalitarian regimes of the left and right. The faltering effort of portions of the military to supplement or supplant civilian leadership between 1917 and 1930 was an almost complete failure and had a sobering effect on most officers. Nevertheless, the impasse into which Spanish political groups had maneuvered themselves by 1936 triggered a reaction more violent than anything the Army or the country had previously experienced. The greater severity of the 1936 reaction, though in no way justifiable, is not difficult to understand in view of the intensified pressures that developed under the Second Republic.

The Franco dictatorship resulting from the Civil War was a reversal of the general course of modern Spanish history, and was to a considerable degree dependent upon temporary conditions. Like some of the fundamental developments a century earlier—the dissolution of the old regime, the overthrow of the constitutional system of 1823, and the liberal victory of 1839–40—it was in large part the result of outside intervention. Without the fascist vogue in European affairs during the 1930's, the Franco regime would hardly have taken the form it assumed during its first eight or nine years. The continuation of the regime and its retention of at least minimal unity and coherence are also due in part to changes in the international situation favorable to its prolongation, as well as to the trauma of the Civil War and the civic apathy that has never been altogether overcome in Spanish society.

Franco has proved a more clever leader and manipulator of the military than most of the prime ministers and generals who preceded him, surpassing in this respect even Azaña and Primo de Rivera. Perhaps the basic reaction among the officers to the prolongation of the dictatorship was a general reversion to professionalism and apolitical feeling. This has paralleled the apolitical trend that has spread through Spanish society as a whole, leaving a political vacuum almost as serious as that of the nineteenth century. Because of this, and because the ultimate basis of power has remained military, there has been some concern among elements of the opposition to emulate their nineteenth-century predecessors by encouraging an anti-Franco coup among the military. Yet leftist critics, whose precursors bitterly condemned the Army's independent political initiative in 1936, have recognized the paradox that under an Army dictatorship the military have become relatively depoliticized and "lack an ideology of their own."[1] In the second half of the twentieth century, as during the preceding one hundred and fifty years, the role of the Spanish military remains dependent not upon the ambition of generals but upon the stability of government institutions and the civic maturity of Spanish society as a whole.

Biographical Sketch of Francisco Franco

FRANCISCO FRANCO was born in El Ferrol on December 4, 1892. He was the scion of an old naval family with early roots in Andalusia that had lived for two centuries in the Galician naval center. His mother's family had minor aristocratic connections, but his father was a paymaster in the Navy's supply system and the household was forced to live on a modest income. Since the elder Franco was something of a rebel and a profligate, the family often endured unnecessary hardship. Franco can hardly be said to have had a happy childhood, and he seemed relieved to escape home in 1907. His cherished hopes of becoming a naval officer were frustrated, for no vacancies were available in the Naval Academy, but his enrollment was arranged in the Infantry Academy at Toledo even though he was some six months under age. Records of his performance at the Academy are not available, but there is no indication that it was particularly distinguished.

Franco was commissioned as a second lieutenant in 1910 at the age of 17. Eighteen months later, the young officer volunteered for service in Morocco—the only path to an active career and rapid promotion. Even in his first skirmishes he showed courage, discipline, and determination. Though not reckless, Franco never shirked his place in the line of fire, and went through numerous encounters with scarcely a scratch. His self-control, pragmatic impersonal attitude, insistence upon order and hierarchy, courageous example, and resourcefulness made him a good platoon and company leader despite his youth. He was one of the few Spanish officers to try to deal seriously with maps, fortifications, and the technical preparation of armed columns. Instead of carousing with whores, cards, and wine, as was the wont of so many africanistas, Franco devoted himself entirely to his work. Though he survived his first four years of combat service unscathed, he was seriously wounded in the abdomen on June 29, 1916, while leading his troops against a rebel position. Despite a pessimistic prognosis, he made a fairly rapid recovery.

After a certain amount of haggling by the Army hierarchy because of his age, he was promoted to major before his twenty-fourth birthday. In 1917, he began a tour of domestic duty as commander of the Infantry brigade at the Oviedo garrison. He applied for admission to the Superior War School in order to supplement his incomplete technical knowledge, but was rejected on the ground that his rank was too high to permit him to register for the studies undertaken by most outstanding young officers of his age. Undismayed, Franco returned to Morocco to participate in organizing the Tercio. Sanjurjo, his commander at Melilla in 1921–22, twice recommended him for promotion to lieutenant colonel, but this proved impossible until after his thirtieth birthday.

Concerning Franco's preeminence among the hard-bitten Tercio members, Arturo Barea has paraphrased the remarks of a veteran Legionnaire as follows:

"You see, Franco.... No, look. The Tercio's rather like being in a penitentiary. The most courageous brute is master of the jail. And something of this sort has happened to that man. He's hated, just as the convicts hate the bravest killer in their jail, and he's obeyed and respected—he imposes himself on all the others —just as the big killer imposes himself on the whole jail. You know how many officers of the Legion have been killed by a shot in the back during an attack. Now, there are many who would wish to shoot Franco in the back, but not one of them has the courage to do it. They're afraid that he might turn his head and see them just when they have taken aim at him."

"But surely it is the same story with Millán Astray."

"Oh, no. One couldn't take a potshot at Millán Astray; he takes too good care of himself. But it wouldn't be difficult to fire at Franco. He takes the lead in an advance, and—well, if somebody's got guts, you just have to admit it. I've seen him walk upright in front of all the others, while they hardly dared to lift their heads from the ground, the bullets fell so thick. And who would shoot him in the back then? You just stay there with your mouth open, half hoping that the Moors'll get him any moment, and half afraid of it, because if they did, you would run away. There's another thing, too: he's much more intelligent than Millán Astray. He knows what he's after. And that's another reason why Millán Astray can't stand him."

"And how did he behave in Melilla?"

"Franco? Believe me, it's sticky going with Franco. You'll get whatever's due to you, and he knows where he's taking you, but as to the treatment you get.... He simply looks blankly at a fellow, with very big and very serious eyes, and says, 'Execute him,' and walks away, just like that. I've seen murderers go white in the face because Franco had looked at them out of the corner of his eye. And he's fussy! God save you if anything's missing from your equipment, or if your rifle isn't clean, or you've been lazy. You know, that man's not quite human and he hasn't got any nerves. And then, he's quite isolated. I believe all the officers detest him because he treats them just as he treats us and isn't friends with any of them. They go on the loose and get drunk—I ask you, what else should they do after two months in the firing line?—and he stays alone in the tent or in barracks, just like one of those old clerks who simply must go to the office, even on Sundays. It's difficult to make him out—it's funny, because he's still so young."*

* Barea, pp. 365–66. Reprinted with permission.

The only book that Franco ever wrote, his *Diario de una Bandera,* was published in 1922 while he was a major in the Tercio. Gossip had it that the Catalan journalist Juan Ferragut served as ghost-writer. There was a good deal of romantic rhetoric in it suitable to the topic, but there was also evidence of Franco's increasing concern for what might be called his "public image." He defended the *mérito* system of promotion as the only sure way of recognizing and improving quality, a view he had expressed in "El Mérito en compaña," a letter sent to the Spanish press in May 1921, during a renewal of the africanista-juntero controversy. Franco seemed to regard the disaster at Annual as evidence of a kind of moral failing, writing: "Let us examine our consciences, let us look at our lethargic virtues, and we will find the crisis in ideals that turned into defeat what ought to have been no more than a minor reverse."* Like most serious-minded officers, he wanted to see the Army supplied with the best and most modern weapons; he approved enthusiastically of the formation of the first squadron of armored cars in May 1922. Franco was no tactical innovator, but he laid great emphasis on the value of proper equipment and the importance of *saber manera* (know-how).†

The first official biography of Franco was by Arrarás. A dozen other eulogies have been published under the censorship of Franco's regime; the most useful are Valdesoto, and Galinsoga and Salgado.

The only attempt at a critical biography has been made by Luis Ramírez (pseud.). While thoroughly undocumented, this analysis is based on considerable investigation into Franco's personal background and family. The author presents a psychological portrait of the young Franco in which the individualistic traits peculiar to the Galician middle-class type, the frustrations of Franco's childhood, and the negative compensation mechanisms underlying the professional characteristics that made him famous are stressed.

* Francisco Franco, *Diario,* p. 191.
† *Ibid.,* p. 181.

Falangist and Carlist Losses, 1937–39

GENERAL OR OFFICIAL statistics on Nationalist losses are not available, save for one or two segments of the Army: for example, Aranda's Galician Corps, which, according to its commander, suffered approximately 30,000 casualties during the course of the conflict. The Excombatientes organization in Madrid collected the following figures on the Falangist and Carlist battalions that served in the Nationalist Army from the beginning of 1937 until the end of the war.

	Total enlistment	Dead	Wounded
Primera Centuria de Falange de Alava	455	101	310
Octava Compañía de Requetés de Alava	371	70	224
Tercio de la Virgen Blanca	1,446	223	437
Tercio de Nuestra Señora de Estíbaliz	516	38	26
Primera Bandera de Burgos (73rd Division)	630	63	315
Primera Bandera de Burgos (62nd Division)	1,400	137	685
Segunda Bandera de Burgos	1,900	181	955
Segunda Bandera de Castilla-Burgos	3,300	322	1,647
Tercera Bandera de Burgos	2,100	184	1,010
Quinta Bandera de Burgos	600	77	290
Sexta Bandera de Burgos	1,450	180	720
Séptima Bandera de Burgos	250	41	125
Bandera "General Mola"	1,000	102	495
Tercio de Santa Gadea	600	62	298
Tercio de Sangüesa-Burgos	600	68	292
Primera Bandera de Badajoz	1,384	24	103
Segunda Bandera de Badajoz	1,374	18	97
Tercera Bandera de Badajoz	1,202	48	236
Cuarta Bandera de Badajoz	1,342	6	59
Quinta Bandera de Badajoz	1,250	20	167
Primera Bandera de Cáceres	2,500	234	726
Segunda Bandera de Cáceres	1,500	19	69
Tercera Bandera de Cáceres	1,300	45	143
Cuarta Bandera de Cáceres	1,700	55	180
Quinta Bandera de Cáceres	1,000	112	348

	Total en-listment	Dead	Wounded
Primera Bandera de Cádiz	3,212	193	389
Segunda Bandera de Cádiz	2,500	19	8
Tercera Bandera de Cádiz	3,100	123	385
Cuarta Bandera de Cádiz	3,500	91	372
Primera Bandera de Castilla	1,095	188	896
Segunda Bandera de Castilla	537	40	117
Tercera Bandera de Castilla	1,504	101	328
Cuarta Bandera de Castilla	2,607	198	1,136
Quinta Bandera de Castilla	683	75	111
Sexta Bandera de Castilla	1,924	242	575
Séptima Bandera de Castilla	827	19	48
Octava Bandera de Castilla	2,320	35	94
Novena Bandera de Castilla	2,667	261	615
Décima Bandera de Castilla	2,743	287	731
Undécima Bandera de Castilla	1,056	15	48
Bandera "Girón"	735	97	147
Tercio "El Alcázar"	1,675	239	643
Tercio "Cristo Rey"	2,077	178	508
Grupo de Zapadores de FET	366	7	45
Primera Bandera de Cataluña	891	3	12
Tercio Monserrat	1,395	269	346
Primera Bandera de Córdoba	1,750	192	382
Segunda Bandera de Córdoba	850	30	119
Tercera Bandera de Córdoba	1,120	50	220
Cuarta Bandera de Córdoba	2,100	290	395
Quinta Bandera de Córdoba	1,450	2	—
Primera Bandera de Granada	2,000	56	70
Segunda Bandera de Granada	1,900	42	60
Tercera Bandera de Granada	2,100	22	31
Cuarta Bandera de Granada	1,800	6	17
Quinta Bandera de Granada	2,000	40	52
Sexta Bandera de Granada	2,000	29	41
Primera Bandera de Huelva	763	9	27
Segunda Bandera de Huelva	698	30	93
Tercera Bandera de Huelva	668	16	52
Cuarta Bandera de Huelva	640	5	23
Tercio "Virgen del Rocío"	801	47	142
Bandera "Virgen de la Cabeza"	916	12	—
Primera Bandera de León	2,800	225	483
Segunda Bandera de León	3,100	332	915
Tercera Bandera de León	2,600	213	681
Cuarta Bandera de León	1,500	76	160
Primera Bandera de Málaga	809	47	130
Segunda Bandera de Málaga	755	18	33
Tercera Bandera de Málaga	761	20	42
Primera Bandera de Las Palmas	384	18	27
Tercera Bandera de Las Palmas	726	14	33
Primera Bandera de Galicia	1,250	145	622
Tercera Bandera de Galicia	900	202	467
Primera Bandera de La Coruña	600	9	23

	Total enlistment	Dead	Wounded
Segunda Bandera de La Coruña	700	76	358
Bandera Legionaria Gallega	290	81	127
Tercio de Nuestra Señora de Valvanera	821	144	501
Bandera Legionaria de Lugo	770	25	15
Bandera de Marruecos	3,684	252	965
Bandera de Orense	2,030	90	230
Primera Bandera de Asturias	917	14	83
Segunda Bandera de Asturias	3,439	839	1,483
Tercera Bandera de Asturias	1,669	247	702
Cuarta Bandera de Asturias	892	46	126
Primera Bandera de Palencia	2,164	245	1,135
Segunda Bandera de Palencia	1,445	35	350
Tercera Bandera de Palencia	2,206	267	1,350
Cuarta Bandera de Palencia	2,106	235	1,254
Primera Bandera de Navarra	5,000	380	3,500
Segunda Bandera de Navarra	7,000	450	4,200
Tercera Bandera de Navarra	800	45	300
Cuarta Bandera de Navarra	3,000	170	1,500
Quinta Bandera de Navarra	6,200	280	3,500
Veintisiete Bandera de Navarra	600	40	120
Tercio de Abárzuza	800	120	300
Tercio de Lácar	12,000	720	7,500
Tercio de Montejurra	10,500	430	5,200
Tercio de Navarra	3,500	240	960
Tercio del Rey	600	40	170
Tercio de San Fermín	1,000	60	350
Tercio de San Miguel	6,300	370	3,800
Tercio de Santiago No. 8	600	30	120
Segunda Bandera de Pontevedra	1,050	9	25
Tercio de Oriamendi	1,505	170	610
Tercio de Nuestra Señora del Camino	2,050	188	845
Tercio de Radio-Teléfonos de Campaña	932	50	175
Primera Bandera de Tenerife	1,460	79	63
Segunda Bandera de Canarias	1,432	56	172
Primera Bandera de Sevilla	3,200	25	210
Segunda Bandera de Sevilla	4,000	81	315
Tercera Bandera de Sevilla	3,450	75	360
Cuarta Bandera de Sevilla	4,300	183	681
Quinta Bandera de Sevilla	3,600	59	304
Sexta Bandera de Sevilla	2,750	17	45
Séptima Bandera de Sevilla	3,700	43	259
Bandera de Soria	1,632	97	370
Primera Bandera de Valencia	1,320	34	102
Tercio de Nuestra Señora de Begoña	1,000	90	304
Primera Bandera de Vizcaya	2,122	64	189
Tercio de Ortiz de Zárate	1,829	66	248
Primera Bandera de Aragón	3,450	152	1,421
Segunda Bandera de Aragón	790	280	496
Tercera Bandera de Aragón	5,050	226	2,354
Cuarta Bandera de Aragón	1,970	68	822

	Total en-listment	Dead	Wounded
Quinta Bandera de Aragón	780	216	418
Sexta Bandera de Aragón	1,860	76	940
Séptima Bandera de Aragón	5,380	263	2,549
Octava Bandera de Aragón	2,050	94	1,136
Novena Bandera de Aragón	3,450	180	2,064
Segunda Bandera de Cruces Negras	677	24	30
	256,147	16,243	80,557

These figures are in some places only approximate, and several dozen units are not included, but they indicate that approximately 25 per cent of the total manpower mobilized by the Nationalist Army originally came from the civilian volunteer units, mainly Falangist and Carlist, and that these volunteers suffered perhaps 25 per cent of the battle casualties. The mortality rate among the volunteers themselves was about 6 per cent, with another 31 per cent wounded.

When these statistics are broken down into regions of recruitment, the proportions are the following:

Region	Per cent dead	Per cent wounded	Per cent of total volunteers	Per cent of total dead	Per cent of total wounded
Navarre	5.8	54.1	19.9	18.3	34.2
Andalusia	3.0	24.6	24.7	11.5	6.5
Castile	8.7	30.5	14.3	19.6	13.9
Aragon	6.3	49.2	9.7	9.6	15.1
Estremadura	4.6	16.3	4.6	3.3	2.4
Galicia	8.3	24.6	3.0	3.9	2.3
Asturias	16.6	34.6	2.7	7.1	3.0
Basque Provinces	4.1	13.4	2.4	1.6	1.0
Canaries	4.2	7.4	1.6	—	—
Spanish Morocco	6.8	26.2	1.4	1.6	1.2
Catalonia	11.9	15.7	.9	1.7	.4

(This tabulation was made by Prof. Juan J. Linz of Columbia University.)

For the Spanish Navy, Díaz de Villegas, p. 95, gives a total of 393 naval officers, 88 NCO's, and 582 sailors killed. Most of the losses among officers were due to the execution of rebels from ships that remained loyal to the Republic. A good many of the deaths among sailors were caused by the sinking of the cruiser *Baleares* in 1938.

Probably the most reliable figure is that of nearly 400 fatalities in the Condor Legion, given by Hauptmann H. H. Meyer in *Die Wehrmacht*. There are a great many discrepancies between reports of losses among the Italians. The fullest account of such losses by a Spaniard, Díaz-Retg's *Les Italiens dans la guerre d'Espagne*, suggests that approximately 50,000

Italians participated, suffering about 14,500 total casualties. Meyer gives 11,058 total Italian casualties, including 3,022 dead. Lower figures are given by official Italian publications, but seem open to greater doubt. The Italian Ministero della Guerra's *Volontari* provides separate Italian casualty figures for each campaign, all of which reach a total of only 1,604 dead and 5,229 wounded. Subsequently a more complete tabulation was published by Rispoli, p. 245, listing 3,252 Italians killed (of whom 178 were airmen), 11,424 wounded, and 225 missing. This agrees roughly with the earlier approximation by Díaz-Retg.

Other accounts of the Italian military involvement in Spain include: Amoroso, *Mortai e Lupi in Catalogna*; Bassi, *Da Cadice ai Pirenei*; Calandra, *Dove il Littorio chiama*; Mortari, *Con gli insorti*; Mosca, *Camiccie nere a Guadalajara*; Segala, *Trincee di Spagna*; Tocci, *Duelli aerei*.

Notes

Complete authors' names, titles, and publication data will be found in the Bibliography, pp. 537–61. The following abbreviations are used in the Notes: BOE, Boletín Oficial del Estado; BOJDN, Boletín Oficial de la Junta de Defensa Nacional; DOMG, Diario Oficial del Ministerio de la Guerra; DOMM, Diario Oficial del Ministerio de la Marina; DSC, Diario de las Sesiones de las Cortes.

Chapter One

1. See the unpublished dissertation by Stewart.
2. Soltó, pp. 25–62.
3. Quoted by Elliott, p. 306.
4. Colón, II, 72–148; Dézert, II, 214ff.
5. The organization of the Spanish Army in the eighteenth century is treated in Barado, *Museo*, II–III; Clonard, V–VI; Ballesteros, VI, 56–77; and Bourgoing, II, 75–113.
6. Oscariz, *Historia*.
7. See Nieto.
8. See Pérez de Guzmán.
9. The most thorough study is in Prieto Llovera.
10. Fernández San Román, pp. 287–88. There is an organizational list in "Sección de Historia Militar."

The bibliography of the War of Independence is extensive. Basic aids to the material in Spanish are Estado Mayor, *Colección*; Ministerio del Ejército; Almirante; Barado, *Literatura*. The two major Spanish accounts are Toreno and Gómez de Arteche. Lovett provides a good survey of political and military developments, and there is a brief general sketch in Priego López. On the major event of the war, the sieges of Zaragoza, see Alcaide Ibeca and Belmas.

11. Quoted as the caption to Equis, *El problema militar*, I.
12. Precise figures for the size of the Officer Corps throughout the nineteenth century are not available, but the number of generals—staffing an army that rarely numbered as many as 100,000 men in peacetime—was approximately as follows:

1792....277	1821....646	1829....522	1836....610
1797....435	1822....696	1830....547	1837....612
1816....835	1823....643	1831....513	1838....596
1817....799	1825....135	1832....591	1839....602
1818....781	1826....427	1833....569	1840....593
1819....801	1827....544	1834....543	1841....598
1820....736	1828....541	1835....593	1842....612

1843....584	1848....655	1853....669	1879....617
1844....647	1849....655	1854....657	1880....600
1845....645	1850....657	1863....550	1881....582
1846....621	1851....629	1872....500	1888....465
1847....637	1852....656	1877....607	

These figures are compiled from: López de Letona, pp. 181–82; Sanjuan, pp. 30–31; and Morote, *La moral,* pp. 17–18. Captain Generals are not included in most of these totals.

13. There is an account of these woes in the anonymous *Examen crítico,* I, 15–19. Cf. Marliani, p. 73.

14. Fernández de Córdova, *Memoria justificativa,* is the government commander's own explanation of his policy. It is criticized in Navarro García, *Obras,* II, 187–212. The problem of supply in the First Carlist War is discussed by Blázquez y Delgado, pp. 173–76. Some of the problems presented by these Carlist columns are shown in Rivero's documented *Manifesto.* The Madrid expedition is recounted from the Carlist side in Lichnowsky, pp. 124–46, and Sánchez, pp. 314–30. Peña e Ibáñez gives a general pro-Carlist account of all three Carlist wars.

15. Official figures at that time indicated twice as many troops, but contemporary accounts indicate the usual discrepancy between theory and reality.

16. Vallecillo provides a copious collection of almost all Spanish military legislation up to the mid-nineteenth century.

17. The first attempt to form a Spanish General Staff was made in 1801, but little or nothing was achieved. New plans were drawn up by Lt. Gen. Joaquín Blake in 1810. These were ignored after the War of Independence. The constitutional regime made a faint effort to develop a General Staff in 1822, but this was nullified the following year by Don Fernando. Under the pressure of the First Carlist War, a General Staff Corps was established in 1834. See Benavides Moro and Yaque, pp. 283–88, 301–22; Suárez Inclán; and Chamorro, which provides extensive material on the Staff members at mid-century.

18. Pavía, *El Ejército del Centro,* pp. 70–71.

19. The military budget during the nineteenth century is discussed to some extent in Blázquez.

20. In 1855, for example, privates drew about 150 pesetas per year, lieutenants 1,100, and major generals 10,500, according to Mezquiriz.

Ordinary farm laborers earned less than 500 pesetas per year, but skilled and semiskilled workers might easily earn 1,000 pesetas or more in Barcelona. In the 1950's, the ratio of a peasant laborer's wages to a lieutenant's salary remained about what it had been a hundred years earlier, but all skilled and semiskilled workers could earn a great deal more in direct income. Salary scales for the 1940's and 1950's are given in the notes for Chap. 22.

21. "Instrucciones sobre el Reclutamiento para Ultramar," Biblioteca Central Militar, doc. no. 4830. Cavalrymen, who were considered part of an elite shock force, were paid 10 to 20 per cent more than soldiers in other sections. Members of the Carabineros (border guards), many of whom were Army veterans, received even higher salaries, and the wages of the approximately 10,000 Civil Guards (see p. 24) were the highest of all. Ordinary Civil Guards—nearly all military veterans—received about five times as much as ordinary soldiers; their officers drew about 50 per cent more than regular Army officers.

22. During the eighteenth century, the government established or subsidized a number of new arms factories and put them under the general supervision of Artillery officers. In neither quantity nor quality did they begin to approach the

output of such enterprises in most Western countries. Cannon and rifles were produced mainly in northern Spain, at small factories whose productive capacity did not exceed 600 rifles per month during the First Carlist War. At that time, most of the Army's material was supplied by Britain. The arms industry is treated in Vigón, *Historia,* III, 511–23.

23. Occasionally the Army expanded beyond this figure, but the official lists were sometimes considerably exaggerated. For example, the 1866 *Cuadro de la composición y organización del Ejército español* gave the total manpower of the Army, including overseas units, supply employees, and 10,673 officers on active duty, as 207,281, whereas there were not many more than half that number of regular troops available.

24. "Reglamento para la organización, orden, y gobierno de la Reserva del Ejército," Biblioteca Central Militar, doc. no. 4943.

25. For example, a royal order of Aug. 3, 1863, transferred a small number of generals to the inactive list, and directed that generals who were unable to mount a horse, or were otherwise physically unfit to assume active command, be retired, but this order was never fully carried out. According to the anonymous but apparently well-informed *El Ejército,* there were active posts for only 222 of the 530 generals nominally on the active list in 1866.

26. The malaise of the Army in 1867 is discussed in Nervo, pp. 191–235.

27. Fernández de Córdova, *Mis Memorias,* III.

28. Quoted by Revesz, pp. 230–31.

29. Mendigorría, *La revolución,* and Sanchiz, *Expedición.* This and all other overseas expeditions of the period are treated in Esteban-Infantes, *Expediciones.* On the political issue, see Bona; Ferrer de Couto, *Reincorporación* and *La Cuestion*; Martin y Oliate; and Núñez.

At one time some 20,000 Spanish troops were serving in Santo Domingo. The only useful military studies of these operations are González Tablas, and Gándara, *Anexión.* According to Gándara's statistics, 486 Spanish troops were killed in skirmishes from August 1863 to June 1865, and 6,854 died of disease.

30. The *casus belli* was minor aggression by local Berber tribesmen in the environs of Ceuta. General Leopoldo O'Donnell, at that time Prime Minister and the dominant political general, took the field himself. During the last two months of 1859 he managed to move 40,000 troops into the Ceuta region. As Commander in Chief, O'Donnell showed himself cool, brave, and circumspect, but his strategy was slow and unimaginative. The Spanish troops were poor marksmen, unskillful at skirmishing and hampered by the broken character of the terrain; yet morale was high, and the recruits showed considerable bravery. Though frequently smaller in physique than their adversaries, the Spaniards were much better organized; and they excelled in bayonet charges, before which the irregular levies of the Sultan could not stand. The latter amounted to between 42,000 and 50,000 men, but lacked modern organization and equipment.

The main Spanish target was Tetuán, chief inland city of northern Morocco. Since there was no road, the twenty-one-mile advance from Ceuta required sixteen days. (Though there were many obstacles involved, this delay was mainly caused by the Army's lack of preparation.) Fortunately for the Spanish, Moroccan leaders tried to defend Tetuán in an ordinary pitched battle, which permitted the Spanish forces to employ coordinated tactics to maximum advantage. In a day-long fight, the Moors were totally routed and Tetuán was occupied. After one more engagement, O'Donnell realized that the Spanish could not press operations further without facing grave logistical problems. The Sultan also was eager for peace, and consequently a treaty was signed in May 1860. It gave Spain a hundred-million-peseta indemnity, as well as the right to occupy territory on the western coast of Morocco (Ifni) and to expand slightly the enclaves at Ceuta and Melilla. The text of the treaty is given in *Servicio Historico,* III, 105–9.

Over a period of six months, 70,000 Spanish troops served in Morocco. Of these, 2,121 were killed or died of wounds and 4,899 died of cholera—a total of 7,020 fatalities, according to the *Memoria,* p. 79. In Spain the popularity of the war was such that the Catalans formed an enthusiastic volunteer battalion that served as a shock unit and endured heavy losses without faltering. When he returned to Madrid, O'Donnell received the most rousing ovation accorded a Spanish leader in fifty years.

The official Spanish military history is in Estado Mayor, *Campañas,* I, 187–329. One of the most objective studies is Joly. Martín Arrúe attempts to refute Ametller. Friedrich Engels wrote an intelligent critique for the *New York Daily Tribune,* Jan. 10, Feb. 18, and Mar. 17, 1860, but Hardman, *The Spanish Campaign,* offers an eyewitness account. The principal literary memoir is Alarcón. Navarro y Rodrigo, *O'Donnell y la guerra,* and Mazade, pp. 205–59, may also be consulted. On the genesis of the enterprise, see Ruperto Aguirre, and Sevilla Andrés, *Africa,* pp. 79–80.

31. *La Gaceta Militar* (Madrid), Aug. 2, 1851.

32. The average life of these papers was approximately one year. An ephemeral newssheet was published by the Cádiz garrison in 1811, but the first regular Army paper was Evaristo San Miguel's ultraliberal *Gaceta Patriótica del Ejército Nacional,* of which some thirty numbers were published at Cádiz in the spring of 1820. A similar journal, *El Guerrero,* was printed briefly at Madrid in 1835, followed for a short period in 1841 by *El Grito del Ejército.* In 1842–43, leaders of the Progressive militia published *España Militar.* Eight other short-lived papers, with such names as *Archivo Militar, Boletín del Ejército,* and *El Militar Español,* appeared between 1841 and 1848.

In their political editorials, these newspapers usually endorsed the liberal position, especially in the early years; but as time went on there was a tendency toward greater conservatism, with considerable emphasis on order. It became more the custom to discuss professional military problems than to try to solve the entire country's political dilemmas. Because of the limited support behind these ventures, none lasted more than four years; but there was no slackening in new attempts. Seven more organs went into print between 1851 and 1858, and fifteen between 1859 and 1874. In 1862, *El Amigo del Soldádo,* which claimed to be the voice of the enlisted man, appeared briefly. The most durable, *El Mundo Militar* (1859–65), perhaps owed its longevity to the fact that it had comparatively less to say about Spanish politics, but made an effort to cover a variety of topics of broader interest. Scattered numbers of some of these papers are available in the Biblioteca Nacional and the Hereroteca Municipal of Madrid.

Chapter Two

1. Finer, in his excellent general analysis of military intervention in politics, has divided the modes of intervention into six categories: (1) normal constitutional channels; (2) collusion and/or competition with civil authorities; (3) intimidation of civil authorities; (4) threats of non-cooperation with or violence toward civilian authorities; (5) failure to defend the civilian authorities; (6) violence. All these modes could, of course, be found to some degree in the nineteenth-century Spanish

experience. Other useful comparative studies of military politics in the modern period include Huntington and Janowitz.

2. Moya and Rey Joly, p. 89.

3. There is a biography by Estasen, *El General Elío.*

4. On these events see Copons, pp. 61–118; Kindelán, *Ejército y política,* p. 156, and Izquierdo Hernández, pp. 725–71.

5. Quoted in Comellas, *Pronunciamientos,* p. 48.

6. The text of the decree is partially quoted in Pintos, p. 66. This study contains considerable material on the discontent and tensions within the Army, especially pp. 19–23 and 258–59.

In 1820, the leaders of the liberal revolt received extraordinary promotions. Moreover, the new Cortes awarded them large grants of money. See Carmen de Burgos, *Gloriosa vida y desdichada muerte de Don Rafael del Riego* (Madrid, 1931), p. 146. According to Elices, *El Gobierno,* p. 328, there were 1,427 special promotions after the successful 1843 rebellion, and 921 following the *vicalvarada* of 1854. General Francisco Serrano, victor at the battle of Alcolea, which broke the power of the Bourbon dynasty, published a general order on Sept. 29, 1868, detailing the special rewards and promotions for the various ranks of his troops. The text is in Vilarrasa and Gatell, II, 345–46. Within less than seven months, 1,635 special promotions were announced, according to *El Correo Militar,* May 24, 1869, cited in Hennessey, p. 45. See Bertrand, *El caballero Prim,* II, 258. Counting the extensive promotions made by the Isabeline regime during its closing months in an effort to ensure loyalty, Elices found that 2,032 promotions in advance of seniority were made in the Spanish Army during the year 1868.

The other side of the coin was the fate awaiting rebels who failed. Many got off surprisingly easy, but the era of pronunciamientos was dotted with the executions of men who did not succeed.

7. Vigón, *Historia,* II, 62.

8. The career of Juan Martín is treated in Hardman, *El Empecinado,* and Fernández Fernández, *El Empecinado.*

9. Espoz y Mina, the first of the outstanding liberal caudillos, wrote his own *Memorias.* "G." [sic], *D. Francisco Espoz y Mina,* is a contemporary biography. Mina's preparation in exile of a later revolt (1830) is the subject of Puyol's *La conspiración.*

10. Similar military conspiracies in France at that time are treated in Guillon.

11. The most extensive history of Spanish Masonry, though unsatisfactory and sometimes exaggerated, is given by Fuente. See Van Halen for an interesting account by a Masonic officer. See also Baroja's *Juan Van Halen.*

12. Comellas, *Pronunciamientos,* pp. 144–45.

13. The principal biographies of Riego are Astur (Enriqueta G. Infanzón); Nard and Pirala; and Burgos. On the motivation for the revolt, see Arzadún, pp. 121ff.

14. The major studies of this insurrection are Comellas, *Los Realistas;* Gambra; and Suárez Verdaguer. See Espinosa for a blow-by-blow account of antiguerrilla operations by the commander of one of the government columns.

15. The best account is by the brother of one of the leaders, Fernández de Córdova, *Mis Memorias,* I, 42–43.

16. The last regular Viceroy, General Joaquín de la Pezuela, was deposed by a rebellion of Army liberals. He wrote in his "Notas": "Accustomed to revolution in Spain, and to deposing their leaders and disobeying the king . . . they committed every kind of disorder. Dissolution, irreligion, and insubordination among commanders and officers were even greater than among the troops. Each one judged

himself capable of commanding an army and a kingdom.... Full of presumption, they murmured against the orders of the command and considered themselves dishonored if they did not win a promotion for the most ordinary service. There was one brigadier, Canterac, who expressed himself as being full of shame because at his age—he was 33—he held such a low rank. These and other conspirators— Valdés, Seoane, Loriga—deprived the commander in chief, Ramírez, of his command. Masonry, which was unknown in Lima and the high Andes, was propagated by those newly arrived from Spain." (Quoted in Rozalejo, pp. 24–25.)

The rebels have told their side of the story in Canterac et al., and in Valdés. See García Camba, II, and the discussion in Woodward.

17. The military, associated with the Revolution and the Empire, were also looked down upon during the Restoration period in France. See Girardet, pp. 7–47.

18. The massive purge of 1823 led to a wholesale Army emigration. It was estimated that military exiles accounted for the great majority of the approximately one thousand émigré Spanish families in London in the mid-1820's (Llorens, pp. 76–84). The principal study of the reaction is in Sarrailh, *La Contre-Révolution*.

19. Llauder, pp. 26–29. Inspector General of Infantry in 1825, Llauder says that he did everything possible to obtain the reinstatement of regular officers, in spite of pressure from the Volunteers.

20. Especially in the campaign of the French-born Conde de España against Catalan traditionalists in 1827. This commander was Captain General of Barcelona from 1827 to 1832, a period usually remembered as a reign of terror against liberals and reactionaries alike. Customary accounts are those given by Pirala, *Guerra civil*, I, 586; Carrera, II, 214–18; Castillo Mayone, *La Ciudadela inquisitorial*. Dissenting opinions are rendered by Fernández de Córdova, *Mis Memorias*, I, 120–22; Bermúdez, "El Teniente," pp. 19–26; and Oleza, *El primer Conde de España*.

21. Ruiz de Morales, pp. 365–75, 424–51; Montes, *Anales históricos*, p. 24.

22. Llauder, pp. 70ff; Bermejo, *Isabel II*, I, 53, 56–57; Sánchez Agesta, pp. 177–86; and Eggers and Feune, p. 133.

23. The details of this pronunciamiento have never been fully clarified. Various explanations are given in Miraflores, I, 211; San Miguel, *Observaciones*; Bermejo, *Isabel II*, I, 299; and *Examen crítico*, II, 129ff. The ideas of the most "advanced" sector of the Army during these years will be found in two other writings of San Miguel, *De la guerra* and *España*.

24. The average tenure in office of a Minister of War during the era of pronunciamientos was approximately two and a half months, as indicated in the following tabulation of appointees:

1814	3	1824	1	1834	2	1844	1	1854	4	1864	3
1815	5	1825	2	1835	8	1845	–	1855	1	1865	2
1816	–	1826	–	1836	7	1846	4	1856	4	1866	2
1817	1	1827	–	1837	9	1847	7	1857	1	1867	–
1818	–	1828	–	1838	9	1848	–	1858	2	1868	3
1819	1	1829	–	1839	1	1849	3	1859	1		
1820	6	1830	–	1840	7	1850	–	1860	–		
1821	5	1831	–	1841	3	1851	2	1861	–		
1822	4	1832	2	1842	2	1852	4	1862	2		
1823	5	1833	2	1843	7	1853	2	1863	2		

(From *Organización y Estado Militar de España*)

25. There is a fairly detailed account in González Llana, II, 332–44.

26. The text is in Bordas, pp. 358–60. *Vindicación del General Maroto* is an

account by the Carlist signator, Rafael Maroto. His role is studied in Gould. The struggles of the Carlist generals against the guerrilleros and *apostólicos* within their camp are treated in Oyarzun; Arizaga; Martínez Villergas, *Desenlace,* pp. 158–92; and Ferrer, *Historia de la última época.*

27. Though this quotation has been widely repeated, there are numerous versions of it and of the revolt. Among others, Fernández Cuesta, Paula, and Pérez, eds., *Causas Formadas;* Massa, pp. 254–75; Guzmán de Leon, I, 725–32; Vigón, *Historia,* III, 108; Bermúdez, *Militares,* p. 24. The rebellion in the Basque country that accompanied the unsuccessful pronunciamiento of 1841 is briefly described by Areilza.

28. According to Fernández de Córdova, *Mis Memorias,* III, 92.

29. Later, after the Moderate reaction, the image of Espartero was rehabilitated among Progressives. There are numerous biographies, mostly laudatory: Segundo, *Espartero;* Sociedad de Ex-Milicianos, *Vida militar;* Hidalgo, *Espartero;* Salmerón, *Historia;* Pirala, *La Regencia;* Nido, *Historia;* Romanones, *Espartero;* Espina, *Espartero;* and Marliani. Karl Marx wrote a trenchant critique of Espartero in the *New York Daily Tribune,* Aug. 19, 1854. Most recently there has appeared Moscardó Cervera's work. Correspondence between Progressive politicians and Espartero in his later years is printed in the Appendix to Olívar, *Isabel II.*

Political relations with Barcelona were of great importance during the climactic phases of Espartero's career. See Buxeres, *Barcelona.* See Antonio Van Halen, sometime Captain General of Catalonia, on the Barcelona revolt of December 1842, which preceded Espartero's downfall, *Diario razonado* and *Refutaciones.* For the rebels, there is *La revolución.*

30. Borrow, pp. 145–50; Bermejo, *Isabel II,* pp. 330–31; Ruiz de Morales, p. 423; Vigón, *Historia,* III, 108.

31. Narváez defended himself in a pamphlet, *Manifiesto en contestación.*

32. To preserve maximum security, this order was formed in secret triangles of three officers each from senior officers downward. Some 400 officers joined the organization in the garrisons of Catalonia alone, according to Sevilla, *Del 19 de marzo al 14 de abril,* p. 41. See Fernández de Córdova, *Mis Memorias,* III, 14–55.

33. Quoted by Bermúdez, *Militares,* p. 31.

34. Letter of May 28, 1845, to Fernández de Córdova: in *Mis Memorias,* III, 105. (Not that so draconian an expedient was employed.)

35. In 1843, Progressive politicians coaxed one of Espartero's principal lieutenants, General Martín Zurbano, into a hopeless and isolated rebellion. There is a eulogistic biography by Chao, *Historia de la vida.*

36. Tettamancy, *La Revolución gallega.* On the Second Carlist War, see Novaliches; Lord; and Oyarzun, pp. 267–78.

37. Diaz Valderrama, *Historia de la Guardia Civil;* Iglesia, *Reseña histórica;* and Ximénez, *Las instituciones.*

38. Quoted by Vigón, *Milicia y política,* pp. 265–66.

39. There is no adequate study of Narváez and his role in Spanish affairs. The least unsatisfactory work is the biography by Revesz, after which there is only Prados and Prados, *Narváez,* and the contemporary anonymous *Historia.* Martínez Villergas, *Paralelo,* is an amusingly invidious attempt to downgrade Narváez's military reputation by comparing him with Espartero. A much better account of the exploits of each of these caudillos in the First Carlist War is given by Chamorro, *Historia,* pp. 111–73, 193–212.

40. Bullón gives an extremely favorable treatment.

41. Quoted in Castell-Florite, pp. 298–99.

42. There are three contemporary accounts—Martos; Bermejo, *Alzamiento;*

Ribot—and one later work, Taxonera, *La revolución*. Apologias were published by three government generals who had been unable to contain the revolt: Gándara, *Manifesto*; Fernández de Córdova, *Memoria*; and Lara, *Aclaraciones*.

43. Montes, pp. 178–86.

44. There has been no adequate study of O'Donnell. Three contemporary works are Castillo, *Historia de la vida militar*; Ibo, *O'Donnell*; and Navarro y Rodrigo, *O'Donnell y su tiempo*. More recent is Melgar, *O'Donnell*.

45. The best biography is the two-volume work by Olívar. Also useful are Orellana, *Historia del General Prim*; Santovenia, *Prim*; Léonardon, *Prim*; and Miquel i Vergés, *El General Prim*. Among the lesser accounts are González Llanos, *Biografía política*; García de Luna, *Prim*; Bellido, *El General Prim*; Agramoent, *Prim*; and Poch, *Prim*. The most detailed treatment of the early part of his career is Giménez, *Historia militar*. Estrada, ed., *Don Juan Prim*, presents a documentary record of Prim's diplomacy in 1861–62.

46. Perhaps the best concentrated account of the San Gil mutiny is in Vigón, *Personaje*, pp. 111–30, 137–40.

47. The most extensive account of the battle is in Leiva, *La Batalla de Alcolea*. The entire range of the rebellion is surveyed in Vilarrasa and Gatell, *Historia de la revolución*; Rubio, *Historia filosófica*; Serrano and Pardo, *Anales*; González Tablas and Toral, *Diario*; and Lara, *Cronista*.

48. Powerful influences prevented a quick and thorough investigation, though during five years of intermittent investigation public prosecutors eventually collected an enormous mass of material. Available evidence indicates that the assassination had first been promoted by the personal aide of the Duc de Montpensier, son of Louis Philippe and brother-in-law of Isabel II, whom some had considered the chief candidate for the Spanish throne until he was frustrated by Prim. Execution of the deed, however, apparently owed much to the radical clique of the Cádiz Republican José Paúl y Angulo, who joined with political archenemies to murder Prim. The head of Serrano's personal escort was apparently also involved in recruiting assassins, but there is no evidence that either Serrano or Montpensier initiated, approved, or even knew of the plot. The most scholarly treatment is in Pedrol, *Los asesinos*. Paúl tried to establish his own innocence in his *Los asesinos del General Prim*.

49. Antonio Ballesteros wrote: "In our opinion, Don Juan Prim had greater ability than any other Spanish statesman of the nineteenth century. His personality stands out among the intellectual mediocrity of his fellow generals." *Historia de España*, VIII, 175.

Chapter Three

1. Consider these figures for the years 1861 through 1863:

	1861	*1862*	*1863*
Total available	135,000	141,000	144,000
Chosen by lot	101,000	97,000	113,000
Rejected for physical reasons	15,000	14,000	14,000
Below minimum height	18,000	17,000	17,000
Legally exempted or paid bounty	34,000	33,000	48,000
Actually drafted	34,000	34,000	35,000

The "legal exemptions" do not appear to have been consistently applied, since the total varied considerably from year to year. The problem of draft exemption is considered in Ayuso, *Abolición,* and in *Trabajos de la comisión de reorganización del Ejército.*

After 1868, debate concerning Army problems mounted rapidly in volume, reaching its climax in 1872–73. This can be followed in a long list of published works which includes Martínez Plowes, *Pensamientos* and *El Ejército;* Mata, *Proyecto;* Elices, *El progreso del Ejército;* Guzmán, *Abolición de quintas;* Milans, *Proyecto de una nueva organización del Ejército;* Morales y Gaspar, *Reorganización del Ejército;* Martínez Pérez, *Proyecto de organización militar;* Primo de Rivera y Sobremonte, *Pas economías;* Ruiz de Quevedo, *Abolición;* San Juan, *Los Ejércitos permanentes y de las quintas;* Pardo Saavedra, *Proyecto de organización del Ejército;* Peña, *Proyecto de ley de reorganización del Ejército;* Sánchez y Solórzano, *Incompatibilidad;* Pérez de la Sala, *Apuntes sobre la abolición de quintas;* Vidart, *La instrucción militar obligatoria;* and such anonymous booklets as *El Ejército permanente y la milicia nacional, Sobre los ejércitos permanentes, ¡Al Ejército!,* and *¡Abajo los Ejércitos permanentes!*

2. This is the judgment of Hennessey, p. 44.

3. *Ibid.,* p. 177.

4. *Ibid.,* p. 190. Total promotions for political reasons in 1873 amounted to 304, according to Elices, *Gobierno,* p. 328.

5. Hennessey, pp. 179–80; Pirala, *Historia contemporánea,* IV, 599–603; Mañé, 188–200.

6. The Carlists had been trying to develop a major revolt since 1869, but not until 1873 did they enjoy much success. Defections from the regular Army were comparatively few. In *Carlismo en Cataluña,* Bolos gives an account of Carlist conspiracy in Catalonia between 1869 and 1872, and includes a long manuscript by an anonymous general indicating that the Carlists were not able to attract many officers in that region. In a letter "to friends," May 20, 1872, Carlist General Rada claimed that the Carlist effort of 1872 would have been quite successful if "a fourth of the obligations undertaken by elements of the Army had been fulfilled" (Pirala, *Historia Contemporanea,* IV, 8–9).

By May 1873, there may have been as many as 60,000 Carlist volunteers under arms, more than at any time in the 1830's. On paper, the Spanish Army had slightly more than 100,000 troops in the peninsula, but 45,000 of them were new recruits. Reinforcements had to be sent to Cuba, most of the new manpower was still in training camps, garrison duty tied up tens of thousands, and other units had to be organized into flying columns to quell the Carlist bands that ranged far afield to the south and east. At first, this left only 20,000 to 25,000 for the Army of the North to use in the field against the main Carlist bases in the Basque country and Navarre. The Third Carlist War was thus in many ways similar to the first, with no quick or easy solution in sight.

The most complete account of military operations is Estado Mayor, *Narración.* Other useful works include Ruiz Dana, *Estudios* and *Estudio crítico;* Llave, *Apuntes;* and Botella, *La Guerra civil.*

7. After the dissolution of the Artillery Corps, its officers had set up a "Junta Directiva" of senior commanders. During the trying months of 1873, the Artillerists made a notable effort to avoid entanglement in party politics, and a letter of September 16 from the Junta explicitly rejected pro-Carlist overtures by a handful of officers. See Vigón, *Personaje,* pp. 151–75.

8. Fernández Almagro, *Historia,* I, 176. On August 5, the statutory size of the Civil Guard was increased nearly 50 per cent, to 30,000 men; and the 80,000 men listed in the territorial reserve were officially mobilized, though many were never actually made to serve.

9. Pavía has recounted this campaign in *La pacificación de Andalucía.*

10. He claimed, somewhat inconsistently, that his real reason for resigning was to protest having been forced to restore the death penalty for mutiny. Hennessey, pp. 223–24.

11. *La España Moderna,* June 1893, quoted in Fernández Almagro, *Historia,* I, 213–14.

12. According to Sánchez Agesta, p. 182.

13. Quoted by Romanones, *Obras,* II, 329.

14. These moves are traced in Hennessey, p. 239.

15. The principal sources are Pavía's own account in a subsequent Cortes speech of March 17, 1876, published as *Descripción,* and Houghton, pp. 3–9, 26–123.

16. There are two biographies of Serrano. His admirer Borrego provides greater detail, while Villa-Urrutia is more critical.

17. *El Ejército,* pp. 2–4.

18. The major study of Cánovas is Fernández Almagro, *Cánovas.*

19. Quoted by Lema, II, 636–40.

20. Vega Inclán, *La última campaña del Marqués del Duero,* is a detailed contemporary account.

21. Pavía, *El Ejército,* p. 12. In 1878, after the appearance of Pavía's book attacking the military administration of Serrano's government, General Serrano Bedoya, the Minister of War in 1874, hurriedly produced a pamphlet, *General en Jefe,* which insisted that the command had improvised with imagination and vigor. Pavía repeated his earlier charges in a counter-pamphlet, *Cuatro palabras.*

22. Rozalejo, pp. 257–58.

23. Compare Rafael Ceballos Escalera (who was quite close to the ultras) to his uncle, Jan. 3, 1875, in Rozalejo, pp. 261–69.

24. The only biography is Ibáñez Marín, *El General Martínez.*

25. Houghton, pp. 287–88.

26. Quoted in Ortega Rubio, I, 178–79.

27. After the reconstitution of their Corps, the Artillery immediately reestablished the strictest discipline and unity to be found in any section of the Army. Though the Artillery officers in the east refused to encourage Martínez Campos, their comrades in the Army of the North were active in helping to form a united front among the field officers to avoid internecine strife between different parts of the military. By making clear to Serrano that most officers did favor Don Alfonso, they helped bring the conflict to a bloodless resolution.

Houghton, one of the keenest observers of the Spanish Army during those years, wrote: "I have noticed how the Artillery officers hold their ground and support each other like an aristocratic, ultraroyalist oligarchy. . . . They know their history, their predecessors, their families. Their manner is cold, distinguished, reserved, almost haughty with the other Corps, always proper with their soldiers. They observe questions of etiquette and discipline with extreme rigor, and certainly from the viewpoint of preparation, tone, and studies, well bear comparison with all European armies. Their barracks and batteries in campaign are models of discipline, cleanliness and military organization. I have had occasion to follow them closely during two years of battle against the Carlists, and can testify that they have contributed greatly to the reestablishment of discipline and the successes of General Serrano against Don Carlos de Borbón."

28. Details of Serrano's effort to retain control are given in Bermejo, *Historia,* III, 1022–24.

29. Fernández Almagro, *Historia política,* I, 246. In a Senate debate five and a half years later, Cánovas and Martínez Campos aired the differences between them over the restoration pronunciamiento. *Sesiones del Senado,* June 11, 1880. See Lema, II, 674–773.

Chapter Four

1. Quoted in Naveros Burgos, p. 114. Similar orders were repeated in a circular to district Captain Generals on February 20, 1875. (Biblioteca no. 4988.)

2. One of the most stern-minded generals, Salamanca, made a detailed demand in the Cortes on April 5, 1876, for interpellation of the government regarding the exaggerated number of promotions during the past year. DSC, CLXXVII, pp. 638–39.

3. Ruiz Dana, *Estudios,* p. 9.

4. Martínez de Campos, *España bélica,* p. 270. Some indication of casualties during 1875 is given in Pérez y Martínez, *Estadística.*

5. Elices, pp. 321–22.

6. Biblioteca no. 4976.

7. Subsequent laws of 1883 and 1889 extended grounds for passing into the Reserve because of old wounds, ill health, or old age. By 1883, there were 173 generals in the Reserve.

8. In addition to the previously existing *Memorial de Ingenieros del Ejército* and *Memorial de Infantería,* between 1877 and 1890 four new professional journals were founded: *Revista Científica Militar, Memorial de Artillería, Revista Militar Española,* and *Revista Técnica de Infantería y Caballería.* After the turn of the century there followed the *Revista de Caballería* and the *Memorial de Caballería.*

9. For example, Moltó, *Apuntes;* González de Mesa, *Reorganización;* Salinas, *Exposición;* González Parrado, *Divagaciones;* and Moya, *La milicia.*

10. Piera and Santos, *Novísima ley.* Cf. Vallés, *Estudio.* To fill up the ranks from the lower classes, it was found necessary to lower the height requirement a trifle more, down to 1.54 meters, or a little over five feet.

11. Navarro Muñoz, pp. 29–42.

12. See Castro Girona, *Jovellar.*

13. Fernández Almagro gives Cánovas' point of view in his *Cánovas,* but deals more fully with Martínez Campos' attitude in his *Historia política,* II, 341–52.

14. Francos Rodríguez, *Canalejas,* 36–37; Sánchez Arjona, p. 27.

15. DSC, Jan. 6, 1883, p. 3329, quoted in Sevilla, *Canalejas,* pp. 137–38.

16. As Canalejas made clear in a speech at the Madrid Army Center in 1893. See *Concepto jurídico.*

17. Prieto y Villarreal, pp. 78–80.

18. Domínguez, *Los hombres.*

19. According to one of the ARM members, Muñoz, pp. 28–29.

20. Siffler-725 [Lt. Miguel Pérez], *Don Manuel Ruiz Zorrilla.* The author of this booklet was organizational secretary of the ARM.

21. Prieto y Villarreal, pp. 94–109; Muñoz, pp. 37–100.

22. *Ibid.,* pp. 127–28.

23. *Ibid.,* p. 133. Cf. García Ladevese, pp. 56–109, which in general seems somewhat less reliable on details.

24. Prieto y Villarreal, pp. 58–62, and Muñoz, pp. 136–78. "Siffler-725" pub-

lished the booklet previously cited to expose his former comrades after he had lost faith. The ARM in turn distributed a statement, "Al Ejército y al Pueblo," in denunciation of Siffler's treachery. The text of this statement is quoted in Fernández Almagro, *Historia política*, II, 575–76.

25. García Ladevese, pp. 125–44.

26. Gómez Chaix, pp. 143–45.

27. *Ibid.*, pp. 146–47.

28. The details are given in Casero, pp. 5–61, and in García Ladevese, pp. 43–47, 185–257.

29. Romanones, "Doña Maria Cristina," in *Obras,* I, 424–25.

30. Letter of Antonio Maura, Aug. 15, 1883, quoted in Maura Gamazo and Fernández, p. 402.

31. DSC, Nov. 19, 1886, IV, 1712.

32. Francos Rodríguez, *Regencia,* p. 105.

33. The full text of the proposal is in DSC, 1887, LXXII, App. 6.

34. Francos Rodríguez, p. 106.

35. *Ibid.*, pp. 147–48.

36. Ortega Rubio, I, 380–82; Fernández Almagro, *Historia política,* II, 40–60.

37. In personal correspondence, Cassola flatly denied such rumors. See Cassola to General Armiñán, Dec. 25, 1888, quoted in Armiñán, *Sánchez Guerra,* pp. 119–21.

38. Quoted in *El Ejército Español,* Jan. 16, 1889.

39. DSC, Jan. 19, 1889, 723–29.

40. DSC, Jan. 21, 1889, 754–60.

41. Romanones, "Sagasta," in *Obras,* I, 104.

42. Prieto y Villarreal, pp. 302–3.

43. Cf. Vigón, *Historia,* III, 147.

44. Cf. Suárez Inclán, p. 147.

45. The "peace budget" was bitterly criticized because it ruled out the purchase of new German Mausers for the Infantry. Cf. Navascués, ¡¡*La Proxima guerra!!* Contemporary studies of Spanish armament, such as Llave's *Estudio,* did not stress the gross inadequacy of the Army's firepower.

46. On the Reserve, see Sánchez Bravo, *Apuntes.*

47. See Alcázar, p. 148.

48. Quoted by Anson, p. 193.

49. *De por qué en España son tan largas las guerras.* These feelings were also reflected in the colonial garrisons. In far-off Manila an Army newspaper, *El Ejército de Filipinas,* featured articles with titles such as "The Army is Necessary for the Life and Progress of the People" (Feb. 18, 1892).

50. Weyler gave an account of his most controversial action in the last Carlist War in his *Memoria justificativa.*

51. See Retana, *Mando del General Weyler.*

52. On Spain's diplomacy in Africa during the years following 1860, see Becker, III, 121–34, 321–32, 641–54, 705–14, *passim;* Sevilla, *Africa,* pp. 131–246; Ibáñez de Ibero, *Política,* pp. 105–22; Cruickshank, which deals mainly with the Madrid conference of 1880; Taviel de Andrade; Mousset, pp. 96–104; García Figueras, *Africa,* pp. 140–41; and Hernández Pacheco and Cordero, *El Sahara español.* Cervera Baviera treats contemporary Morocco from the viewpoint of a Spanish officer.

53. Maura Gamazo, *Alfonso XIII,* I, 181–82. Cf. Cousiño, p. 43.

The command was understandably touchy about criticism. On October 9, 1893,

López Domínguez had instructed Margallo not to let newspaper reporters take any liberties with the Army. (Quoted in Ortega Rubio, II, 415–16.)

54. Fernández Almagro, *Historia política,* II, 220.

55. López Domínguez is quoted as writing in a letter of December 5: "What a pity that the Beni Sicar [a hostile local kabyle] did not predominate and give you a chance to do something, so that the army under your command would have sparkled!" And on the 28th: "You have done the impossible to get the enemy to offer some resistance, but it is clear that they do not want to fight, and although that is disappointing for the Army, you cannot strike someone who will not defend himself. I am losing all hope that we shall have a war." Ibáñez de Ibero, *Política,* p. 127.

56. *Ibid.*

57. The official Spanish military history of this operation is Estado Mayor, *Campañas,* I, 331–473, which states that altogether 44 Spaniards were killed and 206 wounded. There is a brief summary in García Figueras, *Marruecos,* pp. 93–97. Other accounts are in Morote, *Sagasta*; Llanos, *Melilla*; and Rodrigo, *La campaña de Melilla,* which is less technical than Llanos and more completely dominated by patriotic rhetoric.

58. Becker, III, 795–97; Ortega Rubio, II, 254.

59. The same sort of finagling and immobility that made Army reform impossible also prevailed in the Spanish Navy. For example, Isaac Peral's experimental submarine, completed in 1889, remained unperfected because of the obstructive tactics of the naval hierarchy.

Chapter Five

1. True to form, the slave interests spread a rumor that the Captain General was encouraging interracial marriage. See Estorch.

One of the most popular Captain Generals was José Gutiérrez de la Concha, Marqués de la Habana, who held command in 1850–52, 1854–59, and 1874–75. He fostered the oligarchy's economic interests, but also worked to diminish hostility between native Cubans and Spanish officials. Concha published two memoirs, *Memorias* and *La guerra.* For supplementary materials, see Ministerio de Ultramar, *Cuba desde 1850 a 1873.*

Since Spain's experience in Cuba during the later nineteenth century in some ways anticipated that of France in Indo-China and Algeria fifty years later, it is interesting to compare the socially "enlightened" attitudes of some Spanish commanders in Cuba with the roughly similar orientation of a good many of their French counterparts in Algeria during the 1950's.

2. Mola, pp. 933–34.

3. Pirala, *Anales,* I, 385. (Pirala had access to official sources.) The problem of garrisoning Cuba just before the revolt is discussed to some extent by Fernández Golfín, pp. 137–59.

4. Valeriano Weyler made some cogent recommendations about dealing with guerrilla warfare in a *memoria general* of Dec. 10, 1868, partially quoted in Pirala, *Anales,* I, 334–36. However, there were few other instances of tactical understanding among Spanish commanders.

5. The literature on the Ten Years' War is fairly extensive. In addition to the three-volume work by Pirala, which is perhaps the best and most complete nar-

rative, general accounts of the war or portions thereof include Soulère; Guerra; Llofriu; Sedano; García Verdugo; and Moya. Ribó, *Los voluntarios de Cuba,* is an extensive narrative that treats the early activities of the pro-Spanish Cuban auxiliary. For analyses by Spanish commanders, see Acosta and Salamanca. Peláez and Pieltain offer personal memoirs. The best account by a Spanish volunteer is in Escalera. The final phase under Martínez Campos is treated in Ochando, in Flores, and in Navarro Martín.

6. Official casualty figures for the Ten Years' War are not available. Labra has written, p. 165: "I have tried persistently to obtain total casualty figures for Cuba and the peninsula. The government does not have them."

General Jovellar, Colonial Minister from 1876 to 1878, later referred publicly to 140,000 lives lost in the Ten Years' War. The round number of 100,000 deaths has also been used, as in Pirala, *Anales,* VI, 117, and Navarro Muñoz, p. 84. However, Gallego obtained one government list that showed 3,660 Spanish troops killed in battle, but about sixteen times as many—54,754—dead of disease or wounds, with total fatalities amounting to 58,414. See *La insurrección,* p. 59.

7. See Rosell.

8. Salamanca's command is discussed in Gallego, *La insurrección,* pp. 85–125.

9. See Polavieja, *Relación.* Also see Polavieja's letter to his brother-in-law in Fernández Almagro, *Historia política,* II, 742–52.

10. In 1878, Martínez Campos had written to Cánovas from Havana that Christian, humanitarian, and political concerns alike counseled rapid emancipation of the slaves and autonomy for the island. Polavieja understood that Spain's main interest lay in preparing the island to stand alone as a healthy, independent nation capable of warding off the United States. This is stated in his letter to General Ramón Blanco, June 4, 1879 (Polavieja, pp. 32–40). See Fernández Almagro, *En torno,* p. 53.

In this connection it might be appropriate to recall the conciliatory attitude taken by some of the French Army leaders in Indo-China in 1945–46, which contrasted with the intransigent approach of the political leadership. See La Gorce, pp. 375–404.

11. There are several eulogistic Cuban biographies, such as Souza. One of the best Spanish accounts of the development of the revolt is in Gómez.

12. According to the account by Angel de Luque, editor of *El Resumen* during 1895, in *El Diario Universal,* Dec. 30, 1904.

13. *El Globo,* Mar. 18, 1895.

14. *La Correspondencia Militar,* Mar. 19, 1895.

15. Quoted by Tetuán, II, 114–17.

16. Sánchez Bravo, p. 26. This meant that the officer contingent serving in Cuba contained a larger percentage of men from the lower and lower middle classes than did the Officer Corps as a whole. (A study by Peter E. Razzell, cited in Janowitz, p. 56, shows that the British Indian Army had a greater proportion of officers from the middle class and lower class than did the British Home Army.)

17. There were a number of volunteer units with a long history of service under the Spanish flag. The record of one is given by Vesa.

18. Weyler, *Mi mando,* I, 23.

19. For example, early in November 1895 General Echagüe reported: "Antonio Maceo [one of the principal Cuban leaders] was carried away, along with a considerable number of wounded. The enemy forces were 3,000 infantry and more than 800 cavalry. Our column was composed of 1,300 infantry and 300 cavalry. The action lasted seven hours, but the vigor of our troops kept our losses to only

four wounded." This and similar exaggerations led to a circular by Martínez Campos on November 15: "I have seen with disgust that, paying no attention to my orders, commanders still exaggerate the reports of the most insignificant encounters, making brief skirmishes look like regular battles." He demanded accuracy in the future, especially with regard to statistics. (Quoted in Maura Gamazo, *Alfonso XIII*, I, 243.)

20. Nor did such criticism cease with Martínez Campos' recall. See the anonymous book by two Army officers, "A" and "B," *Apuntes*, pp. 38–39.

21. The recruitment law of 1885 altered regulations very little. Though López Domínguez had attempted in 1891 to restrict the practice of paying redemption bounties, there remained numerous exemptions, and *redención a metálica* might still be purchased for 1,500 to 2,000 pesetas, depending on the situation. *Leyes,* pp. 3–31; Alamo, pp. 3–20; Freixa, *Guia de quintas*; Lapoulide, p. 148.

22. On Dec. 27, 1895, Weyler wrote a letter to the editor of *El Mercantil Valenciano,* which had questioned his appointment to the Cuba command because of his reputation for cruelty. Said the general: "I support the idea that it is not necessary to be cruel or reactionary to exercise command with the energy that the salvation of the Fatherland demands on certain occasions, and that this is not opposed to that quality which the highest placed should always have—generosity." (Quoted in Fernández Almagro, *Historia política*, II, 274–75.)

There is no first-rate study of Weyler. Perhaps the least inadequate is Armiñán, *Weyler.* Two other highly favorable biographies, both based in large part on the General's own verbal reminiscences, are Romano, and Weyler y López.

23. One of the few attempts in the United States to right the balance was made by Rea.

24. This has been appreciatively noted by Millis, p. 60.

25. The Spanish garrison had been so shorthanded that, during the campaigns of 1891 and 1894–96, soldiers from the First Engineers Regiment had to be used as ordinary infantrymen. Gallego Ramos, *Zapadores,* pp. 110–11.

26. The problem was not beating the small, poorly armed insurgent bands in the field but rather destroying their base of operations and eliminating support among the native population. Blanco was defended by Serrano, the former rector of the University of Manila, in *Dos palabras.*

27. Fernando Primo de Rivera has given his account in *Memoria.* The military situation and its development are treated in Moya, *Monografía*; Gallego Ramos, *Operaciones*; Monteverde; Reverter; and Sastrón. Guerrero provides a lengthy chronicle of events in both sectors of the colonial war, written from an ultra-Spanish point of view.

28. From the figures published in 1899 by Dr. Angel Larrancerezo in the London medical publication *The Lancet,* and cited in Souza, pp. 271–72. Corral gives one of the best descriptions of the ordeal of the ordinary Spanish soldier.

29. One Spanish Army doctor found that, even if campaign casualties were excluded, the death rate in the Spanish Army was still twice as high as that in the Russian Army, which had the next poorest record. According to this computation, the annual death rate per thousand troops during the years 1886–98 was as follows: Spain, 10.93; Russia, 5.1; France, 4.9; Austria, 4.5; Italy, 4.3; Britain, 3.6; Holland, 3.5; and Germany, 1.5. González Deleito, *Apuntes,* p. 170.

One of the few improvements in Army health matters during these years was the lowering of the suicide rate. According to incomplete Spanish statistics, there had been from 98 to 248 suicides annually during the years 1858–61. But among a force of approximately equal size, such occurrences had been reduced to an average of 43 annually by 1885–87, at least among the peninsular troops, according to two articles by Con y Tres, Aug. 18–Sept. 8, 1892. If these figures are correct, they indicate a rate of suicide only about half as great as that in the French Army of the period.

30. Mola, p. 935.
31. See the impressions of Routier, *L'Espagne en 1897.*
32. Lerroux, *Memorias,* p. 516.
33. Cánovas' political dilemma is accurately described in May, pp. 104–9.
34. Quoted in Ferrer, et al., XXVIII, 216.
35. *La Epoca,* May 17, 1897.
36. DSC, May 21, 1897.
37. Romanones, *Obras,* I, 465–67.
38. Ortega Rubio, III, 171–77.
39. Weyler, *Mi mando,* V.
40. Fernández Almagro, *Historia política,* II, 434.

According to the *Anuario Militar,* the Army expanded during 1897 to an all-time high of 333,297 troops with approximately 23,000 officers. However, official works on Army organization published during those months, such as *La Organización militar* and the textbook by Ruiz Fornells and Melgar, reveal scant understanding of the problems posed by this mobilization.

41. See Romano, p. 143.
42. Melgar, *Don Carlos,* pp. 216–17. Carlist efforts at a military conspiracy within the peninsular garrisons during 1897–98 are treated in Ferrer, et al., XXVIII, 218–19.
43. See Piñeyro, pp. 163–64.
44. The diplomatic genesis of the Spanish-American War is extremely complicated and controversial. The fullest treatment of American diplomacy in this period is by May. Flack's was the first critical American study; Millis's book, cited earlier, remains the classic debunking account. The principal recent American studies are Morgan's *McKinley* and *Road to Empire,* and Offner's dissertation, which are all generally favorable to American policy. The only recent Spanish interpretation is Pabón's brief *El 98.*
45. See Francos' volume of vignettes, *El año.*
46. Martínez de Campos, *España bélica,* p. 356, says that there were 305 Spanish and 447 American casualties at the battle of El Caney–San Juan. There are interesting observations on the battle in Francisco y Díaz, *Nota bibliográfica.*
47. In Spain, a number of volumes were published on this disaster: Cervera, *Guerra hispano-americana;* Benítez, *El manuscrito;* Arderíus, *Santiago de Cuba;* Risco, *Apuntes biográficos;* and Concas, *La Escuadra del Almirante Cervera.* Corzo, *Cervera y su escuadra,* was published in Havana.

The first general Spanish account of the conflict with the United States was that of Urquía y Redecilla. Gómez Núñez, *La Guerra hispano-americana,* provides the most extensive Spanish narrative.

48. Fernández Almagro, *Historia política,* II, 564.

Chapter Six

1. *El Tiempo,* Aug. 16, 1898.
2. Quoted by Fernández Almagro, *Historia política,* II, 573.
3. *Ibid.,* II, 574; Ortega Rubio, IV, 84.

4. Fernández Almagro, *Historia política,* II, 627–28.

5. *Ibid.,* II, 630.

6. Maura Gamazo, II, 63ff. See Pabón, *Cambó,* pp. 181–82.

7. Published in book form by "El Capitán Verdades" (Juan de Urquía) as *Historia negra.*

8. The defense of the final commander in the Philippines, accused of dereliction of duty, was written by Salinas, in *Defensa.* García Alonso, *Defensa,* makes a case for the former commander of the central district of Luzon, who was also examined for failing to fulfill his responsibilities.

9. Quoted in Ortega Rubio, IV, 315–16.

10. *Ibid.,* IV, 316.

11. The military budget had hovered around 150 million pesetas annually during the two decades from 1876 to 1895, dropping temporarily to 115 million under the "peace budget." It went no higher than 177 million in 1898, because approximately 85 per cent of the wartime expenses were borne by an extraordinary budget that sent the national debt to an all-time high. The total cost of the colonial campaigns of 1895–98 was approximately 2,300,000,000 pesetas. The original figures published by the Colonial Ministry on February 10, 1899, were about 3 per cent higher than later figures compiled from the Ministry of Finance and quoted by Romanones in "Las responsabilidades," *Obras,* III, 531.

12. Quoted by Fernández Almagro, *Historia política,* II, 601.

13. DSC, July 15, 1899.

14. The *Anuario Militar* of 1900 listed 471 generals out of a total of 24,705 officers. The count of 110,926 NCO's and recruits includes early dismissals.

15. See Morote, *Sagasta,* p. 119.

16. It is interesting to compare the retirement ages in the German and Spanish armies in 1898–99:

	Spain	Germany		Spain	Germany
Lt. Gen.	72	63	Lt. Col.	60	52
Maj. Gen.	68	60	Major	56	48
Brig. Gen.	66	56	Captain	51	45
Colonel	62	54			

(From Romero Quiñones, pp. 60–61.)

17. See Vigón, *Historia,* III, 266.

18. One plan, Gallego Ramos' *Proyecto,* won a prize from the Madrid daily *El Imparcial* for the best new reorganization sketch. A similar effort was Peyra's *Organización.*

19. See Canella, p. 25.

20. According to Marvaud, p. 196.

21. In 1902, Weyler (then Minister of War) came out for a 25 per cent increase, bringing on an angry interpellation by the Cortes. DCS, November 26, 1902, IV, 1483–87.

22. In his dissertation, *La Tuberculosis,* Dr. González Deleito found that the incidence of tuberculosis was higher in the Spanish Army than in any other European force for which statistics were available. His earlier study, *Higiene social,* noted that the Spanish Army still had not set minimum weight and chest requirements. He concluded that the theoretical nutritional standards of the Tercios of 1600, by which each man was to have been provided with daily rations of two pounds of bread, one pound of meat, and a bottle of wine, were definitely superior to those of the Spanish Army of 1900. In general, these two works corroborate the previous study of Ovilo Canales.

23. As reflected in the autobiography of the supply administrator Amorós, *Biografía,* II.

24. As in a printed lecture by Escartín, *El Ejército en la acción política,* given on January 25, 1905.

25. *Ibid.*

26. Such as Martín y Peinador.

27. Fanjul, p. 10. A constructive feature of this booklet was that it explicitly rejected the self-commiseration to which many within and without the Army were prone, emphasizing instead that "it was the fault of the Spaniards themselves that Spain lost the war and with it all her possessions. . . . There is no doubt that the average citizen's shunning of the most elemental civic duties, as well as his personal egotism and lack of education and patriotic training have been the causes of our disaster, and it is similarly indubitable that all of us are guilty" (*ibid.,* p. 29).

28. This is recounted in one of the first biographies of Don Alfonso, Olmet and García, I, 110–12.

29. Quoted in *ibid.,* I, 212–13.

30. The marginal efforts at Army reform attempted by Weyler are mentioned in Weyler y López, pp. 190–97.

31. The principal source for these events is the memoir of Romanones, who was one of the ministers present. See his "Notas de una vida," in *Obras,* III, 149–50.

32. Fernández Almagro, *Don Alfonso XIII,* p. 18. This is the only serious political history of the reign.

33. Maura Gamazo and Fernández, p. 76.

34. This is mentioned in *El Ejército Español,* November 23, 1905.

35. For the general background, see García Venero, *Nacionalismo catalán,* pp. 251–53.

36. *La Correspondencia Militar* and *El Ejército Español,* November 27, 1905.

37. Fernández Almagro, *Alfonso XIII,* p. 79.

38. Romanones, *Obras,* III, 189–90; Maura and Fernández, pp. 90–91.

39. Olmedo and Cuesta, p. 92. Queipo, then a captain, was a member of this group.

40. Romanones, *Obras,* III, 191; Maura and Fernández, p. 92.

41. Letter to Antonio Maura, November 29, 1905, quoted in Maura and Fernández, pp. 91–92.

42. On the other hand, some of the supposedly Republican machinations of such officers were used in part for purposes of professional and political blackmail. The Portuguese poet Guerra Junqueiro has been quoted as saying: "It's curious. Every time I come to Madrid, I find that the new Minister of War is the general I met on my last visit to the house of Salmerón [the Republican leader]." Ciges, p. 400.

43. See Soldevilla. Fernández Almagro states that this account has never been challenged. See *Alfonso XIII,* pp. 85–86.

44. Fernández Almagro, *Alfonso XIII,* p. 87.

45. Sevilla, *Antonio Maura,* pp. 275–76.

46. Interesting statistics were collected in Larrea, pp. 13–14, 38. The official booklet *Datos relativos* is also useful for these years. The reduction of the Officer Corps by 5,000 between the years 1899 and 1906 was due mainly to the new provisions of 1900 and 1902 facilitating the premature retirement of Reserve officers. During the years 1900–1902, 4,503 of the latter voluntarily retired, though some were not much over 20 years of age. Sánchez Bravo, p. 58.

47. Blázquez, pp. 13, 18.

48. Marvaud, p. 198.

49. The *Anuario Militar* of 1908 listed 14,000 active officers—a considerable increase over recent years.

50. According to a very instructive series of 13 anonymous articles entitled "La Organización del Ejército español mirada por un prusiano," published by the *Revista Técnica de Infantería y Caballería* in 1910–11.

The author found in 1910 that for a minimum of 11,000 officers on active duty, there was a maximum of 115,000 troops; in Germany, less than 20,000 officers commanded 480,000 troops. In peacetime, the German Army required 16 years for promotion to captain by seniority; the Spanish Army, only 9 to 12 years. In Spain, 1,220 officers on the active list were used for routine sedentary functions such as the administration of arsenals, while in Germany these functions were handled by Reserve officers. In the Spanish Infantry, 66 per cent of the colonels, 31.5 per cent of the lieutenant colonels, 80 per cent of the majors, and 42 per cent of the captains were not in active command of troops; the ratio was approximately the same in the Cavalry. Yet junior officers had been promoted with so little seniority that in recent years 1,145 junior Reserve officers had had to be placed on the active list to fill assignments.

51. Blázquez, p. 20.

52. Further information on arms production at this time is given in Vigón, *Historia,* III, 299, 530–35.

53. Equis, p. iv. On p. 130, the author of this heated critique protested: "In a word, so long as the Artillery, Engineering, and General Staff Corps remain as they are [i.e., as entirely separate and isolated Corps, with their regulations distinct from the rest of the Army], Jesus Christ could descend once more to the earth expressly to improve the Spanish Army, and would fail absolutely in the attempt. So long as the problem of the transformation of these Corps is not solved [any effort at reform] will be useless—a thousand times useless—equivalent to throwing into the gutter all the money that the country spends on the Army."

54. A project encouraged by the Liberal Prime Minister of 1910–12, José Canalejas. See Olmet and García, *Canalejas,* p. 221.

55. Articles 267–70 of the *Ley de reclutamiento.* Under the new law an attempt was made to strengthen the Reserve by stipulating that thenceforth members of the First Reserve were to train one month a year; those of the Second Reserve twenty-one days; and those of the Territorial Reserve fifteen days. However, it was not clear that there were funds available to pay for such training.

56. Ministerio del Trabajo, p. xii. In addition, an average of 1.6 per cent of the total had to be released each year because of physical breakdown or incapacity.

57. The percentage of draft dodgers among the total of those liable to service between 1895 and 1914 was as follows:

1895	2.68%	1901	7.15%	1907	9.74%	1911	12.75%
1896	3.56	1902	7.21	1908	10.47	1912	18.92
1897	4.09	1903	7.23	1909	10.31	1913	20.76
1898	4.62	1904	11.92	1910	11.46	1914	22.09
1899	5.58	1905	10.48				

(From Servicio de Estadística, *Estadística de reclutamiento.*)

This figure dropped to an average of 17 per cent during the years 1917–20, according to Jevenois, p. 34.

During the peak years of draft dodging and desertion, the area with the highest annual proportion—approximately 59 per cent—was the Canary Islands. Then came the provinces of Oviedo, 41 per cent; La Coruña, 32 per cent; and Madrid, 29 per cent. Other provinces with a high rate of draft evasion were Málaga, Cádiz, and Almería. Catalonia was the region with the fewest evaders (12 per cent). Of the provinces, Segovia had the lowest rate (3 per cent).

58. The sources cited in the preceding notes give the following figures for draft selection between 1912 and 1920:

Year	Total available	Unfit and draft evaders	Those exempted	Draftees
1912	201,818	89,439	25,501	86,878
1913	217,411	78,923	28,943	109,545
1914	215,765	82,652	30,805	102,308
1915	210,997	75,662	29,554	105,781
1915	217,821	74,746	28,955	114,120
1917	228,520	75,534	29,482	123,504
1918	217,000	67,000	27,059	123,000
1919	209,000	61,000	26,106	122,000
1920	217,000	65,000	28,370	124,000

Given the large number of draft dodgers, exemptees, and redemptioners, it was difficult to find enough regular recruits who could come up to minimum health standards. The laws of 1911–12 specified a minimum height of 150 centimeters, a weight of 48 kilos, and a chest expansion of 75 centimeters; but in 1913 it was necessary to append a subsequent royal decree suppressing the weight requirement.

In 1912, the percentage of usable recruits (excluding the unfit, all those with exemptions, and draft dodgers) was only 43.05, and this fell to an average of only 36 per cent during the years 1915–17. A special committee was established in November 1917 to investigate the problem. Matters improved by 1920, when 57.09 per cent of the potential recruits were found usable. See Romanones, *Obras*, II, 390.

It was not necessarily contradictory that the highest proportion of usable recruits came from the separatist regions (Catalonia and the Basque provinces), for these were socially and economically the most progressive portions of the country.

Another aspect of the problem was revealed by literacy statistics. In 1912, 23.79 per cent of the recruits were classified as illiterate, whereas by 1920 the proportion was 28.12 per cent—an increase perhaps accounted for by more rigorous classification.

59. Romanones, *Obras*, II, 333–39.

Chapter Seven

1. Campoamor's *La actitud de España* and Klinger's dissertation, "Spain's Problem of Alliances," are scholarly studies. See also Reparaz, *Política*; Vidal, *La Politique de l'Espagne au Maroc*; García Figueras, *Marruecos*, pp. 99–112; Ibáñez de Ibero, *Política*, pp. 133–86; Anderson, *The First Moroccan Crisis*; Peyreigne, *Les Influences européennes au Maroc*. The text of the 1904 agreement is given in Hernández de Herrera and García, III, 118–25.

2. *Libro Rojo* (Spanish government "Red Book"), doc. no. 31.

3. See Olmet and García, *El General Marina*, pp. 100–101.

4. The only biography is Maldonado's sketchy *El Roghi*. For more information

see Arnaud, pp. 153–214, 269–85; Usborne, pp. 127–35; Ruiz Albéniz, *El Riff,* pp. 11–144, and *España en el Rif,* pp. 89–111. Official Spanish documents dealing with the Roghi episode are published in the *Libro Rojo.*

5. See García Figueras, *Marruecos,* pp. 116–18.

6. There is little evidence of military planning vis-à-vis Morocco. Publications on the topic were, in general, superficial patriotic booklets like Fernández Fernández, *Nuestros soldados en Africa.* There was occasional discussion of strategy to be used in case the doubtful possibility of a Pyrenean war with France materialized; some plans were made to ensure the defense of outlying regions. See Díaz Fernández, *Defensa de las Islas Canarias,* and the anonymous *Ejército territorial.*

7. According to Brissa, pp. 7–8.

8. The Conde de Romanones, one of the major investors in the Moroccan mines, stoutly denied that military action was undertaken to protect his personal interests, but admitted that such wide credence was given this rumor that even the peasants on his large Guadalajara estates believed that soldiers were dying to protect his profits. See *Obras,* II, 237.

9. Brissa, p. 18.

10. Quoted in Canals, I, 142.

11. Connelly's dissertation provides a thorough study of these events.

12. According to Canals, I, 137.

13. Mola, p. 936.

14. Ruiz Albéniz, for example, who was a close observer of these developments, wrote that the Spanish troops had lost 1,500 men by the end of the month. *España en el Rif,* p. 126.

15. The buildup of the Spanish effort in Morocco is narrated in detail in the Estado Mayor, *Campañas de Marruecos,* official history, II, 5–130.

16. *Ibid.,* II, 131–47.

17. Fernández Almagro, *Alfonso XIII,* p. 141.

18. See La Cierva, p. 146.

19. Estado Mayor, *Campañas,* II, 298. Complete lists of the units involved are given in the Estado Mayor's pamphlet, *Organización,* which shows that some 43,500 troops were in the Melilla area by the end of 1909. The roles of the Navy, Artillery, and Engineers are treated in *La Marina, Crónica,* and Marvá, *Ingenieros.*

The best critique of this campaign was written by the French General de Torcy. Gallego Ramos, *La campaña del Rif,* is a long, rather careful account that also includes the diplomatic antecedents of the campaign, but is deficient in critical analysis. A diary of the early action was prepared by two military professors, García Alvarez and García, *Operaciones,* while Riera, *España en Africa,* narrates the entire operation. López Alarcón, *Melilla, 1909,* and Urquijo, *La campaña del Rif,* are ultra-patriotic in tone. Further references are given in Hernández de Herrera and García, I, 65–88.

The Melilla campaign indicated that the medical services had improved little since the Cuban debacle. By the first months of 1910, nearly one-sixth of the troops in the Melilla zone were on the sick list. (Fernández Almagro, *Alfonso XIII,* p. 156.)

20. Ruiz Albéniz, *España en el Rif,* p. 148.

21. Estado Mayor, *Campañas de Marruecos,* II, 298.

22. Bueno, pp. 25–26.

23. According to Romanones, *Obras,* III, 206, the key meeting in the formation of the anti-Maura bloc was held at the home of López Domínguez. Luque, the most

active intriguer, was widely reported to have muttered in the Cortes: "I don't have the least bit of monarchist sympathy." (Quoted in Fernández Almagro, *Alfonso XIII*, p. 152.)

24. Luque mentioned the planning of this in his prologue to Goded, *Marruecos*, pp. 9–10.

25. When Luque entered Canalejas' Cabinet as War Minister in 1911, one deputy remarked: "The shadow of Pavía has passed through this chamber." Arrarás, *Cruzada*, I, 48.

26. The lengthiest account is in Calvo, pp. 29–65.

27. *Ibid.*, pp. 83–291, and García Figueras, *Marruecos*, pp. 119–23.

28. Estado Mayor, *Campaña del Rif*.

29. Organization of the native units is described in Luis Berenguer. On the history of native auxiliaries in Spanish service in Morocco and Algeria, see Arques and Gibert.

30. The operations of 1911–12 are discussed at length in Estado Mayor, *Campañas*, II, 378–566. See also Hernández de Herrera and García, I, 131–70; Calvo, pp. 293–561; and Arrarás, *Francisco Franco*, pp. 3–11.

31. García Figueras, *Marruecos*, pp. 139–43.

32. Cordero, I, 137–38, 144–48.

33. Forbes, p. 109. This volume, which is largely autobiographical, provides the best account of El Raisuli's career. López Rienda, *Raisuni*, and Ortega, *El Raisuni*, are also useful, but Bermudo-Soriano's *El Raisuni* is quite superficial.

34. Quoted in López Rienda, *Raisuni*, pp. 107–8, and in García Figueras, *Marruecos*, p. 158.

35. See Olmedo and Cuesta, pp. 44–48.

36. Military activities under Alfau's command are treated in Estado Mayor, *Campañas*, II, 683–732.

37. As in Gibert's pamphlet *España y Africa*. Some of the strongest support for an expansionist policy came from the authoritarian ultra-Right. One of the loudest spokesmen of this faction was the Carlist Juan Vázquez de Mella. See his *El problema*.

38. For example, Navarro García's *Estudios militares*.

39. The drastic disparity between French and Spanish accomplishment in Morocco was keenly felt by the more reflective. See González Hontoria, *El Protectorado*.

During the war, German agents were active in the Spanish zone, especially at Melilla, whence efforts were made to bribe Moorish leaders and stir up trouble for France farther south. See Harris, pp. 59–64.

40. The fullest account is in López Rienda, *Raisuni*, pp. 153–61.

41. *Ibid.*, p. 173.

42. One of the most active and independent-minded officers of senior rank, Col. Eduardo López de Ochoa, dashed off a letter to the king from Melilla at the beginning of 1918. He said that if war with Germany should develop he would request permission to lead the first regiment, and added that most officers in his command shared this spirit. López de Ochoa, *Dictadura*, pp. 86–88.

43. This paralleled the Italian inaction in Libya, where only the coastal enclaves were under European control by 1916. Italian conquest of the interior did not begin on a large scale until 1922.

44. López Rienda, *Raisuni*, p. 178.

45. *Ibid.*

46. See Estado Mayor, *Campañas de Marruecos*, II, 807–82. Much of Jordana's final lament is quoted in Hernández de Herrera and García Figueras, I, 244–50.

Chapter Eight

1. Quoted in Cortés, p. 157.
2. *La Correspondencia Militar,* Jan. 12, 1917. See Romanones, *Obras,* III, 343–45.
3. All officers received special supplements for overseas and combat duty. First-year recruits serving in Morocco had their pay raised from 50 to 180 pesetas per year. Under the 1912 law, all who reenlisted in Morocco were to receive not less than 720 pesetas. There were further increments for married soldiers, and for those who undertook to learn Arabic.
4. Sánchez Bravo, pp. 96–97.
5. Vigón, *Historia,* II, 135. A transitory "Junta de Defensa de Ingenieros" had also been formed in the Engineering Corps to protect the professional rights of Army engineers in competition with civilian engineers and architects. Kindelán, *Ejército y política,* p. 187.
6. The importance of the Serrallo standards in crystallizing resentment was mentioned in a circular of the subsequent Junta Superior of Infantry, published in *La Correspondencia Militar,* Oct. 22, 1917.
7. See Mola, pp. 998–1001.
8. According to the first head of the Barcelona Junta, Col. Benito Márquez, in a letter to José Ma. Capo, Oct. 15, 1922, in Márquez and Capo, pp. 5–11.
9. *Ibid.,* p. 24.
10. According to Romanones, *Obras,* III, 368–70.
11. See Pardo Gonzalez, p. 24. Generals were excluded from Junta membership because favoritism and maladministration at the top were among the junteros' chief grievances. Later on, Junta pronouncements tried to gloss over the reasons for this exclusion by claiming that generals were excluded because their rank placed them outside the framework of the various Corps.
12. According to Buxadé, p. 37, an attempt had been made to break up the Juntas several months earlier, when the Madrid generals became worried about efforts to form new Juntas in the capital's garrison. According to this version, Alfau had failed to comply with the earlier order for their dissolution.
13. There are interpretations in Mola, p. 1001, and in *ABC* (Madrid), June 1, 1917.
14. According to Márquez, p. 29, Alfau had asked him on May 24 to have the Juntas suppress the rule excluding generals, and acted only after they refused to do so.
15. The role of the Artillery is discussed in Vigón, *Historia,* III, 245–48.
16. Quoted in Lerroux, *Al servicio,* p. 106.
17. *Ibid.,* pp. 107–10.
18. Buxadé, pp. 58–59.
19. Márquez and Capo, pp. 36–37.
20. *Ibid.,* p. 38.
21. *Ibid.,* pp. 178–80. See also Buxadé, pp. 51–53.
22. Mola, p. 1011.
23. Quoted by Kindelán, *Ejército y política,* p. 191.
24. Quoted by Lerroux, *Al servicio,* pp. 120–21.
25. Quoted by Burgos y Mazo, *Páginas,* pp. 33–39.
26. In a volume of political commentary he published in 1917, the Socialist writer Luis Araquistain stated emphatically that "democracy is not anti-military." *Entre la guerra,* pp. 107–11.

27. The two letters are quoted in Mauro Gamazo and Fernández Almagro, pp. 303–4.

28. Quoted in Buxadé, pp. 98–113.

29. Gustavo Peyra to Maura, June 28, 1917, in Maura Gamazo and Fernández Almagro, pp. 485–86.

30. *Gaceta de Madrid,* July 2, 1917.

31. Lerroux, *Al servicio,* p. 118.

32. The resolutions are quoted in full in *ABC,* Oct. 20, 1917.

33. See Peyra to Maura, July 10, 1917, in Maura Gamazo and Fernández Almagro, pp. 488–89.

34. Márquez and Capo, pp. 203–5; Mola, pp. 1013–14.

35. Quoted in Carretero, p. 162.

36. Márquez and Capo, p. 66.

37. Quoted in Fernández Almagro, *Alfonso XIII,* p. 312.

38. Márquez and Capo, pp. 58–60. In his old age, the Republican leader Lerroux charged that in the summer of 1917 Márquez was "playing a double game, swollen with pride like an Atlas." (*Mis memorias,* p. 166.) This is doubtful. What may have appeared to be duplicity in Márquez was more likely naïveté and ineptness.

39. Burguete's declaration and a subsequent letter of explanation to Márquez are given in Márquez and Capo, pp. 196–200.

40. Quoted in Burgos y Mazo, *Páginas,* pp. 278–83. See also *ABC,* Oct. 20, 1917.

41. *El Heraldo Militar,* Oct. 24, 1917.

42. Miguel Primo de Rivera has been quoted as writing during the summer to a military colleague: "The political arm of the nation is totally corrupted and is the mortal enemy of our institution [the Army]." Márquez and Capo, p. 187. See also Lerroux, *Al servicio,* p. 118.

43. Quoted by Maura Gamazo and Fernández Almagro, p. 307.

44. Buxadé, p. 300.

45. The resolution was later printed in *ABC,* Oct. 20, 1917.

46. *ABC,* Sept. 28, 1917.

47. *ABC,* Oct. 21, 1917. *La Correspondencia Militar* was so well subsidized at this time that it was publishing five daily editions.

48. Márquez and Capo, pp. 216–23.

49. See Burgos y Mazo, *Antología,* pp. 150–55.

50. La Cierva, pp. 184–87.

51. *Ibid.,* pp. 188–92.

52. Sánchez Bravo, pp. 118–22; Pardo González, I, 43.

53. At the time of the last Cabinet crisis Márquez had emphasized: "The Army is no more than the arm of the nation, the executor of the decisions of the public power. The mission of the soldier is not to govern; it is to obey." *El Heraldo de Madrid,* Oct. 24, 1917.

54. Fernández Almagro, *Alfonso XIII,* p. 322. However, Mola, who was a *juntero* from 1917 to 1921, took a rather different view. See *Obras,* p. 1016.

55. Márquez insisted that he had not been expelled, but had resigned. Part of the La Cierva–Márquez correspondence is published in Márquez and Capo, pp. 241–54.

56. La Cierva, p. 196; Arrarás, *Cruzada,* I, 91. Some of these troops were later readmitted to service.

57. According to Salvador Canals, *Crónica de política interior,* cited in Fernández Almagro, *Alfonso XIII,* p. 324.

58. The new Cortes included:

Conservatives		Liberals	
Mauristas and Ciervistas	52	García Prieto	67
Other Regular Conservatives	97	Romanones	41
Independent Conservatives	2	Alba	29
	151	Alcalá Zamora	11
Extremists		Gasset	8
Republicans	18	Misc. Liberals	7
Carlists	9		163
Reformists	9	*Regionalists*	
Socialists	6	Catalans	22
Independents	7	Basques	7
	49	Other Regionalists	3
			32

59. After being forced out of the Infantry Junta Superior, Márquez distributed among several garrisons an open letter in his own defense that failed to produce any effect. Heavy pressure from other Junta leaders forced him to go into retirement. In a letter of March 10, he lamented that the Juntas had been taken over by "one man" (La Cierva) and were becoming the "shroud" of the Patria, rather than its savior. See *La Correspondencia Militar,* March 12, 1918.

60. Of a total of 1,640 delegates, 1,170 voted for continuation of the Juntas. Vigón, *Historia,* II, 168. See Pardo González, I, 44.

61. *El Ejército Español,* March 15, 1918.

62. *ABC,* March 17, 1918.

63. DSC (1918), V, 1848–56.

64. See La Cierva, p. 203.

65. The Classifying Junta was comprised of the chief of the General Staff and four lieutenant generals, and had the power to transfer to the Reserve any general who had seen ten per cent of those at higher rank promoted over his head.

66. This took the form of lectures at the military centers and articles in the military press. Several booklets were also published, such as Marvá, *El Ejército,* and Royo, *La Misión educativa.*

67. One of the loudest voices of anti-leftist alarmism was that of the aged Fernando Primo de Rivera. He wrote a number of articles in *La Correspondencia Militar* and *El Ejército Español* during the winter and spring of 1919, and was made the subject of an interview in *ABC.* These and other materials are found in the pamphlet *Continuación.*

He insisted that the current campaign of the CNT was aimed at social cataclysm, and that the leftists would end by trying to rape all the middle-class women (as he claimed had happened during the Andalusian peasant uprising of 1857). His solution to the social problem was expansion of the Civil Guard, creation of a larger section of rural guards to hold down the peasants, and the encouragement of a volunteer professional Army composed of disciplined patriotic recruits. He held that an Army based on universal conscription was too susceptible to demagogy. Similarly, Fernández de Rota, in ¡*Salvemos a España!,* insisted that only the regular Army could save Spain from leftist revolution.

68. *El Diario Universal,* March 29, 1919; Romanones, *Obras,* III, 386–87.

69. On the events in Barcelona, see Burgos y Mazo, *El verano*; Foix, *El archivo*; García Venero, *Internacionales,* II, 277–81.

70. Burgos y Mazo, *El verano,* p. 461.

71. See Fernández Almagro, *Alfonso XIII*, pp. 364–67.

72. The fullest account of this ministry is in Gallo, *Allendesalazar*.

73. Fernández Almagro, *Alfonso XIII*, p. 369; García Venero, *Internacionales*, II, 321–22.

74. For an interesting commentary by the Maurist writer Tejera, see *Los Parásitos*, pp. 26off.

Chapter Nine

1. During the years 1916–18, a total of 834 Spanish soldiers were killed or died of wounds in Morocco. This was the lowest figure for any comparable period in the Protectorate. See the table on p. 494.

2. Barrera tried to be more "political" in approach than his predecessor Silvestre had been. El Raisuli recommended his promotion to brigadier and his appointment to the Larache command (though the two men later fell out). There is a superficial sketch of Barrera in Martínez de la Riva, *La España*, p. 100. See also Gómez Hidalgo, p. 95.

3. Quoted in Gómez Hidalgo, pp. 93–107.

4. Alfarache, pp. 66–67, and García Figueras, *Marruecos*, pp. 167–68.

5. Berenguer, *La guerra en Marruecos*.

6. He wrote that success in Morocco might best be obtained by "employing against the Moors the most terrible weapons that can be wielded against those infidels—their own greed and inconstancies, jealousies and hatreds, rivalries and ambitions—which always leave them ready for treason and shameful agreements, and incapacitate them for unity behind their own cause." *Ibid.*, p. 7.

7. Quoted by Usborne, p. 245.

8. *Datos relativos*, 1919–20.

9. Beginning in 1919, volunteers were allowed to enlist for a single year of service.

10. Vigón, *Historia*, III, 177.

11. This was frequently mentioned by critics. One of the strongest denunciations is Azpeitua, *Marruecos, la mala semilla*.

12. See Barea, pp. 238–78. The middle section of this autobiography constitutes the most eloquent memoir ever written by a Spanish recruit in Morocco.

13. *Ibid.*, p. 284.

14. The only biography of the founder of the Tercio is Silva, *Millán Astray*. This may be compared with the sketch in Barea. Millán Astray wrote his own eulogy of the unit in *La Legión*, which is paralleled by Micó, *Los caballeros*.

15. These relations were first publicized in an informative article by Indalecio Prieto in *El Liberal* (Bilbao), Aug. 4, 1921, and quoted and commented upon in Gómez Hidalgo, pp. 156–75. See also Alfarache, pp. 54–56.

16. García Figueras, *Marruecos*, p. 173.

17. Berenguer's account of these operations, together with considerable documentation, is given in his *Campañas*, I.

18. Mola, pp. 936–37.

19. Gómez Hidalgo, p. 200.

20. Barea, p. 284.

21. Harris, pp. 113–14.

22. Eza, *Mis responsabilidades*.

23. Quoted in Gómez Hidalgo, pp. 193–99.

24. Quoted in Ruiz Albéniz, *Ecce homo*, pp. 173–92.

25. This is quoted in part by Ruiz Albéniz, *Tánger*, p. 18.

26. There is no thorough study of the career of Abd el-Krim. Roger-Mathieu, ed., *Abd el-Krim*, is often misleading. See also García Figueras, *Marruecos*, pp. 176–77, and Gabrielli, *Abd el-Krim*.

27. Vivero, p. 160.

28. Berenguer's account of these operations is in Campañas, II, 29–34, 50–65. One operation is described in detail by García Figueras in *Primera campaña*.

29. Berenguer, *Campañas*, II, 24.

30. See Bastos, pp. 91–115.

31. According to Vivero, p. 160.

32. *Ibid.*, p. 141.

33. *El Expediente Picasso*, p. 25.

34. Quoted in Vivero, pp. 85–90. On October 25, 1921, the former War Minister Vizconde de Eza read into the *Diario de las Sessiones de las Cortes* a message sent him by Silvestre on May 30, in which the latter recognized that his forces were weak and hardly sufficient for the objectives assigned to them.

35. *ABC*, June 5 and 7, 1921.

36. *El Expediente Picasso*, p. 11.

37. See Ruiz Albéniz, *Ecce homo*, p. 168.

38. Berenguer, *Campañas*, II, 41–42.

39. *El Expediente Picasso*, p. 36.

40. This is the figure for July 21, 1921, read by the Vizconde de Eza in the Cortes on Oct. 25, 1921. *DSC*, Oct. 25, 1921, pp. 3746–59.

41. Cited in Vivero, p. 112.

42. López Rienda, *Raisuni*, pp. 220–23.

43. Vivero, p. 159.

44. The king's wire read: "¡Olé los hombres! El 25 te espero." Fernández Almagro, *Alfonso XIII*, p. 385.

45. Berenguer later published his correspondence with Silvestre from July 15 to July 22, 1921, endeavoring to show that until July 21, Silvestre had not made clear how critical the situation was becoming. *Campañas*, II, 66–76, 238–45.

46. Informed estimates range from 3,000 to 3,500. See Vivero, p. 161; Ruiz Albéniz, *Ecce homo*, p. 356. However, some of the tribesmen were armed with contraband rifles superior in design to those used by the Spanish Infantry.

47. Bastos, pp. 141ff.

48. *El Expediente Picasso*, p. 93.

49. Berenguer, *Campañas*, II, 74–76.

50. *El Expediente Picasso*, p. 95. Ortega y Gasset gives a fairly good description of conditions in the ranks.

51. See *El Ejército y la Armada* (Madrid), Aug. 11, 1921.

52. See Note 40 above.

53. Berenguer, *Campañas*, II, 90.

54. According to Ruiz Albéniz, *Ecce homo*, p. 420.

55. According to La Cierva, p. 265. The Spanish Air Force dated from 1910. Its principal creator was a general of Engineers, Pedro Vives Vich. See Manzano, pp. 320–24. The first planes saw action in the operations at Melilla during 1912. A full squadron was formed at Tetuán in 1913 under Capt. Alfredo Kindelán, marking the second use of air power in modern military history. However, only modest advances were made in subsequent years, and it was not until after 1921 that serious expansion was attempted. There is a brief account of Air Force activity in Morocco during 1921–27 in Acedo, *Aviación*.

56. Fernández Almagro, *Alfonso XIII*, p. 396.
57. Vigon, *Historia*, II, p. 182.
58. Gómez Hidalgo, pp. 241, 115.
59. See Soriano, pp. 175–77.
60. See Goded, pp. 82ff.
61. Many of the Spanish prisoners were badly treated, and some were tortured or murdered. Much of this was beyond the control of Krim himself. In August the Riff leader had returned with full honors to the Spanish lines the corpse of Colonel Gabriel Morales of the Native Bureau, whose sincere, persistent labors had won the Berbers' respect.
62. Mola, p. 1018.
63. Quoted in Fernández Almagro, *Alfonso XIII*, p. 399. In turn, the junteros spread the rumor that Cabanellas was a rank incompetent who had been forced by certain political pressures in the Army to write the letter or face a court-martial for previous dereliction of duty.
64. According to La Cierva, pp. 267–70.
65. Berenguer to Maura, June 28, 1917, in Maura Gamazo and Fernández Almagro, pp. 479–81.
66. *Ibid.*, p. 356.
67. Fernández Almagro, *Alfonso XIII*, p. 412.
68. Maura Gamazo and Fernández Almagro, p. 356.
69. *Ibid.*
70. See La Cierva, pp. 255–56.
71. García Figueras, *Marruecos*, pp. 182–83.
72. Berenguer, *Campañas en el Rif y Yebala*, II, 176–77.
73. García Figueras, *Marruecos*, pp. 183–84.
74. *Ibid.*, p. 184.
75. As was admitted by the War Minister of that period. La Cierva, p. 287.
76. García Figueras, *Marruecos*, p. 184.
77. *El Expediente Picasso*, pp. 295–96.
78. Berenguer, *La guerra*, p. 155.
79. Berenguer's extensive remarks and other material on the campaign for "responsibilities" are given in Ayensa.
80. Fernández Almagro, *Alfonso XIII*, p. 409.
81. *Ibid.*, p. 402.
82. Hernández de Herrera and García Figueras, pp. 423–24.
83. See López Rienda, *Raisuni*, pp. 229–58.
84. García Figueras, *Marruecos*, p. 187.
85. López Rienda, *El escándalo*.
86. *El Expediente Picasso*, pp. 394–96.
87. See Tejera, p. 323.
88. Arrarás, *Cruzada*, I, 121.
89. Fernández Almagro, *Alfonso XIII*, p. 413.
90. According to López de Ochoa, who commanded the Barcelona Infantry garrison in 1922–23, Martínez Anido was terrified of the vengeance of anarchists. He fled the Catalan capital in disguise aboard a third-class railway coach, then hid for three months on a small island in the bay of Bigo. See *Dictadura*, p. 46. Oller Piñol, *Martínez Anido*, is the principal apologia.
91. See Hernández de Herrera and García Figueras, pp. 443–49.
92. Quoted in Hernández Mir, *Dictadura ante la historia*, pp. 28–29.
93. Gabrielli, pp. 48–52.

Chapter Ten

1. Fernández Almagro, *Alfonso XIII*, p. 421.
2. On Primo's background and personality, see Capella, *La verdad de Primo de Rivera*, and Cimadevilla, *El General Primo de Rivera*. A stimulating, though biased, sketch of Primo is given in Queipo, pp. 25–38.
3. A few of these speeches were published for wider distribution, for example his *Conferencia … 8 de marzo de 1919,* which discussed changes in military service and advocated a mixed system of recruiting, greater technical preparation for the regular Army, and, finally, the establishment of a huge territorial Reserve, the Somatén (an idea he was to repeat in 1923–24).
4. Gallo, p. 18.
5. Pardo González, I, 361.
6. See Pérez, *La Dictadura,* and Hernández Mir, *Dictadura ante la historia,* pp. 35–36.
7. Fernández Almagro, *Alfonso XIII*, p. 409.
8. Burgos y Mazo, *Dictadura,* I, 53. It had been rumored that dissident Liberals like Burgos y Mazo would be willing to collaborate in an Aguilera government in order to enact needed reforms.
9. According to Primo de Rivera, in the posthumous *La obra de la Dictadura,* pp. 8–15.
10. Quoted in Alfonso Reyes, p. 52.
11. Arrarás, *Cruzada,* I, 129; Fernández Almagro, *Alfonso XIII*.
12. See Hernández Mir, *Dictadura ante la historia,* pp. 30–31; Pardo González, I, 356–60. In the middle of 1923, "a group of captains" in the Barcelona garrison decided to form a little political organization called La Traza (The Project) which aspired to become, according to its first manifesto in July, "the patriotic union of all Spaniards of good will." Yet they apparently had little to do with Primo de Rivera's subsequent activities and did not directly identify themselves with his dictatorship. When Primo and the king returned from visiting Mussolini in November, they were greeted in Barcelona by Traza members wearing blue shirts. Within a few years, however, the little group had virtually dissolved. Castillo and Alvarez, pp. 115–17.
13. See *La Correspondencia Militar,* Aug. 25–Sept. 1, 1923.
14. See Hernández Mir, *Dictadura en Marruecos,* pp. 60–61.
15. Pardo González, I, 359–60.
16. López de Ochoa, *Dictadura,* pp. 26–27. García Venero, *Cataluña,* pp. 211–13, finds evidence only of a general understanding between Primo and Catalan leaders, but not of a firm agreement.
17. López de Ochoa, *Dictadura,* pp. 22–26. At some point during the summer, apparently during August, the king journeyed south to address a banquet of conservatives at Córdova. In after-dinner conversation, alarm was voiced over parliamentary opposition to certain patriotic projects. According to Federico Fernández Castillejo, who attended the banquet and mentioned the incident in his unpublished "La Segunda República Española," p. 19, the king declared, off the record, that no one need worry, for General Primo de Rivera was preparing a movement that would take care of the problem.
18. Maura Gamazo, *Bosquejo,* pp. 28ff.
19. Hernández Mir, *Dictadura en Marruecos,* pp. 13–14; Pardo González, I, 117–52.

20. The text is quoted in Hernández, *Dictadura en Marruecos,* pp. 16–22. See Maura Gamazo, *Bosquejo,* p. 201.

21. Hernández Mir, *Dictadura en Marruecos,* pp. 37–38. The same work quotes Primo's letters to Gen. Manuel Montero, the military governor of Ceuta, on Sept. 5, 9, and 10, 1923 (pp. 44–45). See Pardo González, I, 364, and Víctor Alba, *La segunda República* (1961), p. 73.

22. If this report is correct, Primo was exaggerating the degree of unanimity among the district Captain Generals.

23. Quoted by Santiago Alba, *L'Espagne et la Dictature,* pp. 13–14.

24. Quoted in *Dos años,* pp. 2–5. Strict censorship was imposed at Barcelona, but one leftist newspaper, *La Libertad,* managed, on the morning of the 13th, to distribute a few copies of a special edition, which said that the Army had revolted to save the king and Army leaders from punishment for responsibilities incurred in Morocco.

25. *Ibid.*

26. Hernández Mir, *Dictadura ante la historia,* p. 71. Further details about the pronunciamiento are given in Martínez de la Riva, *Jornadas,* pp. 1–89, and Martínez Sol, pp. 29–190.

27. Romano, pp. 179–86.

28. He is said to have later remarked: "I wouldn't have exchanged the government's telegram for all the gold in the world!" *Ibid.,* p. 192.

29. Hernández Mir, *Dictadura ante la historia,* p. 85.

30. *Ibid.,* pp. 90–93. Other military spokesmen in Madrid were less reticent. *La Correspondencia Militar* hailed Primo's revolt and ran this banner on its afternoon edition of September 13: "The Army wants to magnify the Fatherland, belittled by the politicians."

31. López de Ochoa, *Dictadura,* p. 31.

32. Pardo González, I, 380.

33. *Ibid.,* I, 392–408; Hernández Mir, *Dictadura ante la historia,* pp. 100–105.

34. Fernández Almagro, *Alfonso XIII,* p. 435.

35. DOMG, Sept. 16, 1923.

36. Hernández Mir, *Dictadura ante la historia,* p. 129.

37. Quoted in Castillo and Alvarez, p. 37.

38. Víctor Alba, *La segunda República,* p. 73.

39. Hernández Mir, *Dictadura ante la historia,* p. 97.

40. DOMG, Sept. 16, 1923.

41. Primo's dealings with the Catalans are discussed in Maura Gamazo, *Bosquejo,* pp. 59–101, and in Joaniquet, *Sala Argemí,* pp. 263–74.

42. López de Ochoa, *Dictadura,* pp. 80–85.

Chapter Eleven

1. Silvela was indignant over innuendos about corruption in Morocco during his tenure, and wrote several letters to the dictator vainly requesting public recognition of his honesty in administering the High Commissioner's budget. Quoted in Villanueva, pp. 48–52.

2. In Primo de Rivera, *La obra,* p. 20.

3. García Figueras, *Marruecos,* pp. 197–98.

4. *Dos años,* pp. 71–72.

5. DOMG, Oct. 9, 1923.

6. *Dos años,* pp. 35–37. Anyone over 23 was eligible. Units were to be established in every province, under the supervision of the Territorial Army Council. DOMG, Sept. 18, 1923.

7. Krim's agents abroad had purchased at least one airplane and had hired a mercenary pilot. With this machine the sheikh proposed to carry the fight to Málaga, the Spanish city nearest his Riffian stronghold. However, Spanish pilots in Morocco practiced low-level strafing, or "Spanish flying," as it was called; during one of these sorties, on March 23, 1924, the budding ace Juan Antonio Ansaldo destroyed Krim's plane on its landing strip near Axdir. See Salmador, pp. 38–43.

8. García Figueras, *Marruecos,* pp. 200–201.

9. These powers were somewhat reduced in a subsequent decree of July 12, 1924. *Dos años,* pp. 258–59, 624–32; Cordero Torres, I, 154–65.

10. According to one unauthenticated document, in the spring of 1924 Primo was still offering Krim full autonomy in the Riff district, provided that his men give up most of their weapons and guarantee safe travel for all through the Riff. According to this source, the Spanish government offered in return to pay for a Berber constabulary force of 3,000 under Krim's command, and to subsidize part of the expenses of the Riff administration. Hernández Mir, *Dictadura ante la historia,* pp. 174–75. Documents concerning Primo's negotiations with Moorish leaders during 1923–24 were collected in Hernández Mir's earlier *Del Rif a Yebala,* pp. 24–127.

11. Cf. Harris, p. 129.

12. Barea, p. 416.

13. Hernández Mir, *Dictadura ante la historia,* p. 180.

14. Hernández Mir, *Dictadura en Marruecos,* p. 161.

15. *Ibid.,* pp. 162–63; Maura Gamazo, *Bosquejo,* p. 157.

16. Hernández Mir, *Dictadura en Marruecos,* p. 163.

17. *Ibid.*

18. Barea, p. 416.

19. Hernández Mir, *Del Rif a Yebala,* p. 172.

20. Maura Gamazo, *Bosquejo,* p. 157.

21. Primo de Rivera, *Pensamiento,* pp. 135–36.

22. Queipo's version of the mess in the Djebala is given in the first part of his *El General Queipo de Llano.* He lists the drastic supply shortages, a consequence of irresponsibility compounded by embezzlement, that he discovered when assigned to inventory the stocks in this area.

23. *Ibid.,* p. 105.

24. *Ibid.,* pp. 106–7.

25. Cf. Primo's interview in *ABC,* Sept. 30, 1924.

26. López de Ochoa, *Dictadura,* pp. 57–58. There is a lengthy account of the evacuation of the Xauen region in Hernández Mir, *Del Rif a Yebala,* pp. 183–244.

27. Primo de Rivera, *Pensamiento,* p. 141.

28. López de Ochoa, *Dictadura,* p. 63.

29. Quoted by Harris, pp. 147–48.

30. Primo de Rivera, *Pensamiento,* p. 141.

31. Barea, p. 356.

32. Sablotny, p. 10. This memoir and Meyer's *Dreitausend Kilometer* are acerbic accounts given by two German recruits, both of whom deserted, of the brutality of life in the Tercio.

33. After his outbursts of the preceding summer, Franco concentrated on his professional duties and contented himself with writing a restrained military critique of the evacuation of Xauen. This essay is quoted in Galinsoga, pp. 100–108.

34. El Raisuli was already severely ill with gout and other maladies. He died several months after being carried away into captivity. There is a rather fascinating eyewitness description of his last public appearance, and of a great many other matters in the rebel zone, in Sheean, *An American Among the Riffi*.

35. Hernández Mir, *Alianza*, pp. 9–159; España, pp. 61–86. On Franco-Spanish relations prior to the events of 1924–25, see Mousset; and see also Laborde.

36. García Figueras, *Marruecos*, p. 207.

37. There is a detailed account of the preparations in Guerrero, Troncoso, and Quintero, *La Columna*, a work by staff officers that chronicles this campaign through the month of November. Cf. Castrillo, pp. 49–54.

38. The confusion attending last-minute adjustments is revealed even in such laudatory accounts as González Ruano and Tarduchy, pp. 124–27.

39. This was confirmed by Col. José Castelló, one of the Army commissioners for native affairs after the pacification. (Conversation with the author in Seville, March 8, 1963.)

40. In *La Victoire*, Laure provides a rather formal exposition of the operations of the two powers. One of the better accounts of the Spanish effort in the latter half of 1925 is given by Goded Llopis, pp. 133–246.

41. On these operations, see Díaz de Villegas, *Lecciones de la experiencia*. The concluding French operations are treated by Damidaux.

It was in this campaign that Millán Astray—who had been promoted to colonel by Primo and had lost one arm in the Djebala in 1924—lost his right eye while leading forces of the Tercio, to whose command he was restored after Franco's promotion to brigadier. Henceforward Millán Astray would be known as "El glorioso mutilado."

42. Maj. Luis Cano Portel, "El Raid de Gomara," *Ejército*, VIII, 91 (August 1947).

43. The only available statistics on the number of dead and missing lost by the Spanish Army in the conquest of the Protectorate are given below:

	Europeans	*Regulares*		*Europeans*	*Regulares*
1916	281	No figures	1922	548	227
1917	183	"	1923	366	142
1918	370	"	1924	3,266	1,091
1919	487	10	1925	399	220
1920	549	12	1926	213	310
1921	10,225	13	1927	195	369
				17,082	2,394

(Taken from the table in Hernández de Herrera and García Figueras, I.) These figures seem fairly accurate for the European forces but are incomplete for the Regulares, whose losses were often high.

The Tercio suffered 8,096 casualties (2,000 dead, 6,096 wounded) among the 20,883 officers and men who served in its nine battalions during seven years of combat in Morocco. The most detailed chronicle is that of Ramas.

44. Letters of May 30, July 21, and August 13, 1926, in Armiñán and Armiñán, pp. 345–50, 373–76, 383–89.

On the Spanish administration of the Protectorate, see the uncritical patriotic compendia by García Figueras, *Protectorado en Marruecos*, and Cordero Torres.

Chapter Twelve

1. López de Ochoa, *Dictadura,* pp. 89–90; Hernández Mir, *Dictadura ante la historia,* p. 264.
2. *Ibid.*
3. DOMG, Feb. 9, 1924.
4. DOMG, July 4, 1926. Cf. Benzo, pp. 203–5.
5. *Dos años,* pp. 219–20.
6. See Fernández Fernández, *Defensa.*
7. Quoted in Hernández Mir, *Dictadura ante la historia,* pp. 239–40.
8. *Ibid.,* pp. 241–42.
9. See Villanueva, pp. 131–32.
10. *Ibid.,* pp. 132–45; Alfarache, p. 49.
11. Miranda, pp. 15–17.
12. *Ibid.,* pp. 47–48.
13. *Ibid.,* pp. 49–50.
14. Acedo, *Calvo Sotelo,* pp. 54–56. Calvo Sotelo's own account of his activity in the Primo de Rivera regime is *Mis servicios al Estado.*
15. Blanco, pp. 19–72; Miranda, pp. 34–38. On the general question of juridical processes, see Salazar, *La Justicia bajo la Dictadura.*
16. Maura Gamazo, *Borquejo,* p. 217.
17. See Burgos y Mazo, *Dictadura,* III, 85.
18. Cf. his letter to Gómez Jordana, June 5, 1925, in Primo de Rivera, *Epistolario,* pp. 131–34.
19. DOMG, Dec. 15, 1925.
20. Fernández Almagro, *Alfonso XIII,* p. 481.
21. The regime's own presentation of its social and economic problem may be found in Pemartín, *Los valores históricos en la dictadura española,* and in Cimadevilla, pp. 113, 152–70.
22. According to López de Ochoa, *Dictadura,* pp. 109–12.
23. There was never opportunity to distribute this manifesto publicly. It is quoted in full in Miranda, pp. 72–76, and Hernández Mir, *Dictadura ante la historia,* pp. 291–94. According to the former, the text of the manifesto was written for Aguilera by the liberal politician Melquiades Alvarez.
24. The fullest account is in Miranda, pp. 54–88. See also López de Ochoa, *Dictadura,* 111–12; Fernández Almagro, *Alfonso XIII,* p. 486.
25. Fernández Almagro, *Alfonso XIII,* p. 487.
26. DOMG, June 10, 1926.
27. Zumarro, pp. 49–50.
28. Vigón, *Historia de la Artillería,* II, 196.
29. Quoted in Zumarro, pp. 52–58. Cf. Fernández Almagro, *Alfonso XIII,* p. 492.
30. DOMG, July 28, 1926. Cf. Vigón, *Historia,* II, 205–6.
31. Vigón, *Historia,* II, 206.
32. *Ibid.,* pp. 207–11.
33. Zumarro, pp. 65–66; Vigón, *Historia,* II, 211–14.
34. DOMG, Sept. 5, 1926.
35. López de Ochoa, *Dictadura,* p. 120.
36. Zumarro, pp. 97–104. The Engineers officers protested in a less conspicuous manner. Nearly all of them sent in individual petitions for retirement or passage

to the Reserve. These were rejected en masse. Three senior Engineers officers who spoke out publicly were placed under arrest. See Benzo, pp. 186–88.

37. DOMG, Nov. 18, 1926.

38. DOMG, Jan. 1, 1927.

39. According to the *Anuario Estadístico,* budget figures just before and during the dictatorship were as follows (in pesetas):

	1922–23	*1923–24*	*1924–25*	*1925–26*
Total	3,044,122,302	3,899,156,243	3,842,347,842	3,525,081,197
Army and				
Morocco	829,625,730	938,103,963	1,074,743,025	848,000,000
Navy	127,120,000	213,934,938	285,588,902	209,087,678

	1927	*1928*	*1929*	*1930*
Total	3,554,740,385	3,784,456,193	4,103,390,547	4,350,000,000
Army and				
Morocco	724,000,000	824,000,000	745,742,828	765,000,000
Navy	222,826,440	264,000,000	227,343,917	302,000,000

(Because of the custom of creating supplementary budgets and special expenditures, it is difficult to obtain precise annual totals, and therefore a margin of error of five per cent or more should be allowed for these figures.)

40. *Anuario Militar,* 1930. This figure does not include some 5,089 *oficiales de complemento* and auxiliaries.

41. Blanco, pp. 137–62; Benzo, pp. 286–92. There had been an earlier investigation of the Ceuta supply depot by a commission under General Bazán in 1923–24. It had prosecuted a few officers at that time, but had not probed deeply.

42. This concern was voiced by the Minister of War, General Juan O'Donnell, in an interview of April 1926. (See Casas Pérez, pp. 73–91.)

43. Franco later went on a brief study tour abroad to observe German military schools in Berlin and Dresden. Many of his subordinates in the Academy—Monasterio, Esteban Infantes, Alonso Vega, Franco Salgado, and Barba Hernández, for example—played prominent roles in the Nationalist Army during the Civil War. The official version of Franco's experience in the Academy is given in Arrarás, *Cruzada,* I, 94, and Galinsoga and Franco, p. 129.

44. The UP's self-image may be found in Pemán, *El hecho y la idea de la Unión Patriótica.*

45. Calvo Sotelo, p. 337.

46. Primo de Rivera, *Pensamiento,* p. 221.

47. *Ibid.,* p. 222.

48. See the table on p. 498.

49. Primo de Rivera, *Actuación ciudadana que corresponde al Ejército.*

50. Letter to Burgos y Mazo (name of author withheld), May 31, 1928, in *Dictadura,* II, 89–92.

51. Miranda, pp. 107–8.

52. *Ibid.,* pp. 110–14; López de Ochoa, *Dictadura,* pp. 151–52.

53. Castro Girona's story, with a collection of documents, was later presented in Farfán and González, *Por los fueros de la verdad.*

54. Burgos y Mazo, *Dictadura,* II, 9–48; Miranda, pp. 119–32.

55. According to López de Ochoa, *Dictadura,* pp. 165–66.

56. But this is denied by Castro Girona in the Farfán-González pamphlet.

57. Rafael Sánchez Guerra, the politician's son, has written his own account, *El movimiento revolucionario de Valencia.* See also Armiñán, *Sánchez Guerra,* and Miranda, pp. 133–52.

58. The only account by a participant is found in Zumarro, pp. 108–93.
59. On the government's reaction, see Barrangó-Solís, pp. 57–61.
60. Primo de Rivera, *Intervenciones,* pp. 59–66.
61. Calvo Sotelo, p. 333.
62. DOMG, Feb. 1, 1929.
63. *Ibid.,* Feb. 20, 1929.
64. The aftermath is discussed in Zumarro, pp. 194–292.
65. DOMG, April 3, 1928.
66. DOMM, Jan. 10, 1929.
67. *Ibid.,* Jan. 15, 1929.
68. *Ibid.,* March 12, 1929.
69. *Ibid.,* Jan. 28, March 13, April 17, 1929.
70. To the very end, Primo protested that the dictatorship was not a dictatorship, and that its program was to follow the regenerationist plans of Joaquín Costa. At the ceremonies inaugurating some new school buildings in the Madrid working-class district of Vallecas in 1929, he said: "The regime is following the policy of the great Costa—marketing and schools, agriculture and elementary education—for which from the beginning its concern was declared. But since the dictatorship has been identified with Costa, he has become a secondary figure for the intellectual vanguardists." Primo made similar remarks repeating his allegiance to Costa at an unveiling of a statue to the reformer at Graus on Sept. 22, 1929. (Quoted in Pérez, pp. 257, 283–85.)
71. Calvo Sotelo, p. 334.
72. *Ibid.,* p. 342.
73. *ABC,* Nov. 5, 1929.
74. In his *Itinerario histórico de la España contemporánea,* pp. 359–86, Aunós also stressed the selfishness of the UPE elements.
75. Calvo Sotelo, pp. 342–49.
76. *Ibid.,* pp. 351–52.
77. Pérez, p. 306.
78. See Burgos y Mazo, *Dictadura,* II, 149–94.
79. Hernández Mir, *Dictadura ante la historia,* pp. 351–53.
80. According to *ibid.,* pp. 358–59.
81. Fernández Almagro, *Alfonso XIII,* p. 540.
82. Maura, p. 29.
83. Ramón Franco mentions this in his *Águilas y garras,* and in the first part of *Madrid bajo las bombas.*
84. Ramón Franco, *Decíamos ayer.*
85. Hernández Mir, *Dictadura ante la historia,* pp. 356–59; Fernández Almagro, *Alfonso XIII,* p. 540.
86. Primo de Rivera, *La obra.*
87. Arrarás, *Cruzada,* I, 204.
88. *Historia de la guerra de España,* pp. 16–17.
89. Burgos y Mazo, *Dictadura,* IV, 194.

Chapter Thirteen

1. Alfarache, p. 73.
2. *El Sol,* Jan. 29, 1930.
3. According to Capt. Fernández Castillejo, Madrid, Jan. 9, 1963.

4. There are six biographies of Mola. The best are Iribarren, *Mola,* and Vigón, *Mola (El Conspirador).*

5. Berenguer, *Dictadura,* p. 50.

6. *Ibid.,* p. 75.

7. On the AMR, see Ramón Franco, *Deciamos ayer,* pp. 163–66.

8. DOMG, Feb. 16, 1930. See Vigón, *Historia,* III, 250.

9. Ramón Franco, *Deciamos ayer,* pp. 163–66.

10. As earlier noted, Queipo had been relieved of his command in Morocco on Sept. 23, 1924, and after he had written complaints to Primo and had become the object of charges by certain other commanders, he was briefly placed under arrest at the end of the year. He was eventually cleared in 1926 and given a new assignment in the peninsula, which he was soon on the verge of losing because of his jokes about Primo's Unión Patriótica. On March 31, 1928, when he would have been in line for promotion to the rank of major general, the Classifying Junta transferred him to that rank on the Reserve list because of his political attitude, thus ending his regular career. See Olmedo and Cuesta, pp. 66–71.

In a letter of April 2, 1925, Primo de Rivera had explained to General Federico Madariaga that the decision not to give Queipo command of a column in the recent Djebala operations had been an administrative one—one not made by the dictator. Primo observed: "But Queipo is his own enemy . . . and since I know Queipo's character, I must assume that he will not leave without wanting to pull down the columns of the temple in an attempt to exalt his own figure by destroying everyone else." Primo de Rivera, pp. 87–90.

11. López de Ochoa would have been Queipo's only rival, but did not contest Queipo's ambition to play the leading role.

12. Quoted in Dámaso Berenguer, *Dictadura,* pp. 228–30.

13. Miranda, p. 54.

14. Dámaso Berenguer, *Dictadura,* pp. 232–33.

15. Ramón Franco, *Madrid,* pp. 131–45, 279–82. Ramón Franco quotes a letter of December 21, 1930, from his brother Francisco, who was representative of the conservative majority of officers opposed to any kind of political initiative. He pleaded with Ramón to come to his senses; whereupon Ramón replied, on January 13, 1931, that Francisco was more conservative than the Conde de Romanones.

16. The salary levels since 1918 had been as follows (in pesetas):

	June 1918	*April 1920*	*June 1926*	*January 1931*
Captain General	30,000	30,000	30,000	30,000
Lieutenant General	25,000	25,000	25,000	27,000
Major General	20,000	20,000	20,000	22,000
Brigadier General	15,000	15,000	15,000	17,000
Colonel	10,000	10,000	12,000	13,000
Lieutenant Colonel	8,000	8,000	10,000	11,000
Major	6,500	6,500	8,000	9,500
Captain	4,500	4,500	6,000	7,500
First Lieutenant	3,000	3,500	4,000	5,000
Second Lieutenant	2,500	3,000	3,500	4,000

These figures are in pesetas per year and are taken from San Martín Losada, *Sueldos* (1927), and San Martín Losada and San Martín, *Almanaque del militar 1951.*

17. Miranda, pp. 60–61.

18. Part of these papers are quoted in Mola, pp. 530–41. A *Vida de Fermín Galán* was written in novelized form by two admirers, Arderíus and Díaz Fernández.

19. Marsá, *La sublevación de Jaca,* is the most direct source. Cf. Ramón Franco, *Madrid,* p. 181. Berenguer later said that Galán precipitated events because of his hatred of the generals and the older leaders. (*Dictadura,* p. 237.)

20. In Zaragoza, General Franco was eager to dissociate himself from his brother Ramón's activities and prove his thorough loyalty to the regime. Without authorization from the Ministry of War, he called out his cadets to assist the forces moving against Galán's rebels.

21. Ramón Franco, *Madrid,* pp. 161–75. The government considered Ramón Franco to be the most dangerous of all the rebel activists during the last months of the monarchy because of his energy and utter audacity (Mola, p. 700).

22. Mola Vidal, *Obras,* p. 577.

23. See Pascazio, p. 99.

24. Maura, p. 136.

25. Arrarás, *Segunda República,* I, 12.

26. See Alcalá, p. 185.

27. La Cierva, p. 365.

28. *Ibid.,* pp. 371–72.

29. *Ibid.,* p. 375.

30. According to an article published by Don Alfonso in *La Nación* (Buenos Aires), May 1, 1932, quoted in Arrarás, *Cruzada,* I, 252. This corresponds to Romanones' account (see *Obras*).

31. Quoted in Alcalá, p. 227.

Chapter Fourteen

1. The only serious effort at a biography of Azaña is Sedwick's work, *The Tragedy of Manuel Azaña.*

2. Azaña, *Estudios de política francesa contemporánea.*

3. *Ibid.,* p. 13.

4. Azaña, *Plumas y palabras,* p. 93.

5. *Ibid.*

6. See Mola, pp. 1028–30, 1054–56.

7. DOMG, April 28, 1931.

8. DOMG, May 26, 1931.

9. DOMG, June 2, 1931; July 26, 1932.

10. DOMG, June 17, 1931.

11. See García Figueras, *Marruecos,* pp. 247–52.

12. Quoted in Galinsoga, pp. 152–64.

13. DOMG, July 14, 1931.

14. *Ibid.,* Dec. 6, 1931.

15. *Ibid.,* May 28, 1932; *Reglamento del Cuerpo de Suboficiales*; and Manteca, *Código del Cuerpo de Suboficiales.*

16. Quoted in Arrarás, *Segunda República,* I, 139.

17. *Ibid.,* p. 140.

18. Azaña, *Una política,* pp. 141–72.

19. *Ibid.,* pp. 237–67.

20. Arrarás, *Segunda República,* I, 369.

21. Azaña, *Una política,* pp. 329–58.
22. *Ibid.,* pp. 281–99.
23. *Ibid.*
24. According to the yearly figures of the *Anuario Militar,* the manpower on the active list of the Spanish Army between 1930 and 1935 varied as follows:

	1930	*1932*	*1933*	*1934*	*1935*
		Peninsular Army			
Generals	163	84	83	83	80
Officers	12,600	7,697	7,773	7,771	7,205
NCO's	7,793	7,149	8,036	8,036	8,337
Troops	109,588	98,218	105,639	105,654	99,020
		Moroccan Army			
Generals	5	3	3	3	3
Officers	2,365	1,756	1,509	1,509	1,401
NCO's	2,477	1,930	1,686	1,686	1,893
Troops (native and European)	56,392	39,844	33,762	33,762	21,455

25. Azaña, *Una política,* pp. 329–58.
26. According to the *Gaceta Oficial,* the total 1931 budget amounted to 3,855,-100,000 pesetas. Army expenses, including those in Morocco, accounted for about 17 per cent of this total. Almost as much (503 million) was spent on public works, with the Navy receiving 272 million and the Ministry of Education only 202 million.

In the original estimate, the total 1932 budget reached 4,684,300,000 pesetas. Army and Moroccan expenses amounted to only 13 per cent of the total, and again were almost equaled by the amount spent on public works (568 million). For the first time in Spanish history, the Ministry of Education, with 265 million, received more than the Army (236 million).

27. Azaña, *Poder y oposición,* I, 119–61. According to the *Gaceta Oficial,* the original 1933 budget amounted to 4,729,000,000 pesetas. The main Army budget was allotted 434 million and the entire Moroccan budget 158 million, for a maximum of less than 13 per cent of the total. The Public Works budget was increased to 873 million and that of the Ministry of Education to 311 million, while the Navy budget stood at 261 million. However, the *Anuario Estadístico de 1933* indicates that in practice the entire budget was eventually reduced by approximately 10 per cent.

28. Azaña, *Poder y oposición,* I, 119–61.
29. Mola, p. 1096.
30. Ministerio de la Guerra, *Dotación de Armamento, Municiones y Material del Ejército de la Península;* Mola, pp. 1098–1100.
31. Peire, *Una política militar expuesta ante las Cortes constituyentes.*
32. Quoted in Vigón, *Historia,* III, 255–56. One of the most extensive published critiques was that of Cebreiros, *Las reformas militares,* which interpreted the comparative statistics in *The League of Nations Armaments Yearbook, 1931* as indicating that, among European states, only Portugal, Germany, and Czechoslovakia were spending less per capita on their armies than Spain was. (This figure did not include Moroccan expenses.)
33. For example, at the end of 1932 Francisco Franco published an article, "Ruud ... Balek!" in the journal *Africa,* protesting that the Moroccan garrison had been reduced below the level of minimum security. See Mola, pp. 1118–20.

Chapter Fifteen

1. Arrarás, *Segunda República,* I, 62–63.
2. Maura, p. 274.
3. Arrarás, *Segunda República,* I, 115.
4. Beltrán, *Preparación,* pp. 82–83.
5. Vegas, p. 11, and Vegas' article in *ABC,* Nov. 2, 1952.
6. Gutiérrez Ravé, p. 79.
7. According to Joaquín Baleztena, former Requeté leader in Navarre. Conversation in Pamplona, Dec. 15, 1958.
8. Galindo, pp. 133–38.
9. The Basque leader José Antonio de Aguirre has written that his movement simply found it impossible to cooperate with monarchist authoritarians. *Libertad y revolución,* pp. 152–57.
10. Galinsoga, p. 156.
11. Lerroux, *Historia,* pp. 144–45.
12. *Ibid.*
13. Azaña, *Una política,* p. 300.
14. Paul Bartel, "Où va l'Espagne?," *Revue Hebdomadaire,* April 9, 1932, quoted in Oudard, p. 27.
15. The only direct account of this is in Ansaldo, pp. 31–35. Ansaldo piloted the plane that carried the conspirators to Italy.
16. Arrarás, *Cruzada,* I, 491.
17. Milego, pp. 153, 490–91.
18. Cf. Goded, *Un faccioso,* p. 15.
19. Burgos y Mazo, *Dictadura,* IV, 195; and *Antología,* pp. 157–59.
20. Arrarás, *Cruzada,* I, 491.
21. Arrarás, *Segunda República,* I, 430.
22. Azaña, *Memorias,* p. 138.
23. Cf. Azaña's remarks in the Cortes on the day following. *Una política,* pp. 539–50.
24. Arrarás, *Cruzada,* I, 492; Lerroux, *Historia,* pp. 145–46.
25. Burgos y Mazo, *Antología,* pp. 161–70.
26. *Ibid.,* p. 160.
27. Cf. González Ruano and Tarduchy, p. 254.
28. Pemán, *Varela,* p. 112. Cf. Marina, pp. 55–59.
29. Goded, *Un faccioso,* pp. 19–20.
30. According to an unpublished memoir by Barrera, quoted in Salmador, pp. 74–77.
31. Esteban-Infantes, *Sublevación,* p. 31.
32. Afterward, when one of the civilian monarchist conspirators was brought to trial, the judge inquired how he had learned exactly when the rebellion would occur and received the reply: "From the night watchman on my street, who had for several weeks been giving me daily information about the successive delays, until at last he told me, 'It's going to be tonight, Don José Félix.'" Ansaldo, p. 35. Cf. Arrarás, *Cruzada,* I, 493–94, which parallels Azaña's remarks.
33. According to Barrera's memoir as quoted by Salmador.
34. Piloted by Ansaldo. Ansaldo, pp. 41–45. Parts of Barrera's account of this are quoted in Salmador, pp. 77–80.
35. Most of the generals on the active list prudently gauged the shallow, chaotic character of the conspiracy. Franco, commanding the Infantry brigade at La

Coruña, arranged to be occupied all day aboard a visiting warship in the harbor so as to avoid meeting the conspirators' emissaries.

36. Esteban-Infantes, *Sanjurjo,* pp. 207, 314–17.

37. González Ruano and Tarduchi, pp. 206–7; Esteban-Infantes, *Sanjurjo,* p. 207; Burgos y Mazo, *Dictadura,* IV, 208–9.

38. There is an extensive account of the revolt in Seville in Arrarás, *Cruzada,* I, 495–524, and an extremely hostile narrative by Gómez Fernández, "*El 52.*"

39. Arrarás, *Cruzada,* I, 532–33.

40. Cf. Azaña, *Memorias,* pp. 184–205.

41. Cf. Cabanellas, *Militarismo.*

42. By the end of 1932, so radical an officer as Major Ramón Franco was beginning to lose much of his sympathy for liberal leftist causes. He later published a booklet, *¡ Villa Cisneros !,* protesting the deportations. Some thirty officers, however, had managed to escape from Río de Oro on the last day of 1932.

43. Salmador, pp. 85–86.

44. These figures are based on Ansaldo's papers, quoted in Salmador, pp. 86–87.

45. According to Beltrán, *Preparación,* pp. 82–86. Ansaldo (p. 48) speaks of three million francs either on deposit or promised.

46. Ansaldo, p. 50; Galindo, p. 166.

47. Quoted in Vigón, *Mola,* p. 79.

48. Ansaldo, pp. 50, 51.

49. *Ibid.*; Salmador, p. 90.

50. Ansaldo, p. 51.

51. The ideological evolution of Calvo Sotelo is discussed in the works by Vegas and Acedo.

52. Ansaldo, pp. 57–58; Salmador, p. 191.

Chapter Sixteen

1. Arrarás, *Segunda República,* II, 254, 278, 357.

2. The only account of the UME ever written is Cacho, *La Unión,* which distorts as much as it explains. There is more precise information in the testimony given by Eduardo Pardo Reina during his trial by court-martial at Valladolid on May 24, 1937, part of the record of which he lent to the author, and which will be referred to hereafter as "Pardo Reina testimony."

3. Pardo Reina testimony.

4. *Ibid.*

5. Hidalgo, *Por qué,* pp. 77–81. Cf. Galinsoga, p. 160.

6. García Figueras, *Santa Cruz.*

7. The text of this agreement is given in William Askew, "Italian Intervention in Spain: The Agreements of March 31, 1934, with the Spanish Monarchist Parties," *Journal of Modern History,* XXIV, 2 (June 1952), 182–83. According to the agreement, Mussolini was willing to obligate himself to the extent of 200 machine guns, 10,000 rifles, 10,000 hand grenades, and 1,500,000 pesetas in cash. The signing of such an agreement was admitted by Antonio Goicoechea in a speech at San Sebastián on November 22, 1937, during which he said that the ultra-right had at that time even been willing to wage a civil war, "if necessary for the safety of Spain." Quoted in the *Manchester Guardian,* Dec. 14, 1937.

During 1934, the Italian government was also in contact with the Estat Catalá group, the extremist wing of Catalan nationalism, which was becoming a sort of Catalan fascist movement. Not satisfied with Catalan autonomy under the Republic, it made plans intermittently for armed insurrection, and hoped for Italian support in the establishment of an independent Catalonia, perhaps under special Italian protection. Cf. Fontana, p. 38. Needless to say, the goals of the monarchists and those of the Estat Catalá were diametrically opposed.

8. According to a conversation with Jaime del Burgo, former Requeté commander, Pamplona, Dec. 16, 1958; further corroborated by Joaquín de Baleztena. Cf. Lizarza Iribarren, p. 35 and Appendix, for further information verifying the agreement of March 31, 1934; and Burgo, *Requetés*.

9. *El Sol* (Madrid), June 24, 1934.

10. Hidalgo, pp. 90–91; Arrarás, *Cruzada*, II, 143–49. Hidalgo accompanied Alcalá Zamora on an official visit to the Balearics during the summer and was much impressed by Franco's military leadership.

11. López de Ochoa, *Campaña*, pp. 26–27.

12. The best military memoir is López de Ochoa's *Campaña*. Llano, *Revolución*, is also useful. Among the pro-left accounts are Canel, *Octubre rojo*; Solano Palacio, *Quince días*; and Villar, *Anarquismo*. For the other side, see "Un testigo imparcial," *Revolución*, and Iglesias, *Asedio*.

Altogether, 88 soldiers and 168 policemen and Guards were killed. The revolutionaries lost more than 900 men, not including those killed in the repression. Part of the miners' success was due to poor leadership on the part of the original military authorities in the region. On February 11, 1935, a military court sentenced Col. Alfredo Navarro, former commander of the Oviedo garrison, to three years' imprisonment, and expulsion from the Officer Corps, for dereliction of duty.

13. Investigation reports were printed in *El Sol*, beginning on October 23, 1934.

14. Villar, *Represión,* published numerous unsigned statements by victims indicating that the great majority of the atrocities were carried out by the Civil Guard.

15. López de Ochoa, *Campaña,* p. 181.

16. Arrarás, *Cruzada*, II, 258–59.

17. Ansaldo, pp. 91–93; Salmador, p. 101.

18. Quoted in Arrarás, *Cruzada*, II, 290. Calvo had begun to make similar statements before returning to Spain: see, for example, the article he published in *La Nación* (Madrid), March 10, 1933, which was reprinted in his *La Voz*, I, 279–85. Correctly judging the Renovación Española group too narrowly monarchist to draw significant support, he obtained the financial aid of wealthy elements to found a new ultra-right movement, the Bloque Nacional. Its Secretary General was the monarchist conspirator and General Staff captain Jorge Vigón. The Bloque Nacional's opening manifesto at the end of 1934 called for a corporate state and spoke of the Army as the "backbone" of the nation. See Joaniquet, *Calvo Sotelo,* pp. 203–8.

19. Lerroux, *Historia*, pp. 344–45, and Hidalgo, *Por qué.*

20. Cf. Romero Cuesta, *Vazquez.*

21. Lerroux, *Historia*, pp. 116–17.

22. *Ibid.,* p. 346.

23. According to Eduardo Pardo Reina in Valladolid, March 11, 1963. Several small ultra-nationalist, pro-military groups were active in Barcelona. In addition to the cliques (La Traza and El Cruzado Español), there was a small, conservative militia group disguised as "The España Club." By 1936, these little bands had at least 300 armed followers. Castillo and Alvarez, pp. 102–5, 117.

24. Prologue to Ruiz de Alda, *Obras,* pp. 36–68. Vaquero (Minister of the Interior in October 1934), II: 6, p. 4; Ledesma, pp. 203–6.

25. Cacho, pp. 23–25. José Antonio drew up a list of men who might serve as Cabinet ministers after a military coup. It was a syncretistic selection of leading names from the extreme right and from the Army, and included Franco, Mola, and Goded. Primo de Rivera, *Textos,* p. 199.

26. Pardo Reina testimony.

27. Cacho, pp. 27–30.

28. Pardo Reina testimony.

29. Cacho, p. 16; Estado Mayor, *Liberación,* pp. 394ff.

30. According to Pardo Reina testimony. This whole maneuver remains unclear, but other sources are not available.

31. One of the rightist deputies, López Cano, read a list of outstanding Masons in the military hierarchy, all supposedly ultra-liberal. Among the major generals, he named Cabanellas, Gómez de Morato, López de Ochoa, Molero, Riquelme, and Villa-Abrille. Among the brigadiers, Castelló, Llano de la Encomienda, Martínez Cabrera, Martínez Monje, Miaja, and Romerales were cited. See *Copia del extracto oficial.*

The fact of Masonic membership seems plausible in the case of almost all these generals, save that by the 1930's Spanish Masons were no longer ultra-liberal, but more or less middle-of-the-road. In 1936, all the generals previously named remained loyal to the regime, with the exception of Cabanellas. If Masonry was still a major bogey to reactionary Spanish Catholics, it had ceased to be decisive in military politics at least a generation earlier.

32. Quoted in Ramos, III, 232.

33. According to Franco's report, in Arrarás, *Franco,* p. 342.

34. March 5, 1935.

35. There is some interesting material on the hiatus in Mola's career in Válgoma, *Mola.*

36. Matorrás, pp. 20–21, 33–34. The author of this volume was at one time a Communist youth leader in Spain.

37. This system is described in Arrarás, *Franco.*

38. Quoted in Arrarás, *Cruzada,* II, 375.

39. DSC, October 2, 1935, pp. 9587–91.

40. Quoted in Arrarás, *Cruzada,* IV, 434.

41. Pardo Reina testimony.

42. *Ibid.*

43. *Ibid.* The right-wing police agent Mauricio Carlavilla intrigued against moderates in the UME, giving Barba Hernández lists of "liberals" to be eliminated, and trying to involve such men in criminal maneuvers through which they might fall into the hands of the authorities.

44. According to Vigón, *Mola,* p. 82.

45. Ansaldo, p. 104.

46. According to the *Gaceta Oficial.* The naval budget had declined steadily, from nearly 261 million pesetas in 1933 to 237 million in 1934 to only 192 million pesetas in 1935. The Moroccan budget fell from 158 million pesetas in 1933 to 64 million in 1935. Expenses of the Ministry of the Interior were drastically slashed, forcing the reduction of police and security activities. One of the few sectors to receive an increase during the *bienio negro* was that of Education: the allotment for that Ministry went up from 311 million in 1933 to 335 million in 1934 to 344 million in 1935.

47. Cf. Arrarás, *Cruzada,* II, 342–400; Arrarás, *Franco,* pp. 206–8; Valdesoto, p. 92. During the preceding year, a general program for reorganization and expan-

sion had been privately drafted by the retired Staff brigadier Pardo González, in *El problema militar.*

48. According to the *Gaceta Oficial,* the Navy, Interior, and several other departments would have been handed major reductions, and the Ministry of Education a small one.

49. Cf. Valdesoto, p. 95; Beltrán, *Preparación,* pp. 113–14.

50. In a letter to Gil Robles, written during March 1937, Franco made it clear that it was the leading generals themselves who had not wanted to be involved in the coup of December 1935: "Neither the duty of discipline nor the situation of Spain—difficult, but not yet of imminent peril—nor the carefulness with which you proceeded during your whole tenure in the Ministry—which did not authorize me for such a task—permitted me to propose what at that time would have seemed to lack justification or belief in the possibility of success, since the Army, which can rebel when such a sacred cause as that of the Fatherland is in imminent danger, cannot give the appearance of arbiter in political disputes nor define the conduct of parties or the powers of the chief of state. Any action at that time would have been condemned to failure as unjustified had the Army undertaken it; and the latter, which now has rebelled to save Spain, was hoping that, if possible, she would be saved through legal channels that would prevent grave and . . . painful upheavals." Quoted in Arrarás, *Cruzada,* II, 401.

51. Cf. Goded, pp. 25–26. Calvo Sotelo was at that time sick in bed with sciatica, but he sent Galarza and Ansaldo to talk with the generals. Even Goded and Fanjul would do nothing unless Gil Robles was willing to issue the order. Ansaldo, p. 111.

52. Maíz, pp. 35–36.

53. López Fernández, pp. 43–44.

54. *Ibid.,* pp. 19–21.

55. *Ibid.,* pp. 32–33.

56. See the study by Venegas, *Las elecciones.* Though many people have tried, it is impossible to be absolutely precise about the 1936 Spanish elections for lack of complete, impartial statistics from all provinces.

57. Pardo Reina testimony. Cf. Maíz, p. 37; Goded, *Un faccioso,* pp. 26–27. Pardo Reina declared that, later that day, *El Norte de Castilla* (Valladolid) published a statement by Portela repeating Franco's pledge of complete support to the government. This further tended to make Madrid officers believe Fanjul and Goded were deceiving them with wild talk.

The garrison in the Catalan capital was confined to barracks, to avoid possible altercations with leftists. The UME Junta in Barcelona had been up all night, awaiting the signal from Madrid that never came. (Castillo and Alvarez, p. 146.)

58. Pla, *Historia de la segunda República española,* IV, 281.

59. Conversation with José María Gil Robles, Madrid, May 10, 1959. Shortly after this crisis, Gil Robles quoted Franco as having said: "Not all the water in the Manzanares could wash out the stain of such a move." Knoblaugh, p. 21.

60. Franco's version is given in Arrarás, *Francisco Franco,* pp. 231–33; Arrarás, *Cruzada,* II, 439–40; Valdesoto, pp. 97–98; and in a letter from his aide, Lt. Col. Carlos Díaz Varela, to José María Iribarren, Feb. 25, 1937, quoted in Iribarren, *Con el general Mola,* pp. 11–13.

61. *Gaceta de la República,* Feb. 18, 1936.

62. Maíz, p. 37.

63. Portela later gave his version in a speech to the wartime rump of the Republican Cortes in Valencia on October 1, 1937. See Fernsworth, pp. 183–84. Franco's account may be found in Arrarás, *Francisco Franco,* pp. 233–35; Arrarás, *Cruzada,* II, 441; Iribarren, *Con el general Mola,* pp. 11–13; and Valdesoto.

64. *El Sol,* Feb. 20, 1936.

Chapter Seventeen

1. Iturralde, I, 405.

2. He is supposed to have given his more liberal acquaintances the impression of complete disillusionment, and has been quoted as saying: "At the present time, I bid farewell to every hope [of collaboration with the generals]. There is nothing one can trust or confide to the military. Those who are not incompetent are, just the same, thieves; you wouldn't believe it. I find it quite repugnant to deal with them." (According to the moderate Socialist leader Zugazagoitia, p. 19.)

3. Arrarás, *Francisco Franco*, pp. 236–39; Beltrán, *Preparación*, pp. 115–16; Beltrán, *Caudillo*, p. 229.

4. Marina, pp. 66–67.

5. Maíz, pp. 50–51; Beltrán, *Preparación*, pp. 116–17; conversation with Brig. Gen. Heli-Rolando Tella, Madrid, January 20, 1963.

6. Cf. Guzmán de Alfarache, pp. 38–39.

7. Pardo Reina testimony.

8. According to Díaz, p. 79. Pardo Reina has calculated that by July 85 per cent of the officers on active duty had affiliated with the UME. The growing strength of the UME was denounced by one of the few active leftist officers, Mangada, in *El Fascismo*.

9. The *Anuario Militar* for 1936 listed just over 8,000 officers on active duty. Of these, 5,282 were in the Infantry, an increase of nearly 20 per cent (mostly new *alféreces*) over the number (4,312) listed for 1932.

10. Redondo and Zavala, p. 345; *Informaciones* (Madrid), July 18, 1956.

11. Arrarás, *Cruzada*, V, 463–64.

12. *Claridad* (Madrid), April 20, 1936. Different terms were used on other occasions, but the idea was much the same.

13. Cf. Sevilla, p. 175.

14. Beltrán, *Caudillo*, p. 244.

15. Pardo Reina testimony.

16. Cf. Arrarás, *Cruzada*, II, 510; Maíz, p. 132; Beltrán, *Preparación*, pp. 126–27, and *Caudillo*, pp. 244–45.

17. On Varela in the 1936 conspiracy see Pemán, *Varela*, pp. 133–55, and Marina, pp. 68–71.

18. López Fernández, p. 39.

19. Or so it seemed to Colonel Segismundo Casado in Madrid, Jan. 29, 1963.

20. Cf. Somoza, pp. 122–23.

21. According to the Pardo Reina testimony. It has not been possible to corroborate this through other sources.

22. The Communists also persisted in their attempts to penetrate the armed forces, though this could be done only at the lowest level. Their sole success seems to have been in the formation of several cells among NCO's in the Marine Infantry, one of the most ultra-liberal sectors of the armed forces. Cf. Arrarás, *Cruzada*, IV, 388.

23. *El Sol*, May 9, 1936; *Claridad*, May 9, 1936.

24. Cf. Redondo and Zavala, pp. 345–47.

25. According to a handwritten note by Sanjurjo, May 31, 1936, quoted in Ferrer's unpublished "Conspiración," pp. 9–10.

26. Lizarza, p. 22; *La Unión* (Seville), July 18, 1937.

27. *La Unión*, July 18, 1937; Copado, p. 82. Some of the preliminaries for this plan were later discovered by the Republican police.

28. Quoted in Ferrer, "Conspiración," p. 10.

29. Maíz, pp. 19–21.

30. Cf. Mola, *Obras,* p. 1167.

31. Quoted in Bernard, pp. 83–87, and Beltrán, *Preparación,* p. 123.

32. Maíz, pp. 69–70.

33. Quoted in Maíz, p. 79.

34. These are quoted in Maíz, pp. 93–95, and Bernard, pp. 80–82. Plans were made for a last redoubt behind the Ebro in case of failure.

35. *La Unión,* July 18, 1937.

36. Iribarren, *Mola* (1945), p. 51n.

37. "Garcilaso" (pseudonym of Raimundo García, Mola's liaison), *Diario de Navarra,* June 23, 1956; Maíz, pp. 103–4; Iribarren, *Mola* (1938), p. 54.

38. Cf. Einhorn, p. 75. After the Civil War began, considerable information on Nazi activities in Spain was obtained when the revolutionaries looted Party headquarters in Madrid and Barcelona. Some of the documents seized were published in Burns, *The Nazi Conspiracy in Spain.*

39. The available evidence on this has been collected in Friedlander's unpublished dissertation, "Rebellion in Spain," pp. 55–56.

40. *Ibid.,* pp. 75–78.

41. Vigón, *Mola,* pp. 93–94.

42. Pérez Salas, p. 80.

43. Cf. Ortiz, pp. 18–19. Details of the conspiracy in Morocco are given in Fernández de Castro, pp. 69–115.

44. Maíz, pp. 100–103; Beltrán, *Preparación,* p. 129.

45. Quoted in Castillo and Alvarez, p. 155.

46. Arrarás, *Cruzada,* III, 449.

47. Quoted in Maíz, p. 168.

48. DSC, June 16, 1936. Despite his disclaimer of monarchist reaction among the military, Calvo's appeals to them in Cortes propaganda statements had become as direct as words could make them. In one of his most celebrated discourses, Calvo declared: "Force of arms—Ortega y Gasset has said it, and no one will object to this testimony—is not brute force, but spiritual; and he even added that the honor of a people is tied to that of its Army. . . . When nations lived in the fortunate age of general unanimity, the Army was no more than a fundamental complement to exterior strength; but today, sapped by profound discord—social, economic, regionalist—they need a strong State, and a strong State does not exist without a powerful Army. . . . When the red hordes of Communism advance, only one brake is conceivable. The strength of the State and the transfusion of military virtues—obedience, discipline, hierarchy—to society itself are necessary to cast out the fetid ferment sowed by Marxism. I call upon the Army and ask that patriotism guide it." Quoted in Arrarás, *Cruzada,* II, 420.

49. Pardo Reina testimony.

50. Knoblaugh, p. 61.

51. Arrarás, *Cruzada,* III, 456–57.

52. Pardo Reina testimony.

53. According to Zugazagoitia, p. 10.

54. Maíz, pp. 132–33.

55. *Ibid.,* pp. 140–42.

56. Quoted in Bernard, p. 91; Maíz, pp. 155–56.

57. Quoted in Bernard, pp. 103–4.

58. Forged evidence of a so-called Communist plot was not manufactured after the rebellion began, but was part of the various maneuvers used for months before

July 17 to provoke counterrevolutionary action. One of these fabrications was intercepted by the Socialists and published in *Claridad* on May 30.

59. During the first months of the Civil War Mola spoke of this in a radio speech from Burgos (published in his *Obras*, pp. 1185–90). It is also mentioned in Iribarren's unpublished "Notas."

60. Quoted in Díaz, p. 82.

61. Ansaldo, p. 121.

62. According to the information that Gil Robles gave Eugenio Vegas Latapié. Conversation in Madrid, Nov. 25, 1958.

63. Maíz, pp. 82, 126.

64. According to Mola's personal secretary, José María Iribarren. Conversation in Pamplona, Dec. 15, 1958.

65. Cf. Arrarás, *Cruzada*, II, 381–83.

66. Quoted in Aznar (1940), p. 31, and in most of the official biographies.

67. Though this would not have been out of character for Franco, the photostat of the letter, though frequently mentioned, has never been produced, so documentary evidence of such a request is lacking.

68. Ansaldo, p. 125.

69. Vigón, *Mola*, p. 97; Bernard, pp. 99–101.

70. *El Pensamiento Alavés* (Vitoria), May 17, 1936.

71. Maíz, p. 207.

72. Vigón, *Mola*, p. 99.

73. Quoted in Bernard, pp. 103–4.

74. "Garcilaso," July 4, 1956; Vigón, *Mola*, pp. 99–100.

75. The monarchist generals who provided information to the *Le Monde* correspondent Jean Créac'h gave him the impression that Franco joined the conspiracy not much earlier than July 9–10. Conversation with Créac'h, Madrid, Jan. 16, 1963. Cf. Ansaldo, p. 125. However, the date of July 15, given in Créac'h, p. 172, is probably too late.

The only one of Franco's official biographers to make passing allusion to the general's slowness in joining the conspiracy is Valdesoto: "From the first days of July, Franco was obligated, as the most distinguished general, to take command of the Army of Africa." (P. 110.)

76. Iribarren, *Con el general Mola*, p. 42.

77. Quoted in Ferrer, "Conspiración," p. 18.

78. *Ibid.*, pp. 24–25.

79. *Ibid.*, pp. 25–27.

80. *Ibid.*, p. 28.

81. Lizarza, pp. 100–102.

82. *Ibid.*, pp. 102–6.

83. *Ibid.*, p. 106.

84. *Ibid.*, p. 107. Corroborated by the Carlist leader José Martínez Berasain; interview in Pamplona, December 15, 1958.

85. *Ibid.*, p. 108.

86. It is absurd to charge, as Spanish rightists frequently have, that the Republican Prime Minister or Minister of the Interior "ordered" this assassination. The truth of the matter seems clearly to have been that the command of the armed forces and the control of public order had largely slipped from the fingers of the government.

87. Quoted in Zugazagoitia, p. 16.

88. *Ibid.*, p. 24.

89. *Ibid.*, p. 9.

90. *Ibid.,* p. 112.

91. It is interesting that nine years later, in a prologue written for the *Obras Completas* (Madrid, 1945) of the Carlist intellectual Victor Pradera, General Franco was pleased to hail the "true Traditionalist spirit" of the "principal leaders" of Carlism, who, he said, had finally offered their support to Mola's conspiracy "solely for God and Spain."

92. The relationship of the Falangists to the rebellion is discussed at greater length in my *Falange,* pp. 108–15.

93. "Garcilaso," July 7, 1956.

94. Beltrán, *Preparación,* pp. 135–36.

95. García Mercadal, I, 31.

96. Iribarren, *Con el general Mola,* pp. 50–53.

97. Iribarren, *Mola* (1938), pp. 92–94; Beltrán, *Preparación,* pp. 231–34.

98. Ansaldo, p. 125.

99. Arrarás, *Cruzada,* IV, 384.

100. Créac'h, p. 175; Beltrán, *Preparación,* pp. 135–36.

101. Iribarren, *Con el general Mola,* pp. 50–53.

102. Iribarren, *Mola* (1945), p. 73.

103. At the last minute, Goded, who was then the military commander of the Balearics, had switched from leading the revolt in Valencia to heading the rebellion at Barcelona. According to rebel accounts, he requested the change on his own initiative. See the account by the General's son, Goded, *Un faccioso;* also see Castillo and Alvarez, pp. 148–49; Iribarren, *Con el general Mola,* p. 41; Beltrán, *Preparación,* p. 131.

According to Indalecio Prieto, during the last weeks of the conspiracy Goded learned of the machinations of monarchist plotters with the Italian government and of the relation between certain rebel officers and Nazi agents. He consequently feared that the conspiracy was becoming badly compromised by plans for German and Italian intervention. He assigned a personal friend, the retired Army officer Hipólito Finat (Marqués de Carvajal), who had a variety of useful political contacts, to bring this matter to the attention of the Madrid authorities and conservative anti-fascists in London and Paris. Finat spoke abroad with Winston Churchill and Albert Sarraut, and attempted to talk with Azaña in Madrid. No agreement was reached with Azaña, however, and Finat abruptly fled from Madrid, fearing arrest. Azaña later complained that Finat's revelations had been too "vague and confused," which was no doubt the case. Indalecio Prieto to Gabriel Jackson, Jan. 31, 1962 (courtesy of Professor Jackson); Friedlander, "Rebellion in Spain," pp. 101–3.

Goded was, by his own lights, an ultra-patriotic nationalist. He was neither fascist nor monarchist, and did not want any foreign powers intervening in Spanish affairs. By mid-July his sense of duty had led him into conflict. His information about conspiratorial maneuvers abroad was, no doubt, imprecise. Though his instinct prompted him to withdraw from the conspiracy, this was easier said than done. It would have meant abandoning the comrades whom he had been inciting to rebellion for several years, and would have presented him with the undesirable alternative of having to rely on the leadership of the Azaña leftists, whom he considered hopelessly incompetent to deal with Spain's problems. Though some commentators suggest that he was shunted to Barcelona by his rivals, it has been conjectured that he did indeed seek the change on his own initiative in order to be in a more vital center where he could adjust to the course of events and play a more influential role.

104. Castillo and Alvarez, p. 147.

105. According to Iribarren, and to Maíz, pp. 231–32. Castillo and Alvarez, p. 147, give a different account.

Chapter Eighteen

1. According to Calleja, pp. 82–83.
2. Arrarás, *Cruzada*, III, 33–35; Fernández de Castro, pp. 171–273. A slightly different version is given in Beltrán, *Preparación*, pp. 165–70, 186–91.
3. For example, this is stated unequivocally in Checa's unpublished "Juicio crítico." Most of the other district commanders refused to join the revolt and in many areas were arrested by the rebels before they could hamper the progress of the rising.
4. Beltrán, *Preparación*, pp. 143–46.
5. Quoted in Valdesoto, pp. 115–17.
6. This was revealed by Franco's wife in the article "¿Qué hacía usted mientras su marido se alzaba en armas?"
7. Details are given in an interesting account by one of the English collaborators, Jerrold, in his *Georgian Adventure*, pp. 370ff. See also Arrarás, *Franco*, pp. 259–81.
8. Cf. Créac'h, p. 175.
9. The best account of the revolt in western Andalusia is in Arrarás, *Cruzada*, III, 159–82, but there are also Garrachón, *De Africa a Cádiz*; Higuera and Molins, I, 73–75; Nunes, pp. 103–4; and Narbona, "Frentes del Sur."
10. Iribarren, *Con el general Mola*, pp. 56–60.
11. According to a questionnaire answered by Joaquín de Baleztena, December 16, 1958.
12. Repeated in Thomas, p. 143.
13. Iribarren, *Mola* (1945), pp. 61–62; Liébana and Orizana, pp. 219–25.
14. Raymundo, *Glorioso Movimiento*; Beltrán, *Preparación*, pp. 201–17; Liébana and Orizana, pp. 165–72.
15. Contreras, *Iniciación*; Beltrán, *Preparación*, pp. 231–38; Liébana and Orizana, pp. 173–94, 205–7, 227–28.
16. Capitán V. M. L., "Ferrol del Caudillo," in *Ejército*, no. 9 (October 1940).
17. Two sharply contrasting accounts of the rebellion in Galicia are the anonymous Republican polemic *Lo que han hecho en Galicia*, and Silva Ferreiro, pp. 31–47.
18. Beltrán, *Preparación*, pp. 271–72.
19. Lizarra, p. 31.
20. The principal rebel sources are Iribarren's *Con el general Mola*, pp. 63–66, and *Mola* (1938), pp. 101–8. Other references, including statements by Martínez Barrio denying the rebel version, are given in Friedlander, pp. 175–78.
21. López Fernández, pp. 63–64.
22. Fernández Ferrer, pp. 18–27, and the excellent section on Spanish military organization in *Enciclopedia*, I, 1147.
23. Zugazagoitia, p. 32.
24. The representative, Pardo Reina, could not reach Sanjurjo before the latter's fatal attempt to fly back to Spain. Pardo Reina testimony.
25. Cf. Arrarás, *Cruzada*, IV, 386–94.
26. Mola had written to one of the Madrid conspirators at the end of June: "In spite of what I say of Miaja, I don't have a bad opinion of him, and therefore

hesitate to believe in the bad qualities generally attributed to him. He was my first captain and I received good counsel from him." *Ibid.,* p. 385.

27. The fullest account is in *ibid.,* pp. 395–493. Cf. Pérez Salas, p. 108, and Jouve, p. 48.

28. According to Indalecio Prieto, *El Socialista,* July 19, 1956.

29. The Army revolt in Barcelona and the role of the anarchist militia are treated from varying viewpoints in Abad, pp. 35ff; Montseny, *De julio a julio;* Lladó, *El 19 de julio;* Lacruz, *El alzamiento;* Goded, Un *faccioso,* pp. 37–59; Pérez Salas, pp. 100–103; Sevilla, *Historia,* p. 270; Jaume Miravittles in Robert Payne, ed., *The Civil War in Spain,* pp. 50–52, 60–66; and Vilarrubias and Lizcano, *Un muerto.*

30. Arrarás, *Cruzada,* IV, 310–17.

31. Iribarren, *Con el general Mola,* p. 63.

32. The fullest account is in Arrarás, *Cruzada,* V, 463–67. The UME group in Valencia had originally directed itself not to Mola but to Goded in the nearby Balearics, later explaining that communication with Goded was easier. But Goded had always been disinclined to accept the offer to lead the Valencia officers, remembering how that garrison had failed to support the conspiracies against Primo de Rivera.

33. Beltrán, *Preparación,* p. 137.

34. Arrarás, *Cruzada,* V, 467–522; Araceli, *Valencia 1936,* pp. 11–31. Carrasco eventually managed to escape to Africa. When he returned to the Nationalist zone he was court-martialed for his indecisiveness in Valencia and sentenced to thirty years' imprisonment, according to the Checa manuscript.

35. Arrarás, *Cruzada,* V, 533–59.

36. *Ibid.,* VI, 20–44.

37. *Ibid.,* VI, 53–100.

38. *Ibid.,* VI, 233–85. Manuel de Irujo's unpublished manuscript, "La Guerra civil en Euzkadi antes del Estatuto" (Bayonne, Jan. 1, 1938), shows that Carrasco was dragged into the conspiracy almost in spite of himself. See Morales, *La guerra civil.*

39. The best account of this fatal crash is by Ansaldo himself, pp. 141–42.

40. *Documents,* pp. 11–13.

41. According to the emissary, the Marqués de Valdeiglesias. Interview in Madrid, February 25, 1959. Cf. Friedlander, p. 219.

42. Kindelán, *La Guerra,* p. 356.

43. The shipment of the first reinforcements and the occupation of the Cádiz-Seville zone are treated in Aznar (1958), I, 142–43; Liébana and Orizana, pp. 155–59; Sánchez del Arco, p. 31; and Alessi, p. 199.

44. The role of the Navy is discussed in Arrarás, *Cruzada,* III, 44–103, and Benavides, *La Escuadra.*

45. Ortiz, pp. 27–46. The Seville air base surrendered to Queipo de Llano's skeleton force on July 19. Since it was the major airfield in southern Spain and had one of the largest stocks of bombs in the peninsula, it was a valuable prize.

Further information on the Nationalist air units early in the conflict may be found in Gomá, *La guerra en el aire,* and Díaz de Villegas, pp. 92–93. The principal personal memoir from the Nationalist Air Force is García Morato, *Guerra en el aire.*

46. Arrarás, *Cruzada,* III, 126. The details of these maneuvers are far from clear. See Friedlander, pp. 215–21.

47. According to the monarchist leader Conde de Vallellano, quoted in the Pardo Reina testimony.

48. The effective use of automatic weapons by the rebels in the mountain fighting north of Madrid is emphasized in the Checa manuscript.

49. Maíz, p. 263.

50. Cf. Cantalupo, p. 63.

51. This is based on information that German officials later gave the American correspondent Charles Foltz. See his *Masquerade in Spain*, pp. 46–47.

52. Secretary of the German Embassy in Madrid to the German Ambassador, July 6, 1936. *Documents*, p. 1.

53. Arrarás, *Cruzada*, III, 115.

54. *Documents*, pp. 3–4.

55. Arrarás, *Cruzada*, III, 127.

56. Lieutenant General Rudolf Bamler, sometime head of German military security in Abwehr III, has testified about the energetic and effective lobbying of Canaris to win support for the Spanish military rebels in general and later for Franco in particular. "Canaris explained everywhere that although Franco was unknown as a politician he deserved full trust and support, for he was a tested man with whom Canaris had worked for many years." Quoted in Colvin, p. 31. See also Abshagen, pp. 30–32, 58–59, 111–14, and Bartz, p. 20.

57. The most thorough discussions of the origins of German and Italian intervention are in Friedlander, pp. 20–27 and 214–34.

58. The official decrees were published in most northern Spanish newspapers and are repeated in Díaz-Plaja, pp. 173–76.

59. Pérez Madrigal, "Veintinueve Años Después"; Arrarás, *Cruzada*, IV, 218.

60. Iribarren, *Con el general Mola*, p. 169.

61. Most of these figures were altogether unknown to the Spanish public. During the following winter a series of cheap booklets were prepared by the writer Rogelio Pérez Olivares and published in Avila to popularize leading military figures. Biographical sketches were published of Mola, Franco, Saliquet, Colonel Ricardo Serrador, and others.

62. Ruiz Vilaplana, pp. 224–26.

63. On the 22d, one of the staff colonels sent Mola's personal secretary, Iribarren, to find four civilians qualified to serve as advisers. With the local Falangist leadership in disarray, the only experienced, reliable politicians to be found were *alfonsino* monarchists. Iribarren, *Con el general Mola*, pp. 106–7.

64. In this connection, the Carlist-dominated Diputación de Navarra was ratified as the provincial government of Navarre. On July 21 it presented Mola with a credit of two million pesetas, as well as undertaking to pay all expenses of Navarrese Requetés.

65. Iribarren, *Con el general Mola*, p. 122.

66. Vigón, *Mola*, p. 199.

67. Aznar (1958), I, 144. Iribarren, *Mola* (1938), p. 132, declares that on July 29 there were only 33,000 cartridges left in the Burgos arsenal. Cf. Arrarás, *Cruzada*, VII, 366.

68. Iribarren, *Mola* (1938), p. 132.

69. *Ibid.*, p. 144; Iribarren, *Con el general Mola*, p. 157.

70. Beumelburg, p. 25.

71. According to the Italian *Informazione Diplomatica* of February, 1939, in Esch, p. 36. By that time Admiral Canaris had apparently been dispatched to Rome by the German government to encourage the Italians to send aid. See Friedlander, pp. 221–25.

72. Bley, p. 15.

73. Bonomi, p. 7. Because of several misfortunes en route, the first squadron

of Italian planes quickly got into the world press. *The Times,* July 31, Aug. 1, 3, 1936; *Manchester Guardian,* Aug. 1, 5, 1936; *Le Temps* (Paris), July 31, 1936. Cf. Belforte, III, 26.

74. Iribarren, *Mola* (1938), p. 135.

75. According to Bley (pp. 31–32), the airlift achieved its maximum load during the days August 7–10. Figures for the total number of troops transported during August vary considerably in German and Spanish accounts, ranging from 8,453 (Beltrán, *Preparación,* p. 200) to 14,000 (Kindelán, *Mis cuadernos,* p. 21). Kropp, whose figures are very precise, says that German planes had moved 8,899 troops by September 1, together with 90 machine guns and 137,660 kilos of ammunition (p. 10). Other accounts include Rohl, pp. 7, 15; Trautloft, p. 17; Stackelberg, p. 23; and Stache, *Legion Condor.*

76. Nationalist publicists have usually avoided mentioning the role of the German and Italian planes. The operation is treated in a great number of accounts, such as *The Times,* Aug. 6, 1936; Aznar (1958), I, 145–55; Arrarás, *Cruzada,* III, 130–40; Belforte, III, 28–29; Díaz de Villegas, p. 136; Oudard, pp. 192–93; Solá and Martel, I, 87–97; Faldella, p. 70; Mattioli, pp. 23–26; and Solmi, p. 43.

Irregular naval operations in the straits are described in Sopranís, *Burlando el bloqueo rojo,* pp. 119, 132–33.

77. At the beginning of the conflict, the Republican Navy retained one battleship (*Jaime I*), three cruisers (*Libertad, Méndez Núñez, Miguel de Cervantes*), sixteen destroyers and gunboats, several minor craft, and the entire submarine fleet. The Nationalist fleet in the first weeks consisted of only one battleship (*España*), one cruiser (*Almirante Cervera*), one destroyer, and a few minor craft. However, in September the Nationalists finished the construction of the new 12,000-ton cruisers *Canarias* and *Baleares,* the most formidable vessels on either side. With German assistance, the old cruiser *Navarra* was repaired and added to the Nationalist fleet, which later received four destroyers and two submarines from the Italian government as well.

On the war at sea, there are Moreno, *La guerra en el mar*; Alonso, *La flota republicana*; Oliveira and Andrés, *La tragedia*; Benavides, *La escuadra*; Ferrari, *Archivo del 'Baleares'*; Fuentes, *El crucero 'Canarias'*; Gay, *Atalayas de Mallorca*; Laviga, *A Madrid*; Pardo Canalis, *Cuando el mar no era un camino*; Valles, *Páginas.*

78. Proportionately, there were even fewer naval officers serving the Republic than there were Army officers. The following figures on "expellees" were published in the *Gaceta de la República* on Aug. 22, 1936:

	Total	*Number expelled*
Admirals	19	17
Ship Captains	31	19
Frigate Captains	65	58
Corvette Captains	128	115
Lieutenants	256	246
Ensigns	172	171
Naval officer candidates	93	90

As in the Army, there was greater unity behind the rebellion among the junior officers than there was in the senior ranks. Of the naval officers "expelled," approximately half were either executed by the Popular Front regime or murdered by mutinous sailors. Blood lust among the mutineers was so strong that even a few pro-Republican officers were murdered. Cf. Benavides, pp. 155–56, 333, and Martín Blázquez, pp. 307–8. Similarly, the rebels purged part of the crews of the vessels under their control (García Mercadal, I, 45).

79. The "pacification" of parts of western Andalusia is recounted in Copado, *Con la Columna Redondo.*

80. Cf. González Pons, "La Batalla de Madrid."

81. Quoted by Martínez Bande, "La Marcha," pp. 3–12.

82. Peirats, I, 148.

83. In the conquest of Badajoz, the Nationalists suffered 285 casualties; the defenders, perhaps 1,000, not counting those who were shot afterward. See Calleja, pp. 99–108.

84. Iribarren, *Con el general Mola,* p. 246.

85. According to Lt. Gen. García Valiño, who commanded many of them. Interview in Madrid, Dec. 2, 1962.

86. Sencourt, p. 149.

87. Moscardó later published his *Diario del Alcázar.* But see Gómez Oliveros, *General Moscardó.*

88. Cardozo, pp. 161–62.

89. The mining operations are discussed in Estado Mayor, *Guerra,* pp. 45–49.

90. There is an extensive literature on the siege of the Alcázar. The most readable and balanced account is Eby, *The Siege of the Alcázar.* The best critique from the Popular Front side is Vilanova, *La defensa del Alcázar,* but see also Southworth, pp. 52–89.

The principal pro-rebel accounts dating from the Civil War period are Muro, *La epopeya del Alcázar;* Moss, *The Siege of the Alcázar;* Arrarás, *Cruzada,* VII, 138–90; Martínez Leal, *El asedio del Alcázar,* a fairly detailed narrative by one of the survivors; and Salamanca, *La vida en el Alcázar,* a diary of the first six weeks of the siege by a Civil Guard officer who was later killed.

According to Martín Blázquez, p. 124, the defenders tried three times to negotiate their surrender to non-militia forces, knowing that the leftist militia would be likely to put them to the knife.

91. The British volunteer Peter Kemp was told by comrades in the rebel army that no prisoners were taken the first day and that the gutters of Toledo ran with blood. Kemp, p. 28.

Chapter Nineteen

1. Cf. Arrarás, *Cruzada,* IV, 315.

2. Quoted in Maíz, pp. 307–10.

3. BOJDN, July 30, 1936.

4. *Ibid.,* Aug. 3, 1936.

5. The official pronouncements during the Civil War of Cardinal Isidro Gomá y Tomás, the Spanish Primate, have been collected in his *Pastorales.*

Iturralde, *El Catolicismo,* II, presents considerable evidence of the acquiescence shown by the Spanish ecclesiastical hierarchy in the fierce repression of the pro-Republican Basque clergy by the Nationalist military authorities.

6. Cf. *El Heraldo de Aragón* (Zaragoza), Aug. 27, 1936.

7. Bonmatí, pp. 229–36.

8. So Don Alfonso told Kemp. See Kemp, p. 25.

9. Créac'h, pp. 175–76.

10. *Documents,* No. 16, p. 16.

11. *Ibid.,* No. 43, pp. 42–43.

12. *Ibid.,* No. 80, pp. 88–89.

13. Knickerbocker, p. 33.

14. BOJDN, Aug. 26, 1936.

15. Créac'h, p. 178.

16. Kindelán, *Mis cuadernos,* pp. 52–53.

17. The precise nature of the political understanding arrived at has not been fully clarified. See Friedlander, "Holy Crusade," pp. 346–56.

18. The only account of this is Kindelán, *Mis cuadernos,* pp. 53–54.

19. Cf. Calleja, p. 116. During the next few years, Yagüe repeated his version of these events to acquaintances. The author has talked with several of them, and their accounts substantially agree. A slightly different, probably somewhat erroneous version is given in Créac'h, pp. 179–80.

20. Kindelán, *Mis cuadernos,* p. 55.

21. This account is based on personal interviews and the versions given in Kindelán, *Mis cuadernos,* pp. 55–56; Créac'h, pp. 181–82; and Vigón, *Mola,* pp. 252–54, all of which differ slightly.

22. Créac'h, pp. 181–82.

23. Foltz, p. 178.

24. BOJDN, Sept. 30, 1936.

25. Foltz, p. 178.

26. Créac'h, pp. 181–82.

27. BOE, Oct. 2, 1936.

28. *Ibid.*

29. BOE, Oct. 6, 1936.

30. According to Mola's secretary, Iribarren. Conversation in Pamplona, December 15, 1958.

31. John Whitaker, p. 105.

32. Franco's other brother, the rebellious aviator Ramón, had been named Spanish Air Attaché in Washington after the February elections. Relieved of that post by the Republican government when the war began, he offered his services to the rebel movement. Franco had never understood the showmanship and devil-may-care libertinism of his younger brother, but at last the two were on the same side. Ramón took a subordinate command in the Nationalist Air Force and was killed in an aerial operation in 1937. Cf. Zwingelstein, p. 156.

33. Serrano Súñer, *Entre Hendaya y Gibraltar.*

34. According to Mola's secretary, Iribarren.

35. One instance of this got into print in the early weeks of the fighting, when the pro-Carlist *Diario de Navarra* (Pamplona) published, on August 26, 1936, a letter from the Civil Guard Captain Joaquín Pelegrí dated August 22 and protesting that one of the triumphs in the current Guipuzcoan campaign for which the Requetés had been given credit was, in fact, won by a mixed battle force of other units. This was reprinted in *La Guerra civil en Guipuzcoa,* by the Falangist volunteer Morales, pp. 113–16.

36. This process, together with the pertinent documents, is presented in Melchor Ferrer's "El General Franco."

37. These developments are discussed in some detail in my *Falange,* pp. 148–73.

38. According to what he later told personal friends.

39. Nor was this merely a matter of speechmaking, for within a few days of the formation of the Burgos Junta, General Gil Yuste, new commander of the

former Fifth Division at Zaragoza, one of the two most important economic centers in rebel hands, had published an order stipulating: "Employers are required to respect the social legislation in effect at the beginning of the movement of national salvation, not reducing a single one of the benefits obtained by the workers up to that date." (*El Noticiero*, Zaragoza, Aug. 1, 1936.)

40. *Documents*, No. 243, p. 267–70.

41. Serrano Súñer, pp. 41–42.

42. Francisco Franco, *Palabras*, pp. 21–31.

43. There is a sketch of Gómez Jordana's career in Prieto, pp. 5–7.

44. Cf. *ABC* (Seville), Sept. 1, 1937.

45. *ABC*, Nov. 5, 1937.

46. A full list of Queipo's makeshift efforts is provided in Ramón-Laca.

47. Cf. his remarks quoted in *The Times*, April 18, 1937.

48. *La Voz de España* (San Sebastián), Aug. 12, 1937; Ruiz Vilaplana, pp. 136–37.

49. Ruiz Vilaplana, p. 134.

50. *ABC*, May 3, 1938.

51. According to Pedro Gamero del Castillo, Serrano's appointee.

52. It might be noted that according to Queipo's staff chief Cuesta Monereo, the Andalusian district furnished 150,000 men for the Nationalist Army in the course of the war.

53. There is a graphic description of these in Langdon-Davies, *Air Raid*.

54. On March 20, Ciano noted that it was Mussolini who had given the order for the most recent raids on Barcelona: "Franco knew nothing about them, and asked yesterday that they should be suspended for fear of complications abroad." Ciano, p. 90.

55. *Documents*, No. 586, pp. 657–63.

56. Francisco Franco, *Palabras*, p. 201.

57. BOE, Apr. 24, 1938.

Chapter Twenty

1. By September 30, 1936, the Nationalist airlift and naval convoys combined had moved 18,185 troops and 362,669 kilos of matériel from Morocco. Kriegswissenschaftlichen Abteilung Luftwaffe, Arbeitsgruppe Spanienkrieg, "Das Unternehmen Feuerzauber" (1940), cited in Dahms, p. 311. Cf. Beumelburg, pp. 23, 26, and Bley, pp. 29, 32. Aznar (1958), I, 158, gives a total of 20,248 troops. By that time Germany had dispatched 54 airplanes (48 Junkers-52 transports and 6 Heinkel-51 medium bombers), 1 8.8 cm. antiaircraft battery, and 28 2 cm. antiaircraft guns. Aznar (1958), I; "Das Unternehmen Feuerzauber," in Merkes, pp. 29, 178. The Italians had sent 31 planes (9 Savoia-81 medium bombers and 22 fighters), 11 batteries of light artillery and antitank guns, and 10 light tanks, thus providing the Nationalists with their first small armored unit. Aznar (1958), I, 515.

2. Asensio, pp. 149–92.

3. On October 10, the Left Socialist Largo Caballero, who had replaced Giral as Republican Prime Minister, signed a decree theoretically placing all militia units under a regular Army staff. However, the few trained officers trying to man the Defense Ministry had already been driven frantic by the militia leaders. General Castelló, the first Minister, early suffered a nervous breakdown, as did several subordinates. For Lt. Col. Hernández Sarabia, Azaña's former military adviser who was serving as Undersecretary, one consolation was to dwell on the past

record of incompetence of the regular Army, whose officers were leading the rebellion. He has been quoted as saying: "Do you think that a lot of idiots who spent half a century disgracing themselves in the face of a handful of Moors have suddenly turned into military geniuses? They are rotten soldiers, as they have always been." Martín Blázquez, p. 173.

4. On October 6, Franco told the German military attaché from Lisbon that during the march from Badajoz to Toledo the Nationalists had killed at least 16,000 Popular Front militia, while the total casualties of his troops, including wounded, were only approximately 1,600. *Documents,* No. 96, pp. 105–7.

Colonel Vicente Rojo, Chief of Staff of the wartime Republican Army, wrote that of one 3,500-man militia column sent out from Madrid in September, only 300 came back. Rojo, *España heroica* (Buenos Aires, 1942), p. 47.

5. The Popular Front militia had the support of several squadrons of Russian armor, including some new T-26 model tanks armed with 45 mm. cannon, which participated in a major counterattack on October 29. This attack was poorly organized. The veteran Nationalist troops did not panic, but learned to concoct new explosives, ancestors of the later "Molotov cocktail," to deal with armored vehicles.

6. Martínez Bande, II, *Ejército,* No. 197 (June 1956), pp. 3–13. Cf. *Documents,* No. 110, pp. 123–25.

7. Calleja, pp. 122–23. Cf. Kindelán, *Mis cuadernos,* p. 37.

8. Sperrle, "Die Legion Condor," in *Die Wehrmacht,* May 30, 1939. Cf. Merkes, pp. 33–35.

9. Kindelán, *Mis cuadernos,* p. 33.

10. Martínez Bande, IV, *Ejército,* No. 207 (April 1957), pp. 9–18.

11. Martínez Bande, "La lucha," pp. 171–202.

12. Martínez Bande, IV. The most complete narrative is Colodney, *The Struggle for Madrid,* which exaggerates somewhat the importance of the International Brigades.

13. John Whitaker, p. 103.

By the end of November, the Nationalist forces outside Madrid still numbered little more than 20,000 men, and were composed of 18 regular Infantry battalions, 6 Banderas of the Tercio, 18 Tabores of Regulares, 8 Falangist Banderas, and 1 battalion of Requetés with 172 guns, according to Martínez Bande, "La lucha." Though some of the Falangist volunteers fought well, their units were not trusted by the professionals. During the March from Seville, even the pro-Falangist Yagüe had refused to have Falangist Banderas indiscriminately included in his columns, for fear that the Falangists might "withdraw from the line" and "panic" his command. (John Whitaker, p. 111.) By contrast, the Republican defenders had only about 95 guns, but by December 26 had increased their infantry strength to 44,313, nearly double that of the Nationalists.

14. The Nationalist attack of December 14–20 is usually known as the battle of Boadilla, from the village before which it was brought to a halt. The best participant's account is Romilly, *Boadilla*. It is treated from varying perspectives in Colodney, pp. 96–97; Lojendio, p. 191; López Muñiz, pp. 54–59; Cardozo, pp. 233–34; and Pacciardi, pp. 104–10.

15. Colodney, pp. 99–105; Lojendio, pp. 193–95; López Fernández, pp. 274–77; and Aznar (1958), pp. 21–25. Incomplete Nationalist statistics indicate that more than 2,500 casualties were suffered in the attacks across the La Coruña highway from November 29 to January 9. The only available Republican records show about 5,500 casualties incurred in repelling them (Martínez Bande, "La lucha").

16. The Catalan Popular Front invested much of its best equipment in this

operation; the matériel might have been better used in trying to break rebel lines in Aragon. At first, however, Nationalist control of Mallorca was seriously threatened. Mussolini had not forgotten the secret clause in the 1926 Italian-Spanish Friendship Treaty promising Italy a base in the Balearics should she become involved in war with France. A staff of military advisers, two air squadrons, units of the Italian Navy, and several shiploads of supplies were dispatched, turning the tide against the Catalans, who had at first held air control with their few planes. Thoroughly disconcerted by air attacks, they evacuated the island on September 3, leaving most of their equipment behind. Higuera and Correa, pp. 159–79; Lojendio, pp. 92–97; and Belforte, III, 44–50. The principal Popular Front apologias are found in Bayo, *Mi desembarco en Mallorca,* and Francisco Soria, *Mallorca.*

17. An Italian Foreign Ministry memo of January 18, 1937, listed 17,422 Italian ground troops in Spain, according to Whealey, p. 29. An Italian Air Ministry report of January 23 placed the total just a bit lower, according to Cattell, p. 4. In general these figures agree with those of the Nationalist Army, which indicate a total of approximately 18,000 Italians in all branches serving in Spain by February 1. Priego, "Intervención," pp. 11–16.

18. The situation at Málaga is described by Koestler in *Dialogue with Death;* Chalmers-Mitchell, *My House in Málaga;* and Gollonet and Morales, *Sangre y fuego.* The Republican commander was Colonel Villalba, former head of the Barbastro garrison, who had tried to play both sides during the conspiracy. According to Italian sources, some 30,000 Spanish and Italian troops, including militia, participated in this brief campaign. Volta, p. 218; Belforte, II, 77–101. Cf. Higuera and Correa, pp. 195–221.

19. Martínez Bande, "Jarama," *Ejército,* No. 246, pp. 47–62.

20. The Nationalists suffered more than 6,000 casualties, while captured Republican records indicate that the latter forces lost about 10,000, including 2,800 casualties in the International Brigades, according to Martínez Bande, *ibid.*

21. *Ibid.*

22. The CTV lost about 1,000 killed, 2,500 wounded, and 800 prisoners or missing, while in the complementary attack Moscardó's division suffered 500 casualties and the Republicans altogether approximately 6,500, according to the materials used by Lago, pp. 23–30. There is a general description of the battle in Colodney, pp. 128–43. In some ways the early pro-Italian account by Deschamps, *La Vérité sur Guadalajara,* was more accurate than contemporary Republican propaganda.

The Republican Colonel Segismundo Casado has stated that some Italians made little effort to fight and noted that a significant number of the Fascist militia who surrendered had been recruited among leftist elements in Italy. (Interview in Madrid, January 29, 1963.) At any rate, the CTV was completely reorganized after this setback.

23. Within the first thirty days of the war draft contingents of the past six years were called up by the rebel command on Mallorca. Cerdó, pp. 23–30.

24. By July 30, 1936, Queipo de Llano had, for example, mobilized all holders of driver's licenses in the Seville area for military transport. Later decrees of September and October required that all workers and employees who volunteered for the Army or militia be paid full wages while serving, though it is not clear that this decree was fulfilled. The texts of most of Queipo's laws are given in Ramón-Laca, *Bajo la férula de Queipo.*

25. Vigón, *Mola,* p. 304.

26. BOJDN, Aug. 8, 10, 26, 1936.

27. Vigón, *Mola,* p. 304.

28. BOE, no. 126, Feb. 23, 1937.

29. BOJDN, Sept. 7, 1936.

30. The only contemporary German account is Funck, " 'Funker' und 'Drohne' hilfen Franco," which notes that German armor specialists manned several squadrons of tanks that fought directly beside the Nationalists in certain engagements during 1936 and 1937, both to instruct the Spanish and to gather information.

31. Quoted in Gil Ossorio, pp. 121–45.

32. *Ibid.*; Díaz de Villegas, p. 96.

During the course of the war, 10,463 *alféreces provisionales* were promoted to first lieutenant, but nearly half of them passed a supplementary 20-day course. In the last year of fighting 497 also took a further course for promotion to captain. Returning officers in these advanced groups as well as special service personnel are probably included in the grand total of 56,000 officers and NCO's that Funck says were trained with German assistance.

33. "Ejercito Nacional. Organización," in *Enciclopedia Universal Ilustrada, Suplemento 1936–1939.* (Hereafter cited as EUI.)

34. *Ibid.*

35. Manuel Hedilla, the interim Falangist chief in 1936–37, recalls that in December 1936 Franco's command was so shorthanded that it even lacked the recruiting staff to drum up reliable volunteers. Hedilla was promised a statue to his memory if the Falangists could find an extra 10,000 volunteers willing to go to the front. He says that these were quickly recruited by Falangist leaders among the poverty-stricken but conservative and Catholic Galician peasants, who were struggling to exist after a bad harvest.

After Navarre, Galicia provided the largest proportionate amount of manpower for the Nationalist Army. A total of 237,385 troops—nearly one-fourth the total recruitment—came from that region, according to the Galician Army Corps commander, Aranda, "La guerra en Asturias y en los frentes de Aragón y Levante (Le Cuerpo de Ejército de Galicia en la Guerra de Liberación)," *La Guerra de Liberación Nacional,* pp. 315–52.

36. This has been talked about frequently, but the only direct reference in Nationalist military literature is Ponte, "Cuando Aragón era yunque," *Ejército,* No. 2 (March 1940).

37. See EUI; cf. Díaz de Villegas, p. 95. These detachments were composed of: 18 battalions of Infantry (12,312 men); 8 Banderas of the Tercio (5,600); 1 machine-gun battalion (500); 1 Falangist Bandera (500); 55 Tabores of Regulares (38,000, of whom 6,800 were Europeans); 8 batteries of Artillery (800); 4 companies of Engineers (400); miscellaneous replacements, including Moors (4,893) and Europeans (1,000).

During the last two years of the war, almost as many Moors were recruited for the Spanish Nationalist Army as had already served in the peninsula, making a grand total of approximately 70,000 Moroccans who participated in the Spanish conflict. Cf. Domenech, p. 43.

38. Records of the Burgos Falange show that of 9,120 volunteers in the Falangist militia of that province prior to April 19, 1937, approximately one-half (4,252) were directly incorporated into the regular Army.

39. See Crespo, *Alféreces provisionales.*

40. There are very few memoirs by individual soldiers in the Nationalist Army, but see Villalba Diéguez, especially pp. 35ff, and Fernández Suárez, *Sentenciado a muerte.*

41. Cf. Faldella, p. 279.

42. Martín Blázquez, p. 306.

43. *Ibid.*, pp. 293–95. However, Col. Segismundo Casado insisted that the "mixed brigade" was purely a Russian creation. Casado, pp. 53, 59.

44. Cf. Casado, p. 88.

45. One section of the Nationalist intelligence network is partially explained by Bertrán, *Experiencias.*

46. Casado, p. 87.

47. The failure of the rebellion in most of the Basque country had left the insurgents' northern flank exposed during the first crucial weeks. Mola had had to dispatch five columns from his slender forces in Navarre to occupy the northeastern province of Guipuzcoa and seal off the French border, an operation completed by early September 1936. One of the Artillery commanders in that campaign later observed: "We did everything as in Africa. Hills and high ground were occupied, small pockets of resistance cleared out, and the forces moved from one limited objective to another, eventually establishing a vague line of demarcation." Martínez de Campos, *Dos batallas*, p. 22.

The Nationalists suffered at least 600 casualties in occupying eastern Guipuzcoa, according to Martínez Bande, "Guipuzcoa," *Ejército*, No. 190, pp. 31–40, and Runy, p. 39.

One of the best of the younger Nationalist commanders, Major Rafael García Valiño, first came to attention in the Guipuzcoa campaign. Like many officers, he had not been privy to the conspiracy (he had in fact been vacationing on the northern coast), but after the rebellion began he quickly made his way to Pamplona. He was placed in charge of a column of Requetés and by the end of the war had been promoted to Corps commander. He has written an account of the entire northern campaign, "La Campaña del Norte," in *Guerra de Liberación Nacional*, pp. 259–314.

48. García Valiño; García Fernández, *Diario*, a military diary by one of the officers of Valiño's First Navarrese Brigade.

49. Ulíbarri, p. 23. The principal general account from the Basque side is Steer, *The Tree of Gernika.* The only major offensive effort by the Basques prior to this time is treated by Martínez Esparza, pp. 23–32.

50. Martínez Bande, "Vizcaya," *Ejército*, No. 212, pp. 23–30.

51. Guernica housed a small mortar factory and the headquarters of one Basque battalion, but its significance was basically moral and psychological. There is no clear evidence that the Nationalist command itself planned the bombardment. Most of the known facts are summarized in Thomas, pp. 419–21.

52. *Documents*, No. 361, p. 410.

53. According to Iribarren. The text of the "Extracto de las Diligencias Instruídas" for the investigation of Mola's death reveals nothing special.

54. Again according to Iribarren.

55. Popular Front losses were heavy; García Valiño has said (in "La Campaña del Norte") that counterattacks in early June cost 2,400 Basque-Asturian dead. Among Nationalist memoirs of this time are Ribas, *El 11º Ligero*, and those of a Requeté chaplain, Cía, *Memorias.* The role of the mixed Italian-Spanish "Fleccie Nere" brigade is treated in Belforte, III, 141–61, and in Piazzoni, pp. 202–6.

56. These figures, only approximate, are based on captured Republican records, and on Nationalist intelligence, which was fairly accurate. Marcos, pp. 47–55.

57. Cf. Zugazagoitia, p. 305.

58. According to Marcos.

59. Rojo, *España Heroica*, pp. 106–11. By this time the Nationalists' allies were learning to make good the qualitative superiority sometimes enjoyed by Russian aircraft in earlier months. Cf. Rougeron, pp. 5, 193–94.

60. Casado, pp. 74–75. The most detailed study, Martínez Bande, "Brunete,"

Revista de Historia Militar, No. 5, pp. 157–97, reports that Republican losses were approximately twice as great as those of the Nationalists, about 24,000 to 12,000.

61. Rojo, p. 111. Casado concurs.

62. The Generalissimo was not alone in this opinion. Juan Vigón, Chief of Staff for the Army of the North, was anxious that the northern offensive be forced to a swift conclusion, in part because of the industrial wealth of this region. Letters to Kindelán, March 1 and July 12, 1937, in his *Mis cuadernos,* pp. 76–78, 93–95.

63. Zugazagoitia, p. 306.

64. Total Nationalist casualties in the two-week Santander campaign were approximately 3,000. Kindelán, *Mis cuadernos,* p. 103. Cf. Camino, "La Batalla de Reinosa."

65. On August 4, 1936, three weeks after the struggle began, Aranda gave up his original plan and withdrew his forces to a defense perimeter 600 to 1,600 meters outside the limits of Oviedo. It was necessary to relinquish contact with other Nationalist outposts in Asturias, which were soon overwhelmed. Aranda's soldiers and local Falangist volunteers kept a tight grip on the capital itself, though at least two-fifths of the city's population favored the Popular Front, according to the Falangist leader Pérez Solís, *Sitio y defensa de Oviedo.*

The miners' militia that assaulted the town often showed great individual bravery and on some occasions outnumbered the defenders by as many as seven to one. However, they lacked ammunition, training, and leadership, and lost most of their original volunteer officers in frontal attacks, as Aranda himself has testified in his "La Guerra en Asturias." The first Nationalist relief column finally broke through from Galicia on October 17, 1936. According to Martínez Bande, "Socorro," pp. 153–77, a total of 20,700 troops were employed in the relief effort, but two-thirds of them had to be used simply to hold open the tenuous supply route from the west. The garrison of Oviedo suffered 70 per cent casualties— about 2,300 men—during the first three months. The relief columns lost 2,600 during the same period. However, it was estimated that by the end of October about three-fourths of the original Popular Front assailants, or nearly 14,000 men, had also been placed on the casualty list, according to Aranda: "Sitio y defensa de Oviedo."

After the city had been relieved, the miners' militia worked harder than ever. After reinforcements had arrived from Santander and Vizcaya, the strongest attempt to take Oviedo began on February 21, 1937. Nearly 40,000 militia, supported by 100 cannon, initiated a series of mass assaults that reached a climax on March 13. Franco's headquarters expected the city to fall, but after six weeks of extremely heavy casualties, the militia began to lose spirit. In "La Guerra en Asturias," Aranda calculated that during the six weeks from February 21 to the end of March 1937 the Republican militia suffered 15,000 casualties. Those of the defenders amounted to 6,182, to which 3,974 more were added by the end of July.

Two more Nationalist accounts that may be consulted are Rivero Sánchez, *Odisea y gesto de Oviedo,* and Carrascal, *Asturias.*

66. A propaganda blurb, "General Aranda," prepared shortly afterward by Armiñán, is the nearest thing to a biography of Aranda that has ever been written.

67. Solano Palacio, *La tragedia del norte,* is one of the few leftist accounts.

68. Kindelán, *Mis cuadernos,* pp. 208–9.

69. EUI states that approximately 7,000 died of wounds.

70. Arrarás, *Cruzada,* IV, 221.

71. Nationalist patriotic literature on the struggle in Aragon includes Colás, *El Movimiento*; Gracia, *Aragón*; and, on the Falangist volunteers, Pablo, *Aquellas Banderas de Aragón*.

Since the beginning of the conflict, the Catalan militia had launched repeated assaults to capture the isolated Nationalist-held provincial capital of Huesca in the Pyrenean foothills to the north. The twenty-month siege of Huesca was not fully lifted until March 1938. The garrison suffered 3,551 total casualties, and 20,458 sick or wounded military and civilians were evacuated, according to Algarra, p. 188.

72. The story of one of these is told by Conill, in *Codo*. Diego, Quintana, and Royo, *Belchite*, is a somewhat fictionalized memoir of the main encounter.

73. Kemp, pp. 155–58.

74. In one sector of the southern Aragon front, 20 to 30 Nationalist soldiers deserted each day during the opening phase of the Belchite battle; they told Republican interrogators of this practice. Pérez Salas, p. 154.

75. Arrarás, *Cruzada*, VII, 542; Aznar (1958), II, 344; Kindelán, *Mis cuadernos*, pp. 107–16.

76. According to the Republican military psychiatrist Emilio Mira. See Mira, p. 73.

77. Count Ciano, the Italian Foreign Minister, noted in his diary on December 20, 1937; "Our commanders are restless, quite rightly. Franco has no idea of synthesis in war. His operations are those of a magnificent battalion commander. His objective is always ground, never the enemy. And he doesn't realize that it is by destruction of the enemy that you win a war." Ciano, *Diary*, p. 46.

By this time, according to Priego, no more than 25,000 of the 35,000 troops in the CTV were Italian. Only the mixed Italian-Spanish "Fleccie" brigades had participated in the counterattack at Belchite, while the only Italian units employed at Teruel were aircraft and artillery.

78. In view of this, on February 2, 1938, Mussolini sent Franco a long-delayed letter urging him to get on with things. (Ciano, *Diary*, pp. 51, 68.) The Generalissimo eventually replied on March 4 that he had had to keep a considerable number of troops in Asturias to track down leftist guerrilleros, but believed that the Republicans were near collapse, politically as well as militarily. (*Ibid.*, p. 83.) It may be inferred that one reason for his lack of haste was that he hoped the internal contradictions of the Popular Front might provoke its collapse.

79. The Nationalists took 17,000 prisoners during January and February, and claim to have buried 14,000 enemy corpses within this period. (Aznar [1958], II, 422.) Their own total casualties apparently amounted to approximately 26,000. (Aranda, "La Guerra en Asturias.")

80. Aranda, "La Guerra en Asturias."

81. *Ibid.*

82. Tank units were sometimes able to achieve breakthroughs. General von Thoma, the chief German Panzer adviser in Spain, said that by the spring of 1938 he had succeeded in forming four tank battalions that totaled 180 vehicles, of which one-third were captured Russian tanks. He remarked after World War II: "General Franco wished to parcel out the tanks among the infantry—in the usual way of generals who belong to the old school. I had to fight this tendency constantly in the endeavor to use the tanks in a concentrated way. The Francoists' successes were largely due to this." Liddell Hart, p. 78. Similarly, González Pons has tried to portray the breakthrough in Aragon as a sort of pre-blitzkrieg in his "La Batalla de Aragón," pp. 60–66. This is misleading. Franco usually had his way, and the terrain of the main Spanish battlefields precluded the significant use of independent armor. García Valiño said that he found the Italian tank units

virtually worthless for opening holes in the enemy line by themselves. Even at the very end of the war, the only armor that the Nationalists had on the southern front consisted of nine captured Russian tanks, according to Lt. Gen. José Cuesta Monereo, "La Guerra en los Frentes del Sur," *Guerra de Liberación Nacional,* pp. 193–258. In general, the aspect of future German tactics most successfully essayed in Spain was aerial attack.

During the first year of the war, foreign observers were impressed by the effectiveness of anti-tank fire, though this was used more by the Germans and Italians against the Russians than vice versa. Cf. Temperley, p. 38. Unsuccessful experiences in Spain did reveal some of the weaknesses of the heavy Russian tanks and helped make possible the formidable T-34 of 1941. The best study of Soviet military experience in Spain is an unpublished dissertation by Robert Plumb, "Soviet Participation in the Spanish Civil War." Non-Communist Republican officers were naturally bitter about Russian experiments. Lt. Col. Checa has said that the third copy of all regular Republican Army reports from the field had as a matter of course to be sent to the Russian advisers.

83. Aranda, "La Guerra en Asturias."

84. Elaborate Nationalist claims were made regarding Republican losses, which were said to amount to 8,000 killed during March, and 7,000 prisoners at Lérida alone, while the Nationalists claim to have suffered only 3,000 casualties in the entire northern sector from March 21 to April 23, 1938. Lojendio, pp. 452–79; Aznar (1958), III, 67–101.

85. According to Rojo, *España heroica,* p. 152.

86. Lojendio, pp. 479–91; Aznar (1958), III, 101–20. Aranda reported that in the advance southeast between March 24 and April 15, 1938, the resistance was so light that the Nationalists suffered only 2,000 total casualties. García Valiño has emphasized to the author the importance of the German and Italian aircraft in making possible this rapid and relatively easy advance.

87. Lojendio, pp. 491–95; Aznar (1958), III, 120–31.

88. Lojendio, pp. 495–508; Aznar (1958), III, 131–48.

89. Arrarás, *Cruzada,* VIII, 79; Aznar (1958), III, 161. By contrast, the Republicans could scarcely mount 200 guns for the defense of the east, and by the summer of 1938 they had only about 125 operational aircraft.

90. Lojendio, pp. 518–26; Aznar (1958), III, 163–69; Rojo, *España heroica,* pp. 159–68, and his ¡*Alerta los pueblos!,* p. 48. In "La Guerra en Asturias," Aranda has written that total Nationalist casualties in the east between April 23 and July 25, 1938, were approximately 15,000—a figure probably more nearly accurate than the much higher Republican claims.

91. As Lojendio, p. 399.

92. Ansaldo, p. 63, cites Vigón, Franco's Chief of Staff, as having condemned this as another example of the Caudillo's circumscribed thinking. Cf. Kindelán, *Mis cuadernos,* p. 191.

93. There is a brief account of the crossing by Urarte, pp. 26–29. The Nationalist division in this sector had earlier suffered heavy losses and had been reinforced with detachments of inexperienced, perhaps somewhat unreliable, conscript troops. Its commander, Colonel Peñarredonda, had a reputation for brutality. Disgraced by his unit's rout at the Ebro, he never again returned to command during the war.

94. Lojendio, pp. 395–406; Rojo, ¡*Alerta los pueblos!,* p. 49; Aznar (1958), III, 178–227.

95. Martínez de Campos, *Dos batallas,* p. 32.

96. Lojendio, pp. 406–16; Aznar (1958), III, 229–40.

97. Kindelán, *Mis cuadernos,* p. 148.

98. *Ibid.*, p. 163.
99. *Ibid.*
100. Ciano, *Diary*, p. 146.
101. Pérez Salas, p. 210.
102. The best account from the Republican side is a memoir by the chief of staff of the Republican 35th Division, Henríquez Caubín, *La Batalla del Ebro.*
103. Moyano, pp. 18–27. Martínez de Campos wrote that altogether some 500 guns were employed by the Nationalists at the Ebro and that when the battle was over, 100 had to be withdrawn from service, while most of the rest were in poor condition (*Dos batallas*, p. 36).
104. Cf. Martínez de Campos, *Dos batallas*, p. 33.
105. Standard Nationalist accounts are Lojendio, pp. 424–34, and Aznar (1958), III, 241–70. See also Marcos, pp. 18–25.
106. According to captured reports, the Republican forces suffered nearly 75,000 casualties; but this figure includes 19,563 prisoners taken by the Nationalists, so actual battle casualties were about even. Cf. Sánchez García, pp. 11–18.
107. Rojo, *España heroica*, pp. 192–93.
108. Aznar (1958), III, 264.
109. According to the figures of Sae, pp. 58–62. It is not entirely clear, however, whether the total of 4,007 includes those who subsequently died of wounds. According to García Valiño, his Maestrazgo Corps lost 1,200 dead. Arrarás, *Cruzada*, VIII, 195, states that altogether, 29 per cent of the wounded Nationalists were able to return to the battle.
110. One aspect of the breakthrough is treated by Salas López, pp. 15–20, who explains that the Nationalists concentrated 500 cannon on a 10-kilometer line from Lérida to Serós.
111. Cuesta Monereo provides a detailed discussion of this in his "La Guerra en Los Frentes del Sur." During most of the war there had been little action on the southern front. From October 1937 to September 1938, the Nationalists incurred only 17,000 casualties in the south, of which more than 2,000 were killed. Most of these losses resulted from a series of limited attacks in 1938 to advance the Nationalist front in northeastern Estremadura and southwestern New Castile.

The Republicans launched a full-scale effort in the Peñarroya district from January 5 to February 4, 1939. The Nationalist defense, though deficient in armor, had the advantage of air control and was further assisted by a heavy rain that began on the third day of the battle. An intercepted Republican report read: "Not only has this been the cause of the paralysis of our maneuver, but the customary difficulty has occurred once more. As soon as the subordinate commanders find themselves in the open field and have to solve the various problems created by combat, indecision appears, accompanied by the slowing down of movement and the establishment of a fixed line. On this occasion, the line is located some three kilometers west of Monterrubio.

"The maneuver could have triumphed. The facts have shown that it was well calculated, but much time has been lost and every passing day makes it more difficult and dangerous."

Cuesta Monereo concludes that it was a serious mistake for the Republican government not to have attempted the proposed accompanying assault that was to have landed west of Málaga. This might have unhinged the entire Nationalist line in the south. Altogether, 92,500 Republicans and 72,000 Nationalists opposed each other in the Peñarroya engagement. Nationalist casualties were 10,500, including over 2,000 dead; those of the Republicans are unknown.

112. Rojo, *¡Alerta los pueblos!*, pp. 274–75.
113. The *casadazo* is described from varying points of view: the account by

Casado; García Pradas, *La traición*; Bouthelier and López Mora, *Ocho días*; Domínguez, *Los vencedores*; Peirats, III, 341–90; Pérez Salas, pp. 240–50; Zugazagoitia, pp. 541–58.

114. Silva, p. 154.

Chapter Twenty-one

1. Quoted in Castillo and Alvarez, p. 153.
2. Knickerbocker, p. 22.
3. BOJDN, July 29, 1936.
4. *Ibid.,* Sept. 1 and 9, 1936.
5. Iribarren, *Con el general Mola,* p. 94. After its publication, this book was immediately suppressed by the Nationalist government, though Mola had personally approved the manuscript before publication and thanked the author for rendering a faithful account.
6. *Ibid.,* p. 212.
7. *Ibid.,* p. 245 (and according to a handwritten correction made in Iribarren's personal copy).
8. Junod, pp. 83ff.
9. Iribarren, *Con el general Mola,* p. 282.
10. *ABC* (Seville), July 22–27, 1936, quoted in Southworth, pp. 178–79, 215.
11. Taylor was at that time correspondent for the *Chicago Tribune* and president of the Anglo-American Press Association. He was also a Catholic, which may have made him more acceptable to the rebels.
12. Hanighen, pp. 60–61.
13. *Ibid.,* p. 65.
14. *Ibid.,* p. 106.
15. John Whitaker, pp. 111–14. Reprinted with permission.
16. Cantalupo, pp. 131–37.
17. Like Balmes and Lapuente, Campins was another senior officer who had once been close to Franco. A decade earlier he had been considered one of the outstanding staff colonels in the Army, and had been used by Franco for part of the technical organization of the Zaragoza Academy.
18. Queipo de Llano told the Portuguese journalist Correia that at the beginning of the war they had shot some 20 other officers in western Andalusia who had refused to join the revolt. Correia, p. 17. These executions of military "traitors to the movement" went on throughout the Civil War.
19. Aralar, p. 13.
20. These figures are largely constructed on the basis of the information provided by Checa during a conversation in Madrid, December 27, 1962. Zugazagoitia, however, would put the figure lower, at no more than 5 per cent.
21. One of the bitterest indictments of the attitude and policy of leftist groups toward potentially pro-Republican Army officers will be found in *Guerra en España,* by Col. Jesús Pérez Salas, who was one of the military men most loyal to the constitutional regime.
22. Alonso, p. 25.
23. Thomas, pp. 169, 631.
24. Jackson, pp. 526–40.
25. Cf. Ruiz Vilaplana, pp. 151–68.
26. During an official trip along the highway between Valladolid and Burgos, Mola found one stretch of road so littered with corpses that he gave an official

order by radio that bodies be dumped at more discreet locations in the future. Martín Blázquez, p. 163.

Regarding the Badajoz slaughter, Juanes wrote in *Por qué fuimos a la guerra* (p. 184) that "together with Marxist militiamen, a number of Carabineros and Civil Guards, whose leaders from the beginning were in open opposition to the Movement, joined the resistance. All of them were justly executed when the troops entered the city, together with some civilian elements who joined the Red forces" (quoted in Foltz, p. 355). Copies of the Juanes book, which had somehow cleared the censor, were soon confiscated. One of the most candid accounts of the Badajoz shootings was written by Mario Neves for the *Diario de Lisboa,* several parts of which are reproduced in Southworth, pp. 182, 184. Newspapers in the Nationalist zone developed a thesaurus of euphemisms to help them in making veiled references to the repression. Cf. *El Adelanto* (Salamanca), July 30, 1936; *ABC,* Aug. 8, 18, 23, 25, 1936; *El Correo Gallego* (Vigo), Aug. 25, 1936; *El Ideal Gallego* (La Coruña), *passim.*

The principal Republican summaries of the White Terror are Gordón, *Crimenes en la retaguardia rebelde,* and the anonymous *Lo que han hecho en Galicia,* for the most part either imprecise or undocumented.

27. Buonacorsi came to the island with the Italian air detachment known as "The Dragons of Death." Even Arrarás, *Cruzada,* IV, 303–4, admits that Buonacorsi's manner was exaggerated, but tries to defend him from worse charges. When visited by the author in Rome in April 1959, Buonacorsi was understandably reluctant to discuss his activity in Mallorca, which ended in December 1936. The British correspondent Lawrence Dundas witnessed part of the repression in Mallorca and estimated the number shot at 3,000. Dundas, pp. 73–77. Cf. Quintana, *Mallorca siempre española.*

28. "It was convenient for the clerical-monarchist forces, jealous of the Falange's expansion, to emphasize its repressive role, thus hiding their own direct involvement in the same task. In this respect, the polemic carried on between the Falange and the Requeté-monarchist group has declared repeatedly—most recently by Radio FE of Valladolid—and without any proof of inaccuracy, that it has never acted as an independent agent of repression in isolation, but rather with the approval of the constituted military authorities." (Ruiz Vilaplana, p. 218.) Georges Bernanos has made the same point concerning the repression on Mallorca in *Les Grands Cimetières sous la lune,* and Edmond Taylor wrote of the contrast between the peculiar sado-masochism of the Tercio and the more simple vengefulness of the Falangists (Hanighen, pp. 67–68).

29. According to the Falangist Territorial Inspector from Seville, Patricio G. de Canales, Valdés said that Falangist national syndicalism meant nothing to him, but that discipline must be restored to save Spain. (Conversation in Madrid, December 29, 1958.)

30. Cf. Liébana and Orizana, pp. 151–54.

31. Arrarás, *Cruzada,* III, 289.

32. At least half a dozen varying accounts of Lorca's death have been rendered. The first report of the Granada repression was given by Robert Neville in the *New York Herald Tribune,* Aug. 21, 1936. There are references to various reports in Thomas, p. 170, but the account given here has been constructed mainly from discussions with Luis Rosales, Madrid, January 11, 1959; Narciso Perales (who reorganized the Granada Falange in the period after Lorca's death), Madrid, January 14, 1959; and the following leaders of the original Granada Falange: José Rosales, March 20, 1959; Cecilio Cirre, March 21, 1959; Santiago Cardell, March 20, 1959; and José López Calero, March 16, 1959. Nationalist representations of the situation in Granada are given in Angel Gollonet Megías and José

Morales López, *Rojo y azul,* and José María Pemán, *ABC,* Dec. 5, 1948. The most extensive treatment of Lorca's death will be found in Schomberg, pp. 102–19, which differs from the version in this text in several respects.

33. Hedilla sent out circulars from Falangist headquarters in Salamanca in November 1936 and January 1937 ordering Falangists to cease participating in the repression. These orders were never fully obeyed; in certain provinces, Falangist bosses were among the leaders in the killings. Hedilla says that he also spoke to Franco in Salamanca but obtained no satisfaction.

34. Cf. *El Diario de Burgos,* Aug. 20, 1937.

35. *Domingo,* Sept. 5, 1937, quoted in Ruiz Vilaplana, p. 235.

36. Mínguez, *Ley de responsabilidades;* Benítez de Lugo, *Responsabilidades.* These are summarized in Clark, I, 132–38.

37. According to the *Anuario Estadístico,* 1944–45.

38. Ciano, in *Documenti,* XII, no. 611, pp. 458–62.

39. Republican Army officers were frequently punished according to their rank and the date at which it had been obtained. According to observers acquainted with the purge, the general rule of thumb was to mete out heavy punishment to those who had ranked as low as sergeant in 1936, when most posts were held by enthusiastic volunteers, or lieutenant in 1937; but NCO's and junior officers commissioned in the latter part of the war, when the Republican Army was somewhat more a technical than a political organization, drew lighter sentences.

40. The prison population in Spain declined as follows: 1941, 233,373; 1942, 159,392; 1943, 124,423; and 1944, 74,095. These figures are for January 1 of each year cited. *Anuario Estadístico,* 1944–45.

41. Foltz, p. 97. Various attempts have been made to calculate the extent of the repression. For example, Souchère, *Explication,* pp. 229–33, endeavors to corroborate such statistics by a careful comparison of official mortality figures in Spain.

Chapter Twenty-two

1. Ciano, in *Documenti,* XII, no. 480, pp. 362–64.

2. BOE, July 25, 1939.

3. Francisco Franco, *Palabras,* p. 299.

4. Knickerbocker, p. 54, had observed of the main rebel columns in the late summer of 1936 "There is a dearth of higher officers.... You seldom see an officer above a captain. On this whole front, the highest-ranking officers are lieutenant colonels and I have not even found one full colonel."

5. The first general postwar salary increase for officers did not become effective until July 1, 1940. It affected the various ranks as follows:

	1936–39 scale	*1940 scale*
Captain General	30,000	50,000
Lieutenant General	27,000	30,000
Major General	22,000	25,000
Brigadier General	17,000	20,000
Colonel	13,000	15,000
Lieutenant Colonel	11,000	13,000
Major	9,500	11,000
Captain	7,500	9,500
First Lieutenant	5,000	7,000
Second Lieutenant	4,000	6,000

(Figures taken from San Martín and San Martín)

6. See Bauer, p. 54.

7. Whealey's unpublished dissertation, "German-Spanish Relations," provides a thorough study of this period.

8. A security officer of the General Staff, Col. Kramer, wrote a report on June 5, 1939, of his conversations with the Spanish generals, among whom he dealt mainly with Aranda and García Valiño. Valiño and Aranda sounded quite pro-German, but also dwelt upon internal Spanish problems such as the lack of elite cadres and the political hostility of most of the urban population. They assured him that the Nationalist regime's only point of unity lay in the figure of the Generalissimo himself. Aranda expressed confidence that he would soon be appointed Chief of Staff, perhaps even Minister of War. Valiño claimed that Franco had promised him the post of High Commissioner of Morocco. *Documents secrets*, III, no. 23, pp. 66–68. These expectations, mostly unfulfilled, are a good example of how the most capable and energetic generals were being strung along by Franco.

9. The military mission is treated in Whealey, pp. 177–92.

10. *Documenti*, XII, no. 333, pp. 268–69.

11. Ciano, *Diary*, p. 100.

12. *Ibid.*, p. 104. It is interesting to note that the retirement age for the newly restored rank of Lieutenant General was set at 70. It has been suggested that this limit was imposed to prevent the former Lt. Gen. Carlos de Borbón, cousin of Alfonso XIII, from enjoying active rank.

One of the lesser monarchist generals, Tella, was expelled from the Army early in 1942. Though a valiant combat officer, he had a reputation as an unbalanced firebrand. It was not unusual for high-ranking military men to use Army facilities for personal profit, but among the scores of colonels and generals abusing such perquisites, the only one singled out for punishment was Tella. He had used a group of Army trucks to transport some private materials in the Burgos district, and was charged with gross abuse of command and involuntarily retired. In the context of the times, this was, as Dionisio Ridruejo has written, "a misdeed of scant importance." *Escrito en España* (Buenos Aires, 1962), p. 105. In later years, Tella collected extensive evidence to prove his innocence of any major wrong-doing.

13. Olmedo and Cuesta, p. 298.

14. Aparicio, pp. 151–53.

15. *Ibid.*

16. Olmedo and Cuesta, pp. 298–320. However, when Franco was awarded the first Gold Medal of the City of Seville on May 6, 1943, he arranged that an identical emblem be awarded to Queipo. In the following year, Queipo finally received his coveted Gran Cruz Laureada. DOME, March 3, 1944.

17. *Documenti*, XII, no. 611, pp. 458–62.

18. *Entre Hendaya y Gibraltar*, p. 124.

19. Yagüe had been promoted to full colonel on December 16, 1936, and was made brigadier in the middle of 1937. However, he was a year older than Franco and about six years older than Varela, and therefore still considered himself somewhat left behind.

20. Before the Civil War, Muñoz Grandes had had the reputation of a strict, efficient professional; his political attitudes were considered to be moderate. Though he apparently joined the UME, there is no evidence that he was actually an active member of the conspiracy, but he was arrested by the Madrid police just as the revolt began. Because of his UME membership, a revolutionary tribunal expelled him from the Republican Army and sentenced him to nine years' im-

prisonment, under the Republican Code of Military Justice, which condemned any officer "who, having knowledge of an attempt to commit this crime [rebellion]," did not "denounce it to his superiors." Such treatment thoroughly embittered the ailing Muñoz Grandes. Though seriously ill from the spring of 1936 to the spring of 1937, he nevertheless reiterated his loyalty to the Republic and eventually persuaded "Papa" Miaja to intercede for him. The Republican commander of the central front sent a statement to court on April 1, 1937, saying that the Republican Army needed officers of "proven competence" and "demonstrated loyalty to the Republic," and asked a full pardon for Muñoz Grandes. This was granted soon afterward. *Gaceta de la República*, no. 112, April 22, 1937. It was expected that he would serve in the Republican Army, but as soon as possible he made his way to the Nationalist zone.

21. Subsequently a "University Militia" of Falangist Youth was established early in 1941. It engaged in paramilitary training, and its graduates were to be entitled to NCO rank. BOE, March 5, 1941; *Fundamentos del Nuevo Estado* (Madrid, 1943), pp. 444–49.

By this time, the schools for alféreces provisionales had been closed, but in 1942 the Reserve officer program of *oficialidad de complemento* was revived and reorganized. It was open to university students who could qualify and were willing to serve two summers plus a special six-month training period. This training entitled them to the rank of Reserve second lieutenant. BOE, April 2, 1942; *Fundamentos del Nuevo Estado*, pp. 449–60.

22. *Documents*, X, no. 87, pp. 97–99. The loyalty of the high command was in no way diminished by a new round of promotions in April 1940, in which twelve colonels were elevated to brigadier and five brigadiers to major general. Two senior monarchist major generals, Kindelán and Ponte, were promoted to the newly restored rank of lieutenant general.

23. Yagüe met his political downfall in mid-1940. Promoted to major general in April of that year, he still dabbled with the notion of a pro-fascist military conspiracy that would replace the present regime with a more militant national revolutionary movement. Though he took no active steps toward rebellion, an aide denounced his furtive maneuvers and conversations. Franco demanded of Yagüe what his real intentions were, and expelled him from the Cabinet in June 1940. See my *Falange*, pp. 212–15.

24. Quoted in Detwiler, p. 36. On the problem of Spain's foreign relations during this period, the unpublished dissertation of Halstead, "Spain, the Powers and the Second World War," should also be consulted.

25. This note of August 10, 1940, from the German High Command, "The Spanish Army at Present," reported that the 25 regular divisions were only 9,000 men strong, though they could be expanded to 12,000 under full mobilization. There was only one Cavalry division and one motorized division, and no fully armored division. There were 20,000 Moors under arms in the Protectorate.

"The Officer Corps is markedly superannuated in the higher ranks. It includes few regular officers, mostly reserve officers retained in service. The officer situation is poor. Owing to the losses of the Civil War a great many of the scheduled positions are unfilled. Only the posts of colonel and lieutenant colonel are filled according to the budget. There is a shortage of majors (50 per cent of budgeted positions), captains (90 per cent of budgeted positions), first and second lieutenants (almost 100 per cent of budgeted positions).

"Platoons are commanded practically throughout by reserve officers. They are released only after completing the 18-month training course for officers on active duty. About 4,000 officers are now attending these courses. In case of war they would immediately rejoin their units and even today they are capable, well-disciplined and dedicated officers. For the creation of an officer corps sufficient for all grades and services (regular engineer officers, e.g., were almost completely wiped out at the beginning of the Civil War) Spain needs, in the opinion of General Martínez Campos, Chief of the Spanish General Staff, 8 years.

"With respect to artillery there are great deficiencies in guns, laying gear, and spare parts. Available guns are mostly worn out.

"There are about 200, mostly light, tanks still fit for war use. Spare parts are lacking.

"The ammunition situation is bad. Spain may at present have ammunition for only a few days.

"The officer, especially if older, often lacks enterprise, tenacity, and sufficient interest in his profession. The young officer promises to become a better one, since the recent war experience and the German example furnished in the Civil War are deeper rooted and alive in him.

"The command is usually sluggish and doctrinaire. The lessons of colonial war are often applied to European conditions in an exaggerated fashion.

"Since in creating a corps of leaders one must resort chiefly to the younger generation, it might take years to make perceptible progress."

Documents, X, no. 326, pp. 461–64.

Military training was meanwhile being regularized by a new draft law promulgated on August 8, 1940, which required two years of active service from all healthy Spanish males over the age of twenty. Volunteers would serve three years, and reductions of from six to twelve months could be obtained by those with previous training. This law set recruitment norms for the next quarter-century.

The pre-1931 Code of Military Justice was re-established *in toto* on July 12, 1940. In a further measure of regularization, the certificates granted during the Civil War permitting officers to hold positions exceeding their official rank were canceled on May 5, 1941. Provisions were made for the retirement at senior rank of those who preferred not to continue in active service at a lower level. Despite murmuring, the measure was generally well received. (Clark, I, 332.)

26. Quoted in Detwiler, p. 71.

27. *Ibid.,* p. 86.

28. Cited in Feis, p. 121.

29. *Documents,* XII, no. 21, pp. 36–37.

30. *Ibid.,* no. 386, pp. 611–15.

31. Report of Col. Kramer, German Air Attaché in Madrid, May 7, 1941, *Documents secrets,* no. 26, pp. 73–78. Aranda had told Kramer that the Superior War College had been ordered to draw up tentative plans for the occupation of Portugal, a move which Aranda did not favor.

32. *Documents secrets,* no. 28, pp. 80–83.

33. Ciano, *Papers,* pp. 460–65.

34. Report of Ambassador von Stohrer, May 8, 1942, *Documents secrets,* 31, pp. 96–101.

35. *Ibid.*

36. Quoted in Mirandet, p. 119.

37. The events leading up to these changes are discussed from another point of view in my *Falange,* pp. 228–37.

38. Créac'h, p. 205.

39. At first Muñoz Grandes was not happy with his new role in Spain, saying that he feared Franco wanted to isolate him politically, according to Ambassador von Moltke in a report of January 15, 1940, subsequently quoted in Edwards and Roa, pp. 25–27.

40. According to Foltz, p. 218.

41. The full text of this letter has been made available from monarchist sources. An abridged version was published in Sánchez-Boxá, pp. 32–33.

The five lieutenant generals who did not sign were Jordana, Vigón, and the recently promoted Muñoz Grandes, Moscardó, and Serrador. Queipo de Llano had been put on the reserve list in February, though at that time he was only 66 years of age. A few weeks after this letter was delivered to Franco, Yagüe was promoted to lieutenant general and made military commander of his native Burgos district. In December, Juan Bautista Sánchez became the fifteenth lieutenant general.

Vigón was especially useful to Franco because, though he had always been a monarchist, his basic loyalty was to the Caudillo. A Cabinet member until 1945, he seems to have kept the Generalissimo well informed about monarchist maneuvers.

42. Créac'h, pp. 207–8.

43. Lt. Gen. Emilio Esteban Infantes, *La División Azul,* provides the best account of the main phase of Spanish participation on the Russian front. A good brief summary is given in "Recuerdo." Because the Blue Division was joined by many highly motivated volunteers, it produced an extensive memoir literature and inspired a number of novels. There is a partial bibliography in Haupt.

44. According to Calleja (p. 202), operations against this first group of maquis lasted from October 4 to November 14, 1944. Some 200 were killed or captured, while the government forces suffered only about 20 casualties. See also Cossías, pp. 61–64.

45. In anticipation of new disturbances within Spain, a new law providing for the trial of "military rebels" by courts-martial had been promulgated on March 2, 1943. The fine print of this decree was so inclusive as to bring nearly anything in the way of political or violent criminal activity under the terms of "military rebellion," even extending some of the previous regulations. Clark, I, 419–22.

46. These maneuvers have been studied in a rather distorted doctoral thesis by John M. Breen, "The Soviet Attempt to Control Spain."

47. This is recounted in detail in Cossías.

48. According to Hughes, p. 210.

49. Statistics on the operation of non-Communist (mainly anarchist) guerrilla units are not available, but the Spanish Communist military leader Enrique Líster has given the following figures for armed Communist actions of all kinds in Spain from 1944 to 1949.

Year	Number of actions
1944	694
1945	783
1946	1,085
1947	1,317
1948	983
1949	509
	5,371

These figures are from Líster, pp. 53–58. It is entirely possible that he has included operations by non-Communist groups as well.

50. Cf. Créac'h, pp. 234–35.

51. Cavanillas, pp. 379–407.

52. It is impossible to be absolutely precise about military expenditure under the Franco regime, because of inaccurate statistics, juggled accounts, and the system of extraordinary budgets that was maintained up to 1946. In 1940, the first regular peacetime budget devoted 1,140,352,376 of a total of 7,161,245,337 pesetas —or approximately 16 per cent—to the Army, not including supplemental appropriations that followed. The naval budget was about one-quarter that of the Army, or some 4 per cent of the total. During the first peacetime years of the regime, considerable emphasis was placed on the Air Force, which received nearly half as much as the Army. By 1943, as the budget expanded to nine and a half billion pesetas, the Army's share increased to more than 19 per cent. The Navy's proportion declined by a fraction, while the Air Force received increasingly less attention, its budget running proportionately about 40 per cent lower than in 1945.

The pressure exerted against the regime in 1944–46 prompted heavier military expenditures. In 1945, when the budget jumped to thirteen-and-a-quarter billion (increasingly inflated) pesetas, the Army was allotted nearly 28 per cent, and the shares of the other two branches were also raised; but in the following year, the Army's proportion was reduced to 23 per cent.

In 1947, the main budget was drastically reduced by more than 15 per cent, but it began to go up again the following year. The absolute totals spent on the armed forces continued to rise, but not much faster than the inflation, and the proportionate cost of military expenditures in the budget as a whole began to decrease. (All figures above are drawn from *Presupuestos*, 1940–49, and the *Anuario Estadístico*, 1940–49.)

Despite persistent inflation, the salaries of the lower ranks remained very low after the Civil War: in the case of privates, only 15 pesetas per month. Salto, pp. 9–35; San Martín, *Sueldos*.

On January 1, 1949, an increased salary scale went into effect for the entire Officer Corps as follows (figures are given in pesetas):

	1941 salary	*1949 salary*
Captain General	50,000	70,000
Lieutenant General	30,000	42,000
Major General	25,000	35,000
Brigadier General	20,000	28,000
Colonel	15,000	21,000
Lieutenant Colonel	13,000	18,200
Major	11,000	15,400
Captain	9,500	13,300
First Lieutenant	7,500	10,500
Second Lieutenant	6,500	9,100

(Figures taken from San Martín and San Martín)

Save for the upper ranks, these were not extraordinary salaries; they barely managed to keep pace with the inflation. However, various subsidies and fringe benefits added 50 per cent or more to the income of officers at certain ranks.

53. Spanish armored equipment in the period immediately following the Civil

War was partially catalogued in Dalias, *Carros de combate*. It consisted of obso-lescent light-machine-gun-bearing German and Italian tanks, with a few similar British models.

54. In 1950 and 1951, the armed forces as a whole received about one-third of slightly increased general budgets, the biggest proportionate raise going to the Navy. In 1952, the total budget jumped to 22,762,147,700 pesetas, and the armed forces enjoyed their proportionate share of the increase. The Army got approxi-mately 19 per cent of the total expenditures, the Air Force nearly 8 per cent, and the Navy about 6 per cent. (*Presupuestos*, 1950–52; *Anuario Estadístico*, 1950–52.)

55. Though lesser officers were not permitted such independent attitudes, it was reported that a Colonel Serrano, sitting as a member of the regime's hand-picked Cortes, protested early in 1952 that the government was spending too much of the nation's slender economic resources on the military. He was said to have been removed from his seat soon after. Créac'h, p. 312.

56. DOMG, January 26, 1952.

57. DOMG, July 18, 1952.

58. Yet it should not be thought that this resulted in an ecstatic wave of pro-Americanism among the Spanish military. There was a considerable amount of resentment over the American military presence in Spain; memories of the ex-clusion policy of 1945–48 still rankled, and the fact that the Spanish were always on the receiving end also created psychological problems.

The clandestine Spanish Communist Party tried to exacerbate national feel-ings of resentment with a barrage of printed and radio propaganda protesting that the 1953 Pact had drawn Spain into the sphere of potential atomic war and made Madrid a prime target for nuclear annihilation.

General Emilio Herrera, one of the creators of the Spanish Air Force and, since 1939, a figure in the Spanish Republican Government-in-exile, also tried to play on these feelings in a letter of November 14, 1953, to his former comrade Gen. Eduardo González Gallarza, Franco's current Minister of the Air Force. "Carta del General Don Emilio Herrera a su antiguo companero de armas Gen-eral Don Eduardo González Gallarza, Ministro del Aire del Gobierno franquista, y que quedó incontestada por éste último."

Another officer who did reply to Herrera's letters some months later expressed the predominant attitude among the military hierarchy: "We are not so vile as to tolerate the sale of our national sovereignty. The catastrophe that you foresee for Spain does not worry us at all; we are absolutely sure that, when the moment of danger arrives, the Caudillo, with his brilliant ability, will take the necessary action to free Spain of any risk." Quoted in *Ibérica*, III, 5 (May 1955).

59. Souchère, *Explication*, p. 273.

60. *Ibid.*, p. 274.

61. These events are discussed in greater detail in Souchère, "The Bankruptcy of Franco's Diplomacy."

It might be noted that the only Moroccan officer in the Spanish Army, Mo-hammed ben-Mizzian, became one of the three generals of the new Moroccan Army.

62. Créac'h, pp. 338–45.

63. A sample of university student opinion was made by the social studies section of the regime's Superior Council of Scientific Investigation in a circular questionnaire that included a request for evaluation of the Spanish military. Of 400 students who answered, 90 per cent were recorded as deeming the military leaders "ignorant, routine, useless," and some 48 per cent were said to have gone so

far as to put them in the category of "woman-chasers, brutal, drunken." Camille
Cianfarra, *New York Times*, January 4 and 7, 1956. However, this opinion poll
has been strongly criticized for poor organization and weak methodology.

64. Créac'h, pp. 362–65.

65. This is discussed in considerable detail in my *Falange*, pp. 250–61.

66. The new scale was as follows:

Rank	Salary in pesetas
Lieutenant General	68,000
Major General	57,700
Brigadier General	48,500
Colonel	41,500
Lieutenant Colonel	37,100
Major	31,300
Captain	25,000
First Lieutenant	19,000
Second Lieutenant	16,150

Sergeants' pay was raised to 14,000 pesetas, an increase of 88 per cent. The ordinary Civil Guard salary was raised, and the Guard was allowed to share with the regular Army special housing and commissary benefits. See San Martín, *Almanaque*.

67. Some of these managed to emigrate, but the majority were apparently returned to Spanish authorities. *La Dépêche de Toulouse*, February 11, 1958; *Ibérica*, VI, 1 (January 1958).

68. The political opposition hailed the formation of the Juntas as an incipient military revolt against the regime, but this seems an exaggeration.

69. A long and forceful critique of the regime that was said to be a Junta manifesto was published *in toto* in *Ibérica*, IV, 10 (October 1956), but its authenticity is not certain.

70. Créac'h, p. 389.

71. Barroso was an example of that minority within the Officer Corps who came from an upper-class background of considerable wealth. He had been military attaché in Paris in 1936 and had met Franco's family at the port of Le Havre when Franco first sent them into safekeeping abroad. During most of the Civil War Barroso served as Chief of Operations at Franco's headquarters.

A sketch of Barroso is given in Arthur Whitaker, pp. 140–42. Its implication that Barroso had made a good deal of money from his position (which would not have been surprising) evoked great protest in official propaganda.

72. Vigón was by far the best literary polemicist in the Army. He had published a series of pro-monarchist articles in the Madrid press during 1955, and had made his ideas about the Spanish military known in several books.

73. Except for the 71-year-old Moscardó, who had been promoted to Captain General in an inactive position two months earlier.

74. The *Escalas Generales* for 1961 listed 721 generals (1 captain general, 46 lieutenant generals, 166 major generals, and 508 brigadiers), but nearly two-thirds were reservists. There were proportionately just as many admirals in the Navy (13 full admirals, 30 vice-admirals, and 62 counter-admirals, for a total of 105).

75. Fernández Hernando, *Reclutamiento*.

76. Following the advent of American military aid in 1953, the proportion of military expenses in the total budget began to decline. The share of the armed

forces fell from 30 per cent in 1953 to 27 per cent in 1955 to 25 per cent in 1957 to 24 per cent in 1959. The ratio between the three services remained approximately the same, with the Army receiving somewhat more than half the total military share, and the Air Force getting less than half as much as the Army, but always a little more than the Navy. *Presupuestos,* 1953–61; *Anuario Estadístico,* 1953–61.

77. According to the *Presupuestos,* the police in Spain had numbered 72,044 in 1935 and cost 6.3 per cent of the total budget (not including urban traffic police). In 1958, they numbered 84,591, an increase slightly less than the proportionate growth of population in the intervening period, and cost 5.3 per cent of the budget.

78. The reliance on courts-martial for the prosecution of political "crimes" was slowly being reduced, but after increased activity by the domestic opposition, a decree of November 26, 1957, restored jurisdiction over all such matters to a "special military judge for subversive activities." A subsequent decree of September 26, 1960, revived a law of 1943 that defined as "military rebellion" politically motivated strikes, the spreading of "false or tendentious" information, and any act detrimental to the prestige of the country's "institutions, government, Army, or police authorities." In practice, however, these rulings were soon relaxed, and were usually not invoked during the strikes that took place in northern Spain between 1962 and 1965. At the beginning of May 1963, the government announced formation of a new civil court and tribunal of public order that would handle all ordinary "political crimes" save those of "terrorism, etc." (*The Times,* May 5, 1963.) The "et cetera" in the official announcement left the usual enormous loophole, but theoretically it was easier thereafter for civilian attorneys and defense witnesses to be employed on behalf of the accused, provided that conditions were what the law termed "favorable."

Most military leaders saw nothing wrong with Army court jurisdiction over civilian dissidents, but there was strong feeling against the arrest of officers by the regular police for nonmilitary offenses. At the end of 1957, Lt. Javier Pradera (progressivist grandson of the Carlist intellectual Víctor Pradera), a member of the Air Force legal corps, was arrested by the political police as a Communist. The Captain General of Madrid, Rodrigo, was said to have been enraged, and dispatched an Air Force platoon to remove him from the regular prison to a special Air Force jail. It is alleged that a ruling by the Cabinet was necessary before the military would allow him to be sent back to the Special Tribunal for political subversion. Cf. *Ibérica,* VI, 2 (February 1958).

The touchiness of the Army command about any discussion of military matters was shown by the fate of a provincial newspaper editor who recommended, in *El Diario Regional* (Valladolid) on November 6, 1964, that the term of compulsory service be greatly reduced. He was immediately removed from his position and arrested, and was later given a six-month suspended sentence.

79. In this Cabinet change, Barroso, in poor health, was replaced as Army Minister by Lt. Gen. Pablo Martín Alonso, another of Franco's *incondicionales.* An africanista, one-time aide-de-camp to Alfonso XIII, and an old Galician acquaintance of the Generalissimo, Martín Alonso had participated in the revolts of 1932 and 1936, but other officers have said that he was reluctant to exercise initiative on both occasions. A brigadier by 1939, he became Director General of Military Education after the Civil War, was promoted to lieutenant general in 1946, then followed Muñoz Grandes as Chief of Franco's Military Household and Captain General of Madrid. Career sketches of Martín Alonso and other leading generals are given in San Martín, *España.*

Known as something of a martinet, Martín Alonso could be trusted to administer his bureaucratic duties without special enterprise or imagination. There is no indication that he ever caused Franco the slightest difficulty. He died unexpectedly after an abdominal operation at the beginning of 1964.

80. During 1963, the peak of speculation occurred at the time of the execution of the Communist leader Grimau. It was rumored that Muñoz Grandes had opposed the ultraconservative (civilian and military) majority in the Cabinet that had voted for Grimau's head, arguing that such a measure would be *contraproducente,* and had opted for the death sentence only to preserve unanimity among the generals in the Cabinet. But it seemed clear that Muñoz Grandes would not contradict Franco unless faced with an absolute crisis, and perhaps not even then. There were vague reports that Army dissidents had approached Lt. Gen. Carlos Asensio, former Army Minister and Chief of Franco's Military Household and of the General Staff, who had very recently retired. When queried about his willingness to head a new military directory, Asensio rejected all propositions, saying that such a solution could not be accepted. Cf. the correspondent of *The Observer,* April 28, 1963.

81. It was lowest in the industrialist-separatist provinces of Barcelona, Vizcaya, and Guipuzcoa, and in Galicia, and also quite low in the provinces of Córdoba and Seville, according to an investigation conducted by Juan J. Linz and reported in his unpublished "Regional Differences in the Social Structure of Spain and their Consequences for Political Integration."

82. As late as the five-year period 1955–60, the average annual rate of illiteracy among new recruits ranged from 12 to 15 per cent (a statistic that might be accepted as minimal). Cavanillas, p. 404.

83. *Pueblo* (Madrid), Feb. 16, 1963.

Conclusion

1. Rafael Moreno, "El Ejército: ¿Monárquico o Democristiano?" *España Libre,* January 1966. Cf. *Mañana,* no. 11, January 1966.

Bibliography

"A" and "B." Apuntes en defensa del honor del Ejército. Madrid, 1898.

Abad de Santillán, Diego. La revolución y la guerra. Barcelona, 1938.

¡Abajo los Ejércitos permanentes! Madrid, 1872.

ABC (Madrid-Seville), 1917–36.

Abshagen, Karl Heinz. Canaris. London, 1956.

Acedo Colunga, Felipe (Lt.). El alma de la Aviación española. Madrid, 1928.

——— (Gen.). José Calvo Sotelo. Barcelona, 1957.

Acosta y Albear, Brig. Gen. Francisco de. Compendio histórico del pasado y presente de Cuba y de su guerra insurreccional hasta el 11 de marzo de 1875. Madrid, 1875.

El Adelanto (Salamanca), 1936.

Agramoent y Cortijo, Francisco. Prim. Madrid, 1931.

Aguirre, José Antonio de. Entre la libertad y la revolución 1930–1935. Bilbao, 1935.

Aguirre, Ruperto. Expedición al Riff. Madrid, 1859.

¡Al Ejército! Madrid, 1871.

Alamo Castillo, Col. Rafael. Compendio de organización y legislación militar. Manresa, 1894.

Alarcón, Pedro Antonio de. Diario de un testigo de la guerra de Africa. 2 vols. Madrid, 1920.

Alba, Santiago. L'Espagne et la Dictature. Paris, 1930.

Alba, Víctor. Historia de la segunda República española. Mexico City, 1961.

Alcaide Ibieca, Agustín. Historia de los sitios que pusieron a Zaragoza en 1808 y 1809 las tropas de Napoleón. 3 vols. Madrid, 1868–78.

Alcalá Galiano, Alvaro. The Fall of a Throne. London, 1933.

Alcazár, Mariano del. López Domínguez. Madrid, 1946.

Alessi, Marco. La Spagna dalla monarchia al governo di Franco. Milan, 1937.

Alfarache, Juan de. Berenguer. Madrid, 1949.

Algarra Ráfegas, Maj. Antonio. El asedio de Huesca. Zaragoza, 1944.

Algo sobre el Ejército territorial de Canarias. Sta. Cruz de Tenerife, 1907.

Almirante, José. Bibliografía militar de España. Madrid, 1876.

Alonso González, Bruno. La flota republicana y la guerra civil española. Mexico City, 1944.

Amador Carrandi, F. Ensayo bibliográfico de las obras y folletos publicados con motivo del Movimiento nacional. Bermeo, 1940.

Ametller y Vilademunt, Brig. Gen. Victoriano. Juicio crítico de la guerra de Africa. Madrid, 1861.

Amorós, Narciso. Biografía. Madrid, n.d.

Amoroso, Lt. Col. Gaetano. Mortai e Lupi in Catalogna. Turin, 1941.

Anderson, Eugene N. The First Moroccan Crisis. Chicago, 1930.

Andrés, Ignacio. El Ejército español. Zaragoza, 1863.

Ansaldo, Juan Antonio. ¿Para qué . . .? (De Alfonso XIII a Juan III). Buenos Aires, 1953.

Anson, Luis María. Acción Española. Zaragoza, 1960.

Anuario Estadístico de España, 1931–65.

Anuario Militar, 1876–1936.

Araceli, Gabriel. Valencia 1936. Zaragoza, 1939.

Aralar, José de. La rebelión militar española y el pueblo vasco. Buenos Aires, 1937.

Aranda, Gen. Antonio. "Sitio y defensa de Oviedo," *Ejército,* No. 8 (August 1940).

Araquistain, Luis de. "The Struggle in Spain," *Foreign Affairs,* April 1934.

Arderíus, Francisco. La Escuadra española en Santiago de Cuba. Barcelona, 1903.

Arderíus, Joaquín, and José Díaz Fernández. Vida de Fermín Galán. Madrid, 1931.

Areilza, José María de. Historia de una conspiración romántica. Madrid, 1950.

Arizaga, José Manuel. Memoria militar y política sobre la guerra en Navarra. Madrid, 1840.

Armiñán, Luis de. Excmo. Sr. General D. Antonio Aranda Mata. Avila, 1937.

———. Sánchez Guerra. Madrid, 1948.

———. Weyler. Madrid, 1946.

———, and José Manuel, eds. Epistolario del dictador. Madrid, 1930.

Arnaud, Dr. Louis. Au temps des "Mehallas": Le Maroc de 1860 à 1912. Casablanca, 1952.

Arques, Enrique, and Narciso Gibert. Los Mogataces. Ceuta-Tetuán, 1928.

Arrarás, Joaquín. Franco. Santiago de Chile, 1938.

———. Historia de la segunda República española. 2 vols. Madrid, 1956–58.

———, ed. Historia de la Cruzada española. 8 vols. Madrid, 1940.

Artola, Miguel. Los afrancesados. Madrid, 1953.

Arzadún, Juan. Fernando VII y su tiempo. Madrid, 1942.

Astur, Eugenia (pseud.). Riego. Oviedo, 1933.

Ayensa, Emilia. Del desastre de Annual a la presidencia del Consejo. Madrid, 1930.

Ayuso, José. Abolición de las quintas. Madrid, 1871.

Azaña, Manuel. En el poder y en la oposición (1932–1934). 2 vols. Madrid, 1934.

———. Una política, 1930–1932. Madrid, 1934.

———. Memorias íntimas. Madrid, 1939.

Aznar, Manuel. Historia militar de la Guerra de España. Madrid, 1940.

Azpeitua, Antonio. Marruecos, la mala semilla. Madrid, 1921.

Ballesteros y Beretta, Antonio. Historia de España y su influencia en la historia universal. 9 vols. Barcelona, 1919–41.

Barado y Font, Francisco. Literatura militar española en el siglo XIX. Madrid, 1889.

———. Museo militar: Historia del Ejército español. 3 vols. Madrid, 1889–95.

Barea, Arturo. The Forging of a Rebel. New York, 1946.

Baroja, Pío. Juan Van Halen. Madrid, 1933.

Barangó-Solís, Fernando. Un movimiento revolucionario: De los sucesos de Ciudad Real al Proceso Sánchez Guerra. Barcelona, 1929.

Bartel, Paul. "Oú va l'Espagne?" *Revue Hebdomadaire,* April 9, 1932.

Bartz, Karl. The Downfall of the German Secret Service. London, 1956.

Bassi, Capt. Maurizio. Da Cadice ai Pirenei. Florence, 1940.

Bastos Ansart, Francisco. El desastre de Annual. Barcelona, 1922.

Bauer, Eddy. Rouge et or. Neuchâtel, 1939.

Bayo, Col. Alberto. Mi desembarco en Mallorca. Guadalajara, Mex., 1944.

Becker, Jerónimo. Historia de las relaciones exteriores de España durante el siglo XIX. 3 vols. Madrid, 1924–26.

Belforte, General Francesco. La guerra civile in Spagna. 4 vols. Milan, 1938–39.

Bellido y Montesinos, Juan. El General Prim en México y Castillejos. Madrid, 1869.

Belmas, Jacques. Journaux des sièges faits ou soutenus par les français dans la péninsule de 1807 à 1814. 4 vols. Paris, 1836–37.

Beltrán Güell, Felipe. Preparación y desarrollo del movimiento nacional. Valladolid, 1938.

———. Caudillo, profetas y soldados. Madrid, 1939.

Benavides, Manuel D. La Escuadra la mandan los cabos. Mexico City, 1944.

Benavides Moro, Gen. Nicolás, and Lt. Col. José A. Yaque Laurel. El Capitán General Don Joaquín Blake y Joyes. Madrid, 1960.

Benítez Francés, Tomás. El manuscrito de un combate o el 3 du julio desde el "Vizcaya." El Ferrol, 1898.

Benítez de Lugo y Reymundo, Luis. Responsabilidades civiles y políticas. Barcelona, 1940.

Benzo, Maj. Eduardo. Al servicio del Ejército. Madrid, 1931.

Berenguer, Lt. Gen. Dámaso. Campañas en el Rif y Yebala 1919–20. Madrid, 1948.

———. De la dictadura a la República. Madrid, n.d.

———. La guerra en Marruecos, ensayo de una adaptación técnica. Madrid, 1918.

Berenguer, Capt. Luis. El Ejército de Marruecos. Tetuán, 1922.

Bermejo, Ildefonso Antonio. Alzamiento popular de 1854. Madrid, 1854.

———. Historia del reinado de Isabel II. 3 vols. Madrid, 1872–74.

———. Historia de la interinidad y guerra civil de España desde 1868. 3 vols. Madrid, 1875–77.

Bermúdez de Castro, Gen. Luis. "El Teniente General Conde de España." *Ejército,* No. 77 (June 1946).

———. Militares románticos. Barcelona, 1950.

Bermudo-Soriano, Eliseo. El Raisuni. Madrid, 1941.

Bernanos, Georges. Les Grands cimetières sous la lune. Paris, 1947.

Bernard, Ino. Mola, mártir de España. Granada, 1938.

Bertrán y Musitu, José. Experiencias de los Servicios de Información del Nordeste de España (S.I.F.N.E.) durante la guerra. Madrid, 1940.

Beumelburg, Werner. Kampf um Spanien: Die Geschichte der Legion Condor. Berlin, 1940.

Biblioteca Central Militar. Archives.

Blanco, Carlos. La Dictadura y los procesos militares. Madrid, 1931.

Blázquez y Delgado Aguilera, Antonio. Historia de la administración militar. Madrid, 1897.

———. Fundamentos de la organización económica del Ejército. Madrid, 1910.

Bley, Wolf. Das Buch der Spanienflieger. Berlin, 1939.

Boletín Oficial de la Junta de Defensa Nacional. 1936.

Boletín Oficial del Estado. 1936–39.

Bolós y Saderra, Joaquín. El Carlismo en Cataluña. Barcelona, 1930.

Bona, Félix de. Cuba, Santo Domingo, y Puerto Rico. Madrid, 1861.

Bonmatí de Codecido, Francisco. El Príncipe Don Juan de España. Valladolid, 1938.

Bonomi, Ruggero. Viva la muerte: Diario dell'Aviación del Tercio. Rome, 1941.

Bordas, Luis. Hechos históricos y memorables acaecidos en España desde la última enfermedad de Fernando VI hasta la conclusión de la guerra de los siete años. Barcelona, 1846.

Borrego, Andrés. Historia de la vida militar y política de Don Francisco Serrano y Domínguez. Madrid, 1892.

Borrow, George. The Bible in Spain. London, 1959.

Botella Carbonell, Juan, ed. La Guerra civil de España de 1872 a 1876 seguida de la insurrección de la isla de Cuba. Barcelona, 1876.

Bourgoing, J. F. Tableau de l'Espagne moderne. 2 vols. Paris, 1807.

Bouthelier, Antonio, and José López Mora. Ocho días: la revuelta comunista, Madrid 5–13 marzo 1939. Madrid, 1940.

Breen, John M. The Soviet Attempt to Control Spain, 1946. Unpublished dissertation. Georgetown University, 1953.

Brissa, José. La revolución de julio en Barcelona. Barcelona, 1910.

Bueno y Núñez de Prado, Maj. Emilio. Historia de la acción de España en Marruecos desde 1904 a 1927. Madrid, 1929.

Bullón de Mendoza, Alfonso. Bravo Murillo y su significación en la política española. Madrid, 1950.

Burgo, Jaime del. Requetés en Navarra antes del alzamiento. Pamplona, 1954.

Burgos, Carmen de. Gloriosa vida y desdichada muerte de Don Rafael del Riego. Madrid, 1931.

Burgos y Mazo, Manuel. Antología política. Valencia, 1944.

———. La Dictadura y los constitucionalistas. 4 vols. Madrid, 1934–35.

———. Páginas históricas de 1917. Madrid, n.d.

———. El verano de 1919 en Gobernación. Cuenca, 1921.

Burns, Emile, ed. The Nazi Conspiracy in Spain. London, 1937.

Buxadé, José. España en crisis: la bullanga misteriosa de 1917. Barcelona, 1918.

Buxeres y Roses, Antonio. Barcelona en julio de 1840. Barcelona, 1884.

Cabanellas, Guillermo. Militarismo y militaradas. Madrid, 1933.

Cacho Zabalza, Antonio. La Unión Militar Española. Alicante, 1940.

Calandra, Aurelio, ed. Dove il Littorio chiama. Rome. 1939.

Calleja, Juan José. Yagüe, un corazón al rojo. Barcelona, 1963.

Calvo, Gonzalo. España en Marruecos. Barcelona, 1913.

Calvo Sotelo, José. Mis servicios al Estado. Madrid, 1931.

———. La voz de un perseguido. 2 vols. Madrid, 1933.

Camino, Maj. Fernando G. "La Batalla de Reinosa," *Ejército*, No. 13 (February 1941).

Campoamor, José María. La actitud de España ante la cuestión de Marruecos (1900–1904). Madrid, 1951.

Canalejas, José. Concepto jurídico de las instituciones militares. Madrid, 1893.

Canals, Salvador. Los sucesos de España en 1909. 2 vols. Madrid, 1910.

Canel, José (pseud.). Octubre rojo en Asturias. Madrid, 1935.

Canella Secades, Francisco de B. Algo sobre la reorganización del Ejército. Córdoba, 1904.

Cantalupo, Roberto. Fu la Spagna. Verona, 1948.

Canterac, José, et al. Copia del oficio que los gefes del Egército nacional pasaron al Excelentísimo Señor Virrey del Perú D. Joaquín de la Pezuela. Madrid, 1821.

Capella, Jacinto. La verdad de Primo de Rivera. Madrid, 1933.

Cardozo, Harold. March of a Nation. New York, 1937.

Carrascal, G. Asturias 18 julio 1936–21 octubre 1937. Valladolid, 1938.

Carrera Pujal, Jaime. Historia política de Cataluña en el siglo XIX. 7 vols. Barcelona, 1957–58.

Carretero, José María. ¿Alfonso XIII fue buen rey? Madrid, 1934.

Casado, Col. Segismundo. The Last Days of Madrid. London, 1939.

Casas Pérez, José de las. El régimen y sus hombres. Madrid, 1926.

Casero, Capitán. Recuerdos de un revolucionario. Valencia, n.d.

Castell-Florite, Marqués de. Domingo Dulce, general isabelino. Barcelona, 1962.

Castillo, José del, and Santiago Alvarez. Barcelona: objetivo cubierto. Barcelona, 1958.

Castillo, Rafael del. Historia de la vida militar y política del Excmo. Sr. Capitán General Don Leopoldo O'Donnell. Cádiz-Madrid, 1860.

Castillo Mayone, Joaquín del. La Ciudadela inquisitorial de Barcelona, o las víctimas inmoladas por el Conde de España. Barcelona, n.d.

Castrillo Mazeres, Francisco. La aportación de España al arte militar. Madrid, 1959.

Castro Girona, Alberto. Jovellar. Madrid, 1947.

Cattell, David T. Soviet Diplomacy and the Spanish Civil War. Los Angeles, 1958.

Cavanillas Prósper, Maj. Gen. Rafael. "El Ejército de Tierra y sus nuevas unidades," El Nuevo Estado Español 1936–1961. Vol. I. Madrid, 1961.

Cebreiros, Lt. Col. Nazario. Las reformas militares. Santander, 1931.

Cerdó Pujol, Lt. Col. Luis. "Mallorca se defiende," Ejército, No. 19 (August 1941).

Cervera, Admiral Pascual. Guerra hispano-americana; colección de documentos. El Ferrol, 1899.

Cervera Baviera, Lt. Julio. Geografía militar de Marruecos. Barcelona, 1884.

Chalmers-Mitchell, Sir Peter. My House in Málaga. London, 1938.

Chamorro y Baquerizo, Pedro, ed. Estado Mayor Central del Ejército español: Historia individual de su cuadro en los años de 1851 a 1856. Madrid, 1856.

———. Historia del ilustre cuerpo de oficiales generales. Madrid, 1851.

Chao, Eduardo. Historia de la vida militar y política de Martín Zurbano. Madrid, 1846.

Cía Navascuez, Policarpo. Memorias del Tercio de Montejurra. Pamplona, 1941.

Ciano, Count Galeazzo. Ciano's Diary, 1937–1938. London, 1952.

———. Ciano's Diplomatic Papers. Malcolm Muggeridge, ed. London, 1948.

Ciges Aparicio, Manuel. España bajo la dinastia de los Borbones. Madrid, 1932.

Cimadevilla, Francisco. El General Primo de Rivera. Madrid, 1944.

Claridad. 1936.

Clark, Clyde L. The Evolution of the Franco Regime. 3 vols. Washington, D.C., 1950.

Clonard, Conde de. Historia orgánica de las Armas de Infantería y Caballería. 6 vols. Madrid, 1851–59.

Colás Laguía, Emilio. El Movimiento patriótico en Aragón. Zaragoza, 1936.

Colodney, Robert G. The Struggle for Madrid. New York, 1958.

Colón de Larriátegui, Félix. Juzgados militares de España y sus Indias. 2 vols. Madrid, 1817.

Colvin, Ian. Master Spy. New York, 1952.

Comellas, José Luis. Los primeros pronunciamientos en España, 1814–20. Madrid, 1958.

———. Los realistas en el primer trienio constitucional, 1820–23. Pamplona, 1958.

Comisión Oficial de Heráldica. Estatuto nobiliario. Madrid, 1945.

Con y Tres, Dr. Elías. *El Ejército de Filipinas,* August 18, 1892, and September 8, 1892.

Concas y Palau, Victor. La Escuadra del Almirante Cervera. Madrid, n.d.

Conill y Mataró, Antonio. Codo. Barcelona, 1944.

Connelly, Joan. The Tragic Week: A Study of Anticlericalism in Spain. Unpublished dissertation. Bryn Mawr, 1963.

Contreras, Juan de. La iniciación en Segovia del Movimiento Nacional. Segovia, 1938.

Copado, Bernabé, S.J. Con la Columna Redondo. Seville, 1937.

Copia del extracto oficial de la sesión oficial celebrada el viernes 15 de febrero de 1935. Madrid, 1935.

Copons y Navia, Lt. Gen. Francisco. Memorias de los años de 1814 y 1820–24. Madrid, 1858.

Cordero Torres, José María. Organización del Protectorado español en Marruecos. 2 vols. Madrid, 1942–43.

Corral, Manuel. ¡El desastre! Barcelona, 1899.

El Correo Gallego. Vigo, 1936.

La Correspondencia Militar. Madrid, 1890–1932.

Cortés Cavanillas, Julián. Alfonso XIII. Madrid, 1959.

Corzo, Isidro. Cervera y su escuadra. Havana, 1901.

Cossías, Tomás. La lucha contra el "maquis" en España. Madrid, 1956.

Cousiño Quiroga, José. El Ejército como elemento indispensable para la vida nacional. Madrid, 1917.

Créac'h, Jean. Le Coeur et l'épée. Paris, 1959.

Crespo, Eduardo. Alféreces provisionales. Madrid, 1955.

Cruickshank, Earl F. Morocco at the Parting of the Ways. Philadelphia, 1935.

Cuadro de la composición y organización del Ejército español. Madrid, 1866.

Dahms, Helmuth Günther. Der spanische Bürgerkrieg, 1936–1939. Tübingen, 1962.

Dalias, Maj. Arturo. Carros de combate reglamentarios en España. Madrid, 1941.

Damidaux, Capt. Charles J. Combats au Maroc, 1925–1926. Paris, 1928.

Datos relativos a la organización, mando y distribución del Ejército y al presupuesto de Guerra. Madrid, 1906–20.

La Dépêche de Toulouse. 1958.

Deschamps, Bernard. La Vérité sur Guadalajara. Paris, 1938.

Detwiler, Donald S. Hitler, Franco und Gibralter: Die Frage des spanischen Eintritts in den Zweiten Weltkrieg. Wiesbaden, 1962.

Dézert, Desdevises du. L'Espagne de l'áncien régime. 3 vols. Paris, 1897–1904.

Diario de las Sesiones de las Cortes, 1876–1923, 1931–36.

Diario Oficial del Ministerio de la Guerra, 1900–1936.

Diario Oficial del Ministerio de la Marina, 1929.

Diario Oficial del Ministerio del Ejército. 1939–63.

El Diario Universal, 1919.

Díaz, Guillermo. Cómo llegó Falange al poder. Buenos Aires, 1942.

Díaz de Villegas, General José. Guerra de liberación. Barcelona, 1957.

Díaz de Villegas, Maj. José, and Capt. Sánchez Pérez. Lecciones de la experiencia. Toledo, 1930.

Díaz Fernández, Manuel. Defensa de las Islas Canarias. Madrid, 1899.

Díaz-Plaja, Fernando, ed. La historia de España en sus documentos. El siglo XX: La Guerra (1936–1939). Madrid, 1963.

Díaz-Retg, Enrique. Les Italiens dans la guerre d'Espagne. Paris, 1939.

Díaz Valderrama, José. Historia de la Guardia Civil. Madrid, 1858.

Diego, Capt. de, Lt. Quintana, and Lt. Royo. Belchite. Barcelona, 1939.

Directorio Militar, dos años de. Madrid, 1925.

Documenti Diplomatici Italiani. Rome, 1952.

Documents on German Foreign Policy, 1918–1945, Series D, III, X, XII. Washington, D.C., 1950.

Documents secrets du Ministère des Affaires Etrangères d'Allemagne. Brussels, 1946.

Domenech Lafuente, Lt. Col. Angel. Un oficial entre moros. Larache, 1948.

Domínguez, Edmundo. Los vencedores de Negrín. Mexico City, 1940.

Domínguez, Fidel. Los hombres de la Izquierda liberal: El Duque de la Torre. Madrid, 1883.

Dundas, Lawrence. Behind the Spanish Mask. London, 1943.

Eby, Cecil D. The Siege of the Alcázar. New York, 1965.

Edwards, Bob, and Augustin Roa. The Spanish Conspirators—After Franco Who? London, 1963.

Eggers, Eduardo R., and Enrique Feune de Colombí. Francisco de Zea Bermúdez y su época, 1779–1850. Madrid, 1958.

Einhorn, Marion. Die ökonomischen Hintergründe der faschistischen deutschen Intervention in Spanien 1936–1939. Berlin, 1962.

El Ejército Español. Madrid, 1905–55.

El Ejército español en 1868. Madrid, 1868.

El Ejército permanente y la milicia nacional, proyecto de una constitución militar. Valladolid, 1868.

Elices Montes, Ramón. El Gobierno y el Ejèrcito en los pueblos libres. Madrid, 1878.

———. El progreso del Ejército. Ponteverda, 1869.

Elliott, John. The Revolt of the Catalans. Cambridge, Eng., 1963.

Enciclopedia Universal Ilustrada, Suplemento 1936–1939.

Engels, Friedrich. Critique for *New York Daily Tribune*, 1860.

Enríquez de Salamanca, Lt. Jesús. La vida en el Alcázar de Toledo. Valladolid, 1937.

Equis, El Capitán (pseud.). El problema militar en España. Burgos, 1916.

Escalera, Juan V. Campaña de Cuba (1869 a 1875): recuerdos de un soldado. Madrid, 1876.

Escartín Lartiga, Eduardo. El Ejército en la acción política. Madrid, 1905.

Esch, Patricia van der. Prelude to War. The Hague, 1951.

España, Juan de. La actuación de España en Marruecos. Madrid, 1926.

Espina, Antonio. Espartero, o ¡ Cúmplase la voluntad nacional! Madrid, 1949.

Espinosa, Gen. Carlos. Diario de los movimientos del Ejército de operaciones del 5º distrito. Madrid, 1822.

Espoz y Mina, Francisco. Memorias. 5 vols. Barcelona, 1851–52.

Estado Mayor Central del Ejército. Narración militar de la Guerra carlista desde 1869 a 1876. 14 vols. Madrid, 1883–89.

———. Organización de las fuerzas del Ejército de operaciones en Melilla. Madrid, 1909.

———. Enseñanzas de la campaña del Rif en 1909. Madrid, 1911.

———. Colección documental del Fraile. 4 vols. Madrid, 1945–50.

———. Historia de la Guerra de Liberación (1936–1939). Madrid, 1945.

————. Historia de las campañas de Marruecos. 2 vols. Madrid, 1947.
————. Guerra de minas en España (1936–1939). Madrid, 1953.
Estasen, Rico de José. El General Elío. Valladolid, 1940.
Esteban-Infantes, Emilio. La División Azul. Barcelona, 1956.
————. Expediciones españolas: siglo XIX. Madrid, 1949.
————. General Sanjurjo. Barcelona, 1957.
————. La sublevación del General Sanjurjo. Madrid, 1933.
Estorch, M. Apuntes para la historia sobre la administración del Marqués de la
    Pezuela en la isla de Cuba. Madrid, 1856.
Estrade, Genaro, ed. Don Juan Prim y su labor diplomática en México. Mexico
    City, 1928.
Examen crítico de las revoluciones de España de 1820 a 1823 y de 1836. Paris,
    1837.
Eza, Vizconde de. Mis responsabilidades en el desastre de Melilla como Ministro
    de la Guerra. Madrid, 1923.

Faldella, Emilio. Venti mesi di guerra in Spagna (luglio 1936–febbraio 1938). Flor-
    ence, 1939.
Fanjul, Capt. Joaquín. Misión social del Ejército. Madrid, 1907.
Farfán, Gerardo, and Pedro González G. de Santiago. Por los fueros de la verdad:
    aclaraciones necesarias para la historia de los sucesos de Valencia. Madrid,
    1930.
Feis, Herbert. The Spanish Story. New York, 1948.
Fernández Almagro, Melchor. Historia del reinado de Don Alfonso XIII. Barce-
    lona, 1936.
————. Historia de la Segunda República española. Madrid, 1940.
————. En torno al 98. Madrid, 1949.
————. Cánovas, su vida y su política. Madrid, 1951.
————. Historia política de la España contemporánea. 2 vols. Madrid, 1956, 1959.
Fernández Cuesta, Nemesio, Francisco de Paula Madrazo, and Juan Pérez Calvo,
    eds. Causas formadas a consecuencia de la sedición militar que tuvo lugar en
    esta corte en la noche del 7 de octubre de 1841. Madrid, 1841.
Fernández de Castro y Pedrera, Rafael. Hacia las rutas de una nueva España (De
    como se preparó y por qué hubo de comenzar en Melilla la santa Cruzada na-
    cional). Melilla, 1940.
Fernández de Córdova, General Fernando. Memoria sobre los sucesos de julio de
    1854. Madrid, 1855.
————. Mis Memorias intimas. 3 vols. Madrid, 1886–89.
Fernández de Córdova, General Luis. Memoria justificativa del General Fernández
    de Córdova. Paris, 1837.
Fernández de Rota, Capt. Antonio. ¡Salvemos a España! Zaragoza, 1920.
Fernández Fernández, León. El Empecinado. Madrid, 1905.
————. Nuestros soldados en Africa. Madrid, 1907.
————. Defensa del coronel Don Francisco Sirvent Betis. Madrid, 1924.
Fernández Ferrer, Col. José. "Guerra de España," *Ejército,* May 16, 1941.
Fernández Golfin, Col. Luis. Breves apuntes sobre las cuestiones más importantes
    de la isla de Cuba. Barcelona, 1866.
Fernández Hernando, Maj. Hieroteo. Reclutamiento, reemplazo y movilización
    de los Ejércitos de España. Madrid, 1959.
Fernández San Román, Brig. Gen. Edouard. Statistique, organisation, et institu-
    tions militaires de l'Armée espagnole. Paris, 1852.

Fernández Suárez, Domingo. Sentenciado a muerte en la España franquista. Havana, 1946.

Fernsworth, Lawrence. Spain's Struggle for Freedom. Boston, 1957.

Ferrari Billoch, F. Archivo del "Baleares." Avila, 1939.

Ferrer, Magín. Historia de la última época . . . del conde de España. Madrid, 1944.

Ferrer, Melchor. "El General Franco y la Comunion Tradicionalista." Unpublished documented manuscript, n.d.

Ferrer, Melchor, *et al.*, eds. Historia del Tradicionalismo español. 30 vols. Seville, 1959.

Ferrer de Couto, José. Reincorporación de Santo Domingo a España. Madrid, 1861.

———. La cuestión de Santo Domingo. Havana, 1864.

Finer, S. E. The Man on Horseback. New York, 1962.

Flack, Horace E. Spanish-American Diplomatic Relations Preceding the War of 1898. Baltimore, 1906.

Flores, Eugenio Antonio. La Guerra de Cuba. Madrid, 1895.

Foix, Pedro. Los archivos del terrorismo blanco. Madrid, 1931.

Foltz, Charles, Jr. The Masquerade in Spain. Boston, 1948.

Fontana, José María. Los catalanes en la guerra de España. Madrid, 1951.

Forbes, Rosita. The Sultan of the Mountains. New York, 1924.

Francisco Soria, Francisco de. Mallorca . . . Por qué fuimos y por qué la abandonamos. Barcelona, 1938.

Francisco y Díaz, Maj. Francisco de. Nota bibliográfica. Madrid, 1909.

Franco, Sra. Carmen Polo de. "¿Qué hacía ud. mientras su marido se alzaba en armas?" Y (Revista para la mujer nacional-sindicalista), June 1938.

Franco, Francisco. Diario de una Bandera. Madrid, 1922.

———. "Ruud . . . Balek!," *Africa*, 1932.

———. Palabras del Caudillo, 19 abril 1937–31 diciembre 1938. Madrid, 1939.

Franco, Maj. Ramón. Aguilas y garras. Madrid, 1929.

———. Deciamos ayer. Madrid, 1931.

———. Madrid bajo las bombas. Madrid, 1931.

———. ¡Villa Cisneros! Madrid, 1933.

Francos Rodríguez, José. La vida de Canalejas. Madrid, 1918.

———. Días de la Regencia. Madrid, 1922.

———. El año de la derrota. Madrid, 1930.

Friedlander, Robert A. "Holy Crusade or Unholy Alliance? Franco's 'National Revolution' and the Moors," *Southwestern Social Science Quarterly*, Vol. XLIV, No. 4 (March 1964).

———. The July 1936 Military Rebellion in Spain: Background and Beginnings. Unpublished dissertation. Northwestern University, 1963.

Freixa y Rabasó, Eusebio. Guía de quintas. Madrid, 1895.

Fuente, Vicente de la. Historia de las sociedades secretas, antiguas y modernas, y especialmente de la Franc-Masonería. 3 vols. Lugo, 1870–71.

Fuentes, Alvaro. El crucero "Canarias" proa a la victoria. Madrid, 1940.

Funck, Oberst Freiherrn von. " 'Funker' und 'Drohne' hilfen Franco," *Die Wehrmacht,* May 1939.

Fundamentos del Nuevo Estado. Madrid, 1943.

"G." D. Francisco Espoz y Mina. Barcelona, 1840.

Gabrielli, Léon. Abd el-Krim et les événements du Rif. Casablanca, 1953.

La Gaceta Militar. Madrid, 1851.

Gaceta de la República. 1936–37.

Galindo Herrero, Santiago. Los partidos monárquicos bajo la Segunda República. Madrid, 1956.

Galinsoga, Luis de, and Lt. Gen. Franco Salgado. Centinela de Occidente. Barcelona, 1956.

Gallego, Tesifonte. La insurrección cubana. Madrid, 1900.

Gallego Ramos, Capt. Eduardo. La campaña del Rif (1909). Madrid, n.d.

———. Operaciones practicadas contra los insurrectos de Cavite. Madrid, 1898.

———. Primer Regimiento de Zapadores. Madrid, 1910.

———. Proyecto de reorganización y mejora del Ejército de tierra. Guadalajara, 1905.

Gallo de Renovales, José. Allendesalazar. Madrid, 1946.

Gambra, Rafael. La primera guerra civil de España. Madrid, 1949.

Gándara, Joaquín de la. Manifesto al pueblo español sobre los sucesos de los días 17, 18, y 19 de julio de 1854. Madrid, 1854.

Gandara, General José de la. Anexión y guerra de Santo Domingo. Madrid, 1884.

García Alonso, Carlos. Defensa del General Monet. Madrid, 1900.

García Alvarez, M., and A. García Pérez. Operaciones en el Rif 1909. Toledo, 1909.

García Camba, Andrés. Memorias para la historia de las armas españolas en el Perú. 2 vols. Madrid, 1846.

García de Luna, Luis. Prim. Madrid, 1866.

García Fernández, Lt. Col. Julio. Diario de operaciones del 3er Batallón de Palencia y 5ª Bandera de Navarra. Burgos, 1939.

García Figueras, Tomás. Primera campaña de Beni Aros. Madrid, 1928.

———. Santa Cruz de Mar Pequeña—Ifni—Sahara: La acción de España en la costa occidental de Africa. Madrid, 1941.

———. Marruecos. Madrid, 1944.

———. Africa en la acción española. Madrid, 1947.

———. España y su protectorado en Marruecos (1912–1956). Madrid, 1957.

García Ladevese, Ernesto. Memorias de un emigrado. Madrid, 1892.

García Mercadel, José. Aire, tierra, y mar. Zaragoza, 1938.

García Morato, Joaquín. Guerra en el aire. Madrid, 1940.

García Pradas, José. La traición de los Stalin: Cómo terminó la guerra de España. New York, 1939.

García Venero, Maximiano. Historia del nacionalismo catalán. Madrid, 1944.

———. Cataluña: síntesis de una región. Madrid, 1954.

———. Historia de las Internacionales en España. 3 vols. Madrid, 1957.

García Verdugo, Vicente. Cuba contra España. Madrid, 1869.

Garcilaso (Raimundo García). *Diario de Navarra*. Pamplona, 1956.

Garrachón Cuesta, Antonio. De Africa a Cádiz y de Cádiz a la España imperial. Cádiz, 1938.

Gay de Montellá, Rafael. Atalayas de Mallorca. Barcelona, 1940.

Gibert, Narciso. España y Africa. Madrid, 1912.

Gil Ossorio, Lt. Col. Fernando. "Oficiales provisionales," *Revista de Historia Militar*, No. 9 (1961).

Giménez y Guited, Francisco. Historia militar y política del General Don Juan Prim. 2 vols. Barcelona, 1860.

Girardet, Raoul. La Société militaire dans la France contemporaine 1815–1939. Paris, 1953.

Goded, Capt. Manuel. Un faccioso cien por cien. Zaragoza, 1938.

Goded Llopis, Gen. Manuel. Marruecos: las etapas de la pacificación. Madrid, 1932.

Gollonet Megías, Angel, and José Morales López. Rojo y azul en Granada. Granada, 1937.
———. Sangre y fuego: Málaga. Granada, 1937.
Gomá, Colonel José. La guerra en el aire. Barcelona, 1958.
Gomá y Tomás, Cardinal Isidro. Pastorales de la guerra de España. Madrid, 1955.
Gómez, Fernando. La insurrección por dentro. Havana, 1897.
Gómez de Arteche y Mora, José. De por qué en España son tan largas las guerras. Barcelona, 1885.
———. Guerra de la Independencia. 14 vols. Madrid, 1868–1903.
Gómez Chaix, Pedro. Ruiz Zorrilla, el ciudadano ejemplar. Madrid, 1934.
Gómez Fernández, Ramiro. "El 52": De General a presidiario. Madrid, 1932.
Gómez Hidalgo, F. Marruecos, la tragedia prevista. Madrid, 1921.
Gómez Núñez, Severo. La Guerra hispano-americana. 5 vols. Madrid, 1899–1902.
Gómez Oliveros, Maj. Benito. General Moscardó. Barcelona, 1956.
González Deleito, Federico. Apuntes de higiene social en el Ejército. Madrid, 1903.
———. La tuberculosis pulmonar en el Ejército español. Madrid, 1905.
González de Mesa, Narciso. Reorganización del Cuerpo Administrativo del Ejército. Havana, 1883.
González Hontoria, Manuel. El protectorado francés en Marruecos y sus enseñanzas para la acción española. Madrid, 1915.
González Llana, Manuel. La España del siglo XIX. Madrid, 1865. Vols. III and XIII.
González Llanos, Francisco. Biografía política y militar del General Prim. Madrid, 1860.
González Parrado, Col. Juan. Divagaciones militares. Madrid, 1886.
González Pons, Col. Enrique. "La Batalla de Madrid," *Ejército*, No. 12 (January 1941).
———. "La Batalla de Aragón, 9 marzo a 15 abril 1938," *Ejército*, No. 22 (November 1941).
González Ruano, César, and Emilio R. Tarduchy. Sanjurjo. Madrid, 1933.
González Sugrañes, Miguel. La República en Barcelona. Barcelona, 1903.
González Tablas, Ramón. Historia de la dominación y última guerra de España en Santo Domingo. 2 vols. Madrid, 1870.
———, and José Toral. Diario de las Operaciones militares de la revolución española. Madrid, 1869.
Gordón Ordás, Félix. Crímenes en la retaguardia rebelde. Havana, 1939.
Gould, Stanton W. General Rafael Maroto and the Carlist War of 1833–40. Unpublished dissertation. University of Chicago, 1953.
Gracia, Vicente P., S.J. Aragón, baluarte de España. Zaragoza, 1938.
La Guerra de liberación española. Zaragoza, 1961.
Guerra y Sánchez, Ramiro. Guerra de los Diez Años 1868–1878. Havana, 1950.
Guerrero, Rafael. Crónica de la guerra de Cuba y de la rebelión de Filipinas. 5 vols. Barcelona, 1895–97.
Guerrero, Santiago, J. M. Troncoso, and B. Quintero. La Columna de Saro en la campaña de Alhucemas. Barcelona, 1926.
Guillon, E. L. M. Les Complots militaires sous la Restauration. Paris, 1895.
Gutiérrez de la Concha, José. Memorias sobre el estado político, gobierno y administración de la isla de Cuba. Madrid, 1853.
———. Memoria sobre la guerra de la isla de Cuba. Madrid, 1877.
Gutiérrez Ravé, José. Diccionario histórico de la guerra de liberación de España. Madrid, 1943.

Guzmán, José. Abolición de quintas y reforma del Ejército. Madrid, 1869.
Guzmán de Alfarache, J. ¡18 de julio! Historia del alzamiento glorioso de Sevilla. Seville, 1937.
Guzmán de León, Antonio. El último Borbón: Historia dramática de Isabel II. 2 vols. Barcelona, 1868–69.

Halen, Antonio van. Diario razonado de los acontecimientos que tuvieron lugar en Barcelona, desde el 13 de noviembre al 22 de diciembre del año de 1842. Madrid, 1843.
———. Refutaciones que hace el Conde de Peracamps. Madrid, 1843.
Halen, Col. Juan van. Memorias. Paris, 1827.
Halstead, Charles R. "Spain, the Powers, and the Second World War." Unpublished dissertation. University of Virginia, 1962.
Hanighen, Frank C., ed. Nothing But Danger. New York, 1939.
Hardman, Frederick. The Spanish Campaign in Morocco. Edinburgh, 1860.
———. El Empecinado visto por un inglés. Madrid, 1931.
Harris, Walter B. France, Spain and the Riff. London, 1927.
Hart, B. H. Liddell. The German Generals Talk. New York, 1958.
Haupt, Werner. "Die 'Blaue Division' in der Literatur," *Wehrwissenschaftliche Rundschau,* Vol. IV (April 1959).
Hennessey, C. A. M. The Federal Republic in Spain. Oxford, 1963.
Henríquez Caubín, Col. Julián. La batalla del Ebro. Mexico City, 1944.
El Heraldo de Madrid. 1917.
El Heraldo Militar. 1905–23.
Hernández de Herrera, Maj. Carlos, and Maj. Tomás García Figueras. Acción de España en Marruecos. 2 vols. Madrid, 1929.
Hernández Mir, Francisco. Alianza contra el Rif. Madrid, 1926.
———. Del Rif a Yebala. Madrid, 1927.
———. La Dictadura ante la historia. Madrid, 1930.
———. La Dictadura en Marruecos. Madrid, 1930.
Hernández Pacheco, F., and José María Cordero Torres. El Sahara español. Madrid, 1962.
Hidalgo, Diego. Por qué fuí lanzado del Ministerio de la Guerra. Madrid, 1934.
Hidalgo, Pedro María. Espartero. León, 1866.
Higuera, Alfonso G. de la, and Luis Molins Correa. Historia de la revolución española. Madrid, 1940.
Historia militar y política de Don Ramón Narváez. Madrid, 1849.
Houghton, Arthur. Les Origines de la restauration des Bourbons en Espagne. Paris, 1890.
How Mussolini Provoked the Spanish Civil War: Documentary Evidence. London, 1938.
Hughes, Emmet J. Report from Spain. New York, 1947.
Huntington, Samuel P. Changing Patterns of Military Politics. New York, 1962.

Ibáñez de Ibero, Carlos. Méndez Núñez. Madrid, 1946.
———. Política mediterránea de España 1704–1951. Madrid, 1952.
Ibáñez Marín, José. El General Martínez Campos y su monumento. Madrid, n.d.
Ibo Alfaro, Manuel. Apuntes para la historia de Don Leopoldo O'Donnell. Madrid, 1867.
El Ideal Gallego. La Coruña, 1936–37.
Iglesia, E. Reseña histórica de la Guardia Civil. Madrid, 1898.
Iglesias Somoza, Eraclio. Asedio y defensa de la cárcel de Oviedo. Vitoria, 1935.

Informaciones (Madrid), July 1956.

Iribarren, José María. Con el general Mola. Zaragoza, 1937.

———. Mola. Zaragoza, 1938, Madrid, 1939. 2d. ed., Madrid, 1945.

———. Notas sobre la preparación y peripecias desdichadas de mi libro *Con el general Mola.* Unpublished. Pamplona, 1944.

Irujo, Manuel de. "La Guerra civil en Euzkadi antes del Estatuto." Unpublished manuscript.

Iturralde, Juan de (pseud.). El Catolicismo y la cruzada de Franco. 2 vols. Paris, 1958, 1961.

Izquierdo Hernández, Manuel. Antecedentes y comienzos del reinado de Fernando VII. Madrid, 1963.

Jackson, Gabriel. The Spanish Republic and the Civil War, 1931–1939. Princeton, 1965.

Janowitz, Morris. The Military in the Political Development of the New Nations. Chicago, 1964.

Jerrold, Douglas. Georgian Adventure. London, 1939.

Jevenois, Pedro. El servicio militar de los españoles de ultramar. Madrid, 1925.

Joaniquet, Aurelio. Calvo Sotelo. Santander, 1939.

———. Alfonso Sala Argemí. Madrid, 1955.

Joly, A. Historia crítica de la guerra de Africa en 1859–60. Madrid, 1910.

Jouve, Marguérite. Vu, en Espagne, Février 1936–Février 1937. Paris, 1937.

Juanes, José. Por qué fuimos a la guerra. Avila, 1937.

Juliá Téllez, Eduardo. Historia del movimiento libertador de España en la provincia gaditana. Cádiz, 1944.

Junod, Marcel. Le Troisième combattant. Paris, 1947.

Kemp, Peter. Mine Were of Trouble. London, 1957.

Kindelán, Gen. Alfredo. Mis cuadernos de guerra. Madrid, 1945.

———. Ejército y política. Madrid, 1957.

Klinger, Wallace R. Spain's Problem of Alliances. Unpublished dissertation, University of Pennsylvania, 1946.

Knickerbocker, H. R. The Siege of Alcazar. Philadelphia, 1936.

Knoblaugh, H. Edward. Correspondent in Spain. London, 1937.

Koestler, Arthur. Dialogue with Death. London, 1937.

Kropp, Major Albert. So kämpfen deutsche Soldaten. Berlin, 1939.

Laborde, Jules. Il y a toujours des Pyrénées. Paris, 1918.

Labra, Rafael María de. La reforma política en Ultramar (1868–1900). Madrid, 1902.

La Cierva y Peñafiel, Juan de. Notas de mi vida. Madrid, 1955.

Lacruz, Francisco. El alzamiento, la revolución, y el terror en Barcelona. Barcelona, 1943.

Lago García, Lt. Col. Ramiro. "La Batalla de Guadalajara," *Ejército,* No. 60 (January 1945).

La Gorce, Paul-Marie de. The French Army. New York, 1963.

Langdon-Davies, John. Air Raid. London, 1938.

Lapoulide, Juan L., ed. Ley reformada de reclutamiento y reemplazo del Ejército. Madrid, 1896.

Lara, Juan de. Aclaraciones sobre los acontecimientos militares de Madrid en los días 17 y 18 de julio de 1854. Madrid, 1855.

Lara, M. M. de. El cronista de la revolución española de 1868. Barcelona, 1869.

Largo Caballero, Francisco. Discursos a los trabajadores. Madrid, 1936.
Larrancerezo, Dr. Angel. Article in *The Lancet*. 1899.
Larrea, Francisco. Fortalecimiento y mejora del Ejército español. Madrid, 1906.
Laure, Lt. Col. A. M. E. La Victoire franco-espagnole dans le Rif. Paris, 1927.
Laviga Mediano, Lt. Félix. A Madrid por la mar. Zaragoza, 1938.
League of Nations Armaments Yearbook 1931.
Ledesma Ramos, Ramiro. ¿ Fascismo en España ? Madrid, 1935.
Leiva y Muñoz, Francisco de. La Batalla de Alcolea. Córdoba, 1879.
Lema, Marqués de. De la revolución a la restauración. 2 vols. Madrid, 1927.
Léonardon, Henri. Prim. Paris, 1910.
Lerroux, Alejandro. Al servicio de la República. Madrid, 1930.
———. La pequeña historia. Buenos Aires, 1945.
———. Mis memorias. Madrid, 1963.
Ley de reclutamiento y reemplazo del Ejército conforme a la de bases de 29 de junio de 1911 y la de 25 de diciembre de 1912 . . . Madrid, 1916.
Leyes constitutiva del Ejército y orgánica del Estado Mayor Central. Madrid, 1894.
Lichnowsky, Prince Felix. Recuerdos de la guerra carlista 1837–39. Madrid, 1942.
Liébana, José Manuel, and G. Orizana. El Movimiento Nacional. Valladolid, 1937.
Linz, Juan J. "An Authoritarian Regime: Spain," E. Allardt and Y. Littunen, eds., Cleavages, Ideologies, and Party Systems. Helsinki, 1964.
Líster, Enrique. "Lessons of the Spanish Guerrilla War (1939–1951)," *World Marxist Review* (February 1965).
Lizarra, Antonio de. Los vascos y la República española. Buenos Aires, 1944.
Lizarza Iribarren, Antonio. Memorias de la conspiración. Pamplona, 1957.
Lladó i Figueres, Josep María. El 19 de julio a Barcelona. Barcelona, 1938.
Llano Roza de Ampudia, Aurelio de. La revolución en Asturias octubre 1934. Oviedo, 1935.
Llanos, Adolfo. Melilla. Madrid, 1894.
Llauder, Gen. Manuel. Memorias documentadas. Madrid, 1844.
Llave y García, Joaquín de la. Apuntes sobre la última guerra en Cataluña, 1872–1875. Barcelona, n.d.
Llave y García, Col. Joaquín de la. Estudio sobre nuestra artillería de plaza. Madrid, 1892.
Llofriu y Sagrera, Eusebio. Historia de la insurrección y guerra de la isla de Cuba. 4 vols. Madrid, 1870–72.
Llord, Josep. Campanya montemolinista de Catalunya, o Guerra dels matiners, setembre de 1846 a mayo de 1849. Barcelona, 1926.
Llorens Castillo, Vicente. Liberales y románticos: una emigración española en Inglaterra, 1823–34. Mexico City, 1954.
Lo que han hecho en Galicia. Paris, 1938.
Lojendio, Col. Luis María de. Operaciones militares de la guerra de España 1936–1939. Barcelona, 1940.
López Alarcón, Enrique. Melilla, 1909. Madrid, 1910.
López de Letona, Maj. Gen. Antonio. Estudios críticos sobre el Estado militar de España. Madrid, 1866.
López de Ochoa, Gen. Eduardo. De la Dictadura a la República. Barcelona, 1932.
———. Campaña militar de Asturias en octubre de 1934. Madrid, 1936.
López Fernández, Capt. Antonio. Defensa de Madrid. Mexico City, 1945.
López Muñiz, Col. E. M. La batalla de Madrid. Madrid, 1943.
López Rienda, Rafael. El escándalo del millón de Larache. Madrid, 1922.

———. Raisuni. Madrid, 1923.
Loredo Aparicio, José. La piedad de Franco. Mexico City, 1946.
Lovett, Gabriel. Napoleon and the Birth of Modern Spain. 2 vols. New York, 1965.
Luque, Angel de. *El Diario Universal*. Madrid, December 30, 1904.

Maíz, Félix. Alzamiento en España. Pamplona, 1956.
Maldonado, Eduardo. El Roghi. Melilla, 1949.
Mañé y Flaquer, Juan. La rebelión de 1868 juzgada por sus autores. Barcelona, 1876.
Mangada Roseñorn, Col. Julio. El Fascismo en el Ejército a la Unión de Militares Españoles. Madrid, 1936.
Manteca Pérez, Luis, ed. Código del Cuerpo de Suboficiales. Madrid, 1933.
Manzano, Rafael. Los grandes capitanes españoles. Barcelona, 1926.
Marcos, Lt. Col. Santiago Mateo. "El servicio rojo en la batalla de Brunete," *Ejército*, No. 28 (May 1942).
Marina, Gen. Francisco J. General Varela. Barcelona, 1958.
Mario de Coca, Gabriel. Anti-Caballero. Madrid, 1936.
Marliani, Manuel. Regencia de D. Baldomero Espartero y sucesos que la prepararon. Madrid, 1870.
Maroto, Rafael. Vindicación del General Maroto. Madrid, 1846.
Márquez, Col. Benito, and José Maria Capo. Las Juntas Militares de Defensa. Barcelona, 1923.
Marsá, Graco. La sublevación de Jaca. Madrid, 1930.
Martín Arrué, Francisco. La Guerra de Africa de 1859 a 1860. Madrid, 1898.
Martín Blázquez, Capt. José. I Helped to Build an Army. London, 1939.
Martín y Oliate, Cayetano. España y Santo Domingo. Toledo, 1864.
Martín y Peinador, León. El Ejército ha de ser el sostén de la Patria. Segovia, 1903.
Martínez Bande, Maj. J. M. "Campaña de Guipuzcoa (julio–septiembre 1936)," *Ejército*, No. 190 (November 1955).
———. "La Marcha sobre Madrid," *Ejército*, No. 194 (March 1956).
———. "Campaña del Norte—Vizcaya," *Ejército*, No. 212 (September 1957).
———. "Socorro a Oviedo (julio–octubre, 1936)," *Revista de Historia Militar*, No. 1 (1957).
———. "Batalla de Brunete," *Revista de Historia Militar*, No. 5 (1959).
———. "La Batalla del Jarama," *Ejército*, No. 246 (July 1960).
———. "La lucha en torno a Madrid en el invierno de 1936–1937: Las operaciones para la rectificación del flanco izquierda nacional," *Revista de Historia Militar*, No. 11 (1962).
Martínez Barrado, José Antonio. Cómo se creó una Bandera de Falange. Zaragoza, 1939.
Martínez de Campos, Lt. Gen. Carlos. España bélica: siglo XIX. Madrid, 1961.
———. Dos batallas de la Guerra de Liberación de España. Madrid, n.d.
Martínez de la Riva, Ramón. Las jornadas triunfales de un golpe de Estado. Madrid, 1923.
———. La España de hoy. Madrid, 1926.
Martínez Esparza, Gen. José. "El sitio de Villarreal de Alava," *Ejército*, No. 111 (April 1949).
Martínez Leal, Maj. Alfredo. El asedio del Alcázar de Toledo. Toledo, 1937.
Martínez Pérez, Francisco. Proyecto de organización militar. Madrid, 1871.
Martínez Plowes, Juan. Pensamientos sobre la organización del Ejército español. Madrid, 1866.
———. El Ejército sin quintas. Zaragoza, 1871.

Martínez Sol, Ramón. De Canalejas al Tribunal de Responsabilidades. Madrid, 1933.

Martínez Villergas, Juan. Desenlace de la guerra civil. Madrid, 1851.

——. Paralelo entre la vida militar de Espartero y la de Narváez. Madrid, 1851.

Martos, Cristino. La revolución de julio en 1854. Madrid, 1854.

Marvá y Mayer, José. Las Tropas de Ingenieros en la campaña de Melilla. Madrid, 1909.

——. El Ejército y la Armada y la cultura nacional. Madrid, 1919.

Marvaud, Angel. L'Espagne au XXe siècle. Paris, 1913.

Marx, Karl. Article in *New York Daily Tribune*. August 19, 1854.

Massa y Sanguinetti, Carlos. Vida militar y política de Diego de León. Madrid, 1845.

Mata y Alós, Francisco de. Proyecto de la organización de la reserva del Ejército. Madrid, 1867.

Matorrás, Enrique. El comunismo en España. Madrid, 1935.

Mattioli, Guido. L'Aviazione legionaria in Spagna. Rome, 1938.

Maura, Miguel. Así cayó Alfonso XIII. Mexico City, 1962.

Maura Gamazo, Gabriel. Historia crítica del reinado de Don Alfonso XIII durante su menoridad. 2 vols. Barcelona, 1919.

——. Bosquejo histórico de la Dictadura. Madrid, 1930.

——, and Melchor Fernández Almagro. Por qué cayó Alfonso XIII. Madrid, 1948.

May, Ernest R. Imperial Democracy. New York, 1961.

Mazade, Charles de. Les Révolutions de l'Espagne contemporaine, 1854–68. Paris, 1869.

Melgar, Francisco, Conde de. Veinte años con D. Carlos. Madrid, 1940.

——. O'Donnell. Madrid, 1946.

Memoria administrativa de la campaña de Africa. Madrid, 1862.

Mendigorría, Marqués de. La revolución de Roma y la expedición a Italia de 1849. Madrid, 1882.

Merkes, Manfred. Die deutsche Politik gegenüber dem spanischen Bürgerkrieg 1936–1939. Bonn, 1961.

Meyer, Walter. Dreitausend Kilometer barfuss durch Afrika. Stuttgart, 1929.

Mezquiriz y Ecalain, José de. Tarifa de sueldos líquidos. Madrid, 1855.

Micó y España, Carlos. Los caballeros de la Legión. Madrid, 1922.

Milans del Bosch, Gen. Lorenzo. Proyecto de una nueva organización del Ejército español. Madrid, 1869.

Milego, Julio. El General Barrera. Madrid, 1935.

Millán Astray, José. La Legión. Madrid, 1923.

Millis, Walter. The Martial Spirit. Cambridge, 1931.

Mínguez de Rico, Manuel, ed. Ley de responsabilidades políticas y de depuración de funcionarios públicos. Madrid, 1939.

Ministerio del Ejército. Guerra de la Independencia, 1808–1814: Diccionario bibliográfico, 3 vols. Madrid, 1944–52.

Ministerio de la Guerra. Dotación de Armamento, Municiones y Material del Ejército de la Península. Madrid, September 24, 1932.

Ministerio de Trabajo, Comercio e Industria. Estadística del reclutamiento y reemplazo del trienio 1918–1920. Madrid, 1923.

Ministerio de Ultramar. Cuba desde 1850 a 1873: colección de informes, memorias, proyectos y antecedentes. Madrid, 1873.

Ministero della Guerra. Volontari del Esercito nella Guerra di Spagna. Milan, 1939.

Mira, Emilio. Psychiatry in War. New York, 1943.

Miraflores, Marqués de. Memorias para escribir la historia contemporánea. Madrid, 1843.

Miranda, Vicente Marco. Las conspiraciones contra la Dictadura. Madrid, 1930.

Mola Vidal, Gen. Emilio. Obras completas. Valladolid, 1940.

Moltó y Díaz-Berrio, Remigio. Apuntes sobre algunas reformas de indispensable necesidad en el Ejército. Madrid, 1881.

Montes, Pedro Domingo. Anales históricos de la revolución política en España. Madrid, 1870.

Monteverde y Sedano, Lt. Col. Federico. Campaña de Filipinas: La División Lachambre 1897. Madrid, 1898.

Montseny, Federica. De julio a julio. Barcelona, 1937.

Morales, M. La Guerra civil en Guipuzcoa, julio–agosto 1936. Valladolid, 1937.

Morales y Gaspar, Patricio. Indicaciones sobre la reorganización del Ejército español. Zaragoza, 1870.

Morales Lopez, José María. Rojo y azul en Granada. Granada, 1937.

Moreno, Adm. Francisco. La guerra en el mar. Barcelona, 1957.

Moreno, Rafael. "El Ejército: ¿Monárquico o Democristiano?" *España Libre,* January 1966.

Morgan, H. Wayne. William McKinley and His America. Syracuse, N.Y., 1963.

———. America's Road to Empire: The War with Spain and Overseas Expansion. New York, 1965.

Morote, Luis. La moral de la derrota. Madrid, 1900.

———. Sagasta, Melilla, Cuba. Paris, 1908.

Mortari, Curio. Con gli insorti in Marocco e Spagna. Milan, 1937.

Mosca, Luigi. Camiccie nere a Guadalajara. Naples, 1941.

Moscardó, Gen. José. Diario del Alcázar. Madrid, 1943.

Moscardó Cervera, Frederic. Valéncia i el General Espartero. Valencia, 1955.

Moss, Geoffrey M. The Siege of the Alcázar. London, 1937.

Mousset, Albert. L'Espagne dans la politique mondiale. Paris, 1923.

Moya y Jiménez, Francisco de. La milicia y sus excesos. Valladolid, 1889.

———. Mongrafía militar de Mindanao. Madrid, 1895.

———. Consideraciones militares sobre la campaña de Cuba. Madrid, 1901.

———, and Celestino Rey Joly. El Ejército y la Marina en las Cortes de Cádiz. Cádiz, 1912.

Moyano, Maj. Ignacio. "De la batalla del Ebro: La acción de la Artillería," *Ejército,* No. 23 (December 1941).

Muñoz Epelde, Melchor. Memorias de un amnistiado. Badajoz, 1901.

Muro Zegri, Diego. La epopeya del Alcázar. Valladolid, 1937.

Narbona, Francisco. "Frentes del Sur," *Temas españoles,* No. 24 (Madrid, 1953).

Nard, Francisco, and Antonio Pirala. Vida militar y política de Don Rafael de Riego. Alicante, 1923.

Narváez, Ramón María. Manifiesto en contestación a las acusaciones del capitán general Conde de Luchana. Madrid, 1839.

Navarro García, Gen. Modesto. Estudios militares (Aplicados al caso hipotético de una lucha con Francia). Madrid, 1916.

———. Obras. Madrid, 1916.

Navarro Martín, Antonio. Opúsculo sobre la pacificación de Cuba. Mexico City, 1878.

Navarro Muñoz, Fabián. Apuntes para un ensayo de organización militar de España. Madrid, 1884.

Navarro y Rodrigo, Carlos María. O'Donnell y la guerra de Africa. Madrid, 1868.

———. O'Donnell y su tiempo. Madrid, 1869.

554   *Bibliography*

Navascués, Maj. Felipe de. ¡ La próxima guerra ! Madrid, 1895.
Navero Burgos, José Miguel. El Marqués de la Vega de Armijo. Madrid, 1947.
Nervo, Baron de. L'Espagne en 1867. Paris, 1868.
Nido y Segalerva, Juan del. Historia política y parlamentaria de S. A. D. Baldomero Espartero. Madrid, 1916.
Nieto Lanzos, Abelardo. El General Ricardos. Madrid, 1946.
El Norte de Castilla. Valladolid, 1936.
Novaliches, Marqués de. Memoria sobre la guerra de Cataluña. Madrid, 1851.
Nunes, Leopoldo. A Guerra em Espanha. Lisbon, 1936.
Núñez de Arce, Gaspar. Santo Domingo. Madrid, 1865.

Ochando, Tomás. El General Martínez Campos en Cuba. Madrid, 1878.
Offner, John L. President McKinley and the Origins of the Spanish-American War. Unpublished dissertation. Pennsylvania State University, 1957.
Oleza, José de. El primer Conde de España. Madrid, 1944.
Olívar Bertrand, Rafael. El caballero Prim. 2 vols. Barcelona, 1951.
———. Así cayó Isabel II. Barcelona, 1955.
Oliveira, Mauricio, and José Andrés Vázquez. La tragedia española en el mar. 4 vols. Cádiz, 1938–39.
Oller Piñol, Juan. Martínez Anido, su vida y su obra. Madrid, 1943.
Olmedo Delgado, Antonio and Lt. Gen. José Cuesta Monereo. El General Queipo de Llano. Barcelona, 1957.
Olmet, Luis Antón de, and Antonia García Caraffa. Canalejas. Madrid, 1913.
———. Alfonso XIII. 2 vols. Madrid, 1913–14.
———. El General Marina. Madrid, n.d.
Orellana, Francisco J. Historia del General Prim. 3 vols. Barcelona, 1872.
"La Organización del Ejército español mirada por un prusiano," *Revista Técnica de Infantería y Caballería,* X–XI (1910–11).
La Organización militar de España. Madrid, 1898.
Organización y Estado Militar de España y Ultramar en el 1º de enero de 1869. Madrid, 1869.
Ortega, Manuel L. El Raisuni. Madrid, 1917.
Ortega y Gasset, Eduardo. Annual. Madrid, 1922.
Ortega Rubio, Juan. Historia de la Regencia de María Cristina Habsbourg Lorena. 5 vols. Madrid, 1905–6.
Ortiz de Villajos, C. G. De Sevilla a Madrid: Ruta libertadora de la Columna Castejón. Granada, 1937.
Oscariz, Javier de. Historia de las milicias provinciales. Madrid, 1851.
Otero Enríquez, Santiago. La nobleza en el Ejército: estudio histórico de legislación nobiliaria militar, 1500–1865. Madrid, 1915.
Oudard, Georges. Chemises noires, brunes, vertes en Espagne. Paris, 1938.
Ovilo Canales, Felipe. La decadencia del Ejército: estudio de higiene social. Madrid, 1899.
Oyarzun, Román. Historia del carlismo. Madrid, 1939.

Pablo Muñoz, José de. Aquellas Banderas de Aragón. Valencia, 1942.
Pabón, Jesús. Cambó, 1876–1918. Barcelona, 1951.
———. El 98, acontecimiento internacional. Madrid, 1952.
Pacciardi, Randolfo. Il Battaglione Garibaldi. Lugano, 1948.
Palacio, Solano. Quince días de comunismo libertario en Asturias. Barcelona, 1936.
Pardo Canales, Dr. Julio. Cuando el mar no era un camino. Zaragoza, 1937.
Pardo González, General Cándido. Al servicio de la verdad. Madrid, 1930.

————. El problema militar de España. Madrid, 1934.

Pardo Saavedra, Victor. Proyecto de organización del Ejército. Madrid, 1872.

Pascazio, Nicola. La rivoluzione di Spagna. Rome, 1933.

Patrón de Sopranís, Alfonso. Burlando el bloqueo rojo. Jerez, 1937.

Paúl y Angulo, José. Los asesinos del General Prim y la política en España. Paris, 1886.

Pavía y Rodríguez de Albuquerque, Gen. Manuel. Cuatro palabras a los folletos de . . . D. José de los Reyes y D. Francisco Bedoya. Madrid, 1878.

————. Descripción del acto del 3 de enero de 1874. Madrid, 1878.

————. El Ejército del Centro. Madrid, 1878.

————. La pacificación de Andalucía. Madrid, 1878.

Payne, Robert, ed. The Civil War in Spain. New York, 1962.

Payne, Stanley G. Falange: A History of Spanish Fascism. Stanford, 1961.

Pedrol Ríus, Antonio. Los Asesinos del General Prim. Madrid, 1960.

Peira y Fernández-Fontecha, Antonio, and José de Santos y Fernández Laza, eds. Novísima ley de reclutamiento y reemplazo del Ejército. Madrid, 1878.

Peirats, José. La C.N.T. en la revolución española. 3 vols. Toulouse, 1958.

Peire, Tomás. Una política militar expuesta ante las Cortes constituyentes. Madrid, 1933.

Peláez, Antonio. Contestación del General D. Antonio Peláez. Madrid, 1869.

Pemán, José María. El hecho y la idea de la Unión Patriótica. Madrid, 1930.

————. Vida del Capitán General Varela. Cádiz, 1954.

Pemartín, José. Los valores históricos en la dictadura española. Madrid, 1929.

Peña, Nicolás de la. Proyecto de ley de reorganización del Ejército y la política. Madrid, 1872.

Peña e Ibáñez, Juan José. Las guerras carlistas. San Sebastián, 1940.

El Pensamiento Alavés. Vitoria, 1936.

Pérez, Dionisio. La Dictadura a través de sus notas oficiosas. Madrid, 1930.

Pérez de Guzmán y Gallo, Juan. El dos de mayo de 1808 en Madrid. Madrid, 1908.

Pérez de la Sala, Pedro. Apuntes sobre la abolición de quintas. Madrid, 1873.

Pérez Madrigal, Joaquín. "Veintinueve años después," *¡ Qué pasa !*, July 1965.

Pérez Salas, Jesús. Guerra en España, 1936–1939. Mexico City, 1947.

Pérez Solís, Oscar. Sitio y defensa de Oviedo. Valladolid, 1938.

Pérez y Martínez, Vicente. Estadística del movimiento de enfermos y heridos ocurrido en las fuerzas del norte y de la izquierda desde mayo de 1875 a fin de marzo de 1876. Madrid, 1877.

Peyra Anglada, Gustavo. Estudio de una organización del Ejército. Barcelona, 1905.

Peyreigne, Charles. Les Influences européennes au Maroc avant la Conférence d'Algésiras. Toulouse, 1908.

Piazzoni, Sandro. Las tropas "Flechas Negras" en la guerra de España. Barcelona, 1941.

Pieltain, Gen. Cándido. La isla de Cuba desde mediados de abril a fines de octubre de 1873. Madrid, 1879.

Piñeyro, Enrique. Cómo acabó la dominación de España en América. Paris, n.d.

Pintos Vieites, María del Carmen. La Política de Fernando VII entre 1814 y 1820. Pamplona, 1958.

Pirala, Antonio. Historia de la guerra civil. 6 vols. Madrid, 1868.

————. Historia contemporánea. Anales desde 1843 hasta la conclusión de la última guerra civil. 6 vols. Madrid, 1877.

————. La Regencia de Espartero. Madrid, 1890.

————. Anales de la Guerra de Cuba. 3 vols. Madrid, 1895.

Plá, José. Cambó. 3 vols. Barcelona, 1929–30.
———. Historia de la segunda República española. 4 vols. Barcelona, 1941.
Poch Noguer, José. Prim. Barcelona, 1934.
Polavieja, General Camilo. Relación documentada de mi política en Cuba. Madrid, 1898.
Prados López, Manuel, and José Prados López. Narváez, el espadón de Loja. Madrid, 1952.
Presupuestos Generales de los Gastos del Estado. 1940–62.
Priego López, Col. Juan. Guerra de la Independencia (1808–1814): síntesis político-militar. Madrid, 1947.
———. "La intervención extranjera," *Ejército,* No. 206 (March, 1957).
Prieto, Tomás. Soldados de España. Madrid, 1946.
Prieto, Indalecio. El Liberal. Bilbao, August 4, 1921.
Prieto Llovera, Brig. Gen. Patricio. El Grande de España Capitán General Castaños. Madrid, 1958.
Prieto y Villarreal, Emilio. Ruiz Zorrilla desde su expulsión de España hasta su muerte (1875–1895). Madrid, 1903.
Primo de Rivera, Fernando. Memoria del Teniente General Primo de Rivera acerca de su gestión en Filipinas. Madrid, 1898.
———. Articles in *La Correspondencia Militar* and in *El Ejército Español.* 1919.
———. Continuación a las opiniones del General Primo de Rivera. Guadalajara, 1919.
Primo de Rivera, José Antonio. Textos inéditos y epistolario. Madrid, 1956.
Primo de Rivera, Miguel. Conferencia del general Primo de Rivera del 8 de marzo de 1919. Madrid, 1919.
———. Actuación ciudadana que corresponde al Ejército, 26 de octubre de 1927. Madrid, 1927.
———. El pensamiento de Primo de Rivera. Madrid, 1929.
———. Intervenciones en la Asamblea Nacional. Madrid, 1930.
———. La obra de la Dictadura: Primo de Rivera. Sus cuatro ultimos articulos. Madrid, 1930.
Primo de Rivera y Sobremonte, Rafael. Las economías en los gastos públicos. Madrid, 1871.
Puyol, Julio. La conspiración de Espoz y Mina. Madrid, 1932.

Queipo de Llano, General Gonzalo. El General Queipo de Llano perseguido por la dictadura. Madrid, 1930.
Quintana, Lorenzo. Mallorca siempre española. Cádiz, 1938.
Quintana Martínez, Eduardo. Crónica artillera de la campaña de Melilla de 1909. Madrid, 1910.
———. La Marina de Guerra española en Africa. Cádiz, 1912.

Ramas Izquierdo, Sgt. Federico. La Legión: Historia de guerra (1º septiembre 1920 al 12 octubre 1927). Ceuta, 1933.
Ramírez, Luis (pseud.). Francisco Franco. Paris, 1964.
Ramón-Laca, Julio. Bajo la férula de Queipo. Seville, 1939.
Ramos Oliveira, Antonio. Historia de España. 3 vols. Mexico City, 1952.
Raymundo, Francisco J. de. Cómo se inició el Glorioso Movimiento Nacional en Valladolid y la gesta heroica del Alto del León. Valladolid, 1937.
Rea, George B. Facts and Fakes about Cuba. New York, 1897.
Redondo, Gen. Luis, and Maj. Juan de Zavala. El Requeté. Barcelona, 1957.

Reflexiones sobre el proyecto de ley constitutiva del Ejército presentadas al Gobierno por la Junta auxiliar de milicias. Madrid, 1821.

Reglamento del Cuerpo de Suboficiales (Creado por Ley de 5 de julio de 1934). Madrid, 1935.

Reparaz, Gonzalo de. Política de España en Africa. Barcelona, 1907.

Retana, Wenceslao E. Mando del General Weyler en Filipinas 5 junio 1888–17 noviembre 1891. Madrid, 1896.

Reverter Delmas, Emilio. La insurrección de Filipinas en 1896. Barcelona, 1899.

Revesz, Andrés. Un dictador liberal: Narváez. Madrid, 1953.

La revolución y bombardeo de Barcelona en 1842, escrita por un sargento primero, que era en aquella época del Batallón de Artillería de la Milicia Nacional de esta ciudad. Barcelona, 1843.

Reyes, Alfonso. Momentos de España. Mexico City, 1947.

Ribas de Piña, Col. Miguel. El 11º Ligero durante el primer año triunfal. Santander, 1938.

Ribó, José Joaquín. Historia de los voluntarios de Cuba. 2 vols. Madrid, 1872–74.

Ribot y Fontseré, Antonio. La revolución de julio en Madrid. Madrid, 1854.

Ridruejo, Dionisio. Escrito en España. Buenos Aires, 1962.

Riera, Augusto. España en Africa: Crónica de la Campaña de 1909. Barcelona, 1910.

Risco, P. Alberto. Apuntes biográficos del excelentísimo señor don Pascual Cervera Topete. Toledo, 1920.

Rispoli, Tullio. La Spagna dei Legionari. Rome, 1942.

Rivero, Gen. Felipe. Manifesto del General Felipe Rivero sobre las operaciónes ejecutadas en Andalucía. Bilbao, 1837.

Rivero Sánchez, Manuel. Odisea y gesta de Oviedo (18 julio 1936–21 octubre 1937). Las Palmas, 1938.

Rodrigo Nocedal, Ramón G. La campaña de Melilla. Madrid, 1894.

Roger-Mathieu, J., ed. Mémoires d'Abd-el-Krim. Paris, 1927.

Rohl, Hermann. Deutsche Flieger über Spanien. Rentlingen, 1939.

Rojo, Col. Vicente. ¡ Alerta los pueblos ! Buenos Aires, 1939.

———. España heroica. Buenos Aires, 1942.

Romano, Julio. Weyler, el hombre de hierro. Madrid, 1934.

Romanones, Conde de. Espartero, el general del pueblo. Madrid, 1932.

———. Obras completas. 3 vols. Madrid, 1953.

Romero Cuesta, José. El Sargento Vázquez. Madrid, 1936.

Romero Quiñones, Ubaldo. Principios de organización racional y productiva del Ejército. Guadalajara, 1899.

Romilly, Esmond. Boadilla. London, 1937.

Rosell Planas, Rebeca. Factores económicos, políticos y sociales de la Guerra Chiquita. Havana, 1953.

Rougeron, C. Les Enseignements aériens de la guerre d'Espagne. Paris, 1939.

Routier, Gaston. L'Espagne en 1897. Paris, 1897.

Royo Villanova, Antonio. La misión educativa del Ejército. Madrid, 1919.

Rozalejo, Marqués de. El Conde de Cheste. Madrid, 1935.

Rubio, Carlos. Historia filosófica de la revolución española. 2 vols. Madrid, 1869.

Ruiz Albéniz, Victor. El Riff. Madrid, 1912.

———. España en el Rif. Madrid, 1921.

———. Ecce homo: las responsabilidades del desastre. Madrid, 1922.

———. Tánger y la colaboración franco-española en Marruecos. Madrid, 1927.

Ruiz Dana, Gen. Pedro. Estudios sobre la guerra civil en el norte de 1872 a 1876. Madrid, 1876.

———. Estudio crítico sobre la última guerra civil. 2 vols. Madrid, 1887.

Ruiz de Alda, Julio. Obras completas. Barcelona, 1939.

Ruiz de Morales, Joaquín. Historia de la Milicia Nacional. Madrid, 1855.

Ruiz de Quevedo, Eugenio. Abolición de las quintas. Madrid, 1871.

Ruiz Fornells, Enrique, and Alfredo Melgar Mata. Organización militar de España y algunas potencias extranjeras. Toledo, 1897.

Ruiz Vilaplana, Antonio. Doy fe: Un año de actuación en la España de Franco. Paris, 1938.

Runy, Doctor. Irún, llave del norte. Santander, 1939.

Sablotny, Richard. Legionnaire in Morocco. Los Angeles, 1940.

Sae y Fernández Casariego, Maj. Enrique. "De la Batalla del Ebro: Estadística Sanitaria," *Ejército,* No. 36 (January 1941).

Salamanca, Gen. Manuel. Apuntes de la guerra de Cuba. Havana, 1934.

Salas, López, Capt. Fernando de. "Rotura del Frente Catalán por Serós," *Ejército,* No. 102 (July 1948).

Salazar Alonso, Rafael. La Justicia bajo la Dictadura. Madrid, 1930.

Salinas y Angulo, Ignacio. Exposición de las funciones del Estado Mayor en paz y en guerra. 2 vols. Madrid, 1883.

——— (Brig. Gen.). Defensa del General Jáudenes. Madrid, 1899.

Salmador, Victor G. Juan Antonio Ansaldo. Montevideo, 1962.

Salmerón y Alonso, Francisco. Historia del señor D. Baldomero Espartero. Madrid, 1870.

Salto García-Margallo, Maj. Antonio. Contabilidad interior de los cuerpos. Madrid, 1943.

Sánchez, R. Historia de Don Carlos y de los principales sucesos de la guerra civil en España. Madrid, 1844.

Sánchez Agesta, Luis. Historia del constitucionalismo español. Madrid, 1955.

Sánchez Arjona, Fernando. Canalejas. Madrid, 1947.

Sánchez-Boxá, G. Don Juan, le roi qu'on veut pour l'Espagne. Toulouse, 1946.

Sánchez Bravo, Angel. Apuntes para la historia de la Escala de Reserva del Ejército. Cuenca, 1929.

Sánchez del Arco, Manuel. El sur de España en la reconquista de Madrid. Seville, 1951.

Sánchez García, Lt. Col. Carlos. "Batalla del Ebro," *Ejército,* No. 211 (August 1957).

Sánchez Guerra, Rafael. El movimiento revolucionario de Valencia. Madrid, 1930.

Sánchez y Solórzano, Mauro. Incompatibilidad del Ejército y la política. Madrid, 1872.

Sanchíz, J. Expedición española a Italia, 1849. 2 vols. Madrid, 1856–58.

Sanjuan y Valero, Lt. Col. Pascual. Consideraciones escritas sobre la necesidad de los Ejércitos permanentes y de las quintas. Madrid, 1871.

San Martín Losada, Eduardo. Sueldos, haberes y gratificaciones del personal del Ejército. Madrid, 1927.

———. Sueldos, haberes y gratificaciones del personal del Ejército. Madrid, 1943.

———, and José Ignacio San Martín López. Almanaque del militar 1951. Madrid, 1951.

———. España y su glorioso Ejército. Madrid, 1952.

———. Almanaque del militar. Madrid, 1957.

San Miguel, Gen. Evaristo. De la guerra civil de España. Madrid, 1836.

———. Breves observaciones sobre los sucesos de agosto de 1836 y sus resultados. Madrid, 1838.

———. España en octubre de 1838. Madrid, 1839.

Santovenia, Emeterio S. Prim, el caudillo estadista. Madrid, 1933.

Sarrailh, Jean. La Contre-Révolution sous la Régence de Madrid. Bordeaux, 1930.

Sastrón, Manuel. La insurrección de Filipinas y Guerra hispano-americano en el archipiélago. Madrid, 1901.

Schomberg, Jean. Federico García Lorca: L'homme, l'oeuvre. Paris, 1954.

Sección de Historia Militar. Estados de la organización y fuerza de los Ejércitos españoles beligerantes en la península durante la guerra de España contra Bonaparte. Barcelona, 1822.

Sedano, Carlos de. Cuba: estudios políticos. Madrid, 1872.

Sedwick, Frank. The Tragedy of Manuel Azaña and the Fate of the Spanish Republic. Columbus, Ohio, 1963.

Segala, Renzo. Trincee di Spagna. Milan, 1938.

Segundo Flórez, José, ed. Espartero. 4 vols. Madrid, 1844–45.

Sencourt, Robert. Spain's Ordeal. New York, 1940.

Serrano, Nicolás María. Dos palabras de justicia debidas al General Blanco. Madrid, 1897.

———, and Melchor Pardo. Anales de la Guerra Civil: España desde 1868 a 1876. Madrid, 1875 (sic).

Serrano Bedoya, Gen. Francisco. El General en Jefe del Ejército del Centro y el Ministro de la Guerra durante el mes de septiembre de 1874. Madrid, 1878.

Serrano Suñer, Ramón. Entre Hendaya y Gibraltar. Mexico City, 1945.

Servicio General de Estadística. Estadística del reclutamiento y reemplazo del Ejército Trienio 1912–1914. Madrid, 1915.

Servicio Histórico Militar. Acción de España en Africa. Madrid, 1941.

Sevilla Andrés, Diego. Historia política de la zona roja. Madrid, 1954.

———. Antonio Maura. Barcelona, 1954.

———. Del 19 de marzo al 14 de abril. Valencia, 1959.

———. Africa en la política española del siglo XIX. Madrid, 1960.

———. Canalejas. Barcelona, 1956.

Sheean, Vincent. An American among the Riffi. New York, 1926.

Siffler-725, pseud. of Lt. Miguel Pérez. Don Manuel Ruiz Zorrilla ante la A.R.M. Madrid, 1883.

Silva, Gen. Carlos de. General Millán Astray. Barcelona, 1956.

Silva Ferreiro, M. Galicia y el Movimiento Nacional. Santiago de Compostela, 1938.

Sobre los ejércitos permanentes y el sistema de guerra. Madrid, 1868.

El Socialista, 1956.

Sociedad de Ex-Milicianos de Madrid. Vida militar y política de Espartero. 3 vols. Madrid, 1844.

El Sol, 1930–36.

Solá, Víctor María de, and Carlos Martel. Estelas gloriosas de la escuadra azul. Cádiz, 1937.

Solano Palacio, Fernando. La tragedia del norte (Asturias mártir). Barcelona, 1938.

Soldevilla, Fernando. El año político 1906. Madrid, 1907.

Solmi, Arrigo. Lo stato nuovo nella Spagna di Franco. Milan, 1940.

Soltó y Montes, Brig. Gen. Joaquín de. "Los grandes tercios viejos de la Infantería española," *Revista de Historia Militar,* No. 11 (1962).

Somoza Silva, Lázaro. El General Miaja. Mexico City, 1944.

Soriano, Rodrigo. España bajo el sable. Santiago de Chile, 1926.

Souchère, Elena de la. "The Bankruptcy of Franco's Diplomacy," *Ibérica,* Vol. IV, Nos. 6–7 (June–July 1956).

———. Explication de l'Espagne. Paris, 1962.
Soulère, Emilio Augusto. Historia de la insurrección de Cuba. 2 vols. Barcelona, 1879–80.
Southworth, Herbert R. Le Mythe de la croisade de Franco. Paris, 1963.
Souza, Benigno. Máximo Gómez el Generalísimo. Havana, 1936.
Sperrle, Gen. Hans. "Die Legion Condor," in *Die Wehrmacht*, May 30, 1939.
Stache, Rudolf. Armee mit geheimen Auftrag: Die deutsche Legion Condor in Spanien. Bremen, n.d.
Stackelberg, Karl Georg von. Legion Condor. Berlin, 1939.
Steer, G. L. The Tree of Gernika. London, 1938.
Stewart, Paul R., Jr. The Army of the Catholic Kings, 1474–1516. Unpublished dissertation. University of Illinois, 1962.
Suárez Inclán, Col. Pío. Organización del Cuerpo de Estado Mayor. Madrid, 1912.
Suárez Verdaguer, Federico. La crisis política del antiguo régimen en España. Madrid, 1950.

Taviel de Andrade, Enrique. Cuestión de Marruecos. Madrid, 1888.
Taxonera, Luciano. La revolución del 54. Madrid, 1881.
Tejera, Domingo. Los parásitos del trono. Seville, 1930.
Temperley, Maj. Gen. A. C. "Military Lessons of the Spanish Civil War," *Foreign Affairs*, XVI, No. 1 (October 1937).
Le Temps (Paris), 1936.
"Un testigo imparcial." Revolución en Asturias. Madrid, 1934.
Tettamancy, C. La revolución gallega. La Coruña, 1908.
Tetuán, Duque de. Apuntes para la defensa de la política internacional y gestión diplomática del Gobierno Liberal-Conservador desde el 28 de marzo de 1895 a 29 de septiembre de 1897. Madrid, 1902.
Thomas, Hugh. The Spanish Civil War. New York, 1961.
Tocci, Valentino. Duelli aerei. Rome, 1938.
Torcy, General de. Los españoles en Marruecos en 1909. Madrid, 1911.
Toreno, Conde de. Historia del levantamiento, guerra, y revolución de España. 3 vols. Paris, 1838.
Trabajos de la comisión de reorganización del Ejército. Madrid, 1873.
Trautloft, Hannes. Als Jagdflieger in Spanien. Berlin, n.d.

Ulíbarri, General Gámir de. Guerra de España, 1936–1939. Paris, 1939.
Urarte Eznarriaga, Capt. Emilio de. "Los pontoneros rojos en al paso del Ebro," *Ejército,* No. 18 (July 1941).
Urquía, Juan de (pseud., El Capitán Verdades). Historia negra. Barcelona, 1899.
———. La guerra hispano-americana. Barcelona, 1899.
Urquijo, Fernando de. La campaña del Rif en 1909. Madrid, n.d.
Usborne, Vice-Adm. C. V. The Conquest of Morocco. London, 1936.

Valdés, Jerónimo. Exposición que dirige al rey don Fernando VII don Jerónimo Valdés sobre las causas que motivaron las pérdidas del Perú. Madrid, 1894.
Valdesoto, Fernando de. Francisco Franco. Madrid, 1943.
Válgoma, Carlos de la. Mola. Madrid, n.d.
Vallecillo, Antonio, ed. Legislación militar de España antigua y moderna. 29 vols. Madrid, 1853–56.
Vallés, Camilo. Estudio sobre la organización militar de España. Madrid, 1881.
Valles Collantes, Francisco. Páginas de gloria de la Marina española. Cádiz, 1938.
Vaquero, Eloy. *Mensaje* (New York, 1958).

Vázquez de Mella, Juan. El problema hispano-morroquí. Madrid, 1914.
Vega Inclán, Miguel de la. Relación histórica de la última campaña del Marqués del Duero. Madrid, 1874.
Vegas Latapié, Eugenio. Escritos políticos. Madrid, n.d.
Venegas, José. Las elecciones del Frente Popular. Buenos Aires, 1942.
Vergés, José Miquel i. El General Prim en España y en México. Mexico City, 1949.
Vesa y Fillart, Antonio. Historia del Regimiento de Caballería de Jaruco. Barcelona, 1908.
Vidal, Emile. La Politique de l'Espagne au Maroc. Montpellier, 1913.
Vidart, Louis. La instrucción militar obligatoria. Madrid, 1873.
———. La fuerza armada. Madrid, 1876.
Vigón, Lt. Gen. Jorge. Un personaje español del siglo XIX (El Cuerpo de Artillería). Madrid, 1930.
———. Historia de la Artillería española. 3 vols. Madrid, 1947.
———. Milicia y política. Madrid, 1947.
———. Cien años en la vida del Ejército Español. Madrid, 1956.
———. Mola (El Conspirador). Barcelona, 1957.
Vilanova Fuentes, Antonio. La defensa del Alcázar de Toledo. Mexico City, 1963.
Vilarrasa, Eduardo María, and José Ildefonso Gatell. Historia de la revolución de septiembre. 2 vols. Barcelona, 1875.
Vilarrubias, F. A., and J. F. Lizcano. Un muerto. Madrid, 1961.
Villalba Diéguez, Fernando. Diario de guerra (1938–1939). Madrid, 1939.
Villanueva, Francisco. La Dictadura militar. Madrid, 1930.
Villar, Manuel. El anarquismo en la insurrección de Asturias. Buenos Aires, 1936.
———. La represión de octubre. Barcelona, 1936.
Villa-Urrutia, Marqués de. El General Serrano. Madrid, 1929.
Vivero, Augusto. El derrumbamiento. Madrid, 1922.
Volta, Sandro. Spagna a ferro e fuoco. Florence, 1937.

Welles, Benjamin. Spain, the Gentle Anarchy. New York, 1965.
Weyler, Valeriano. Memoria justificativa del General Weyler. Palma de Mallorca, 1875.
———. Mi mando en Cuba. 5 vols. Madrid, 1910–11.
Weyler y López Puga, Valeriano. En el archivo de mi abuelo. Madrid, 1946.
Whealey, Robert H. German–Spanish Relations, January–August 1939. Unpublished dissertation. University of Michigan, 1963.
Whitaker, Arthur P. Spain and Defense of the West. New York, 1961.
Whitaker, John. We Cannot Escape History. New York, 1943.
Woodward, Margaret. Spanish Apathy and American Independence. Unpublished dissertation. University of Chicago, 1964.
Woznicki, Robert. Historia de las Bases Conjuntas Hispano-Americanas, 1951–1960. Unpublished dissertation. University of Madrid, 1961.

Ximénez de Sandoval, C. Las instituciones de seguridad pública. Madrid, 1958.

Zugazagoitia, Julián. Historia de la guerra de España. Buenos Aires, 1940.
Zumarro, Alejandro. Los sucesos de Ciudad Real por un condenado a muerte. Madrid, 1933.
Zwingelstein, André. Au pays de la terreur rouge. Paris, 1937.

Index

Index